MAPPING THE SOCIAL LANDSCAPE

Mapping the Social Landscape

Readings in Sociology

Fourth Edition

SUSAN J. FERGUSON
Grinnell College

Boston   Burr Ridge, IL   Dubuque, IA   Madison, WI   New York   San Francisco   St. Louis
Bangkok   Bogotá   Caracas   Kuala Lumpur   Lisbon   London   Madrid   Mexico City
Milan   Montreal   New Delhi   Santiago   Seoul   Singapore   Sydney   Taipei   Toronto

The McGraw·Hill Companies

 **Higher Education**

MAPPING THE SOCIAL LANDSCAPE: READINGS IN SOCIOLOGY, FOURTH EDITION
Published by McGraw-Hill, a business unit of The McGraw-Hill Companies, Inc., 1221 Avenue
of the Americas, New York, NY 10020. Copyright © 2005, 2002, 1999, 1996 by The McGraw-Hill
Companies, Inc. All rights reserved. No part of this publication may be reproduced or distributed in any form or by any means, or stored in a database or retrieval system, without the
prior written consent of The McGraw-Hill Companies, Inc., including, but not limited to, any
network or other electronic storage or transmission, or broadcast for distance learning.

   Some ancillaries, including electronic and print components, may not be available to customers outside the United States.

ISBN 0-07-287899-1

2 3 4 5 6 7 8 9 0 FGR/FGR 0 9 8 7 6 5 4

Editor-in-chief: *Emily Barrosse*
Publisher: *Phillip A. Butcher*
Sponsoring editor: *Sherith Pankratz*
Marketing manager: *Dan Loch*
Production services manager: *Jennifer Mills*
Production service: *Publishing Support Services*
Manuscript editor: *Margaret Moore*
Art director: *Jeanne M. Schreiber*
Design manager: *Cassandra Chu*
Cover designer: *Yvo Riezebos*
Interior designer: *Linda M. Robertson*
Production supervisor: *Tandra Jorgensen*

The text was set in 10/12 Book Antiqua by G&S Typesetters, Inc., and printed on acid-free 45#
New Era Matte by Quebecor Fairfield.

Cover images: Bikes, © fStop/ Veer; Subway, © PhotoAlto Photography/ Veer; Umbrellas,
© DigitalVision Photography/ Veer; Woman, Photomondo/Getty Images/ PhotoDisc

Library of Congress Cataloging-in-Publication Data
Mapping the social landscape: readings in sociology / [edited by] Susan J. Ferguson.—4th ed.
   p. cm
   Includes bibliographical references.
      ISBN 0-07-287899-1 (softcover)
   1. Social institutions.   2. Socialization.   3. Equality.   4. Social change.   5. Sociology.
I. Ferguson, Susan J.
HM826.M36 2005
301—dc22   2004040330

www.mhhe.com

With love to my grandmother, Edna Catherine Clark, who always believed that an education would open the doors of the world to me. She was right.

Preface

As the title suggests, *Mapping the Social Landscape* is about exploration and discovery. It means taking a closer look at a complex, ever-changing social world in which locations, pathways, and boundaries are not fixed. Because sociology describes and explains our social surroundings, it enables us to understand this shifting landscape. Thus, sociology is about discovering society and discovering ourselves. The purpose of this anthology is to introduce the discipline of sociology and to convey the excitement and the challenge of the sociological enterprise.

Although a number of readers in introductory sociology are already available for students, I have yet to find one that exposes students to the broad diversity of scholarship, perspectives, and authorship that exists within the field of sociology. This diversity goes beyond recognizing gender, racial-ethnic, and social class differences to acknowledging a plurality of voices and views within the discipline. Like other anthologies, this one includes classic works by authors such as Karl Marx, Max Weber, Talcott Parsons, and C. Wright Mills; in addition, however, I have drawn from a wide range of contemporary scholarship, some of which provides newer treatments of traditional concepts. This diversity of viewpoints and approaches should encourage students to evaluate and analyze the sociological ideas and research findings presented.

In addition, because I find it invaluable in my own teaching to use examples from personal experiences to enable students to see the connection between "private troubles and public issues," as C. Wright Mills phrased it, I have included in this collection a few personal narratives to help students comprehend how social forces affect individual lives. Thus, this anthology includes classic as well as contemporary writings, and the voices of other social scientists who render provocative sociological insights. The readings also exemplify functionalist, conflict, and symbolic interactionist perspectives and different types of research methodology. Each article is preceded by a brief headnote that sets the context within which the reader can seek to understand the sociological work. Thus, the selections communicate an enthusiasm for sociology while illustrating sociological concepts, theories, and methods.

During the past 30 years, sociology has benefited from a rich abundance of creative scholarship, but many of these original works have not been adequately presented in textbooks or readers. I believe an introductory anthology needs to reflect the new questions concerning research and theory within the discipline. Moreover, I find that students enjoy reading the actual words and research of sociologists. This anthology, therefore, includes many cutting-edge pieces of sociological scholarship and some very recent publications by recognized social analysts. Current issues are examined, including childhood school cliques, teen pregnancy, depression and identity, gangs, the tattoo subculture, gay and lesbian families, TV talk shows, working at McDonald's, the effects of globalization, racism in the United States, the Internet, poverty, military boot camps, teen suicide, eating disorders, elite boarding schools, and the political influence of corporate PACs. In essence, I have attempted not to break new ground but, rather, to compile a collection that provides a fresh, innovative look at the discipline of sociology.

Changes to the Fourth Edition

With this fourth edition, I maintain a balance of classical and contemporary readings. In addition to many of the classic pieces that appeared in the third edition, I have included Kingsley Davis and Wilbert Moore's classic work on some principles of stratification. I also have brought back Talcott Parsons' classic selection on the social structure of medicine. Both of these classic pieces are wonderful "lead" articles for the sections they are in, and they lay the groundwork for enhanced sociological understanding. Other changes I have made to this fourth edition include the addition of 18 selections of contemporary sociological research that illustrate analyses of timely social issues and the intersections among race, social class, and gender. These new selections examine cosmetic surgery, women in racist groups, a prison riot, rape on college campuses, the working poor, racial dynamics at the slaughterhouse, Native Americans and casinos, HIV/AIDS in Africa, religion in the United States, working mothers, Iraq and the war against terrorism, and multiracial identities. Among these readings are some selections that I consider to be contemporary classics in that they provide an overview of the discipline of sociology or a specific content area. These readings include an essay by Michael Schwalbe on how the social world works; a now classic work by Michael Omi and Howard Winant on the social construction of race in the United States; and an essay by Amitai Etzioni on community building. Based on reviewers' comments, I also have added a separate section on the institution of the mass media, which highlights the work of Marty Marger and Gregory Mantsios, as well as an excerpt from Todd Gitlin's new book, *Media Unlimited: How the Torrent of Images and Sounds Overwhelms Our Lives* (2001). I also have extensively revised the sections on race, health and medicine, and social change. I think the students will find the newer pieces in these sections more accessible and interesting. Of course, for all of the readings, I have tried to choose selections that are compelling to students and demonstrate well the diversity within the discipline of sociology. Please note that I welcome feedback from professors and students on this edition of *Mapping the Social Landscape*. You can e-mail me at Grinnell College. My e-mail address is fergusos @grinnell.edu.

Supplemental Learning Materials

I have written an accompanying test manual that contains numerous examination and discussion questions for each reading. As the editor of this anthology, I developed these items with the goal of helping instructors test students' understanding of key concepts and themes. The Instructor's Manual can be obtained from your local McGraw-Hill representative. In addition, there is a Web site for this book that links to additional information and resources. It can be found at www.mhhe.com/ferguson4.

Acknowledgments

The completion of this book involved the support and labor of many people. I would like to begin by acknowledging my former sociology editor, Serina Beauparlant of Mayfield Publishing Company, who challenged me, almost 10 years ago, to take on this project. Much of Serina's vision is contained within the structure of this book. Over the years we have spent many hours on the telephone debating the strengths and weaknesses of various readings. Serina, if I am a clutch hitter, then you are the phenomenal batting coach. I could not have asked for a more thoughtful and attentive sociology editor. Thank you for initiating this project with me.

I also am indebted to the Grinnell College faculty secretaries, Karen Groves, Linda Price, and Stephanie Puls, for their time typing and copying portions of the manuscript. My student assistants, Andrew Greenlee, Margaret Hainline, Stacie Kossoy, Bridget LaVelle, Joa Taylor, and Jessica Ward, also need to be commended for copying material, carrying innumerable pounds of books between my office and the library, or helping me to write questions and find Web sites for the supplemental learning materials. I am especially indebted to Grinnell College for its generous research support.

Over the past 10 years, 60 sociologists have reviewed earlier drafts of the manuscript and provided me with valuable observations concerning the readings and teaching introductory sociology. First and foremost, I want to acknowledge the early insights of Agnes Riedmann, who suggested several key pieces in the first draft. I also appreciate the suggestions for selections made by Joan Ferrante, Annette Lareau, and Michael Messner.

My special thanks go to Arnold Arluke, Northeastern University; Joanne M. Badagliacco, University of Kentucky; Gary L. Brock, Southwest Missouri State University; Tom Gerschick, Illinois State University; Thomas B. Gold, University of California at Berkeley; Jack Harkins, College of DuPage; Paul Kamolnick, East Tennessee State University; Peter Kivisto, Augustana College; Fred Kniss, Loyola University; Diane E. Levy, University of North Carolina at Wilmington; Peter Meiksins, Cleveland State University; Roslyn Arlin Mickelson, University of North Carolina at Charlotte; and Carol Ray, San Jose State University, for their feedback on the first edition of the manuscript. Your detailed comments were enormously helpful in the tightening and refining of the manuscript. Moreover, your voices reflect the rich and varied experiences with teaching introductory sociology.

For the second edition, I would like to thank the following reviewers: Angela Danzi, State University of New York at Farmingdale; Diane Diamond, State University of New York at Stony Brook; Yvonne Downs, State University of New York at Fredonia; Kay Forest, Northern Illinois University; Bob Granfield, University of Denver; Susan Greenwood, University of Maine; Kate Hausbeck, University of Nevada at Las Vegas; Arthur J. Jipson, Miami University; James Jones, Mississippi State University; Carolyn A. Kapinus, Penn State University; J. Richard Kendrick, Jr., State University of New York at Cortland; M. Kris McIlwaine, University of Arizona; Kristy McNamara, Furman University; Tracy Ore, St. Cloud State University; Denise Scott, State University of New York at Geneseo; Maynard Seider, Massachusetts College of Liberal Arts; Thomas Soltis, Westmoreland County Community College; Martha Thompson, Northeastern Illinois University; Huiying Wei-Arthus, Weber State University; Adam S. Weinberg, Colgate University; Amy S. Wharton, Washington State University; and John Zipp, University of Akron.

For the third edition, I would like to thank the following reviewers: Stephen Adair, Central Connecticut State University; Javier Auyero, State University of New York at Stony Brook; David K. Brown, Illinois State University; Kay B. Forest, Northern Illinois University; Angela J. Hattery, Wake Forest University; Karen Honeycutt, Keene State University; Neal King, Belmont University; Judith N. Lasker, Lehigh University; Rosemary F. Powers, Eastern Oregon University; Melissa Riba, Michigan State University; Deirdre Royster, University of Massachusetts, Amherst; James T. Salt, Lane Community College; H. Lovell Smith, Loyola College in Maryland; and Thomas Soltis, Westmoreland County Community College.

For the fourth edition, I would like to thank the following reviewers: Kevin J. Delaney, Temple University; Patricia L. Gibbs, Foothill College; Rebecca Klatch, University of California, San Diego; David Rohall, University of New Hampshire; Patricia Shropshire, Michigan State University; Thomas Soltis, Westmoreland County Community College; Kevin A. Tholin, Indiana University, South Bend; and several anonymous reviewers. All of your comments were extremely helpful to me during the revision process.

Finally, at McGraw-Hill, I would like to recognize the creative and patient efforts of several individuals, including Cassandra Chu, Marty Granahan, Dan Loch, Jen Mills, Sherith Pankratz, and Amy Shaffer. I also want to acknowledge the detailed work of the copyeditor, Margaret Moore, and the production management skills of Vicki Moran. Thank you both for whipping my manuscript into shape!

Contents

Preface   vii

Part I   THE SOCIOLOGICAL PERSPECTIVE   1

1. C. Wright Mills
   THE PROMISE   1
   —*classic piece on the sociological imagination*

2. Donna Gaines
   TEENAGE WASTELAND: Suburbia's Dead-End Kids   7
   —*applying the sociological imagination to teen suicide*

3. Mary Romero
   INTERSECTION OF BIOGRAPHY AND HISTORY:
   My Intellectual Journey   20
   —*applying the sociological imagination to domestic service*

SOCIAL RESEARCH

4. Michael Schwalbe
   FINDING OUT HOW THE SOCIAL WORLD WORKS   36
   —*a summary of what it means to be sociologically mindful*

5. Craig Haney, W. Curtis Banks, and Philip G. Zimbardo
   INTERPERSONAL DYNAMICS IN A SIMULATED PRISON   47
   —*classic piece on the research design of Zimbardo's famous
   experiment*

6. Elaine Bell Kaplan
   NOT OUR KIND OF GIRL   57
   —*participant observation research among African American
   teen mothers*

Part II   CULTURE   66

7. Anne M. Velliquette and Jeff B. Murray
    THE NEW TATTOO SUBCULTURE   66
        —the tattoo subculture and meanings of body adornment

8. Elijah Anderson
    THE CODE OF THE STREETS   79
        —an exploration of street culture

9. Eugenia Kaw
    "OPENING" FACES: The Politics of Cosmetic Surgery
    and Asian American Women   91
        *—the influence of gender and racial stereotypes on the
        beauty culture*

10. Haunani-Kay Trask
    LOVELY HULA HANDS: Corporate Tourism and the
    Prostitution of Hawaiian Culture   111
        —an examination of cultural exploitation

Part III   SOCIALIZATION   119

11. Judith Lorber
    "NIGHT TO HIS DAY": The Social Construction of Gender   119
        —the socialization of gender identity

12. Michael Messner
    BOYHOOD, ORGANIZED SPORTS, AND THE
    CONSTRUCTION OF MASCULINITIES   132
        —the social construction of masculinity

13. Robert Granfield
    MAKING IT BY FAKING IT: Working-Class Students
    in an Elite Academic Environment   147
        —working-class identity and law school socialization

14. Gwynne Dyer
    ANYBODY'S SON WILL DO   161
        —resocialization into the total institution of the military

Part IV   GROUPS AND SOCIAL STRUCTURE   173

15. Patricia A. Adler and Peter Adler
    PEER POWER: Clique Dynamics among School Children   173
        *—a study of the structure and interactional dynamics among
        school children's groups*

16. Martín Sánchez Jankowski
    GANG BUSINESS: Making Ends Meet   189
        —a functional analysis of a primary group

17. Kathleen M. Blee
    BECOMING A RACIST: Women in Contemporary Ku
    Klux Klan and Neo-Nazi Groups   200
        —an illustration of secondary group membership

18. Mark Colvin
    DESCENT INTO MADNESS: The New Mexico State
    Prison Riot   214
        —an example of social structure breaking down

Part V   DEVIANCE, CRIME, AND SOCIAL CONTROL   230

19. David L. Rosenhan
    ON BEING SANE IN INSANE PLACES   230
        —classic piece on labeling and social deviance

20. Penelope A. McLorg and Diane E. Taub
    ANOREXIA NERVOSA AND BULIMIA: The Development
    of Deviant Identities   241
        —the social construction of deviant identities

21. Philippe Bourgois
    IN SEARCH OF RESPECT: Selling Crack in El Barrio   253
        —an ethnographic study of drug dealing in the inner city

22. A. Ayres Boswell and Joan Z. Spade
    FRATERNITIES AND COLLEGIATE RAPE CULTURE:
    Why Are Some Fraternities More Dangerous Places
    for Women?   265
        —the social organization of crime

Part VI   SOCIAL INEQUALITY

279

SOCIAL CLASS

23. Kingsley Davis, Wilbert E. Moore, and Melvin Tumin
SOME PRINCIPLES OF STRATIFICATION
—*classic pieces on the functions of social stratification*

279

24. G. William Domhoff
WHO RULES AMERICA? The Corporate Community
and the Upper Class
—*the lifestyles and social institutions of the upper class*

289

25. Melvin L. Oliver and Thomas M. Shapiro
BLACK WEALTH / WHITE WEALTH: A New Perspective
on Racial Inequality
—*a sociology of wealth and racial inequality*

303

26. Barbara Ehrenreich
NICKEL-AND-DIMED: On (Not) Getting By in America
—*an exploration of the lives of the working poor*

318

GENDER

27. Barbara Risman
GENDER AS STRUCTURE
—*a review of four theories that explain sex and gender*

332

28. Christine L. Williams
THE GLASS ESCALATOR: Hidden Advantages for
Men in the "Female" Professions
—*an examination of sex typing and job segregation*

342

29. Yen Le Espiritu
THE RACIAL CONSTRUCTION OF ASIAN AMERICAN
WOMEN AND MEN
—*an examination of racist and sexist images in U.S. culture*

353

30. Myra Sadker and David Sadker
FAILING AT FAIRNESS: Hidden Lessons
—*gender inequality in the institution of education*

366

RACE AND ETHNICITY

31. Michael Omi and Howard Winant
RACIAL FORMATIONS IN THE UNITED STATES   380
    —*the social construction of race*

32. Jennifer Lee and Frank D. Bean
BEYOND BLACK AND WHITE: Remaking Race in America   390
    —*how race is measured by the U.S. government*

33. Lillian B. Rubin
"IS THIS A WHITE COUNTRY, OR WHAT?"   398
    —*working-class families talk about race and ethnicity*

34. Charlie LeDuff
AT A SLAUGHTERHOUSE, SOME THINGS NEVER DIE   410
    —*an examination of the racial dynamics at one workplace site*

Part VII   SOCIAL INSTITUTIONS   421

POWER AND POLITICS

35. C. Wright Mills
THE POWER ELITE   421
    —*classic piece on the power elite*

36. Dan Clawson, Alan Neustadtl, and Mark Weller
DOLLARS AND VOTES: How Business Campaign
Contributions Subvert Democracy   429
    —*an application of Mills' power elite*

37. Donald L. Barlett and James B. Steele
PLAYING THE POLITICAL SLOTS: American Indians
and Casinos   443
    —*the politics of and profiteering from gambling on reservations*

MASS MEDIA

38. Martin N. Marger
THE MASS MEDIA AS A POWER INSTITUTION   452
    —*an examination of power and the mass media*

39. Gregory Mantsios
MEDIA MAGIC: Making Class Invisible   463
    —*how the mass media distorts social class*

40. Todd Gitlin
MEDIA UNLIMITED: How the Torrent of Images
and Sounds Overwhelms Our Lives   472
    —*the globalization of American media*

THE ECONOMY AND WORK

41. Karl Marx and Friedrich Engels
MANIFESTO OF THE COMMUNIST PARTY   482
    —*classic piece on the relationship between the capitalists
    and the workers*

42. William Julius Wilson
WHEN WORK DISAPPEARS: The World of the New
Urban Poor   488
    —*current analysis of inner-city joblessness*

43. Robin Leidner
OVER THE COUNTER: McDonald's   501
    —*an ethnographic study of routinization in work*

RELIGION

44. Max Weber
THE PROTESTANT ETHIC AND THE SPIRIT
OF CAPITALISM   517
    —*classic piece on the influence of religion on other social
    institutions*

45. Mark Chaves
ABIDING FAITH   524
    —*the current status of religion among Americans*

46. Kathleen S. Lowney
BARING OUR SOULS: TV Talk Shows and the Religion
of Recovery   530
    —*an analysis of religious revivalism and morality on TV talk shows*

HEALTH AND MEDICINE

47. Talcott Parsons
    THE SOCIAL STRUCTURE OF MEDICINE 540
    —*classic piece on the functions of health and illness in society*

48. Johanna McGeary
    DEATH STALKS A CONTINENT 545
    —*an examination of the AIDS epidemic in Africa*

49. David A. Karp
    ILLNESS AND IDENTITY 559
    —*an interview study of people with depression*

EDUCATION

50. Mary Crow Dog and Richard Erdoes
    CIVILIZE THEM WITH A STICK 573
    —*education as an institution of social control*

51. Peter W. Cookson, Jr., and Caroline Hodges Persell
    PREPARING FOR POWER: Cultural Capital and Curricula
    in America's Elite Boarding Schools 581
    —*an examination of elite education*

52. Ann Arnett Ferguson
    BAD BOYS: Public Schools in the Making of
    Black Masculinity 592
    —*racial and gender stereotyping in American schools*

THE FAMILY

53. Judith Stacey
    GAY AND LESBIAN FAMILIES ARE HERE 601
    —*changing definitions of family*

54. Ann Crittenden
    THE MOMMY TAX 614
    —*the income discrimination faced by working mothers*

55. Arlie Russell Hochschild
    THE TIME BIND: When Work Becomes Home and
    Home Becomes Work 625
    —*how individuals combine their work and home lives*

Part VIII   SOCIAL CHANGE   637

56. George Ritzer
    THE McDONALDIZATION OF SOCIETY   637
       —*a contemporary theory of social change*

57. Conrad L. Kanagy and Donald B. Kraybill
    HOW WILL THE INTERNET CHANGE SOCIETY?   646
       —*an examination of the social change being caused by computers*

58. Charles Derber
    THE WILDING OF AMERICA: Iraq and the War against
    Terrorism   654
       —*war as an extreme example of social change*

59. Amitai Etzioni
    COMMUNITY BUILDING: Steps toward a Good Society   665
       —*one sociologist's vision of needed social change*

60. Allan G. Johnson
    WHAT CAN WE DO? Becoming Part of the Solution   673
       —*social change strategies to deal with privilege and oppression*

Tell me the landscape in which you live, and I will tell you who you are.

José Ortega y Gasset

PART I
The Sociological Perspective

1

THE PROMISE

C. WRIGHT MILLS

The initial three selections examine the sociological perspective. The first of these is written by C. Wright Mills (1916–1962), a former professor of sociology at Columbia University. During his brief academic career, Mills became one of the best known and most controversial sociologists. He was critical of the U.S. government and other social institutions where power was unfairly concentrated. He also believed that academics should be socially responsible and speak out against social injustice. The excerpt that follows is from Mills' acclaimed book *The Sociological Imagination*. Since its original publication in 1959, this text has been a required reading for most introductory sociology students around the world. Mills' sociological imagination perspective not only compels the best sociological analyses but also enables the sociologist and the individual to distinguish between "personal troubles" and "public issues." By separating these phenomena, we can better comprehend the sources of and solutions to social problems.

Nowadays men often feel that their private lives are a series of traps. They sense that within their everyday worlds, they cannot overcome their troubles, and in this feeling, they are often quite correct: What ordinary men are directly aware of and what they try to do are bounded by the private orbits in which they live; their visions and their powers are limited to the close-up scenes of job, family, neighborhood; in other milieux, they move vicariously and remain spectators. And the more aware they become,

This article was written in 1959 before scholars were sensitive to gender inclusivity in language. The references to masculine pronouns and men are, therefore, generic to both males and females and should be read as such. Please note that I have left the author's original language in this selection and other readings. —*Editor*

From *The Sociological Imagination*, pp. 3–13. Copyright © 1959, 2000 by Oxford University Press, Inc. Reprinted with the permission of Oxford University Press.

however vaguely, of ambitions and of threats which transcend their immediate locales, the more trapped they seem to feel.

Underlying this sense of being trapped are seemingly impersonal changes in the very structure of continent-wide societies. The facts of contemporary history are also facts about the success and the failure of individual men and women. When a society is industrialized, a peasant becomes a worker; a feudal lord is liquidated or becomes a businessman. When classes rise or fall, a man is employed or unemployed; when the rate of investment goes up or down, a man takes new heart or goes broke. When wars happen, an insurance salesman becomes a rocket launcher; a store clerk, a radar man; a wife lives alone; a child grows up without a father. Neither the life of an individual nor the history of a society can be understood without understanding both.

Yet men do not usually define the troubles they endure in terms of historical change and institutional contradiction. The well-being they enjoy, they do not usually impute to the big ups and downs of the societies in which they live. Seldom aware of the intricate connection between the patterns of their own lives and the course of world history, ordinary men do not usually know what this connection means for the kinds of men they are becoming and for the kinds of history making in which they might take part. They do not possess the quality of mind essential to grasp the interplay of man and society, of biography and history, of self and world. They cannot cope with their personal troubles in such ways as to control the structural transformations that usually lie behind them.

Surely it is no wonder. In what period have so many men been so totally exposed at so fast a pace to such earthquakes of change? That Americans have not known such catastrophic changes as have the men and women of other societies is due to historical facts that are now quickly becoming "merely history." The history that now affects every man is world history. Within this scene and this period, in the course of a single generation, one-sixth of mankind is transformed from all that is feudal and backward into all that is modern, advanced, and fearful. Political colonies are freed; new and less visible forms of imperialism installed. Revolutions occur; men feel the intimate grip of new kinds of authority. Totalitarian societies rise and are smashed to bits—or succeed fabulously. After two centuries of ascendancy, capitalism is shown up as only one way to make society into an industrial apparatus. After two centuries of hope, even formal democracy is restricted to a quite small portion of mankind. Everywhere in the underdeveloped world, ancient ways of life are broken up and vague expectations become urgent demands. Everywhere in the overdeveloped world, the means of authority and of violence become total in scope and bureaucratic in form. Humanity itself now lies before us, the super-nation at either pole concentrating its most coordinated and massive efforts upon the preparation of World War Three.

The very shaping of history now outpaces the ability of men to orient themselves in accordance with cherished values. And which values? Even when they do not panic, men often sense that older ways of feeling and thinking have collapsed and that newer beginnings are ambiguous to the point of moral stasis. Is it any wonder that ordinary men feel they cannot cope with the larger worlds with which they are so suddenly confronted? That they cannot understand the meaning of their epoch for their own lives? That—in defense of selfhood—they become morally insensible, trying to remain altogether private men? Is it any wonder that they come to be possessed by a sense of the trap?

It is not only information that they need—in this Age of Fact, information often dominates their attention and overwhelms their capacities to assimilate it. It is not only the skills of reason that they need—although their struggles to acquire these often exhaust their limited moral energy.

What they need, and what they feel they need, is a quality of mind that will help them to use information and to develop reason in order to achieve lucid summations of what is going on in the world and of what may be happening within themselves. It is this quality, I am going to contend, that journalists and scholars, artists and publics, scientists and editors are coming to expect of what may be called the sociological imagination.

The sociological imagination enables its possessor to understand the larger historical scene in terms of its meaning for the inner life and the external career of a variety of individuals. It enables him to take into account how individuals, in the welter of their daily experience, often become falsely conscious of their social positions. Within that welter, the framework of modern society is sought, and within that framework the psychologies of a variety of men and women are formulated. By such means the personal uneasiness of individuals is focused upon explicit troubles and the indifference of publics is transformed into involvement with public issues.

The first fruit of this imagination—and the first lesson of the social science that embodies it—is the idea that the individual can understand his own experience and gauge his own fate only by locating himself within his period, that he can know his own chances in life only by becoming aware of those of all individuals in his circumstances. In many ways it is a terrible lesson; in many ways a magnificent one. We do not know the limits of man's capacities for supreme effort or willing degradation, for agony or glee, for pleasurable brutality or the sweetness of reason. But in our time we have come to know that the limits of "human nature" are frighteningly broad. We have come to know that every individual lives, from one generation to the next, in some society; that he lives out a biography, and that he lives it out within some historical sequence. By the fact of his living he contributes, however minutely, to the shaping of this society and to the course of its history, even as he is made by society and by its historical push and shove.

The sociological imagination enables us to grasp history and biography and the relations between the two within society. That is its task and its promise. To recognize this task and this promise is the mark of the classic social analyst. It is characteristic of Herbert Spencer—turgid, polysyllabic, comprehensive; of E. A. Ross—graceful, muckraking, upright; of Auguste Comte and Emile Durkheim; of the intricate and subtle Karl Mannheim. It is the quality of all that is intellectually excellent in Karl Marx; it is the clue to Thorstein Veblen's brilliant and ironic insight, to Joseph Schumpeter's many-sided constructions of reality; it is the basis of the psychological sweep of W. E. H. Lecky no less than of the profundity and clarity of Max Weber. And it is the signal of what is best in contemporary studies of man and society.

No social study that does not come back to the problems of biography, of history and of their intersections within a society, has completed its intellectual journey. Whatever the specific problems of the classic social analysts, however limited or however broad the features of social reality they have examined, those who have been imaginatively aware of the promise of their work have consistently asked three sorts of questions:

1. What is the structure of this particular society as a whole? What are its essential components, and how are they related to one another? How does it differ from other varieties of social order? Within it, what is the meaning of any particular feature for its continuance and for its change?

2. Where does this society stand in human history? What are the mechanics by which it is changing? What is its place within and its meaning for the development of humanity as a whole? How does any particular feature we are examining affect, and how is it affected by, the historical period in which it moves? And this period—what are its essential features? How does it differ from other periods? What are its characteristic ways of history making?

3. What varieties of men and women now prevail in this society and in this period? And what varieties are coming to prevail? In what ways are they selected and formed, liberated and repressed, made sensitive and blunted? What kinds of "human nature" are revealed in the conduct and character we observe in this society in this period? And what is the meaning for "human nature" of each and every feature of the society we are examining?

Whether the point of interest is a great power state or a minor literary mood, a family, a prison, a creed—these are the kinds of questions the best social analysts have asked. They are the intellectual pivots of classic studies of man in society—and they are the questions inevitably raised by any mind possessing the sociological imagination. For that imagination is the capacity to shift from one perspective to another—from the political to the psychological; from examination of a single family to comparative assessment of the national budgets of the world; from the theological school to the military establishment; from considerations of an oil industry to studies of contemporary poetry. It is the capacity to range from the most impersonal and remote transformations to the most intimate features of the human self—and to see the relations between the two. Back of its use there is always the urge to know the social and historical meaning of the individual in the society and in the period in which he has his quality and his being.

That, in brief, is why it is by means of the sociological imagination that men now hope to grasp what is going on in the world, and to understand what is happening in themselves as minute points of the intersections of biography and history within society. In large part, contemporary man's self-conscious view of himself as at least an outsider, if not a permanent stranger, rests upon an absorbed realization of social relativity and of the transformative power of history. The sociological imagination is the most fruitful form of this self-consciousness. By its use men whose mentalities have swept only a series of limited orbits often come to feel as if suddenly awakened in a house with which they had only supposed themselves to be familiar. Correctly or incorrectly, they often come to feel that they can now provide themselves with adequate summations, cohesive assessments, comprehensive orientations. Older decisions that once appeared sound now seem to them products of a mind unaccountably dense. Their capacity for astonishment is made lively again. They acquire a new way of thinking, they experience a transvaluation of values: in a word, by their reflection and by their sensibility, they realize the cultural meaning of the social sciences.

———————

Perhaps the most fruitful distinction with which the sociological imagination works is between "the personal troubles of milieu" and "the public issues of social structure." This distinction is an essential tool of the sociological imagination and a feature of all classic work in social science.

Troubles occur within the character of the individual and within the range of his immediate relations with others; they have to do with his self and with those limited areas of social life of which he is directly and personally aware. Accordingly, the statement and the resolution of troubles properly lie within the individual as a biographical entity and within the scope of his immediate milieu—the social setting that is directly open to his personal experience and to some extent his willful activity. A trouble is a private matter: Values cherished by an individual are felt by him to be threatened.

Issues have to do with matters that transcend these local environments of the individual and the range of his inner life. They have to do with the organization of many such milieux into the institutions of a historical society as a whole, with the ways in which various milieux overlap and interpenetrate to form the larger structure of social and historical life. An issue is a public matter: Some value cherished by publics is felt to be threatened. Often there is a debate about what that value really is and about what it is that really threatens it. This debate is often without focus if only because it is the very nature of an issue, unlike even widespread trouble, that it cannot very well be defined in terms of the immediate and everyday environments of ordinary men.

An issue, in fact, often involves a crisis in institutional arrangements, and often too it involves what Marxists call "contradictions" or "antagonisms."

In these terms, consider unemployment. When, in a city of 100,000, only one man is unemployed, that is his personal trouble, and for its relief we properly look to the character of the man, his skills, and his immediate opportunities. But when in a nation of 50 million employees, 15 million men are unemployed, that is an issue, and we may not hope to find its solution within the range of opportunities open to any one individual. The very structure of opportunities has collapsed. Both the correct statement of the problem and the range of possible solutions require us to consider the economic and political institutions of the society, and not merely the personal situation and character of a scatter of individuals.

Consider war. The personal problem of war, when it occurs, may be how to survive it or how to die in it with honor; how to make money out of it; how to climb into the higher safety of the military apparatus; or how to contribute to the war's termination. In short, according to one's values, to find a set of milieux and within it to survive the war or make one's death in it meaningful. But the structural issues of war have to do with its causes; with what types of men it throws up into command; with its effects upon economic and political, family and religious institutions, with the unorganized irresponsibility of a world of nation-states.

Consider marriage. Inside a marriage a man and a woman may experience personal troubles, but when the divorce rate during the first four years of marriage is 250 out of every 1,000 attempts, this is an indication of a structural issue having to do with the institutions of marriage and the family and other institutions that bear upon them.

Or consider the metropolis—the horrible, beautiful, ugly, magnificent sprawl of the great city. For many upper-class people, the personal solution to "the problem of the city" is to have an apartment with private garage under it in the heart of the city, and forty miles out, a house by Henry Hill, garden by Garrett Eckbo, on a hundred acres of private land. In these two controlled environments—with a small staff at each end and a private helicopter connection—most people could solve many of the problems of personal milieux caused by the facts of the city. But all this, however splendid, does not solve the public issues that the structural fact of the city poses. What should be done with this wonderful monstrosity? Break it all up into scattered units, combining residence and work? Refurbish it as it stands? Or, after evacuation, dynamite it and build new cities according to new plans in new places? What should those plans be? And who is to decide and to accomplish whatever choice is made? These are structural issues; to confront them and to solve them requires us to consider political and economic issues that affect innumerable milieux.

Insofar as an economy is so arranged that slumps occur, the problem of unemployment becomes incapable of personal solution. Insofar as war is inherent in the nation-state system and in the uneven industrialization of the world, the ordinary individual in his restricted milieu will be powerless—with or without psychiatric aid—to solve the troubles this system or lack of system imposes upon him. Insofar as the family as an institution turns women into darling little slaves and men into their chief providers and un-weaned dependents, the problem of a satisfactory marriage remains inca-pable of purely private solution. Insofar as the overdeveloped megalopolis and the overdeveloped automobile are built-in features of the overdeveloped society, the issues of urban living will not be solved by personal ingenuity and private wealth.

What we experience in various and specific milieux, I have noted, is often caused by structural changes. Accordingly, to understand the changes of many personal milieux we are required to look beyond them. And the num-ber and variety of such structural changes increase as the institutions within which we live become more embracing and more intricately connected with one another. To be aware of the idea of social structure and to use it with sen-sibility is to be capable of tracing such linkages among a great variety of mi-lieux. To be able to do that is to possess the sociological imagination.

2

TEENAGE WASTELAND
Suburbia's Dead-End Kids

DONNA GAINES

This reading by Donna Gaines is excerpted from her internationally ac-claimed book *Teenage Wasteland: Suburbia's Dead-End Kids* (1990). *Rolling Stone* declared *Teenage Wasteland* "the best book on youth culture," and it is a required reading for university course lists in several disciplines. Gaines is a journalist, cultural sociologist, and New York State certified social worker. An international expert on youth violence and culture, Gaines has been in-terviewed extensively in newspapers, for documentaries, on radio and on television. Professor Gaines also has taught sociology at Barnard College of Columbia University and at the Graduate Faculty of New School University.

This excerpt is an example of sociological research that employs C. Wright Mills' sociological imagination and, specifically, his distinction between personal troubles and public issues. As Gaines illustrates, when one teenager commits suicide it is a personal tragedy, but when groups of teenagers form a suicide pact and successfully carry it out, suicide becomes a matter of public concern. In order to explain adequately why this incident occurred, Gaines examines both the history and the biography of suburban teens.

In Bergenfield, New Jersey, on the morning of March 11, 1987, the bodies of four teenagers were discovered inside a 1977 rust-colored Chevrolet Camaro. The car, which belonged to Thomas Olton, was parked in an unused garage in the Foster Village garden apartment complex, behind the Foster Village Shopping Center. Two sisters, Lisa and Cheryl Burress, and their friends, Thomas Rizzo and Thomas Olton, had died of carbon monoxide poisoning.

Lisa was 16, Cheryl was 17, and the boys were 19—they were suburban teens, turnpike kids like the ones in the town I live in. And thinking about them made me remember how it felt being a teenager too. I was horrified that it had come to this. I believed I understood why they did it, although it wasn't a feeling I could have put into words.

You could tell from the newspapers that they were rock and roll kids. The police had found a cassette tape cover of AC/DC's *If You Want Blood, You've Got It* near the bodies. Their friends were described as kids who listened to thrash metal, had shaggy haircuts, wore lots of black and leather. "Dropouts," "druggies," the papers called them. Teenage suburban rockers whose lives revolved around their favorite bands and their friends. Youths who barely got by in school and at home and who did not impress authority figures in any remarkable way. Except as fuck-ups.

My friends, most of whom were born in the 1950s, felt the same way about the kids everyone called "burnouts." On the weekend following the suicides, a friend's band, the Grinders, were playing at My Father's Place, a Long Island club. That night the guys dedicated a song, "The Kids in the Basement," to the four teens from Bergenfield—"This is for the suicide kids." In the weeks following the suicide pact, a number of bands in the tri-state area also dedicated songs to them. Their deaths had hit close to home. . . .

A week or two after the suicide pact, *The Village Voice* assigned me to go to Bergenfield. Now this was not a story I would've volunteered for. . . . But one day my editor at the *Voice* called to ask if I wanted to go to Bergenfield. She knew my background—that I knew suburbia, that I could talk to kids. By now I fully embraced the sociologist's ethical commitment to the "rights of the researched," and the social worker's vow of client confidentiality. As far as suicidal teenagers were concerned, I felt that if I couldn't help them, I didn't want to bother them.

But I was really pissed off at what I kept reading. How people in Bergenfield openly referred to the four kids as "troubled losers." Even after they were dead, nobody cut them any slack. "Burnouts," "druggies," "dropouts." Something was wrong. So I took the opportunity.

From the beginning, I believed that the Bergenfield suicides symbolized a tragic defeat for young people. Something was happening in the larger society that was not yet comprehended. Scholars spoke ominously of "the postmodern condition," "societal upheaval," "decay," "anomie." Meanwhile, American kids kept losing ground, showing all the symptoms of societal neglect. Many were left to fend for themselves, often with little success. The news got worse. Teenage suicides continued, and still nobody seemed to be getting the point.

Now, in trying to understand this event, I might have continued working within the established discourse on teenage suicide. I might have carried on the tradition of obscuring the bigger picture, psychologizing the Bergenfield suicide pact, interviewing the parents of the four youths, hounding their friends for the gory details. I might have spent my time probing school records, tracking down their teachers and shrinks for insights, focusing on their personal histories and intimate relationships. I might have searched out the individual motivations behind the words left in the note written and signed by each youth on the brown paper bag found with their bodies on March 11. But I did not.

Because the world has changed for today's kids. We also engaged in activities that adults called self-destructive. But for my generation, "doing it" meant having sex; for them, it means committing suicide.

"Teenage suicide" was a virtually nonexistent category prior to 1960. But between 1950 and 1980 it nearly tripled, and at the time of the Bergenfield suicide pact it was described as the second leading cause of death among America's young people; "accidents" were the first. The actual suicide rate among people aged 15 to 24—the statistical category for teenage suicide—is estimated to be even higher, underreported because of social stigma. Then there are the murky numbers derived from drug overdoses and car crashes, recorded as accidents. To date, there are more than 5,000 teen suicides annually, accounting for 12 percent of youth mortalities. An estimated 400,000 adolescents attempt suicide each year. While youth suicide rates leveled off by 1980, by mid-decade they began to increase again. Although they remained lower than adult suicide rates, the acceleration at which youth suicide rates increased was alarming. By 1987, we had books and articles detailing "copycat" and "cluster" suicides. Teenage suicide was now described as an epidemic.

Authors, experts, and scholars compiled the lists of kids' names, ages, dates, and possible motives. They generated predictive models: Rural and suburban white kids do it more often. Black kids in America's urban teenage wastelands are more likely to kill each other. Increasingly, alcohol and drugs are involved. In some cases, adults have tried to identify the instigating factor as a lyric or a song—Judas Priest, Ozzy Osbourne. Or else a popular film about the subject—the suicide of a celebrity; too much media attention or not enough.

Some kids do it violently: drowning, hanging, slashing, jumping, or crashing. Firearms are still the most popular. Others prefer to go out more peacefully, by gas or drug overdose. Boys do it more than girls, though girls try it more often than boys. And it does not seem to matter if kids are rich or poor.

Throughout the 1980s, teenage suicide clusters appeared across the country—six or seven deaths, sometimes more, in a short period of time in a single community. In the boomtown of Plano, Texas. The fading factory town of Leominster, Massachusetts. At Bryan High School in a white, working-class suburb of Omaha, Nebraska. A series of domino suicides among Arapaho Indian youths at the Wind River Reservation in Wyoming. Six youth suicides in the county of Westchester, New York, in 1984; five in 1985 and seven in 1986.

Sometimes they were close friends who died together in pacts of two. In other cases, one followed shortly after the other, unable to survive apart. Then there were strangers who died alone, in separate incidents timed closely together.

The Bergenfield suicide pact of March 11 was alternately termed a "multiple-death pact," a "quadruple suicide," or simply a "pact," depending on where you read about it. Some people actually called it a *mass* suicide because the Bergenfield case reminded them of Jonestown, Guyana, in 1978, where over 900 followers of Jim Jones poisoned themselves, fearing their community would be destroyed.

As experts speculated over the deaths in Bergenfield, none could recall a teenage suicide pact involving four people dying together; *it was historically unique.*

I wondered, did the "burnouts" see themselves as a community under siege? Like Jim Jones' people, or the 960 Jews at Masada who jumped to their deaths rather than face defeat at the hands of the Romans? Were the "burnouts" of Bergenfield choosing death over surrender? Surrender to what? Were they martyrs? If so, what was their common cause?

Because the suicide pact was a *collective act,* it warrants a social explanation—a portrait of the "burnouts" in Bergenfield as actors within a particular social landscape.

For a long time now, the discourse of teenage suicide has been dominated by atomizing psychological and medical models. And so the larger picture of American youth as members of a distinctive generation with a unique collective biography, emerging at a particular moment in history, has been lost.

The starting-off point for this research, then, is a teenage suicide pact in an "upper-poor" white ethnic suburb in northern New Jersey. But, of course, the story did not begin and will not end in Bergenfield.

Yes, there were specific sociocultural patterns operating in Bergenfield through which a teenage suicide pact became objectively possible. Yes, there were particular conditions which influenced how the town reacted to the event. Yes, there were reasons—that unique constellation of circumstances congealed in the lives of the four youths in the years, weeks, and days prior to March 11—that made suicide seem like their best alternative.

Given the four youths' personal histories, their losses, their failures, their shattered dreams, the motivation to die in this way seems transparent. Yet, after the suicide pact, in towns across the country, on television and in the press, people asked, "Why did they do it?" But I went to Bergenfield with other questions.

This was a suicide pact that involved close friends who were by no accounts obsessed, star-crossed lovers. What would make four people want to die together? Why would they ask, in their collective suicide note, to be waked and buried together? Were they part of a suicide cult?

If not, what was the nature of the *social* bond that tied them so closely? What could be so intimately binding that in the early morning hours of March 11 not one of them could stop, step back from the pact they had made to say, "Wait, I can't do this"? Who were these kids that everybody called "burnouts"?

"Greasers," "hoods," "beats," "freaks," "hippies," "punks." From the 1950s onward, these groups have signified young people's refusal to cooperate. In the social order of the American high school, teens are expected to do what they are told—make the grade, win the prize, play the game. Kids who refuse have always found something else to do. Sometimes it kills them; sometimes it sets them free.

In the 1980s, as before, high school kids at the top were the "preps," "jocks," or "brains," depending on the region. In white suburban high schools in towns like Bergenfield, the "burnouts" are often the kids near the bottom—academically, economically, and socially.

To outsiders, they look tough, scruffy, poor, wild. Uninvolved in and unimpressed by convention, they create an alternative world, a retreat, a refuge. Some burnouts are proud; they "wave their freak flags high." They call themselves burnouts to flaunt their break with the existing order, as a form of resistance, a statement of refusal.

But the meaning changes when "burnout" is hurled by an outsider. Then it hurts. It's an insult. Everyone knows you don't call somebody a burnout to their face unless you are looking for a fight. At that point, the word becomes synonymous with "troubled loser," "druggie"—all the things the press and some residents of the town called the four kids who died together in Tommy Olton's Camaro.

How did kids in Bergenfield *become* "burnouts," I wondered. At what point were they identified as outcasts? Was this a labeling process or one of self-selection? What kinds of lives did they have? What resources were available for them? What choices did they have? What ties did these kids have to the world outside Bergenfield? Where did their particular subculture come from? Why in the 1980s, the Reagan years, in white, suburban America?

What were their hopes and fears? What did heavy metal, Satan, suicide, and long hair mean to them? Who were their heroes, their gods? What saved them and what betrayed them in the long, cold night?

And what was this "something evil in the air" that people spoke about? Were the kids in Bergenfield "possessed"? Was the suicide pact an act of cowardice by four "losers," or the final refuge of kids helplessly and hopelessly trapped? How different was Bergenfield from other towns?

Could kids be labeled to death? How much power did these labels have? I wanted to meet other kids in Bergenfield who were identified as "burnouts" to find out what it felt like to carry these labels. I wanted to understand the existential situation they operated in—not simply as hapless losers, helpless victims, or tragic martyrs, but also as *historical actors* determined in their choices, resistant, defiant.

Because the suicide pact in Bergenfield seemed to be a symptom of something larger, a metaphor for something more universal, I moved on from there to other towns. For almost two years I spent my time reading thrash magazines, seeing shows, and hanging out with "burnouts" and "dirtbags" as well as kids who slip through such labels. . . .

From the beginning, I decided I didn't want to dwell too much on the negatives. I wanted to understand how alienated kids survived, as well as how they were defeated. How did they maintain their humanity against what I now felt were impossible odds? I wondered. What keeps young people together when the world they are told to trust no longer seems to work? What motivates them to be decent human beings when nobody seems to respect them or take them seriously? . . .

Joe's[1] been up for more than a day already. He's fried, his clothes are getting crusty, and he points to his armpits and says he smells (he doesn't). He's broke, he misses his girlfriend. He says he can't make it without someone. His girlfriend dumped him last year. He's gone out with other girls, but it's not the same. And he knows he can't win in this town. He's got a bad name. What's the use. He's tried it at least six times. Once he gashed at his vein with an Army knife he picked up in Times Square. He strokes the scars.

Tonight, he says, he's going to a Bible study class. Some girl he met invited him. Shows me a God pamphlet, inspirational literature. He doesn't want anyone to know about this, though. He thought the Jesus girl was nice. He's meeting her at seven. Bobby comes back in the room with Nicky, looking for cigarettes.

Later in the living room Joe teases Doreen. Poking at her, he gets rough. Bobby monitors him. "Calm down, Joe." We are just sitting around playing music, smoking cigarettes. Fooling around. "Did you see those Jesus freaks down at Cooper's Pond the other day?" Randy laughs. Nicky tells Joe to forget it. Jesus chicks won't just go with you; you have to date them for a long time, pretend you're serious about them. They don't fuck you right away. "It's not worth the bother."

Suicide comes up again. Joan and Susie have razor scars. The guys make Susie show me her freshly bandaged wrists. I look at her. She's such a beautiful girl. She's sitting there with her boyfriend, Randy, just fooling around. I ask her quietly, "Why are you doing this?" She smiles at me seductively. She doesn't say anything. What the fuck is this, erotic? Kicks? Romantic? I feel cold panic.

Nicky slashed his wrists when his old girlfriend moved out of state. His scars are much older. I motion to him about Susie. Discreetly he says, "It's best just to ignore it, don't pay too much attention." Throughout the afternoon I try every trick I know to get Susie to talk to me. She won't. She's shy, quiet; she's all inside herself.

And I really don't want to push too hard. The kids say they're already going nuts from all the suicide-prevention stuff. You can't panic. But I have to figure out if this is a cult, a fad, a hobby, or something I'm supposed to report to the police. I'm afraid to leave.

I wonder, do they know the difference between vertical and horizontal cuts? Don't their parents, their teachers, the cops, and neighbors see this shit going on? Maybe they feel as confused as I do. Maybe this is why they didn't see it coming here, and in the other towns. You can't exactly go around strip-searching teenagers to see if they have slash wounds. . . .

After the suicide pact, parents complained that the kids really did need somewhere to go when school let out. The after-school activities were limited to academics, sports, or organized school clubs. Even with part-time after-school jobs, a number of the town's young people did not find the conventional activities offered by the town particularly intriguing.

But according to established adult reasoning, if you didn't get absorbed into the legitimate, established routine of social activity, you'd be left to burn out on street corners, killing time, getting wasted. It was impossible for anyone to imagine any autonomous activity that nonconforming youth en masse might enjoy that would not be self-destructive, potentially criminal, or meaningless.

Parents understood that the lack of "anything to do" often led to drug and alcohol abuse. Such concerns were aired at the volatile meeting in the auditorium of Bergenfield High School. It was agreed that the kids' complaint of "no place to go" had to be taken seriously. Ten years ago, in any suburban town, teenagers' complaints of "nothing to do" would have been met with adult annoyance. But not anymore.

In Bergenfield, teenage boredom could no longer be dismissed as the whining of spoiled suburban kids. Experts now claimed that national rates of teenage suicide were higher in suburbs and rural areas because of teen isolation and boredom. In Bergenfield, adults articulated the fact that many local kids did hang out on street corners and in parks looking for drugs because things at home weren't too good.

Youngsters have always been cautioned by adults that the devil would make good use of their idle hands. But now they understood something else: boredom led to drugs, and boredom could kill. Yet it was taken for granted that if you refused to be colonized, if you ventured beyond the boundaries circumscribed by adults, you were "looking for trouble." But in reality, it was adult organization of young people's social reality over the last few hundred years that had *created* this miserable situation: one's youth as wasted years. Being wasted and getting wasted. Adults often wasted kids' time with meaningless activities, warehousing them in school; kids in turn wasted their own time on drugs. Just to have something to do.

So by now whenever kids hang out, congregating in some unstructured setting, adults read *dangerousness*. Even if young people are talking about serious things, working out plans for the future, discussing life, jobs, adults just assume they are getting wasted. They are. . . .

For the duration of my stay, in almost every encounter, the outcast members of Bergenfield's youth population would tell me these things: The cops are dicks, the school blows, the jocks suck, Billy Milano (lead singer of now defunct S.O.D.—Stormtroopers of Death) was from a nearby town, and Iron Maiden had dedicated "Wasted Years" to the Burress sisters the last time the band played Jersey. These were their cultural badges of honor, unknown to the adults.

Like many suburban towns, Bergenfield is occupationally mixed. Blue-collar aristocrats may make more money than college professors, and so one's local class identity is unclear. Schools claim to track kids in terms of "ability," and cliques are determined by subculture, style, participation, and refusal.

Because the myth of a democratized mass makes class lines in the suburbs of the United States so ambiguous to begin with, differences in status become the critical lines of demarcation. And in the mostly white, mainly Christian town of Bergenfield, where there are neither very rich nor very poor people, this sports thing became an important criterion for determining "who's who" among the young people.

The girls played this out, too, as they always have, deriving their status by involvement in school (as cheerleaders, in clubs, in the classroom). And just as important, by the boys they hung around with. They were defined by who they were, by what they wore, by where they were seen, and with whom.

Like any other "Other," the kids at the bottom, who everybody here simply called burnouts, were actually a conglomerate of several cliques— serious druggies, Deadheads, dirtbags, skinheads, metalheads, thrashers, and punks. Some were good students, from "good" families with money and prestige. In any other setting all of these people might have been bitter rivals, or at least very separate cliques. But here, thanks to the adults and the primacy of sports, they were all lumped together—united by virtue of a common enemy, the jocks. . . .

For a bored, ignored, lonely kid, drug oblivion may offer immediate comfort; purpose and adventure in the place of everyday ennui. But soon it has a life of its own—at a psychic and a social level, the focus of your life becomes *getting high* (or *well* as some people describe it). Ironically, the whole miserable process often begins as a positive act of self-preservation.

Both the dirts and the burnt may understand how they are being fucked over and by whom. And while partying rituals may actually celebrate the refusal to play the game, neither group has a clue where to take it beyond the parking lot of 7-Eleven.

So they end up stranded in teenage wasteland. They devote their lives to their bands, to their friends, to partying; they live in the moment. They're going down in flames, taking literally the notion that "rust never sleeps," that it is "better to burn out than fade away." While left-leaning adults have valorized the politically minded punks and right-wing groups have engaged some fascistic skins, nobody really thinks too much about organizing dirts or burnouts. Law enforcement officials, special education teachers, and drug treatment facilities are the adults who are concerned with these kids.

Such wasted suburban kids are typically not politically "correct," nor do they constitute an identifiable segment of the industrial working class. They are not members of a specific racial or ethnic minority, and they have few political advocates. Only on the political issues of abortion and the death penalty for minors will wasted teenage girls and boys be likely to find adults in their corner.

Small in numbers, isolated in decaying suburbs, they aren't visible on any national scale until they are involved in something that really horrifies us, like a suicide pact, or parricide, or incest, or "satanic" sacrifice. For the most part, burnouts and dirtbags are anomic small-town white boys and girls, just trying to get through the day. Their way of fighting back is to have enough fun to kill themselves before everything else does. . . .

In the scheme of things, average American kids who don't have rich or well-connected parents have had these choices: Play the game and try to get ahead. Do what your parents did—work yourself to death at a menial job and find solace in beer, God, or family. Or take risks, cut deals, or break the law. The Reagan years made it hard for kids to "put their noses to the grindstone" as their parents had. Like everyone, these people hoped for better lives. But they lived in an age of inflated expectations and diminishing returns. Big and fast money was everywhere, and ever out of reach. America now had an economy that worked sort of like a cocaine high—propped up by hot air and big debt. The substance was absent. People's lives were like that too, and at times they were crashing hard.

In the meantime, wherever you were, you could still dream of becoming spectacular. A special talent could be your ticket out. Long Island kids had role models in bands like the Crumbsuckers, Ludichrist, Twisted Sister, Steve Vai, and Pat Benatar. North Jersey was full of sports celebrities and rock millionaires—you grew up hoping you'd end up like Mike Tyson or Jon Bon Jovi. Or like Keith Richards, whose father worked in a factory; or Ozzy, who also came from a grim English factory town, a hero who escaped the drudge because he was spectacular. This was the hip version of the American dream.

Kids who go for the prize now understand there are only two choices—rise to the top or crash to the bottom. Many openly admit that they would rather end it all now than end up losers. The nine-to-five world, corporate grunt life, working at the same job for 30 years, that's not for them. They'd prefer to hold out until the last possibility and then just piss on it all. The big easy or the bottomless pit, but never the everyday drone. And as long as there are local heroes and stories, you can still believe you have a chance to emerge from the mass as something larger than life. You can still play the great lottery and dream.

Schools urge kids to make these choices as early as possible, in a variety of ways. In the terse words of the San Francisco hardcore band MDC, "There's no such thing as cheating in a loser's game." Many kids who start out as nobody from nowhere with nothing will end up that way. Nevertheless, everyone pretends that everything is possible if you give it your best shot. We actually believe it. While educators hope to be as efficient as possible in figuring out where unspectacular students can plug into the workforce, kids try to play at being one in a million, some way of shining, even if it's just for a while. . . .

Girls get slightly different choices. They may hope to become spectacular by virtue of their talents and their beauty. Being the girlfriend of a guy in a band means you might get to live in his mansion someday if you stick it out with him during the lean years. You might just end up like Bon Jovi's high school sweetheart, or married to someone like Cinderella's lead singer—he married his hometown girlfriend and helped set her up in her own business. These are suburban fairy tales.

Around here, some girls who are beautiful and talented hope to become stars, too, like Long Island's local products Debbie Gibson and Taylor Dayne. Some hope to be like actress Heather Locklear and marry someone really hot like Motley Crüe's drummer, Tommy Lee. If you could just get to the right place at the right time.

But most people from New Jersey and Long Island or anywhere else in America don't end up rich and famous. They have some fun trying, though, and for a while life isn't bad at all.

Yet, if you are unspectacular—not too book-smart, of average looks and moderate creative ability—there have always been places for you. Much of your teachers' efforts will be devoted to your more promising peers, and so will your nation's resources. But your parents will explain to you that this is the way it is, and early on, you will know to expect very little from school.

There are still a few enclaves, reservations. The shop and crafting culture of your parents' class of origin is one pocket of refuge. In the vocational high school, your interests are rewarded, once you have allowed yourself to be dumped there. And if the skills you gather there don't really lead to anything much, there's always the military.

Even though half the kids in America today will never go to college, the country still acts as if they will. At least, most schools seem to be set up to prepare you for college. And if it's not what you can or want to do, their attitude is tough shit, it's your problem.

And your most devoted teachers at vocational high school will never tell you that the training you will get from them is barely enough to get your foot in the door. You picture yourself getting into something with a future only to find that your skills are obsolete, superficial, and the boss prefers people with more training, more experience, more promise. So you are stuck in dead-end "youth employment jobs," and now what?

According to the William T. Grant Commission on Work, Family and Citizenship, 20 million people between the ages of 16 and 24 are not likely to go to college. The "forgotten half," as youth advocates call them, will find jobs in service and retail. But the money is bad, only half that of typical manufacturing jobs. The good, stable jobs that don't require advanced training have been disappearing rapidly. From 1979 to 1985 the U.S.A. suffered a net loss of 1.7 million manufacturing jobs. What's left?

In my neighborhood, the shipping and warehousing jobs that guys like the Grinders took, hedging their bets against rock stardom, are now seen as "good jobs" by the younger guys at Metal 24. I am regularly asked to . . . "find out if they're hiring" down at [the] shipping company. Dead-end kids around here who aren't working with family are working "shit jobs."

The skills used in a typical "shit job" . . . involve slapping rancid butter on stale hard rolls, mopping the floor, selling Lotto tickets, making sure shelves and refrigerators are clean, sorting and stacking magazines, taking delivery on newspapers, and signing out videos. They are also advised to look out for shoplifters, to protect the register, and to be sure that the surveillance camera is running. Like most kids in shit jobs, they are most skilled at getting over on the boss and in developing strategies to ward off boredom. It is not unusual to see kids at the supermarket cash register or the mall clothing shop standing around with a glazed look in their eyes. And you will often hear them complain of boredom, tiredness, or whine, "I can't wait to get out of here." Usually, in shit jobs this is where it begins and ends. There aren't many alternatives.

Everywhere, such kids find getting into a union or having access to supervisory or managerial tracks hard to come by. Some forms of disinvestment are more obvious than others. In a company town, you will be somewhat clear about what is going on. At the end of the 1980s, the defense industry of Long Island seemed threatened; people feared that their lives would soon be devastated.

But the effect of a changing economic order on most kids only translates into scrambling for a new safety zone. It is mostly expressed as resentment against entrepreneurial foreigners (nonwhites) and as anomie—a vague sense of loss, then confusion about where they might fit in. . . .

So where are we going? Some people fear we are polarizing into a two-class nation, rich and poor. More precisely, a privileged knowledge-producing class and a low-paid, low-status service class. It is in the public high school that this division of labor for an emergent postindustrial local economy is first articulated. At the top are the kids who will hold jobs in a highly competitive technological economic order, who will advance and be respected if they cooperate and excel.

At the bottom are kids with poor basic skills, short attention spans, limited emotional investment in the future. Also poor housing, poor nutrition, bad schooling, bad lives. And in their bad jobs they will face careers of unsatisfying part-time work, low pay, no benefits, and no opportunity for advancement.

There are the few possibilities offered by a relative—a coveted place in a union, a chance to join a small family business in a service trade, a spot in a small shop. In my neighborhood, kids dream of making a good score on the cop tests, working up from hostess to waitress. Most hang out in limbo hoping to get called for a job in the sheriff's department, or the parks, or sanitation. They're on all the lists, although they know the odds for getting called are slim. The lists are frozen, the screening process is endless.

Meantime they hold jobs for a few months here and there, or they work off the books, or at two bad jobs at once. . . .

When he gave the eulogy at his godson's funeral, Tommy Olton's uncle Richard was quoted as saying, "When I held you in my arms at your baptism, I wanted it to be a fresh start, for you to be more complete than we had ever been ourselves, but I wonder if we expected too much. In thinking only of ourselves, maybe we passed down too great a burden."

Trans-historically, cross-culturally, humans have placed enormous burdens on their young. Sometimes these burdens have been primarily economic: The child contributes to the economy of the family or tribe. Sometimes the burden has been social—the child is a contribution to the immortality of our creed. Be fruitful and multiply.

But the spiritual burden we pass on to the child may be the most difficult to bear. We do expect them to fulfill an incompleteness in ourselves, in our world. Our children are our vehicle for the realization of unfulfilled human dreams: our class aspirations, our visions of social justice and world peace, of a better life on earth.

Faith in the child, in the next generation, helps get us through this life. Without this hope in the future *through the child* we could not endure slavery, torture, war, genocide, or even the ordinary, everyday grind of a "bad life." The child-as-myth is an empty slate upon which we carve our highest ideals. For human beings, the child is God, utopia, and the future incarnate. The Bergenfield suicide pact ruptured the sacred trust between the generations. It was a negation.

After I had been to Bergenfield, people asked me, "Why did they do it?" People want to know in 25 words or less. But it's more complicated than that. I usually just say, "They had bad lives," and try to explain why these lives ended where, when, and how they did. But I still wonder, at what point are people pushed over the line?

On the surface the ending of the four kids' bad lives can be explained away by the "case history" approach. Three of the four had suicidal or self-destructive adult role models: the suicide of Tommy Olton's father, the drug-related death of the Burress sisters' father. Tommy Rizzo, along with his three friends, had experienced the recent loss of a beloved friend, Joe Major. Before Joe, the death of three other local "burnouts." Then there was the chronic drug and alcohol abuse, an acknowledged contributing factor in suicide. Families ruptured by divorce, death, estrangement. Failure at school.

But these explanations alone would not add up to a suicide pact among four kids. If they did, the teenage suicide rate would be much, much higher. The personal problems experienced by the four kids were severe, painful, but by the 1980s, they were no longer remarkable.

For a while I wondered if the excessive labeling process in Bergenfield was killing off the "burnouts." Essentially, their role, their collective identity in their town was that of the "nigger" or "Jew." Us and Them, the One and the Other. And once they were constituted as "burnouts" by the town's hegemonic order, the kids played out their assigned role as self-styled outcasts with irony, style, and verve.

Yes, Bergenfield was guilty of blaming the victim. But only slightly more guilty than any other town. Labeling, blaming the victim, and conferring rewards on more cooperative kids was cruel, but also not remarkable in the eighties.

As I felt from the beginning, the unusually cloying geography of Bergenfield seemed somehow implicated in the suicide pact. The landscape appeared even more circumscribed because of the "burnouts'" lack of legitimate space in the town: they were too old for the [roller skating] Rink, and the Building [an abandoned warehouse taken over by the teens] was available for criminal trespass only. Outcast, socially and spatially, for years the "burnouts" had been chased from corner to parking lot, and finally, to the garage bays of Foster Village. They were nomads, refugees in the town of their birth. *There was no place for them.* They felt unloved, unwanted, devalued, disregarded, and discarded.

But this little town, not even two miles long from north to south, was just a dot on a much larger map. It wasn't the whole world. Hip adults I know, friends who grew up feeling like outcasts in their hometown, were very sympathetic to the plight of the "burnouts." Yet even they often held out one last question, sometimes contemptuously: "Why didn't they *just leave?*" As if the four kids had failed even as outcasts. My friends found this confusing. "No matter how worthless the people who make the rules say you are, you don't have to play their game. You can always walk and not look back," they would argue. People who feel abject and weird in their hometown simply move away.

But that has always been a class privilege. The townies are the poor kids, the wounded street warriors who stay behind. And besides, escape was easier for everyone 20 years ago. American society had safety nets then that don't exist now—it's just not the same anymore.

During the eighties, dead-end kids—kids with personal problems and unspectacular talents living in punitive or indifferent towns with a sense of futility about life—became more common. There were lots of kids with bad lives. They didn't all commit suicide. But I believe that in another decade, Tommy Rizzo, Cheryl Burress, Tommy Olton, and Lisa Burress would not have "done it." They might have had more choices, or choices that really meant something to them. Teenage suicide won't go away until kids' bad lives do. Until there are other ways of moving out of bad lives, suicide will remain attractive.

ENDNOTE

[1] As I promised the kids I met hanging out on the streets of Bergen County and on Long Island, "No names, no pictures." Names such as "Joe," "Eddie," and "Doreen" are fictitious, changed to protect their privacy.

3

INTERSECTION OF BIOGRAPHY AND HISTORY
My Intellectual Journey

MARY ROMERO

This selection by Mary Romero is another example of C. Wright Mills' sociological imagination. Romero is a professor in the School of Justice Studies at Arizona State University, where she teaches sociology and Chicano studies. In this excerpt, Romero explains how biography and history influenced her investigation of domestic service work done by Chicanas. In particular, she describes her research process, which involved reinterpreting her own and others' domestic service experiences within the larger work history of Mexican Americans and the devaluation of housework. Thus, this selection is from the introduction to Romero's 1992 book, *Maid in the U.S.A.*, a study of domestic work and the social interactions between domestics and their employers.

When I was growing up many of the women whom I knew worked cleaning other people's houses. Domestic service was part of my taken-for-granted reality. Later, when I had my own place, I considered housework something you did before company came over. My first thought that domestic service and housework might be a serious research interest came as a result of a chance encounter with live-in domestics along the U.S.–Mexican border. Before beginning a teaching position at the University of Texas at El Paso, I stayed with a colleague while apartment hunting. My colleague had a live-in domestic to assist with housecleaning and cooking. Asking around, I learned that live-in maids were common in El Paso, even among apartment and condominium dwellers. The hiring of maids from Mexico was so common that locals referred to Monday as the border patrol's day off because the agents ignored the women crossing the border to return to their employers' homes after their weekend off. The practice of hiring undocumented Mexican women as domestics, many of whom were no older than fifteen, seemed strange to me. It was this strangeness that raised the topic of domestic service as a question and made problematic what had previously been taken for granted.

I must admit that I was shocked at my colleague's treatment of the 16-year-old domestic whom I will call Juanita. Only recently hired, Juanita was still adjusting to her new environment. She was extremely shy, and her timidity was made even worse by constant flirting from her employer. As far as I could see, every attempt Juanita made to converse was met with teasing so that the conversation could never evolve into a serious discussion. Her employer's sexist, paternalistic banter effectively silenced the domestic, kept her constantly on guard, and made it impossible for her to feel comfortable at work. For instance, when she informed the employer of a leaky faucet, he shot her a look of disdain, making it clear that she was overstepping her boundaries. I observed other encounters that clearly served to remind Juanita of her subservient place in her employer's home.

Although Juanita was of the same age as my colleague's oldest daughter and but a few years older than his two sons, she was treated differently from the other teenagers in the house. She was expected to share her bedroom with the ironing board, sewing machine, and other spare-room types of objects.[1] More importantly, she was assumed to have different wants and needs. I witnessed the following revealing exchange. Juanita was poor. She had not brought toiletries with her from Mexico. Since she had not yet been paid, she had to depend on her employer for necessities. Yet instead of offering her a small advance in her pay so she could purchase the items herself and giving her a ride to the nearby supermarket to select her own toiletries, the employer handled Juanita's request for toothbrush, toothpaste, shampoo, soap, and the like in the following manner. In the presence of all the family and the houseguest, he made a list of the things she needed. Much teasing and joking accompanied the encounter. The employer shopped for her and purchased only generic brand items, which were a far cry from the brand-name products that filled the bathroom of his 16-year-old daughter. Juanita looked at the toothpaste, shampoo, and soap with confusion; she may never have seen generic products before, but she obviously knew that a distinction had been made.

One evening I walked into the kitchen as the employer's young sons were shouting orders at Juanita. They pointed to the dirty dishes on the table and pans in the sink and yelled "WASH!" "CLEAN!" Juanita stood frozen next to the kitchen door, angry and humiliated. Aware of possible repercussions for Juanita if I reprimanded my colleague's sons, I responded awkwardly by reallocating chores to everyone present. I announced that I would wash the dishes and the boys would clear the table. Juanita washed and dried dishes alongside me, and together we finished cleaning the kitchen. My colleague returned from his meeting to find us in the kitchen washing the last pan. The look on his face was more than enough to tell me that he was shocked to find his houseguest—and future colleague—washing dishes with the maid. His embarrassment at my behavior confirmed my suspicion that I had violated the normative expectations of class behavior within the home. He attempted to break the tension with a flirtatious and sexist remark to Juanita which served to excuse her from the kitchen and from any further discussion.

The conversation that followed revealed how my colleague chose to interpret my behavior. Immediately after Juanita's departure from the kitchen, he initiated a discussion about "Chicano radicals" and the Chicano movement. Although he was a foreign-born Latino, he expressed sympathy for *la causa*. Recalling the one Chicano graduate student he had known to obtain a Ph.D. in sociology, he gave several accounts of how the student's political behavior had disrupted the normal flow of university activity. Lowering his voice to a confidential whisper, he confessed to understanding why Marxist theory has become so popular among Chicano students. The tone of his comments and the examples that he chose made me realize that my "outrageous" behavior was explained, and thus excused, on the basis of my being one of those "Chicano radicals." He interpreted my washing dishes with his maid as a symbolic act; that is, I was affiliated with *los de abajo*.

My behavior had been comfortably defined without addressing the specific issue of maids. My colleague then further subsumed the topic under the rubric of "the servant problem" along the border. (His reaction was not unlike the attitude employers have displayed toward domestic service in the United States for the last hundred years.)[2] He began by providing me with chapter and verse about how he had aided Mexican women from

Juarez by helping them cross the border and employing them in his home. He took further credit for introducing them to the appliances found in an American middle-class home. He shared several funny accounts about teaching country women from Mexico to use the vacuum cleaner, electric mixer, and microwave (remember the maid scene in the movie *El Norte*?) and implicitly blamed them for their inability to work comfortably around modern conveniences. For this "on-the-job training" and introduction to American culture, he complained, his generosity and goodwill had been rewarded by a high turnover rate. As his account continued, he assured me that most maids were simply working until they found a husband. In his experience they worked for a few months or less and then did not return to work on Monday morning after their first weekend off. Of course it never dawned on him that they may simply have found a job with better working conditions.

The following day, Juanita and I were alone in the house. As I mustered up my best Spanish, we shared information about our homes and families. After a few minutes of laughter about my simple sentence structure, Juanita lowered her head and in a sad, quiet voice told me how isolated and lonely she felt in this middle-class suburb literally within sight of Juarez. Her feelings were not the consequence of the work or of frustrations with modern appliances, nor did she complain about the absence of Mexican people in the neighborhood; her isolation and loneliness were in response to the norms and values surrounding domestic service. She described the situation quite clearly in expressing puzzlement over the social interactions she had with her employer's family: Why didn't her employer's children talk to her or include her in any of their activities when she wasn't working? Her reaction was not unlike that of Lillian Pettengill, who wrote about her two-year experience as a domestic in Philadelphia households at the turn of the century: "I feel my isolation alone in a big house full of people." [3]

Earlier in the day, Juanita had unsuccessfully tried to initiate a conversation with the 16-year-old daughter while she cleaned her room. She was of the same age as the daughter (who at that moment was in bed reading and watching TV because of menstrual cramps—a luxury the maid was not able to claim). She was rebuffed and ignored and felt that she became visible only when an order was given. Unable to live with this social isolation, she had already made up her mind not to return after her day off in Juarez. I observed the total impossibility of communication. The employer would never know why she left, and Juanita would not know that she would be considered simply another ungrateful Mexican whom he had tried to help.

After I returned to Denver, I thought a lot about the situations of Juanita and the other young undocumented Mexican women living in country club areas along the border. They worked long days in the intimacy of American middle-class homes but were starved for respect and positive social interaction. Curiously, the employers did not treat the domestics as "one of the family," nor did they consider themselves employers. Hiring a domestic was likely to be presented within the context of charity and good works; it was considered a matter of helping "these Mexican women" rather than recognized as a work issue.

I was bothered by my encounter along the border, not simply for the obvious humanitarian reasons, but because I too had once worked as a domestic, just as my mother, sister, relatives, and neighbors had. As a teenager, I cleaned houses with my mother on weekends and vacations. My own working experience as a domestic was limited because I had always been accompanied by my mother or sister instead of working alone. Since I was a day worker, my time in the employer's home was limited and I was able to return to my family and community each day. In Juanita's situation as a live-in domestic, there was no distinction between the time on and off work. I wondered whether domestic service had similarly affected my mother, sister, and neighbors. Had they too worked beyond the agreed-upon time? Did they have difficulty managing relationships with employers? I never worked alone and was spared the direct negotiations with employers. Instead, I cooperated with my mother or sister in completing the housecleaning as efficiently and quickly as possible.

I could not recall being yelled at by employers or their children, but I did remember anger, resentment, and the humiliation I had felt at kneeling to scrub other people's toilets while they gave step-by-step cleaning instructions. I remember feeling uncomfortable around employers' children who never acknowledged my presence except to question where I had placed their belongings after I had picked them up off the floor to vacuum. After all, my experience was foreign to them; at the age of 14 I worked as a domestic while they ran off to swimming, tennis, and piano lessons. Unlike Juanita, I preferred to remain invisible as I moved around the employer's house cleaning. Much later, I learned that the invisibility of workers in domestic service is a common characteristic of the occupation. Ruth Schwartz Cowan has commented on the historical aspect of invisibility:

> The history of domestic service in the United States is a vast, unresolved puzzle, because the social role "servant" so frequently carries with it the unspoken adjective *invisible.* In diaries and letters, the "invisible" servant becomes visible only when she departs employment ("Mary left today"). In statistical series, she appears only when she is employed full-time, on a live-in basis; or when she is willing to confess the nature of her employment to a census taker, and (especially since the Second World War) there have frequently been good reasons for such confessions to go unmade.[4]

Although I remained invisible to most of the employers' family members, the mothers, curiously enough, seldom let me move around the house invisibly, dusting the woodwork and vacuuming carpets. Instead, I was subjected to constant supervision and condescending observations about "what a good little girl I was, helping my mother clean house." After I had moved and cleaned behind a hide-a-bed and Lazy-boy chair, vacuumed three floors including two sets of stairs, and carried the vacuum cleaner up and down-stairs twice because "little Johnny" was napping when I was cleaning the bedrooms—I certainly didn't feel like a "little girl helping mother." I felt like a domestic worker!

There were employers who attempted to draw parallels between my ado-lescent experience and their teenagers' behavior: they'd point to the messy bedrooms and claim, "Well, you're a teenager, you understand clothes, books, papers, and records on the floor." Even at 14, I knew that being sloppy and not picking up after yourself was a privilege. I had two brothers and three sis-ters. I didn't have my own bedroom but shared a room with my sisters. Not one of us would think of leaving our panties on the floor for the others to pick up. I didn't bother to set such employers straight but continued to clean in si-lence, knowing that at the end of the day I would get cash and confident that I would soon be old enough to work elsewhere.

Many years later, while attending graduate school, I returned to domes-tic service as an "off-the-record" means to supplement my income. Graduate fellowships and teaching assistantships locked me into a fixed income that frequently was not enough to cover my expenses.[5] So once again I worked alongside my mother for seven hours as we cleaned two houses. I earned about 50 dollars for the day. Housecleaning is strenuous work, and I returned home exhausted from climbing up and down stairs, bending over, rubbing, and scrubbing.

Returning to domestic service as a graduate student was awkward. I tried to reduce the status inconsistency in my life by electing to work only in houses from which families were absent during the day. If someone appeared while I worked, I ignored their presence as they did mine. Since working arrangements had been previously negotiated by my mother, I had limited face-to-face interactions with employers. Most of the employers knew I was a graduate student, and fortunately, most seemed reluctant to ask me too many questions. Our mutual silence served as a way to deal with the status incon-sistency of a housewife with a B.A. hiring an ABD to clean her house.

I came to El Paso with all of these experiences unquestioned in my mem-ory. My presuppositions about domestic service were called into question only after observing the more obviously exploitative situation in the border town. I saw how vulnerable undocumented women employed as live-in do-mestics are and what little recourse they have to improve their situation, short of finding another job. Experiencing Juanita's shame and disgust at my colleague's sons' behavior brought back a flood of memories that eventually influenced me to study the paid housework that I had once taken for granted. I began to wonder professionally about the Chicanas employed as domestics that I had known throughout my own life: how vulnerable were they to ex-ploitation, racism, and sexism? Did their day work status and U.S. citizenship provide protection against degradation and humiliation? How did Chicanas go about establishing a labor arrangement within a society that marked them as racial and cultural inferiors? How did they deal with racial slurs and sexist remarks within their employers' homes? How did Chicanas attempt to negotiate social interactions and informal labor arrangements with employers and their families?

An Exploratory Study

The Research Process

Intending to compare my findings with the research on U.S. minority women employed as domestics, I chose to limit my study to Chicanas, that is, women of Mexican descent born and raised in the United States. Although many women born in Mexico and living in the United States consider themselves Chicanas, my sample did not include women born outside the United States. My major concern in making this distinction was to avoid bringing into the analysis immigration issues that increase the vulnerability of the women employed as domestics. I wanted to keep conditions as constant as possible to make comparisons with the experiences Judith Rollins, Bonnie Thornton Dill, and Soraya Moore Coley report among African American women and with Evelyn Nakano Glenn's study of Japanese American women.[6] In order to duplicate similar residential and citizenship characteristics of these studies, I restricted my sample to Chicanas living in Denver whose families had migrated from rural areas of New Mexico and Colorado. All of the women interviewed were U.S. citizens and lived in Denver most of their adult lives.

I began the project by soliciting the cooperation of current and former domestics from my own family. I relied on domestics to provide entree into informal networks. These networks turned out to be particularly crucial in gaining access to an occupation that is so much a part of the underground economy. My mother, sister, and sister-in-law agreed to be interviewed and to provide names of relatives, friends, and neighbors. I also identified Chicana domestics in the community with the assistance of outreach workers employed by local churches and social service agencies. The snowball sampling was achieved by asking each interviewee to recommend other Chicana domestics as potential interviewees.

The women were extremely cautious about offering the names of friends and relatives. In most cases, they contacted the person first and only then gave me the name and telephone number. This actually turned out to be quite helpful. Potential interviewees had already heard about my study from someone who had been interviewed. They had a general idea of the questions I was going to ask and in some cases a little background information about who I was. However, on three occasions, I called women to ask for an interview and was confronted with resistance and shame. The women expressed embarrassment at being identified by their work—as a "housekeeper" or "cleaning lady." I responded by sharing my research interests in the occupation and in the relationship between work and family. I also shared my previous experience as a domestic.[7] One woman argued with me for 20 minutes about conducting research on an occupation that was low status, suggesting instead that I study Chicana lawyers or doctors, that is, "another occupation that presents our people in a more positive light." Another woman denied ever having worked as a domestic even though several women, including her sister-in-law, had given me her name as someone currently employed as a domestic.

The stigma of domestic service was a problem during the interviews as well. From the outset, it was very important for each woman to establish herself as someone more than a private household worker. Conducting non-structured, free-flowing, and open-ended interviews allowed the women to establish multiple identities, particularly diffuse family and community roles.

The interviews were conducted in the women's homes, usually while sitting in the living room or at the dining room table with the radio or television on in the background. Although family members peeked in, for the most part there were few interruptions other than an occasional telephone call. From time to time, the women called to their husbands in the other room to ask the name of a street where they had once lived or the year the oldest son had been born in order to figure out when they had left and returned to work. The average interview lasted two hours, but I often stayed to visit and chat long after the interview was over. They told me about their church activities and plans to remodel the house and asked me for my opinion on current Chicano politics. Some spread out blankets, tablecloths, and pillow covers to exhibit their needlework. They showed me pictures of their children and grandchildren, giving me a walking tour of living rooms and bedrooms where wedding and high school portraits hung. As each one was identified, I learned more about their lives.

I conducted 25 open-ended interviews with Chicanas living and working in the greater Denver metropolitan area. The most visible Chicano communities in Denver are in the low-income neighborhood located in the downtown area or in one of two working-class neighborhoods in the northern and western areas of the city. I interviewed women from each of these communities. I asked them to discuss their overall work histories, with particular emphasis on their experiences as domestics. I probed for detailed information on domestic work, including strategies for finding employers, definitions of appropriate and inappropriate tasks, the negotiation of working conditions, ways of doing housework efficiently, and the pros and cons of domestic service. The accounts included descriptions of the domestics' relationships with white middle-class mistresses and revealed Chicanas' attitudes toward their employers' lifestyles.

All of the interviewees' families of orientation were from northern New Mexico or southern Colorado, where many of them had lived and worked on small farms. Some of the women had arrived in Denver as children with their parents, others as young brides, and still others as single women to join siblings and cousins in Denver's barrios. Several women recalled annual migrations to northern Colorado to pick sugar beets, prior to their permanent relocation to Denver. In some cases, the women's entire families of orientation had migrated to Denver; in others, parents and siblings had either remained behind or migrated to other cities. Many older women had migrated with their husbands after World War II, and several younger women interviewed had arrived at the same time, as children. Women who had migrated as single adults typically had done so in the last 10 or 15 years. Now they were married and permanently living in Denver. . . .

Historical Background

After the Mexican American War, Mexicans were given the option to maintain their Mexican citizenship and leave the country or become U.S. citizens. Many reluctantly chose the latter in order to keep their homes. Although the Treaty of Guadalupe Hidalgo was supposed to guarantee land grant provisions to those who chose to remain in occupied territory, legal and illegal maneuvers were used to eliminate communal usage of land and natural resources. Between 1854 and 1930, an estimated 2,000,000 acres of private land and 1,700,000 acres of communal land were lost.[8] In the arid Southwest, small plots were insufficient to continue a subsistence-based farming economy, thus the members of the Hispano community were transformed from landowners to wage laborers. Enclosure of the common lands forced Mexicans from their former economic roles, "freed" Mexicans for wage labor, and established a racially stratified labor force in the Southwest.

As early as 1900, the Hispano farming and ranching communities of northern New Mexico and southern Colorado began to lose their population. A combination of push-pull factors conspired to force rural Hispanos off the land and attracted them to urban areas like Denver. Rural northern New Mexico and southern Colorado experienced drastic depopulation as adults left to find jobs. During the Depression, studies conducted in cooperation with the Works Progress Administration (WPA) noted the desperate situation:

> The Tewa Basin Study by the U.S. Department of Agriculture showed that in 11 Spanish-American villages containing 1,202 families, an average of 1,110 men went out of the villages to work for some part of each year prior to 1930. In 1934, only 157 men out of 1,202 families had found outside work.[9]

Migration in search of jobs became a way of life for many families. New Mexicans and southern Coloradans joined the migratory farm labor stream from Texas, California, and Mexico. World War II further depopulated the rural villages as people flocked to the cities in response to job openings in defense plants and related industries. Postwar migration from New Mexico was estimated to be one-fifth of the 1940 rural Chicano population.[10] This pattern continued in the following decades. For instance, Thomas Malone found that during the decade of the 1950s, only one of seven northern counties in New Mexico had not experienced a decrease in its former predominantly Spanish-speaking population.[11] By 1960, 61 percent of the population had been urbanized,[12] and between 1950 and 1960, an additional 24 percent left their rural communities.[13]

Perhaps because research on population movement among Chicanos has been so overwhelmingly concerned with emigration from Mexico, this type of internal population movement among Chicanos has not been well studied. What research is available has focused primarily on male workers and the relationship between urbanization and acculturation.[14] Chicanas have been either ignored or treated simply as family members—mothers, daughters, or wives, accompanying male relatives in search of work—rather than as wage earners in their own right. Nevertheless, for many women migration to an urban area made it necessary that they enter the labor market. Domestic service became a significant occupation in the experience.

Profile of Chicana Household Workers

Only the vaguest statistical data on Chicana private household workers are available; for the most part these workers remain a doubly hidden population. The reasons are themselves instructive. Domestic workers tend to be invisible because paid domestic work has not been one of the occupations recorded in social science surveys, and the U.S. Census Bureau uses a single code lumping together all private household workers, including launderers, cooks, housekeepers, child-care workers, cleaners, and servants. Even when statistics on domestics can be teased out of the census and labor data bases, they are marred by the common practice of underreporting work in the informal sector. Unlike some of the private household workers in the East, Chicana domestics are not unionized and remain outside the "counted" labor force. Many private household workers are not included in the statistics collected by the Department of Labor. The "job" involves an informal labor arrangement made between two people, and in many cases payment is simply a cash transaction that is never recorded with the Internal Revenue Service (IRS).

Governmental undercounting of Chicanos and Mexican immigrants in the United States further adds to the problem of determining the number of Chicanas and Mexicanas employed as private household workers. For many, domestic service is part of the underground economy, and employing undocumented workers is reported neither to the IRS nor to the Immigration and Naturalization Service (INS), thus making another source of statistical information unreliable. Chicanos continue to be an undercounted and obscure population. Problems with the categorization of domestics have been still further complicated by changing identifiers for the Mexican American population: Mexican, Spanish-speaking, Hispanic, Spanish-surnamed, and the like make it impossible to segment out the Chicano population.

The 25 Chicanas whom I interviewed included welfare recipients as well as working-class women, ranging in age from 29 to 68. Thirteen of the 25 women were between 29 and 45 years old. The remaining 12 were over 52 years old. All the women had children, and the older women also had grandchildren. The smallest family consisted of one child, and the largest family had seven children. The average was three children. All but one of the women had been married. Five of the women were single heads of households, two of them were divorced, and the other three were single, separated, or widowed. The married women were currently living with husbands employed in blue-collar positions, such as construction and factory work. At the time of the interview, the women who were single heads of households were financially supporting no more than two children.

Educational backgrounds ranged from no schooling to completion of high school. Six women had completed high school, and seven had no high school experience, including one who had never attended school at all. The remaining 12 had at least a sixth-grade education. Although the least educated were the older women, eight of the women under 42 had not completed high school. The youngest woman with less than an eighth-grade education was 53 years old. The 12 women over 50 averaged eight years of schooling. Three of the high school graduates were in their early thirties, two were in their early forties, and one was 57 years old. Although one woman preferred to be interviewed in Spanish, all the women spoke English.

Work experience as a private household worker ranged from five months to 30 years. Women 50 years and older had worked in the occupation from eight to 30 years, while four of the women between the ages of 33 and 39 had worked as domestics for 12 years. Half of the women had worked for more than 10 years as private household workers. Only three women had worked as domestics prior to marriage; each of these women had worked in live-in situations in rural areas in Colorado. Several years later, after marriage and children, they returned as day workers. All the other women, however, had turned to nonresidential day work in response to a financial crisis; in the majority of cases, it was their first job after marriage and having children. Some of the women remained domestics throughout their lives, but others moved in and out of domestic work. Women who returned to domestic service after having other types of jobs usually did so following a period of unemployment.

The work histories revealed that domestic service was only one of several low-paying, low-status jobs the women had held during their lives. They had been hired as waitresses, laundresses, janitors, farmworkers, nurse's aides, fast-food servers, cooks, dishwashers, receptionists, school aides, cashiers, baby-sitters, salesclerks, factory workers, and various types of line workers in poultry farms and car washes. Almost half of the women had worked as janitors in hospitals and office buildings or as hotel maids. About one-fourth of the women had held semiskilled and skilled positions such as beauticians, typists, and medical-record clerks. Six of the women had worked only as domestics.

Paid and Unpaid Domestic Work

In describing their daily routine activities, these Chicanas drew my attention to the interrelationship between paid and unpaid housework. As working women, Chicana private household workers face the "double day" or "second shift," but in their case both days consisted of the same types of tasks. Paid housework done for an employer was qualitatively different from housework done for their own families.

In the interviews, Chicanas described many complexities of domestic service. They explained how they used informal networks to find new employers for themselves and for relatives and friends. As they elaborated on the advantages and disadvantages of particular work arrangements and their reasons for refusing certain household tasks, I soon realized that these women not only knew a great deal about cleaning and maintaining homes, but they understood the influence of social relationships on household tasks. Analysis of the extensive planning and negotiation involved in the informal and underground arrangements of domestic service highlighted the significance of the social relationships surrounding housework.

Their work histories included detailed explanations of beginning, returning to, and continuing in domestic service. In the discussions, I began to understand the paradox of domestic service: On the one hand, cleaning houses is degrading and embarrassing; on the other, domestic service can be higher paying, more autonomous, and less dehumanizing than other low-status, low-skilled occupations. Previous jobs in the beet fields, fast-food restaurants, car washes, and turkey farms did not offer annual raises, vacations, or sick leave. Furthermore, these jobs forced employees to work long hours and to keep rigid time schedules, and they frequently occurred outside or in an unsafe work environment. Unlike the other options available, domestic service did have the potential for offering flexible work schedules and autonomy. In most cases, domestic service also paid much more. Although annual raises, vacation, and social security were not the norm for most Chicanas in domestic service, there remained the possibility that such benefits could be negotiated with employers. Furthermore, as former farmworkers, laundresses, and line workers, the women found freedom in domestic work from exposure to dangerous pesticides, poor ventilation, and other health risks. This paradox foreshadowed a critical theoretical issue, the importance of understanding the social process that constructs domestic service as a low-status occupation.

Stigma as a perceived occupational hazard of domestic service emerged during the initial contact and throughout most of the interviews. The stigma attached to domestic service punctuated the interviews. I knew that many women hid their paid household labor from the government, but I did not realize that this secrecy encompassed neighbors, friends, and even extended family members. Several women gave accounts that revealed their families' efforts to conceal their employment as domestics. Children frequently stated that their mothers "just did housework," which was ambiguous enough to define them as full-time homemakers and not necessarily as domestics.

Faced with limited job opportunities, Chicanas selected domestic service and actively sought to make the most of the situation. In comparison with other jobs they had held, domestic service usually paid more and offered greater flexibility in arranging the length of the workday and workweek. Although other jobs did not carry the stigma of servitude, workers were under constant supervision, and the work was similarly low status. Therefore, the women who chose domestic service over other low-paying, low-status jobs based their selection on the occupation that offered some possibility of control. Their challenge was to structure the work so as to reap the most benefits: pay, work hours, labor, and autonomy. Throughout the interviews, the women emphasized job flexibility as the major advantage of domestic service over previous jobs. Nonrigid work schedules allowed time to do their own housework and fulfill family obligations, such as caring for sick children or attending school functions. By stressing the benefits gained by doing day work, Chicanas diffused the low status in their work identities and emphasized their family and community identities. The ways in which they arranged both work and family revealed coping strategies used to deal with the stigma, and this drew me to analyze housework as a form of labor having both paid and unpaid manifestations.

The conventional social science separation of work and family is an analytical construct and is not found in the lived reality of Chicana domestics. Invariably the interviewees mixed and intertwined discussions of work and family. Moreover, the actual and practical relationships between work and family were explicit in their descriptions of daily activities: The reasons for seeking employment included the family's financial situation and the desire to raise its standard of living; earning extra money for the household was viewed as an extension of these women's roles as mothers and wives; arranging day work involved planning work hours around the children's school attendance, dentist and doctor appointments, and community and church activities; in some cases, young mothers even took their preschool-age children with them to work. The worlds of paid and unpaid housework were not disconnected in the lives of these women.

Attending to the importance of the relationship between paid and unpaid domestic work led me to ponder new questions about the dynamics of buying and selling household labor. How does housework differ when it is paid work? How does the housewife role change when part of her work is allocated to another woman? What is the range of employer–employee relationship in domestic service today? And is there a difference in the type of relationships developed by employed and unemployed women buying household labor?

The importance of attending to both paid and unpaid housework in re-searching domestic service became more apparent as I began presenting my research to academic audiences. When I read papers on the informal labor market or on family and community networks used to find work, some of my colleagues responded as women who employed domestics. Frequently, question-and-answer sessions turned into a defense of such practices as hiring undocumented workers, not filing income taxes, or gift giving in lieu of raises and benefits. Although I was aware that as working women, many academics employed someone to clean their houses, I was not prepared for scholars and feminists to respond to my scholarly work as housewives or em-ployers. I was also surprised to discover that many of the maternalistic prac-tices traditionally found in domestic service were common practices in their homes. The recurring responses made me realize that my feminist colleagues had never considered their relationships with the "cleaning woman" on the same plane as those with secretaries, waitresses, or janitors; that is, they thought of the former more or less in terms of the mistress–maid relation-ship. When, through my research, I pointed out the contradiction, many still had difficulty thinking of their homes—the haven from the cruel academic world—as someone's workplace. Their overwhelming feelings of discomfort, guilt, and resentment, which sometimes came out as hostility, alerted me to the fact that something more was going on.

Although written over a decade ago, Margaret Mead's depiction of the middle-class woman's dilemma still seems to capture the contradictory feel-ings and attitudes that I hear among feminists today.

> Traveling around the country, I meet a great many young wives and mothers who are struggling with the problem that seems to have no solu-tion—how to hold down two full-time jobs at once. . . . As I listen I real-ize how many of them—guiltily but wistfully—yearn for the bygone days of servants. . . . They are guilty because they don't quite approve of anyone's working as a servant in someone else's home.[15]

In a society that espouses egalitarian values, we can expect yearnings "for the bygone days of servants" to be experienced as a contradiction. A century ago, Jane Addams discussed the awkward feelings and apprehensiveness aca-demic women feel:

> I should consider myself an unpardonable snob if, because a woman did my cooking, I should not hold myself ready to have her for my best friend, to drive, to read, to attend receptions with her, but that friendship might or might not come about, according to her nature and mine, just as it might or might not come about between me and my college col-league. On the other hand, I would consider myself very stupid if merely

because a woman cooked my food and lived in my house I should insist upon having a friendship with her, whether her nature and mine responded to it or not. It would be folly to force the companionship of myself or my family upon her when doubtless she would vastly prefer the companionship of her own friends and her own family.[16]

In her book on black domestics and white employers in the South, Susan Tucker addresses the deeper psychological and class factors involved in hiring servants.

Most studies of domestic work maintain that the prime motivation for hiring a servant is the enhancement of the employer's image as a superior being. Yet, many women certainly must feel some discomfort, even when paying a decent wage, about the possibility of such a motivation. . . . There are many conflicting principles and traditions surrounding the employment of a socially and economically disadvantaged woman who goes daily into a wealthy home. One might feel discomfort if one were aware of any number of different types of ideas—feminist, egalitarian, religious.[17]

Domestic service must be studied because it raises a challenge to any feminist notion of "sisterhood." A growing number of employed middle- and upper-middle-class women escape the double-day syndrome by hiring poor women of color to do housework and child care. David Katzman underscored the class contradiction:

Middle-class women, the employers, gained freedom from family roles and household chores and assumed or confirmed social status by the employment of a servant. . . . The greater liberty of these middle-class women, however, was achieved at the expense of working-class women, who, forced to work, assumed the tasks beneath, distasteful to, or too demanding for the family members.[18]

Housework is ascribed on the basis of gender, and it is further divided along class lines and, in most cases, by race and ethnicity. Domestic service accentuates the contradiction of race and class in feminism, with privileged women of one class using the labor of another woman to escape aspects of sexism.

ENDNOTES

[1] The conditions I observed in El Paso were not much different from those described by D. Thompson in her 1960 article, "Are Women Bad Employers of Other Women?" *Ladies' Home Journal:* "Quarters for domestic help are usually ill placed for quiet. Almost invariably they open from pantry or kitchen, so that if a member of the family goes to get a snack at night he wakes up the occupant. And the live-in maid has nowhere to receive a caller except in the kitchen or one [of] those tiny rooms." "As a general rule anything was good enough for a maid's room. It became a catchall for

furniture discarded from other parts of the house. One room was a cubicle too small for a regular-sized bed." Cited in Linda Martin and Kerry Segrave, *The Servant Problem: Domestic Workers in North America* (Jefferson, NC: McFarland, 1985), p. 25.

[2] David Katzman addresses the "servant problem" in his historical study of domestic service, *Seven Days a Week: Women and Domestic Service in Industrializing America* (Chicago: University of Illinois Press, 1981). Defined by middle-class housewives, the problem includes both the shortage of servants available and the competency of women willing to enter domestic service. Employers' attitudes about domestics have been well documented in women's magazines. Katzman described the topic as "the bread and butter of women's magazines between the Civil War and World War I"; moreover, Martin and Segrave, *The Servant Problem*, illustrate the continuing presence of articles on the servant problem in women's magazines today.

[3] Lillian Pettengill's account *Toilers of the Home: The Record of a College Woman's Experience As a Domestic Servant* (New York: Doubleday, 1903) is based on two years of employment in Philadelphia households.

[4] Ruth Schwartz Cowan, *More Work for Mother: The Ironies of Household Technology from the Open Hearth to the Microwave* (New York: Basic Books, 1983), p. 228.

[5] Earning money as domestic workers to pay college expenses not covered by scholarships is not that uncommon among other women of color in the United States. Trudier Harris interviewed several African American women public school and university college teachers about their college-day experiences in domestic service. See *From Mammies to Militants: Domestics in Black American Literature* (Philadelphia: Temple University Press, 1982), pp. 5–6.

[6] Judith Rollins, *Between Women: Domestics and Their Employers* (Philadelphia: Temple University Press, 1985); Bonnie Thornton Dill, "Across the Boundaries of Race and Class: An Exploration of the Relationship between Work and Family among Black Female Domestic Servants" (Ph.D. dissertation, New York University, 1979): Judith Rollins, "'Making Your Job Good Yourself': Domestic Service and the Construction of Personal Dignity," in *Women and the Politics of Empowerment*, ed. Ann Bookman and Sandra Morgen (Philadelphia: Temple University Press, 1988), pp. 33–52; Soraya Moore Coley, "'And Still I Rise': An Exploratory Study of Contemporary Black Private Household Workers" (Ph.D. dissertation, Bryn Mawr College, 1981); Evelyn Nakano Glenn, *Issei, Nisei, War Brides: Three Generations of Japanese American Women in Domestic Service* (Philadelphia: Temple University Press, 1986).

[7] In some cases, it was important to let women know that my own background had involved paid housework and that my mother and sister were currently employed full-time as private household workers. Sharing this information conveyed that my life had similarities to theirs and that I respected them. This sharing of information is similar to the concept of "reciprocity" (R. Wax, "Reciprocity in Field Work," in *Human Organization Research: Field Relationships and Techniques,* ed. R. N. Adams and J. J. Preiss [New York: Dorsey, 1960], pp. 90–98).

[8] Clark Knowlton, "Changing Spanish-American Villages of Northern New Mexico," *Sociology and Social Research* 53 (1969): 455–75.

[9] Nancie Gonzalez, *The Spanish-Americans of New Mexico* (Albuquerque: University of New Mexico Press, 1967), p. 123.

[10] William W. Winnie, "The Hispanic People of New Mexico" (Master's thesis, University of Florida, 1955).

[11] Thomas J. Malone, "Recent Demographic and Economic Changes in Northern New Mexico," *New Mexico Business* 17 (1964): 4–14.

[12] Donald N. Barrett and Julian Samora, *The Movement of Spanish Youth from Rural to Urban Settings* (Washington, DC: National Committee for Children and Youth, 1963).

[13] Clark Knowlton, "The Spanish Americans in New Mexico," *Sociology and Social Research* 45 (1961): 448–54.

[14] See Paul A. Walter, "The Spanish-Speaking Community in New Mexico," *Sociology and Social Research* 24 (1939): 150–57; Thomas Weaver, "Social Structure, Change and Conflict in a New Mexico Village" (Ph.D. dissertation, University of California, 1965); Florence R. Kluckhohn and Fred L. Stodtbeck, *Variations in Value Orientations* (Evanston, IL: Row, Peterson, 1961); Frank Moore, "San Jose, 1946: A Study in Urbanization" (Master's thesis, University of New Mexico, 1947); Donald N. Barrett and Julian Samora, *The Movement of Spanish Youth* (Washington, DC: National Committee for Children and Youth, 1963).

[15] Margaret Mead, "Household Help," *Redbook Magazine*, October 1976, pp. 42, 45, 47.

[16] See page 545 of Jane Addams, "A Belated Industry," *American Journal of Sociology* 1 (1896): 536–50.

[17] Susan Tucker, *Telling Memories among Southern Women: Domestic Workers and Their Employers in the Segregated South* (Baton Rouge: Louisiana State University Press, 1988), p. 231.

[18] David Katzman, *Seven Days a Week* (Chicago: University of Illinois Press, 1981), pp. 269–70.

SOCIAL RESEARCH

4

FINDING OUT HOW THE SOCIAL WORLD WORKS

MICHAEL SCHWALBE

Most sociologists agree that the best way to learn about research is through hands-on experience gained by conducting a study. The research process, examined in the next three readings, often turns up new questions and challenges for the researcher. The first reading is by Michael Schwalbe, a professor of sociology at North Carolina State University, and is excerpted from his 1998 book, *The Sociologically Examined Life: Pieces of the Conversation*. In this selection, Schwalbe explains the advantages of utilizing systematic research

---

to study the social world. Schwalbe also summarizes the kinds of questions sociologists often ask and argues that it is important to be "sociologically mindful" whenever addressing social research.

W ithout looking up any statistics, can you say whether there are more poor black people or poor white people in the United States? A common mistake, because blacks are often represented as being poor, is to say that there are more poor black people than poor white people. But blacks make up only about 12 percent of the U.S. population. And even though the rate of poverty is higher among blacks (about 30 percent) than among whites (about 15 percent), there are so many more white people in the United States that whites still make up the majority of those living in poverty. . . . A few facts and a bit of logic make this easy to figure out.

So logical deduction is one way to know things, or to find out the implications of what we know. Much of what we know comes straight from others. It is passed on to us by parents, teachers, friends, and so on. We can also know things from personal experience or observation, from systematic research, and from mystical revelation. It is possible, too, that some knowledge is instinctive, as, for example, when an infant "knows" that it should suck on whatever is put in its mouth.

It is interesting to think about where our knowledge comes from. What usually concerns us more, however, is how to be sure that our knowledge is valid and reliable. Each source of knowledge has limitations in these respects. Part of being sociologically mindful is being aware of these limitations.

Logical deduction, for instance, is a fine way to elaborate our knowledge—except that if our *premises* are wrong, then our conclusions will also be wrong; we will simply reason our way to further ignorance. One strength of logical deduction, however, is that others can check up on our assumptions and our reasoning, and thus correct us if we go astray.

Relying on what others tell us is necessary and is often a good way to learn, but how do we know that what others tell us is right? Surely you have had the experience of being told—by a parent, teacher, or mentor—something that later turned out to be wrong. Then there is the problem of deciding between different versions of the truth that come to us from sources that seem equally credible. How do we decide who is right?

Personal experience and observation are good sources of knowledge, except that it is easy to misjudge and overgeneralize from these sources. For example, your own observations might tell you that the sun revolves around the earth, or that all Lithuanians are slobs because both of the Lithuanians you've met in your life were a bit slobby, or that there is no ruling class in the United States because you've never seen it gathered in one place, or that crime is rising because you were just robbed. The problem in each case is not that you don't know what you've seen, but that what you've seen isn't enough to support the conclusion you reached. . . .

Advantages of Systematic Research

Careful research is perhaps the best way to create valid and reliable knowledge about the state of the social world and how it works. It is the best way for several reasons. First, by using standard, widely accepted means of finding things out, we can control personal biases. If we can do this, we are less likely to mistake what we would like to be true for what is really true.

Suppose, for example, I believe that democratic work organizations are better than authoritarian ones and would therefore like to believe that they are also more efficient. My bias would be to look only for evidence that supports my belief. But if I use a standard method of assessing efficiency, and use it carefully and fairly to compare democratic and authoritarian work organizations, I will have to accept whatever I find. My bias would thus be canceled out, or at least controlled.

Second, research can get us beyond personal experience and casual observation, because to re-*search* is to look beyond what is obvious to us from where we stand. It is to look for ideas and information that might challenge the common sense that gets us through daily life. It means considering the quality and correctness of knowledge created by others, even if we find their knowledge irritating. All this can be difficult, because our usual habit is to settle comfortably into believing-that we already know what is right.

A third reason for doing research is that it lets us check up on each other. If we use methods that others agree are proper, they can look at our results and say, "Hmmm, yes, you did it right; these results must be correct." Or they can say, "Ah, you went astray here at this point, so your conclusions are not trustworthy." We can make the same judgments when others offer us knowledge they have created. In this way, by working together, we can do better at dispelling illusions and, in the long run, creating knowledge that is valid and reliable.

Perhaps you noticed that I had only good things to say about knowledge that comes from research. Does this mean that one should accept as true whatever is published in a scientific or scholarly journal? No. Knowledge from any source should be critically interrogated. Careful research is just a way to avoid problems that are common when knowledge is created in other ways. And if research is not done properly, it can yield as much foolishness as any other method.

The larger point here is that we should be mindful, to the extent we can, of where our own knowledge comes from. We can be mindful in this way by asking ourselves how we know what we claim to know. Is some piece of knowledge a result of logical deduction? (If so, have we reasoned correctly? How do we know that our premises are correct?) Is some piece of knowledge a hand-me-down from others? (If so, where did *their* knowledge come from? How can we be sure it is correct?) Is some piece of knowledge a result of personal experience or observation? (If so, are we claiming to know more than our personal experience can warrant? Is it possible that we have observed only what we want to believe is true, or that our observations have been limited in some crucial way?)

The point of asking ourselves these questions is not to arrive at a paralyzing state of doubt about what we know, but to more wisely decide how much faith to put in what we know. If we can do this, we can open ourselves to new knowledge without fear of surrendering our minds to yet another fishy belief system. Being sociologically mindful, we can get a better view of what is coming at us by way of new knowledge and where it is coming from. We can also see what is worth catching.

The Kinds of Questions We Can Ask

All attempts to create knowledge are responses to questions, and knowledge must be created in a way that suits the question. For example, if you asked, "How much does this book weigh?" the proper way to get an answer is to weigh it. How many words does it contain? Count them. Will it fly like a boomerang? Give it the right kind of throw and observe the result. These are *empirical* questions, which means that they are answerable by measuring, counting, or looking to see what happens.

But suppose you asked, "Is the cover of this book beautiful?" What then? You could ask ten artists for their opinions. What if seven said it was ugly, two were ambivalent, and one thought it was beautiful? In this case no measuring stick will settle the matter, because you have asked an *aesthetic* question—a question about what is subjectively pleasing to the senses—and aesthetic questions are not answerable with data. We can try to say why something strikes us as ugly or beautiful, tasteful or crass, but no evidence or logic will prove us right and others wrong.

Here is another kind of question: Was it worthwhile for me to write this [article], considering that I might have been doing other useful things with my time? Again, this is not an empirical question, since there is no way to get an answer by measuring, counting, or observing. It is a *moral* question, since it calls for a judgment about what is right to do. I could say why it seemed to me a good thing to write this [article], but my reasons would be based on moral precepts and on my sense of how the future is likely to unfold. There is no data I can show, no standard analysis, to prove that my answer is right. All I can do is to offer reasonable arguments.

There are also questions of *interpretation,* the most simple of which is "What does this thing mean?" Such questions often arise when we confront works of art. We might look at a painting or read a novel and wonder what the writer or artist wanted us to understand. But any fact, object, gesture, phrase, or behavior—anything that has meaning—can raise a question of interpretation.

Sometimes we can get an answer by asking for clarification. Perhaps the writer or artist can tell us what s/he meant (although writers and artists can't always fully explain what their work means). Or perhaps there is expert opinion available to help us make sense of things. Other times there might be so much ambiguity that no clear interpretation can be nailed down. All anyone can do then is to give reasons to support the plausibility of a particular interpretation.

You can perhaps see now that research is better suited to answering some questions than others. It is a good way to answer empirical questions. It can also be useful for answering interpretive questions, because we can sometimes dig up evidence that supports the plausibility of an interpretation. And although it is wise to search for ideas and information to help guide our moral and aesthetic judgments, research will not tell us which judgments are correct.

It is good to be mindful of the kind of question we are facing. Sometimes we get into fruitless debates because we are not clear about this. There is no point, for example, in trading opinions about the correct answer to a simple empirical question. Are crime rates rising? Go to the library and look up the best answer you can find. If it is the answer to an empirical question that is in dispute, we should stop disputing and go get the answer.

Interpreting the Answers to Empirical Questions

Sometimes the answer to an empirical question can create a great deal of interpretive trouble. For example, to ask "What are the rates of poverty among blacks and whites living in the United States?" is to ask an empirical question. We can look up the answers because someone else (the U.S. Census Bureau) has already done the counting and the arithmetic. As I noted earlier, the poverty rate among blacks is about 30 percent and among whites it is about 15 percent (these figures fluctuate somewhat and can also vary depending on how poverty is defined). But what do these figures mean? How can we interpret them?

I once presented these figures during a discussion of racial inequality. The class suddenly got quiet. No one wanted to comment on the meaning of the percentages. When I pressed for some reaction, a white student said, "I think no one is talking because the figures are embarrassing." Did he mean that the figures were embarrassing because they pointed out a failure to overcome racial inequality? I wasn't sure, so I asked him to be more explicit. "The figures are embarrassing," he said with some hesitation, "to black students." I was baffled by this.

After further conversation, it became clear that the student who spoke about the figures being "embarrassing to black students" saw the figures as evidence of black inferiority. His presumption was that the poverty rate of a group was an indicator of the capability of people in that group. I saw the figures as evidence of racism and discrimination. In this case, the facts about poverty rates were clear, but they did not speak for themselves. The same facts lent themselves to nearly opposite interpretations.

To support my interpretation, I might have said that in the United States, millions of people, black and white, are poor because they can't find jobs that pay a decent wage, or they can't find jobs at all. Sometimes the jobs available in an area don't match people's skills. Or else the jobs disappear when employers move factories to foreign countries where they can pay workers less. And so people can end up poor, or very nearly poor, even though they are able and willing to work.

I might have added that the higher poverty rate among blacks is a result of factories being closed down in inner cities in the North, where a lot of the black population is concentrated. It's a result of schools that do not serve black children well. It's a result of discrimination in hiring and network advantages enjoyed by whites. In some cases, part of the problem is a lack of marketable skills, but that's because access to education and training is limited, not because people's natural abilities are limited.

I might have said all this—and probably did—but was it enough to establish my interpretation as correct? Although I am sure that my statement helped some people see why the white student's interpretation was wrong, others who preferred to hold onto that interpretation could point out, correctly, that I had not really *proven*—by anything I'd said or any evidence I'd shown—that blacks were not inferior to whites. All I had done was to suggest that "black inferiority" was not a plausible explanation—if other things were taken into account, if those other things were true, and if no significant counterevidence was being overlooked.

My interpretation was not, however, a matter of opinion. My interpretation was based on previously answered empirical questions. Have jobs disappeared in areas heavily populated by blacks? Do employers discriminate against blacks? Do whites enjoy network advantages when it comes to getting jobs? Do schools serve black kids as well as they serve white kids? Is there a lack of access to education and job training? With knowledge of the answers to these empirical questions, we can determine which interpretation of the poverty-rate figures is most likely to be correct. . . .

Mindful Skepticism

Once, during a discussion of the benefits of education, a black woman said she was outraged to learn that, on the average, a high-school diploma was likely to yield higher earnings (by mid-life) for a white man than a college degree was likely to yield for a black woman. When she said this, another student, a white male said, "I don't believe it. How can you possibly know that?" Before she could answer, I said, "She probably read the article that was assigned for today. If you look on page 34 in the text, you'll see a table that shows what she's referring to." He paged through his book and found the table. After studying it for a few moments, he harumphed and said, "Well, anybody can make up numbers."

As a teacher, I was irritated by this response, because it meant this: "No matter what information I am presented with, if it does not suit my prior beliefs, if it does not make me comfortable, I will discount it, so I can continue to believe what I want to believe." An attitude like this leaves little room for education to make a dent. I wondered why this student would bother to study anything at all, or read any books at all, if he was so intent on being unchanged.

And yet I could not say that his attitude was entirely foolish. Numbers are often cooked up to mislead us, and numbers can be wrong because of honest mistakes, so it is reasonable to be skeptical of numbers, whatever the source. Is there any way to tell which numbers are right? Yes, it can be done; it just requires training. Since most people do not have such training, however, it is understandable that they might say, "I can't tell what's right or wrong, so I'm going to treat all statistics as hogwash."

This is clearly not a mindful response to the situation. It is like saying, "I can't read, so I am going to treat all books as hogwash." It would be better to learn to read and to learn also what is necessary to distinguish the hog from the wash. This is hard but not impossible. What helps is being mindfully, rather than indiscriminately, skeptical of new information.

One of the difficulties in learning about the social world is that we must rely on information created and filtered by others. We can't check out everything for ourselves, even if we know how. This being the case, we must pay attention to how information (in the form of words or numbers) is created, by whom, for what purposes. We must ask, Who stands to benefit if this information is accepted as true? Being mindful in these ways puts us on alert against fraud, yet it does not cut us off from learning.

We should also seek alternative views, since this can help us see the limits of our own knowledge. A bit of conventional knowledge—that "Columbus discovered America," for instance—seems simple and true until an alternative is suggested: "Columbus launched a brutal invasion of an already populated continent." This is not just a different way to describe the same events, but a different way of seeing what those events were. If we try out this alternative view, we can look at what passes for conventional knowledge and see that it is, at the very least, contestable.

What is conventional and what is alternative depends, of course, on where you stand. A view that you consider alternative might seem conventional to someone else. Recognizing this relativity of perspectives is part of being sociologically mindful. But there is more to it. Being sociologically mindful, we can also see that these alternative perspectives create the possibility of understanding the world more fully, because they give us more angles from which to view it.

Perhaps by looking for and seriously considering alternative views— and there are always multiple alternatives—we will eventually get closer to a better version of the truth. That is something to aim for. In the meantime, it is wise to consider alternative views because doing so can help us see how competing versions of the truth are created. In this way we can learn more about how others see the world, how we have come to see the world, and what more we might see if we are willing to suffer a bit of uncertainty.

Partial Truth and Inevitable Uncertainty

The student who said, "Anyone can make up numbers," did not want to suffer uncertainty. Perhaps he was afraid that if he let go of what he already believed, he would end up lost, not knowing what to believe. He did not know how to be mindfully skeptical.

Part of what we fear is losing what we think is the truth. If we are sociologically mindful, however, we know that we never possess the absolute, complete truth. What we have is a head full of humanly-created images, representations, and accounts that seem to pretty well make sense of the world as we know it. Why not stand ready, as we see and experience more of the world, to invent or borrow new ways of making sense?

If we can admit that there is more to the world than we have yet seen or experienced—and more than we could see and experience in a lifetime— perhaps we can also say to ourselves, "In anticipation of learning more about the world, as I surely will do, I will treat my current beliefs as provisional and explore alternative ways of making sense of things, because one of these ways might come in handy some day."

To adopt this stance toward knowledge does not mean flitting from one belief to another. It is like the deliberate movement of wading upstream in a river. To move ahead you must take gentle steps, making sure of your footing before you shift your weight forward. You must stay flexible and lean into the current. If you rush or lose concentration, you will end up all wet. So you pay attention, moving mindfully when it makes sense to move.

Being sociologically mindful, we know that we never get to the whole truth about the social world. All the truths that we invent or borrow—all the images, representations, and accounts we come upon—are partial views of a whole that is unknowable because it is always changing in ways that run ahead of our ability to understand. We thus need not fear that new ideas and information will wrest the truth from us. They might, however, give us a larger, more complex, and unruly truth to contend with, and that can be unsettling.

For some people it is scary to think of never being sure of having it right. Imagining that one has it right, now and forever, is comforting. The problem, however, is that other people see things differently, and when conflicts arise, others will neither happily conform to the version of truth that comforts us nor lay down their knowledge to embrace ours. And so, if we want to understand and get along with others, we must be willing to seriously consider their perspectives and to tolerate the uncertainty that comes with this openness.

Perpetual Inquiry and Conversation

I have been recommending a mindful skepticism toward all knowledge—that which we already possess and that which strikes us as new and strange. In this way we can avoid the dead ends of nihilism ("There is no truth. Anyone can make up numbers. You might as well believe what you want.") and fanaticism ("There is only one truth and my people know it! All other beliefs are false or insane!"). These are dead ends because they make conversation pointless and offer no hope of resolving conflict.

A mindful skepticism toward knowledge keeps us inquiring, observing, and trying to make better sense of things; it keeps us trying to create more accurate, complete, and useful representations; it keeps us open to new information; and it keeps us connected to others as we try to do all this. Conversation is both a means to this end and an end in itself—at least it is if we believe that it is better to try to understand others than to ignore or to hurt them. Be mindfully skeptical, then, of all knowledge, including that which I have offered in this [article]. After fair consideration, take and use what is helpful for making sense and for keeping the conversation going.

Curiosity, Care, and Hope

If you could live forever, would life get boring? Some people might say, "Yes, because it would be the same old thing, day after day, forever." But here is another possibility: Life would get more *interesting* because as one learned more about the world, one would see more complexities, more mysteries, more problems to be solved, and more things to be done. Why might some people see life as holding such great promise? I think it is because they are full of curiosity, care, and hope.

If there is no curiosity about the nature of things and how they work, then the world will seem like a drab backdrop against which life is endured until it is over. If there is no care about anything outside one's self or beyond one's time, then it will seem pointless to worry about things that don't matter for getting through the day. Without hope, it will seem pointless to invest much effort in analyzing the social world. So it seems that we need curiosity, care, and hope to spark a desire to pay attention to the social world, to try to understand it as it is, and to use this awareness to pursue change.

Sometimes the conditions of people's lives do not inspire much curiosity, care, or hope. There might be so much day-to-day hardship and sameness, and so few prospects for change, that people limit their attention to each day's tasks and fleeting amusements. Other people might be so comfortable that they too lose interest in critically examining the world beyond their coccoon of privilege. Under these conditions, people are not likely to develop much sociological mindfulness. Then again, perhaps the process can be turned around. Perhaps a lesson in mindfulness can spark curiosity, care, and hope.

Being mindful that the world is a complex and mysterious place, and that penetrating these mysteries is satisfying, ought to arouse our curiosity. Being mindful of how our actions affect others' experiences of joy and suffering ought to encourage feelings of care. And being mindful of how human action creates the world ought to give us hope that we can make the world a better place. Obviously these are expressions of my own wishes, yet I have tried to do more than put them forth as wishes.

I have tried to show how much there is to be curious about: the many connections, patterns, contingencies, appearances, and interdependencies that constitute the social world; all the ways that people try to solve problems together and end up creating cultural habits; the ways that some people create social arrangements to benefit themselves at the expense of others; and all the ways that people create the images, accounts, and representations that make up our knowledge of social reality. We could study these matters forever and always be learning something new.

I have also shown that sociological mindfulness gives us reasons for caring. The more we pay attention to and understand connections, interdependencies, and contingencies, the better we can see how *our* ways of thinking and acting affect *others'* chances for good lives. We can see, too, that what others think and do affects us as well. Being sociologically mindful helps us see how this is true in a way that goes beyond what is obvious in everyday life as we interact with others who are close to us.

And just as we care about the others who are close to us, we can, if we are sociologically mindful, come to care about the distant others whose lives are intertwined with ours. At the least, we can thus see new reasons for caring about the social arrangements that bind us to others, for better or worse.

Perhaps you are thinking, "What about hope? It seems that 'being sociologically mindful' just makes us aware of how messed up the social world is. How is *that* supposed to inspire hope?" Actually, mere awareness of problems—inequalities, exploitation, the suffering of others—is not supposed to inspire hope. It is supposed to inspire outrage and a desire to change things. Unfortunately, when awareness of problems is combined with feelings of powerlessness, the result is often despair.

Being sociologically mindful, however, we know that the social world is, for all its seeming solidity, a social construction. All the ideas, habits, arrangements, and so on that make up the social world are human creations. We know, too, that the social world keeps going as it does because of the beliefs people share and because of how they keep doing things together on an everyday basis. If we are mindful of all this, we can see that the problems that exist now need not exist forever; they are all within our power to overcome.

Of course it will not be easy, because many powerful people benefit from the arrangements that cause problems for so many others. There is also the problem of changing the arrangements that are devised to keep things from changing. Yet the possibility of change always exists, if only people can organize to make it happen, and that is a good reason for hope.

Mindfulness can get us out of the rut of despair by reminding us that we cannot change a society overnight by ourselves. It is silly to say, "I failed to bring about a revolution this week, even though I tried very hard. That proves it's hopeless. I guess I'll give up and just march along with everyone else." Yet many people fall into this kind of trap. The way out is through awareness that change requires working with others to challenge existing arrangements and to create new ones. We cannot do it alone.

There is no point in despairing because we cannot single-handedly change the world. Of course we can't. We can, however, try to find or organize others who recognize a need for change and are willing to work for it. It is amazing how being in community with others can help alleviate the despair that arises from failed dreams of heroism.

Sociological mindfulness also reminds us that we *can* change a small part of the social world single-handedly. If we treat others with more respect and compassion, if we refuse to participate in re-creating inequalities even in little ways, if we raise questions about official representations of reality, if we refuse to work in destructive industries, then we are making change. We do not have to join a group or organize a protest to make these kinds of changes. We can make them on our own, by deciding to live differently.

Perhaps our modest efforts will reverberate with others and inspire them to live differently. Or perhaps no one will notice, or they will notice but think we are strange. And so you might think, "If no one is going to notice that I am a superior moral being, then what is the point? Why bother to be different and risk ridicule?" That is one way to look at it. Being sociologically mindful, however, suggests a different thought: "I cannot be sure that *anything* I do will change things for the better, yet I can be sure that if I do not at least *try*, then I will fail to do what I think is right and will be contributing to keeping things the same. Therefore I will opt to do what is right, whether much or little comes of it."

In the end, sociological mindfulness must be about more than studying how the social world works. It must also do more than inspire curiosity, care, and hope—although these we cannot do without. If it is to be worth practicing, sociological mindfulness must help us change ourselves and our ways of doing things together so that we can live more peacefully and productively with others, without exploitation, disrespect, and inequality. Sociological mindfulness is a way to see where we are and what needs to be done. It is a path to heartful membership in a conversation that ought to have no end.

RELATED READINGS

Kuhn, Thomas. 1970. *The Structure of Scientific Revolutions.* 2d ed. Chicago: University of Chicago Press.

Lofland, John and Lyn H. Lofland. 1995. *Analyzing Social Settings.* 3d ed. Belmont, CA: Wadsworth.

Maxwell, Nicholas. 1984. *From Knowledge to Wisdom.* New York: Basil Blackwell.

O'Hear, Anthony. 1989. *An Introduction to the Philosophy of Science*. New York: Oxford University Press.
Thomas, Jim. 1993. *Doing Critical Ethnography*. Newbury Park, CA: Sage.
Winch, Peter. 1958. *The Idea of a Social Science and Its Relations to Philosophy*. London: Routledge and Kegan Paul.

5

INTERPERSONAL DYNAMICS IN A SIMULATED PRISON

CRAIG HANEY • W. CURTIS BANKS
PHILIP G. ZIMBARDO

Ethical questions concerning social research are a rather recent discussion in the history of social science. It was not until the 1960s and early 1970s that we began to question research protocols and the effects of social experiments on humans. This second reading in the social research section, by Craig Haney, W. Curtis Banks, and Philip G. Zimbardo, reviews the research methodology used in Zimbardo's famous prison study conducted in 1971. Zimbardo, a professor of psychology at Stanford University, was fascinated with the social dynamics of prisons, especially the social interaction that takes place between guards and prisoners. The selection below takes us inside the research world of the prison environment and reveals many ethical and logistical concerns about using social experiments to study human behavior.

Although we have passed through many periods of so-called prison "reform," in which physical conditions within prisons have improved and in which the rhetoric of rehabilitation has replaced the language of punitive incarceration, the social institution of prison has continued to fail. On purely pragmatic grounds, there is substantial evidence that prisons really neither "rehabilitate" nor act as a deterrent to future crime—in America, recidivism rates upwards of 75 percent speak quite decisively to these criteria. And, to perpetuate what is additionally an economic failure, American

Abridged from Craig Haney, W. Curtis Banks, and Philip G. Zimbardo, "Interpersonal Dynamics in a Simulated Prison," *International Journal of Criminology and Penology*, 1973, *1*. 69–97. Reprinted with permission from Craig Haney.

taxpayers alone must provide an expenditure for "corrections" of 1.5 billion dollars annually. On humanitarian grounds as well, prisons have failed: our mass media are increasingly filled with accounts of atrocities committed daily, man against man, in reaction to the penal system or in the name of it.

Attempts at explaining the deplorable condition of our penal system, and its dehumanizing effects upon prisoners and guards, characteristically focus upon what can be called the *dispositional hypothesis.* Rarely expressed explicitly, it is central to a prevalent nonconscious ideology: The state of the social institution of prison is due to the "nature" of the people who administrate it, or the "nature" of the people who populate it, or both. The dispositional hypothesis has been embraced by the proponents of the prison status quo (blaming violence on the criminal dispositions of prisoners), as well as by its critics (attributing brutality of guards and staff to their sadistic personality structures). The appealing simplicity of this proposition localizes the source of prison riots, recidivism, and corruption in these "bad seeds" and not in the conditions of the "prison soil." The system itself goes on essentially unchanged, its basic structure unexamined and unchallenged.

A critical evaluation of the dispositional hypothesis, however, cannot be made directly through observation in existing prison settings, since such naturalistic observation necessarily confounds the acute effects of the environment with the chronic characteristics of the inmate and guard populations. To partial out the situational effects of the prison environment per se from those attributable to a priori dispositions of its inhabitants requires a research strategy in which a "new" prison is constructed, comparable in its fundamental social-psychological milieu to existing prison systems but entirely populated by individuals who are undifferentiated in all essential dimensions from the rest of society.

Such was the approach taken in the present empirical study, namely, to create a prisonlike situation in which the guards and inmates were initially comparable and characterized as being "psychologically healthy," and then to observe the patterns of behavior which resulted and to record the cognitive, emotional, and attitudinal reactions that emerged.

No specific hypotheses were advanced other than the general one that assignment to the treatment of "guard" or "prisoner" would result in significantly different reactions on behavioral measures of interaction, emotional measures of mood state and pathology, and attitudes toward self, as well as other indices of coping and adaptation to this extreme situation.

Method

The effects of playing the role of "guard" or "prisoner" were studied in the context of an experimental simulation of a prison environment. The research design was a relatively simple one, involving as it did only a single treatment variable, the random assignment to either a "guard" or "prisoner" condition.

These roles were enacted over an extended period of time (nearly one week) within an environment which had been physically constructed to closely resemble a prison. Central to the methodology of creating and maintaining the psychological state of imprisonment was the functional simulation of significant properties of "real prison life" (established through information from former inmates, correctional personnel, and texts).

Subjects

The 22 subjects who participated in the experiment were selected from an initial pool of 75 respondents who answered a newspaper ad asking for male volunteers to participate in a psychological study of "prison life," in return for payment of $15 per day. Those who responded to the notice completed an extensive questionnaire concerning their family background, physical and mental health history, prior experience, and attitudinal propensities with respect to any possible sources of psychopathology (including their involvements in crime). Each respondent who completed the background questionnaire was interviewed by one of two experimenters. Finally, the 24 subjects who were judged to be *most stable* (physically and mentally) were selected to participate in the study. On a random basis, half of the subjects were assigned the role of "guard," half were assigned to the role of "prisoner."

The subjects were normal, healthy males attending colleges throughout the United States who were in the Stanford [University] area during the summer. They were largely of middle-class background and Caucasians (with the exception of one Asian subject). Initially they were strangers to each other, a selection precaution taken to avoid the disruption of any preexisting friendship patterns and to mitigate against any transfer of previously established relationships or patterns of behavior into the experimental situation.

Procedure

Role Instructions   All subjects had been told that they would be randomly assigned either the guard or the prisoner role, and all had voluntarily agreed to play either role for $15 per day for up to two weeks. They signed a contract guaranteeing a minimally adequate diet, clothing, housing, and medical care, as well as the financial remuneration, in return for their stated "intention" of serving in the assigned role for the duration of the study.

It was made explicit in the contract that those assigned to be prisoners should expect to be under surveillance (have little or no privacy) and to have some of their basic civil rights suspended during their imprisonment. They were aware that physical abuse was explicitly prohibited. Subjects were given no other information about what to expect and no instructions about behavior "appropriate" for the prisoner role. Those actually assigned to this treatment were informed by phone to be available at their place of residence on a given Sunday, when we would start the experiment.

The subjects assigned to be guards attended an orientation meeting on the day prior to the induction of the prisoners. At this time they were introduced to the principal investigators, the "superintendent" of the prison (P.G.Z.) and an undergraduate research assistant who assumed the administrative role of "warden." They were told that we were attempting to simulate a prison environment within the limits imposed by pragmatic and ethical considerations. Their assigned task was to "maintain the reasonable degree of order within the prison necessary for its effective functioning," although the specifics of how this duty might be implemented were not explicitly detailed. To involve the subjects in their roles even before the first prisoner was incarcerated, the guards assisted in the final phases of completing the prison complex—putting the cots in the cells, posting signs on the walls, setting up the guards' quarters, and moving furniture, water coolers, and refrigerators.

The guards generally believed that we were interested primarily in studying the behavior of prisoners. Of course, we were also concerned with effects which enacting the role of guard in this environment would have on their behavior and subjective states. For this reason, they were given few explicit instructions on what it meant to be a guard and were left to "fill in" their own definitions of the role. A notable exception was the explicit and categorical prohibition against the use of physical punishment or aggression, which we emphasized from the outset of the study.

The prisoner subjects remained in the mock prison 24 hours a day for the duration of the study. Three were arbitrarily assigned to each of the three cells, and two others were on standby call at their homes. The guard subjects worked on three-man, eight-hour shifts, remaining in the prison environment only during their work shifts and going about their usual routines at other times. The one subject assigned to be a standby guard withdrew just before the simulation phase began. Final data analysis, then, is based on 11 prisoners and 10 guards.

Physical Aspects of the Prison   The prison was built in a 35-foot section of a basement corridor in the psychology building at Stanford University. It was partitioned by two fabricated walls, one of which was fitted with the only entrance door to the cell block; the other contained a small observation screen. Three small cells (6 × 9 feet) were made from converted laboratory rooms by replacing the usual doors with steel-barred doors painted black and removing all furniture. A cot (with mattress, sheet, and pillow) for each prisoner was the only furniture in the cells. A small closet across from the cells served as a solitary confinement facility; its dimensions were extremely small (2 × 2 × 7 feet), and it was unlit.

In addition, several rooms in an adjacent wing of the building were used as guards' quarters (to change in and out of uniform or for rest and relaxation), a bedroom for the "warden" and "superintendent," and an interview-testing room. Concealed video recording equipment was located in the testing room and behind the observation screen at one end of the "yard," where there was also sufficient space for several observers.

Uniforms   In order to promote feelings of anonymity in the subjects, each group was issued uniforms. For the guards, this consisted of plain khaki shirts and trousers, a whistle, a police nightstick (wooden baton), and reflecting sunglasses which made eye contact impossible. The prisoners' uniforms were loosely fitting muslin smocks with an identification number on front and back. A light chain and lock were placed around one ankle. On their feet they wore rubber sandals, and their hair was covered with a nylon stocking made into a cap. Each prisoner was also issued a toothbrush, soap, soapdish, towel, and bed linen. No personal belongings were allowed in the cells. The outfitting of both prisoners and guards in this manner served to enhance group identity and reduce individual uniqueness within the two groups.

Induction Process   With the cooperation of the Palo Alto City Police Department, all of the subjects assigned to the prisoner treatment were unexpectedly "arrested" at their residences. A police officer charged them with either suspicion of burglary or armed robbery, advised them of their legal rights, handcuffed them, thoroughly searched them (often as curious neighbors looked on), and carried them off to the police station in the rear of the police car. At the station they went through the standard booking routines of being fingerprinted, having an identification file prepared, and then being placed in a detention cell. Subsequently, each prisoner was blindfolded and driven by one of the experimenters and a subject-guard to our mock prison. Throughout the entire arrest procedure, the police officers involved maintained a formal, serious attitude, avoiding answering any questions of clarification as to the relation of this "arrest" to the mock prison study.

Upon arrival at our experimental prison, each prisoner was stripped, sprayed with a delousing preparation (deodorant spray), and made to stand alone, naked, in the cell yard before being outfitted. After being given their uniforms and having an I.D. picture ("mug shot") taken, each prisoner was put in his cell.

Administrative Routine   When all the cells were occupied, the warden greeted the prisoners and read them the rules of the institution (developed the previous day by the guards and the warden). They were to be memorized and to be followed. Prisoners were to be referred to only by the number of their uniforms, in a further effort to depersonalize them.

The prisoners were served three bland meals per day, were allowed three supervised toilet visits, and were given two hours daily for the privilege of reading or letter writing. Work assignments were issued for which the prisoners were to receive an hourly wage to constitute their $15 daily payment. Two visiting periods per week were scheduled, as were movie rights and exercise periods. Three times a day all prisoners were lined up for a "count" (one on each guard work-shift). The initial purpose of the count was to ascertain that all prisoners were present and to test them on their knowledge of the rules and of their I.D. numbers. The first perfunctory counts lasted only about 10 minutes, but on each successive day (or night) they were spontaneously increased in duration by the guards until some lasted several hours. Many of the preestablished features of administrative routine were modified or abandoned by the guards, and some privileges were forgotten by the staff over the course of study.

Data Collection: Dependent Measures

The exploratory nature of this investigation and the absence of specific hypotheses led us to adopt the strategy of surveying as many behavioral and psychological manifestations of the prison experience on the guards and the prisoners as was possible. The dependent measures were of two general types: (1) transactions between and within each group of subjects, recorded on video- and audiotape as well as directly observed, and (2) individual reactions on questionnaires, mood inventories, personality tests, daily guard shift reports, and postexperimental interviews.

Data collection was organized around the following sources:

1. *Videotaping*   Using the concealed video equipment, about 12 hours of recordings were made of daily, regularly occurring events such as the counts and meals, as well as unusual interactions such as a prisoner rebellion; visits from a priest, a lawyer, and parents; parole board meetings; and others.

2. *Audio recording*   Concealed microphones recorded over 30 hours of verbal interactions between guards and prisoners in the prison yard, as well as some within the cells and in the testing-interview room.

3. *Rating scales*   Mood adjective checklists and sociometric measures were administered on several occasions to assess emotional changes in affective state and interpersonal dynamics among the guard and prisoner groups.

4. *Individual difference scales*   Prior to the start of the simulation, all subjects had completed a series of paper-and-pencil personality tests selected to provide dispositional indicators of interpersonal behavior styles—the F scale of Authoritarian Personality (Adorno, Frenkel-Brunswik, Levinson, and Sanford 1950) and the Machiavellianism Scale (Christie and Geis 1970)—and to isolate areas of possible personality pathology through the newly developed Comrey Personality Scale (Comrey 1970).

5. *Personal observations*   The guards made daily reports of their observations after each shift, the experimenters kept informal diaries, and all subjects completed postexperimental questionnaires of their reactions to the experience about a month after the study was over.

Data Analysis: Video Recordings

Special analyses were required only of the video and audio material. The other data sources were analyzed following established scoring procedures.

Since the present discussion is based primarily on the videotaped material, details of this analysis are outlined here.

There were 25 relatively discrete incidents identifiable on the tapes of prisoner–guard interactions. Each incident or scene was scored for the presence of nine behavioral (and verbal) categories by two judges who had not been involved with the simulation study. These categories were defined as follows:

- ▼ *Question* All questions asked, requests for information or assistance (excluding rhetorical questions).
- ▼ *Command* An order to commence or abstain from a specific behavior, directed to either individuals or groups. Also generalized orders; e.g., "Settle down."
- ▼ *Information* A specific piece of information proffered by anyone, whether requested or not, dealing with any contingency of the simulation.
- ▼ *Individuating reference* Positive: use of a person's real name, nickname, or allusion to special positive physical characteristics. Negative: use of prison number, title, generalized "you," or reference to derogatory characteristic.
- ▼ *Threat* Verbal statement of contingent negative consequences of a wide variety; e.g., no meal, long count, pushups, lock-up in hole, no visitors.
- ▼ *Deprecation/insult* Use of obscenity, slander, malicious statement directed toward individuals or groups, e.g., "You lead a life of mendacity," "You guys are really stupid."
- ▼ *Resistance* Any physical resistance, usually prisoners to guards, such as holding onto beds, blocking doors, shoving guard or prisoner, taking off stocking caps, refusing to carry out orders.
- ▼ *Help* Person physically assisting another (excludes verbal statements of support); e.g., guard helping another to open door, prisoner helping another prisoner in cleanup duties.
- ▼ *Use of instruments* Use of any physical instrument to either intimidate, threaten, or achieve specific end; e.g., fire extinguisher, batons, whistles.

Results

The results of the present experiment support many commonly held conceptions of prison life and validate anecdotal evidence supplied by articulate ex-convicts. The environment of arbitrary custody had great impact upon *the affective states* of both guards and prisoners as well as upon *the interpersonal processes* between and within those role-groups.

In general, guards and prisoners showed a marked decrease in positive affect or emotion, and their overall outlook became increasingly negative. As the experiment progressed, prisoners expressed intentions to do harm to others more frequently. For both prisoners and guards, self-evaluations were more deprecating as the experience of the prison environment became internalized.

Overt behavior was generally consistent with the subjective self-reports and affective expressions of the subjects. While guards and prisoners were essentially free to engage in any form of interaction (positive or negative, supportive or affrontive, etc.), the characteristic nature of their encounters tended to be negative, hostile, affrontive, and dehumanizing. Prisoners immediately adopted a generally passive style of responding, while guards assumed a very active initiative role in all interactions. Throughout the experiment, commands were the most frequent form of verbal behavior and, generally, verbal exchanges were strikingly impersonal, with few references to individual identity. Although it was clear to all subjects that the experimenters would not permit physical violence to take place, varieties of less direct aggressive behavior were observed frequently (especially on the part of guards). In fact, varieties of verbal affronts became the most frequent form of interpersonal contact between guards and prisoners.

The most dramatic evidence of the impact of the mock prison upon the participants was seen in the gross reactions of five prisoners who had to be released from the study because of extreme emotional depression, crying, rage, or acute anxiety. The pattern of symptoms was quite similar in four of the subjects and began as early as the second day of imprisonment. The fifth subject was released after being treated for a psychosomatic rash which covered portions of his body. Of the remaining prisoners, only two said they were unwilling to forfeit all the money they had earned in return for being "paroled" from the study. When the experiment was terminated prematurely after only six days, all the remaining prisoners were delighted by their unexpected good fortune; in contrast, most of the guards seemed to be distressed by the decision to stop the experiment. It appeared to us that the guards had become sufficiently involved in their roles so that they now enjoyed the extreme control and power they exercised and were reluctant to give it up. One guard, who did report being personally upset at the suffering of the prisoners, claimed to have considered asking to change his role to become one of them—but never did so. None of the guards ever failed to come to work on time for their shift, and indeed, on several occasions guards remained on duty voluntarily and uncomplainingly for extra hours—without additional pay.

The extreme reactions which emerged in both groups of subjects provide clear evidence of the power of the social forces operating in this pathological setting. There were, however, individual differences observed in *styles* of coping with this stressful experience, as well as varying degrees of success in adaptation to it. While all were somewhat adversely affected by it, half the prisoners did "endure" the oppressive atmosphere—at least in the sense that they remained until the study was completed. Not all of the guards resorted to the overt and inventive forms of hostility employed by others. Some guards were tough but fair ("played by the rules"), some went far beyond their roles to engage in cruelty and harassment, while a few were passive and rarely instigated any coercive control over the prisoners. It is important to emphasize, however, that at some time during the six days *all* guards participated in what could be characterized as sadistic treatment of prisoners. . . .

Representative Personal Statements

Much of the flavor and impact of this prison experience has been unavoidably lost in the relatively formal, objective analyses outlined in [other papers]. The following quotations taken from interviews, conversations, and questionnaires provide a more personal view of what it was like to be a prisoner or guard in the "Stanford County Prison" experiment.

GUARDS' COMMENTS

They [the prisoners] seemed to lose touch with the reality of the experiment—they took me so seriously.

I didn't interfere with any of the guards' actions. Usually if what they were doing bothered me, I would walk out and take another duty.

. . . looking back, I am impressed by how little I felt for them.

They [the prisoners] didn't see it as an experiment. It was real and they were fighting to keep their identity. But we were always there to show them just who was boss.

I was tired of seeing the prisoners in their rags and smelling the strong odors of their bodies that filled the cells. I watched them tear at each other, on orders given by us.

Acting authoritatively can be fun. Power can be a great pleasure.

During the inspection, I went to cell 2 to mess up a bed which the prisoner had made and he grabbed me, screaming that he had just made it, and he wasn't going to let me mess it up. He grabbed my throat, and although he was laughing I was pretty scared. I lashed out with my stick and hit him in the chin (although not very hard) and when I freed myself I became angry.

PRISONERS' COMMENTS

The way we were made to degrade ourselves really brought us down, and that's why we all sat docile toward the end of the experiment.

I realize now (after it's over) that no matter how together I thought I was inside my head, my prison behavior was often less under my control than I realized. No matter how open, friendly, and helpful I was with other prisoners I was still operating as an isolated, self-centered person, being rational rather than compassionate.

I began to feel I was losing my identity, that the person I call _____ *, the person who volunteered to get me into this prison (because it was a prison to me, it still is a prison to me, I don't regard it as an experiment or a simulation . . .) was distant from me, was remote until finally I wasn't that person, I was 416. I was really my number and 416 was really going to have to decide what to do.*

I learned that people can easily forget that others are human.

Debriefing Encounter Sessions

Because of the unexpectedly intense reactions (such as the above) generated by this mock prison experience, we decided to terminate the study at the end of six days rather than continue for the second week. Three separate encounter sessions were held, first for the prisoners, then for the guards, and finally for all participants together. Subjects and staff openly discussed their reactions, and strong feelings were expressed and shared. We analyzed the moral conflicts posed by this experience and used the debriefing sessions to make explicit alternative courses of action that would lead to more moral behavior in future comparable situations.

Follow-ups on each subject over the year following termination of the study revealed that the negative effects of participation had been temporary, while the personal gain to the subjects endured.

Conclusions and Discussion

It should be apparent that the elaborate procedures (and staging) employed by the experimenters to ensure a high degree of "mundane realism" in this mock prison contributed to its effective functional simulation of the psychological dynamics operating in "real" prisons. We observed empirical relationships in the simulated prison environment which were strikingly isomorphic to the internal relations of real prisons, corroborating many of the documented reports of what occurs behind prison walls. Most dramatic and distressing to us were the ease with which sadistic behavior could be elicited from individuals who were not "sadistic types" and the frequency with which acute emotional breakdowns could occur in persons selected precisely for their emotional stability.

Authors' Note: This research was funded by an ONR grant: N00014-67-A-0112-0041 to Professor Philip G. Zimbardo.

The ideas expressed in this paper are those of the authors and do not imply endorsement of ONR or any sponsoring agency. We wish to extend our thanks and appreciation for the contributions to this research by David Jaffe who served as "warden" and pretested some of the variables in the mock prison situation. In addition, Greg White provided invaluable assistance during the data reduction phase of this study. Many others (most notably Carolyn Burkhart, Susie Phillips, and Kathy Rosenfeld) helped at various stages of the experiment, with the construction of the prison, prisoner arrest, interviewing, testing, and data analysis—we extend our sincere thanks to each of these collaborators. Finally, we especially wish to thank Carlo Prescott, our prison consultant, whose personal experience gave us invaluable insights into the nature of imprisonment.

REFERENCES

Adorno, T. W., E. Frenkel-Brunswik, D. J. Levinson, and R. N. Sanford. 1950. *The Authoritarian Personality.* New York: Harper.
Christie, R., and F. L. Geis, eds. 1970. *Studies in Machiavellianism.* New York: Academic Press.
Comrey, A. L. 1970. *Comrey Personality Scales.* San Diego, CA: Educational and Industrial Testing Service.

6

NOT OUR KIND OF GIRL

ELAINE BELL KAPLAN

Social research is concerned with the definition and assessment of social phenomena. Many social concepts such as teen pregnancy are difficult to study because of stereotyping and ideological pronouncements that blame the victim for the social problem. For example, this selection by Elaine Bell Kaplan is taken from her dissertation research in which she challenges the myths of black teenage motherhood and reveals the complex interaction of social factors such as racism, social class, and gender relations that influence black teenagers to become mothers. Kaplan, an associate professor of sociology at the University of Southern California, revised her dissertation into the 1995 book *Not Our Kind of Girl: Unraveling the Myths of Black Teenage Pregnancy.* The excerpt below summarizes the ethnographic research methods Kaplan used to find and interview African American teen mothers.

"If we want to solve the problems of the Black community, we have to do something about illegitimate babies born to teenage mothers." The caller, who identified himself as Black, was responding to a radio talk show discussion about the social and economic problems of the Black

---

From Elaine Bell Kaplan. 1995. *Not Our Kind of Girl: Unraveling the Myths of Black Teenage Motherhood.* Berkeley: University of California Press, pp. xviii–xxiii, 10–26. Copyright © 1997 Regents of the University of California. Used with permission from the publisher.

community. According to this caller's view, Black teen mothers' children grow up in fatherless households with mothers who have few moral values and little control over their offspring. The boys join gangs; the girls stand a good chance of becoming teen mothers themselves. The caller's perspective captures the popular view of many Americans: that marital status and age-appropriate sexual behavior ensure the well-being of the family and the community. . . .

According to mainstream ideology, men who through hard work have moved up the career ladder and provide their families with decent food on the dinner table, clothes on their backs, and an occasional family vacation have achieved the American Dream. Women's achievements are measured by their marriage and child rearing, done in proper order and at an appropriate age. Teenage girls are expected to replicate these values by refraining from sexual relations before adulthood and marriage.

Certainly, such traditional ideas held sway over the Black community I knew. Two decades ago unmarried teenagers with babies were a rare and unwelcome presence in my Harlem community. These few girls would be subjected to gossip about their lack of morals and stigmatized if they were on welfare. But by the 1980s so many young Black girls were pushing strollers around inner-city neighborhoods that they became an integral part of both the reality and the myth concerning the sexuality of Black underclass culture and Black family values. These Black teenage mothers did not fit in with the American ethic of hard work and strong moral character. . . .

If this conservative ideology is extended to teen mothers, their situation can be explained only as a result of aberrant moral character. If Black adolescent girls fail to achieve, something in their nature prevents them from doing so. As president, Ronald Reagan often urged teenage mothers to "just say no" so that taxpayers would no longer be forced to pay for their sexual behavior. The "Just Say No" slogan invoked by the Reagan and Bush administrations in the 1980s was utilized in the 1990s by both Black and White conservatives in the attempt "to change welfare as we know it." If these politicians have their way, teenage mothers will be shunned, hidden, and ignored.

As I made my way through East Oakland and downtown Richmond [California] to interview teen mothers,* I witnessed a different scenario from the one devised by politicians. Teenage mothers are housed in threatening, drug-infested environments, schooled in jail-like institutions, and obstructed from achieving the American Dream. In our ostensibly open society, teenage mothers are disqualified from full participation and are marked as deviant. Black teenage girls aged fourteen, fifteen, and sixteen—many of them just

---

*Except when necessary for clarification, all teenage mothers and older women who were previously teenage mothers will for the sake of brevity be referred to as teen mothers—a term they use. When appropriate the teen mothers' own mothers will be referred to as adult mothers. All names and places have been changed to protect confidentiality.

beginning to show an adolescent interest in wearing makeup, dressing in the latest fashions, and reading teen magazines—are stigmatized. These teen mothers attempt to cope as best they can by redefining their situation in terms that involve the least damage to their self-respect.

Are Black teenage mothers responsible for the socioeconomic problems besetting the Black community, as the radio show caller would have us believe? Do Black teenage mothers have different moral values than most Americans? Do they have babies in order to collect welfare, as politicians suggest? Do the families of Black teenage mothers condone their deviant behavior, as the popular view contends? Or, as William J. Wilson's economic theory suggests, is Black teenage motherhood simply a response to the economic problems of the Black community? Black teenage girls confront a world in which gender norms, poverty, and racism are intertwined. Accordingly, to answer questions about these young mothers, we must sort out a host of complex economic and social problems that pervade their lives. I hope the questions I have asked and the answers given will provide portraits of real teenage mothers involved in real experiences.

The reality of these teenage mothers is that they have had to adopt strategies for survival that seem to them to make sense within their social environment but are as inadequate for them as they were for teenage mothers in the past.

These ethnographic pictures illuminate the way structural contradictions act on psychological well-being and the way people construct and reconstruct their lives in order to cope on a daily basis. One issue that comes through quite clearly in this study, and one that is often overlooked by politicians and various studies on Black teenage mothers, is that these teenagers know what constitutes a successful life. Black teenage mothers . . . struggle against being considered morally deviant, underclass, and unworthy.

If we are to understand the stories of these teenage mothers and generalize from their experiences in any significant way, we must place them within the current theoretical and political discussions concerning Black teenage mothers. As T. S. Eliot noted long ago, reality is often more troubling than myth.

What is begging for our attention is the fact that adolescence is a time when Black girls, striving for maturity, lose the support of others in three significant ways. First, they are abandoned by the educational system; second, they become mere sexual accompanists for boys and men; third, these problems create a split between the girls and their families and significant others. What is needed to understand the losses, the stresses, and the large and small violences that render such teenage girls incapable of successfully completing their adolescent tasks, is a gender, race, and class analysis. When early motherhood is added to these challenges, they become insurmountable. The adolescent mothers I saw were deprived of every resource needed for any human being to function well in our society: education, jobs, food, medical care, a secure place to live, love and respect, the ability to securely connect with others. In addition, these girls were silenced by the insidious and insistent stereotyping of them as promiscuous and aberrant teenage girls. . . .

Talking to Teen Mothers

I began my search to understand the rise in Black motherhood by interviewing two teen mothers referred to me by friends. They came to my house early one Saturday morning and stayed for three hours. Although I had prepared a series of general questions, the young women had so much more to say that I was compelled to create a more extensive set. Next, the director of a local family planning center let me attend a teen parent meeting, where I left a letter of introduction inviting those who were interested in my project to contact me. These teen mothers referred me to others. Eventually, I created a list of fifteen teen mothers.

The director of the family planning center also introduced me to Mary Higgins, the director of the Alternative Center in East Oakland. The Center operated with a grant from a large charity organization that allowed it to develop outreach programs geared to the needs of the local teenage population. These programs included an alternative school, day care, self-esteem development, parenting skills training, and personal counseling. Mary in turn introduced me to Ann Getty, a counselor at the center. Through Ann I met Claudia Wilson, a counselor for the Richmond Youth Counseling program. A short time after that meeting, I began to work as a volunteer consultant for the Alternative Center and to attend meetings with counselors and others who visited the center.

Through my contacts at the center, in the autumn of 1985 I met DeVonya Smalls and twenty of the sample of thirty-two teen mothers who participated in this study. The rest of my sample was drawn from other contacts I made in a network of community workers at the Richmond Youth Service Agency and through my work as a volunteer consultant there. The youth agency's counselors introduced me to teenage mothers who lived in the downtown Richmond area. As a consultant, I was able to talk extensively with the adolescents who took part in teen mother programs.

After several months of making contacts, losing some, and making new ones, I was able to pull together the sample of thirty-two teenage mothers. Of this sample, I "hung out" with a core group of seven teen mothers for a period of seven months, including sixteen-year-old DeVonya Smalls. The other six teen mothers who participated were sixteen-year-old Susan Carter, a mother of a two-month-old baby, who was living with her mother and sister in East Oakland; seventeen-year-old Shana Leeds, a mother with a nine-month-old baby, who was living with a family friend in downtown Richmond; and eighteen-year-old Terry Parks, a mother of a two-year-old, who was sharing her East Oakland apartment with twenty-year-old Dana

Little and her five-year-old son. The group also included twenty-year-old Diane Harris, who had become pregnant at seventeen and within months had exchanged a middle-class lifestyle for that of a welfare mother and was now living in a run-down apartment in East Oakland; Lois Patterson, a twenty-seven-year-old mother of two and long-term welfare recipient, who was living with her extended family in a small, crowded house in East Oakland; and Evie Jenkins, a forty-three-year-old mother of two, who was living on monthly disability insurance in a housing project near downtown Richmond. Like Diane Harris, Evie lost her middle-class status when she became a teenage welfare mother at age seventeen.

I accompanied these women to the Alternative Center, to the welfare office, and to visits with their mothers. Some of the teen mothers could not find private places to talk, so we talked in the back seat of my car, over lunch or dinner in coffee shops, in a shopping mall, at teenage program meetings, or while moving boxes to a new apartment—in other words, anywhere they would let me join them.

Interviewing the teen mothers on a regular basis was difficult: they frequently moved, appointments were missed, telephones were disconnected. One day I tried to call five mothers about planned participant observation sessions only to find all their telephones disconnected. A few mothers were willing to be interviewed because they thought they would benefit in some way. One mother let me interview her because she thought I had access to housing and could get her an apartment. Another thought I would be able to get her into a teen parent program. A few mothers did not bother returning my telephone calls once they discovered I could not pay them.

I did not pay the teen mothers or the others for taking part in these interviews. In exchange for their information, I told the teen mothers about my own family, gave out information about welfare assistance and teen parent programs, and drove them to various stores. I helped De Vonya Smalls move into her first apartment. I went out with the teen mothers to eat Chinese food, shared takeout dinners, and bought potato chips and sodas for, so it seemed, everyone's sisters, brothers, and cousins. I was in some homes so often that the families began to treat me like a friend.

I found myself caught up in the teen mothers' lives more than I had planned. I was able to capture changes in their lives. I watched a teen mother break up with her baby's father. I witnessed DeVonya Smalls and Shana Leeds move in and out of three different homes. I saw Shana Leeds go through the process of applying for AFDC. I sat through long afternoons with Diane Harris discussing her baby's "womanizing" father, only to attend their wedding a few months later.

I also talked to everyone else I could, including the teen mothers' mothers, Black and White teenage girls who were not mothers, teachers, counselors, directors of teen programs, social workers, and Planned Parenthood counselors. Many have definite views about teenage mothers, some representing a more conservative voice than we usually hear in the Black community.

Sadly, most of the teen mothers' fathers and their babies' fathers were not involved in their lives in any significant way. The teen mothers' lack of knowledge about the babies' fathers' whereabouts made it impossible for me to interview the men. The few men who were still involved with the teen mothers refused to be interviewed. The best I could do was to observe some of the dynamics between two teen fathers and mothers.

Personal Histories

The teen mothers' ages ranged from fourteen to forty-three. Seventeen of them were currently teen mothers (aged fourteen to nineteen), and fifteen were older women who had previously been teen mothers (aged twenty to forty-three). The presence of the two age groups enabled me to appreciate the dynamic quality and long-term effects of teenage pregnancy on the mothers. The current teen mothers brought to the study a "here and now" aspect: I witnessed some of the family drama as it unfolded. The older women brought a sense of history and their reflective skills; the problems of being a teenage mother did not disappear when the teenage mothers became adults. The older women's stories served two goals for this [study]: to show that the black community has a history of not condoning teenage motherhood, and to locate emerging problems within the structural changes of our society that have affected everyone in recent years. . . .

As a group, the teen mothers' personal histories reveal both common and not-so-common patterns among teenage mothers. The youngest teen mother was fourteen and the oldest was eighteen at the time of their first pregnancies. Seventeen teen mothers were currently receiving welfare aid. But contrary to the commonly held assumption that welfare mothers beget welfare mothers, only five teen mothers reported that their families had been on welfare for longer than five years. Twenty-four of the teen mothers had grown up in families headed by a single mother—a common pattern among teenage mothers. Thirteen reported that their mothers had been teenage mothers. Unlike other studies that focus on poor teenage mothers, this study also included five middle-class and three working-class teenage mothers whose parents were teachers, civil service managers, or nursing assistants. Nine of the teen mothers were attending high school (of whom six were attending alternative high school). Several had taken college courses, and two had managed to obtain a college degree.

Along with capturing an ethnographic snapshot of the seven teen mothers, I conducted semistructured interviews in which I asked all the teen mothers specific questions about their experiences before, during, and after their pregnancies. I asked questions about various common perceptions: the idea of passive and promiscuous teenage girls, the role of men in their lives, the notion of strong cultural support for their pregnancies, the concept of extended family support networks, and the idea that teenage mothers have babies in order to receive welfare aid. Each teenage mother was interviewed for two to two and one-half hours. I audiotaped and transcribed all of the interviews.

I transcribed the material verbatim except for names and other identifying markers, which were changed during the transcription. I coded each teen mother on background variables and patterns. I read and reread my fieldnotes, supporting documents, and relevant literature. For [my research] I chose those quotations that would best represent typical responses, overall categories, and major themes. I used quotations from the core sample of seven as well as from the larger sample of thirty-two to include a wide range of responses.

Whenever possible I have tried to capture the teen mothers' emotional responses to the questions or issues. Often a teen mother would express through a sigh or a laugh feelings about some issue that contradicted her verbal response. For instance, when Terry Parks laughed as she described her feelings about being on welfare, I added a note about her laughter because it indicated to me that she was embarrassed about the subject. Without that notation, I would not have been able to communicate the emotional intensity with which she said the word "welfare" as she talked about her welfare experiences.

Through the Ethnographic Lens

I use an ethnographic approach to provide an intricate picture of how gender and poverty dictate the lives of these young teenage mothers and how societal gender, race, and class struggles are played out at the personal level. An ethnographic approach can bridge the gap between the sociological discussion of field research and the actual field experience. Studying these women through the lens of ethnography helped me move the teen mothers' personal stories to an objective level of analysis. The ethnographic method allowed the teen mothers to express to me personal information that was close to the heart. The method also allowed me to bring these Black teenage mothers into sociology's purview, to better understand them as persons, to make their voices heard, and to make their lives important to the larger society. The interviews and observations show that Black teenage girls' experiences are structural and troublesome. At all times I have attempted to make these teen mothers' stories real and visible by presenting the teen mothers' own words with as little editing as possible and by revealing their own insights into the interlocking structures of gender, race, and class.

The Insider Interviewer

I could not walk easily into some teen mothers' lives. Being close to the people being interviewed made me both pleased and tense. Being an insider—someone sharing the culture, community, ethnicity, or gender background of the study participants—has its advantages and disadvantages. When the interviewer can identify with the class and ethnic background of the person being interviewed, there is a greater chance of establishing rapport. The person will express a greater range of attitudes and opinions, especially when the opinions to be expressed are somewhat opposed to general public opinion. The situation is more complex when interviewees are asked to reveal information that may serve the researcher's interest but not that of the group involved. "Don't wash dirty linen in public," they remind the researcher.

The most difficult questions I faced, as do most insider interviewers, had to do with the politics of doing interviews in my own community. As an insider I had to decide whether making certain issues public would benefit the group at the same time that it served my research goals. I imagine that these interviews will raise questions. How will the White community perceive Black families if I discuss the conflicts between teen mothers and their mothers, or fathers who refuse to support their children, or the heavy negative sanctioning of these teen mothers by some in the Black community? My work would be taken out of context, several people warned me.

Every Black researcher who works on issues pertaining to her or his community grapples with these questions. We think about the possibility that our findings may contradict what the Black community wants outsiders to know. Some researchers select nonthreatening topics. Others romanticize Black life despite the evidence that life is hard for those on the bottom. And others simply adopt a code of silence, taking a position similar to that of the Black college teacher who in another context made the point to me, "I'm socialized to bear my pain in silence and not go blabbing about my problems to White folks, let alone strangers."

Being an insider did not help me gain the confidence of the teen mothers and others immediately. Most were suspicious of researchers. I lost a chance to interview one group of teen mothers involved in a special school project because the counselors who worked with them did not like the way a White male researcher had treated the teen mothers previously. Indeed, these teen mothers had the right to be suspicious. What these girls and women say about their lives can be used against them by public policy makers, since the Black community is often blamed for its own social and economic situations.

But overall, being a Black woman was helpful, because eventually the teen mothers, realizing we had much in common, stopped being suspicious of me and began to talk candidly of their lives. Occasionally I could not find a baby-sitter and had to bring my little boy along. I found my son's presence helped reduce the aloofness of my role as researcher and the powerlessness of the teens' position as interview subjects. I was surprised at how helpful my son was in breaking through the first awkward moments. We made him the topic of discussion—mothers can always compare child-care problems. His presence also helped me counter some of the teenagers' tendencies to deny problems. When I talked to DeVonya Smalls about my son's effects on my own schedule, like having to get up at five in the morning instead of at seven, she relaxed and told me about her efforts to study for a test while her baby cried for attention. She also admitted to doing poorly in school.

I decided to study these teenage mothers because Black teenage mothers are not going away, no matter how much we ignore, romanticize, or remain silent about their lives. I strongly disagree with approaches that let the group's code of silence supersede the need to understand the problems and issues of Black teenage mothers. That kind of false ideology only perpetuates the myths about Black teenage motherhood and causes researchers to neglect larger sociological issues or fail to ask pertinent questions about the lives of these mothers. In the name of racial pride, then, we essentially overlook how the larger society shares a great deal of responsibility for these problems. The only way to reduce the number of teenage pregnancies or to improve the lives of teenage mothers is to understand the societal causes by examining the realities of these girls' lives. The time had arrived, as Nate Hare put it, for an end to the unrealistic view of Black lives.

PART II
Culture

7

_____

THE NEW TATTOO SUBCULTURE

ANNE M. VELLIQUETTE • JEFF B. MURRAY

Culture is defined as the shared ways of a human social group. This definition includes the ways of thinking, understanding, and feeling that have been gained through common experience in social groups and are passed on from one generation to another. Thus, culture reflects the social patterns of thought, emotions, and practices that arise from social interaction within a given society. In this reading, the first of four to explore culture, Anne Velliquette and Jeff Murray explore the social and symbolic meanings of body adornment in the new tattoo subculture. A *subculture* is defined as a system of values, attitudes, modes of behavior, and lifestyles of a social group that is distinct from, but related to, the dominant culture of a society. In particular, this ethnographic study investigates what tattoos, as cultural objects, signify for both the tattooist (the service provider) and the tattooee (the client).

In the past, what you were determined what you looked like. Today, what you choose to look like expresses who—or indeed what—you would like to be. The choice is yours.

—TED POLHEMUS

Humans are the only known species that deliberately alters its appearance through the customization of our bodies (Randall and Polhemus 1996). At the most basic level, we get up every morning and make decisions about what to wear. The customization of our bodies, however, goes far beyond the clothing we choose to wear as a "second skin" (Randall and Polhemus 1996:79). At the surface level, our skin can be tattooed, pierced, branded, scarred, and adorned with jewelry, cosmetics, and various articles of clothing. Our hair can also be creatively modified and adorned. Beyond redefining our surface appearance, we can also alter the body's actual

_____

Reprinted by permission from Anne M. Velliquette and Jeff B. Murray.

shape through techniques such as body building and plastic surgery. In all cultures, human beings spend time and effort customizing the body strictly for the sake of appearance (Randall and Polhemus 1996). This customization often involves not only time and energy, but pain and discomfort (Myers 1992; Randall and Polhemus 1996). This leads to an engaging question: Why do human beings of all cultures alter their natural inherited appearance?

In most societies, the likely reason for altering the body is that such alteration provides a vehicle for self-expression (Finkelstein 1991; Randall and Polhemus 1996; Velliquette, Murray, and Creyer 1998). Permanent as well as temporary forms of body adornment may signify a wide array of symbolic meanings. For example, permanent forms of body decoration (e.g., tattoos, piercings, and scarification) have been known to represent emblems of accomplishment, group membership, social status, personal identity, or a willingness to endure pain in order to please a lover (Bohannan 1988; Drewal 1988; Gathercole 1988; Gritton 1988; Sanders 1988; Velliquette et al. 1998). Temporary forms of body adornment also provide an invaluable means of self-expression. Our personal choice in clothing, hairstyle, body shape, and use of objects may display various identity features such as gender, status, values, interests, and a particular approach to life. Clearly, body adornment has become a way for human beings to present their desired self-image to others (Blumer 1969; Finkelstein 1991; Goffman 1959). Thus, understanding the way that individuals use nonverbal signs and symbols to construct, revise, and maintain symbolic meaning is important for the construction of self-identity.

Focusing on one type of body adornment, this article presents an ethnographic account of symbolic meaning as expressed by two segments of the *New Tattoo Subculture*,[1] the tattooist (the service provider) and the tattooee (the client). Although it is difficult to assess the number of people participating in the new tattoo subculture, it has been estimated that 12 to 20 million Americans have joined the ranks of the tattooed (Blouin 1996; Velliquette et al. 1998). This is not surprising given that in 1996, tattoo studios were among the top six growth businesses in the United States (American Business Information, Inc. 1996; Velliquette et al. 1998). During the 1990s, observers have also witnessed sharp increases in the sale of tattoo ink, books, magazines, videos, special clothing designed to show off the decorated body, and other tattoo-related odds and ends, as well as the expansion of tattoo associations and conventions, the growth of state regulations, and an increase in the number of advertisements featuring tattooed models and celebrities (Ball 1996; Blouin 1996; Krakow 1994; Peterson 1996).

Tattooing's recent popularity, as well as the increased interest in the tattoo as popular culture (e.g., Gap and Polo ads featuring tattoos, and a tattooed Barbie doll by Mattel), leads to some interesting research questions. What is it about the tattoo as a cultural object that draws people to participate in this subculture? In what ways is the tattoo used as a form of expression?

What is involved in the experience of acquiring a tattoo? What transpires during the service interaction between the tattooist and tattooee? To address these questions, we begin with a brief discussion of the literature on tattooing as an art form, its rich history, and its cultural and subcultural roots. Next, we summarize the ethnographic method used for data collection. Following this summary, we offer an ethnographic account of the tattoo subculture in order to demonstrate the symbolic nature of the act of tattooing. We draw from our own experiences and observations (including fieldwork at two tattoo studios, a tattoo museum/archive, and a tattoo convention) to illustrate ways in which the tattoo is used as a form of expression. We also consider the process itself via interactions between tattooists and their clients. Finally, we consider emergent aspects of this research that may further illustrate what has been described as the New Tattoo Subculture.

Tattooing: Yesterday and Today

Tattoo is a word loaded with rich visual associations summoning images that range from circus sideshow freaks or tribal warriors to WWII sailors, the Holocaust, street gangs, criminals, or the more recent association of media stars and athletes (Velliquette et al. 1998). With such vivid associations spanning across decades, it becomes clear that tattoos have a long and fascinating history. . . . The practice of tattooing is one of the oldest art forms discovered by archaeologists (Ball 1996; Randall and Polhemus 1996). The word *tattoo* is derived from the Tahitian word *ta-tu* meaning "to strike." A *ta* was a sharp, jagged piece of antler or bone. Different types of bones, or *tas*, were used to create different designs by tapping or pushing ink, usually made from vegetable or fruit dyes, into the flesh (Ball 1996; Randall and Polhemus 1996). Because it is usually only the bones and not the skin of our distant ancestors that remain intact, it is impossible to determine just how old the tattoo really is. The oldest irrefutable evidence of tattooing entered the archaeological record only a few years ago, when the complete body of an Iceman was found frozen in a glacier in the Alps. Some 5,000 years old, this ancient hunter's body was adorned with 15 tattoos (Randall and Polhemus 1996). In order to appreciate the history of tattooing, one must appreciate its social logic and functions.

The social-symbolic role that tattoos have played in society varies a great deal, depending on factors such as historical period, geography, economic development, innovation, and cultural diffusion. In ancient societies, tattoos, as well as other forms of permanent body modification, were most commonly associated with permanency in one's life (e.g., gender and maturity), lifelong social connections (e.g., tribe membership), or a celebrated appearance style that showed considerable continuity through dozens of generations (Randall and Polhemus 1996; Sanders 1988). The permanency of the tattoo symbolized premodern society's need for social integration, order, and stability (Randall and Polhemus 1996). . . . The current trend in tattooing has been explained as serving a number of social-symbolic roles: as a mark of affiliation to express group commitment and belonging (e.g., the logo worn by Harley Davidson riders), as a mark of personal identity (e.g., a symbol that represents a unique personal experience), as a mark of resistance (e.g., a symbol that violates consumption codes), or as a mark of identity change (e.g., a symbol that emulates a media image) (Randall and Polhemus 1996; Sanders 1988; Velliquette et al. 1998).

The recent popular interest in tattoos, along with remarkable changes in the practices and styles of tattooing, has attracted a number of new artists, some of them classically trained at prestigious art institutes (e.g., the tattoo artist Jamie Summers; see Rubin 1988:256). The role the artist/tattooist plays becomes an important part of this "Tattoo Renaissance" (Rubin 1988:233). The tattooist engages in *impression management*[2] to set the stage for an artistic service encounter. For example, the tattooist sets an artistic tone by impressing upon the client that her shop is a studio, that her work is art, and that her identity is an artist (Sanders 1989). Thus tattooists who view themselves as artists are continually engaged in legitimation talk in order to neutralize the stigma that has been historically associated with tattooing (Sanders 1989). As tattoo artists legitimize their work as art, it seems that they in turn decrease the stigma for the consumer. This increased recognition of tattooing as an art form has not only led to its development as a creative medium for some artists, it has also led to a new creative form of expression for the consumer (Rubin 1988; Velliquette et al. 1998). The consumer engages in experiential consumption, and through negotiated order with the artist, the consumer embarks upon a symbolic journey where the choice in artist, design, colors, and body location are all linked to the consumer's personal experiences and sense of identity (Sanders 1988).

In summary, a review of literature suggests two central a priori themes: *collective legitimization* and *self-identity*. These themes are not mutually exclusive, but rather are intertwined analytical categories that are useful for the framework of discovery. Further, to allow for a discussion of several aspects of interaction, several "sensitizing concepts" are introduced within each theme (Blumer 1969:147–48). . . .

Ethnographic Method and Setting

Tattooing is one topic that "demands a plunge into the waters, not a comfortable observer's beach chair at the side of the ocean" (Steward 1990:198). According to Blumer (1969) and Hebdige (1979), immersion in the field (or hovering close) produces some of the most compelling and evocative accounts of subculture and human interaction. Given the symbolic complexity associated with the artist-client interaction, the choice of design, and the act of becoming tattooed, we decided to use ethnographic interviews and participant observation as our primary data-gathering techniques.

We collected the majority of the text for this study over a six-month period in 1996. We returned to the field in 1997 for approximately two to three months in order to follow up on questions regarding support for both a priori and emerging themes grounded in the data. The text consists of over 400 pages of typed fieldnotes composed immediately after each participant observation in the everyday activities of two tattoo studios. Generally, we spent two to four hours at a time, at least once a week, in one of the studios, helping to maintain files of tattoo designs, working behind the front desk, sitting with customers as they were tattooed, assisting with some technical procedures, interviewing customers, and interviewing artists when they were not tattooing. . . . In addition to participating in the studios, we collected fieldnotes and took photographs at a 1996 national tattoo convention and two tattoo artwork museum gallery exhibitions. Further, in order to gain more historical appreciation, we traveled to the Tattoo Archive in Berkeley, California. The Tattoo Archive is a national museum of tattoo history and collectibles. We spent four days collecting relevant information and interviewing the curator.

Although the primary goal of ethnography is immersion in the lifeworlds and everyday experiences of a group of people, the researcher inevitably remains an outsider (Emerson, Fretz, and Shaw 1995). Since both "outsider" and "insider" perspectives are important in this type of research (Rubin 1988:11, n. 2), we decided to reinforce an insider's perspective by becoming tattooed. I (first author) chose a *cat* (ankle) for my first tattoo and a *butterfly* (lower front hip) for my second. . . . I carefully recorded the details of this experience in a private journal. These notes also became part of the text. . . .

Findings from the Field

As expected, we found support for many of the *collective legitimization* issues that had been discussed in previous literature on tattooing. For example, we found that tattooists often tried to convince their clients that tattooing is an art form and that "tattoos aren't just for bikers anymore" (fieldnotes January 31, 1996). The tattooists worked hard to legitimize their field of work by becoming certified, referring to themselves as artists, attending national tattoo conventions, showing their work at local art galleries, and studying other artists in the field. The artists often conversed about different tattoo artists' reputations in the field, often ranking them in terms of their favorites. . . . The artists also discussed how bored they get with customer-requested designs that do not allow them to use their creative, artistic talent. One artist referred to these simplistic, uncreative designs as "cartoon characters." This artist hated these simple designs because she felt "like a kid coloring in a coloring book. . . . Something you do when you're five years old" (fieldnotes April 15, 1997).

The artist says to me, "The owner is tired of doing the small cartoon characters like the tazmanian devil. . . . She hates doing that shit. She is into the big pieces that she can really get creative with. . . . You know, custom work." (fieldnotes April 9, 1997)

We also found that the artists worked hard to impress upon their clients that their studios were clean and met all of the health department's regulations. Several neutralization tactics were employed by the artists to change the perceptions of those individuals who viewed tattooing as deviant and tattoo shops as dirty, underground holes where deviants hung out. The following passage represents an attempt to neutralize the tattooing experience:

The male artist calls the Irish man back to the room and I stay to watch. The artist sits him down in the chair and shows him the needles that will be used. The artist tells him they are clean, new needles and that they are sealed in the bags. I ask the artist to repeat what he said and he says, "I like to let the customers see that the needles are new and sterile. I would want to see that if I were the customer." The artist then cuts open the sealed bags to get the needles out. (fieldnotes March 1, 1997)

The owners of the tattoo studios worked hard to legitimize their businesses further by creating a clinical atmosphere. For example, in the client rooms where tattooing took place, there were several glass jars on the counter filled with supplies (e.g., cotton, disposable razors, gauze), paper towels, antiseptic cleaning sprays, lotions, ointments, and tattooing equipment (e.g., guns, disposable ink trays, and ink). Some of the equipment was displayed on the wall (e.g., pliers and parts to the gun). There were also boxes of surgical gloves on the counter, a washing sink, and a hazardous waste container for disposal of needles and other infectious material. The room had an appearance similar to that of a doctor's office.

Although the tattoo artists employed these neutralization tactics, a certain amount of stigma remained, as viewed and expressed by a few informants. One informant described how he thought others would react to his tattoos in his profession: "I know it is not totally acceptable. I would catch crap if I ever showed up here in the future to teach with my tattoos hanging out. . . . They would lay down and die!" (fieldnotes April 17, 1997). Several customers stated that there are levels of social acceptance for various kinds of tattoos. One informant explained how the sun design she wanted on her hip was more socially acceptable than a skull and crossbones on a person's chest. To further illustrate the stigma associated with tattoos, we provide the following quoted passage:

I want to get it where I can cover it up. You know, so my mom won't see it. My mom hates tattoos. She lives in a place where she associates all tattoos with gang members. (fieldnotes March 1, 1997)

As discussed in the literature, collective legitimization is a process of *impression management* (Goffman 1959). Early in the ethnography, it became apparent that, in many respects, tattooists are performers. We often observed tattooists putting on a public display of professionalism. For example, tattooists often impressed upon their clients that they were artistic, friendly, and most of all technically competent and sterile. The following passage is representative of this theme:

> The artist and I continue to talk and she tells me, "I was so nervous when I had to do my first tongue piercing." She then tells me she was shaking when she did it, which made the guy nervous. Then the artist said, "You really have to pretend like you know what the hell you are doing." (fieldnotes February 15, 1997)

Within the studio setting, we observed the tattooists spending their time in two different regions: the front stage and the back stage areas of the shop. In the front stage, "permanent cosmetic/tattoo artist" certificates were hung on the wall in the lobby. The walls in the lobby area were covered with photographs of tattoos given to previous clients: the best and most unique work made the "wall." The wall attracted customers who were entering the shop and added to the credibility of the artists. Also included in the front stage region were the rooms where clients became tattooed. In the front stage region, including both the lobby and the tattoo rooms, we often observed tattooists engaging in what Goffman (1959:80) refers to as "team performance."

> The artist is finishing a large, colorful, elaborate design with a horse, clouds, and moon on a woman's arm. The artist calls the other artist in to come and look at the work. The female artist says, "This design is a dual effort between me and _____." The male artist had done the outline the week before and now the female artist was adding color. They were both happy with the results of their work. They complimented one another's artistic work (telling each other how good they were) in front of the client. (fieldnotes March 1, 1997)

Another important concept related to impression management is emotion management. The artists often managed their emotions when in the presence of clients. The artists typically refrained from displaying disappointment, anger, disgust, or impatience when interacting with their customers.

> A guy came in looking for someone to quote him a price on some touch-up work. The owner asked him where he got the tattoo done and he replied, "By a friend of mine in Oklahoma City. He is a paraplegic and he does real good work. I just don't want to have to drive to OK City to have it touched up." After he left the owner said, "He thought that was a good tattoo?" She then said, "It was hard not to laugh!! You really have to control yourself from laughing in situations like that." (fieldnotes March 28, 1997)

The tattooists usually segregated their audiences by keeping conversations like this one within the circle of the other artists. However, a few instances were observed where this segregation did not take place and customers were allowed to hear backstage talk:

> The male artist assists this time on a tongue piercing. The owner talks to the male artist about piercing and tells him the first time she did a navel, she was extremely nervous. She says this in front of the customer as if he is not there. She then says, "The only way to really practice is to just get in there and do one." The customer then asks with a nervous tone of voice, "Is this your first one?" He says this with surprise and anxiety. She said, "Oh no, I have done many, I am just saying that this is really the only way to get used to it." The male artist then tells the guy (as if to calm him down), "Everything we are using on you is sterile." The guy sits still as the two artists pierce his tongue and the client's friend and I watch. (field-notes March 19, 1997)

In the tattoo studio, the artists attempted to gain and maintain control during the service encounter by *negotiating order* (Strauss and Corbin 1990). The artists claimed that the average client's lack of experience and knowledge necessitated the need for the artist to be in control at all times to ensure a successful interaction. . . .

As we observed, most negotiations appeared to go smoothly during artist–client interactions. A working consensus was usually achieved, because most clients seemed to realize the artist's role as the expert in the situation.

> The female customer then said, "It is not the pain I am worried about. . . . I just want to know where it will look best." The owner replies, "Well, ankles are a nice place because the skin is so smooth and tight there, so it is easier to tattoo a nice design on the ankle. The skin is stretched tight on the ankle unlike the spongy skin of the breast, stomach, back or hip area." The owner then also tells her that the "shoulders [back] make a nice canvas as well." The artist refers to the skin as canvas for the ink. . . . The girl continues to ask the owner for advice on colors, size, and location. (field-notes February 15, 1997)

It appeared to us that most interactions were controlled by the artists. It was discovered rather quickly that the customer is literally in the tattooist's hands.

> The artist didn't like the way she had drawn the leaf. She said she had kind of made a mistake when tattooing it. I asked her about making mistakes. She said, "It happens. . . . When you make a mistake, you just cover it up. The customer won't ever know." I thought about this and realized that the customer usually can't see what is going on up-close during the process and that they probably wouldn't know if a mistake had been made. (fieldnotes February 22, 1997)

Although most interactions and negotiations went smoothly, there were instances where this was not the case. The artists labeled the clients involved in the unsuccessful interactions as "bad clients" and the customers involved in the successful interactions as "good clients." The following passages provide examples of "bad clients" as defined by the artists:

> The owner explains, "This chick came in the other day for a navel piercing and she had the dirtiest belly button I had ever seen! It took me five minutes to pick all of the shit out of it! I thought about charging her extra just for that!" (fieldnotes April 9, 1997)

> The artist defines bad customers: "The ones where price is the most important thing. . . . The customers that will let you run with it and do whatever you want to, those are the great ones. . . . Unfortunately there aren't many of those. . . . Most people say, "I can only afford 50 dollars' worth." I sometimes give them a few free colors just to make it look better. . . . The whiny ones are bad too, when you step on your pedal and you're not even touching them and they are like, 'Ow! Quit!' you know. . . . You just feel like slapping them." (fieldnotes April 15, 1997)

It was very common for customers to bring friends with them for support during the tattooing procedure. The social support often helped the potential client with such decisions as choice of design, size, colors, and body location. Friends offered further support by engaging in conversation to keep the client's mind off the painful procedure. We also observed this type of conversational support between the artists and their clients. One artist described how she felt this conversational support was part of the job:

> *You get to talk to a lot of people. Sitting there with them for an hour or an hour and a half, you get to talking and make new friends. We're actually like bartenders you know, people cry on our shoulder. . . . You usually know their life story by the time they leave.* (fieldnotes April 15, 1997)

The second a priori theme identified in the literature reveals how tattoos are used to reinforce one's *self-identity*. We discovered that the use of tattoos to express one's inner self was probably the most commonly stated motivation for acquiring a tattoo. In this context, the tattoo becomes an extension of the person, symbolizing the person's narrative story. One informant described how becoming tattooed "is more of a reflection of who you think you are" (fieldnotes April 17, 1997). As one artist explained, "The tattoo is already there inside those who really want it, it is already a part of them, the tattoo artist just brings it out" (fieldnotes July 12, 1996). . . . One of the informants, who had acquired tattoos from 35 different artists, described his tattoos as a "scrapbook" symbolizing his life story:

> I asked him if there was one he favored or if any particular one had great meaning. He said, "They all do." He told me that he considers his tattoo

art work "his personal scrapbook." Each and every tattoo remir formant of a person, place, time or period in his life. A perso book of one's life or self. (fieldnotes July 12, 1996)

During the ethnography, we discovered that customers choose tattoos to represent who they are in different ways. Some choose symbols for personal distinction, whereas others choose symbols for integration purposes. Both cases contributed to an expression of identity: the former case seemed to represent one's personal identity whereas the latter case represented one's social identity. One informant described how tattoos distinguish him from others in a crowd (and help create a sense of personal identity):

> *When you make the decision, 'I'm going to be a person with a tattoo,' you know you are different from most people. . . . Just the bottom line, standing in the line at Wal-Mart, I know I'm different. . . . It is fun being different, it is even more fun being more different.* (fieldnotes April 17, 1997)

Other examples from interviews in which the tattoo symbolized the owner's personal identity include a Mickey Mouse tattooed to the informant's arm because his grandfather called him "Mickey"; a butterfly tattooed to the client's hip symbolizing her given name; a rattlesnake design chosen in memory of being bitten and almost dying; a rose tattooed on the wrist for every child born and a butterfly tattooed on the ankle for every family member who had died; and a cat design that reflected a woman's long history of living with and loving cats. There were other instances where the design seemed to represent the client's social identity (integration):

> Back at the counter, a young man (30s) with an Irish accent comes in and asks to see the hog file. The owner asks him to clarify what kind of hog and he says, "You know, a razorback." Shortly after that remark he says, "I am not getting a hog because of THE Razorbacks basketball team, the hog is part of my family crest. It looks just like the razorback, only it's not running. . . . It is just standing there." I ask him where he is from and he says, "Dublin." He then tells me that every family name has a crest and that his has the hog in the design. (fieldnotes March 1, 1997)

Often the process of becoming tattooed could be explained as experiential consumption (Holbrook and Hirschman 1982), where the event was tied to a meaningful experience. The following passages are representative of this concept:

> The two girls who were best friends got matching tattoos on vacation in Mexico to bond their friendship. I ask her why the tribal piece and she says, "I don't know, we didn't really care what the design was. . . . We just wanted something simple . . . to represent our friendship." (fieldnotes April 15, 1997)

A young woman comes in (WF 20) with her mother to get a tattoo of a moon and fairy. She tells me that she had drawn the design herself. This will be her fourth tattoo as she has gotten one every year for her birthday since she was 16 years old. (fieldnotes March 19, 1997)

As discovered in this ethnography, tattoos are consumed for many different reasons. Most informants agreed, however, that tattoos are a form of self-expression, a way to communicate to others some aspect of the wearer's self-identity. . . .

Discussion and Conclusions

The preceding review of literature and ethnographic account suggests some feasible answers to the research questions stated in the introduction: What is it about the tattoo as a cultural object that draws people to participate in the tattoo subculture? In what ways is the tattoo used as a form of expression? What is involved in the experience of acquiring a tattoo? What transpires during the service interaction between the tattooist and tattooee? The a priori and emergent themes suggest that there are many reasons why individuals are drawn to participate in the new tattoo subculture. A subculture "signifies a way of life of a group of people" and is "characterized by interaction, continuity, and outsider and insider definitions of distinctiveness" (Prus 1996: 85). The tattoo subculture is no different in that the tattoo as a cultural object attracts people who want to express difference as well as integration. In this realm, the tattoo indicates the separate domains to which its wearers belong, while it expresses unity and connects otherwise diverse domains. For example, as we discovered in this ethnography, the tattoo was a common bond among all informants regardless of social class or background. Further, the tattoo was a form of distinction, separating the informants from the rest of society, or the non-tattooed.

Another reason that members are drawn to this subculture can be attributed to the phenomenon of certain objects becoming so firmly associated with an individual that they are understood as literal extensions of that individual's being. The tattoo as a cultural object is a "document that describes our past, an image that reflects our present, and a sign that calls us into the future" (Richardson 1989). Informants used tattoos to express symbolically the meanings they attached to themselves from past, present, and future perspectives. In other words, tattoos were used both to reflect one's past or current identity and to construct and revise one's future identity. Two of the most important themes used to represent this idea are *self-identity* and *simulated self*. Following the ideas presented under the self-identity theme, most informants used the tattoo to express the inner self, "to bring a little bit or a lot of their inner self out for others to see" (fieldnotes March 31, 1996). In this sense, tattoos were extensions of self-conceptions. In contrast, with the simulated self, informants believed that by adopting a symbol, they were changing their images and becoming someone different.

We conclude by stating that it is important and most "useful to examine subcultures by understanding the identities people achieve as participants, the activities deemed consequential in that context, the bonds participants develop with one another, and the sorts of commitments the people involved make with respect to the setting at hand" (Prus 1996:85). This study has achieved such a thorough examination of the new tattoo subculture. If the implications of the examples surveyed in this research can be summarized into a single idea, that idea would be the importance of cultural objects in constituting culture and human relations. Cultural artifacts, such as the tattoo, have properties and tendencies that in an era where material culture is rapidly increasing, deserve to be investigated in their own right.

ENDNOTES

[1] The modifier *New* signifies the recent expansion of popular interest in tattooing as a form of marking identity (Krakow 1994; Lautman 1994; Randall and Polhemus 1996; Velliquette et al. 1998).

[2] Erving Goffman (1959) argues that in everyday life, there is a clear understanding that first impressions are important and seldom overlooked. Those in service occupations have many motives for trying to control the impression they present during the service encounter. This process is called *impression management.*

REFERENCES

American Business Information, Inc. 1996. "1996 Business Changes Report." Omaha, NE: Marketing Research Division. Jeff Ferris, Project Manager.

Ball, Keith, ed. 1996. "Skin and Bones: Tools of the Trade." *Tattoo* 82 (June): 76–79.

Blouin, Melissa, ed. 1996. "Tattoo You: Health Experts Worried about Artful Trend." *Northwest Arkansas Times,* July 14, p. C4.

Blumer, Herbert. 1969. *Symbolic Interactionism: Perspective and Method.* Englewood Cliffs, NJ: Prentice-Hall.

Bohannan, Paul. 1988. "Beauty and Scarification amongst the Tiv." Pp. 77–82 in *Marks of Civilization,* edited by Arnold Rubin. Los Angeles: Museum of Cultural History.

Drewal, Henry John. 1988. "Beauty and Being: Aesthetics and Ontology in Yoruba Body Art." Pp. 83–96 in *Marks of Civilization,* edited by Arnold Rubin. Los Angeles: Museum of Cultural History.

Emerson, Robert M., Rachael I. Fretz, and Linda L. Shaw. 1995. *Writing Ethnographic Fieldnotes.* Chicago: University of Chicago Press.

Finkelstein, Joanne. 1991. *The Fashioned Self.* Philadelphia: Temple University Press.

Gathercole, Peter. 1988. "Contexts of Maori Moko." Pp. 171–78 in *Marks of Civilization,* edited by Arnold Rubin. Los Angeles: Museum of Cultural History.

Goffman, Erving. 1959. *The Presentation of Self in Everyday Life.* New York: Doubleday.

Gritton, Joy. 1988. "Labrets and Tattooing in Native Alaska." Pp. 181–90 in *Marks of Civilization,* edited by Arnold Rubin. Los Angeles: Museum of Cultural History.

Hebdige, Dick. 1979. *Subculture: The Meaning of Style.* New York: Routledge.

Holbrook, Morris B. and Elizabeth C. Hirschman. 1982. "The Experiential Aspects of Consumption: Consumer Fantasies, Feelings, and Fun." *Journal of Consumer Research* 9 (September): 132–40.

Krakow, Amy. 1994. *Total Tattoo Book.* New York: Warner Books.

Lautman, Victoria. 1994. *The New Tattoo.* New York, London, and Paris: Abbeville Press.

Myers, James. 1992. "Nonmainstream Body Modification: Genital Piercing, Branding, Burning, and Cutting." *Journal of Contemporary Ethnography* 21(3): 267–306.

Peterson, Andrea. 1996. "Parents Spur Laws against Tattoos for Kids." *Wall Street Journal,* September, pp. B1–B2.

Prus, Robert. 1996. *Symbolic Interaction and Ethnographic Research: Intersubjectivity and the Study of Human Lived Experience.* Albany: State University of New York Press.

Randall, Housk and Ted Polhemus. 1996. *The Customized Body.* London and New York: Serpent's Tail.

Richardson, Miles. 1989. "The Artifact as Abbreviated Act: A Social Interpretation of Material Culture." Pp. 172–78 in *The Meaning of Things,* edited by Ian Hodder. London: Unwin Hyman.

Rubin, Arnold. 1988. "The Tattoo Renaissance." Pp. 233–62 in *Marks of Civilization,* edited by Arnold Rubin. Los Angeles: Museum of Cultural History.

Sanders, Clinton R. 1988. "Drill and Frill: Client Choice, Client Typologies, and Interactional Control in Commercial Tattoo Settings." Pp. 219–33 in *Marks of Civilization,* edited by Arnold Rubin. Los Angeles: Museum of Cultural History.

———. 1989. "Organizational Constraints on Tattoo Images: A Sociological Analysis of Artistic Style." Pp. 232–41 in *The Meaning of Things,* edited by Ian Hodder. London: Unwin Hyman.

Steward, Samuel M. 1990. *Bad Boys and Tough Tattoos: A Social History of the Tattoo with Gangs, Sailors, and Street Corner Punks, 1950–1965.* New York: Harrington Park Press.

Strauss, Anselm and Juliet Corbin. 1990. *Basics of Qualitative Research: Grounded Theory Procedures and Techniques.* Beverly Hills, CA: Sage Publications.

Velliquette, Anne M., Jeff B. Murray, and Elizabeth H. Creyer. 1998. "The Tattoo Renaissance: An Ethnographic Account of Symbolic Consumer Behavior." *Advances in Consumer Research* 25:461–67.

8

THE CODE OF THE STREETS

ELIJAH ANDERSON

In this selection, adapted from *Streetwise: Race, Class, and Change in an Urban Community* (1990), Elijah Anderson demonstrates how cultural values create new standards for behavior. Anderson, a professor of sociology and director of the Philadelphia Ethnography Project at the University of Pennsylvania, is an expert on the sociology of black America. The ethnographic study below analyzes the social norms governing street behavior and violence in the inner city. The resulting "code" is a complex system of norms, dress, rituals, and expected behavior. In order to survive within the subculture of the inner city, children and adults must learn the code and adapt their lives accordingly.

Of all the problems besetting the poor inner-city black community, none is more pressing than that of interpersonal violence and aggression. It wreaks havoc daily with the lives of community residents and increasingly spills over into downtown and residential middle-class areas. Muggings, burglaries, carjackings, and drug-related shootings, all of which may leave their victims or innocent bystanders dead, are now common enough to concern all urban and many suburban residents. The inclination to violence springs from the circumstances of life among the ghetto poor—the lack of jobs that pay a living wage, the stigma of race, the fallout from rampant drug use and drug trafficking, and the resulting alienation and lack of hope for the future.

Simply living in such an environment places young people at special risk of falling victim to aggressive behavior. Although there are often forces in the community which can counteract the negative influences, by far the most powerful being a strong, loving, "decent" (as inner-city residents put it) family committed to middle-class values, the despair is pervasive enough to have spawned an oppositional culture, that of "the streets," whose norms are often consciously opposed to those of mainstream society. These two orientations—decent and street—socially organize the community, and their coexistence has important consequences for residents, particularly children

From *The Code of the Streets*. Originally in *The Atlantic Monthly* 273, no. 5 (May 1994): 81–94. Copyright © 1994 by Elijah Anderson. Reprinted with the permission of the author.

growing up in the inner city. Above all, this environment means that even youngsters whose home lives reflect mainstream values—and the majority of homes in the community do—must be able to handle themselves in a street-oriented environment.

This is because the street culture has evolved what may be called a code of the streets, which amounts to a set of informal rules governing interpersonal public behavior, including violence. The rules prescribe both a proper comportment and a proper way to respond if challenged. They regulate the use of violence and so allow those who are inclined to aggression to precipitate violent encounters in an approved way. The rules have been established and are enforced mainly by the street-oriented, but on the streets the distinction between street and decent is often irrelevant; everybody knows that if the rules are violated, there are penalties. Knowledge of the code is thus largely defensive; it is literally necessary for operating in public. Therefore, even though families with a decency orientation are usually opposed to the values of the code, they often reluctantly encourage their children's familiarity with it to enable them to negotiate the inner-city environment.

At the heart of the code is the issue of respect—loosely defined as being treated "right," or granted the deference one deserves. However, in the troublesome public environment of the inner city, as people increasingly feel buffeted by forces beyond their control, what one deserves in the way of respect becomes more and more problematic and uncertain. This in turn further opens the issue of respect to sometimes intense interpersonal negotiation. In the street culture, especially among young people, respect is viewed as almost an external entity that is hard-won but easily lost, and so must constantly be guarded. The rules of the code in fact provide a framework for negotiating respect. The person whose very appearance—including his clothing, demeanor, and way of moving—deters transgressions feels that he possesses, and may be considered by others to possess, a measure of respect. With the right amount of respect, for instance, he can avoid "being bothered" in public. If he is bothered, not only may he be in physical danger but he has been disgraced or "dissed" (disrespected). Many of the forms that dissing can take might seem petty to middle-class people (maintaining eye contact for too long, for example), but to those invested in the street code, these actions become serious indications of the other person's intentions. Consequently, such people become very sensitive to advances and slights, which could well serve as warnings of imminent physical confrontation.

This hard reality can be traced to the profound sense of alienation from mainstream society and its institutions felt by many poor inner-city black people, particularly the young. The code of the streets is actually a cultural adaptation to a profound lack of faith in the police and the judicial system. The police are most often seen as representing the dominant white society and not caring to protect inner-city residents. When called, they may not respond, which is one reason many residents feel they must be prepared to take extraordinary measures to defend themselves and their loved ones against those who are inclined to aggression. Lack of police accountability has in fact been incorporated into the status system: The person who is believed capable of "taking care of himself" is accorded a certain deference, which translates into a sense of physical and psychological control. Thus the street code emerges where the influence of the police ends and personal responsibility for one's safety is felt to begin. Exacerbated by the proliferation of drugs and easy access to guns, this volatile situation results in the ability of the street-oriented minority (or those who effectively "go for bad") to dominate the public spaces.

Decent and Street Families

Although almost everyone in poor inner-city neighborhoods is struggling financially and therefore feels a certain distance from the rest of America, the decent and the street family in a real sense represent two poles of value orientation, two contrasting conceptual categories. The labels "decent" and "street," which the residents themselves use, amount to evaluative judgments that confer status on local residents. The labeling is often the result of a social contest among individuals and families of the neighborhood. Individuals of the two orientations often coexist in the same extended family. Decent residents judge themselves to be so while judging others to be of the street, and street individuals often present themselves as decent, drawing distinctions between themselves and other people. In addition, there is quite a bit of circumstantial behavior—that is, one person may at different times exhibit both decent and street orientations, depending on the circumstances. Although these designations result from so much social jockeying, there do exist concrete features that define each conceptual category.

Generally, so-called decent families tend to accept mainstream values more fully and attempt to instill them in their children. Whether married couples with children or single-parent (usually female) households, they are generally "working poor" and so tend to be better off financially than their street-oriented neighbors. They value hard work and self-reliance and are willing to sacrifice for their children. Because they have a certain amount of faith in mainstream society, they harbor hopes for a better future for their children, if not for themselves. Many of them go to church and take a strong interest in their children's schooling. Rather than dwelling on the real hardships and inequities facing them, many such decent people, particularly the increasing number of grandmothers raising grandchildren, see their difficult situation as a test from God and derive great support from their faith and from the church community.

Extremely aware of the problematic and often dangerous environment in which they reside, decent parents tend to be strict in their child-rearing practices, encouraging children to respect authority and walk a straight moral line. They have an almost obsessive concern about trouble of any kind and remind their children to be on the lookout for people and situations that might lead to it. At the same time, they are themselves polite and considerate of others, and teach their children to be the same way. At home, at work, and in church, they strive hard to maintain a positive mental attitude and a spirit of cooperation.

So-called street parents, in contrast, often show a lack of consideration for other people and have a rather superficial sense of family and community. Though they may love their children, many of them are unable to cope with the physical and emotional demands of parenthood and find it difficult to reconcile their needs with those of their children. These families, who are more fully invested in the code of the streets than the decent people are, may aggressively socialize their children into it in a normative way. They believe in the code and judge themselves and others according to its values. . . .

Campaigning for Respect

[The] realities of inner-city life are largely absorbed on the streets. At an early age, often even before they start school, children from street-oriented homes gravitate to the streets, where they "hang"—socialize with their peers. Children from these generally permissive homes have a great deal of latitude and are allowed to "rip and run" up and down the street. They often come home from school, put their books down, and go right back out the door. On school nights, eight- and nine-year-olds remain out until nine or ten o'clock (and teenagers typically come in whenever they want to). On the streets they play in groups that often become the source of their primary social bonds. Children from decent homes tend to be more carefully supervised and are thus likely to have curfews and to be taught how to stay out of trouble.

When decent and street kids come together, a kind of social shuffle occurs in which children have a chance to go either way. Tension builds as a child comes to realize that he must choose an orientation. The kind of home he comes from influences but does not determine the way he will ultimately turn out—although it is unlikely that a child from a thoroughly street-oriented family will easily absorb decent values on the streets. Youths who emerge from street-oriented families but develop a decency orientation almost always learn those values in another setting—in school, in a youth group, in church. Often it is the result of their involvement with a caring "old head" (adult role model).

In the street, through their play, children pour their individual life experiences into a common knowledge pool, affirming, confirming, and elaborating on what they have observed in the home and matching their skills against those of others. And they learn to fight. Even small children test one another, pushing and shoving, and are ready to hit other children over circumstances not to their liking. In turn, they are readily hit by other children, and the child who is toughest prevails. Thus the violent resolution of disputes, the hitting and cursing, gains social reinforcement. The child in effect is initiated into a system that is really a way of campaigning for respect.

In addition, younger children witness the disputes of older children, which are often resolved through cursing and abusive talk, if not aggression or outright violence. They see that one child succumbs to the greater physical and mental abilities of the other. They are also alert and attentive witnesses to the verbal and physical fights of adults, after which they compare notes and share their interpretations of the event. In almost every case the victor is the person who physically won the altercation, and this person often enjoys the esteem and respect of onlookers. These experiences reinforce the lessons the children have learned at home: Might makes right, and toughness is a virtue, while humility is not. In effect they learn the social meaning of fighting. When it is left virtually unchallenged, this understanding becomes an ever more important part of the child's working conception of the world. Over time the code of the streets becomes refined.

Those street-oriented adults with whom children come in contact—including mothers, fathers, brothers, sisters, boyfriends, cousins, neighbors, and friends—help them along in forming this understanding by verbalizing the messages they are getting through experience: "Watch your back." "Protect yourself." "Don't punk out." "If somebody messes with you, you got to pay them back." "If someone disses you, you got to straighten them out." Many parents actually impose sanctions if a child is not sufficiently aggressive. For example, if a child loses a fight and comes home upset, the parent might respond, "Don't you come in here crying that somebody beat you up; you better get back out there and whup his ass. I didn't raise no punks! Get back out there and whup his ass. If you don't whup his ass, I'll whup your ass when you come home." Thus the child obtains reinforcement for being tough and showing nerve.

While fighting, some children cry as though they are doing something they are ambivalent about. The fight may be against their wishes, yet they may feel constrained to fight or face the consequences—not just from peers but also from caretakers or parents, who may administer another beating if they back down. Some adults recall receiving such lessons from their own parents and justify repeating them to their children as a way to toughen them up. Looking capable of taking care of oneself as a form of self-defense is a dominant theme among both street-oriented and decent adults who worry about the safety of their children. There is thus at times a convergence in their child-rearing practices, although the rationales behind them may differ.

Self-Image Based on "Juice"

By the time they are teenagers, most youths have either internalized the code of the streets or at least learned the need to comport themselves in accordance with its rules, which chiefly have to do with interpersonal communication.

The code revolves around the presentation of self. Its basic requirement is the display of a certain predisposition to violence. Accordingly, one's bearing must send the unmistakable if sometimes subtle message to "the next person" in public that one is capable of violence and mayhem when the situation requires it, that one can take care of oneself. The nature of this communication is largely determined by the demands of the circumstances but can include facial expressions, gait, and verbal expressions—all of which are geared mainly to deterring aggression. Physical appearance, including clothes, jewelry, and grooming, also plays an important part in how a person is viewed; to be respected, it is important to have the right look.

Even so, there are no guarantees against challenges because there are always people around looking for a fight to increase their share of respect—or "juice," as it is sometimes called on the street. Moreover, if a person is assaulted, it is important, not only in the eyes of his opponent but also in the eyes of his "running buddies," for him to avenge himself. Otherwise, he risks being "tried" (challenged) or "moved on" by any number of others. To maintain his honor, he must show he is not someone to be "messed with" or "dissed." In general, the person must "keep himself straight" by managing his position of respect among others; this involves in part his self-image, which is shaped by what he thinks others are thinking of him in relation to his peers.

Objects play an important and complicated role in establishing self-image. Jackets, sneakers, gold jewelry, reflect not just a person's taste, which tends to be tightly regulated among adolescents of all social classes, but also a willingness to possess things that may require defending. A boy wearing a fashionable, expensive jacket, for example, is vulnerable to attack by another who covets the jacket and either cannot afford to buy one or wants the added satisfaction of depriving someone else of his. However, if the boy forgoes the desirable jacket and wears one that isn't "hip," he runs the risk of being teased and possibly even assaulted as an unworthy person. To be allowed to hang with certain prestigious crowds, a boy must wear a different set of expensive clothes—sneakers and athletic suit—every day. Not to be able to do so might make him appear socially deficient. The youth comes to covet such items—especially when he sees easy prey wearing them.

In acquiring valued things, therefore, a person shores up his identity—but since it is an identity based on having things, it is highly precarious. This very precariousness gives a heightened sense of urgency to staying even with peers, with whom the person is actually competing. Young men and women who are able to command respect through their presentation of self—by allowing their possessions and their body language to speak for them—may not have to campaign for regard but may, rather, gain it by the force of their manner. Those who are unable to command respect in this way must actively campaign for it—and are thus particularly alive to slights.

One way of campaigning for status is by taking the possessions of others. In this context, seemingly ordinary objects can become trophies imbued with symbolic value that far exceeds their monetary worth. Possession of the trophy can symbolize the ability to violate somebody—to "get in his face," to take something of value from him, to "dis" him, and thus to enhance one's own worth by stealing someone else's. The trophy does not have to be something material. It can be another person's sense of honor, snatched away with a derogatory remark. It can be the outcome of a fight. It can be the imposition of a certain standard, such as a girl's getting herself recognized as the most beautiful. Material things, however, fit easily into the pattern. Sneakers, a pistol, even somebody else's girlfriend, can become a trophy. When a person can take something from another and then flaunt it, he gains a certain regard by being the owner, or the controller, of that thing. But this display of ownership can then provoke other people to challenge him. This game of who controls what is thus constantly being played out on inner-city streets, and the trophy—extrinsic or intrinsic, tangible or intangible—identifies the current winner.

An important aspect of this often violent give-and-take is its zero-sum quality. That is, the extent to which one person can raise himself up depends on his ability to put another person down. This underscores the alienation that permeates the inner-city ghetto community. There is a generalized sense that very little respect is to be had, and therefore everyone competes to get what affirmation he can of the little that is available. The craving for respect that results gives people thin skins. Shows of deference by others can be highly soothing, contributing to a sense of security, comfort, self-confidence, and self-respect. Transgressions by others which go unanswered diminish these feelings and are believed to encourage further transgressions. Hence one must be ever vigilant against the transgressions of others or even *appearing* as if transgressions will be tolerated. Among young people, whose sense of self-esteem is particularly vulnerable, there is an especially heightened concern with being disrespected. Many inner-city young men in particular crave respect to such a degree that they will risk their lives to attain and maintain it.

The issue of respect is thus closely tied to whether a person has an inclination to be violent, even as a victim. In the wider society, people may not feel required to retaliate physically after an attack, even though they are aware that they have been degraded or taken advantage of. They may feel a great need to defend themselves *during* an attack, or to behave in such a way as to deter aggression (middle-class people certainly can and do become victims of street-oriented youths), but they are much more likely than street-oriented people to feel that they can walk away from a possible altercation with their self-esteem intact. Some people may even have the strength of character to flee, without any thought that their self-respect or esteem will be diminished.

In impoverished inner-city black communities, however, particularly among young males and perhaps increasingly among females, such flight would be extremely difficult. To run away would likely leave one's self-esteem in tatters. Hence people often feel constrained not only to stand up and at least attempt to resist during an assault but also to "pay back"—to seek revenge—after a successful assault on their person. This may include going to get a weapon or even getting relatives involved. Their very identity and self-respect, their honor, is often intricately tied up with the way they perform on the streets during and after such encounters. This outlook reflects the circumscribed opportunities of the inner-city poor. Generally, people outside the ghetto have other ways of gaining status and regard, and thus do not feel so dependent on such physical displays.

By Trial of Manhood

On the street, among males these concerns about things and identity have come to be expressed in the concept of "manhood." Manhood in the inner city means taking the prerogatives of men with respect to strangers, other men, and women—being distinguished as a man. It implies physicality and a certain ruthlessness. Regard and respect are associated with this concept in large part because of its practical application: If others have little or no regard for a person's manhood, his very life and those of his loved ones could be in jeopardy. But there is a chicken-and-egg aspect to this situation: One's physical safety is more likely to be jeopardized in public *because* manhood is associated with respect. In other words, an existential link has been created between the idea of manhood and one's self-esteem, so that it has become hard to say which is primary. For many inner-city youths, manhood and respect are flip sides of the same coin; physical and psychological well-being are inseparable, and both require a sense of control, of being in charge.

The operating assumption is that a man, especially a real man, knows what other men know—the code of the streets. And if one is not a real man, one is somehow diminished as a person, and there are certain valued things one simply does not deserve. There is thus believed to be a certain justice to the code, since it is considered that everyone has the opportunity to know it. Implicit in this is that everybody is held responsible for being familiar with the code. If the victim of a mugging, for example, does not know the code and so responds "wrong," the perpetrator may feel justified even in killing him and may feel no remorse. He may think, "Too bad, but it's his fault. He should have known better."

So when a person ventures outside, he must adopt the code—a kind of shield, really—to prevent others from "messing with" him. In these circumstances it is easy for people to think they are being tried or tested by others even when this is not the case. For it is sensed that something extremely valuable is at stake in every interaction, and people are encouraged to rise to the occasion, particularly with strangers. For people who are unfamiliar with the code—generally, people who live outside the inner city—the concern with respect in the most ordinary interactions can be frightening and incomprehensible. But for those who are invested in the code, the clear object of their demeanor is to discourage strangers from even thinking about testing their manhood. And the sense of power that attends the ability to deter others can be alluring even to those who know the code without being heavily invested in it—the decent inner-city youths. Thus a boy who has been leading a basically decent life can, in trying circumstances, suddenly resort to deadly force.

Central to the issue of manhood is the widespread belief that one of the most effective ways of gaining respect is to manifest "nerve." Nerve is shown when one takes another person's possessions (the more valuable the better), "messes with" someone's woman, throws the first punch, "gets in someone's face," or pulls a trigger. Its proper display helps on the spot to check others who would violate one's person and also helps to build a reputation that works to prevent future challenges. But since such a show of nerve is a forceful expression of disrespect toward the person on the receiving end, the victim may be greatly offended and seek to retaliate with equal or greater force. A display of nerve, therefore, can easily provoke a life-threatening response, and the background knowledge of that possibility has often been incorporated into the concept of nerve.

True nerve exposes a lack of fear of dying. Many feel that it is acceptable to risk dying over the principle of respect. In fact, among the hard-core street-oriented, the clear risk of violent death may be preferable to being "dissed" by another. The youths who have internalized this attitude and convincingly display it in their public bearing are among the most threatening people of all, for it is commonly assumed that they fear no man. As the people of the community say, "They are the baddest dudes on the street." They often lead an existential life that may acquire meaning only when they are faced with the possibility of imminent death. Not to be afraid to die is by implication to have few compunctions about taking another's life. Not to be afraid to die is the quid pro quo of being able to take somebody else's life— for the right reasons, if the situation demands it. When others believe this is one's position, it gives one a real sense of power on the streets. Such credibility is what many inner-city youths strive to achieve, whether they are decent or street-oriented, both because of its practical defensive value and because of the positive way it makes them feel about themselves. The difference between the decent and the street-oriented youth is often that the decent youth makes a conscious decision to appear tough and manly; in another setting—with teachers, say, or at his part-time job—he can be polite and deferential. The street-oriented youth, on the other hand, has made the concept of manhood a part of his very identity; he has difficulty manipulating it—it often controls him.

Girls and Boys

Increasingly, teenage girls are mimicking the boys and trying to have their own version of "manhood." Their goal is the same—to get respect, to be recognized as capable of setting or maintaining a certain standard. They try to achieve this end in the ways that have been established by the boys, including posturing, abusive language, and the use of violence to resolve disputes, but the issues for the girls are different. Although conflicts over turf and status exist among the girls, the majority of disputes seem rooted in assessments of beauty (which girl in a group is "the cutest"), competition over boyfriends, and attempts to regulate other people's knowledge of and opinions about a girl's behavior or that of someone close to her, especially her mother.

A major cause of conflicts among girls is "he say, she say." This practice begins in the early school years and continues through high school. It occurs when "people," particularly girls, talk about others, thus putting their "business in the streets." Usually one girl will say something negative about another in the group, most often behind the person's back. The remark will then get back to the person talked about. She may retaliate or her friends may feel required to "take up for" her. In essence this is a form of group gossiping in which individuals are negatively assessed and evaluated. As with much gossip, the things said may or may not be true, but the point is that such imputations can cast aspersions on a person's good name. The accused is required to defend herself against the slander, which can result in arguments and fights, often over little of real substance. Here again is the problem of low self-esteem, which encourages youngsters to be highly sensitive to slights and to be vulnerable to feeling easily "dissed." To avenge the dissing, a fight is usually necessary.

Because boys are believed to control violence, girls tend to defer to them in situations of conflict. Often if a girl is attacked or feels slighted, she will get a brother, uncle, or cousin to do her fighting for her. Increasingly, however, girls are doing their own fighting and are even asking their male relatives to teach them how to fight. Some girls form groups that attack other girls or take things from them. A hard-core segment of inner-city girls inclined toward violence seems to be developing. As one 13-year-old girl in a detention center for youths who have committed violent acts told me, "To get people to leave you alone, you gotta fight. Talking don't always get you out of stuff." One major difference between girls and boys: Girls rarely use guns. Their fights are therefore not life-or-death struggles. Girls are not often willing to put their lives on the line for "manhood." The ultimate form of respect on the male-dominated inner-city street is thus reserved for men.

"Going for Bad"

In the most fearsome youths, such a cavalier attitude toward death grows out of a very limited view of life. Many are uncertain about how long they are going to live and believe they could die violently at any time. They accept this fate; they live on the edge. Their manner conveys the message that nothing intimidates them; whatever turn the encounter takes, they maintain their attack—rather like a pit bull, whose spirit many such boys admire. The demonstration of such tenacity "shows heart" and earns their respect.

This fearlessness has implications for law enforcement. Many street-oriented boys are much more concerned about the threat of "justice" at the hands of a peer than at the hands of the police. Moreover, many feel not only that they have little to lose by going to prison but that they have something to gain. The toughening-up one experiences in prison can actually enhance one's reputation on the streets. Hence the system loses influence over the hard core who are without jobs, with little perceptible stake in the system. If mainstream society has done nothing *for* them, they counter by making sure it can do nothing *to* them.

At the same time, however, a competing view maintains that the true nerve consists in backing down, walking away from a fight, and going on with one's business. One fights only in self-defense. This view emerges from the decent philosophy that life is precious, and it is an important part of the socialization process common in decent homes. It discourages violence as the primary means of resolving disputes and encourages youngsters to accept nonviolence and talk as confrontational strategies. But "if the deal goes down," self-defense is greatly encouraged. When there is enough positive support for this orientation, either in the home or among one's peers, then nonviolence has a chance to prevail. But it prevails at the cost of relinquishing a claim to being bad and tough, and therefore sets a young person up as at the very least alienated from street-oriented peers and quite possibly a target of derision or even violence.

Although the nonviolent orientation rarely overcomes the impulse to strike back in an encounter, it does introduce a certain confusion and so can prompt a measure of soul-searching, or even profound ambivalence. Did the person back down with his respect intact or did he back down only to be judged a "punk"—a person lacking manhood? Should he or she have acted? Should he or she have hit the other person in the mouth? These questions beset many young men and women during public confrontations. What is the "right" thing to do? In the quest for honor, respect, and local status—which few young people are uninterested in—common sense most often prevails, which leads many to opt for the tough approach, enacting their own particular versions of the display of nerve. The presentation of oneself as rough and tough is very often quite acceptable until one is tested. And then that presentation may help the person pass the test, because it will cause fewer questions to be asked about what he did and why. It is hard for a person to explain why he lost the fight or why he backed down. Hence many will strive to appear to "go for bad," while hoping they will never be tested. But when they are tested, the outcome of the situation may quickly be out of their hands, as they become wrapped up in the circumstances of the moment.

An Oppositional Culture

The attitudes of the wider society are deeply implicated in the code of the streets. Most people in inner-city communities are not totally invested in the code, but the significant minority of hard-core street youths who are have to maintain the code in order to establish reputations, because they have— or feel they have—few other ways to assert themselves. For these young people the standards of the street code are the only game in town. The extent to which some children—particularly those who through upbringing have become most alienated and those lacking in strong and conventional social support—experience, feel, and internalize racist rejection and contempt from mainstream society may strongly encourage them to express contempt for the more conventional society in turn. In dealing with this contempt and rejection, some youngsters will consciously invest themselves and their considerable mental resources in what amounts to an oppositional culture to preserve themselves and their self-respect. Once they do, any respect they might be able to garner in the wider system pales in comparison with the re-spect available in the local system; thus they often lose interest in even at-tempting to negotiate the mainstream system.

At the same time, many less alienated young blacks have assumed a street-oriented demeanor as a way of expressing their blackness while really embracing a much more moderate way of life; they, too want a nonviolent set-ting in which to live and raise a family. These decent people are trying hard to be part of the mainstream culture, but the racism, real and perceived, that they encounter helps to legitimate the oppositional culture. And so on occa-sion they adopt street behavior. In fact, depending on the demands of the sit-uation, many people in the community slip back and forth between decent and street behavior.

A vicious cycle has thus been formed. The hopelessness and alienation many young inner-city black men and women feel, largely as a result of en-demic joblessness and persistent racism, fuels the violence they engage in. This violence serves to confirm the negative feelings many whites and some middle-class blacks harbor toward the ghetto poor, further legitimating the oppositional culture and the code of the streets in the eyes of many poor young blacks. Unless this cycle is broken, attitudes on both sides will become increasingly entrenched, and the violence, which claims victims black and white, poor and affluent, will only escalate.

9

"OPENING" FACES
The Politics of Cosmetic Surgery
and Asian American Women

EUGENIA KAW

Sociologists are interested in how culture limits our free choice and shapes social interaction. Because each of us is born into a particular culture that has certain norms and values, our personal values and life expectations are profoundly influenced by our culture. For example, what are the values of American culture? Many scholars agree that dominant U.S. values are achievement, Judeo-Christian morals, material comfort, patriotism, and in-dividualism. In the selection excerpted below, Eugenia Kaw, a Ph.D. can-didate in the Anthropology Graduate Program at Princeton University, examines how the racial and gender stereotypes of the dominant culture influence standards of beauty. Specifically, Kaw examines why Asian Amer-ican women are using cosmetic surgery to alter their appearances in order to look more Caucasian and to better conform to the values and norms of the beauty culture in the United States.

Ellen, a Chinese American in her forties, informed me she had had her upper eyelids surgically cut and sewed by a plastic surgeon twenty years ago in order to get rid of "the sleepy look," which her naturally "puffy" eyes gave her. She pointed out that the sutures, when they healed, became a crease above the eye which gave the eyes a more "open appear-ance." She was quick to tell me that her decision to undergo "double-eyelid" surgery was not so much because she was vain or had low self-esteem, but rather because the "undesirability" of her looks before the surgery was an undeniable fact.

During my second interview with Ellen, she showed me photos of her-self from before and after her surgery in order to prove her point. When Stacy, her twelve-year-old daughter, arrived home from school, Ellen told me she wanted Stacy to undergo similar surgery in the near future because Stacy has only single eyelids and would look prettier and be more successful in life

---

Reprinted with permission from the author.

if she had a fold above each eye. Ellen brought the young girl to where I was sitting and said, *"You see, if you look at her you will know what I mean when I say that I had to have surgery done on my eyelids. Look at her eyes. She looks just like me before the surgery."* Stacy seemed very shy to show me her face. But I told the girl truthfully that she looked fine and beautiful the way she was. Immediately she grinned at her mother in a mocking, defiant manner, as if I had given her courage, and put her arm up in the manner that bodybuilders do when they display their bulging biceps.

As empowered as Stacy seemed to feel at the moment, I could not help but wonder how many times Ellen had shown her "before" and "after" photos to her young daughter with the remark that "Mommy looks better after the surgery." I also wondered how many times Stacy had been asked by Ellen to consider surgically "opening" her eyes like "Mommy did." And I wondered about the images we see on television and in magazines and their often negative, stereotypical portrayal of "squinty-eyed" Asians (when Asians are featured at all). I could not help but wonder how normal it is to feel that an eye without a crease is undesirable and how much of that feeling is imposed. And I shuddered to think how soon it might be before twelve-year-old Stacy's defenses gave away and she allowed her eyes to be cut.

The permanent alteration of bodies through surgery for aesthetic purposes is not a new phenomenon in the United States. As early as World War I, when reconstructive surgery was performed on disfigured soldiers, plastic surgery methods began to be refined for purely cosmetic purposes (that is, not so much for repairing and restoring but for transforming natural features a person is unhappy with). Within the last decade, however, an increasing number of people have opted for a wide array of cosmetic surgery procedures, from tummy tucks, facelifts, and liposuction to enlargement of chests and calves. By 1988, two million Americans had undergone cosmetic surgery (Wolf 1991:218), and a 69 percent increase had occurred in the number of cosmetic surgery procedures between 1981 and 1990, according to the ASPRS, or American Society of Plastic and Reconstructive Surgeons (n.d.).

Included in these numbers are an increasing number of cosmetic surgeries undergone by people like Stacy who are persons of color (American Academy of Cosmetic Surgery press release, 1991). In fact, Asian Americans are more likely than any other ethnic group (white or nonwhite) to pursue cosmetic surgery. ASPRS reports that over thirty-nine thousand of the aesthetic procedures performed by its members in 1990 (or more than 6 percent of all procedures performed that year) were performed on Asian Americans, who make up 3 percent of the U.S. population (Chen 1993:15). Because Asian Americans seek cosmetic surgery from doctors in Asia and from doctors who specialize in fields other than surgery (e.g., ear, nose, and throat specialists and opthamologists), the total number of Asian American patients is undoubtedly higher (Chen 1993:16).

The specific procedures requested by different ethnic groups in the United States are missing from the national data, but newspaper reports and medical texts indicate that Caucasians and nonwhites, on the average, seek significantly different types of operations (Chen 1993; Harahap 1982; Kaw 1993; LeFlore 1982; McCurdy 1990; Nakao 1993; Rosenthal 1991). While Caucasians primarily seek to augment breasts and to remove wrinkles and fat through such procedures as facelifts, liposuction, and collagen injection, African Americans more often opt for lip and nasal reduction operations; Asian Americans more often choose to insert an implant on their nasal dorsum for a more prominent nose or undergo double-eyelid surgery whereby parts of their upper eyelids are excised to create a fold above each eye, which makes the eye appear wider.

Though the American media, the medical establishment, and the general public have debated whether such cosmetic changes by nonwhite persons reflect a racist milieu in which racial minorities must deny their racial identity and attempt to look more Caucasian, a resounding no appears to be the overwhelming opinion of people in the United States. Many plastic surgeons have voiced the opinion that racial minorities are becoming more assertive about their right to choose and that they are choosing not to look Caucasian. Doctors say that nonwhite persons' desire for thinner lips, wider eyes, and pointier noses is no more than a wish to enhance their features in order to attain "balance" with all their other features (Kaw 1993; Merrell 1994; Rosenthal 1991).

Much of the media and public opinion also suggests that there is no political significance inherent in the cosmetic changes made by people of color which alter certain conventionally known, phenotypic markers of racial identity. On a recent Phil Donahue show where the racially derogatory nature of blue contact lenses for African American women was contested, both white and nonwhite audience members were almost unanimous that African American women's use of these lenses merely reflected their freedom to choose in the same way that Bo Derek chose to wear corn rows and white people decided to get tans (Bordo 1990). Focusing more specifically on cosmetic surgery, a *People Weekly* magazine article entitled "On the Cutting Edge" (January 27, 1992, p. 3) treats Michael Jackson (whose nose has become narrower and perkier and whose skin has become lighter through the years) as simply one among many Hollywood stars whose extravagant and competitive lifestyle has motivated and allowed them to pursue cosmetic self-enhancement. Clearly, Michael Jackson's physical transformation within the last decade has been more drastic than Barbara Hershey's temporary plumping of her lips to look younger in *Beaches* or Joan Rivers's facelift, yet his reasons for undergoing surgery are not differentiated from those of Caucasian celebrities; the possibility that he may want to cross racial divides through surgery is not an issue in the article.

When critics speculate on the possibility that a person of color is attempting to look white, they often focus their attack on the person and his or her apparent lack of ethnic pride and self-esteem. For instance, a *Newsweek* article, referring to Michael Jackson's recent television interview with Oprah

Winfrey, questioned Jackson's emphatic claim that he is proud to be a black American: "Jackson's dermatologist confirmed that the star has vitiligo, a condition that blocks the skin's ability to produce pigment . . . [however,] most vitiligo sufferers darken their light patches with makeup to even the tone. Jackson's makeup solution takes the other tack: less ebony, more ivory" (Fleming and Talbot 1993:57). Such criticisms, sadly, center around Michael Jackson the person instead of delving into his possible feelings of oppression or examining society as a potential source of his motivation to alter his natural features so radically.

. . . Based on structured, open-ended interviews with Asian American women like Ellen who have or are thinking about undergoing cosmetic surgery for wider eyes and more heightened noses, I attempt to convey more emphatically the lived social experiences of people of color who seek what appears to be conventionally recognized Caucasian features. Rather than mock their decision to alter their features or treat it lightly as an expression of their freedom to choose an idiosyncratic look, I examine everyday cultural images and social relationships which influence Asian American women to seek cosmetic surgery in the first place. Instead of focusing, as some doctors do (Kaw 1993), on the size and width of the eyelid folds the women request as indicators of the women's desire to look Caucasian, I examine the cultural, social, and historical sources that allow the women in my study to view their eyes in a negative fashion—as "small" and "slanted" eyes reflecting a "dull," "passive" personality, a "closed" mind, and a "lack of spirit" in the person. I explore the reasons these women reject the natural shape of their eyes so radically that they willingly expose themselves to a surgery that is at least an hour long, costs one thousand to three thousand dollars, entails administering local anesthesia and sedation, and carries the following risks: "bleeding and hematoma," "hemorrhage," formation of a "gaping wound," "discoloration," scarring, and "asymmetric lid folds" (Sayoc 1974:162–66).

In our feminist analyses of femininity and beauty, we may sometimes find it difficult to account for cosmetic surgery without undermining the thoughts and decisions of women who opt for it (Davis 1991). However, I attempt to show that the decision of the women in my study to undergo cosmetic surgery is often carefully thought out. Such a decision is usually made only after a long period of weighing the psychological pain of feeling inadequate prior to surgery against the possible social advantages a new set of features may bring. Several of the women were aware of complex power structures that construct their bodies as inferior and in need of change, even while they simultaneously reproduced these structures by deciding to undergo surgery (Davis 1991:33).

I argue that as women and as racial minorities, the psychological burden of having to measure up to ideals of beauty in American society falls especially heavy on these Asian American women. As women, they are constantly bombarded with the notion that beauty should be their primary goal (Lakoff and Scherr 1984; Wolf 1991). As racial minorities, they are made to feel inadequate by an Anglo American–dominated cultural milieu that has historically both excluded them and distorted images of them in such a way that they themselves have come to associate those features stereotypically identified with their race (i.e., small, slanty eyes, and a flat nose) with negative personality and mental characteristics.

In a consumption-oriented society such as the United States, it is often tempting to believe that human beings have an infinite variety of needs which technology can endlessly fulfill, and that these needs, emerging spontaneously in time and space, lack any coherent patterns, cultural meanings, or political significance (Bordo 1990; Goldstein 1993; O'Neill 1985:98). However, one cannot regard needs as spontaneous, infinite harmless, and amorphous without first considering what certain groups feel they lack and without first critically examining the lens with which the larger society has historically viewed this lack. Frances C. MacGregor, who between 1946 and 1959 researched the social and cultural motivations of such white ethnic minorities as Jewish and Italian Americans to seek rhinoplasty, wrote, "The statements of the patients . . . have a certain face validity and explicitness that reflect both the values of our society and the degree to which these are perceived as creating problems for the deviant individual" (MacGregor 1967:129).

Social scientific analyses of ethnic relations should include a study of the body. As evident in my research, racial minorities may internalize a body image produced by the dominant culture's racial ideology and, because of it, began to loathe, mutilate, and revise parts of their bodies. Bodily adornment and mutilation (the cutting up and altering of essential parts of the body; see Kaw 1993) are symbolic mediums most directly and concretely concerned with the construction of the individual as social actor or cultural subject (Turner 1980). Yet social scientists have only recently focused on the body as a central component of social self-identity (Blacking 1977; Brain 1979; Daly 1978; Lock and Scheper-Hughes 1990; O'Neill 1985; Turner 1980; Sheets-Johnstone 1992). Moreover, social scientists, and sociocultural anthropologists in particular, have not yet explored the ways in which the body is central to the everyday experience of racial identity.

Method and Description of Subjects

In this article, I present the findings of an ethnographic research project completed in the San Francisco Bay Area. I draw on data from structured interviews with doctors and patients, basic medical statistics, and relevant newspaper and magazine articles. The sampling of informants for this research was not random in the strictly statistical sense since informants were difficult to find. Both medical practitioners and patients treat cases of cosmetic surgery as highly confidential, as I later discuss in more detail. To find a larger, more random sampling of Asian American informants, I posted fliers and placed advertisements in various local newspapers. Ultimately, I was able to conduct structured, open-ended interviews with eleven Asian American women, four of whom were referred to me by the doctors in my study and six by mutual acquaintances; I found one through an advertisement. Nine had had cosmetic surgery of the eye or the nose; one recently considered a double-eyelid operation; one is considering undergoing double-eyelid operation in the next few years. The women in my study live in the San Francisco Bay Area, except for two who reside in the Los Angeles area. Five were operated on by doctors who I also interviewed for my study, while four had their operations in Asia—two in Seoul, Korea, one in Beijing, China, and one in Taipei, Taiwan. Of the eleven women in my study, only two (who received their operations in China and in Taiwan) had not lived in the United States prior to their operations. The ages of the Asian American women in my study range from eighteen to seventy-one; one woman was only fifteen at the time of her operation. Their class backgrounds are similar in that they were all engaged in middle-class, white-collar occupations: there were three university students, one art student, one legal assistant, one clerk, one nutritionist, one teacher, one law student, and two doctors' assistants.

Although I have not interviewed Asian American men who have or are thinking of undergoing cosmetic surgery, I realize that they too undergo double-eyelid and nose bridge operations. Their motivations are, to a large extent, similar to those of the women in my study (Iwata 1991). Often their decision to undergo surgery also follows a long and painful process of feeling marginal in society (Iwata 1991). I did not purposely exclude Asian American male patients from my study; rather, none responded to my requests for interviews.

To understand how plastic surgeons view the cosmetic procedures performed on Asian Americans, five structured, open-ended interviews were conducted with five plastic surgeons, all of whom practice in the Bay Area. I also examined several medical books and plastic surgery journals which date from the 1950s to 1990. And I referenced several news releases and informational packets distributed by such national organizations as the American Society of Plastic and Reconstructive Surgeons, an organization which represents 97 percent of all physicians certified by the American Board of Plastic Surgery.

To examine popular notions of cosmetic surgery, in particular how the phenomenon of Asian American women receiving double-eyelid and nose bridge operations is viewed by the public and the media, I have referenced relevant newspaper and magazine articles.

I obtained national data on cosmetic surgery from various societies for cosmetic surgeons, including the American Society of Plastic and Reconstructive Surgeons. Data on the specific types of surgery sought by different ethnic groups in the United States, including Asian Americans, were missing from the national statistics. At least one public relations coordinator told me that such data are unimportant to plastic surgeons. To compensate for this lack of data, I asked the doctors in my study to provide me with figures from their respective clinics. Most told me they had little data on their cosmetic patients readily available.

Colonization of Asian American Women's Souls: Internalization of Gender and Racial Stereotypes

Upon first talking with my Asian American women informants, one might conclude that the women were merely seeking to enhance their features for aesthetic reasons and that there is no cultural meaning or political significance in their decision to surgically enlarge their eyes and heighten their noses. As Elena, a twenty-one-year-old Chinese American who underwent double-eyelid surgery three years ago from a doctor in my study, stated: *"I underwent my surgery for personal reasons. It's not different from wanting to put makeup on. . . . I don't intend to look Anglo-Saxon. I told my doctor, 'I would like my eyes done with definite creases on my eyes, but I don't want a drastic change.'"* Almost all the other women similarly stated that their unhappiness with their eyes and nose was individually motivated and that they really did not desire Caucasian features. In fact, one Korean American woman, Nina, age thirty-four, stated she was not satisfied with the results of her surgery from three years ago because her doctor made her eyes "too round" like that of Caucasians. One might deduce from such statements that the women's decision to undergo cosmetic surgery of the eye and nose is harmless and may be even empowering to them, for their surgery provides them with a more permanent solution than makeup for "personal" dissatisfactions they have about their features.

However, an examination of their descriptions of the natural shape of their eyes and nose suggests that their "personal" feelings about their features reflect the larger society's negative valuation and stereotyping of Asian features in general. They all said that "small, slanty" eyes and a "flat" nose suggest, in the Asian person, a personality that is "dull," "unenergetic," "passive," and "unsociable" and a mind that is narrow and "closed." For instance, Elena said, *"When I look at other Asians who have no folds and their eyes are slanted and closed, I think of how they would look better more awake."* Nellee, a twenty-one-year-old Chinese American, said that she seriously considered surgery for double eyelids in high school so that she could "avoid the stereotype of the 'oriental bookworm'" who is "dull and doesn't know how to have fun." Carol, a thirty-seven-year-old Chinese American who received double eyelids seven years ago, said: *"The eyes are the window of your soul . . . [yet] lots of oriental people have the outer corners of their eyes a little down, making them look tired. [The double eyelids] don't make a big difference in the size of our eyes but they give your eyes more spirit."* Pam, a Chinese American, age forty-four, who received double-eyelid surgery from another doctor in my study, stated, *"Yes.*

Of course. Bigger eyes look prettier. . . . Lots of Asians' eyes are so small they become little lines when the person laughs, making the person look sleepy." Likewise, Annie, an eighteen-year-old Korean American woman who had an implant placed on her nasal dorsum to build up her nose bridge at age fifteen, said: *"I guess I always wanted that sharp look—a look like you are smart. If you have a roundish kind of nose it's like you don't know what's going on. If you have that sharp look, you know, with black eyebrows, a pointy nose, you look more alert. I always thought that was cool."* The women were influenced by the larger society's negative valuation of stereotyped Asian features in such a way that they evaluated themselves and Asian women in general with a critical eye. Their judgments were based on a set of standards, stemming from the eighteenth- and nineteenth-century European aesthetic ideal of the proportions in Greek sculpture, which are presumed by a large amount of Americans to be within the grasp of every woman (Goldstein 1993:150, 160).

Unlike many white women who may also seek cosmetic surgery to reduce or make easier the daily task of applying makeup, the Asian American women in my study hoped more specifically to ease the task of creating with makeup the illusion of features they do not have as women who are Asian. Nellee, who has not yet undergone double-eyelid surgery, said that at present she has to apply makeup everyday *"to give my eyes an illusion of a crease. When I don't wear makeup I feel my eyes are small."* Likewise, Elena said that before her double-eyelid surgery she checked almost every morning in the mirror when she woke up to see if a fold had formed above her right eye to match the more prominent fold above her left eye: *"[on certain mornings] it was like any other day when you wake up and don't feel so hot, you know. My eye had no definite folds, because when Asians sleep their folds change in and out—it's not definite."* Also, Jo, a twenty-eight-year-old Japanese American who already has natural folds above each eye but wishes to enlarge them through double-eyelid surgery, explained:

> *I guess I just want to make a bigger eyelid [fold] so that they look bigger and not slanted. I think in Asian eyes it's the inside corner of the fold [she was drawing on my notebook] that goes down too much. . . . Right now I am still self-conscious about leaving the house without any makeup on, because I feel just really ugly without it. I try to curl my eyelashes and put on mascara. I think it makes my eyes look more open. But surgery can permanently change the shape of my eyes. I don't think that a bigger eyelid fold will actually change the slant but I think it will give the perception of having less of it, less of an Asian eye.*

For the women in my study, their oppression is a double encounter: one under patriarchal definitions of femininity (i.e., that a woman should care about the superficial details of her look), and the other under Caucasian standards of beauty. The constant self-monitoring of their anatomy and their continuous focus on detail exemplify the extent to which they feel they must measure up to society's ideals.

In the United States, where a capitalist work ethic values "freshness," "a quick wit," and assertiveness, many Asian American women are already disadvantaged at birth by virtue of their inherited physical features which society associates with dullness and passivity. In this way, their desire to look more spirited and energetic through the surgical creation of folds above each eye is of a different quality from the motivation of many Anglo Americans seeking facelifts and liposuction for a fresher, more youthful appearance. Signs of aging are not the main reason Asian American cosmetic patients ultimately seek surgery of the eyes and the nose; often they are younger (usually between eighteen and thirty years of age) than the average Caucasian patient (Kaw 1993). Several of the Asian American women in my study who were over thirty years of age at the time of their eyelid operation sought surgery to get rid of extra folds of skin that had developed over their eyes due to age; however, even these women decided to receive double eyelids in the process. When Caucasian patients undergo eyelid surgery, on the other hand, the procedure is almost never to create a double eyelid (for they already possess one); in most cases, it is to remove sagging skin that results from aging. Clearly, Asian American women's negative image of their eyes and nose is not so much a result of their falling short of the youthful, energetic beauty ideal that influences every American as it is a direct product of society's racial stereotyping.

The women in my study described their own features with metaphors of dullness and passivity in keeping with many Western stereotypes of Asians. Stereotypes, by definition, are expedient caricatures of the "other," which serve to set them apart from the "we"; they serve to exclude instead of include, to judge instead of accept (Gilman 1985:15). Asians are rarely portrayed in the American print and electronic media. For instance, Asians (who constitute 3 percent of the U.S. population) account for less than 1 percent of the faces represented in magazine ads, according to a 1991 study titled "Invisible People" conducted by New York City's Department of Consumer Affairs (cited in Chen 1993:26). When portrayed, they are seen in one of two forms, which are not representative of Asians in general: as Eurasian-looking fashion models and movie stars (e.g., Nancy Kwan, who played Suzie Wong) who already have double eyelids and pointy noses; and as stereotypically Asian characters such as Charlie Chan, depicted with personalities that are dull, passive, and nonsociable (Dower 1986; Kim 1986; Ramsdell 1983; Tajima 1989). The first group often serves as an ideal toward which Asian American women strive, even when they say they do not want to look Caucasian. The second serves as an image from which they try to escape.

Asian stereotypes, like all kinds of stereotypes, are multiple and have changed throughout the years; nevertheless they have maintained some distinct characteristics. Asians have been portrayed as exotic and erotic (as epitomized by Suzie Wong, or the Japanese temptress in the film *The Berlin Affair*), and especially during the U.S. war in the Pacific during World War II, they were seen as dangerous spies and mad geniuses who were treacherous and stealthy (Dower 1986; Huhr and Kim 1989). However, what remains consistent in the American popular image of Asians is their childishness, narrow-mindedness, and lack of leadership skills. Moreover, these qualities have long been associated with the relatively roundish form of Asian faces, and in particular with the "puffy" smallness of their eyes. Prior to the Japanese attack on Pearl Harbor, for instance, the Japanese were considered incapable of planning successful dive bombing attacks due to their "myopic," "squinty" eyes. During the war in the Pacific, their soldiers were caricatured as having thick horn-rimmed glasses through which they must squint to see their targets (Dower 1986). Today, the myopic squinty-eyed image of the narrow-minded Asian persists in the most recent stereotype of Asians as "model minorities" (as eptimoized in the Asian exchange student character in the film *Sixteen Candles*). The term *model minority* was first coined in the 1960s when a more open-door U.S. immigration policy began allowing an unprecedented number of Asian immigrants into the United States, many of whom were the most elite and educated of their own countries (Takaki 1989). Despite its seemingly complimentary nature, *model minority* refers to a person who is hardworking and technically skilled but desperately lacking in creativity, worldliness, and the ability to assimilate into mainstream culture (Huhr and Kim 1989; Takaki 1989). Representations in the media, no matter how subtle, of various social situations can distort and reinforce one's impressions of one's own nature (Goffman 1979).

Witnessing society's association of Asian features with negative personality traits and mental characteristics, many Asian Americans become attracted to the image of Caucasian, or at least Eurasian, features. Several of the women in my study stated that they are influenced by images of fashion models with Western facial types. As Nellee explained: *"I used to read a lot of fashion magazines which showed occidental persons how to put makeup on. So I used to think a crease made one's eyes prettier. It exposes your eyelashes more. Right now they all go under the hood of my eyes."* Likewise, Jo said she thought half of her discontent regarding her eyes is a self-esteem problem, but she blames the other half on society: *"When you look at all the stuff that they portray on TV and in the movies and in Miss America pageants, the epitome of who is beautiful is that all-American look. It can even include African Americans now but not Asians."* According to Jo, she is influenced not only by representations of Asians as passive, dull, and narrow-minded, but also by a lack of representation of Asians in general because society considers them un-American, unassimilable, foreign, and to be excluded.

Similar images of Asians also exist in East and Southeast Asia, and since many Asian Americans are immigrants from Asia, they are likely influenced by these images as well. Multinational corporations in Southeast Asia, for example, consider the female work force biologically suited for the most monotonous industrial labor because they claim the "Oriental girl" is "diligent" and has "nimble fingers" and a "slow-wit" (Ong 1987:151). In addition, American magazines and films have become increasingly available in many parts of Asia since World War II, and Asian popular magazines and electronic media depict models with Western facial types, especially when advertising Western products. In fact, many of my Asian American women informants possessed copies of such magazines, available in various Asian stores and in Chinatown. Some informants, like Jane, a twenty-year-old Korean American who underwent double-eyelid surgery at age sixteen and nasal bridge surgery at age eighteen, thumbed through Korean fashion magazines which she stored in her living room to show me photos of the Western and Korean models who she thought looked Caucasian, Eurasian, or had had double-eyelid and nasal bridge surgeries. She said these women had eyes that were too wide and noses that were too tall and straight to be on Asians. Though she was born and raised in the United States, she visits her relatives in Korea often. She explained that the influences the media had on her life in Korea and in the United States were, in some sense, similar: *"When you turn on the TV [in Korea], you see people like Madonna and you see MTV and American movies and magazines. In any fashion magazine you don't really see a Korean-type woman; you see Cindy Crawford. My mother was telling me that when she was a kid, the ideal beauty was someone with a totally round, flat face. Kind of small and five feet tall. I guess things began to change in the 1950s when Koreans started to have a lot of contact with the West."* The environment within which Asian women develop a perspective on the value and meaning of their facial features is most likely not identical in Asia and the United States, where Asian women are a minority, but in Asia one can still be influenced by Western perceptions of Asians.

Some of the women in my study maintained that although racial inequality may exist in many forms, their decision to widen their eyes had little to do with racial inequality; they were attempting to look like other Asians with double eyelids, not like Caucasians. Nina, for example, described a *beautiful woman as such: "Her face should not have very slender eyes like Chinese, Korean, or Japanese but not as round as Europeans. Maybe Filipino, Thai, or other Southeast Asian faces are ideal. Basically I like an Asian's looks. . . . I think Asian eyes [not really slender ones] are sexy and have character."* The rest of her description, however, makes it more difficult for one to believe that the Asian eyes she is describing actually belong on an Asian body: *"The skin should not be too dark . . . and the frame should be a bit bigger than that of Asians."* Southeast Asians, too, seek cosmetic surgery for double eyelids and nose bridges. One doctor showed me "before" and "after" photos of many Thai, Indonesian, and Vietnamese American women, who, he said, came to him for wider, more definite creases so that their eyes, which already have a double-eyelid, would look deeper-set.

In the present global economy, where the movement of people and cultural products is increasingly rapid and frequent and the knowledge of faraway places and trends is expanding, it is possible to imagine that cultural exchange happens in a multiplicity of directions, that often people construct images and practices that appear unconnected to any particular locality or culture (Appadurai 1990). One might perceive Asian American women in my study as constructing aesthetic images of themselves based on neither a Caucasian ideal nor a stereotypical Asian face. The difficulty with such constructions, however, is that they do not help Asian Americans to escape at least one stereotypical notion of Asians in the United States—that they are "foreign" and "exotic." Even when Asians are considered sexy, and attractive in the larger American society, they are usually seen as exotically sexy and attractive (Yang and Ragaz 1993:21). Since their beauty is almost always equated with the exotic and foreign, they are seen as members of an undifferentiated mass of people. Even though the women in my study are attempting to be seen as individuals, they are seen, in some sense, as less distinguishable from each other than white women are. As Lumi, a Japanese former model recently told *A. Magazine: The Asian American Quarterly,* "I've had bookers tell me I'm beautiful, but that they can't use me because I'm 'type.' All the agencies have their one Asian girl, and any more would be redundant" (Chen 1993:21).

The constraints many Asian Americans feel with regard to the shape of their eyes and nose are clearly of a different quality from almost every American's discontent with weight or signs of aging; it is also different from the dissatisfaction many women, white and nonwhite alike, feel about the smallness or largeness of their breasts. Because the features (eyes and nose) Asian Americans are most concerned about are conventional markers of their racial identity, a rejection of these markers entails, in some sense, a devaluation of not only oneself but also other Asian Americans. It requires having to imitate, if not admire, the characteristics of another group more culturally dominant than one's own (i.e., Anglo Americans) in order that one can at least try to distinguish oneself from one's own group. Jane, for instance, explains that looking like a Caucasian is almost essential for socioeconomic success: *"Especially if you go into business, or whatever, you kind of have to have a Western facial type and you have to have like their features and stature—you know, be tall and stuff. So you can see that [the surgery] is an investment in your future."*

Unlike those who may want to look younger or thinner in order to find a better job or a happier social life, the women in my study must take into consideration not only their own socioeconomic future, but also more immediately that of their offspring, who by virtue of heredity, inevitably share their features. Ellen, for instance, said that *"looks are not everything. I want my daughter, Stacy, to know that what's inside is important too. Sometimes you can look beautiful because your nice personality and wisdom inside radiate outward, such as in the way you talk and behave."* Still, she has been encouraging twelve-year-old Stacy to have double-eyelid surgery because she thinks "having less sleepy looking eyes would make a better impression on people and help her in the future with getting jobs." Ellen had undergone cosmetic surgery at the age of twenty on the advice of her mother and older sister and feels she has benefited. Indeed, all three women in the study under thirty who have actually undergone cosmetic surgery did so on the advice of their mother and in their mother's presence at the clinic. Elena, in fact, received her double-eyelid surgery as a high school graduation present from her mother, who was concerned for her socioeconomic future. The mothers, in turn, are influenced not so much by a personal flaw of their own which drives them to mold and perfect their daughters as by a society that values the superficial characteristics of one race over another.

A few of the women's dating and courtship patterns were also affected by their negative feelings toward stereotypically Asian features. Jo, for example, who is married to a Caucasian man, said she has rarely dated Asian men and is not usually attracted to them, partly because they look too much like her: *"I really am sorry to say that I am not attracted to Asian men. And it's not to say that I don't find them attractive on the whole. But I did date a Japanese guy once and I felt like I was holding my brother's hand [she laughs nervously]."*

A Mutilation of the Body

Although none of the women in my study denied the fact of racial inequality, almost all insisted that the surgical alteration of their eyes and nose was a celebration of their bodies, reflecting their right as women and as minorities to do what they wished with their bodies. Many, such as Jane, also said the surgery was a rite of passage or a routine ceremony, since family members and peers underwent the surgery upon reaching eighteen. Although it is at least possible to perceive cosmetic surgery of the eyes and nose for many Asian Americans as a celebration of the individual and social bodies, as in a rite of passage, this is clearly not so. My research has shown that double-eyelid and nasal bridge procedures performed on Asian Americans do not hold, for either the participants or the larger society, cultural meanings that are benign and spontaneous. Rather, these surgeries are a product of society's racial ideologies, and for many of the women in my study, the surgeries are a calculated means for socioeconomic success. In fact, most describe the surgery as something to "get out of the way" before carrying on with the rest of their lives.

Unlike participants in a rite of passage, these Asian American women share little *communitas* (an important element of rites of passage) with each other or with the larger society. Arnold Van Gennup defined rites of passage as "rites which accompany every change of place, state, social position, and age" (quoted in Turner 1969:94). These rites create an almost egalitarian type of solidarity (communitas) between participants and between the participants and a larger social group. A body modification procedure which is an example of such a rite is the series of public head-scarification rituals for pubescent boys among the Kabre of Togo, West Africa (Brain 1979:178). The final scars they acquire make them full adult members of their group. Their scarification differs considerably from the cosmetic surgery procedures of Asian American women in my study in at least two of its aspects: (1) an egalitarian bond is formed between the participants (between and among those who are doing the scarring and those who are receiving it); and (2) both the event and the resulting feature (i.e., scars) signify the boy's incorporation into a larger social group (i.e., adult men), and therefore, both are unrelentingly made public.

The Asian American women who undergo double-eyelid and nasal bridge surgeries do not usually create bonds with each other or with their plastic surgeons. Their surgery, unlike the scarification rite of the Kabre, is a private event that usually occurs in the presence of the patient, the doctor, and the doctor's assistants only. Moreover, there is little personal connection between doctor and patient. Though a few of the Asian American women in my study were content with their surgery and with their doctors, most describe their experience on the operating table as one of fear and loneliness, and some described their doctors as impersonal, businesslike, and even tending toward profit-making. Annie, for instance, described the fear she felt being alone with the doctor and his assistants in the operating room, when her mother suddenly left the room because she could not bear to watch:

> They told me to put my thumbs under my hips so I didn't interfere with my hands. I received two anesthesia shots on my nose—this was the only part of the operation that hurt, but it hurt! I closed my eyes. I didn't want to look. I didn't want to see like the knives or anything. I could feel like the snapping of scissors and I was aware when they were putting that thing up my nose. My mom didn't really care. They told her to look at my nose. They were wondering if I wanted it sharper and stuff. She said, "Oh no. I don't want to look" and just ran away. She was sitting outside. I was really pissed.

Elena described her experience of surgery in a similar manner: "*I had no time to be nervous. They drugged me with valium, I think. I was awake but drugged, conscious but numb. I remember being on the table. They [doctor and nurses] continued to keep up a conversation. I would wince sometimes because I could feel little pinches. He [the doctor] would say, 'Okay. Pumpkin, Sweetheart, it will be over soon.' . . . I didn't like it, being called Pumpkin and being touched by a stranger. . . . I wanted to say Shut up! to all three people.*" Clearly, the event of surgery did not provide an opportunity or the atmosphere for the women in my study to forge meaningful relationships with their doctors.

Asian American women who undergo cosmetic surgery also have a very limited chance of bonding with each other by sharing experiences of the surgery, because unlike participants in a Kabre puberty rite, these women do not usually publicize either their operation or their new features. All informed me that apart from me and their doctors, few people knew about their surgery since at the most they had told three close friends and/or family members about it. As Annie stated, *"I don't mind if people found out [that I had a nose operation], but I won't go around telling them."* Jane explained: *"It's nothing to be ashamed of, not at all, but it's not something you brag about either. . . . To this day my boyfriend doesn't notice I had anything done. That makes me feel pretty good. It's just that you want to look good, but you don't want them [other people] to know how much effort goes into it."* In fact, all the women in my study said they wanted a "better" look, but one that was not so drastically different from the original that it looked "unnatural." Even those who underwent revision surgeries to improve on their first operation said they were more at ease and felt more effective in social situations (with boyfriends, classmates and employers) after their primary operation, mainly because they looked subtly "better," not because they looked too noticeably different from the way they used to look. Thus, it is not public awareness of these women's cosmetic surgery or the resulting features which win them social acceptance. Rather, the successful personal concealment of the operation and of any glaring traces of the operation (e.g., scars or an "unnatural" look) is paramount for acceptance. Clearly, the alteration of their features is not a rite of passage celebrating the incorporation of individual bodies into a larger social body; rather, it is a personal quest by marginal people seeking acceptance in a society where the dominant culture's ideals loom large and are constraining. The extent to which the Asian American women have internalized society's negative valuation of their natural features is best exemplified by the fact that these women feel more self-confident in social interactions as a result of this slight alteration of their eyelids—that is, with one minor alteration in their whole anatomy—which others may not even notice.

Medicine and the "Disembodiment" of the Asian American Female Consumer

Some sectors of the medical profession fail to recognize that Asian American women's decision to undergo cosmetic surgery of the eyelid and the nose is not so much triggered by a simple materialistic urge to feel better with one more status item that money can buy as much as it is an attempt to heal a specific doubt about oneself which society has unnecessarily brought on. For instance, one doctor in my study stated the following about double-eyelid surgery on Asian American women: *"It's like when you wear certain shoes, certain clothes, or put certain makeup on, well—why do you wear those? Why this brand of clothes and not another? . . . You can label these things different ways, but I think that it [the double-eyelid surgery of Asian Americans] is just a desire to look better. You know, it's like driving a brand-new car down the street or having something bought from Nordstrom."* By viewing cosmetic surgery and items bought from a department store as equally arbitrary, plastic surgeons, like economists, sometimes assume that the consumer (in this case, the cosmetic surgery client) is disembodied (O'Neill 1985:103). They view her as an abstract, nonhuman subject whose choice of items is not mediated by any historical circumstances, symbolic meaning, or political significance.

With "advances" in science and technology and the proliferation of media images, the number of different selves one can become appears arbitrary and infinite to many Americans, including the women in my study. Thus, many of them argue, as do some plastic surgeons (see Kaw 1993), that the variation in the width of the crease requested by Asian Americans (from six to ten millimeters) is indicative of a whole range of personal and idiosyncratic styles in double-eyelid operations. The idea is that the women are not conforming to any standard, that they are molding their own standards of beauty. However, they ignore that a primary goal in all double-eyelid operations, regardless of how high or how far across the eyelid the crease is cut, is to have a more open appearance of the eye, and the trend in all cases is to create a fold where there was none. These operations are an instance of the paradoxical "production of variety within standardization" in American consumer culture (Goldstein 1993:152). Thus, there is a double bind in undergoing a double-eyelid operation. On the one hand, the women are rebelling against the notion that one must be content with the physical features one is born with, that one cannot be creative in molding one's own idea of what is beautiful. On the other hand, they are conforming to Caucasian standards of beauty.

The women in the study seem to have an almost unconditional faith that science and technology will help them feel satisfied with their sense of self. And the plastic surgery industry, with its scientific advances and seemingly objective stance, makes double-eyelid surgery appear routine, necessary, and for the most part, harmless (Kaw 1993). The women in my study had read advertisements of cosmetic surgery clinics, many of them catering to their specific "needs." In my interviews with Nellee, who had once thought about having double-eyelid surgery, and Jo, who is thinking about it for the near future, I did not have to tell them that the operation entailed creating a crease on the upper eyelid through incision and sutures. They told me. Jo, for instance, said, *"I know the technology and it's quite easy, so I am not really afraid of it messing up."*

Conclusion: Problem of Resistance in a Culture Based on Endless Self-Fashioning

My research has shown that Asian American women's decision to undergo cosmetic surgery for wider eyes and more prominent noses is very much influenced by society's racial stereotyping of Asian features. Many of the women in my study are aware of the racial stereotypes from which they suffer. However, all have internalized these negative images of themselves and of other Asians, and they judge the Asian body, including their own, with the critical eye of the oppressor. Moreover, almost all share the attitude of certain sectors of the media and medicine in regard to whether undergoing a surgical operation is, in the end, harmful or helpful to themselves and other Asian Americans; they say it is yet another exercise of their freedom of choice.

The American value of individualism has influenced many of the women to believe that the specific width and shape they choose for their eyelid folds and nose bridges indicate that they are molding their own standards of beauty. Many said they wanted a "natural" look that would be uniquely "in balance" with the rest of their features. However, even those such as Jane, who openly expressed the idea that she is conforming to a Western standard of beauty, emphasized that she is not oppressed but rather empowered by her surgical transformation: *"Everything is conforming as I see it. It's just a matter of recognizing it. . . . Other people—well, they are also conforming to something else. Nothing anybody has ever done is original. And it's very unlikely that people would go out and be dressed in any way if they hadn't seen it somewhere. So I don't think it's valid to put a value judgment on [the type of surgery I did]. I'm definitely for self-improvement. So if you don't like a certain part of your body, there's no reason not to change it."*

The constraints Asian American women in my study feel every day with regard to their natural features are a direct result of unequal race relationships in the United States. These women's apparent lack of concern for their racial oppression is symptomatic of a certain postmodern culture arising in the United States which has the effect of hiding structural inequalities from public view (Bordo 1990). In its attempt to celebrate differences and to shun overgeneralizations and totalizing discourses that apparently efface diversity among people in modern life, this postmodern culture actually obscures differences; that is, by viewing differences as all equally arbitrary, it effaces from public consciousness historically determined differences in power between groups of people. Thus, blue contact lenses for African American women, and double eyelids and nose bridges for Asian women are both seen as forms of empowerment and indistinguishable in form and function from perms for white women, corn rows on Bo Derek, and tans on Caucasians. All cosmetic changes are seen in the same way—as having no cultural meaning and no political significance. In this process, what is trivialized and obscured is the difficult, and often frustrated struggle with which subordinate groups must assert their difference as something to be proud of in the face of dominant ideologies (Bordo 1990:666).

With the proliferation of scientific and technological industries, the many selves one can become appear infinite and random. Like the many transformations of the persona of Madonna throughout her career or the metamorphosis of Michael Jackson's face during his "Black and White" video, the alteration of bodies through plastic surgery has become for the American public simply another means of self-expression and self-determination. As

Ellen said, *"You can be born Chinese. But if you want to look like a more desirable one, and if surgery is available like it is now, then why not do it?"* She said that instead of having to undergo the arduous task of placing thin strips of transparent plastic tape over the eyelids to create a temporary crease (a procedure which, she said, many Asians unhappy with single eyelids used to do), Asians now have the option to permanently transform the shape of their eyes.

Thus, instead of becoming a battleground for social and cultural resistance, the body has become a playground (Bordo 1990:667). Like Michael Jackson's lyrics in the song "Man in the Mirror" ("If you want to make the world a better place, then take a look at yourself and make a change"; Jackson 1987), it is ambiguous whether political change and social improvement are best orchestrated through changing society or through an "act of creative interpretation" (Bordo 1990) of the superficial details of one's appearance. The problem and dilemma of resistance in U.S. society are best epitomized in this excerpt of my interview with Jo, the twenty-eight-year-old law student who is thinking of having double-eyelid surgery:

> *Jo: In my undergraduate college, every Pearl Harbor Day I got these phone calls and people would say, "Happy Pearl Harbor Day," and they made noises like bombs and I'd find little toy soldiers at my dorm door. Back then, I kind of took it as a joke. But now, I think it was more malicious. . . . [So] I think the surgery is a lot more superficial. Affecting how society feels about a certain race is a lot more beneficial. And it goes a lot deeper and lasts a lot longer.*
>
> *Interviewer:* Looking into the future, do you think you will do both?
>
> *Jo: Yeah* [nervous laughter]. *I do. I do.*

Jo recognizes that undergoing double-eyelid surgery, that is, confirming the undesirability of Asian eyes, is in contradiction to the work she would like to do as a teacher and legal practitioner. However, she said she cannot easily destroy the negative feelings she already possesses about the natural shape of her eyes.

Implications: Asian Americans and the American Dream

The psychological burden of having constantly to measure up has been often overlooked in the image of Asian Americans as model minorities, as people who have achieved the American dream. The model minority myth assumes not only that all Asian Americans are financially well-to-do, but also that those Asian Americans who are from relatively well-to-do, non-working-class backgrounds (like many of the women in my study) are free from the everyday constraints of painful racial stereotypes (see Takaki 1989; Huhr and Kim 1989). As my research has shown, the cutting up of Asian Americans' faces through plastic surgery is a concrete example of how, in modern life, Asian Americans, like other people of color, can be influenced by the dominant culture to loathe themselves in such a manner as to begin mutilating and revising parts of their body.

Currently, the eyes and nose are those parts of the anatomy which Asian Americans most typically cut and alter since procedures for these are relatively simple with the available technology. However, a few of the women in my study said that if they could, they would also want to increase their stature, and in particular, to lengthen their legs; a few also suggested that when safer implants were found, they wanted to augment their breasts; still others wanted more prominent brow bridges and jawlines. On the one hand, it appears that through technology women can potentially carve an endless array of new body types, breaking the bounds of racial categories. On the other hand, these desired body types are constructed in the context of the dominant culture's beauty ideals. The search for the ideal body may have a tremendous impact, in terms of racial discrimination, on patterns of artificial genetic selection, such as occurs at sperm banks, egg donation centers, and in the everyday ritual of courtship.

REFERENCES

American Society of Plastic and Reconstructive Surgeons (ASPRS). N.d. "Estimated Number of Cosmetic Surgery Procedures Performed by ASPRS Members in 1990." Pamphlet.

Appadurai, Arjun. 1990. "Disjuncture and Difference in the Global Cultural Economy." *Public Culture* 2(2):1–24.

Blacking, John. 1977. *The Anthropology of the Body.* London: Academic Press.

Bordo, Susan. 1990. "Material Girl: The Effacements of Postmodern Culture." *Michigan Quarterly Review* 29:635–76.

Brain, Robert. 1979. *The Decorated Body.* New York: Harper and Row.

Chen, Joanne. 1993. "Before and After: For Asian Americans, the Issues Underlying Cosmetic Surgery Are Not Just Skin Deep." *A Magazine: The Asian American Quarterly* 2(1):15–18, 26–27.

Daly, Mary. 1978. *Gyn/ecology: The Metaethics of Radical Feminism.* Boston: Beacon Press.

Davis, Kathy. 1991. "Remaking the She-Devil: A Critical Look at Feminist Approaches to Beauty." *Hypatia* 6(2):21–43.

Dower, John. 1986. *War without Mercy: Race and Power in the Pacific War.* New York: Pantheon.

Fleming, Charles and Mary Talbot. 1993. "The Two Faces of Michael Jackson." *Newsweek,* February 22, p. 57.

Gilman, Sander L. 1985. *Difference and Pathology: Stereotypes of Sexuality, Race and Madness.* Ithaca, NY: Cornell University Press.

Goffman, Erving. 1979. *Gender Advertisement.* Cambridge: Harvard University Press.

Goldstein, Judith. 1993. "The Female Aesthetic Community." *Poetics Today* 14(1): 143–63.

Harahap, Marwali. 1982. "Oriental Cosmetic Blepharoplasty." Pp. 79–97 in *Cosmetic Surgery for Non-white Patients,* edited by Harold Pierce. New York: Grune & Stratton.

Huhr, Won Moo and Kwant Chung Kim. 1989. "The 'Success' Image of Asian Americans: Validity, and Its Practical and Theoretical Implications." *Ethnic and Racial Studies* 12(4):512–37.

Iwata, Edward. 1991. "Race without Face." *San Francisco Image Magazine,* May, pp. 51–55.

Jackson, Michael. 1987. "Man in the Mirror." On *Bad.* Epic Records, New York.

Kaw, Eugenia. 1993. "Medicalization of Racial Features: Asian American Women and Cosmetic Surgery." *Medical Anthropology Quarterly* 7(1):74–89.

Kim, Elaine. 1986. "Asian-Americans and American Popular Culture." In *Dictionary of Asian-American History,* edited by Hyung-Chan Kim. New York: Greenwood Press.

Lakoff, Robin T. and Raquel L. Scherr. 1984. *Face Value: The Politics of Beauty.* Boston: Routledge & Kegan Paul.

LeFlore, Ivens C. 1982. "Face Lift, Chin Augmentation and Cosmetic Rhinoplasty in Blacks." In *Cosmetic Surgery for Non-white Patients,* edited by Harold Pierce. New York: Grune & Stratton.

Lock, Margaret and Nancy Scheper-Hughes. 1990. "A Critical-Interpretive Approach in Medical Anthropology: Rituals and Routines of Discipline and Dissent." Pp. 47–72 in *Medical Anthropology: Contemporary Theory and Method,* edited by Thomas Johnson and Carolyn Sargent. New York: Praeger.

McCurdy, John A. 1990. *Cosmetic Surgery of the Asian Face.* New York: Thieme Medical Publishers.

MacGregor, Frances C. 1967. "Social and Cultural Components in the Motivations of Persons Seeking Plastic Surgery of the Nose." *Journal of Health and Social Behavior* 8(2):125–35.

Merrell, Kathy H. 1994. "Saving Faces." *Allure,* January, pp. 66–68.

Nakao, Annie. 1993. "Faces of Beauty: Light Is Still Right." *San Francisco Examiner and Chronicle,* April 11, p. D4.

O'Neill, John. 1985. *Five Bodies.* Ithaca, NY: Cornell University Press.

Ong, Aihwa. 1987. *Spirits of Resistance and Capitalist Discipline: Factory Women in Malaysia.* Albany: State University of New York Press.

Ramsdell, Daniel. 1983. "Asia Askew: U.S. Best-sellers on Asia. 1931–1980." *Bulletin of Concerned Asian Scholars* 15(4):2–25.

Rosenthal, Elisabeth. 1991. "Ethnic Ideals: Rethinking Plastic Surgery." *New York Times,* September 25, p. B7.

Sayoc, B. T. 1974. "Surgery of the Oriental Eyelid." *Clinics in Plastic Surgery* 1(1): 157–71.

Sheets-Johnstone, Maxine, ed. 1992. *Giving the Body Its Due.* Albany: State University of New York Press.

Tajima, Renee E. 1989. "Lotus Blossoms Don't Bleed: Images of Asian Women." Pp. 308–17 in *Making Waves: An Anthology of Writings by and about Asian American Women,* edited by Diane Yeh-Mei Wong. Boston: Beacon Press.

Takaki, Ronald. 1989. *Strangers from a Different Shore.* Boston: Little, Brown.

Turner, Terence. 1980. "The Social Skin." Pp. 112–14 in *Not Work Alone,* edited by J. Cherfas and R. Lewin. London: Temple Smith.

Turner, Victor. 1969. *The Ritual Process: Structure and Anti-Structure.* Chicago: Aldine.

Wolf, Naomi. 1991. *The Beauty Myth: How Images of Beauty Are Used Against Women.* New York: Morrow.

Yang, Jeff and Angelo Ragaz. 1993. "The Beauty Machine." *A. Magazine: The Asian American Quarterly* 2(1):20–21.

10

LOVELY HULA HANDS
Corporate Tourism and the Prostitution
of Hawaiian Culture

HAUNANI-KAY TRASK

Many U.S. racial-ethnic groups, including Native Americans, Latinos, and African Americans, have experienced cultural exploitation. Exploitation occurs when aspects of a subculture, such as its beliefs, rituals, and social customs, are commodified and marketed without the cultural group's permission. This selection by Haunani-Kay Trask explores the cultural commodification and exploitation of Hawaiian culture. Trask, a descendant from the Pi'ilani line of Maui and the Kahakumakaliua line of Kaua'i, is a professor of Hawaiian studies at the University of Hawai'i at Manoa. In this excerpt, taken from her 1993 book, *From a Native Daughter: Colonialism and Sovereignty in Hawai'i* Trask argues that several aspects of Polynesian and Hawaiian cultures, including their language, dress, and dance forms, have been marketed as products for the mass consumption of tourists.

I am certain that most, if not all, Americans have heard of Hawai'i and have wished, at some time in their lives, to visit my native land. But I doubt that the history of how Hawai'i came to be territorially incorporated, and economically, politically, and culturally subordinated to the United States is known to most Americans. Nor is it common knowledge that Hawaiians have been struggling for over 20 years to achieve a land base and some form of political sovereignty on the same level as American Indians. Finally, I would imagine that most Americans could not place Hawai'i or any other Pacific island on a map of the Pacific. But despite all this appalling ignorance, five million Americans will vacation in my homeland this year *and* the next, and so on into the foreseeable capitalist future. Such are the intended privileges of the so-called American standard of living: ignorance of, and yet power over, one's relations to native peoples.

Thanks to postwar American imperialism, the ideology that the United States has no overseas colonies and is, in fact, the champion of self-determination the world over holds no greater sway than in the United States itself. To most Americans, then, Hawai'i is *theirs:* to use, to take, and, above all, to fantasize about long after the experience.

Just five hours away by plane from California, Hawai'i is a thousand light-years away in fantasy. Mostly a state of mind, Hawai'i is the image of escape from the rawness and violence of daily American life. Hawai'i—the word, the vision, the sound in the mind—is the fragrance and feel of soft kindness. Above all, Hawai'i is "she," the Western image of the native "female" in her magical allure. And if luck prevails, some of "her" will rub off on you, the visitor.

This fictional Hawai'i comes out of the depths of Western sexual sickness which demands a dark, sin-free native for instant gratification between imperialist wars. The attraction of Hawai'i is stimulated by slick Hollywood movies, saccharine Andy Williams music, and the constant psychological deprivations of maniacal American life. Tourists flock to my native land for escape, but they are escaping into a state of mind while participating in the destruction of a host people in a native place.

To Hawaiians, daily life is neither soft nor kind. In fact, the political, economic, and cultural reality for most Hawaiians is hard, ugly, and cruel.

In Hawai'i, the destruction of our land and the prostitution of our culture are planned and executed by multinational corporations (both foreign-based and Hawai'i-based), by huge landowners (like the missionary-descended Castle and Cook—of Dole Pineapple fame—and others) and by collaborationist state and county governments. The ideological gloss that claims tourism to be our economic savior and the "natural" result of Hawaiian culture is manufactured by ad agencies (like the state-supported Hawai'i Visitors' Bureau) and tour companies (many of which are owned by the airlines), and spewed out to the public through complicitous cultural engines like film, television and radio, and the daily newspapers. As for the local labor unions, both rank and file and management clamor for more tourists while the construction industry lobbies incessantly for larger resorts. . . .

My use of the word *tourism* in the Hawai'i context refers to a mass-based, corporately controlled industry that is both vertically and horizontally integrated such that one multinational corporation owns an airline, the tour buses that transport tourists to the corporation-owned hotel where they eat in a corporation-owned restaurant, play golf and "experience" Hawai'i on corporation-owned recreation areas, and eventually consider buying a second home built on corporation land. Profits, in this case, are mostly repatriated back to the home country. In Hawai'i, these "home" countries are Japan, Taiwan, Hong Kong, Canada, Australia, and the United States. . . .

With this as a background on tourism, I want to move now into the area of cultural prostitution. "Prostitution" in this context refers to the entire institution which defines a woman (and by extension the "female") as an object of degraded and victimized sexual value for use and exchange through the medium of money. The "prostitute" is then a woman who sells her sexual capacities and is seen, thereby, to possess and reproduce them at will, that is, by her very "nature." The prostitute and the institution which creates and maintains her are, of course, of patriarchal origin. The pimp is the conduit of exchange, managing the commodity that is the prostitute while acting as the guard at the entry and exit gates, making sure the prostitute behaves as a prostitute by fulfilling her sexual–economic functions. The victims participate in their victimization with enormous ranges of feeling, including resistance and complicity, but the force and continuity of the institution are shaped by men.

There is much more to prostitution than my sketch reveals but this must suffice for I am interested in using the largest sense of this term as a metaphor in understanding what has happened to Hawaiian culture. My purpose is not to exact detail or fashion a model but to convey the utter degradation of our culture and our people under corporate tourism by employing "prostitution" as an analytic category.

Finally, I have chosen four areas of Hawaiian culture to examine: our homeland, or *one hānau* that is Hawai'i, our lands and fisheries, the outlying seas and the heavens; our language and dance; our familial relationships; and our women.

Nā Mea Hawai'i—Things Hawaiian

The *mo'ōlelo,* or history of Hawaiians, is to be found in our genealogies. From our great cosmogonic genealogy, the *Kumulipo,* derives the Hawaiian identity. The "essential lesson" of this genealogy is "the interrelatedness of the Hawaiian world, and the inseparability of its constituent parts." Thus, "the genealogy of the land, the gods, chiefs, and people intertwine one with the other, and with all aspects of the universe."[1]

In the *mo'ōlelo* of Papa and Wākea, earth-mother and sky-father, our islands are born: Hawai'i, Maui, O'ahu, Kaua'i, and Ni'ihau. From their human offspring came the *taro* plant and from the taro came the Hawaiian people. The lessons of our genealogy are that human beings have a familial relationship to land and to the *taro,* our elder siblings or *kua'ana.*

In Hawai'i, as in all of Polynesia, younger siblings must serve and honor elder siblings who, in turn, must feed and care for their younger siblings. Therefore, Hawaiians must cultivate and husband the land which will feed and provide for the Hawaiian people. This relationship of people to land is called *mālama 'āina* or *aloha 'āina,* care and love of the land.

When people and land work together harmoniously, the balance that results is called *pono.* In Hawaiian society, the *ali'i* or chiefs were required to maintain order, abundance of food, and good government. The *maka'āinana* or common people worked the land and fed the chiefs; the *ali'i* organized production and appeased the gods.

Today, *mālama 'āina* is called stewardship by some, although that word does not convey spiritual and genealogical connections. Nevertheless, to love and make the land flourish is a Hawaiian value. *'Āina,* one of the words for land, means *that which feeds. Kama'āina,* a term for native-born people, means *child of the land.* Thus is the Hawaiian relationship to land both familial and reciprocal.

Our deities are also of the land: Pele is our volcano, Kāne and Lono our fertile valleys and plains, Kanaloa our ocean and all that lives within it, and so on with the 40,000 and 400,000 gods of Hawai'i. Our whole universe, physical and metaphysical, is divine.

Within this world, the older people or *kūpuna* are to cherish those who are younger, the *mo'opuna.* Unstinting generosity is a value and of high status. Social connections between our people are through *aloha,* simply translated as love but carrying with it a profoundly Hawaiian sense that is, again, familial and genealogical. Hawaiians feel *aloha* for Hawai'i whence they come and for their Hawaiian kin upon whom they depend. It is nearly impossible to feel or practice *aloha* for something that is not familial. This is why we extend familial relations to those few non-natives whom we feel understand and can reciprocate our *aloha.* But *aloha* is freely given and freely returned; it is not and cannot be demanded, or commanded. Above all, *aloha* is a cultural feeling and practice that works among the people and between the people and their land.

The significance and meaning of *aloha* underscores the centrality of the Hawaiian language or *'ōlelo* to the culture. *'Ōlelo* means both language and tongue; *mo'ōlelo,* or history, is that which comes from the tongue, that is, a story. *Haole* or white people say we have oral history, but what we have are stories passed on through the generations. These are different from the *haole* sense of history. To Hawaiians in traditional society, language had tremendous power, thus the phrase, *i ka 'ōlelo ke ola; i ka 'ōlelo ka make*—in language is life, in language is death.

After nearly 2,000 years of speaking Hawaiian, our people suffered the near extinction of our language through its banning by the American-imposed government in 1896. In 1900, Hawai'i became a territory of the United States. All schools, government operations, and official transactions were thereafter conducted in English, despite the fact that most people, including non-natives, still spoke Hawaiian at the turn of the century.

Since 1970, *'ōlelo Hawai'i,* or the Hawaiian language, has undergone a tremendous revival, including the rise of language immersion schools. The state of Hawai'i now has two official languages, Hawaiian and English, and the call for Hawaiian language speakers and teachers grows louder by the day.[2]

Along with the flowering of Hawaiian language has come a flowering of Hawaiian dance, especially in its ancient form, called *hula kahiko.* Dance academies, known as *hālau,* have proliferated throughout Hawai'i as have *kumu hula,* or dance masters, and formal competitions where all-night presentations continue for three or four days to throngs of appreciative listeners. Indeed, among Pacific Islanders, Hawaiian dance is considered one of the finest Polynesian art forms today.

Of course, the cultural revitalization that Hawaiians are now experiencing and transmitting to their children is as much a *repudiation* of colonization by so-called Western civilization in its American form as it is a *reclamation* of our past and our own ways of life. This is why cultural revitalization is often resisted and disparaged by anthropologists and others: they see very clearly that its political effect is de-colonization of the mind. Thus our rejection of the nuclear family as the basic unit of society and of individualism as the best form of human expression infuriates social workers, the churches, the legal system, and educators. Hawaiians continue to have allegedly "illegitimate" children, to *hānai* or adopt both children and adults outside of sanctioned Western legal concepts, to hold and use land and water in a collective form rather than a private property form, and to proscribe the notion and the value that one person should strive to surpass and therefore outshine all others.

All these Hawaiian values can be grouped under the idea of *'ohana,* loosely translated as family, but more accurately imagined as a group of both closely and distantly related people who share nearly everything, from land and food to children and status. Sharing is central to this value since it prevents individual decline. Of course, poverty is not thereby avoided, it is only shared with everyone in the unit. The *'ohana* works effectively when the *kua'ana* relationship (elder sibling/younger sibling reciprocity) is practiced.

Finally, within the *'ohana,* our women are considered the lifegivers of the nation, and are accorded the respect and honor this status conveys. Our young women, like our young people in general, are the *pua,* or flower of our *lāhui,* or our nation. The renowned beauty of our women, especially their sexual beauty, is not considered a commodity to be hoarded by fathers and brothers but an attribute of our people. Culturally, Hawaiians are very open and free about sexual relationships, although Christianity and organized religion have done much to damage these traditional sexual values.

With this understanding of what it means to be Hawaiian, I want to move now to the prostitution of our culture by tourism.

Hawai'i itself is the female object of degraded and victimized sexual value. Our *'āina,* or lands, are not any longer the source of food and shelter, but the source of money. Land is now called real estate, rather than our mother, *Papa.* The American relationship of people to land is that of exploiter to exploited. Beautiful areas, once sacred to my people, are now expensive resorts; shorelines where net fishing, seaweed gathering, and crabbing occurred are more and more the exclusive domain of recreational activities: sunbathing, windsurfing, jet skiing. Now, even access to beaches near hotels is strictly regulated or denied to the local public altogether.

The phrase *mālama 'āina*—to care for the land—is used by government officials to sell new projects and to convince the locals that hotels can be built with a concern for "ecology." Hotel historians, like hotel doctors, are stationed in-house to soothe the visitors' stay with the pablum of invented myths and tales of the "primitive."

High schools and hotels adopt each other and funnel teenagers through major resorts for guided tours from kitchens to gardens to honeymoon suites in preparation for postsecondary jobs in the lowest-paid industry in the state. In the meantime, tourist appreciation kits and movies are distributed through the state department of education to all elementary schools. One film, unashamedly titled "What's in It for Me?," was devised to convince locals that tourism is, as the newspapers never tire of saying, "the only game in town."

Of course, all this hype is necessary to hide the truth about tourism, the awful exploitative truth that the industry is the major cause of environmental degradation, low wages, land dispossession, and the highest cost of living in the United States.

While this propaganda is churned out to local residents, the commercialization of Hawaiian culture proceeds with calls for more sensitive marketing of our native values and practices. After all, a prostitute is only as good as her income-producing talents. These talents, in Hawaiian terms, are the *hula;* the generosity, or *aloha,* of our people; the *u'i* or youthful beauty of our women and men; and the continuing allure of our lands and waters, that is, of our place, Hawai'i.

The selling of these talents must produce income. And the function of tourism and the state of Hawai'i is to convert these attributes into profits.

The first requirement is the transformation of the product, or the cultural attribute, much as a woman must be transformed to look like a prostitute, that is, someone who is complicitous in her own commodification. Thus *hula* dancers wear clownlike make-up, don costumes from a mix of Polynesian cultures, and behave in a manner that is smutty and salacious rather than powerfully erotic. The distance between the smutty and the erotic is precisely the distance between Western culture and Hawaiian culture. In the hotel version of the *hula,* the sacredness of the dance has completely evaporated while the athleticism and sexual expression have been packaged like ornaments. The purpose is entertainment for profit rather than a joyful and truly Hawaiian celebration of human and divine nature.

But let us look at an example that is representative of literally hundreds of images that litter the pages of scores of tourist publications. From an Aloha Airlines booklet—shamelessly called the "Spirit of Aloha"—there is a characteristic portrayal of commodified *hula* dancers, one male and one female. The costuming of the female is more South Pacific—the Cook Islands and Tahiti—while that of the male is more Hawaiian. (He wears a Hawaiian loincloth called a *malo.*) The ad smugly asserts the hotel dinner service as a *lū'au,* a Hawaiian feast (which is misspelled) with a continuously open bar, lavish "island" buffet, and "thrilling" Polynesian revue. Needless to say, Hawaiians did not drink alcohol, eat "island" buffets, or participate in "thrilling" revues before the advent of white people in our islands.

But back to the advertisement. Lahaina, the location of the resort and once the capital of Hawai'i, is called "royal" because of its past association with our *ali'i*, or chiefs. Far from being royal today, Lahaina is sadly inundated by California yuppies, drug addicts, and valley girls.

The male figure in the background is muscular, partially clothed, and unsmiling. Apparently, he is supposed to convey an image of Polynesian sexuality that is both enticing and threatening. The white women in the audience can marvel at this physique and still remain safely distant. Like the black American male, this Polynesian man is a fantasy animal. He casts a slightly malevolent glance at our costumed maiden whose body posture and barely covered breasts contradict the innocent smile on her face.

Finally, the "wondrous allure" referred to in the ad applies to more than just the dancers in their performances; the physical beauty of Hawai'i "alive under the stars" is the larger reference.

In this little grotesquerie, the falseness and commercialism fairly scream out from the page. Our language, our dance, our young people, even our customs of eating are used to ensnare tourists. And the price is only a paltry $39.95, not much for two thousand years of culture. Of course, the hotel will rake in tens of thousands of dollars on just the *lū'au* alone. And our young couple will make a pittance.

The rest of the magazine, like most tourist propaganda, commodifies virtually every part of Hawai'i: mountains, beaches, coastlines, rivers, flowers, our volcano goddess, Pele, reefs and fish, rural Hawaiian communities, even Hawaiian activists.

The point, of course, is that everything in Hawai'i can be yours, that is, you the tourist, the non-native, the visitor. The place, the people, the culture, even our identity as a "native" people is for sale. Thus, the magazine, like the airline that prints it, is called *Aloha*. The use of this word in a capitalist context is so far removed from any Hawaiian cultural sense that it is, literally, meaningless.

Thus, Hawai'i, like a lovely woman, is there for the taking. Those with only a little money get a brief encounter; those with a lot of money, like the Japanese, get more. The state and counties will give tax breaks, build infrastructure, and have the governor personally welcome tourists to ensure they keep coming. Just as the pimp regulates prices and guards the commodity of the prostitute, so the state bargains with developers for access to Hawaiian land and culture. Who builds the biggest resorts to attract the most affluent tourists gets the best deal: more hotel rooms, golf courses, and restaurants approved. Permits are fast-tracked, height and density limits are suspended, new groundwater sources are miraculously found.

Hawaiians, meanwhile, have little choice in all this. We can fill up the unemployment lines, enter the military, work in the tourist industry, or leave Hawai'i. Increasingly, Hawaiians are leaving, not by choice but out of economic necessity.

Our people who work in the industry—dancers, waiters, singers, valets, gardeners, housekeepers, bartenders, and even a few managers—make between $10,000 and $25,000 a year, an impossible salary for a family in Hawai'i. Psychologically, our young people have begun to think of tourism as the only employment opportunity, trapped as they are by the lack of alternatives. For our young women, modeling is a "cleaner" job when compared to waiting on tables, or dancing in a weekly revue, but modeling feeds on tourism and the commodification of Hawaiian women. In the end, the entire employment scene is shaped by tourism.

Despite their exploitation, Hawaiians' participation in tourism raises the problem of complicity. Because wages are so low and advancement so rare, whatever complicity exists is secondary to the economic hopelessness that drives Hawaiians into the industry. Refusing to contribute to the commercialization of one's culture becomes a peripheral concern when unemployment looms.

Of course, many Hawaiians do not see tourism as part of their colonization. Thus tourism is viewed as providing jobs, not as a form of cultural prostitution. Even those who have some glimmer of critical consciousness don't generally agree that the tourist industry prostitutes Hawaiian culture. To me, this is a measure of the depth of our mental oppression: We can't understand our own cultural degradation because we are living it. As colonized people, we are colonized to the extent that we are unaware of our oppression. When awareness begins, then so too does de-colonization. Judging by the growing resistance to new hotels, to geothermal energy and manganese nodule mining which would supplement the tourist industry, and to increases in the sheer number of tourists, I would say that de-colonization has begun, but we have many more stages to negotiate on our path to sovereignty.

My brief excursion into the prostitution of Hawaiian culture has done no more than give an overview. Now that you have heard a native view, let me just leave this thought behind. If you are thinking of visiting my homeland, please don't. We don't want or need any more tourists, and we certainly don't like them. If you want to help our cause, pass this message on to your friends.

ENDNOTES

Author's Note: "Lovely Hula Hands" is the title of a famous and very saccharine song written by a *haole* who fell in love with Hawai'i in the pre-statehood era. It embodies the worst romanticized views of *hula* dancers and Hawaiian culture in general.

[1] Lilikalā Kame'eleihiwa, *Native Land and Foreign Desires* (Honolulu: Bishop Museum Press, 1992), p. 2.

[2] See Larry Kimura, 1983. "Native Hawaiian Culture," in *Native Hawaiians Study Commission Report,* Vol. 1 (Washington, DC: U.S. Department of the Interior), pp. 173–97.

PART III

Socialization

11

"NIGHT TO HIS DAY"
The Social Construction of Gender

JUDITH LORBER

In this and the following three selections, we examine socialization, the process of learning cultural values and norms. *Socialization* refers to those social processes through which an individual becomes integrated into a social group by learning the group's culture and his or her roles in that group. It is largely through this process that an individual's concept of self is formed. Thus, socialization teaches us the cultural norms, values, and skills necessary to survive in society. Socialization also enables us to form social identities and an awareness about ourselves as individuals. The following reading by Judith Lorber, a professor emerita of sociology and women's studies at Brooklyn College and the Graduate School, City University of New York, is taken from her comprehensive study *Paradoxes of Gender* (1993). Here, Lorber examines socialization and how we learn our gender identities following birth.

[Gethenians] do not see each other as men or women. This is almost impossible for our imagination to accept. What is the first question we ask about a newborn baby?

—URSULA LE GUIN

Talking about gender for most people is the equivalent of fish talking about water. Gender is so much the routine ground of everyday activities that questioning its taken-for-granted assumptions and presuppositions is like thinking about whether the sun will come up.[1] Gender is so pervasive that in our society we assume it is bred into our genes. Most people find it hard to believe that gender is constantly created and re-created out of

---

From *Paradoxes of Gender*, pp. 13–15 and 17–27. Copyright © 1993 by Yale University Press. Reprinted by permission.

119

human interaction, out of social life, and is the texture and order of that social life. Yet gender, like culture, is a human production that depends on everyone constantly "doing gender" (West and Zimmerman 1987).

And everyone "does gender" without thinking about it. Today, on the subway, I saw a well-dressed man with a year-old child in a stroller. Yesterday, on a bus, I saw a man with a tiny baby in a carrier on his chest. Seeing men taking care of small children in public is increasingly common—at least in New York City. But both men were quite obviously stared at—and smiled at, approvingly. Everyone was doing gender—the men who were changing the role of fathers and the other passengers, who were applauding them silently. But there was more gendering going on that probably fewer people noticed. The baby was wearing a white crocheted cap and white clothes. You couldn't tell if it was a boy or a girl. The child in the stroller was wearing a dark blue T-shirt and dark print pants. As they started to leave the train, the father put a Yankee baseball cap on the child's head. Ah, a boy, I thought. Then I noticed the gleam of tiny earrings in the child's ears, and as they got off, I saw the little flowered sneakers and lace-trimmed socks. Not a boy after all. Gender done.

Gender is such a familiar part of daily life that it usually takes a deliberate disruption of our expectations of how women and men are supposed to act to pay attention to how it is produced. Gender signs and signals are so ubiquitous that we usually fail to note them—unless they are missing or ambiguous. Then we are uncomfortable until we have successfully placed the other person in a gender status; otherwise, we feel socially dislocated. In our society, in addition to man and woman, the status can be *transvestite* (a person who dresses in opposite-gender clothes) and *transsexual* (a person who has had sex-change surgery). Transvestites and transsexuals carefully construct their gender status by dressing, speaking, walking, gesturing in the ways prescribed for women or men—whichever they want to be taken for—and so does any "normal" person.

For the individual, gender construction starts with assignment to a sex category on the basis of what the genitalia look like at birth.[2] Then babies are dressed or adorned in a way that displays the category because parents don't want to be constantly asked whether their baby is a girl or a boy. A sex category becomes a gender status through naming, dress, and the use of other gender markers. Once a child's gender is evident, others treat those in one gender differently from those in the other, and the children respond to the different treatment by feeling different and behaving differently. As soon as they can talk, they start to refer to themselves as members of their gender. Sex doesn't come into play again until puberty, but by that time, sexual feelings and desires and practices have been shaped by gendered norms and expectations. Adolescent boys and girls approach and avoid each other in an elaborately scripted and gendered mating dance. Parenting is gendered, with different expectations for mothers and for fathers, and people of different genders work at different kinds of jobs. The work adults do as mothers and fathers and as low-level workers and high-level bosses, shapes women's and men's life experiences, and these experiences produce different feelings, consciousness, relationships, skills—ways of being that we call feminine or masculine.[3] All of these processes constitute the social construction of gender.

Gendered roles change—today fathers are taking care of little children, girls and boys are wearing unisex clothing and getting the same education, women and men are working at the same jobs. Although many traditional social groups are quite strict about maintaining gender differences, in other social groups they seem to be blurring. Then why the one-year-old's earrings? Why is it still so important to mark a child as a girl or a boy, to make sure she is not taken for a boy or he for a girl? What would happen if they were? They would, quite literally, have changed places in their social world.

To explain why gendering is done from birth, constantly and by everyone, we have to look not only at the way individuals experience gender but at gender as a social institution. As a social institution, gender is one of the major ways that human beings organize their lives. Human society depends on a predictable division of labor, a designated allocation of scarce goods, assigned responsibility for children and others who cannot care for themselves, common values and their systematic transmission to new members, legitimate leadership, music, art, stories, games, and other symbolic productions. One way of choosing people for the different tasks of society is on the basis of their talents, motivations, and competence—their demonstrated achievements. The other way is on the basis of gender, race, ethnicity—ascribed membership in a category of people. Although societies vary in the extent to which they use one or the other of these ways of allocating people to work and to carry out other responsibilities, every society uses gender and age grades. Every society classifies people as "girl and boy children," "girls and boys ready to be married," and "fully adult women and men," constructs similarities among them and differences between them, and assigns them to different roles and responsibilities. Personality characteristics, feelings, motivations, and ambitions flow from these different life experiences so that the members of these different groups become different kinds of people. The process of gendering and its outcome are legitimated by religion, law, science, and the society's entire set of values. . . .

Western society's values legitimate gendering by claiming that it all comes from physiology—female and male procreative differences. But gender and sex are not equivalent, and gender as a social construction does not flow automatically from genitalia and reproductive organs, the main physiological differences of females and males. In the construction of ascribed social statuses, physiological differences such as sex, stage of development, color of skin, and size are crude markers. They are not the source of the social statuses of gender, age grade, and race. Social statuses are carefully constructed through prescribed processes of teaching, learning, emulation, and enforcement. Whatever genes, hormones, and biological evolution contribute to human social institutions is materially as well as qualitatively transformed by social practices. Every social institution has a material base, but culture and social practices transform that base into something with qualitatively different patterns and constraints. The economy is much more than producing food and goods and distributing them to eaters and users; family and kinship are not the equivalent of having sex and procreating; morals and religions cannot be equated with the fears and ecstasies of the brain; language goes far beyond the sounds produced by tongue and larynx. No one eats "money" or "credit"; the concepts of "god" and "angels" are the subjects of theological disquisitions; not only words but objects, such as their flag, "speak" to the citizens of a country.

Similarly, gender cannot be equated with biological and physiological differences between human females and males. The building blocks of gender are *socially constructed statuses*. Western societies have only two genders, "man" and "woman." Some societies have three genders—men, women, and *berdaches* or *hijras* or *xaniths*. Berdaches, hijras, and xaniths are biological males who behave, dress, work, and are treated in most respects as social women; they are therefore not men, nor are they female women; they are, in our language, "male women."[4] There are African and American Indian societies that have a gender status called *manly hearted women*—biological females who work, marry, and parent as men; their social status is "female men" (Amadiume 1987; Blackwood 1984). They do not have to behave or dress as men to have the social responsibilities and prerogatives of husbands and fathers; what makes them men is enough wealth to buy a wife.

Modern Western societies' *transsexuals* and *transvestites* are the nearest equivalent of these crossover genders, but they are not institutionalized as third genders (Bolin 1987). Transsexuals are biological males and females who have sex-change operations to alter their genitalia. They do so in order to bring their physical anatomy in congruence with the way they want to live and with their own sense of gender identity. They do not become a third gender; they change genders. Transvestites are males who live as women and females who live as men but do not intend to have sex-change surgery. Their dress, appearance, and mannerisms fall within the range of what is expected from members of the opposite gender, so that they "pass." They also change genders, sometimes temporarily, some for most of their lives. Transvestite women have fought in wars as men soldiers as recently as the nineteenth century; some married women, and others went back to being women and married men once the war was over.[5] Some were discovered when their wounds were treated; others not until they died. In order to work as a jazz musician, a man's occupation, Billy Tipton, a woman, lived most of her life as a man. She died at 74, leaving a wife and three adopted sons for whom she was husband and father, and musicians with whom she had played and traveled, for whom she was "one of the boys" (*New York Times* 1989).[6] There have been many other such occurrences of women passing as men to do more prestigious or lucrative men's work (Matthaei 1982:192–93).[7]

Genders, therefore, are not attached to a biological substratum. Gender boundaries are breachable, and individual and socially organized shifts from one gender to another call attention to "cultural, social, or aesthetic dissonances" (Garber 1992:16). These odd or deviant or third genders show us what we ordinarily take for granted—that people have to learn to be women and men. Men who cross-dress for performances or for pleasure often learn from women's magazines how to "do femininity" convincingly (Garber 1992: 41–51). Because transvestism is direct evidence of how gender is constructed, Marjorie Garber (1992) claims it has "extraordinary power . . . to disrupt, expose, and challenge, putting in question the very notion of the 'original' and of stable identity" (p. 16).

Gender Bending

It is difficult to see how gender is constructed because we take it for granted that it's all biology, or hormones, or human nature. The differences between women and men seem to be self-evident, and we think they would occur no matter what society did. But in actuality, human females and males are physiologically more similar in appearance than are the two sexes of many species of animals and are more alike than different in traits and behavior (Epstein 1988). Without the deliberate use of gendered clothing, hairstyles, jewelry, and cosmetics, women and men would look far more alike.[8] Even societies that do not cover women's breasts have gender-identifying clothing, scarification, jewelry, and hairstyles.

The ease with which many transvestite women pass as men and transvestite men as women is corroborated by the common gender misidentification in Westernized societies of people in jeans, T-shirts, and sneakers. Men with long hair may be addressed as "miss," and women with short hair are often taken for men unless they offset the potential ambiguity with deliberate gender markers (Devor 1987, 1989). Jan Morris, in *Conundrum,* an autobiographical account of events just before and just after a sex-change operation, described how easy it was to shift back and forth from being a man to being a woman when testing how it would feel to change gender status. During this time, Morris (1975) still had a penis and wore more or less unisex clothing; the context alone made the man and the woman:

> Sometimes the arena of my ambivalence was uncomfortably small. At the Travellers' Club, for example, I was obviously known as a man of sorts— women were only allowed on the premises at all during a few hours of the day, and even then were hidden away as far as possible in lesser rooms or alcoves. But I had another club, only a few hundred yards away, where I was known only as a woman, and often I went directly from one to the other, imperceptibly changing roles on the way—"Cheerio, sir,"

the porter would say at one club, and "Hello, madam," the porter would greet me at the other. (P. 132)

Gender shifts are actually a common phenomenon in public roles as well. Queen Elizabeth II of England bore children, but when she went to Saudi Arabia on a state visit, she was considered an honorary man so that she could confer and dine with the men who were heads of a state that forbids unrelated men and women to have face-to-unveiled face contact. In contemporary Egypt, lower-class women who run restaurants or shops dress in men's clothing and engage in unfeminine aggressive behavior, and middle-class educated women of professional or managerial status can take positions of authority (Rugh 1986:131). In these situations, there is an important status change: These women are treated by the others in the situation as if they are men. From their own point of view, they are still women. From the social perspective, however, they are men.[9]

In many cultures, gender bending is prevalent in theater or dance—the Japanese kabuki are men actors who play both women and men; in Shakespeare's theater company, there were no actresses—Juliet and Lady Macbeth were played by boys. Shakespeare's comedies are full of witty comments on gender shifts. Women characters frequently masquerade as young men, and other women characters fall in love with them; the boys playing these masquerading women, meanwhile, are acting out pining for the love of men characters.[10] . . .

But despite the ease with which gender boundaries can be traversed in work, in social relationships, and in cultural productions, gender statuses remain. Transvestites and transsexuals do not challenge the social construction of gender. Their goal is to be feminine women and masculine men (Kando 1973). Those who do not want to change their anatomy but do want to change their gender behavior fare less well in establishing their social identity. . . .

Paradoxically, then, bending gender rules and passing between genders does not erode but rather preserves gender boundaries. In societies with only two genders, the gender dichotomy is not disturbed by transvestites, because others feel that a transvestite is only transitorily ambiguous—is "really a man or woman underneath." After sex-change surgery, transsexuals end up in a conventional gender status—a "man" or a "woman" with the appropriate genitals (Eichler 1989). When women dress as men for business reasons, they are indicating that in that situation, they want to be treated the way men are treated; when they dress as women, they want to be treated as women:

By their male dress, female entrepreneurs signal their desire to suspend the expectations of accepted feminine conduct without losing respect and reputation. By wearing what is "unattractive" they signify that they are not intending to display their physical charms while engaging in public activity. Their loud, aggressive banter contrasts with the modest demeanor that attracts men. . . . Overt signalling of a suspension of the rules preserves normal conduct from eroding expectations. (Rugh 1986:131)

For Individuals, Gender Means Sameness

Although the possible combinations of genitalia, body shapes, clothing, mannerisms, sexuality, and roles could produce infinite varieties in human beings, the social institution of gender depends on the production and maintenance of a limited number of gender statuses and of making the members of these statuses similar to each other. Individuals are born sexed but not gendered, and they have to be taught to be masculine or feminine.[11] As Simone de Beauvoir said: "One is not born, but rather becomes, a woman . . . ; it is civilization as a whole that produces this creature . . . which is described as feminine" ([1949] 1953:267).

Children learn to walk, talk, and gesture the way their social group says girls and boys should. Ray Birdwhistell (1970:39–46), in his analysis of body motion as human communication, calls these learned gender displays *tertiary* sex characteristics and argues that they are needed to distinguish genders because humans are a weakly dimorphic species—their only sex markers are genitalia. Clothing, paradoxically, often hides the sex but displays the gender.

In early childhood, humans develop gendered personality structures and sexual orientations through their interactions with parents of the same and opposite gender. As adolescents, they conduct their sexual behavior according to gendered scripts. Schools, parents, peers, and the mass media guide young people into gendered work and family roles. As adults, they take on a gendered social status in their society's stratification system. Gender is thus both ascribed and achieved (West and Zimmerman 1987).

The case of the male child who was gender-reassigned and raised as a girl after a botched circumcision destroyed his penis, who then chose to become a boy when he became a teenager, seems to clinch the argument that biology trumps socialization (Colapinto 2000). Money and Ehrhardt (1972) claimed that this case was a natural experiment in whether you could raise a male as a girl because the child in question had an identical twin, who was being raised as a boy. But this case can be read as the rejection of a devalued gender status as much as it can the inevitable emergence of bodily and psychological hard-wiring.

The child chose to reject the reassigned sex status on reaching puberty, when hormones and further genital surgery were prescribed by doctors to create additional feminization. According to the original account of the case, the mother said early on that her gender-reassigned daughter was a tomboy (Money and Ehrhardt 1972:118–23). But the mother had also been a tomboy, and she acknowledged that the behavior she was imposing on her daughter was more restrictive than what she demanded of her son. Femininity never had any appeal for "Joan." Colapinto (1997:68) quotes Joan's identical twin brother as saying, "'When I say there was nothing feminine about Joan,' Kevin laughs, 'I mean there was *nothing* feminine. She walked like a guy. She talked about guy things, didn't give a crap about cleaning house, getting married, wearing makeup. . . . We both wanted to play with guys, build forts and have snowball fights and play army.'" Enrolled in Girl Scouts, Joan was miserable. "I remember making daisy chains and thinking, 'If this is the most exciting thing in Girl Scouts, forget it,' John says. 'I kept thinking of the fun stuff my brother was doing in Cubs.'"

Is this rejection of conventional "girl things" the result of internal masculinization or the gender resistance of a rebellious child? Being a man is a preferred status in many societies, so it is not surprising for those with ambiguous genitalia to prefer that gender identity (Herdt and Davidson 1988). More research needs to be done on the life histories of intersexed adolescents and adults in today's less gender-fixed climate to see to what extent they have chosen to go against their sex assignment as infants and how their lives compare to transsexuals who opt to have genital surgery to change their sex.

People go along with the imposition of gender norms because the weight of morality as well as immediate social pressure enforces them. Consider how many instructions for properly gendered behavior are packed into this mother's admonition to her daughter: "This is how to hem a dress when you see the hem coming down and so to prevent yourself from looking like the slut I know you are so bent on becoming" (Kincaid 1978).

Gender norms are inscribed in the way people move, gesture, and even eat. In one African society, men were supposed to eat with their "whole mouth, wholeheartedly, and not, like women, just with the lips, that is half-heartedly, with reservation and restraint" (Bourdieu [1980] 1990:70). Men and women in this society learned to walk in ways that proclaimed their different positions in the society:

> The manly man . . . stands up straight into the face of the person he approaches, or wishes to welcome. Ever on the alert, because ever threatened, he misses nothing of what happens around him. . . . Conversely, a well brought-up woman . . . is expected to walk with a slight stoop, avoiding every misplaced movement of her body, her head or her arms, looking down, keeping her eyes on the spot where she will next put her foot, especially if she happens to have to walk past the men's assembly. (P. 70)

Many cultures go beyond clothing, gestures, and demeanor in gendering children. They inscribe gender directly into bodies. In traditional Chinese society, mothers bound their daughters' feet into three-inch stumps to enhance their sexual attractiveness. Jewish fathers circumcise their infant sons to show their covenant with God. Women in African societies remove the clitoris of prepubescent girls, scrape their labia, and make the lips grow together to preserve their chastity and ensure their marriageability. In Western societies, women augment their breast size with silicone and reconstruct their faces with cosmetic surgery to conform to cultural ideals of feminine beauty. . . .

Most parents create a gendered world for their newborn by naming, birth announcements, and dress. Children's relationships with same-gendered and different-gendered caretakers structure their self-identifications and personalities. Through cognitive development, children extract and apply to their own actions the appropriate behavior for those who belong in their own gender, as well as race, religion, ethnic group, and social class, rejecting what is not appropriate. If their social categories are highly valued, they value themselves highly; if their social categories are low status, they lose self-esteem (Chodorow 1974). Many feminist parents who want to raise androgynous children soon lose their children to the pull of gendered norms (Gordon 1990: 87–90). My son attended a carefully nonsexist elementary school, which didn't even have girls' and boys' bathrooms. When he was seven or eight years old, I attended a class play about "squares" and "circles" and their need for each other and noticed that all the girl squares and circles wore makeup, but none of the boy squares and circles did. I asked the teacher about it after the play, and she said, "Bobby said he was not going to wear makeup, and he is a powerful child, so none of the boys would either." In a long discussion about conformity, my son confronted me with the question of who the conformists were, the boys who followed their leader or the girls who listened to the woman teacher. In actuality, they both were, because they both followed same-gender leaders and acted in gender-appropriate ways. (Actors may wear makeup, but real boys don't.)

For human beings there is no essential femaleness and maleness, femininity or masculinity, womanhood or manhood, but once gender is ascribed, the social order constructs and holds individuals to strongly gendered norms and expectations. Individuals may vary on many of the components of gender and may shift genders temporarily or permanently, but they must fit into the limited number of gender statuses their society recognizes. In the process, they re-create their society's version of women and men: "If we do gender appropriately, we simultaneously sustain, reproduce, and render legitimate the institutional arrangements. . . . If we fail to do gender appropriately, we as individuals—not the institutional arrangements—may be called to account (for our character, motives, and predispositions)" (West and Zimmerman 1987:146).

The gendered practices of everyday life reproduce a society's view of how women and men should act (Bourdieu [1980] 1990). Gendered social arrangements are justified by religion and cultural productions and backed by law, but the most powerful means of sustaining the moral hegemony of the dominant gender ideology is that the process is made invisible; any possible alternatives are virtually unthinkable (Foucault 1972; Gramsci 1971).[12]

For Society, Gender Means Difference

The pervasiveness of gender as a way of structuring social life demands that gender statuses be clearly differentiated. Varied talents, sexual preferences, identities, personalities, interests, and ways of interacting fragment the individual's bodily and social experiences. Nonetheless, these are organized in Western cultures into two and only two socially and legally recognized gender statuses, "man" and "woman."[13] In the social construction of gender, it does not matter what men and women actually do; it does not even matter if they do exactly the same thing. The social institution of gender insists only that what they do is *perceived* as different.

If men and women are doing the same tasks, they are usually spatially segregated to maintain gender separation, and often the tasks are given different job titles as well, such as executive secretary and administrative assistant (Reskin 1988). If the differences between women and men begin to blur, society's "sameness taboo" goes into action (Rubin 1975:178). At a rock and roll dance at West Point in 1976, the year women were admitted to the prestigious military academy for the first time, the school's administrators "were reportedly perturbed by the sight of mirror-image couples dancing in short hair and dress gray trousers," and a rule was established that women cadets could dance at these events only if they wore skirts (Barkalow and Raab 1990:53).[14] Women recruits in the U.S. Marine Corps are required to wear makeup—at a minimum, lipstick and eye shadow—and they have to take classes in makeup, hair care, poise, and etiquette. This feminization is part of a deliberate policy of making them clearly distinguishable from men Marines. Christine Williams (1989) quotes a 25-year-old woman drill instructor as saying: "A lot of the recruits who come here don't wear makeup; they're tomboyish or athletic. A lot of them have the preconceived idea that going into the military means they can still be a tomboy. They don't realize that you are a *Woman* Marine" (pp. 76–77).[15]

If gender differences were genetic, physiological, or hormonal, gender bending and gender ambiguity would occur only in hermaphrodites, who are born with chromosomes and genitalia that are not clearly female or male. Since gender differences are socially constructed, all men and all women can enact the behavior of the other, because they know the other's social script: "'Man' and 'woman' are at once empty and overflowing categories. Empty because they have no ultimate, transcendental meaning. Overflowing because even when they appear to be fixed, they still contain within them alternative, denied, or suppressed definitions" (Scott 1988:49). Nonetheless, though individuals may be able to shift gender statuses, the gender boundaries have to hold, or the whole gendered social order will come crashing down.

Paradoxically, it is the social importance of gender statuses and their external markers—clothing, mannerisms, and spatial segregation—that makes gender bending or gender crossing possible—or even necessary. The social viability of differentiated gender statuses produces the need or desire to shift statuses. Without gender differentiation, transvestism and transsexuality would be meaningless. You couldn't dress in the opposite gender's clothing if all clothing were unisex. There would be no need to reconstruct genitalia to match identity if interests and lifestyles were not gendered. There would be no need for women to pass as men to do certain kinds of work if jobs were not typed as "women's work" and "men's work." Women would not have to dress as men in public life in order to give orders or aggressively bargain with customers.

Gender boundaries are preserved when transsexuals create congruous autobiographies of always having felt like what they are now. The transvestite's story also "recuperates social and sexual norms" (Garber 1992:69). In the transvestite's normalized narrative, he or she "is 'compelled' by social and economic forces to disguise himself or herself in order to get a job, escape repression, or gain artistic or political 'freedom'" (Garber 1992:70). The "true identity," when revealed, causes amazement over how easily and successfully the person passed as a member of the opposite gender, not a suspicion that gender itself is something of a put-on.

ENDNOTES

[1] Gender is, in Erving Goffman's (1983) words, an aspect of *Felicity's Condition:* "any arrangement which leads us to judge an individual's . . . acts not to be a manifestation of strangeness. Behind Felicity's Condition is our sense of what it is to be sane" (p. 27). Also see Bem 1993; Frye 1983, pp. 17–40; Goffman 1977.

[2] In cases of ambiguity in countries with modern medicine, surgery is usually performed to make the genitalia more clearly male or female.

[3] See J. Butler 1990 for an analysis of how doing gender *is* gender identity.

[4] On the hijras of India, see Nanda 1990; on the xaniths of Oman, Wikan 1982, pp. 168–86; on the American Indian berdaches, W. L. Williams 1986. Other societies that have similar institutionalized third-gender men are the Koniag of Alaska, the Tanala of Madagascar, the Mesakin of Nuba, and the Chukchee of Siberia (Wikan 1982, p. 170).

[5] Durova 1989; Freeman and Bond 1992; Wheelwright 1989.

[6] Gender segregation of work in popular music still has not changed very much, according to Groce and Cooper 1990, despite considerable androgyny in some very popular figures. See Garber 1992 on the androgyny. She discusses Tipton on pp. 67–70.

[7] In the nineteenth century, not only did these women get men's wages, but they also "had male privileges and could do all manner of things other women could not: open a bank account, write checks, own property, go anywhere unaccompanied, vote in elections" (Faderman 1991, p. 44).

[8] When unisex clothing and men wearing long hair came into vogue in the United States in the mid-1960s, beards and mustaches for men also came into style again as gender identifications.

[9] For other accounts of women being treated as men in Islamic countries, as well as accounts of women and men cross-dressing in these countries, see Garber 1992, pp. 304–52.

[10] Dollimore 1986; Garber 1992, pp. 32–40; Greenblatt 1987, pp. 66–93; Howard 1988. For Renaissance accounts of sexual relations with women and men of ambiguous sex, see Lacqueur 1990, pp. 134–39. For modern accounts of women passing as men that other women find sexually attractive, see Devor 1989, pp. 136–37; Wheelwright 1989, pp. 53–59.

[11] For an account of how a potential man-to-woman transsexual learned to be feminine, see Garfinkel 1967, pp. 116–85, 285–88. For a gloss on this account that points out how, throughout his encounters with Agnes, Garfinkel failed to see how he himself was constructing his own masculinity, see Rogers 1992.

[12] The concepts of moral hegemony, the effects of everyday activities (praxis) on thought and personality, and the necessity of consciousness of these processes before political change can occur are all based on Marx's analysis of class relations.

[13] Other societies recognize more than two categories, but usually no more than three or four (Jacobs and Roberts 1989).

[14] Carol Barkalow's book has a photograph of 11 first-year West Pointers in a math class, who are dressed in regulation pants, shirts, and sweaters, with short haircuts. The caption challenges the reader to locate the only woman in the room.

[15] The taboo on males and females looking alike reflects the U.S. military's homophobia (Bérubé 1989). If you can't tell those with a penis from those with a vagina, how are you going to determine whether their sexual interest is heterosexual or homosexual unless you watch them having sexual relations?

REFERENCES

Amadiume, Ifi. 1987. *Male Daughters, Female Husbands: Gender and Sex in an African Society.* London: Zed Books.

Barkalow, Carol, with Andrea Raab. 1990. *In the Men's House.* New York: Poseidon Press.

Beauvoir, Simone de. [1949] 1953. *The Second Sex,* translated by H. M. Parshley. New York: Knopf.

Bem, Sandra Lipsitz. 1993. *The Lenses of Gender: Transforming the Debate on Sexual Inequality.* New Haven, CT: Yale University Press.

Bérubé, Allan. 1989. "Marching to a Different Drummer: Gay and Lesbian GIs in World War II." In *Hidden from History: Reclaiming the Gay and Lesbian Past,* edited by Martin Bauml Duberman, Martha Vicinus, and George Chauncey Jr. New York: New American Library.

Birdwhistell, Ray L. 1970. *Kinesics and Context: Essays on Body Motion Communication.* Philadelphia: University of Pennsylvania Press.

Blackwood, Evelyn. 1984. "Sexuality and Gender in Certain Native American Tribes: The Case of Cross-Gender Females." *Signs* 10:27–42.

Bolin, Anne. 1987. "Transsexualism and the Limits of Traditional Analysis." *American Behavior Scientist* 31:41–65.

Bourdieu, Pierre. [1980] 1990. *The Logic of Practice.* Stanford, CA: Stanford University Press.

Butler, Judith. 1990. *Gender Trouble: Feminism and the Subversion of Identity.* New York: Routledge.

Chodorow, Nancy. 1974. "Family Structure and Feminine Personality." In *Woman, Culture and Society,* edited by Michelle Zimbalist Rosaldo and Louise Lamphere. Stanford, CA: Stanford University Press.

Colapinto, John. 1997. "The True Story of John/Joan." *Rolling Stone,* December 11, pp. 54–97.

————.2000. *As Nature Made Him: The Boy Who Was Raised as a Girl.* New York: Harper-Collins.

Devor, Holly. 1987. "Gender Blending Females: Women and Sometimes Men." *American Behavior Scientist* 31:12–40.

————. 1989. *Gender Blending: Confronting the Limits of Duality.* Bloomington: University of Indiana Press.

Dollimore, Jonathan. 1986. "Subjectivity, Sexuality, and Transgression: The Jacobean Connection." *Renaissance Drama,* n.s. 17:53–81.

Durova, Nadezhda. 1989. *The Cavalry Maiden: Journals of a Russian Officer in the Napoleonic Wars,* translated by Mary Fleming Zirin. Bloomington: Indiana University Press.

Eichler, Margrit. 1989. "Sex Change Operations: The Last Bulwark of the Double Standard." In *Feminist Frontiers II,* edited by Laurel Richardson and Verta Taylor. New York: Random House.

Epstein, C. F. 1988. *Deceptive Distinctions: Sex, Gender and the Social Order.* New Haven, CT: Yale University Press.

Faderman, Lillian. 1991. *Odd Girls and Twilight Lovers: A History of Lesbian Life in Twentieth-Century America.* New York: Columbia University Press.

Foucault, Michel. 1972. *The Archeology of Knowledge and the Discourse on Language,* translated by A. M. Sheridan Smith. New York: Pantheon.

Freeman, Lucy and Alma Halbert Bond. 1992. *America's First Woman Warrior: The Courage of Deborah Sampson.* New York: Paragon.

Frye, Marilyn. 1983. *The Politics of Reality: Essays in Feminist Theory.* Trumansburg, NY: Crossing Press.

Garber, Marjorie. 1992. *Vested Interests: Cross-Dressing and Cultural Anxiety.* New York: Routledge.

Garfinkel, Harold. 1967. *Studies in Ethnomethodology.* Englewood Cliffs, NJ: Prentice-Hall.

Goffman, Erving. 1977. "The Arrangement between the Sexes." *Theory and Society* 4:301–33.

————. 1983. "Felicity's Condition." *American Journal of Sociology* 89:1–53.

Gordon, Tuula. 1990. *Feminist Mothers.* New York: New York University Press.

Gramsci, Antonio. 1971. *Selections from the Prison Notebooks,* translated and edited by Quintin Hoare and Geoffrey Nowell Smith. New York: International Publishers.

Greenblatt, Stephen. 1987. *Shakespearean Negotiations: The Circulation of Social Energy in Renaissance England.* Berkeley: University of California Press.

Groce, Stephen B. and Margaret Cooper. 1990. "Just Me and the Boys? Women in Local-Level Rock and Roll." *Gender & Society* 4:220–29.

Herdt, Gilbert and Julian Davidson. 1988. "The Sambia 'Turnim-Man': Sociocultural and Clinical Aspects of Gender Formation in Male Pseudohermaphrodites with 5α-Reductase Deficiency in Papua, New Guinea." *Archives of Sexual Behavior* 17:33–56.

Howard, Jean E. 1988. "Crossdressing, the Theater, and Gender Struggle in Early Modern England." *Shakespeare Quarterly* 39:418–41.

Jacobs, Sue-Ellen and Christine Roberts. 1989. "Sex, Sexuality, Gender, and Gender Variance." In *Gender and Anthropology,* edited by Sandra Morgen. Washington, DC: American Anthropological Association.

Kando, Thomas. 1973. *Sex Change: The Achievement of Gender Identity among Feminized Transsexuals.* Springfield, IL: Charles C. Thomas.

Kincaid, Jamaica. 1978. "Girl." *The New Yorker,* June 26.

Lacqueur, Thomas. 1990. *Making Sex: Body and Gender from the Greeks to Freud.* Cambridge, MA: Harvard University Press.

Lorber, Judith. 2001. "Feminist Theories of the Body." Pp. 214–15 in *Gender Inequality: Feminist Theories and Politics,* 2d ed., Los Angeles: Roxbury.

Matthaei, Julie A. 1982. *An Economic History of Woman's Work in America.* New York: Schocken.

Money, John and Anke A. Ehrhardt. 1972. *Man and Woman, Boy and Girl.* Baltimore, MD: Johns Hopkins University Press.

Morris, Jan. 1975. *Conundrum.* New York: Signet.

Nanda, Serena. 1990. *Neither Man nor Woman: The Hijras of India.* Belmont, CA: Wadsworth.

New York Times. 1989. "Musician's Death at 74 Reveals He Was a Woman." February 2.

Reskin, Barbara F. 1988. "Bringing the Men Back In: Sex Differentiation and the Devaluation of Women's Work." *Gender & Society* 2:58–81.

Rogers, Mary R. 1992. "They Were All Passing: Agnes, Garfinkel, and Company." *Gender & Society* 6:169–91.

Rubin, Gayle. 1975. "The Traffic in Women: Notes on the Political Economy of Sex." In *Toward an Anthropology of Women,* edited by Rayna Rapp Reiter. New York: Monthly Review Press.

Rugh, Andrea B. 1986. *Reveal and Conceal: Dress in Contemporary Egypt.* Syracuse, NY: Syracuse University Press.

Scott, Joan Wallach. 1988. *Gender and the Politics of History.* New York: Columbia University Press.

West, Candace and Don Zimmerman. 1987. "Doing Gender." *Gender & Society* 1:125–51.

Wheelwright, Julie. 1989. *Amazons and Military Maids: Women Who Cross-Dressed in Pursuit of Life, Liberty and Happiness.* London: Pandora Press.

Wikan, Unni. 1982. *Behind the Veil in Arabia: Women in Oman.* Baltimore, MD: Johns Hopkins University Press.

Williams, Christine L. 1989. *Gender Differences at Work: Women and Men in Nontraditional Occupations.* Berkeley: University of California Press.

Williams, Walter L. 1986. *The Spirit and the Flesh: Sexual Diversity in American Indian Culture.* Boston: Beacon Press.

12

BOYHOOD, ORGANIZED SPORTS, AND THE CONSTRUCTION OF MASCULINITIES

MICHAEL MESSNER

An important point about socialization is that societal values, identities, and social roles are learned and *not* instinctual. We have to learn the social norms and behaviors our society expects from us. In this reading, published in 1990, Michael Messner challenges the notion that gender identity formation is biological or natural. Instead, Messner examines how masculinity is learned

From *Journal of Contemporary Ethnography* (formerly *Urban Life*), Vol. 18, No. 4, January 1990, pp. 416–44. Copyright © 1990 by Sage Publications, Inc. Reprinted by permission of Sage Publications, Inc.

through socialization, especially through the participation of boys and men in organized sports. Messner, professor of sociology and gender studies at the University of Southern California, has studied men, masculinity, and sports for over 10 years.

I view gender identity not as a "thing" that people "have," but rather as a *process of construction* that develops, comes into crisis, and changes as a person interacts with the social world. Through this perspective, it becomes possible to speak of "gendering" identities rather than "masculinity" or "femininity" as relatively fixed identities or statuses.

There is an agency in this construction: People are not passively shaped by their social environment. As recent feminist analyses of the construction of feminine gender identity have pointed out, girls and women are implicated in the construction of their own identities and personalities, both in terms of the ways that they participate in their own subordination and the ways that they resist subordination (Benjamin 1988; Haug 1987). Yet this self-construction is not a fully conscious process. There are also deeply woven, unconscious motivations, fears, and anxieties at work here. So, too, in the construction of masculinity. Levinson et al. (1978) have argued that masculine identity is neither fully "formed" by the social context, nor is it "caused" by some internal dynamic put into place during infancy. Instead, it is shaped and constructed through the interaction between the internal and the social. The internal gendering identity may set developmental "tasks," may create thresholds of anxiety and ambivalence, yet it is only through a concrete examination of people's interactions with others within social institutions that we can begin to understand both the similarities and differences in the construction of gender identities.

In this study, I explore and interpret the meanings that males themselves attribute to their boyhood participation in organized sport. In what ways do males construct masculine identities within the institution of organized sports? In what ways do class and racial differences mediate this relationship and perhaps lead to the construction of different meanings, and perhaps different masculinities? And what are some of the problems and contradictions within these constructions of masculinity?

Description of Research

Between 1983 and 1985, I conducted interviews with 30 male former athletes. Most of the men I interviewed had played the (U.S.) "major sports"—football, basketball, baseball, track. At the time of the interview, each had been retired from playing organized sports for at least five years. Their ages ranged from 21 to 48, with the median, 33; 14 were black, 14 were white, and 2 were Hispanic; 15 of the 16 black and Hispanic men had come from poor or working-class families, while the majority (9 of 14) of the white men had come from middle-class or professional families. All had at some time in their lives based their identities largely on their roles as athletes and could therefore be said to have had "athletic careers." Twelve had played organized sports through high school, 11 through college, and 7 had been professional athletes. Though the sample was not randomly selected, an effort was made to see that the sample had a range of difference in terms of race and social class backgrounds, and that there was some variety in terms of age, types of sports played, and levels of success in athletic careers. Without exception, each man contacted agreed to be interviewed.

The tape-recorded interviews were semistructured and took from one and one-half to six hours, with most taking about three hours. I asked each man to talk about four broad eras in his life: (1) his earliest experiences with sports in boyhood, (2) his athletic career, (3) retirement or disengagement from the athletic career, and (4) life after the athletic career. In each era, I focused the interview on the meanings of "success and failure," and on the boy's/man's relationships with family, with other males, with women, and with his own body.

In collecting what amounted to life histories of these men, my overarching purpose was to use feminist theories of masculine gender identity to explore how masculinity develops and changes as boys and men interact within the socially constructed world of organized sports. In addition to using the data to move toward some generalizations about the relationship between "masculinity and sport," I was also concerned with sorting out some of the variations among boys, based on class and racial inequalities, that led them to relate differently to athletic careers. I divided my sample into two comparison groups. The first group was made up of 10 men from higher-status backgrounds, primarily white, middle-class, and professional families. The second group was made up of 20 men from lower-status backgrounds, primarily minority, poor, and working-class families.

Boyhood and the Promise of Sports

Zane Grey once said, "All boys love baseball. If they don't they're not real boys" (as cited in Kimmel 1990). This is, of course, an ideological statement: In fact, some boys do *not* love baseball, or any other sports, for that matter. There are millions of males who at an early age are rejected by, become alienated from, or lose interest in organized sports. Yet all boys are, to a greater or lesser extent, judged according to their ability, or lack of ability, in competitive sports (Eitzen 1975; Sabo 1985). In this study I focus on those males who did become athletes—males who eventually poured thousands of hours into the development of specific physical skills. It is in boyhood that we can discover the roots of their commitment to athletic careers.

How did organized sports come to play such a central role in these boys' lives? When asked to recall how and why they initially got into playing sports, many of the men interviewed for this study seemed a bit puzzled: After all, playing sports was "just the thing to do." A 42-year-old black man who had played college basketball put it this way:

> *It was just what you did. It's kind of like, you went to school, you played athletics, and if you didn't, there was something wrong with you. It was just like brushing your teeth: It's just what you did. It's part of your existence.*

Spending one's time playing sports with other boys seemed as natural as the cycle of the seasons: baseball in the spring and summer, football in the fall, basketball in the winter—and then it was time to get out the old baseball glove and begin again. As a black 35-year-old former professional football star said:

> *I'd say when I wasn't in school, 95 percent of the time was spent in the park playing. It was the only thing to do. It just came as natural.*

And a black 34-year-old professional basketball player explained his early experiences in sports:

> *My principal and teacher said, "Now if you work at this you might be pretty damned good." So it was more or less a community thing—everybody in the community said, "Boy, if you work hard and keep your nose clean, you gonna be good." 'Cause it was natural instinct.*

"It was natural instinct." "I was a natural." Several athletes used words such as these to explain their early attraction to sports. But certainly there is nothing "natural" about throwing a ball through a hoop, hitting a ball with a bat, or jumping over hurdles. A boy, for instance, may have amazingly dexterous inborn hand-eye coordination, but this does not predispose him to a career of hitting baseballs any more than it predisposes him to a life as a brain surgeon. When one listens closely to what these men said about their early experiences in sports, it becomes clear that their adoption of the self-definition of "natural athlete" was the result of what Connell (1990) has called "a collective practice" that constructs masculinities. The boyhood development of masculine identity and status—truly problematic in a society that offers no official rite of passage into adulthood—results from a process of interaction with people and social institutions. Thus, in discussing early motivations in sports, men commonly talk of the importance of relationships with family members, peers, and the broader community.

Family Influences

Though most of the men in this study spoke of their mothers with love, respect, even reverence, their descriptions of their earliest experiences in sports are stories of an exclusively male world. The existence of older brothers or uncles who served as teachers and athletic role models—as well as sources of competition for attention and status within the family—was very common. An older brother, uncle, or even close friend of the family who was a successful athlete appears to have acted as a sort of standard of achievement against whom to measure oneself. A 34-year-old black man who had been a three-sport star in high school said:

> *My uncles—my Uncle Harold went to the Detroit Tigers, played pro ball—all of 'em, everybody played sports, so I wanted to be better than anybody else. I knew that everybody in this town knew them—their names were something. I wanted my name to be just like theirs.*

Similarly, a black 41-year-old former professional football player recalled:

> *I was the younger of three brothers and everybody played sports, so consequently I was more or less forced into it. 'Cause one brother was always better than the next brother and then I came along and had to show them that I was just as good as them. My oldest brother was an all-city ballplayer, then my other brother comes along—he's all-city and all-state—and then I have to come along.*

For some, attempting to emulate or surpass the athletic accomplishments of older male family members created pressures that were difficult to deal with. A 33-year-old white man explained that he was a good athlete during boyhood, but the constant awareness that his two older brothers had been better made it difficult for him to feel good about himself, or to have fun in sports:

> *I had this sort of reputation that I followed from the playgrounds through grade school, and through high school. I followed these guys who were all-conference and all-state.*

Most of these men, however, saw their relationship with their athletic older brothers and uncles in a positive light; it was within these relationships that they gained experience and developed motivations that gave them a competitive "edge" within their same-aged peer group. As a 33-year-old black man describes his earliest athletic experiences:

> *My brothers were role models. I wanted to prove—especially to my brothers— that I had heart, you know, that I was a man.*

When asked, "What did it mean to you to be 'a man' at that age?" he replied:

> *Well, it meant that I didn't want to be a so-called scaredy-cat. You want to hit a guy even though he's bigger than you to show that, you know, you've got this macho image. I remember that at that young an age, that feeling was exciting to me. And that carried over, and as I got older, I got better and I began to look around me and see, well hey! I'm competitive with these guys, even though I'm younger, you know? And then of course all the compliments come—and I began to notice a change, even in my parents—especially in my father—he was proud*

of that, and that was very important to me. He was extremely important. . . .
He showed me more affection, now that I think of it.

As this man's words suggest, if men talk of their older brothers and uncles mostly as role models, teachers, and "names" to emulate, their talk of their relationships with their fathers is more deeply layered and complex. Athletic skills and competition for status may often be learned from older brothers, but it is in boys' relationships with fathers that we find many of the keys to the emotional salience of sports in the development of masculine identity.

Relationships with Fathers

The fact that boys' introductions to organized sports are often made by fathers who might otherwise be absent or emotionally distant adds a powerful emotional charge to these early experiences (Osherson 1986). Although playing organized sports eventually came to feel "natural" for all of the men interviewed in this study, many needed to be "exposed" to sports, or even gently "pushed" by their fathers to become involved in activities like Little League baseball. A white 33-year-old man explained:

> *I still remember it like it was yesterday—Dad and I driving up in his truck, and I had my glove and my hat and all that—and I said, "Dad, I don't want to do it." He says, "What?" I says, "I don't want to do it." I was nervous. That I might fail. And he says, "Don't be silly. Lookit: There's Joey and Petey and all your friends out there." And so Dad says, "You're gonna do it, come on." And in my memory he's never said that about anything else; he just knew I needed a little kick in the pants and I'd do it. And once you're out there and you see all the other kids making errors and stuff, and you know you're better than those guys, you know: Maybe I* do *belong here. As it turned out, Little League was a good experience.*

Some who were similarly "pushed" by their fathers were not so successful as the aforementioned man had been in Little League baseball, and thus the experience was not altogether a joyous affair. One 34-year-old white man, for instance, said he "inherited" his interest in sports from his father, who started playing catch with him at the age of four. Once he got into Little League, he felt pressured by his father, one of the coaches, who expected him to be the star of the team:

> *I'd go 0-for-four sometimes, strike out three times in a Little League game, and I'd dread the ride home. I'd come home and he'd say, "Go in the bathroom and swing the bat in the mirror for an hour," to get my swing level. . . . It didn't help much, though, I'd go out and strike out three or four times again the next game too [laughs ironically].*

When asked if he had been concerned with having his father's approval, he responded:

Failure in his eyes? Yeah, I always thought that he wanted me to get some kind of [athletic] scholarship. I guess I was afraid of him when I was a kid. He didn't hit that much, but he had a rage about him—he'd rage, and that voice would just rattle you.

Similarly, a 24-year-old black man described his awe of his father's physical power and presence, and his sense of inadequacy in attempting to emulate him:

My father had a voice that sounded like rolling thunder. Whether it was intentional on his part or not, I don't know, but my father gave me a sense, an image of him being the most powerful being on earth, and that no matter what I ever did I would never come close to him. . . . There were definite feelings of physical inadequacy that I couldn't work around.

It is interesting to note how these feelings of physical inadequacy relative to the father lived on as part of this young man's permanent internalized image. He eventually became a "feared" high school football player and broke school records in weight-lifting. . . .

Using sports activities as a means of identifying with and "living up to" the power and status of one's father was not always such a painful and difficult task for the men I interviewed. Most did not describe fathers who "pushed" them to become sports stars. The relationship between their athletic strivings and their identification with their fathers was more subtle. A 48-year-old black man, for instance, explained that he was not pushed into sports by his father, but was aware from an early age of the community status his father had gained through sports. He saw his own athletic accomplishments as a way to connect with and emulate his father:

I wanted to play baseball because my father had been quite a good baseball player in the Negro leagues before baseball was integrated, and so he was kind of a model for me. I remember, quite young, going to a baseball game he was in—this was before the war and all—I remember being in the stands with my mother and seeing him on first base, and being aware of the crowd. . . . I was aware of people's confidence in him as a serious baseball player. I don't think my father ever said anything to me like "play sports." . . . [But] I knew he would like it if I did well. . . . His admiration was important. . . . He mattered. . . .

First experiences in sports might often come through relationships with brothers or other male relatives, and the early emotional salience of sports was often directly related to a boy's relationship with his father. The sense of commitment that these young boys eventually made to the development of athletic careers is best explained as a process of development of masculine gender identity and status in relation to same-sex peers.

Masculine Identity and Early Commitment to Sports

When many of the men in this study said that during childhood they played sports because "it's just what everybody did," they of course meant that it was just what *boys* did. They were introduced to organized sports by older brothers and fathers, and once involved, found themselves playing within an exclusively male world. Though the separate (and unequal) gendered worlds of boys and girls came to appear as "natural," they were in fact socially constructed. Thorne's observations of children's activities in schools indicated that rather than "naturally" constituting "separate gendered cultures," there is considerable interaction between boys and girls in classrooms and on playgrounds. When adults set up legitimate contact between boys and girls, Thorne observed, this usually results in "relaxed interactions." But when activities in the classroom or on the playground are presented to children as sex-segregated activities and gender is marked by teachers and other adults ("boys line up here, girls over there"), "gender boundaries are heightened, and mixed-sex interaction becomes an explicit arena of risk" (Thorne 1986: 70). Thus, sex-segregated activities such as organized sports as structured by adults, provide the context in which gendered identities and separate "gendered cultures" develop and come to appear natural. For the boys in this study, it became "natural" to equate masculinity with competition, physical strength, and skills. Girls simply did not (could not, it was believed) participate in these activities.

Yet it is not simply the separation of children, by adults, into separate activities that explains why many boys came to feel such a strong connection with sports activities, while so few girls did. As I listened to men recall their earliest experiences in organized sports, I heard them talk of insecurity, loneliness, and especially a need to connect with other people as a primary motivation in their early sports strivings. As a 42-year-old white man stated, "The most important thing was just being out there with the rest of the guys— being friends." Another 32-year-old interviewee was born in Mexico and moved to the United States at a fairly young age. He never knew his father, and his mother died when he was only nine years old. Suddenly he felt rootless, and threw himself into sports. His initial motivations, however, do not appear to be based on a need to compete and win:

> *Actually, what I think sports did for me is it brought me into kind of an instant family. By being on a Little League team, or even just playing with all kinds of different kids in the neighborhood, it brought what I really wanted, which was some kind of closeness. It was just being there, and being friends.*

Clearly, what these boys needed and craved was that which was most problematic for them: connection and unity with other people. But why do these young males find *organized sports* such an attractive context in which to establish "a kind of closeness" with others? . . . For the boy who both seeks and fears attachment with others, the rule-bound structure of organized sports can promise to be a safe place in which to seek nonintimate attachment with others within a context that maintains clear boundaries, distance, and separation.

Competitive Structures and Conditional Self-Worth

Young boys may initially find that sports gives them the opportunity to experience "some kind of closeness" with others, but the structure of sports and athletic careers often undermines the possibility of boys learning to transcend their fears of intimacy, thus becoming able to develop truly close and intimate relationships with others (Kidd 1990; Messner 1987). The sports world is extremely hierarchical, and an incredible amount of importance is placed on winning, on "being number one." For instance, a few years ago I observed a basketball camp put on for boys by a professional basketball coach and his staff. The youngest boys, about eight years old (who could barely reach the basket with their shots), played a brief scrimmage. Afterward, the coaches lined them up in a row in front of the older boys who were sitting in the grandstands. One by one, the coach would stand behind each boy, put his hand on the boy's head (much in the manner of a priestly benediction), and the older boys in the stands would applaud and cheer, louder or softer, depending on how well or poorly the young boy was judged to have performed. The two or three boys who were clearly the exceptional players looked confident that they would receive the praise they were due. Most of the boys, though, had expressions ranging from puzzlement to thinly disguised terror on their faces as they awaited the judgments of the older boys.

This kind of experience teaches boys that it is not "just being out there with the guys—being friends," that ensures the kind of attention and connection that they crave; it is being *better* than the other guys—*beating* them—that is the key to acceptance. Most of the boys in this study did have some early successes in sports, and thus their ambivalent need for connection with others was met, at least for a time. But the institution of sport tends to encourage the development of what Schafer (1975) has called "conditional self-worth" in boys. As boys become aware that acceptance by others is contingent upon being good—a "winner"—narrow definitions of success, based upon performance and winning, become increasingly important to them. A 33-year-old black man said that by the time he was in his early teens

> it was expected of me to do well in all my contests—I mean by my coaches, my peers, and my family. So I in turn expected to do well, and if I didn't do well, then I'd be very disappointed.

The man from Mexico, discussed above, who said that he had sought "some kind of closeness" in his early sports experiences began to notice in his early teens that if he played well, was a *winner,* he would get attention from others:

> *It got to the point where I started realizing, noticing that people were always there for me, backing me all the time—sports got to be really fun because I always had some people there backing me. Finally my oldest brother started going to all my games, even though I had never really seen who he was [laughs]— after the game, you know, we never really saw each other, but he was at all my baseball games, and it seemed like we shared a kind of closeness there, but only in those situations. Off the field, when I wasn't in uniform, he was never around.*

By high school, he said, he felt "up against the wall." Sports hadn't delivered what he had hoped it would, but he thought if he just tried harder, won one more championship trophy, he would get the attention he truly craved. Despite his efforts, this attention was not forthcoming. And, sadly, the pressures he had put on himself to excel in sports had taken most of the fun out of playing.

For many of the men in this study, throughout boyhood and into adolescence, this conscious striving for successful achievement became the primary means through which they sought connection with other people (Messner 1987). But it is important to recognize that young males' internalized ambivalences about intimacy do not fully determine the contours and directions of their lives. Masculinity continues to develop through interaction with the social world—and because boys from different backgrounds are interacting with substantially different familial, educational, and other institutions, these differences will lead them to make different choices and define situations in different ways. Next, I examine the differences in the ways that boys from higher- and lower-status families and communities related to organized sports.

Status Differences and Commitments to Sports

In discussing early attractions to sports, the experiences of boys from higher- and lower-status backgrounds are quite similar. Both groups indicate the importance of fathers and older brothers in introducing them to sports. Both groups speak of the joys of receiving attention and acceptance among family and peers for early successes in sports. Note the similarities, for instance, in the following descriptions of boyhood athletic experiences of two men. First, a man born in a white, middle-class family:

> *I loved playing sports so much from a very early age because of early exposure. A lot of the sports came easy at an early age, and because they did, and because you were successful at something, I think that you're inclined to strive for that gratification. It's like, if you're good, you like it, because it's instant gratification. I'm doing something that I'm good at and I'm gonna keep doing it.*

Second, a black man from a poor family:

> *Fortunately I had some athletic ability, and, quite naturally, once you start do-ing good in whatever it is—I don't care if it's jacks—you show off what you do. That's your ability, that's your blessing, so you show it off as much as you can.*

For boys from both groups, early exposure to sports, the discovery that they had some "ability," shortly followed by some sort of family, peer, and community recognition, all eventually led to the commitment of hundreds and thousands of hours playing, practicing, and dreaming of future stardom. Despite these similarities, there are also some identifiable differences that begin to explain the tendency of males from lower-status backgrounds to develop higher levels of commitment to sports careers. The most clear-cut difference was that while men from higher-status backgrounds are likely to describe their earliest athletic experiences and motivations almost exclusively in terms of immediate family, men from lower-status backgrounds more commonly describe the importance of a broader community context. For instance, a 46-year-old man who grew up in a "poor working class" black family in a small town in Arkansas explained:

> *In that community, at the age of third or fourth grade, if you're a male, they expect you to show some kind of inclination, some kind of skill in football or basketball. It was an expected thing, you know? My mom and my dad, they didn't push at all. It was the general environment.*

A 48-year-old man describes sports activities as a survival strategy in his poor black community:

> *Sports protected me from having to compete in gang stuff, or having to be good with my fists. If you were an athlete and got into the fist world, that was your business, and that was okay—but you didn't have to if you didn't want to. People would generally defer to you, give you your space away from trouble.*

A 35-year-old man who grew up in "a poor black ghetto" described his boyhood relationship to sports similarly:

> *Where I came from, either you were one of two things: You were in sports or you were out on the streets being a drug addict, or breaking into places. The guys who were in sports, we had it a little easier, because we were accepted by both groups. . . . So it worked out to my advantage, 'cause I didn't get into a lot of trouble—some trouble, but not a lot.*

The fact that boys in lower-status communities faced these kinds of reali-ties gave salience to their developing athletic identities. In contrast, sports were important to boys from higher-status backgrounds, yet the middle-class environment seemed more secure, less threatening, and offered far more options. By the time most of these boys got into junior high or high school, many had made conscious decisions to shift their attentions away from athletic careers to educational and (nonathletic) career goals. A 32-year-old white college athletic director told me that he had seen his chance to pursue a pro baseball career as "pissing in the wind" and, instead, focused on education. Similarly, a 33-year-old white dentist who was a three-sport star in high school decided not to play sports in college so he could focus on getting into dental school. As he put it,

> *I think I kind of downgraded the stardom thing. I thought it was small potatoes. And sure, that's nice in high school and all that, but on a broad scale, I didn't think it amounted to all that much.*

This statement offers an important key to understanding the construction of masculine identity within a middle-class context. The status that this boy got through sports had been *very* important to him, yet he could see that "on a broad scale," this sort of status was "small potatoes." This sort of early recognition is more than a result of the oft-noted middle-class tendency to raise "future-oriented" children (Rubin 1976; Sennett and Cobb 1973). Perhaps more important, it is that the *kinds* of future orientations developed by boys from higher-status backgrounds are consistent with the middle-class context. These men's descriptions of their boyhoods reveal that they grew up immersed in a wide range of institutional frameworks, of which organized sports was just one. And—importantly—they could see that the status of adult males around them was clearly linked to their positions within various professions, public institutions, and bureaucratic organizations. It was clear that access to this sort of institutional status came through educational achievement, not athletic prowess. A 32-year-old black man who grew up in a professional-class family recalled that he had idolized Wilt Chamberlain and dreamed of being a pro basketball player, yet his father discouraged his athletic strivings:

> *He knew I liked the game. I loved the game. But basketball was not recommended; my dad would say, "That's a stereotyped image for black youth. . . . When your basketball is gone and finished, what are you gonna do? One day, you might get injured. What are you gonna look forward to?" He stressed education.*

Similarly, a 32-year-old man who was raised in a white, middle-class family, had found in sports a key means of gaining acceptance and connection in his peer group. Yet he was simultaneously developing an image of himself as a "smart student" and becoming aware of a wide range of nonsports life options:

> *My mother was constantly telling me how smart I was, how good I was, what a nice person I was, and giving me all sorts of positive strokes, and those positive strokes became a self-motivating kind of thing. I had this image of myself as smart, and I lived up to that image.*

It is not that parents of boys in lower-status families did not also encourage their boys to work hard in school. Several reported that their parents "stressed books first, sports second." It's just that the broader social context—education, economy, and community—was more likely to *narrow* lower-status boys' perceptions of real-life options, while boys from higher-status backgrounds faced an expanding world of options. For instance, with a different socioeconomic background, one 35-year-old black man might have become a great musician instead of a star professional football running back. But he did not. When he was a child, he said, he was most interested in music:

> *I wanted to be a drummer. But we couldn't afford drums. My dad couldn't go out and buy me a drum set or a guitar even—it was just one of those things; he was just trying to make ends meet.*

But he *could* afford, as could so many in his socioeconomic condition, to spend countless hours at the local park, where he was told by the park supervisor

> *that I was a natural—not only in gymnastics or baseball—whatever I did, I was a natural. He told me I shouldn't waste this talent, and so I immediately started watching the big guys then.*

In retrospect, this man had potential to be a musician or any number of things, but his environment limited his options to sports, and he made the best of it. Even within sports, he, like most boys in the ghetto, was limited:

> *We didn't have any tennis courts in the ghetto—we used to have a lot of tennis balls, but no racquets. I wonder today how good I might be in tennis if I had gotten a racquet in my hands at an early age.*

It is within this limited structure of opportunity that many lower-status young boys found sports to be *the* place, rather than *a* place, within which to construct masculine identity, status, the relationships. A 36-year-old white man explained that his father left the family when he was very young and his mother faced a very difficult struggle to make ends meet. As his words suggest, the more limited a boy's options, and the more insecure his family situation, the more likely he is to make an early commitment to an athletic career:

> *I used to ride my bicycle to Little League practice—if I'd waited for someone to pick me up and take me to the ball park I'd have never played. I'd get to the ball park and all the other kids would have their dad bring them to practice or games. But I'd park my bike to the side and when it was over I'd get on it and go home. Sports was the way for me to move everything to the side—family problems, just all the embarrassments—and think about one thing, and that was sports. . . . In the third grade, when the teacher went around the classroom and asked everybody, "What do you want to be when you grow up?," I said, "I want to be a major league baseball player," and everybody laughed their heads off.*

This man eventually did enjoy a major league baseball career. Most boys from lower-status backgrounds who make similar early commitments to athletic careers are not so successful. As stated earlier, the career structure of organized sports is highly competitive and hierarchical. In fact, the chances of attaining professional status in sports are approximately 4:100,000 for a white man, 2:100,000 for a black man, and 3:1 million for a Hispanic man in the United States (Leonard and Reyman 1988). Nevertheless, the immediate rewards (fun, status, attention), along with the constricted (nonsports) structure of opportunity, attract disproportionately large numbers of boys from lower-status backgrounds to athletic careers as their major means of constructing a masculine identity. These are the boys who later, as young men, had to struggle with "conditional self-worth," and, more often than not, occupational dead ends. Boys from higher-status backgrounds, on the other hand, bolstered their boyhood, adolescent, and early adult status through their athletic accomplishments. Their wider range of experiences and life chances led to an early shift away from sports careers as the major basis of identity (Messner 1989).

Conclusion

The conception of the masculinity-sports relationship developed here begins to illustrate the idea of an "elective affinity" between social structure and personality. Organized sports is a "gendered institution"—an institution constructed by gender relations. As such, its structure and values (rules, formal organization, sex composition, etc.) reflect dominant conceptions of masculinity and femininity. Organized sports is also a "gendering institution"—an institution that helps to construct the current gender order. Part of this construction of gender is accomplished through the "masculinizing" of male bodies and minds.

Yet boys do not come to their first experiences in organized sports as "blank slates," but arrive with already "gendering" identities due to early developmental experiences and previous socialization. I have suggested here that an important thread running through the development of masculine identity is males' ambivalence toward intimate unity with others. Those boys who experience early athletic successes find in the structure of organized sport an affinity with this masculine ambivalence toward intimacy: The rule-bound, competitive, hierarchical world of sport offers boys an attractive means of establishing an emotionally distant (and thus "safe") connection with others. Yet as boys begin to define themselves as "athletes," they must learn that in order to be accepted (to have connection) through sports, they must be winners. And in order to be winners, they must construct relationships with others (and with themselves) that are consistent with the competitive and hierarchical values and structure of the sports world. As a result, they often develop a "conditional self-worth" that leads them to construct more instrumental relationships with themselves and others. This ultimately exacerbates their difficulties in constructing intimate relationships with others. In effect, the interaction between the young male's preexisting internalized ambivalence toward intimacy with the competitive, hierarchical institution of sport has resulted in the construction of a masculine personality that is characterized by instrumental rationality, goal-orientation, and difficulties with intimate connection and expression (Messner 1987).

This theoretical line of inquiry invites us not simply to examine how social institutions "socialize" boys, but also to explore the ways that boys' already-gendering identities interact with social institutions (which, like organized sport, are themselves the product of gender relations). This study has also suggested that it is not some singular "masculinity" that is being constructed through athletic careers. It may be correct, from a psychoanalytic perspective, to suggest that all males bring ambivalences toward intimacy to their interactions with the world, but "the world" is a very different place for males from different racial and socioeconomic backgrounds. Because males have substantially different interactions with the world, based on class, race, and other differences and inequalities, we might expect the construction of masculinity to take on different meanings for boys and men from differing backgrounds (Messner 1989). Indeed, this study has suggested that boys from higher-status backgrounds face a much broader range of options than do their lower-status counterparts. As a result, athletic careers take on different meanings for these boys. Lower-status boys are likely to see athletic careers as *the* institutional context for the construction of their masculine status and identities, while higher-status males make an early shift away from athletic careers toward other institutions (usually education and nonsports careers). A key line of inquiry for future studies might begin by exploring this irony of sports careers: Despite the fact that "the athlete" is currently an example of an exemplary form of masculinity in public ideology, the vast majority of boys who become most committed to athletic careers are never well rewarded for their efforts. The fact that class and racial dynamics lead boys from higher-status backgrounds, unlike their lower-status counterparts, to move into nonsports careers illustrates how the construction of different kinds of masculinities is a key component of the overall construction of the gender order.

REFERENCES

Benjamin, J. 1988. *The Bonds of Love: Psychoanalysis, Feminism and the Problem of Domination.* New York: Pantheon.

Connell, R. W. 1990. "An Iron Man: The Body and Some Contradictions of Hegemonic Masculinity." In *Sport, Men and the Gender Order: Critical Feminist Perspectives,* edited by M. A. Messner and D. F. Sabo. Champaign, IL: Human Kinetics.

Eitzen, D. S. 1975. "Athletics in the Status System of Male Adolescents: A Replication of Coleman's *The Adolescent Society.*" *Adolescence* 10:268–76.

Haug, F. 1987. *Female Sexualization.* London: Verso.

Kidd, B. 1990. "The Men's Cultural Centre: Sports and the Dynamic of Women's Oppression / Men's Repression." In *Sport, Men and the Gender Order: Critical Feminist*

Perspectives, edited by M. A. Messner and D. F. Sabo. Champaign, IL: Human Kinetics.

Kimmel, M. S. 1990. "Baseball and the Reconstitution of American Masculinity: 1880 – 1920." In *Sport, Men and the Gender Order: Critical Feminist Perspectives,* edited by M. A. Messner and D. F. Sabo. Champaign, IL: Human Kinetics.

Leonard, W. M., II, and J. M. Reyman. 1988. "The Odds of Attaining Professional Athlete Status: Refining the Computations." *Sociology of Sport Journal* 5:162–69.

Levinson, D. J. et al. 1978. *The Seasons of a Man's Life.* New York: Ballantine.

Messner, M. 1987. "The Meaning of Success: The Athletic Experience and the Development of Male Identity." Pp. 193–210 in *The Making of Masculinities: The New Men's Studies,* edited by H. Brod. Boston: Allyn & Unwin.

——. 1989. "Masculinities and Athletic Careers." *Gender and Society* 3:71–88.

Osherson, S. 1986. *Finding Our Fathers: How a Man's Life Is Shaped by His Relationship with His Father.* New York: Fawcett Columbine.

Rubin, L. B. 1976. *Worlds of Pain: Life in the Working Class Family.* New York: Basic Books.

Sabo, D. 1985. "Sport, Patriarchy and Male Identity: New Questions about Men and Sport." *Arena Review* 9:2.

Schafer, W. E. 1975. "Sport and Male Sex Role Socialization." *Sport Sociology Bulletin* 4:47–54.

Sennett, R. and J. Cobb. 1973. *The Hidden Injuries of Class.* New York: Random House.

Thorne, B. 1986. "Girls and Boys Together . . . but Mostly Apart: Gender Arrangements in Elementary Schools." Pp. 167–84 in *Relationships and Development,* edited by W. W. Hartup and Z. Rubin. Hillsdale, NJ: Erlbaum.

13

MAKING IT BY FAKING IT
Working-Class Students in an Elite
Academic Environment

ROBERT GRANFIELD

Learning an occupation is a common form of adult socialization. Occupational socialization occurs during formal education, during job training, and during time spent on the job. Every profession has a set of values that it wants its colleagues to embrace. For example, to become a doctor one needs to learn the skills and knowledge of practicing medicine as well as the attitudes and values of the medical profession. Medical students experience

From *Journal of Contemporary Ethnography* (formerly *Urban Life*), Vol. 20, No. 3, October 1991, 331–51. Copyright © 1991 by Sage Publications, Inc. Reprinted by permission of Sage Publications, Inc.

an intense period of professional socialization during the years, almost a decade, they spend in medical school and residency. Law students are socialized as well, and the following reading by Robert Granfield (1991), an associate professor of sociology at the University of Denver, discusses how working-class students are socialized into elite law schools and into the legal profession.

Research on stigma has generated significant insights into the complex relationship between self and society. The legacy of Goffman's (1963) seminal work on the subject can be found in studies on alcoholism, mental illness, homosexuality, physical deformities, and juvenile delinquency. Even the literature on gender and racial inequality has benefited from an emphasis on stigma. Goffman's attention to the social processes of devaluation and the emerging self-concepts of discredited individuals not only created research opportunities for generations of sociologists but contributed to a humanistic ideology that viewed stigma assignment and its effects as unjust.

One of the most vibrant research programs that emerged from Goffman's classic work has been in the area of stigma management. A host of conceptual terms have been employed to describe the process through which discreditable individuals control information about themselves so as to manage their social identity. Concepts such as passing, deviance disavowal, accounts, disclaimers, and covering have often been used in analyzing accommodations and adjustments to deviance, as Pfuhl's (1986) review shows. These tactics, while offering rewards associated with being seen as normal, frequently contribute to psychological stress. Possessing what Goffman (1963:5) referred to as "undesired differentness" often has significant consequences for one's personal identity as well as for available life chances. . . .

In this article, I focus on class stigma by examining a group of highly successful, upwardly mobile, working-class students who gained admission to a prestigious Ivy League law school in the East. While upward mobility from the working class occurs far less often within elite branches of the legal profession (Heinz and Laumann 1982; Smigel 1969) or corporate management (Useem and Karabel 1986), a certain amount of this type of mobility does take place. Working-class aspirants to the social elite, however, must accumulate cultural capital (Bourdieu and Passeron 1990; Cookson and Persell 1985) before they are able to transcend their status boundaries.

First, this article examines the ways in which working-class students experience a sense of differentness and marginality within the law school's elite environment. Next, I explore how these students react to their emerging class stigma by managing information about their backgrounds. I then demonstrate that the management strategies contribute to identity ambivalence and consider the secondary forms of adjustment students use to resolve this tension. Finally, I discuss why an analysis of social class can benefit from the insights forged by Goffman's work on stigma.

Setting and Methodology

The data analyzed for this article were collected as part of a much larger project associated with law school socialization (Granfield 1989). The subjects consist of students attending a prestigious, national law school in the eastern part of the United States. The school has had a long reputation of training lawyers who have become partners in major Wall Street law firms, Supreme Court judges, United States presidents and other politicians, heads of foundations, and . . . [have assumed many] other eminent leadership positions. Throughout the school's history, it has drawn mostly on the talents of high-status males. It was not until the second half of the twentieth century that women, minorities, and members of the lower classes were allowed admission into this esteemed institution (Abel 1989).

Most of the students attending the university at the time the study was being conducted were white and middle class.[1] The overwhelming majority are the sons and daughters of the professional-managerial class. Over 70 percent of those returning questionnaires had Ivy League or other highly prestigious educational credentials. As one would expect, fewer working-class students possessed such credentials.

A triangulated research design (Fielding and Fielding 1986) was used to collect the data. The first phase consisted of extensive fieldwork at the law school from 1985 to 1988, during which time I became a "peripheral member" (Adler and Adler 1987) in selected student groups. My activities while in the field consisted of attending classes with students, participating in their Moot Court[2] preparations, studying with students on campus, and at times, in their apartments, lunching with them, becoming involved in student demonstrations over job recruiting and faculty hiring, attending extracurricular lectures presented on campus, and participating in orientation exercises for first-year students. Throughout the entire fieldwork phase, I assumed both overt and covert roles. During the observation periods in classrooms, I recorded teacher-student interactions that occurred.

To supplement these observations, I conducted in-depth interviews with 103 law students at various stages in their training. Both personal interviews and small-group interviews with three or four students were recorded. The interviews lasted approximately two hours each and sought to identify the lived process through which law students experience legal training.

Finally, I administered a survey to 50 percent of the 1,540 students attending the law school. The survey examined their backgrounds, motives for attending law school, subjective perceptions of personal change, expectations about future practice, and evaluations of various substantive areas of practice. Over half (391) of the questionnaires were returned—a high rate of response for a survey of six pages requiring approximately 30 minutes of the respondent's time.

For this article, a subset of working-class students was selected for extensive analysis. Of the 103 students interviewed for the larger study, 23 came from working-class backgrounds, none of these from either the labor aristocracy or the unstable sectors of the working class. Typical parental occupations include postal worker, house painter, factory worker, fireman, dock worker, and carpenter. Many of these students were interviewed several times during their law school career. Many of the students selected for interviews were identified through questionnaires, while others were selected through the process of snowball sampling (Chadwick, Bahr, and Albrecht 1984).

Feeling Out of Place

Working-class students entered this elite educational institution with a great deal of class pride. This sense of class pride is reflected in the fact that a significantly larger proportion of working-class students reported entering law school for the purposes of contributing to social change than their non-working-class counterparts (see Granfield and Koenig 1990). That these students entered law school with the desire to help the downtrodden suggests that they identified with their working-class kin. In fact, students often credited their class background as being a motivating factor in their decision to pursue a career in social justice. One third-year student, whose father worked as a postal worker, recalled her parental influence:

> *I wanted a career in social justice. It seemed to me to be a good value for some-one who wanted to leave this world a little better than they found it. My parents raised me with a sense that there are right things and wrong things and that maybe you ought to try to do some right things with your life.*

A second-year student said that he was influenced by the oppressive experiences that his father endured as a factory laborer. Coming to law school to pursue a career in a labor union, this student explained, "I was affected by my father, who had a job as a machinist. My father believes that corporations have no decency. I would term it differently, but we're talking about the same thing." Identifying with their working-class heritage produced not only a sense of pride but a system of values and ideals that greatly influenced their initial career objectives.

However, identification with the working class began to diminish soon after these students entered law school. Not long after arriving, most working-class students encountered an entirely new moral career. Although initially proud of their accomplishments, they soon came to define themselves as different and their backgrounds a burden. Lacking the appropriate cultural capital (Bourdieu 1984) associated with their more privileged counterparts, working-class students began to experience a crisis in competency. Phrases such as "the first semester makes you feel extremely incompetent," "the first year is like eating humble pie," and "I felt very small, powerless, and dumb" were almost universal among these working-class students. Some students felt embarrassed by their difficulty in using the elaborated speech codes (Bernstein 1977) associated with the middle class. One working-class woman said that she was very aware of using "proper" English, adding that "it makes me self-conscious when I use the wrong word or tense. I feel that if I had grown up in the middle class, I wouldn't have lapses. I have difficulty expressing thoughts while most other people here don't."

The recognition of their apparent differentness is perhaps best noted by examining the students' perception of stress associated with the first year of studies. Incoming working-class students reported significantly higher levels of personal stress than did their counterparts with more elite backgrounds. Much of this anxiety came from fears of academic inadequacy. Despite generally excellent college grades and their success in gaining admission to a nationally ranked law school, these students often worried that they did not measure up to the school's high standards. Nearly 62 percent of the first-year working-class students reported experiencing excessive grade pressure, compared to only 35 percent of those students from higher social class backgrounds.

In the words of Sennett and Cobb (1973), this lack of confidence is a "hidden injury of class," a psychological burden that working-class students experienced as they came to acquire the "identity beliefs" associated with middle-class society. While most students experience some degree of uncertainty and competency crisis during their first year, working-class students face the additional pressure of being cultural outsiders. Lacking manners of speech, attire, values, and experiences associated with their more privileged counterparts, even the most capable working-class student felt out of place:

> *I had a real problem my first year because law and legal education are based on upper-middle-class values. The class debates had to do with profit maximization, law and economics, atomistic individualism. I remember in class we were talking about landlords' responsibility to maintain decent housing in rental apartments. Some people were saying that there were good reasons not to do this. Well, I think that's bullshit because I grew up with people who lived in apartments with rats, leaks, and roaches. I feel really different because I didn't grow up in suburbia.*

Another student, a third-year working-class woman, felt marginalized because even her teachers assumed class homogeneity:

> *I get sensitive about what professors have to say in class. I remember in a business class the professor seemed to assume that we all had fathers that worked in business and that we all understood about family investments. He said, "You're all pretty much familiar with this because of your family background."*

I remember thinking, doesn't he think there's any people in this law school who come from a working-class background?

Such experiences contributed to a student's sense of living in an alien world. The social distance these students experienced early in their law school career produced considerable discomfort.

This discomfort grew more intense as they became increasingly immersed into this new elite world. Within a short span of time, these students began to experience a credential gap vis-à-vis other students who possessed more prestigious academic credentials. A first-year male student who attended a state school in the Midwest explained:

I'm not like most people here. I didn't go to prestigious schools. I'm a bit of a minority here because of that. When I got here I was really intimidated by the fact of how many Yale and Harvard people there were here.

At times, working-class law students were even embarrassed by their spouse's lower status. One first-year student described how her husband's credential gap caused her some anxiety:

People would ask me what my husband did and I would say he works for Radio Shack. People would be surprised. That was hard. Lately, we haven't done as much with [law school] people.

Thus, students sometimes pruned contacts that would potentially result in stigma disclosure. In general, then, as working-class students progressed through law school, they began to adopt a view of themselves as different. The recognition of this difference subsequently led them to develop techniques of adjusting to their perceived secondary status.

Faking It

The management of identity has critical strategic importance not only for group affiliation and acceptance but for life chances. Stigma limits one's opportunities to participate in social life as a complete citizen, particularly so for those possessing gender or racial stigmas. However, because of the visibility of these stigmas, a person's adjustment to second-class citizenship is accomplished typically through either role engulfment in which a person accepts a spoiled identity (Schur 1971) or through direct confrontation where assignment of secondary status is itself challenged (Schur 1980). Rarely are these groups able to employ the concealment tactics typical among those groups whose stigma is not overtly visible.

Unlike gender or racial stigma, however, individuals often adjust to class stigma by learning to conceal their uniqueness. The practice of concealing one's class background, for instance, is not unusual. Certainly, members of the elite frequently learn that it is in "bad taste" to flaunt their privileged background and that it is more gracious to conceal their eminent social status (Baltzell 1958). Similarly, individuals who experience downward mobility often attempt to maintain their predecline image by concealing loss of status. Camouflaging unemployment in the world of management by using such terms as "consultant" and by doctoring résumés are ways that downwardly mobile executives "cover" their spoiled status (Newman 1988). Concealing one's social class circumstances and the stigma that may be associated with it assist individuals in dealing with any rejection and ostracism that may be forthcoming were the person's actual status known.

Initially, students who took pride in having accomplished upward mobility openly displayed a working-class presentation of self. Many went out of their way to maintain this presentation. One first-year student who grew up in a labor union family in New York explained that "I have consciously maintained my working-class image. I wear work shirts or old flannel shirts and blue jeans every day." During his first year, this student flaunted his working-class background, frequently also donning an old army jacket, hiking boots, and a wool hat. Identifying himself as part of the "proletarian left," he tried to remain isolated from what he referred to as the "elitist" law school community.

This attempt to remain situated in the working class, however, not only separated these students from the entire law school community but alienated them from groups that shared their ideological convictions. While much of the clothing worn by non-working-class students suggests resistance to being identified as a member of the elite, working-class students become increasingly aware of their differentness. Although these students identify with the working class, others, despite their appearance, possess traits and lifestyles that are often associated with more privileged groups (see Lurie 1983; Stone 1970). One first-year woman who described herself as "radical" complained that the other law school radicals were really "a bunch of upper-class white men." Subsequently, working-class students must disengage from their backgrounds if they desire to escape feeling discredited.

Working-class students disengaged from their previous identity by concealing their class backgrounds. Just as deviants seek to manage their identity by "passing" as nondeviants (Goffman 1963), these working-class law students often adopted identities that were associated with the more elite social classes.[3] Concealment allowed students to better participate in the culture of eminence that exists within the law school and reap available rewards.

This concealment meant, for instance, that students needed to acquire new dress codes. As Stone (1970) illustrated, appearance signifies identity and exercises a regulatory function over the responses of others. Such cultural codes pertaining to appearance often are used to exclude individuals from elite social positions (Bourdieu 1984; Jackell 1988; Lamont and Lareau 1988). Although working-class students lacked the cultural capital of higher social classes, they began to realize that they could successfully mimic their more privileged counterparts. Like undistinguished prep school students (Cookson and Persell 1985), working-class law students learned how to behave in an upper-class world, including how to dress for a new audience whose favorable appraisal they must cultivate. One second-year male discussed this process:

> *I remember going to buy suits here. I went to Brooks Brothers for two reasons. One, I don't own a suit. My father owns one suit, and it's not that good. Second, I think it's important to look good. A lot of my friends went to Brooks Brothers, and I feel it's worth it to do it right and not to have another hurdle to walk in and have the wrong thing on. It's all a big play act. . . . During my first year, I had no luck with interviews. I was in my own little world when I came here. I wished I had paid more attention to the dressing habits of second- and third-year students.*

Being in their own "working-class world" forced these students to begin recognizing the importance of different interpersonal skills. A second-year woman commented that

> *I have really begun to see the value of having good social skills. I think that is one of the ways that law firms weed out people. In order to get jobs you have to have those social skills. I'm real conscious of that when I go out on interviews now.*

The recognition among working-class students that they were able to imitate upper-class students increasingly encouraged them to conceal their backgrounds. One second-year student, whose father worked as a house painter, boasted of his mastery of "passing":

> *I generally don't tell people what my father does or what my mother does. I notice that I'm different, but it's not something other people here notice because I can fake it. They don't notice that I come from a blue-collar background.*

Paying attention to the impression that one presents becomes extremely important for the upwardly mobile working-class student.

These students were sometimes assisted in their performances by professional career counselors employed by the law school. These professionals gave students instructions on how to present themselves as full-fledged members of this elite community. Students were taught that unless they downplayed their social class background, the most lucrative opportunities would be denied them. A third-year woman from a working-class area in Boston recalled learning this new norm of presentation:

> *I'm sort of proud that I'm from South Boston and come from a working-class background. During my second year, however, I wasn't having much luck with my first interviews. I went to talk with my adviser about how to change my résumé a bit or how to present myself better. I told my adviser that on the interviews I was presenting myself as a slightly unusual person with a different*

background. We talked about that, and he told me that it probably wasn't a good idea to present myself as being a little unusual. I decided that he was right and began to play up that I was just like them. After that, the interviews and offers began rolling in. I began to realize that they [interviewers] really like people who are like themselves.

Recognizing that job recruiters seek homogeneity is an important lesson that upwardly mobile working-class students must learn if they are to gain admission into high status and financially rewarding occupations.[4] Kanter (1977) demonstrated, for instance, that managers come to reward those who resemble themselves. More recently, Jackell (1988) documented how the failure of managers to "fit in" resulted in suspicion and subsequent exclusion from advancement. Fitting in is particularly important in prestigious law firms which tend to resemble the high-status clients they represent (Abel 1989). During interviews, however, working-class law students faced a distinct disadvantage, as the interviewers who actively pursued new recruits rarely posed questions about the student's knowledge of law.[5] Most seemed intent on finding students who fit into the law firm's corporate structure. The entire recruitment process itself, from the initial interview to "fly out," represents ceremonial affirmation of these students' elite status in which they need only demonstrate their "social" competence. Working-class students typically found such interactions stressful. One third-year student explained her experiences:

They [the recruiters] didn't test my knowledge of law. They were interested in finding out what kind of person I was and what my background was. I tried to avoid talking about that and instead stressed the kind of work I was interested in. I think that most firms want a person who they can mold, that fits into their firm.

Some of the most successful working-class students enjoyed the accolades bestowed on them because of their hard work and natural abilities. In speaking of her success, a third-year student on law review said that when she entered law school, it never occurred to her that she would clerk for the Supreme Court and then work for a major Wall Street law firm, adding that "once you begin doing well and move up the ladder and gain a whole new set of peers, then you begin to think about the possibilities." However, such success comes at a price, particularly for working-class students of color. Although having achieved success, many of these students continued to feel like outsiders. One such student, a third-year black male, reflected on what he considered the unfortunate aspects of affirmative action programs:

I have mixed feelings about the law review because of its affirmative action policies. On the one hand, I think it's good that minorities are represented on the law review. On the other hand, there's a real stigma attached to it. Before law school, I achieved by my own abilities. On law review, I don't feel I get respect. I find myself working very hard and getting no respect. Other students don't work as hard. I spend a lot of time at the review because I don't want to turn in a bad assignment. I don't want them [other law review members] to think that I don't have what it takes.

Students who perceived themselves as outsiders frequently overcompensated for their failings because they felt judged by the "master status" associated with their social identity. This reaction to class stigma is typical among working-class students in educational institutions. In addition to developing their educational skills, working-class students are confronted with learning social skills as well. This makes succeeding particularly difficult for these students and is a task fraught with the fear of being discovered as incompetent (Sennett and Cobb 1973).

Ambivalence

Despite their maneuvers, these working-class students had difficulty transcending their previous identity. The attempt by these students to manage their stigma resulted in what Goffman (1963:107) termed "identity ambivalence." Working-class students who sought to exit their class background could neither embrace their group nor let it go. This ambivalence is often felt by working-class individuals who attain upward mobility into the professional-managerial class (Steinitz and Solomon 1986). Many experience the "stranger in paradise" syndrome, in which working-class individuals feel like virtual outsiders in middle-class occupations (Ryan and Sackrey 1984). Such experiences frequently lead to considerable identity conflict among working-class individuals who attempt to align themselves with the middle class.

The working-class law students in my sample typically experienced identity conflicts on their upward climb. Not only did they feel deceptive in their adjustment strategies, but many felt the additional burden of believing they had "sold out" their own class and were letting their group down. Like other stigmatized individuals who gain acceptance among dominant groups (Goffman 1963), these students often felt they were letting down their own group by representing elite interests. One third-year female student ruefully explained:

My brother keeps asking me whether I'm a Republican yet. He thought that after I finished law school I would go to work to help people, not work for one of those firms that do business. In a way, he's my conscience. Maybe he's right. I've got a conflict with what I'm doing. I came from the working class and wanted to do public interest law. I have decided not to do that. It's been a difficult decision for me. I'm not completely comfortable about working at a large firm.

Another student, who grew up on welfare, expressed similar reservations about his impending career in law:

I'm not real happy about going to a large firm. I make lots of apologies. I'm still upset about the fact that my clients are real wealthy people, and it's not clear as to what the social utility of that will be.

Like the previous example, this student experienced a form of self-alienation as a result of his identity ambivalence. Students often experience a sense of guilt as they transcend their working-class backgrounds. Such guilt, however, needs to be abated if these students are to successfully adjust to their new reference group and reduce the status conflict they experience. For these working-class students, making the primary adjustment to upward mobility required strategies of accommodation in personal attitudes regarding their relationship to members of less privileged social classes. Secondary identity adjustments were therefore critical in helping students mitigate the ambivalence they experienced over their own success and subsequent separation from the working class.

Resolving Ambivalence

Although accommodation strategies were typical throughout the entire student body,[6] working-class students at this law school were more likely to employ particular types of strategies to help manage their identity. Students sought to manage their ambivalence by remaining "ideologically" distanced from the very social class their elite law school credential had facilitated alignment with. Many of these students became deliberate role models, unreservedly immersing themselves in higher social classes for that specific purpose. Such adjustments might be thought of as political since they were intended to directly challenge the domination of social elites. A black working-class student described how his actions would benefit the less fortunate:

I get slammed for being a corporate tool. People feel that I have sold out. I'm irritated by that. For years, blacks have been treated as slaves, sharecroppers, or porters. So I think that whether I want to be a partner at Cravath or to be an NAACP defense attorney, either of these positions are politically correct. We need black people with money and power. I think that I can make significant contributions to black causes.

For many students who experienced ambivalence, working in elite law firms was seen as the best way to help those they left behind. Other students redefined the value of large corporate law firms for the opportunities that such positions offered in contributing to social change. One third-year student suggested:

I used to think that social change would come about by being an activist. That's why I originally wanted to do public interest law. But you really can't accomplish much by doing this. The hiring partner at [a major New York law firm]

convinced me that this is the only way to get things done. He served as the un-
der secretary of state in the [former president's] administration. He made sense
when he told me that if I wanted to contribute to social change I had to become
an important person.

Students became less convinced that directly serving the less-privileged social classes would effectively resolve the problems that concerned them. A
third-year student explained how disenchanted she had become with public
interest law:

I used to think that you could do good things for people. . . . I don't think that
anymore. I'm no longer troubled by the idea of being a corporate lawyer as op-
posed to a public interest one. I'm still concerned about social problems like
poverty or poor housing, but I'm not sure that being a public interest attorney
is the way to resolve those things. The needs of the people that public interest
lawyers serve are just beyond what I can do as an attorney. I think I can do more
good for people if I commit myself to working with community groups or activi-
ties in the bar during my spare time.

The offering of such accounts helps students resolve the contradiction they
experience by choosing a large law firm practice, as does the practical planning to use one's spare time (e.g., to do community activities). Unfortunately,
given the structure of contemporary large law firms, spare time is a rarity
(Nelson 1988; Spangler 1986). Adopting these new definitions regarding the
pursuit of effective social change means that working-class students need not
feel penitent over their upward mobility. Such strategies, of course, are attractive, as they suggest that the student is becoming elite not solely because
he or she is striving for personal reward and success but as a means to best
pursue the noble ideals of public service and social activism.

A more drastic accommodation involved avoidance of those who reminded working-class students of their social obligations toward helping the
less fortunate. Just associating with individuals whose career path was
geared toward helping the downtrodden caused considerable uneasiness in
working-class students who had decided to enter large law firms. One third-
year student said that he had begun to avoid law students who had retained
their commitment to work with the poor:

It's taken for granted here that you can work for a large firm and still be a good
person. The people who don't reinforce that message make me uncomfortable now.
Frankly, that's why I'm not hanging out with the public interest people. They re-
mind me of my own guilt.

In some cases, avoidance turned into open hostility. Another third-year student described how she now saw other students who remained committed to
their ideals of helping the less fortunate: "They're so single-minded at times
and I think a little naive. They've really pushed me away from wanting to do

public interest work as a full-time occupation." Condemning her condemners helped this student neutralize the guilt she felt over working for a corporate law firm.

Conclusion

Upwardly mobile working-class students in this study, as well as in others, interpret and experience their social class from the perspective of stigma. However, since the stigma of being a member of the lower classes is thought to be just, upwardly mobile working-class students frequently construct identities in which they seek to escape the taint associated with their affiliation. Overcoming this stigma is therefore considered an individual rather than a collective effort. As was demonstrated in this study, such efforts often involve managing one's identity in the ways that Goffman outlined. Research that explores identity struggles as they relate to class could offer further extensions of Goffman's comments on stigma. Such research also has potential value in contributing to our understanding of working-class movements in the United States. Indeed, exploring the experience of class from the perspective of stigma and its management could offer great insight into the social psychology of working-class disempowerment.

ENDNOTES

Author's Note: Partial funding for this research was provided by the Woodrow Wilson Foundation.

[1] The following are the percentage distributions of social class background on the random sample of questionnaire returnees I collected for the larger project: upper class (2.8), upper-middle (44.6), middle (30.0), lower-middle (8.0), working (13.1), and lower (0.5).

[2] This is a first-year exercise in which students select a case to argue in front of a three-person panel consisting of a law professor, a third-year student, and an invited guest from the legal community. First-year students prepare their cases for several months in advance before formally presenting their oral argument.

[3] Similar findings were reported by Domhoff and Zweigenhaft (1991) in which they described the experiences of black students who were enrolled in elite prep schools as a result of affirmative action.

[4] Students are actively pursued. During the 1987 recruitment seasons at the law school, an average of 44 recruiters from commercial law firms conducted interviews with students each day. This represents nearly one law firm for each law student eligible to interview. In most cases, law firms are looking to hire more than one student.

[5] A study of hiring policies among large law firms found that "personal characteristics" ranked second among the criteria for selecting new lawyers (see Buller and Beck-Dudley 1990).

[6] Many students are confronted with identity conflicts that stem from the separation of personal values from professional roles. This is felt most among those students

who entered law school with social activist ideals (for further discussion of this, see Granfield 1986, 1989, 1992).

REFERENCES

Abel, R. 1989. *American Lawyers.* New York: Oxford University Press.
Adler, P. and P. Adler. 1987. *Membership Roles in Field Research.* Newbury Park, CA: Sage.
Baltzell, E. D. 1958. *Philadelphia Gentlemen.* New York: Free Press.
Bernstein, B. 1977. *Class Codes and Control.* Vol. 3, *Towards a Theory of Educational Transmission.* London: Routledge & Kegan Paul.
Bourdieu, P. 1984. *Distinction: A Social Critique of the Judgment of Taste.* Cambridge, MA: Harvard University Press.
Bourdieu, P. and J. C. Passeron. 1990. *Reproduction in Education, Society and Culture.* London: Routledge & Kegan Paul.
Buller, P. and C. Beck-Dudley. 1990. "Performance, Policies and Personnel." *American Bar Association Journal* 76:94.
Chadwick, B., H. Bahr, and S. Albrecht. 1984. *Social Science Research Methods.* Englewood Cliffs, NJ: Prentice-Hall.
Cookson, P. and C. Persell. 1985. *Preparing for Power: America's Elite Boarding Schools.* New York: Basic Books.
Domhoff, G. W. and R. Zweigenhaft. 1991. *Blacks in the White Establishment: A Study of Race and Class in America.* New Haven, CT: Yale University Press.
Fielding, N. and J. Fielding. 1986. *Linking Data.* Beverly Hills, CA: Sage.
Goffman, E. 1963. *Stigma: Notes on the Management of Spoiled Identity.* Englewood Cliffs, NJ: Prentice-Hall.
Granfield, R. 1986. "Legal Education As Corporate Ideology: Student Adjustment to the Law School Experience." *Sociological Forum* 1:514–23.
———. 1989. "Making the Elite Lawyer: Culture and Ideology in Legal Education." Ph.D. dissertation, Northeastern University, Boston.
———. 1992. *Making Elite Lawyers.* New York: Routledge, Chapman & Hall.
Granfield, R. and T. Koenig. 1990. "From Activism to Pro Bono: The Redirection of Working Class Altruism at Harvard Law School." *Critical Sociology* 17:57–80.
Heinz, J. and E. Laumann. 1982. *Chicago Lawyers: The Social Structure of the Bar.* New York: Russell Sage.
Jackell, R. 1988. *Moral Mazes: The World of the Corporate Manager.* New York: Oxford University Press.
Kanter, R. 1977. *Men and Women of the Corporation.* New York: Basic Books.
Lamont, M. and A. Lareau. 1988. "Cultural Capital: Allusions, Gaps and Glissandos in Recent Theoretical Development." *Sociological Theory* 6:153–68.
Lurie, A. 1983. *The Language of Clothes.* New York: Vintage.
Nelson, R. 1988. *Partners with Power: The Social Transformation of the Large Law Firm.* Berkeley: University of California Press.
Newman, K. 1988. *Falling from Grace: The Experience of Downward Mobility in the American Middle Class.* New York: Free Press.
Pfuhl, E. 1986. *The Deviance Process.* Belmont, CA: Wadsworth.
Ryan, J. and C. Sackrey. 1984. *Strangers in Paradise: Academics from the Working Class.* Boston: South End Press.
Schur, E. 1971. *Labeling Deviant Behavior.* New York: Harper & Row.
———. 1980. *The Politics of Deviance.* Englewood Cliffs, NJ: Prentice-Hall.
Sennett, R. and R. Cobb. 1973. *The Hidden Injuries of Class.* New York: Random House.
Smigel, E. 1969. *The Wall Street Lawyer.* Bloomington: Indiana University Press.

Spangler, E. 1986. *Lawyers for Hire: Salaried Professionals at Work.* New Haven, CT: Yale University Press.

Steinitz, V. and E. Solomon. 1986. *Starting Out: Class and Community in the Lives of Working Class Youth.* Philadelphia: Temple University Press.

Stone, G. 1970. "Appearance and the Self." Pp. 394–414 in *Social Psychology through Symbolic Interaction,* edited by G. Stone and H. Farberman. New York: Wiley.

Useem, M. and J. Karabel. 1986. "Paths to Corporate Management." *American Sociological Review* 51:184–200.

14

ANYBODY'S SON WILL DO

GWYNNE DYER

An important point about socialization is that if culture is learned, it also can be unlearned. Sociologists call this process *resocialization.* This situation occurs when an individual gives up one way of life and one set of values for another. Examples of resocialization include the experience of new immigrants, of a person changing careers, of someone joining a feminist consciousness-raising group, or of an individual undergoing a religious conversion, such as a woman entering a convent to become a nun or a person being initiated into a cult. The following reading by journalist Gwynne Dyer is from his 1985 book, *War: Past, Present, and Future.* Here, Dyer focuses on the intense resocialization civilians experience during military basic training.

You think about it and you know you're going to have to kill but you don't understand the implications of that, because in the society in which you've lived murder is the most heinous of crimes . . . and you are in a situation in which it's turned the other way round. . . . When you do actually kill someone the experience, my experience, was one of revulsion and disgust. . . .

I was utterly terrified—petrified—but I knew there had to be a Japanese sniper in a small fishing shack near the shore. He was firing in the other direction at Marines in another battalion, but I knew as soon as he picked off the people there—there was a window on our side—that he would start picking

From *War: Past, Present, and Future,* pp. 101–105, 108–16, and 125. Copyright © 1985 by Media Resources. Reprinted with the permission of Crown Publishers, a division of Random House, Inc.

us off. And there was nobody else to go . . . and so I ran towards the shack and broke in and found myself in an empty room. . . .

There was a door which meant there was another room and the sniper was in that—and I just broke that down. I was just absolutely gripped by the fear that this man would expect me and would shoot me. But as it turned out he was in a sniper harness and he couldn't turn around fast enough. He was entangled in the harness so I shot him with a .45, and I felt remorse and shame. I can remember whispering foolishly, "I'm sorry" and then just throwing up. . . . I threw up all over myself. It was a betrayal of what I'd been taught since a child.

—WILLIAM MANCHESTER

Yet he did kill the Japanese soldier, just as he had been trained to—the revulsion only came afterward. And even after Manchester knew what it was like to kill another human being, a young man like himself, he went on trying to kill his "enemies" until the war was over. Like all the other tens of millions of soldiers who had been taught from infancy that killing was wrong, and had then been sent off to kill for their countries, he was almost helpless to disobey, for he had fallen into the hands of an institution so powerful and so subtle that it could quickly reverse the moral training of a lifetime.

The whole vast edifice of the military institution rests on its ability to obtain obedience from its members even unto death—and the killing of others. It has enormous powers of compulsion at its command, of course, but all authority must be based ultimately on consent. The task of extracting that consent from its members has probably grown harder in recent times, for the gulf between the military and the civilian worlds has undoubtedly widened: Civilians no longer perceive the threat of violent death as an everyday hazard of existence, and the categories of people whom it is not morally permissible to kill have broadened to include (in peacetime) the entire human race. Yet the armed forces of every country can still take almost any young male civilian and turn him into a soldier with all the right reflexes and attitudes in only a few weeks. Their recruits usually have no more than twenty years' experience of the world, most of it as children, while the armies have had all of history to practice and perfect their techniques.

Just think of how the soldier is treated. While still a child he is shut up in the barracks. During his training he is always being knocked about. If he makes the least mistake he is beaten, a burning blow on his body, another on his eye, perhaps his head is laid open with a wound. He is battered and bruised with flogging. On the march . . . they hang heavy loads round his neck like that of an ass.

—Egyptian, ca. 1500 B.C.[1]

The moment I talk to the new conscripts about the homeland I strike a land mine. So I kept quiet. Instead, I try to make soldiers of them. I give them hell from morning to sunset. They begin to curse me, curse the army, curse the state. Then they begin to curse together, and become a truly cohesive group, a unit, a fighting unit.

—Israeli, ca. A.D. 1970[2]

All soldiers belong to the same profession, no matter what country they serve, and it makes them different from everybody else. They have to be different, for their job is ultimately about killing and dying, and those things are not a natural vocation for any human being. Yet all soldiers are born civilians. The method for turning young men into soldiers—people who kill other people and expose themselves to death—is basic training. It's essentially the same all over the world, and it always has been, because young men everywhere are pretty much alike.

Human beings are fairly malleable, especially when they are young, and in every young man there are attitudes for any army to work with: the inherited values and postures, more or less dimly recalled, of the tribal warriors who were once the model for every young boy to emulate. Civilization did not involve a sudden clean break in the way people behave, but merely the progressive distortion and redirection of all the ways in which people in the old tribal societies used to behave, and modern definitions of maleness still contain a great deal of the old warrior ethic. The anarchic machismo of the primitive warrior is not what modern armies really need in their soldiers, but it does provide them with promising raw material for the transformation they must work in their recruits.

Just how this transformation is wrought varies from time to time and from country to country. In totally militarized societies—ancient Sparta, the samurai class of medieval Japan, the areas controlled by organizations like the Eritrean People's Liberation Front today—it begins at puberty or before, when the young boy is immersed in a disciplined society in which only the military values are allowed to penetrate. In more sophisticated modern societies, the process is briefer and more concentrated, and the way it works is much more visible. It is, essentially, a conversion process in an almost religious sense—and as in all conversion phenomena, the emotions are far more important than the specific ideas. . . .

Armies know this. It is their business to get men to fight, and they have had a long time to work out the best way of doing it. All of them pay lip service to the symbols and slogans of their political masters, though the amount of time they must devote to this activity varies from country to country. . . . Nor should it be thought that the armies are hypocritical—most of their members really do believe in their particular national symbols and slogans. But their secret is that they know these are not the things that sustain men in combat.

What really enables men to fight is their own self-respect, and a special kind of love that has nothing to do with sex or idealism. Very few men have died in battle, when the moment actually arrived, for the United States of

America or for the sacred cause of Communism, or even for their homes and families; if they had any choice in the matter at all, they chose to die for each other and for their own vision of themselves. . . .

The way armies produce this sense of brotherhood in a peacetime environment is basic training: a feat of psychological manipulation on the grand scale which has been so consistently successful and so universal that we fail to notice it as remarkable. In countries where the army must extract its recruits in their late teens, whether voluntarily or by conscription, from a civilian environment that does not share the military values, basic training involves a brief but intense period of indoctrination whose purpose is not really to teach the recruits basic military skills, but rather to change their values and their loyalties. "I guess you could say we brainwash them a little bit," admitted a U.S. Marine drill instructor, "but you know they're good people."

The duration and intensity of basic training, and even its major emphases, depend on what kind of society the recruits are coming from, and on what sort of military organization they are going to. It is obviously quicker to train men from a martial culture than from one in which the dominant values are civilian and commercial, and easier to deal with volunteers than with reluctant conscripts. Conscripts are not always unwilling, however; there are many instances in which the army is popular for economic reasons. . . .

It's easier if you catch them young. You can train older men to be soldiers; it's done in every major war. But you can never get them to believe that they like it, which is the major reason armies try to get their recruits before they are 20. There are other reasons too, of course, like the physical fitness, lack of dependents, and economic dispensability of teenagers, that make armies prefer them, but the most important qualities teenagers bring to basic training are enthusiasm and naiveté. Many of them actively want the discipline and the closely structured environment that the armed forces will provide, so there is no need for the recruiters to deceive the kids about what will happen to them after they join.

> *There is discipline. There is drill. . . . When you are relying on your mates and they are relying on you, there's no room for slackness or sloppiness. If you're not prepared to accept the rules, you're better off where you are.*
> —British army recruiting advertisement, 1976

> *People are not born soldiers, they become soldiers. . . . And it should not begin at the moment a new recruit is enlisted into the ranks, but rather much earlier, at the time of the first signs of maturity, during the time of adolescent dreams.*
> —*Red Star* (Soviet army newspaper), 1973

Young civilians who have volunteered and have been accepted by the Marine Corps arrive at Parris Island, the Corps's East Coast facility for basic training, in a state of considerable excitement and apprehension: Most are aware that they are about to undergo an extraordinary and very difficult experience. But they do not make their own way to the base; rather, they trickle in to Charleston airport on various flights throughout the day on which their training platoon is due to form, and are held there, in a state of suppressed but mounting nervous tension, until late in the evening. When the buses finally come to carry them the 76 miles to Parris Island, it is often after midnight—and this is not an administrative oversight. The shock treatment they are about to receive will work most efficiently if they are worn out and somewhat disoriented when they arrive.

The basic training organization is a machine, processing several thousand young men every month, and every facet and gear of it has been designed with the sole purpose of turning civilians into Marines as efficiently as possible. Provided it can have total control over their bodies and their environment for approximately three months, it can practically guarantee converts. Parris Island provides that controlled environment, and the recruits do not set foot outside it again until they graduate as Marine privates 11 weeks later.

> *They're allowed to call home, so long as it doesn't get out of hand—every three weeks or so they can call home and make sure everything's all right, if they haven't gotten a letter or there's a particular set of circumstances. If it's a case of an emergency call coming in, then they're allowed to accept that call; if not, one of my staff will take the message. . . .*
>
> *In some cases I'll get calls from parents who haven't quite gotten adjusted to the idea that their son had cut the strings—and in a lot of cases that's what they're doing. The military provides them with an opportunity to leave home but they're still in a rather secure environment.*
>
> —Captain Brassington, USMC

For the young recruits, basic training is the closest thing their society can offer to a formal rite of passage, and the institution probably stands in an unbroken line of descent from the lengthy ordeals by which young males in precivilized groups were initiated into the adult community of warriors. But in civilized societies it is a highly functional institution whose product is not anarchic warriors, but trained soldiers.

Basic training is not really about teaching people skills; it's about changing them so that they can do things they wouldn't have dreamt of otherwise. It works by applying enormous physical and mental pressure to men who have been isolated from their normal civilian environment and placed in one where the only right way to think and behave is the way the Marine Corps wants them to. The key word the men who run the machine use to describe this process is *motivation.*

> *I can motivate a recruit and in third phase, if I tell him to jump off the third deck, he'll jump off the third deck. Like I said before, it's a captive audience and I can train that guy; I can get him to do anything I want him to do. . . . They're good kids and they're out to do the right thing. We get some bad kids, but you know,*

we weed those out. But as far as motivation—here, we can motivate them to do anything you want, in recruit training.

—USMC drill instructor, Parris Island

The first three days the raw recruits spend at Parris Island are actually relatively easy, though they are hustled and shouted at continuously. It is during this time that they are documented and inoculated, receive uniforms, and learn the basic orders of drill that will enable young Americans (who are not very accustomed to this aspect of life) to do everything simultaneously in large groups. But the most important thing that happens in "forming" is the surrender of the recruits' own clothes, their hair—all the physical evidence of their individual civilian identities.

During a period of only 72 hours, in which they are allowed little sleep, recruits lay aside their former lives in a series of hasty rituals (like being shaven to the scalp) whose symbolic significance is quite clear to them even though they are quite deliberately given absolutely no time for reflection, or any hint that they might have the option of turning back from their commitment. The men in charge of them know how delicate a tightrope they are walking, though, because at this stage the recruits are still newly caught civilians who have not yet made their ultimate inward submission to the discipline of the Corps.

> *Forming Day One makes me nervous. You've got a whole new mob of recruits, you know, 60 or 70 depending, and they don't know anything. You don't know what kind of a reaction you're going to get from the stress you're going to lay on them, and it just worries me the first day. . . .*
>
> *Things could happen, I'm not going to lie to you. Something might happen. A recruit might decide he doesn't want any part of this stuff and maybe take a poke at you or something like that. In a situation like that it's going to be a spur-of-the-moment thing and that worries me.*

—USMC drill instructor

But it rarely happens. The frantic bustle of forming is designed to give the recruit no time to think about resisting what is happening to him. And so the recruits emerge from their initiation into the system, stripped of their civilian clothes, shorn of their hair, and deprived of whatever confidence in their own identity they may previously have had as 18-year-olds, like so many blanks ready to have the Marine identity impressed upon them.

The first stage in any conversion process is the destruction of an individual's former beliefs and confidence, and his reduction to a position of helplessness and need. It isn't really as drastic as all that, of course, for three days cannot cancel out 18 years; the inner thoughts and the basic character are not erased. But the recruits have already learned that the only acceptable behavior is to repress any unorthodox thoughts and to mimic the character the Marine Corps wants. Nor are they, on the whole, reluctant to do so, for they *want* to be Marines. From the moment they arrive at Parris Island, the vague notion that has been passed down for a thousand generations that masculinity means being a warrior becomes an explicit article of faith, relentlessly preached: To be a man means to be a Marine.

There are very few 18-year-old boys who do not have highly romanticized ideas of what it means to be a man, so the Marine Corps has plenty of buttons to push. And it starts pushing them on the first day of real training: The officer in charge of the formation appears before them for the first time, in full dress uniform with medals, and tells them how to become men.

> *The United States Marine Corps has 205 years of illustrious history to speak for itself. You have made the most important decision in your life . . . by signing your name, your life, your pledge to the Government of the United States, and even more importantly, to the United States Marine Corps—a brotherhood, an elite unit. In 10.3 weeks you are going to become a member of that history, those traditions, this organization—if you have what it takes. . . .*
>
> *All of you want to do that by virtue of your signing your name as a man. The Marine Corps says that we build men. Well, I'll go a little bit further. We develop the tools that you have—and everybody has those tools to a certain extent right now. We're going to give you the blueprints, and we are going to show you how to build a Marine. You've got to build a Marine—you understand?*
>
> —Captain Pingree, USMC

The recruits, gazing at him in awe and adoration, shout in unison, "Yes, sir!" just as they have been taught. They do it willingly, because they are volunteers—but even conscripts tend to have the romantic fervor of volunteers if they are only 18 years old. Basic training, whatever its hardships, is a quick way to become a man among men, with an undeniable status, and beyond the initial consent to undergo it, it doesn't even require any decisions.

> *I had just dropped out of high school and I wasn't doing much on the street except hanging out, as most teenagers would be doing. So they gave me an opportunity—a recruiter picked me up, gave me a good line, and said that I could make it in the Marines, that I have a future ahead of me. And since I was living with my parents, I figured that I could start my own life here and grow up a little.*
>
> —USMC recruit, 1982

> *I like the hand-to-hand combat and . . . things like that. It's a little rough going on me, and since I have a small frame I would like to become deadly, as I would put it. I like to have them words, especially the way they've been teaching me here.*
>
> —USMC recruit (from Brooklyn), Parris Island, 1982

The training, when it starts, seems impossibly demanding physically for most of the recruits—and then it gets harder week by week. There is a constant barrage of abuse and insults aimed at the recruits, with the deliberate purpose of breaking down their pride and so destroying their ability to resist the transformation of values and attitudes that the Corps intends them to undergo. At the same time, the demands for constant alertness and for instant obedience are continuously stepped up, and the standards by which the dress and behavior of the recruits are judged become steadily more unforgiving. But it is all carefully calculated by the men who run the machine, who think and talk in terms of the stress they are placing on the recruits: "We take so many c.c.'s of stress and we administer it to each man—they should be a little bit scared and they should be unsure, but they're adjusting." The aim is to keep the training arduous but just within most of the recruits' capability to withstand. One of the most striking achievements of the drill instructors is to create and maintain the illusion that basic training is an extraordinary challenge, one that will set those who graduate apart from others, when in fact almost everyone can succeed.

There has been some preliminary weeding out of potential recruits even before they begin basic training, to eliminate the obviously unsuitable minority, and some people do "fail" basic training and get sent home, at least in peacetime. The standards of acceptable performance in the U.S. armed forces, for example, tend to rise and fall in inverse proportion to the number and quality of recruits available to fill the forces to the authorized manpower levels. (In 1980, about 15% of Marine recruits did not graduate from basic training.) But there are very few young men who cannot be turned into passable soldiers if the forces are willing to invest enough effort in it.

Not even physical violence is necessary to effect the transformation, though it has been used by most armies at most times.

> *It's not what it was 15 years ago down here. The Marine Corps still occupies the position of a tool which the society uses when it feels like that is a resort that they have to fall to. Our society changes as all societies do, and our society felt that through enlightened training methods we could still produce the same product—and when you examine it, they're right. . . . Our 100 c.c.'s of stress is really all we need, not two gallons of it, which is what used to be. . . . In some cases with some of the younger drill instructors it was more an initiation than it was an acute test, and so we introduced extra officers and we select our drill instructors to "fine-tune" it.*
>
> —Captain Brassington, USMC

There is, indeed, a good deal of fine-tuning in the roles that the men in charge of training any specific group of recruits assume. At the simplest level, there is a sort of "good cop–bad cop" manipulation of recruits' attitudes toward those applying the stress. The three younger drill instructors with a particular serial are quite close to them in age and unremittingly harsh in their demands for ever higher performance, but the senior drill instructor, a man almost old enough to be their father, plays a more benevolent and understanding part and is available for individual counseling. And generally off-stage, but always looming in the background, is the company commander, an impossibly austere and almost godlike personage.

At least these are the images conveyed to the recruits, although of course all these men cooperate closely with an identical goal in view. It works: In the end they become not just role models and authority figures, but the focus of the recruits' developing loyalty to the organization.

> *I imagine there's some fear, especially in the beginning, because they don't know what to expect. . . . I think they hate you at first, at least for a week or two, but it turns to respect. . . . They're seeking discipline, they're seeking someone to take charge, 'cause at home they never got it. . . . They're looking to be told what to do and then someone is standing there enforcing what they tell them to do, and it's kind of like the father-and-son game, all the way through. They form a fatherly image of the DI whether they want to or not.*
>
> —Sergeant Carrington, USMC

Just the sheer physical exercise, administered in massive doses, soon has recruits feeling stronger and more competent than ever before. Inspections, often several times daily, quickly build up their ability to wear the uniform and carry themselves like real Marines, which is a considerable source of pride. The inspections also help to set up the pattern in the recruits of unquestioning submission to military authority: Standing stock-still, staring straight ahead, while somebody else examines you closely for faults is about as extreme a ritual act of submission as you can make with your clothes on.

But they are not submitting themselves merely to the abusive sergeant making unpleasant remarks about the hair in their nostrils. All around them are deliberate reminders—the flags and insignia displayed on parade, the military music, the marching formations and drill instructors' cadenced calls—of the idealized organization, the "brotherhood" to which they will be admitted as full members if they submit and conform. Nowhere in the armed forces are the military courtesies so elaborately observed, the staffs' uniforms so immaculate (some DIs change several times a day), and the ritual aspects of military life so highly visible as on a basic training establishment.

Even the seeming inanity of close-order drill has a practical role in the conversion process. It has been over a century since mass formations of men were of any use on the battlefield, but every army in the world still drills its troops, especially during basic training, because marching in formation, with every man moving his body in the same way at the same moment, is a direct physical way of learning two things a soldier must believe: that orders have to be obeyed automatically and instantly, and that you are no longer an individual, but part of a group.

The recruits' total identification with the other members of their unit is the most important lesson of all, and everything possible is done to foster it. They spend almost every waking moment together—a recruit alone is an anomaly to be looked into at once—and during most of that time they are enduring shared hardships. They also undergo collective punishments, often for the misdeed or omission of a single individual (talking in the ranks, a bed not swept under during barracks inspection), which is a highly effective way of suppressing any tendencies toward individualism. And, of course, the DIs place relentless emphasis on competition with other "serials" in training: There may be something infinitely pathetic to outsiders about a marching group of anonymous recruits chanting, "Lift your heads and hold them high, 3313 is a-passin' by," but it doesn't seem like that to the men in the ranks.

Nothing is quite so effective in building up a group's morale and solidarity, though, as a steady diet of small triumphs. Quite early in basic training, the recruits begin to do things that seem, at first sight, quite dangerous: descend by ropes from 50-foot towers, cross yawning gaps hand-over-hand on high wires (known as the Slide for Life, of course), and the like. The common denominator is that these activities are daunting but not really dangerous: The ropes will prevent anyone from falling to his death off the rappelling tower, and there is a pond of just the right depth—deep enough to cushion a falling man, but not deep enough that he is likely to drown—under the Slide for Life. The goal is not to kill recruits, but to build up their confidence as individuals and as a group by allowing them to overcome apparently frightening obstacles.

> *You have an enemy here at Parris Island. The enemy that you're going to have at Parris Island is in every one of us. It's in the form of cowardice. The most rewarding experience you're going to have in recruit training is standing on line every evening, and you'll be able to look into each other's eyes, and you'll be able to say to each other with your eyes: "By God, we've made it one more day! We've defeated the coward."*
>
> —Captain Pingree, USMC

> *Number on deck, sir, 45 . . . highly motivated, truly dedicated, rompin', stompin', bloodthirsty, kill-crazy United States Marine Corps recruits, SIR!*
>
> —Marine chant, Parris Island, 1982

If somebody does fail a particular test, he tends to be alone, for the hurdles are deliberately set low enough that most recruits can clear them if they try. In any large group of people there is usually a goat: someone whose intelligence or manner or lack of physical stamina marks him for failure and contempt. The competent drill instructor, without deliberately setting up this unfortunate individual for disgrace, will use his failure to strengthen the solidarity and confidence of the rest. When one hapless young man fell off the Slide for Life into the pond, for example, his drill instructor shouted the usual invective—"Well, get out of the water. Don't contaminate it all day"—and then delivered the payoff line: "Go back and change your clothes. You're useless to your unit now."

"Useless to your unit" is the key phrase, and all the recruits know that what it means is "useless *in battle*." The Marine drill instructors at Parris Island know exactly what they are doing to the recruits, and why. They are not rear-echelon people filling comfortable jobs, but the most dedicated and intelligent NCOs the Marine Corps can find; even now, many of them have combat experience. The Corps has a clear-eyed understanding of precisely what it is training its recruits for—combat—and it ensures that those who do the training keep that objective constantly in sight.

The DIs "stress" the recruits, feed them their daily ration of synthetic triumphs over apparent obstacles, and bear in mind all the time that the goal is to instill the foundations for the instinctive, selfless reactions and the fierce group loyalty that is what the recruits will need if they ever see combat. They are arch-manipulators, fully conscious of it, and utterly unashamed. These kids have signed up as Marines, and they could well see combat; this is the way they have to think if they want to live.

> *I've seen guys come to Vietnam from all over. They were all sorts of people that had been scared—some of them had been scared all their life and still scared. Some of them had been a country boy, city boys—you know, all different kinds of people—but when they got in combat they all reacted the same—99 percent of them reacted the same. . . . A lot of it is training here at Parris Island, but the other part of it is survival. They know if they don't conform—conform I call it, but if they don't react in the same way other people are reacting, they won't survive. That's just it. You know, if you don't react together, then nobody survives.*
>
> —USMC drill instructor, Parris Island, 1982

> *When I went to boot camp and did individual combat training, they said if you walk into an ambush what you want to do is just do a right face—you just turn right or left, whichever way the fire is coming from, and assault. I said, "Man, that's crazy. I'd never do anything like that. It's stupid." . . .*
>
> *The first time we came under fire, on Hill 1044 in Operation Beauty Canyon in Laos, we did it automatically. Just like you look at your watch to see what time it is. We done a right face, assaulted the hill—a fortified position with concrete bunkers emplaced, machine guns, automatic weapons—and we took it. And we killed—I'd estimate probably 35 North Vietnamese soldiers in the assault, and we only lost three killed. I think it was about two or three, and about eight or ten wounded. . . .*
>
> *But you know, what they teach you, it doesn't faze you until it comes down to the time to use it, but it's in the back of your head, like, What do you do when you come to a stop sign? It's in the back of your head, and you react automatically.*
>
> —USMC sergeant, 1982

Combat is the ultimate reality that Marines—or any other soldiers, under any flag—have to deal with. Physical fitness, weapons training, battle drills, are all indispensable elements of basic training, and it is absolutely essential that the recruits learn the attitudes of group loyalty and interdependency which will be their sole hope of survival and success in combat. The training inculcates or fosters all of those things, and even by the halfway point in the 11-week course, the recruits are generally responding with enthusiasm to their tasks. . . .

In basic training establishments, . . . the malleability is all one way: in the direction of submission to military authority and the internalization of military values. What a place like Parris Island produces when it is successful, as it usually is, is a soldier who will kill because that is his job.

ENDNOTES

[1] Leonard Cottrell, *The Warrior Pharaohs* (London: Evans Brothers, 1968).
[2] Samuel Rolbart, *The Israeli Soldier* (New York: A. S. Barnes, 1970), p. 206.

PART IV

Groups and Social Structure

15

PEER POWER
Clique Dynamics among School Children

PATRICIA A. ADLER • PETER ADLER

The following four selections explore groups and social structure. The basic components of social structure are the roles and social statuses of individuals. Over the course of a lifetime, people occupy numerous statuses and roles. A *status* is a social position an individual holds within a group or a social system. A *role* is a set of expectations about the behavior assigned to a particular social status. Each role helps to define the nature of interaction with others and contributes to social organization by creating patterns of interpersonal and group relationships. Because we modify social roles more than we do our social statuses, roles are the dynamic aspect of social status. In the first reading, Patricia and Peter Adler investigate the social roles and social statuses children hold in social cliques. Of particular interest to the Adlers is how social hierarchies are formed and how power is distributed among the friendship groups of third- to sixth-grade students.

A dominate feature of children's lives is the clique structure that organizes their social world. The fabric of their relationships with others, their levels and types of activity, their participation in friendships, and their feelings about themselves are tied to their involvement in, around, or outside the cliques organizing their social landscape. Cliques are, at their base, friendship circles, whose members tend to identify each other as mutually connected.[1] Yet they are more than that; cliques have a hierarchical structure, being dominated by leaders, and are exclusive in nature, so that not all individuals who desire membership are accepted. They function as bodies of power within grades, incorporating the most popular individuals, offering the most exciting social lives, and commanding the most interest and attention from classmates (Eder and Parker 1987). As such, they represent a vibrant component of the preadolescent experience, mobilizing powerful forces that produce important effects on individuals.[2] . . .

In this [reading] we look at these dynamics and their association, at the way clique leaders generate and maintain their power and authority (leadership, power/dominance), and at what it is that influences followers to comply so readily with clique leaders' demands (submission). These interactional dynamics are not intended to apply to all children's friendship groups, only those (populated by one-quarter to one-half of the children) that embody the exclusive and stratified character of cliques.

Techniques of Inclusion

The critical way that cliques maintained exclusivity was through careful membership screening. Not static entities, cliques irregularly shifted and evolved their membership, as individuals moved away or were ejected from the group and others took their place. In addition, cliques were characterized by frequent group activities designed to foster some individuals' inclusion (while excluding others). Cliques had embedded, although often unarticulated, modes for considering and accepting (or rejecting) potential new members. These modes were linked to the critical power of leaders in making vital group decisions. Leaders derived power through their popularity and then used it to influence membership and social stratification within the group. This stratification manifested itself in tiers and subgroups within cliques composed of people who were hierarchically ranked into levels of leaders, followers, and wannabes. Cliques embodied systems of dominance, whereby individuals with more status and power exerted control over others' lives.

Recruitment

. . . Potential members could be brought to the group by established members who had met and liked them. The leaders then decided whether these individuals would be granted a probationary period of acceptance during which they could be informally evaluated. If the members liked them, the newcomers would be allowed to remain in the friendship circle, but if they rejected them, they would be forced to leave.

Tiffany, a popular, dominant girl, reflected on the boundary maintenance she and her best friend Diane, two clique leaders, had exercised in fifth grade:

Q: Who defines the boundaries of who's in or who's out?

Tiffany: Probably the leader. If one person might like them, they might introduce them, but if one or two people didn't like them, then they'd start to get everyone up. Like in fifth grade, there was Dawn Bolton and she was new. And the girls in her class that were in our clique liked her, but Diane and I didn't like her, so we kicked her out. So then she went to the other clique, the Emily clique.

Timing was critical to recruitment. The beginning of the year, when classes were being reconstructed and people formed new social configurations, was the major time when cliques considered additions. Once these alliances were set, cliques tended to close their boundaries once again and stick to socializing primarily within the group. Kara, a fifth-grade girl, offered her view: *"In the fall, right after school starts, when everyone's lining up and checking each other out, is when people move up, but not during the school year. You can move down during the school year, if people decide they don't like you, but not up."* . . .

Most individuals felt that invitation to membership in the popular clique represented an irresistible offer. They repeatedly asserted that the popular group could get anybody they wanted to join them. One of the strategies used was to try to select new desirables and go after them. This usually meant separating the people from their established friends. Melody, an unpopular fourth-grade girl, described her efforts to hold on to her best friend who was being targeted for recruitment by the popular clique:

> *She was saying that they were really nice and stuff. I was really worried. If she joined their group, she would have to leave me. She was over there, and she told me that they were making fun of me, and she kind of sat there and went along with it. So I kind of got mad at her for doing that. "Why didn't you stick up for me?" She said, "Because they wouldn't like me anymore."*

Melody subsequently lost her friend to the clique.

When clique members wooed someone to join them, they usually showed only the better side of their behavior. It was not until they had the new person firmly committed to the group that the shifts in behavior associated with leaders' dominance and status stratification activities began. Diane recalled her inclusion into the popular clique and its aftermath:

> *In fifth grade I came into a new class and I knew nobody. None of my friends from the year before were in my class. So I get to school, a week late, and Tiffany comes up to me and she was like, 'Hi Diane, how are you? Where were you? You look so pretty.' And I was like, wow, she's so nice. And she was being so nice for like two weeks, kiss-ass major. And then she started pulling her bitch moves. Maybe it was for a month that she was nice. And so then she had clawed me into her clique and her group, and so she won me over that way, but then she was a bitch to me once I was inside it, and I couldn't get out because I had no other friends. 'Cause I'd gone in there and already been accepted into the popular clique, so everyone else in the class didn't like me, so I had nowhere else to go.*

Eder (1985) also notes that popular girls are often disliked by unpopular people because of their exclusive and elitist manner (as befits their status).

Application

A second way for individuals to gain initial membership into a clique occurred through their actively seeking entry (Blau 1964). . . . According to Rick, a fifth-grade boy who was in the popular clique but not a central member, application for clique entry was more easily accomplished by individuals than groups. He described the way individuals found routes into cliques:

> *It can happen any way. Just you get respected by someone, you do something nice, they start to like you, you start doing stuff with them. It's like you just kind of follow another person who is in the clique back to the clique, and he says, "Could this person play?" So you kind of go out with the clique for a while and you start doing stuff with them, and then they almost like invite you in. And then soon after, like a week or so, you're actually in. It all depends. . . . But you can't bring your whole group with you, if you have one. You have to leave them behind and just go in on your own.*

Successful membership applicants often experienced a flurry of immediate popularity. Because their entry required clique leaders' approval, they gained associational status.

Friendship Realignment

Status and power in a clique were related to stratification, and people who remained more closely tied to the leaders were more popular. Individuals who wanted to be included in the clique's inner echelons often had to work regularly to maintain or improve their position.

Like initial entry, this was sometimes accomplished by people striving on their own for upward mobility. In fourth grade, Danny was brought into the clique by Mark, a longtime member, who went out of his way to befriend him. After joining the clique, however, Danny soon abandoned Mark when Brad, the clique leader, took an interest in him. Mark discussed the feelings of hurt and abandonment this experience left him with:

> *I felt really bad, because I made friends with him when nobody knew him and nobody liked him, and I put all my friends to the side for him, and I brought him into the group, and then he dumped me. He was my friend first, but then Brad wanted him. . . . He moved up and left me behind, like I wasn't good enough anymore.*

The hierarchical structure of cliques, and the shifts in position and relationships within them, caused friendship loyalties within these groups to be less reliable than they might have been in other groups. People looked toward those above them and were more susceptible to being wooed into friendship with individuals more popular than they. When courted by a higher-up, they could easily drop their less popular friends.

Cliques' stratification hierarchies might motivate lower-echelon members to seek greater inclusion by propelling themselves toward the elite inner circles, but membership in these circles was dynamic, requiring active effort to sustain. More popular individuals had to put repeated effort into their friendship alignments as well, to maintain their central positions relative to people just below them, who might rise up and gain in group esteem. Efforts to protect themselves from the potential incursions of others took several forms, among them co-optation, position maintenance, follower realignment, and membership challenge, only some of which draw upon inclusionary dynamics.

Follower realignment involved the perception that other clique members were gaining in popularity and status and might challenge leaders' position. But instead of trying to hold them in place (position maintenance) or exclude them from the group (membership challenge), leaders shifted their base of support; they incorporated lesser but still loyal members into their activities, thereby replacing problematic supporters with new ones. . . .

Co-optation involved leaders diminishing others' threats to their position by drawing them into their orbit, increasing their loyalty, and diminishing their independence. Clique members gaining in popularity were sometimes given special attention. At the same time, leaders might try to cut out their rivals' independent base of support from other friends.

Darla, a fourth grader, had occupied a second-tier leadership position with Kristy, her best friend. She explained what happened when Denise, the clique leader, came in and tore their formerly long-standing friendship apart:

> *Me and Kristy used to be best friends, but she [Denise] hated that. 'Cause even though she was the leader, we were popular and we got all the boys. She didn't want us to be friends at all. But me and Kristy were, like, getting to be a threat to her, so Denise came in the picture and tore me and Kristy apart, so we weren't even friends. She made Kristy make totally fun of me and stuff. And they were so mean to me. . . .*

. . . Hence, friendship realignment involved clique members' abandoning previous friendships or plowing through existing ones in order to assert themselves into relationships with those in central positions. These actions were all geared toward improving instigators' positions and thus their inclusion. Their outcome, whether anticipated or not, was often the separation of people and the destruction of their relationships.

Ingratiation

Currying favor with people in the group, like previous inclusionary endeavors, can be directed either upward (supplication) or downward (manipulation). Addressing the former, Dodge et al. (1983) note that children often begin their attempts at entry into groups with low-risk tactics; they first try to become accepted by more peripheral members, and only later do they direct their gaze and inclusion attempts toward those with higher status. The children we observed did this as well, making friendly overtures toward clique followers and hoping to be drawn by them into the center.

The more predominant behavior among group members, however, involved currying favor with the leader to enhance their popularity and attain greater respect from other group members. One way they did this was by imitating the style and interests of the group leader. Marcus and Adam, two fifth-grade boys, described the way borderline people would fawn on their clique and its leader to try to gain inclusion:

> Marcus: *Some people would just follow us around and say, "Oh yeah, whatever he says, yeah, whatever his favorite kind of music is, is my favorite kind of music."*
>
> Adam: *They're probably in a position where they want to be more in because if they like what we like, then they think more people will probably respect them. Because if some people in the clique think this person likes their favorite group, say it's REM, or whatever, so it's say Bud's [the clique leader's], this person must know what we like in music and what's good and what's not, so let's tell him that he can come up and join us after school and do something.*

Fawning on more popular people not only was done by outsiders and peripherals but was common practice among regular clique members, even those with high standing. Darla, the second-tier fourth-grade girl mentioned earlier, described how, in fear, she used to follow the clique leader and parrot her opinions:

> *I was never mean to the people in my grade because I thought Denise might like them and then I'd be screwed. Because there were some people that I hated that she liked and I acted like I loved them, and so I would just be mean to the younger kids, and if she would even say, 'Oh she's nice,' I'd say, 'Oh yeah, she's really nice!'*

Clique members, then, had to stay abreast of the leader's shifting tastes and whims if they were to maintain status and position in the group. Part of their membership work involved a regular awareness of the leader's fads and fashions, so that they could accurately align their actions and opinions with the current trends in a timely manner. (See also Eder and Sanford 1986.)

Besides outsiders supplicating to insiders and insiders supplicating to those of higher standing, individuals at the top had to think about the effects of their actions on their standing with those below them. While leaders did not have to explicitly imitate the style and taste of their followers, they did have to act in a way that held their adulation and loyalty. This began with people at the top making sure that those directly below them remained firmly placed where they could count on them. Any defection, especially by the more popular people in a clique, could seriously threaten their standing.

Leaders often employed manipulation to hold the attention and loyalty of clique members.[3] Another manipulative technique involved acting different ways toward different people. Rick recalled how Brad, the clique leader in fifth grade, used this strategy to maintain his position of centrality: *"Brad would always say that Trevor is so annoying. 'He is such an idiot, a stupid baby,' and everyone would say, 'Yeah, he is so annoying. We don't like him.' So they would all be mean to him. And then later in the day, Brad would go over and play with Trevor and say that everyone else didn't like him, but that he did. That's how Brad maintained control over Trevor."* Brad employed similar techniques of manipulation to ensure that all the members of his clique were similarly tied to him. Like many leaders, he would shift his primary attention among the different clique members, so that everyone experienced the power and status associated with his favor. Then, when they were out of favor, his followers felt relatively deprived and strove to regain their privileged status. This ensured their loyalty and compliance.

To a lesser degree, clique members curried friendship with outsiders. Although they did not accept them into the group, they sometimes included them in activities and tried to influence their opinions. While the leaders had their in-group followers, lower-status clique members, if they cultivated them well, could look to outsiders for respect, admiration, and imitation. This attitude and behavior were not universal, however; some popular cliques were so disdainful and mean to outsiders that nonmembers hated them. Diane, Tiffany, and Darla, three popular girls who had gone to two different elementary schools, reflected on how the grade school cliques to which they had belonged displayed opposing relationships with individuals of lesser status:

> Darla: *We hated it if the dorks didn't like us and want us to be with them. 'Cause then we weren't the popularest ones 'cause we always had to have them look up to us, and when they wouldn't look up to us we would be nice to them.*
>
> Diane: *The medium people always hated us.*
>
> Tiffany: *They hated us royally, and we hated them back whenever they started.*
>
> Darla: *Sometimes we acted like we didn't care, but it bothered me.*
>
> Tiffany: *We always won, so it didn't matter.*

Thus, while there were notable exceptions (see Eder 1985), many popular clique members strove to ingratiate themselves with people less popular than they, from time to time, to ensure that their dominance and adulation extended beyond their own boundaries, throughout the grade.

Techniques of Exclusion

Although inclusionary techniques reinforced individuals' popularity and prestige while maintaining the group's exclusivity and stratification, they failed to contribute to other, essential, clique features such as cohesion and integration, the management of in-group and out-group relationships, and submission to clique leadership. These features are rooted, along with further sources of domination and power, in cliques' exclusionary dynamics.

Out-Group Subjugation

When they were not being nice to try to keep outsiders from straying too far from their realm of influence, clique members predominantly subjected outsiders to exclusion and rejection.[4] They found sport in picking on these lower-status individuals. As one clique follower remarked, "*One of the main things is to keep picking on unpopular kids because it's just fun to do."* Eder (1991) notes that this kind of ridicule, where the targets are excluded and not enjoined to participate in the laughter, contrasts with teasing, where friends make fun of each other in a more lighthearted manner but permit the targets to remain included in the group by also jokingly making fun of themselves. Diane, a clique leader in fourth grade, described the way she acted toward outsiders: *"Me and my friends would be mean to the people outside of our clique. Like, Eleanor Dawson, she would always try to be friends with us, and we would be like, 'Get away, ugly.'"*

Interactionally sophisticated clique members not only treated outsiders badly but managed to turn others in the clique against them. Parker and Gottman (1989) observe that one of the ways people do this is through gossip. Diane recalled the way she turned all the members of her class, boys as well as girls, against an outsider:

> *I was always mean to people outside my group like Crystal, and Sally Jones; they both moved schools. . . . I had this gummy bear necklace, with pearls around it and gummy bears. She [Crystal] came up to me one day and pulled my necklace off. I'm like, "It was my favorite necklace," and I got all of my friends, and all the guys even in the class, to revolt against her. No one liked her. That's why she moved schools, because she tore my gummy bear necklace off and everyone hated her. They were like, "That was mean. She didn't deserve that. We hate you."*

Turning people against an outsider served to solidify the group and to assert the power of the strong over the vulnerability of the weak. Other classmates tended to side with the dominant people over the subordinates, not only because they admired their prestige but also because they respected and feared the power of the strong.

Insiders' ultimate manipulation in leading the group to pick on outsiders involved instigating the bullying and causing others to take the blame. Davey, the fifth-grade clique follower mentioned earlier, described, with some mystery and awe, the skilled maneuvering of Joe, his clique leader: *"He'd start a fight and then he would get everyone in it, 'cause everyone followed him, and then he would get out of it so he wouldn't get in trouble."*

Q: How'd he do that?

Davey: One time he went up to this kid Morgan, who nobody liked, and said, "Come on Morgan, you want to talk about it?" and started kicking him, and then everyone else started doing it. Joe stopped and started watching, and then some parapro[fessional] came over and said, "What's going on here?" And then everyone got in trouble except for him.

Q: Why did he pick on Morgan?

Davey: 'Cause he couldn't do anything about it, 'cause he was a nerd.

Getting picked on instilled outsiders with fear, grinding them down to accept their inferior status and discouraging them from rallying together to challenge the power hierarchy.[5] In a confrontation between a clique member and an outsider, most people sided with the clique member. They knew that clique members banded together against outsiders, and that they could easily become the next target of attack if they challenged them. Clique members picked on outsiders with little worry about confrontation or repercussion. They also knew that their victims would never carry the tale to teachers or administrators (as they might against other targets; see Sluckin 1981) for fear of reprisal. As Mike, a fifth-grade clique follower, observed, *"They know if they tell on you, then you'll 'beat them up,' and so they won't tell on you, they just kind of take it in, walk away."*

In-Group Subjugation

Picking on people within the clique's confines was another way to exert dominance. More central clique members commonly harassed and were mean to those with weaker standing.[6] Many of the same factors prompting the ill treatment of outsiders motivated high-level insiders to pick on less powerful insiders. Rick, a fifth-grade clique follower, articulated the systematic organization of downward harassment:

> *Basically the people who are the most popular, their life outside in the playground is picking on other people who aren't as popular, but are in the group. But the people just want to be more popular so they stay in the group, they just kind of stick with it, get made fun of, take it. . . . They come back everyday, you do more ridicule, more ridicule, more ridicule, and they just keep taking it because they want to be more popular, and they actually like you but you don't like them. That goes on a lot, that's the main thing in the group. You make fun of someone, you get more popular, because insults is what they like, they like insults.*

The finger of ridicule could be pointed at any individual but the leader. It might be a person who did something worthy of insult, it might be someone who the clique leader felt had become an interpersonal threat, or it might be someone singled out for no apparent reason (see Eder 1991). Darla, the second-tier fourth grader discussed earlier, described the ridicule she encountered and her feelings of mortification when the clique leader derided her hair:

> *Like I remember, she embarrassed me so bad one day. Oh my God, I wanted to kill her! We were in music class and we were standing there and she goes, "Ew! what's all that shit in your hair?" in front of the whole class. I was so embarrassed, 'cause, I guess I had dandruff or something.[7]*

Often, derision against insiders followed a pattern, where leaders started a trend and everyone followed it. This intensified the sting of the mockery by compounding it with multiple force. Rick analogized the way people in cliques behaved to the links on a chain: *"Like it's a chain reaction, you get in a fight with the main person, then the person right under him will not like you, and the person under him won't like you, and et cetera, and the whole group will take turns against you. A few people will still like you because they will do their own thing, but most people will do what the person in front of them says to do, so it would be like a chain reaction. It's like a chain; one chain turns, and the other chain has to turn with them or else it will tangle."*

Compliance

Going along with the derisive behavior of leaders or other high-status clique members could entail either active or passive participation. Active participation occurred when instigators enticed other clique members to pick on their friends. For example, leaders would often come up with the idea of placing phony phone calls to others and would persuade their followers to do the dirty work. They might start the phone call and then place followers on the line to finish it, or they might pressure others to make the entire call, thus keeping one step distant from becoming implicated, should the victim's parents complain.

Passive participation involved going along when leaders were mean and manipulative, as when Trevor submissively acquiesced in Brad's scheme to convince Larry that Rick had stolen his money. Trevor knew that Brad was hiding the money the whole time, but he watched while Brad whipped Larry into a frenzy, pressing him to deride Rick, destroy Rick's room and possessions, and threaten to expose Rick's alleged theft to others. It was only when Rick's mother came home, interrupting the bedlam, that she uncovered the money and stopped Larry's onslaught. The following day at school, Brad and Trevor could scarcely contain their glee. As noted earlier, Rick was demolished by the incident and cast out by the clique; Trevor was elevated to the status of Brad's best friend by his co-conspiracy in the scheme.

Many clique members relished the opportunity to go along with such exclusive activities, welcoming the feelings of privilege, power, and inclusion. Others were just thankful that they weren't the targets. This was especially true of new members, who, as Sanford and Eder (1984) describe, often feel unsure about their standing in a group. Marcus and Adam, two fifth-grade clique followers introduced earlier, expressed their different feelings about such participation:

Q: What was it like when someone in your group got picked on?
Marcus: If it was someone I didn't like or who had picked on me before, then I liked it. It made me feel good.
Adam: I didn't really enjoy it. It made me feel better if they weren't picking on me. But you can't do too much about it, so you sort of get used to it.

Like outsiders, clique members knew that complaining to persons in authority did them no good. Quite the reverse, such resistance tactics made their situation worse, as did showing their vulnerabilities to the aggressors.[8]

Kara, a popular fifth-grade girl, explained why such declarations had the opposite effect from that intended: *"Because we knew what bugged them, so we could use it against them. And we just did it to pester 'em, aggravate 'em, make us feel better about ourselves. Just to be shitty."*

When people saw their friends in tenuous situations, they often reacted in a passive manner. Popular people who got in fights with other popular people might be able to count on some of their followers for support, but most people could not command such loyalty. Jeff, a fifth-grade boy, explained why people went along with hurtful behavior:

> *It's a real risk if you want to try to stick up for someone because you could get rejected from the group or whatever. Some people do, and nothing happens because they're so high up that other people listen to them. But most people would just find themselves in the same boat. And we've all been there before, so we know what that's like.*

Clique members thus went along with picking on their friends, even though they knew it hurt, because they were afraid (see also Best 1983). They became accustomed to living within a social world where the power dynamics could be hurtful, and accepted it.

Stigmatization

Beyond individual incidents of derision, clique insiders were often made the focus of stigmatization for longer periods of time. Unlike outsiders who commanded less enduring interest, clique members were much more involved in picking on their friends, whose discomfort more readily held their attention. Rick noted that the duration of this negative attention was highly variable: *"Usually at certain times, it's just a certain person you will pick on all the time, if they do something wrong. I've been picked on for a month at a time, or a week, or a day, or just a couple of minutes, and then they will just come to respect you again."* When people became the focus of stigmatization, as happened to Rick, they were rejected by all their friends. The entire clique rejoiced in celebrating their disempowerment. They would be made to feel alone whenever possible. Their former friends might join hands and walk past them through the play yard at recess, physically demonstrating their union and the discarded individual's aloneness.

Worse than being ignored was being taunted. Taunts ranged from verbal insults to put-downs to singsong chants. Anyone who could create a taunt was favored with attention and imitated by everyone (see Fine 1981). Even outsiders, who would not normally be privileged to pick on a clique member, were able to elevate themselves by joining in on such taunting (see Sanford and Eder 1984).

The ultimate degradation was physical. Although girls generally held themselves to verbal humiliation of their members, the culture of masculinity gave credence to boys' injuring each other (Eder and Parker 1987; Oswald et al. 1987; Thorne 1993). Fights would occasionally break out in which boys were punched in the ribs or stomach, kicked, or given black eyes. When this happened at school, adults were quick to intervene. But after hours or on the school bus, boys could be hurt. Physical abuse was also heaped on people's homes or possessions. People spit on each other or others' books or toys, threw eggs at their family's cars, and smashed pumpkins in front of their house.

Expulsion

While most people returned to a state of acceptance following a period of severe derision (see Sluckin 1981 for strategies children use to help attain this end), this was not always the case. Some people became permanently excommunicated from the clique. Others could be cast out directly, without undergoing a transitional phase of relative exclusion. Clique members from any stratum of the group could suffer such a fate, although it was more common among people with lower status.

When Davey, mentioned earlier, was in sixth grade, he described how expulsion could occur as a natural result of the hierarchical ranking, where a person at the bottom rung of the system of popularity was pushed off. He described the ordinary dynamics of clique behavior:

> Q: How do clique members decide who they are going to insult that day?
>
> Davey: *It's just basically everyone making fun of everyone. The small people making fun of smaller people, the big people making fun of the small people. Nobody is really making fun of people bigger than them because they can get rejected, because then they can say, "Oh yes, he did this and that, this and that, and we shouldn't like him anymore." And everybody else says, "Yeah, yeah, yeah," 'cause all the lower people like him, but all the higher people don't. So the lowercase people just follow the highercase people. If one person is doing something wrong, then they will say, "Oh yeah, get out, good-bye."*

Being cast out could result either from a severely irritating infraction or from individuals standing up for their rights against the dominant leaders. Sometimes expulsion occurred as a result of breakups between friends or friendship realignments leading to membership challenges (mentioned earlier), where higher-status people carried the group with them and turned their former friends into outcasts. . . .

On much rarer occasions, high-status clique members or even leaders could be cast out of the group (see Best 1983). One sixth-grade clique leader, Tiffany, was deposed by her former lieutenants for a continued pattern of petulance and self-indulgent manipulations:

> Q: Who kicked you out?
>
> Tiffany: *Robin and Tanya. They accepted Heidi into their clique, and they got rid of me. They were friends with her. I remember it happened in one blowup in the cafeteria. I asked for pizza and I thought I wasn't getting enough*

ENDNOTES

[1]See Hallinan (1979), Hubbell (1965), Peay (1974), and Varenne (1982) for a discussion of cliques' sociometric characteristics.

[2]They are primary groups, offering individuals the opportunity to select close friendships of their own choosing (Elkin and Handel 1989), to learn about society, to practice their behavior, and to evolve their selves and identities. Autonomous from the world of adults (Fine 1981), they are often forged in opposition to adult values (Elkin and Handel 1989), with a culture of resistance to adult standards (Corsaro 1985). They thus encompass a robust form of children's peer culture that is both unique in its own right yet at the same time a staging ground for future adult behavior.

[3]Oswald, Krappmann, Chowdhuri, and von Salisch (1987) note that one way children assert superiority over others and indebt them with loyalty is to offer them "help," either materially or socially.

[4]Hogg and Abrams (1988) find that denigrating out-group members enhances a group's solidarity and improves the group status of people participating in such denigration. This tendency is particularly strong where two groups perceive themselves to be in conflict or competition.

[5]Eder and Sanford (1986) and Merten (1994) note the same tendency among adolescent peer groups in middle school.

[6]Eder (1991) also notes that when insiders pick on other members of their clique, this can have good-natured overtones, indicating that they like them.

[7]Eder and Sanford (1986) and Eder and Parker (1987) discuss the importance of physical appearance, particularly hair, in adhering to group norms and maintaining popularity.

[8]Merten (1994, 1996) discusses the dilemma faced by children who are picked on, who would like to report the problem to a teacher but cannot do so out of fear that the teacher's intervention would incur the wrath of others. He notes the consequences for one boy whose mother complained to other parents about the way their children treated her son: when these others came to school the next day, they ridiculed the boy even more, taunting and deriding him for being a tattletale.

[9]Bigelow, Tesson, and Lewko (1996) also note this "Lord of the Flies" phenomenon.

REFERENCES

Best, Raphaela. 1983. *We've All Got Scars*. Bloomington: Indiana University Press.

Bigelow, Brian J., Geoffrey Tesson, and John H. Lewko. 1996. *Learning the Rules*. New York: Guilford Press.

Blau, Peter M. 1964. *Exchange and Power in Social Life*. New York: Wiley.

Corsaro, William A. 1985. *Friendship and Peer Culture in the Early Years*. Norwood, NJ: Ablex.

Davies, Bronwyn. 1982. *Life in the Classroom and Playground: The Accounts of Primary School Children*. London: Routledge and Kegan Paul.

Dodge, Kenneth A., David C. Schlundt, Iris Schocken, and Judy D. Delugach. 1983. "Social Competence and Children's Sociometric Status: The Role of Peer Group Entry Strategies." *Merrill-Palmer Quarterly* 29:309–36.

Eder, Donna. 1985. "The Cycle of Popularity: Interpersonal Relations among Female Adolescents." *Sociology of Education* 58:154–65.

———. 1991. "The Role of Teasing in Adolescent Peer Group Culture." Pp. 181–97 in *Sociological Studies of Child Development*, vol. 1, edited by P. A. Adler and P. Adler. Greenwich, CT: JAI Press.

Eder, Donna and Stephen Parker. 1987. "The Cultural Production and Reproduction of Gender: The Effect of Extracurricular Activities on Peer-Group Culture." *Sociology of Education* 60:200–213.

Eder, Donna and Stephanie Sanford. 1986. "The Development and Maintenance of Interactional Norms among Early Adolescents." Pp. 283–300 in *Sociological Studies of Child Development*, vol. 1, edited by P. A. Adler and P. Adler. Greenwich, CT: JAI Press.

Elkin, Frederick and Gerald Handel. 1989. *The Child and Society*. 5th ed. New York: Random House.

Fine, Gary Alan. 1981. "Friends, Impression Management, and Preadolescent Behavior." Pp. 29–52 in *The Development of Children's Friendships*, edited by S. Asher and J. Gottman. New York: Cambridge University Press.

Hallinan, Maureen. 1979. "Structural Effects on Children's Friendships and Cliques." *Social Psychology Quarterly* 42:43–54.

Hogg, Michael A. and Dominic Abrams. 1988. *Social Identifications*. New York: Routledge.

Hubbell, Charles H. 1965. "An Input-Output Approach to Clique Identification." *Sociometry* 28:377–99.

Merten, Don E. 1994. "The Cultural Context of Aggression: The Transition to Junior High School." *Anthropology and Education Quarterly* 25:29–43.

———. 1996. "Visibility and Vulnerability: Responses to Rejection by Nonaggressive Junior High School Boys." *Journal of Early Adolescence* 16:5–26.

Oswald, Hans, Lothar Krappmann, Irene Chowdhuri, and Maria von Salisch. 1987. "Gaps and Bridges: Interactions between Girls and Boys in Elementary School." Pp. 205–23 in *Sociological Studies of Child Development*, vol. 1, edited by P. A. Adler and P. Adler. Greenwich, CT: JAI Press.

Parker, Jeffrey G. and John M. Gottman. 1989. "Social and Emotional Development in a Relational Context." Pp. 95–131 in *Peer Relationships in Child Development*, edited by T. J. Berndt and G. W. Ladd. New York: Wiley.

Peay, Edmund R. 1974. "Hierarchical Clique Structures." *Sociometry* 37:54–65.

Sanford, Stephanie and Donna Eder. 1984. "Adolescent Humor during Peer Interaction." *Social Psychology Quarterly* 47:235–43.

Sluckin, Andy. 1981. *Growing Up in the Playground*. London: Routledge and Kegan Paul.

Thorne, Barrie. 1993. *Gender Play*. New Brunswick, NJ: Rutgers University Press.

Varenne, Herve. 1982. "Jocks and Freaks: The Symbolic Structure of the Expression of Social Interaction among American Senior High School Students." Pp. 210–35 in *Doing the Ethnography of Schooling*, edited by G. Spindler. New York: Holt, Rinehart, and Winston.

16

GANG BUSINESS
Making Ends Meet

MARTÍN SÁNCHEZ JANKOWSKI

This selection by Martín Sánchez Jankowski is excerpted from his book *Islands in the Street: Gangs and American Urban Society* (1991). Sánchez Jankowski, a professor of sociology at the University of California at Berkeley, studies the *primary group* of social gangs that exist in urban settings across the United States. Examples of other primary groups are families, friendship cliques, sororities and fraternities, neighborhood coffee klatches, and small work groups. Thus, primary groups emerge when people live or work closely together. As this reading by Sánchez Jankowski shows, gangs are similar to other primary groups in that they are small, intimate, and informal. Sánchez Jankowski also argues that, contrary to the stereotype of gang culture, gangs have some social values that are similar to those of other American groups, including a work ethic and an entrepreneurial spirit.

Cunning and deceit will serve a man better than force to rise from a base condition to great fortune.

—NICCOLÒ MACHIAVELLI, THE DISCOURSES (1517?)

If there is one theme that dominates most studies of gangs, it is that gangs are collectives of individuals who are social parasites, and that they are parasitic not only because they lack the skills to be productive members of society but, more important, because they lack the values, particularly the work ethic, that would guide them to be productive members of society.[1] However, one of the most striking factors I observed was how much the entrepreneurial spirit, which most Americans believe is the core of their productive culture, was a driving force in the worldview and behavior of gang members.[2] If entrepreneurial spirit denotes the desire to organize and manage business interests toward some end that results in the accumulation of capital, broadly defined, nearly all the gang members that I studied possessed, in varying degrees, five attributes that are either entrepreneurial in character or that reinforce entrepreneurial behavior.

Martín Sánchez Jankowski, *Islands in the Street: Gangs and American Urban Society*, pp. 101–105, 119–26. Copyright © 1991 The Regents of the University of California. Reprinted by permission of the University of California Press.

The first of these entrepreneurial attitudes is competitiveness. Most gang members I spoke with expressed a strong sense of self-competence and a drive to compete with others. They believed in themselves as capable of achieving some level of economic success and saw competition as part of human nature and an opportunity to prove one's self-worth. This belief in oneself often took on a dogmatic character, especially for those individuals who had lost in some form of economic competition. The losers always had ready excuses that placed the blame on something other than their own personal inadequacy, thereby artificially reinforcing their feelings of competence in the face of defeat.[3]

Gang members' sense of competitiveness also reflected their general worldview that life operates under Social Darwinist principles. In the economic realm, they believed there is no ethical code that regulates business ventures, and this attitude exempted them from moral constraints on individual economic-oriented action.[4] The views of Danny provide a good example of this Social Darwinist outlook. Danny was a 20-year-old Irish gang member from Boston:

> *I don't worry about whether something is fair or not when I'm making a business deal. There is nothing fair or unfair, you just go about your business of trying to make a buck, and if someone feels you took advantage of him, he has only himself to blame. If someone took advantage of me, I wouldn't sit around belly-aching about it, I'd just go and try to get some of my money back. One just has to ask around here [the neighborhood] and you'd find that nobody expects that every time you're going to make a business deal, that it will be fair—you know, that the other guy is not going to be fair, hell, he is trying to make money, not trying to be fair. This is the way those big business assholes operate too! The whole thing [the system] operates this way. . . .*

The second entrepreneurial attribute I observed is the desire and drive to accumulate money and material possessions. Karl Marx, of course, described this desire as the "profit motive" and attributed it primarily to the bourgeoisie.[5] There is a profit-motive element to the entrepreneurial values of gang members, but it differs significantly from Marx's analysis of the desire to accumulate material and capital for their own sake, largely divorced from the desire to improve one's material condition. Nor is gang members' ambition to accumulate material possessions related to a need for achievement, which the psychologist David McClelland identifies as more central to entrepreneurial behavior in certain individuals than the profit motive per se.[6] Rather, the entrepreneurial activity of gang members is predicated on their more basic understanding of what money can buy.[7] The ambition to accumulate capital and material possessions is related, in its initial stages (which can last for a considerable number of years), to the desire to improve the comfort of everyday living and the quality of leisure time.

This desire, of course, is shared by most people who live in low-income neighborhoods. Some of them resign themselves to the belief that they will never be able to secure their desires. Others attempt to improve their life situation by using various "incremental approaches," such as working in those jobs that are made available to them and saving their money, or attempting to learn higher-level occupational skills. In contrast, the entrepreneurs of low-income neighborhoods, especially those in gangs, attempt to improve their lives by becoming involved in a business venture, or a series of ventures, that has the potential to create large changes in their own or their family's socioeconomic condition.

The third attribute of entrepreneurial behavior prevalent in gangs is status-seeking. Mirroring the dominant values of the larger society, most gang members attempt to achieve some form of status with the acquisition of possessions. However, most of them cannot attain a high degree of status by accumulation alone. To merit high status among peers and in the community, gang members must try, although most will be unsuccessful, to accumulate a large number of possessions and be willing to share them. Once gang members have accumulated sufficient material possessions to provide themselves with a relative level of comfort or leisure above the minimal, they begin to seek the increase in status that generosity affords. (For philanthropic purposes, accumulating cash is preferable to accumulating possessions, because the more money one has, the more flexibility one has in giving away possessions.)

The fourth entrepreneurial attribute one finds among gang members is the ability to plan. Gang members spend an impressive amount of time planning activities that will bring them fortune and fame, or, at least, plenty of spending money in the short term. At their grandest, these plans have the character of dreams, but as the accounts of renowned business tycoons show, having big dreams has always been a hallmark of entrepreneurial endeavors.[8] At the other end of the spectrum are short-range plans (also called small scams) that members try to pull on one another, usually to secure a loan. . . .

Gang members also engage in intermediary and long-range planning. A typical intermediary plan might concern modest efforts to steal some type of merchandise from warehouses, homes, or businesses. Because most of the sites they select are equipped with security systems, a more elaborate plan involving more time is needed than is the case for those internal gang scams just described. Long-range planning and organization, sometimes quite elaborate, are, as other studies have reported, at times executed with remarkable precision.[9]

Finally, the fifth entrepreneurial attribute common among gang members is the ability to undertake risks. Generally, young gang members (nine to fifteen years of age) do not understand risk as part of a risk-reward calculus, and for this age group, risk-taking is nearly always pursued for itself, as an element of what Thrasher calls the "sport motive,"[10] the desire to test oneself. As gang members get older, they gradually develop a more sophisticated understanding of risk-taking, realizing that a certain amount of risk is

necessary to secure desired goals. Now they attempt to calculate the risk factors involved for nearly every venture, measuring the risk to their physical
well-being, money, and freedom. Just like mainstream businessmen, they
discover that risk tends to increase proportionally to the level of innovation
undertaken to secure a particular financial objective. Most of these older
gang members are willing to assume risks commensurate with the subjective
"value" of their designated target, but they will not assume risks just for the
sake of risk-taking. . . .

Economic Activity: Accumulating

With a few exceptions, nearly all the literature on gangs focuses on their economic delinquency.[11] This is a very misleading picture, however, for although gangs operate primarily in illegal markets, they also are involved in
legal markets. Of the 37 gangs observed in the present study, 27 generated
some percentage of their revenues through legitimate business activity. It is
true that gangs do more of their business activity in the illegal markets, but
none of them wants to be exclusively active in these markets.[12]

In the illegal market, gangs concentrate their economic activities primarily in goods, services, and recreation. In the area of goods, gangs have
been heavily involved in accumulating and selling drugs, liquor, and various
stolen products such as guns, auto parts, and assorted electronic equipment.
These goods are sometimes bought and sold with the gang acting as the
wholesaler and/or retailer. At other times, the gang actually produces the
goods it sells. For example, while most gangs buy drugs or alcohol and retail
them, a few gangs manufacture and market homemade drugs and moonshine liquor. Two gangs (one African American and one Irish) in this study
had purchased stills and sold their moonshine to people on the street, most
of whom were derelicts, and to high school kids too young to buy liquor
legally.[13] Three other gangs (two Puerto Rican and one Dominican) made a
moonshine liquor from fermented fruit and sold it almost exclusively to
teenagers. Both types of moonshine were very high in alcohol, always above
one hundred proof. While sales of this liquor were not of the magnitude to
create fortunes, these projects were quite surprisingly capable of generating
substantial amounts of revenue.

The biggest money-maker and the one product nearly every gang tries to
market is illegal drugs.[14] The position of the gang within the illegal drug market varies among gangs and between cities. In New York, the size of the gang
and how long it has been in existence have a great deal to do with whether it
will have access to drug suppliers. The older and larger gangs are able to buy
drugs from suppliers and act as wholesalers to pushers. They shun acting as
pushers (the lowest level of drug sales) themselves because there are greater
risks and little, if any, commensurate increase in profit. In addition, because
heroin use is forbidden within most gangs, the gang leaders prefer to es-

tablish attitudes oriented to the sale rather than the consumption of drugs within the organization. In the past, when the supply was controlled by the Italian Mafia, it was difficult for gangs to gain access to the quantity of drug supplies necessary to make a profit marketing them. In the past ten years, though, the Mafia has given way (in terms of drug supply) to African American, Puerto Rican, and Mexican syndicates.[15] In addition, with the increased popularity of cocaine in New York, the African American, Puerto Rican, and Dominican syndicates' connections to Latin American sources of cocaine supply rival, and in many cases surpass, those of Mafia figures.[16] With better access to supplies, gangs in New York have been able to establish a business attitude toward drugs and to capitalize on the opportunities that drugs now afford them.

Some gangs have developed alternative sources of supply. They do so in two ways. Some, particularly the Chicano gangs, have sought out pharmacies where an employee can be paid off to steal pills for the gang to sell on the street.[17] Other gangs, particularly in New York, but also some in Los Angeles, have established "drug mills" to produce synthetic drugs such as LSD (or, more recently, crack cocaine) for sale on the street. The more sophisticated drug mills, which are controlled by various organized crime families, manufacture a whole line of drugs for sale, including cut heroin, but gangs are almost never involved in them. Those gangs that have established a production facility for generating drugs, no matter how crude it may be, generate sizable sums of money. Whether a gang is able to establish a sophisticated production and distribution system for drug sales depends on the sophistication of the gang organization and the amount of capital available for start-up purposes.

Stolen guns are another popular and profitable product. Gangs sometimes steal guns and then redistribute them, but most often they buy them from wholesale gun peddlers and then resell them. Sometimes the gangs will buy up a small number of shotguns and then cut the barrel and stock down to about 13 to 15 inches in length and then sell them as "easily concealable." A prospective buyer can get whatever gun he wants if he is willing to pay the going price. In the present study, the Irish gangs have been, commercially speaking, the most involved with guns, often moving relatively large shipments, ranging from sawed-off shotguns to fully automatic rifles and pistols of the most sophisticated types.[18] It was reported that these guns were being moved, with the help of the Irish social clubs, to the Catholics of Northern Ireland for their struggle with the Protestants there. No matter what the destination, rather large sums of money were paid to the Irish gangs for their efforts in acquiring the weapons or in helping move them. Although all the gangs studied were involved in the sale of illegal guns, illegal gun sales constituted a larger proportion of the economic activities of Irish gangs than they did for the others.

Gangs in all three cities were also involved in the selling of car parts. All the parts sold were stolen, some stolen to fill special orders from customers and others stolen and reworked in members' home garages into customized parts for resale. Business was briskest in Los Angeles, where there is a large market, especially among the low-rider clientele, for customized auto parts.[19] The amount of money made from stolen auto parts varies according to the area, whether or not the gang has an agent to whom to sell the parts, and the types of parts sold. On the whole, revenues from stolen auto parts are not nearly as high as those from selling illegal drugs, guns, or liquor, and so less time is devoted by gangs to this activity.

Gangs' business activities also include a number of services, the three most common being protection, demolition (usually arson), and indirect participation in prostitution. Protection is the most common service, both because there is a demand for it in the low-income areas in which gangs operate and because the gangs find it the easiest service to deliver, since it requires little in the way of resources or training. Gangs offer both personal and business protection. Nearly all the gangs had developed a fee schedule according to the type of protection desired. Most, but certainly not all, of the protection services offered by the gangs in this study involved extortion. Usually the gang would go into a store and ask the owner if he felt he needed protection from being robbed. Since it was clear what was being suggested, the owner usually said yes and asked how much it would cost him. When dealing with naive owners, those who did not speak English very well or did not know American ghetto customs, or with owners who flatly resisted their services, the gang would take time to educate or persuade them to retain its services. In the case of the immigrants (most of whom were Asian or Near Eastern), the gang members would begin by explaining the situation, but usually such owners did not understand, and so the gang would demonstrate its point by sending members into the store to steal. Another tactic was to pay a dope addict to go in and rob the store. After such an incident occurred, the gang would return and ask the owner if he now needed protection. If he refused, the tactics were repeated, and almost all the owners were finally convinced. However, for those owners who understood and resisted from the start, more aggressive tactics were used, such as destruction of their premises or harassment of patrons. More often than not, continued pressure brought the desired result. However, it should be noted that in the vast majority of cases, no coercion was needed, because store owners in high-crime areas were, more often than not, happy to receive protection. As one owner said to me: "I would need to hire a protection company anyway, and frankly the gang provides much more protection than they could ever do."

Gangs also offer their services as enforcers to clients who need punishment administered to a third party. Small-time hustlers or loan sharks, for example, hired some gangs to administer physical coercion to borrowers delinquent in their repayments. More recently one gang offered and apparently was hired by a foreign government to undertake terrorist attacks against the government and people of the United States.[20] Although that was an extreme case, nearly all gangs seek enforcement contracts because the fee is usually high, few resources have to be committed, and relatively little in the way of planning (compared to other projects) is needed.

The permanent elimination of or damage to property is another service gangs offer. This more often than not involves arson, and the buildings hit are commonly dilapidated. The gangs' clients are either landlords who want to torch the building to get the insurance money or residents who are so frustrated by the landlord's unwillingness to provide the most basic services that they ask the gang to retaliate. In both cases, there is usually much preliminary discussion of the project within the gang. These service jobs require a good deal of discussion and planning because there is the potential to hurt someone living in the building or to create enormous hardship if people have no alternative place to live, and the gang will do almost anything to avoid injuring people in its community. The gangs of New York have had the most business along these lines, particularly in the South Bronx, but arson is a service offered in Detroit, Chicago, and Philadelphia as well. As one gang leader from the Bronx said:

> You just don't bomb or torch any building that someone wants down. You got to find out who lives there, if they got another place to go, if they would be for takin' out the building and if they'd be OK with the folks [law enforcement authorities]. Then you got to get organized to get everybody out and sometimes that ain't many people and sometimes it is. If there is lots of people in the building, we'd just pass [refuse] on the job. . . . Now if we can work all these things out, we take the job and we deliver either a skeleton [outer walls are standing, but nothing else] or a cremation [just ashes].

Many potential clients know that a gang will refuse to burn down a building in its neighborhood if some type of harm will come to residents of its community, and so they contract with a gang from another area to do the job. Such incidents always ignite a war not only between the affected gangs but also between the communities. Take the example of the Hornets, a gang from one borough in New York that had contracted to set on fire a building in another borough. Although no one was killed in the fire, a few people were slightly burned, and of course everyone who lived in the building became homeless. At the request of a number of residents, the Vandals, a gang from the affected area, began to investigate and found out who had contracted to torch the building and which gang had been responsible. Then, at the request of an overwhelming majority of the community, the Vandals retaliated by burning down a building in the culprit gang's community. Hipper, a 20-year-old member of the Vandals, said:

> We got to protect our community, they depend on us and they want us to do something so this [the burning of an apartment building in the neighborhood] don't happen again. . . . We be torchin' one of their buildings. I hope this don't

hurt anybody, but if we don't do this, they be back hurting the people in our com-
munity and we definitely don't be letting that happen!

This is an excellent example of the bond that exists between the community and the gang. There is the understanding, then, among the community that the gang is a resource that can be counted on, particularly in situations where some form of force is necessary. Likewise, the gang knows that its legitimacy and existence are tied to being integrated in and responsible to community needs.

Prostitution is one illegal service in which gangs do not, for the most part, become directly involved. Gangs will accept the job of protecting pimps and their women for a fee (15, or 40 percent, of the gangs in this study had), and in this way they become indirectly associated with the prostitution business. Yet they generally avoid direct involvement because they feel protective of the females in their communities, and their organizations are wary of being accused by neighborhood residents of exposing female members of the community to the dangers associated with prostitution.

The last type of illegal ecomomic activity in which all of the gangs in the present study were involved has to do with providing recreation. Some gangs establish numbers games in their neighborhoods. One New York gang had rented what had been a small Chinese food take-out place and was running numbers from the back where the kitchen had once been. (When I first observed the place, I thought it was a Chinese take-out and even proposed we get some quick food from it, which met with much laughter from the members of the gang I was with.) This gang became so successful that it opened up two other numbers establishments. One had been a pizza place (and was made to look as though it still served pizza slices); the other was a small variety store, which still functioned in that capacity, but also housed the numbers game in the back rooms.

Setting up gambling rooms is another aspect of the recreation business. Eleven of the gangs (or 30 percent) rented small storefronts, bought tables and chairs, and ran poker and/or domino games. The gang would assume the role of the "house," receiving a commission for each game played. Some of the gangs bought slot machines and placed them in their gambling rooms. Five (or 14 percent) of the gangs had as many as fifteen machines available for use.

Finally, ten gangs (27 percent), primarily those with Latino members, rented old buildings and converted them to accommodate cockfights. The gang would charge each cock owner a fee for entering his bird and an entrance fee for each patron. All of these ventures could, at various times, generate significant amounts of capital. The exact amount would depend on how often they were closed by the police and how well the gang managed the competition in its marketplace.

Turning to the legal economic activities undertaken by gangs, I observed that two ran "mom and pop" stores that sold groceries, candy, and soft drinks. Three gangs had taken over abandoned apartment buildings, reno-vated them, and rented them very cheaply—not simply because the accom-modations were rather stark, but also because the gang wanted to help the less fortunate members of its community. The gangs also used these build-ings to house members who had nowhere else to live. Undertaken and gov-erned by social as much as economic concerns, these apartment ventures did not generate much income.

Interestingly, the finances of these legal activities were quite tenuous. The gangs that operated small grocery stores experienced periodic failures during which the stores had to be closed until enough money could be ac-quired (from other sources) to either pay the increased rent, rebuild shelf stock, or make necessary repairs. For those gangs who operated apartment buildings, in every case observed, the absence of a deed to the building or the land forced the gang to relinquish its holdings to either the city or a new land-lord who wanted to build some new structure. Though there was a plentiful supply of abandoned buildings, most gangs lost interest in the renovation-and-rental business because such projects always created a crisis in their cap-ital flow, which in turn precipitated internal bickering and conflict.

Other legal economic activities undertaken by the gangs I studied were automobile and motorcycle repair shops, car parts (quasi junkyards), fruit stands, and hair shops (both barber and styling). However, most of these ventures contributed only very modest revenues to the gangs' treasuries. Furthermore, the gang leadership had difficulty keeping most of the legal economic activities functioning because the rank and file were, by and large, not terribly enthusiastic about such activities. Rank-and-file resistance to most of these activities was of three sorts: members did not want to commit regularly scheduled time to any specific ongoing operation; members felt that the legal activities involved considerable overhead costs that lowered the profit rate; and members calculated that the time required to realize a large profit was far too long when compared to illegal economic activity. Thus, when such projects were promoted by the gang leadership and under-taken by the rank and file, they were done under the rubric of community service aid projects. The comments of Pin, a 19-year-old African American gang member from New York, are representative of this general position on legal economic activity:

> *No, I don't go for those deals where we [the gang] run some kind of hotel out of an old building or run some repair shop or something like that. When you do that you can't make no money, or if you do make something it so small and takes so long to get it that it's just a waste of our [the gang's] money. But when the leadership brings it up as a possibility, well, sometimes I vote for it because I figure you got to help the community, many of them [people in the community] say they sort of depend on our help in one way or another, so I always say this is*

one way to help the community and me and the brothers go along with it. But
everybody knows you can't make no money on shit like this.

ENDNOTES

[1] Nearly all studies of gangs incorporate this theme into their analysis. One of the exceptions is Cloward and Ohlin, *Delinquency and Opportunity,* which argues that many delinquents have the same values as other members of American society. However, even Cloward and Ohlin incorporate some of the conventional argument by accepting the premise that gang members' skills to compete in the larger society have been retarded by a lack of opportunity.

[2] See Charles Sabel, *Work and Politics* (Cambridge: Cambridge University Press, 1987), pp. 1–30, on the importance of worldviews in affecting the behavior of individuals in industrial organizations and politics.

[3] David Matza mentions a comparable tendency among delinquents to deny guilt associated with wrongdoing when he discusses the delinquent's belief that he is nearly always the victim of a "bum rap" (see Matza, *Delinquency and Drift* [New Brunswick, NJ: Transaction Books], pp. 108–10).

[4] I use the term *economic oriented action* the way Weber does: "Action will be said to be 'economical oriented' so far as, according to its subjective meaning, it is concerned with the satisfaction of a desire for 'utilities' *(Nutzleistung)*" (Weber, *Economy and Society* 1:63).

[5] See Karl Marx, *The Economic and Philosophical Manuscripts of 1844,* 4th rev. ed. (Moscow: Progress Publishers, 1974), p. 38.

[6] See David C. McClelland, *The Achieving Society* (New York: Free Press, 1961), pp. 233–37.

[7] See Lee Rainwater, *What Money Buys: Inequality and the Social Meanings of Income* (New York: Basic Books, 1974). Also see Richard P. Coleman and Lee Rainwater, *Social Standing in America: New Dimensions of Class* (New York: Basic Books, 1978), pp. 29–45.

[8] See the accounts of successful entrepreneurs from poor families who dreamed of grandeur and became America's most renowned business tycoons in Matthew Josephson, *The Robber Barons: The Great American Capitalists, 1861–1901* (New York: Harcourt, Brace & World, 1962), especially the chapter titled "What Young Men Dream," pp. 32–49.

[9] See Thrasher, *The Gang,* p. 86.

[10] Ibid., p. 86.

[11] Both the theoretical and empirical literature focus on the gang's criminal activity. For theoretical discussions, see Kornhauser, *Social Sources of Delinquency,* pp. 51–61. For empirical studies, see nearly all of the classic and contemporary work on gangs. A sample of this literature would include Thrasher, *The Gang;* Herman Schwendinger and Julia Schwendinger, *Adolescent Subcultures and Delinquency* (New York: Praeger, 1985); Cloward and Ohlin, *Delinquency and Opportunity;* Cohen, *Delinquent Boys.* Two exceptions are Horowitz, *Honor and the American Dream,* and Vigil, *Barrio Gangs.*

[12] There are two factors that have encouraged gangs to be more active in illegal markets. First, gangs, like organized crime syndicates, attempt to become active in many economic activities that are legal. However, because so much of the legal market is controlled by groups that have established themselves in strategic positions (because they entered that market a considerable time in the past), gangs have

found it difficult at best to successfully penetrate many legal markets. Further, there are financial incentives that have encouraged gangs to operate in the illegal market. These include the fact that costs are relatively low, and while personal risk (in terms of being incarcerated and/or physically hurt) is rather high, high demand along with high risk can produce greater profit margins. Despite the fact that these two factors have encouraged gangs to be more active in the illegal market, it is important to emphasize that nearly all the gangs studied attempted to, and many did, conduct business in the legal market as well.

[13] The Schwendingers indicate that "youthful tastes regulate the flow of goods and services in the [adolescent] market" and gangs do take advantage of these tastes. See Schwendinger and Schwendinger, *Adolescent Subcultures and Delinquency*, p. 286.

[14] See Fagan, "Social Organization of Drug Use and Drug Dealing among Urban Gangs," pp. 633–67; and Jerome H. Skolnick, *Forum: The Social Structure of Street Drug Dealing* (Sacramento: Bureau of Criminal Statistics/Office of the Attorney General, 1989).

[15] See Francis A. J. Ianni, *Black Mafia: Ethnic Succession in Organized Crime* (New York: Simon & Schuster, 1974). Also see Moore, *Homeboys*, pp. 86–92, 114–16.

[16] See Peter Lupsha and K. Schlegel, "The Political Economy of Drug Trafficking: The Herrera Organization (Mexico and the United States)" (paper presented at the Latin American Studies Association, Philadelphia, 1979).

[17] This paying off of employees for drug supplies began, according to Joan Moore, in Los Angeles in the 1940s and 1950s (see Moore, *Homeboys*, pp. 78–82).

[18] These gangs can procure fully automatic M-16s, Ingrams, and Uzzis.

[19] Low riders are people, nearly all of whom are of Mexican descent, who drive customized older automobiles (1950s and 1960s models are preferred), one of the characteristics being that the springs for each wheel are cut away so that the car rides very low to the ground. Some of these cars have hydraulic systems that can be inflated at the flip of a switch so that the car can ride low to the ground at one moment and at the normal level the next. For a discussion of the importance of customized automobiles in Los Angeles, especially among Chicano youth, see Schwendinger and Schwendinger, *Adolescent Subcultures and Delinquency*, pp. 234–45.

[20] The El Rukn gang in Chicago was recently indicted and convicted of contracting with the Libyan government to carry out terrorist acts within the United States. See *Chicago Tribune*, November 3, 4, 6, 7, 1987.

REFERENCES

Cloward, Richard A. and Lloyd B. Ohlin. 1960. *Delinquency and Opportunity: A Theory of Delinquent Gangs*. New York: Free Press.

Cohen, Albert K. 1955. *Delinquent Boys: The Culture of the Gang*. Glencoe, IL: Free Press.

Coleman, Richard P. and Lee Rainwater. 1978. *Social Standing in America: New Dimensions of Class*. New York: Basic Books.

Fagan, Jeffery. 1989. "The Social Organization of Drug Use and Drug Dealing among Urban Gangs." *Criminology* 27, no. 4 (November): 633–70.

Horowitz, Ruth. 1983. *Honor and the American Dream: Culture and Identity in a Chicano Community*. New Brunswick: Rutgers University Press.

Ianni, Francis, A. J. 1974. *Black Mafia: Ethnic Succession in Organized Crime*. New York: Simon & Schuster.

Josephson, Matthew. 1962. *The Robber Barons: The Great American Capitalists, 1861–1901*. New York: Harcourt, Brace & World.

Kornhauser, Ruth Rosner. 1978. *Social Sources of Delinquency: An Appraisal of Analytic Models.* Chicago: University of Chicago Press.

Lupsha, Peter and K. Schlegel. 1979. "The Political Economy of Drug Trafficking: The Herrera Organization (Mexico and the United States)." Paper presented at a meeting of the Latin American Studies Association, Philadelphia.

McClelland, David C. 1961. *The Achieving Society.* New York: Free Press.

Marx, Karl. 1974. *The Economic and Philosophical Manuscripts of 1844.* 4th rev. ed. Moscow: Progress Publishers.

Matza, David. 1990. *Delinquency and Drift.* New Brunswick, NJ: Transaction Books.

Moore, Joan W. 1978. *Homeboys: Gangs, Drugs, and Prisons in the Barrios of Los Angeles.* Philadelphia: Temple University Press.

Rainwater, Lee. 1970. *Behind Ghetto Walls: Black Family Life in a Federal Slum.* Chicago: Aldine Press.

———. 1974. *What Money Buys: Inequality and the Social Meanings of Income.* New York: Basic Books.

Thrasher, Frederic. 1928. *The Gang: A Study of 1303 Gangs in Chicago.* Chicago: University of Chicago Press.

Vigil, James Diego. 1988. *Barrio Gangs: Street Life and Identity in Southern California.* Austin: University of Texas Press.

Weber, Max. 1978. *Economy and Society: An Outline of Interpretive Sociology.* Edited by Guenther Roth and Claus Wittich. Berkeley: University of California Press.

17

BECOMING A RACIST
Women in Contemporary Ku Klux Klan and Neo-Nazi Groups

KATHLEEN M. BLEE

This reading by Kathleen Blee, a professor of sociology at the University of Pittsburgh, is taken from Blee's 2002 book, *Inside Organized Racism: Women in the Hate Movement.* As part of her research on organized racist groups in the United States, Blee interviews women members active in the Ku Klux Klan, neo-Nazi groups, Christian identity sects, and white-power skinhead gangs in order to understand why women are joining these groups. Sociologists often debate whether racist groups and gangs are primary or secondary groups. *Secondary groups* tend to be larger, less intimate, and more formal

From *Gender & Society,* Volume 10, No. 6, Dec. 1996, pp. 680–702. Copyright © 1996 by Sage Publications, Inc. Reprinted by permission of Sage Publications, Inc.

than primary groups. Moreover, most secondary groups are utilitarian in that they serve some function. Depending on how intimate and informal the racist group is and how important it is to the individual members would determine which category it falls in. In this selection, Blee looks at what causes American women to join racist groups and how membership in these groups changes the women's sense of self.

The study of organized racism is deeply, but invisibly, gendered. From the Reconstruction-era Ku Klux Klan to contemporary neo-Nazis, the committed racist appears as male. Women racists exist in shadow, lurking behind husbands and boyfriends. A recent social psychology of modern racist activists gives an account of Raymond, a longtime adherent of violent white supremacy. At the edge of Raymond's story appears his "dreadfully myopic" girlfriend:

> Rosandra would stoop over the sink in the gloom, doing dishes. I have never seen a dish sink so poorly lit; there was perhaps a fifteen-watt bulb. Given that bad light and her terrible vision, she would have to bring the plate within a few inches of her eyes to see it well enough to wash it. Rosandra became pregnant almost at once: Raymond "didn't believe in" contraception. (Ezekiel 1995:244)

Nothing in this narrative allows the reader to understand Rosandra's place, if any, in the racist movement, nor her motivation to maintain a relationship with Raymond. She appears directionless, manipulated, and victimized.

This depiction of Rosandra is typical of scholarly and popular media accounts of women in racist groups. Women are seen as apolitical in their own right, attached to the racist movement only through the political affiliations of their husbands, boyfriends, or fathers. The logic is circular: Organized racism is a male province. Women who join must be the ideological appendages of racist men. Thus, women's attitudes, actions, and motivations are derivative, incidental, and not worthy of scholarly consideration. What is important about organized racism is knowable by studying men.

As a result of such reasoning, scholarship on women in modern racist groups in the United States is virtually nonexistent . . .

The lack of specific attention to contemporary U.S. women racist activists has two consequences that limit our ability to understand the modern racist movement and that undermine efforts to design effective strategies against the politics of organized racial, religious, and ethnic bigotry. First, the common (but unexamined) assumption that women are not active in the racist movement, or that such movements are restricted to men, has made it difficult to explain the adherence of substantial numbers of women to organized racism today. In the past decade, the number of racist groups in the United States has increased dramatically,[1] which is due in large part to efforts to broaden and diversify membership beyond the small enclaves of Southern white male supporters who traditionally formed the nucleus of militant racism (Center for Democratic Renewal 1990–94; Ridgeway 1990; Rose 1992; Southern Poverty Law Center 1985–95, 1990–95). Such strategies, and the resultant public visibility of organized racism, have shaped a modern racist movement in which women constitute an estimated 25 percent of the membership (and nearly 50 percent of new recruits) in many groups.[2] . . .

Second, the exclusive attention to men in organized racist movements has deformed theoretical understanding of the process whereby individuals become racial activists. Explanations of rightist affiliation tend to take several forms. Some theories interpret right-wing participation as an outgrowth of individual or collective social-psychological factors. Perhaps the most noted of these is Adorno, Frenkel-Brunswik, Levinson, and Sanford's (1950) thesis that individuals with low tolerance for ambiguity and a high need for rigid, stereotyped views (i.e., the "authoritarian personality") are attracted to the uncomplicated, authoritative, and conspiratorial ideologies that characterize right-wing extremism. Hofstadter's (1965) frequently cited characterization of a "paranoid style" in rightist politics also emphasizes the connection between psychological factors and political ideologies of the Right by suggesting that the conspiratorial claims that buttress many right-wing political arguments represent the projection of individual pathologies into public life.

Such works have engendered familiar understandings of adherence to extremist right-wing movements as the outgrowth of authoritarian parenting, educational deficits, personal ignorance, or irrational prejudices, and led to the presumption that most participants in rightist politics are irrational, frustrated, or deluded (Brinkley 1993). Although explanations based on deficiencies and pathologies remain standard in commonsense understandings of far-right politics, they have lost favor with researchers, in part because such theories have been unable to explain the variation among, and the historically rapid growth and decline of, right-wing extremist groups in the United States and elsewhere (see Billig 1978:46–47). . . .

In this article, I attempt to address these problems by examining what happens when women join racist movements—how women reconcile the male-oriented agendas of the racist movement with understandings of themselves and their gendered self-interests. By so doing, I situate the political actions of women racists in rational, if deplorable, understandings of self and society.

Methodology

Data are from in-depth interviews with 34 women racist activists conducted between September 1994 and October 1995. I began this study by collecting and reading a one-year series of all newsletters, magazines, flyers, and recordings of music and speeches published by every currently active self-proclaimed white power, white supremacist, white separatist, Ku Klux Klan, skinhead, Nazi/neo-Nazi, and similar group that I could identify through existing lists of racist groups, through personal contacts with self-proclaimed racist activists, and through reference in racist periodicals.[3] This resulted in a collection of publications by more than 100 different groups,[4] most with items issued at least two or more times during the year. Through these publications, I identified all groups that claimed significant numbers of women members or that identified at least one woman as a spokesperson or leader. These groups became a sampling frame for this study. From this list of groups, I selected approximately 30 that varied in regional location, age of member, and type of group.

This approach allowed me to identify groups with women activists but did not produce names of specific members since racist activists generally use aliases or code names (e.g., "Viking Mary") in their publications. I was able to make contact and secure interviews with several women activists directly through their groups. Such a direct approach was, however, inadvisable for most groups because they are highly suspicious and hostile to unknown outsiders. To secure the majority of interviews, I relied on a more indirect approach, using personal networks, including parole officers, correctional officials, newspaper reporters, other racist activists and former activists, federal and state gang task forces, attorneys, other researchers, and my own contacts with individuals in this movement to make contacts with individual members of the targeted groups. Initial interviews with a few key informants gave me additional entrée to other racist activists. Throughout, I continued to select respondents from groups in the original sample list rather than by pursuing a snowball sample or a sample of convenience to ensure variability in experience and perspective. As much as possible, I selected respondents of disparate ages who held different positions or had varying levels of commitment to the racist movement.

Respondents included 4 leaders who are known both within the movement and outside, 10 leaders who are not known publicly, and 20 rank-and-file members of racist groups. They ranged in age from 16 to 90, with a median age of 24. In general, members of the Ku Klux Klan groups were older and skinheads were younger, but one informant, the editor of a skinhead newsletter, was in her 80s and several Klanswomen were in their early 20s. The respondents lived in 15 different states, with the greatest concentrations in Georgia (6), Oklahoma (5), Oregon (4), and Florida (4). They were dispersed across regions as well, with 11 from the South, 10 from the West Coast, 10 from the Midwest, and 3 from the East Coast. . . .

Findings

What happens when women join racist groups? What is it about their lives, as they reveal them, that seems to coincide with the agenda of racist politics? How do they tailor their understanding of self or of racial politics to "make sense" of racist commitments? Life histories reveal some of the means by which women activists establish a rational basis for their participation in racist groups through strategies of conversion, selective adoption, and resignation. Each strategy represents attempts by women activists to create coherent personal narratives by actively reconfiguring the "fit" between themselves and the goals of the racist movement.

Conversion

One way that women activists create a rational basis for their involvement in organized racism is by retrospectively constructing their entry into racial politics as the outgrowth of dramatic personal transformation. Reflecting back on an earlier, nonpolitical life, these women come to view their current political commitments as the result of a single sensational event or series of events through which their personal goals and beliefs became fused with the agendas of the racial movement. In the life histories, accounts of personal transformation typically take the form of a conversion story, not unlike the accounts of those who have been converted to religion, sobriety, or feminism (see Bearman and Stovel 1993; Brereton 1991; Cain 1991; Goldberg 1990; Hart 1992). As converts to racial activism, these women construct the stories of their lives as narratives of passage from racial naïveté to racist enlightenment. In such conversion stories, the more mundane details of actual recruitment to racist groups fall to the wayside. What is highlighted—indeed, what is remembered—in the life narratives is a sense of self-transformation.

Such racial "awareness" is more often a *consequence* of association with members of racist groups than a *cause* motivating participation. Of the 34 respondents, more than one-third (13) were recruited into the movement by friends or acquaintances (such as fellow "bikers"): another 10 were convinced to join by parents, siblings, cousins, or children.[5] Three were recruited through a husband or boyfriend. Only 8 (less than one-quarter) sought out contact with the racist movement themselves, on the basis of prior ideological conviction. For most, conversion to the principles of racist activism followed from personal association with other racists and from participation in racist actions, not the reverse. Conversion stories thus cannot be taken as a literal account of ideological transformation but rather provide respondents with an ordered and agentic undergirding to what otherwise might seem a disorderly, even chaotic, series of life events and decisions (see Rosenthal 1991:36). And they accord intent, calculation, and meaning to radically changing self-identities. . . .

Related abstractly as rationales for subsequent racial activism, respondents' conversion stories imply a singular and personal experience that crystallized understanding and prompted a voyage of discovery, a passage from darkness into light. In the conversion narratives, activists claim that this experience made them acutely aware that Jews—or African Americans or government agents—caused and controlled the economy, or politics—or even the minutiae of daily life. For nearly all informants, the narrative of conversion pivoted on a single dramatic life event—a near-death experience, loss of a loved one, even the death of a pet—an ordeal that clarified perception, sharpened value priorities, and seemed to reveal the racial and ethnic dynamics of history.

Alice,[6] a 23-year-old racist skinhead, interviewed on death row in a Southern state where she was incarcerated for a series of murders and robberies, cited a car accident as her personal turning point, after which *"it's like, my whole attitude changed . . . my mind focused more on white supremacy." "Since the day I was born,"* Alice recalled, she had been taught racist attitudes by her parents, but, like them, she had never felt the inclination to act on those beliefs until she awoke from a coma after her car accident. In Alice's narrative, descriptions of the loss of control she felt as a hospital patient — *"IVs in my arms, tubes in my nose"* — blurred together with images of African American nurses surrounding her bedside, probing and invading her body. Assertions of self against institutional dehumanization and bodily invasion thus took on a racialized cast for which her earlier belief system served as an ideological template: *"I said [to the African American nurses] 'don't touch me. Don't get near me . . . leave me alone.'"* It was this incident, she concluded, that brought her into permanent "racial awareness" and that set the stage for her subsequent involvement in neo-Nazi gangs. Indeed, Alice's narrative of life after her hospitalization reflected this new sense of racial commitment. Speaking of a cousin who married an African American man, she recalled that before the accident she saw family loyalty as more important than racial background, but after her racial "awakening," *"that was it . . . I walked out the door and I haven't spoken to her since."*

Other conversion-by-near-death stories embedded the antecedents, rather than the outcomes, of personal catastrophe in racial terms. Typical of this was the life history narrative of Judy, a very prominent middle-aged Aryan leader on the East Coast. For her, racial commitment was born when she was seriously injured in a hit-and-run accident while living in an impoverished area of Cleveland. . . .

. . . According to Judy's account, . . . her ability to maintain harmony and to ignore the retrospectively obvious proclivity of her African American neighbors for crime and indolence had depended on racial naïveté. Once she became more "aware," such unconscious acceptance was no longer possible. The car accident then became the narrative moment that destroyed Judy's innocence and began a process of self-transformation. Key to this process was her certainty that "they" were responsible for the accident. Although she acknowledges that she did not see the driver who hit her, Judy nonetheless maintained that it "must have been" an African American man from a neighboring house. *"I ignored them, but then I was hit by that car . . . I swear they hit me on purpose . . . because I would not have anything to do with them."*

As in Alice's account, Judy's racist action followed, almost unbidden, from racial awakening: *"Of course, after I got hit by a car, that was it . . . I started getting into politics."* An African American driver was the only possibility that seemed to make sense of this otherwise random tragedy, to accord it intent and purpose. In addition, such a racial lens made sense of her other hardships of her financial marginality and limited opportunities. Such racialized understanding, however, did not come incrementally or as the result of Judy's economic frustrations alone. Rather, Judy relates the process of becoming a racist as a sudden, metamorphic process. The world was now revealed as purposeful, conspiratorial, and rent by deep racial fissures. Such understanding then furnished Judy with a sense of purpose. From that point, she relates, her life's mission was one of devotion to furthering white, Aryan supremacy and African American subordination.

Jan, a 55-year-old Nazi from a small midwestern city, related a similar story, describing her complicated medical history in increasingly conspiratorial tones, as a prototype of the struggle between Aryan and Jew. Consider Jan's memory of the operating room when she was being prepared for surgery:

> *There was nobody in there. No instruments, nothing. Then a man appeared from behind me and said he's my anesthesiologist. We started talking, I sat on that operating table, that iron metal thing, and he said, "Where are you from?" I said, I'm from Germany. I had long blond hair and my face was clear, wonderful complexion. At that time still I believed and trusted completely. . . . He said, "Well, I'm gonna give you the anesthesia now." I inhaled and realized that I couldn't exhale . . . he was just sitting there watching me . . . I wanted to say, I can't breathe, [but] I had no more voice.*

In this account, Jan's German (Aryan) naïveté is counterposed against a disembodied but menacing presence who can literally take away her voice and her breath. Much later in the story, Jan gives the explanation for this encounter, simultaneously providing causality and plot to the narrative of her life story. She relates her discovery that the anesthesiologist was Jewish, that, in fact, the hospital—along with the media, the government, nearly everything—was owned and controlled by Jews. Jews are both sinister and invisible, Jan concludes. That is the key to their awesome power to control the fate of unsuspecting Aryans.

If such stories reveal one common way that activists mold themselves to the ideologies of racist groups, it is also clear that they are not reliable accounts of actual political recruitment or ideological conversion. On the contrary, virtually all informants, when pressed to construct chronological life histories, reveal a pattern of recruitment to racial-based politics quite at odds with the pattern of conversion-by-striking event described in more abstract accounts. The Cleveland activist's accident, for example, was not simply the blinding moment of awareness that she recounts in her life history but also one that brought her into contact with a locally prominent neo-Nazi who offered to take her in during her convalescence. Similarly, it was in the process of investigating a medical malpractice claim that the middle-aged Nazi activist became acquainted with a local white power activist who monitored local hospitals and doctors.

Thus, these conversion stories are best understood as *learned* narratives, retrospectively formatted by the political, ideological, and even stylistic conventions of racist group imagery. They have the monocausal structure of racist ideology in which the world is sharply divided between friend and foe and historical agency is assigned to specific groups, usually Jews or African Americans. Racial activists thus learn to align themselves with racial goals, in part, by transforming their understandings of self. . . .

Selective Adoption

A second way that women create coherent narratives of their involvement in the racist movement is by transforming their sense of the goals of organized racism. Just as through "conversion" women adjust themselves to conform more closely to the goals of the racial movement, women racial activists also transform their understandings of racial activism by selectively disregarding aspects of the ideologies or agendas of racial groups that are at variance with their personal goals or allegiances. For these women, "collective identity"— what Gamson refers to as the process of defining "being part of a 'we' who can do something" (1992:84)—is highly fragmentary, based on the selective adoption of group agendas and identities. This discrepancy between personal and group understandings and identities explains why the organizational texts and public propaganda of racist groups often differ in significant ways from individual members' attitudes and political motivations and even from members' perceptions of the group's goals and agendas.

Life history narratives indicate that many women members undergo a fairly convoluted and incomplete process of political and rhetorical socialization into organized racism. This is reflected in the shallow explanations that activists provide for their participation, such as a middle-aged midwestern Klanswoman who said she joined the Klan because *"you can meet celebrities . . . you know, [referring to talk show Klansmen] people you see on television."* But it is obvious also in the pains that informants take to point out their disagreements with the racist movement overall or even with their particular group. Several Klanswomen confided their support for legal abortion and their disagreement with the Klan's negative stand on homosexuality. A young neo-Nazi leader on the West Coast disclosed that her best friend was married to an African American and that their children play together. And an Aryan supremacist in New England told of her involvement in a lesbian-dominated goddess-worship group, dismissing the suggestion that this runs counter to the antihomosexual politics of her group by saying, *"Oh, we're just great friends . . . none of us really believe in the label thing."* Almost one-third (11) of the informants volunteered information on mixed-race or homosexual family members with whom they were on friendly terms.[7]

Even the attitudes of very committed racists do not always mirror the groups to which they are dedicated. Nearly all informants (29), including those in leadership positions, dissented from at least part of the organizational doctrine, typically based on personal experiences such as having family members or work colleagues of another race, religion, nationality, or sexual orientation. Several Klanswomen complained that their Klan chapters were too male oriented, too sexist. Others complained that movement men only want women to have white babies; one countered that she tells young women recruits to *"get an education and be somebody first."* Women in groups with rigidly male-dominant ideologies, as expected, were more likely to dispute their organizational positions than were women in groups with more gender-inclusive philosophies.

A variant of this tendency toward selective adoption is the belief that race, religion, and ethnicity can only be known through actions. People who are "on your side" therefore are *necessarily* white, Aryan, or Christian—regardless of their appearance. Conversely, those who wrong you must be nonwhite, non-Aryan, or Jewish. Such a logic is evident in a number of interviews where respondents sought to distinguish someone's *true* racial identity from their superficial racial markings. When a Southern neo-Nazi described her best friend, an African American man, for instance, she explained that, as a confidante, he was "really white." Having an interracial friendship thus did not disturb her racist beliefs because she assigned race on the basis of loyalty, not skin color.

Adherence to organized racism, therefore, does not presuppose complete ideological transformation. Rather, at least some recruits selectively disregard, transform, or choose to violate the very principles that appear central to the mission and agenda of racist groups. And such ideological distancing is intensely gendered. It allows these respondents to participate in racist groups whose goals and agendas—largely forged by the beliefs of male racist leaders—are not fully consonant with the lives and relationships of women recruits. As women enter racial politics, they adopt the ideas that least threaten their own lives and personal commitments; the rest are simply ignored.

Surprisingly, such apparent inconsistencies rarely seem to threaten either the ideological coherence of the group or members' allegiance to the group's overall agendas. At least in part, this is due to the relatively fluid and disorganized nature of many contemporary racist groups in which dissent from organizational doctrine is widespread and fairly accepted among subgroups of members, like these women activists.[8] Indeed, ideological flexibility may be key to the ability of racist groups at this stage of development to recruit from among mainstream white populations.

Resignation

A third narrative strategy is resignation. Stories of men's political commitment—on the Left or Right—typically convey a tone of excitement, of self-
satisfaction. Ezekiel (1995) comments on such a sense of personal fulfillment
through racist political action: "Organizing is the leader's jones. He has to
have it. Like every jones, it is his world, his lover, his identity. Without it he
is nothing; when engaged, he is God" (p. 64).

This sense of satisfaction and lack of reservation, widely reported among
male racist leaders (Billig 1978; Hasselbach 1996; also Luchterhand and
Wieland 1981) and evident in the self-aggrandizing autobiographies that
pepper the literature of contemporary racist groups, is not found among
women racist activists. Racial "enlightenment" is presented, at best, in terms
of passive resignation, more often in despair—as a burden, an onerous responsibility, an unwanted obligation. There is little bluster, almost no swag-
ger, among these women when they are discussing their racial mission. In
contrast to Billig's (1978) interview with a male member of the British National Front who was anxious to impart the party line to others, these racist
women were much more reluctant to see political knowledge as preferable to
ignorance. As one Nazi member put it, *"It's painful, it hurts, it's all consuming
when you have the knowledge."* Another commented, *"If I had to do it over again,
I wouldn't want to know anything."* A member of an Aryan supremacist group
stated, *"It's hard feeling this duty to alert other people."*

Although almost one-half (16) of the respondents said that they had tried
to recruit others into the movement, almost everyone was hesitant, or even
negative, about the possibility of enlisting immediate family members, especially their own children or prospective children. As one Nazi survivalist
stated, *"I won't teach my children to be political . . . I don't want them to have that
burden."* A Klanswoman said that she *"wouldn't encourage anyone to join, it's
just something I did."*

Many respondents took pains to deny their own racial activism. Even
highly visible racial leaders claimed that they were not activists, that they
tried not to be "too active," or that they were active only when it was "necessary for survival." As one prominent Aryan supremacist commented when
discussing her own affiliation with a violent racist group, *"I was in kind of an
unaware state [when I joined]."*

Even when activists described acts of personal political agency—searching out what they invariably called "the truth" in literature or through
movement contacts—their descriptions of these activities were passive, even
despondent. Political histories, especially from those involved with gender-
traditional groups like the Klan or Christian Identity sects, were related primarily in terms of victimization.

These women racists also present themselves as victims of public perception, unjustly characterized negatively by the world at large. A white

separatist complained that she needed to hide her real feelings about African Americans and Jews for fear of losing her job. A Nazi protested that she didn't "like the way people view me as a hater." An Aryan supremacist said, *"People look at us as though we are sick, as though we are the problem of society."* To counter this, informants routinely distance themselves from what they claim are more extreme elements of the movement, claiming, as a Klanswoman did, that their group "is no different than being in the Girl Scouts" but that, conversely, "most of the [other] people in the movement have too much hate." Similarly, a skinhead related a story of another woman racist leader who *"used to tell me people that had brown hair and brown eyes [like me] were just filth and trash and wasn't worthy of being around. She really scared me."* More commonly, women object to the restrictions placed on their racial activities by movement men or complain about the disparaging remarks about women that pervade much racist literature and the conversation of male racist leaders.[9]

It is not a sense of ideological passion or the desire to spread racist ideas and thereby change the world that characterizes the ways in which women understand their role in organized racism. Rather, a sense of hopelessness pervades both descriptions of the "degenerate" society that surrounds them and the possibilities for changing that situation. For them, racism is a politic of despair. Male racial activists talk of becoming empowered by racial knowledge and racial activism, boasting of their connections to violence and their abilities to change undesired situations (e.g., Billig 1978:226–27). For women, the talk is very different. Activism is seen solely as a recourse for protecting their children or themselves from a troubled society that they have come to understand in racialized terms, but a means that stands little chance of success. As a white supremacist said, *"I would like my future to be a little house on the prairie picture . . . but it will not be like that. I think we'll be struggling my whole life . . . surrounded by immorality and corruption."* Activism thereby is a defensive stance. It does not deliver a sense of self-satisfaction and power. For these women, the racist movement promises the possibility for fending off the social forces that they see as threatening to engulf them and their families, but it promises, and delivers, little to them personally.

The emotional resignation found among these women activists reflects a final form of "sense making." To the extent that racist politics does not deliver obvious and tangible rewards for women activists, they construct their participation in the movement as involuntary, automatic, and unconscious. Consider the passive nature of the political narrative related by a 19-year-old Rocky Mountain state racist skinhead:

Q: Do you remember the first thing that brought you in [to the white supremacist movement]?

A: Uh, well, they used to have like Bible Studies here, the white supremacists here . . . I went to them even though I'm not necessarily all for the Bible, but I went there and started getting involved with them, and they would have like demonstrations and marches and stuff around here. So I started going with them to offer support and then . . . well, a friend of mine went to one of their meetings one time and she told me about it and then I went to it the next week, and then I started getting involved in it and stuff.

Little in this narrative suggests the sense of confidence, self-direction, or personal agency that is often assumed to be a compensation for participation in social movements (Gamson 1992:186). Rather, this informant presents racial involvement as something that just happened *to* her, the end result of a series of minor actions chosen without a particular political objective.

Making sense of racial politics by denying personal agency is a common response of those involved in political causes that are widely condemned and serves to normalize the consequences of involvement. Rosenthal (1991:39) found such assertions in a study of Germans who witnessed World War II but did not face persecution. The narratives of women racist activists, however, express more than just self-justifications. Instead, the declarations of resignation convey both hopelessness in the face of outside social or political forces and powerlessness to reconcile the contradiction between what they see as lofty movement goals of white, Aryan supremacy and the actual experience of white, Aryan women within the racist movement. All activists concur that the movement's abstract goals of racial purity are laudatory, but many also indicate that the process of working toward these goals provides them little gratification. It is in this sense that the resignation of women racial activists— their expressions of self-denigration, emotional pain, victimization, and lack of awareness—represents a gendered response to experiences within male-defined racist politics.

Implications

The inclusion of women into an analysis of racist movements, and the explication of how women reconcile their perceived interests with those of the racist movement, suggests several implications about the process whereby people become members of organized hate groups. First, the divergent understandings and incorporations of movement goals by members highlight the multidimensionality of political positions within organized racism. Even within the most extreme racist groups, there is no simple relationship between gender, or sexual orientation or abortion politics, and the ideologies of race, nation, morality, or family that we typically bundle together as "right wing" or "reactionary" (Yohn 1994). Not all members favor gender inequality, oppose abortion, or favor the death penalty for homosexuality. Indeed, the organizing momentum of the racist movement in recent years, and its ability to attract substantial numbers of women recruits, may reflect its ability to accommodate some measure of ideological dissension within its ranks even while maintaining a facade of political unity.

Second, this analysis indicates that women's involvement in organized racism is more rational, and less capricious, than earlier research suggests. Women's entrance into organized racism is not a simple matter of their obliviousness to the political agenda of racist groups nor of personal gullibility on the part of individual recruits. Rather, women work to create a rational connection between themselves and the goals of racist politics.

This reconceptualization also has implications for political organizing. If the conditions of women's participation in organized racism indeed are social and rational, rather than psychological and irrational, then it should be possible to design political measures to counter the recruitment of women by racist groups, even to recruit women away from racial politics. Further, if the narratives through which women construct an understanding of the intersection of their personal biographies and the politics of racist organizing are themselves gendered, it is the case that antiracist organizing also needs to be gendered. We cannot counter the appeal of racist groups to some women, or lure women from these groups, by assuming that racial activism is gender neutral. Rather, it is clear that women's understandings of their racial activism rest on a foundation of fear of bodily threat, a valuation of personal relationships, and a sense of personal passivity that may differ significantly from the self-evaluations of male racists, and these need to be addressed in effective antiracist politics.

Given the paucity of research on women in racist groups, it is premature to posit specific strategies, but some general guidelines can be inferred from the findings of this research. Most important, if personal allegiances are as important as ideological commitments to many women racist activists, then relationships whose nature is at variance with racist goals (e.g., interracial friendships) are a possible route for "conversion" *out* of racist politics. Moreover, to the extent that women experience their participation in racist politics through a lens of resignation and despair, alternative political agendas that empower, rather than restrict, women members may be attractive. Finally, given the critical role of personal recruitment into racial politics, tactics that seek to disrupt or prevent contacts between racial activists and potential recruits are critical. At present, the racist movement is enjoying considerable success in recruiting women. However, well-designed strategic efforts by antiracist activists can play a considerable role in reversing this trend.

ENDNOTES

[1] Although many of the new racist groups are small—often consisting of little more than a handful of members with a post office box—some command substantial numbers of members. (See periodic reports from the Center for Democratic Renewal, P.O. Box 50469, Atlanta, GA 30302, and the Southern Poverty Law Center, 400 Washington Avenue, Montgomery, AL 36104).

[2] These estimates are based on private discussions between the author and several national and regional Ku Klux Klan and neo-Nazi leaders. Secret and transient memberships of these groups make it impossible to verify these figures, but they gener-

ally coincide with information provided by state police officials and national anti-racist, anti-Semitic monitoring groups such as the Center for Democratic Renewal and the Southern Poverty Law Center.

[3] Lists of contemporary racist groups exist in the Wilcox Collection at the University of Kansas, but the ephemeral nature of many groups and their constant relocation to evade authorities make any list outdated almost as soon as it is published.

[4] Because racist groups change their names and memberships very quickly, it is impossible to tell exactly how many distinct groups are represented in this list.

[5] Family ties were a common route into racial activism, but by no means were all racial activists raised in white supremacist households. More than one-third of my informants identify their parents' ideological leanings as progressive or leftist.

[6] This, and all names, are pseudonyms. All informants were promised anonymity, so names and locations of interviews are not reported here.

[7] Such sentiments should not be confused with the fraudulent expressions of affinity for victims that are frequently found in retrospectives of war or violent activity (e.g., Luchterhand and Wieland 1981:281).

[8] By contrast, dissent within the tightly organized Nazi party after the mid-1930s was possible only among intimate groups, if at all (Peukert 1982:77).

[9] Although it is beyond the scope of this article, several studies examine the contradictions between the desire for female participation in racist/fascist movements and the idealization of apolitical maternal women in the ideologies of these movements (see Blee 1991; Koonz 1984).

REFERENCES

Adorno, T. W., Else Frenkel-Brunswik, Daniel J. Levinson, and R. Nevitt Sanford. 1950. *The Authoritarian Personality*. New York: Harper.

Bearman, Peter and Katherine Stovel. 1993. "Becoming a Nazi: Models of Identity Formation." Paper presented at the annual meeting of the American Sociological Association, August, Miami, FL.

Billig, Michael. 1978. *Fascists: A Social Psychological View of the National Front*. London: Academic Press.

Blee, Kathleen M. 1991. *Women of the Klan: Racism and Gender in the 1920s*. Berkeley: University of California Press.

Brereton, Virginia L. 1991. *From Sin to Salvation: Stories of Women's Conversions, 1800 to the Present*. Bloomington: Indiana University Press.

Brinkley, Alan. 1993. "The Problem of American Conservatism." Paper presented at the annual meeting of the Organization of American Historians, April, Anaheim, CA.

Cain, Carole. 1991. "Personal Stories: Identity Acquisition and Self-Understanding in Alcoholics Anonymous." *Ethos* 19:210–53.

Center for Democratic Renewal. 1990–94. *The Monitor*. Published bimonthly by the Center for Democratic Renewal.

Ezekiel, Raphael. 1995. *The Racist Mind: Portraits of American Neo-Nazis and Klansmen*. New York: Viking.

Gamson, William A. 1992. *Talking Politics*. New York: Cambridge University Press.

Goldberg, David T. 1990. "The Social Formation of Racist Discourse." In *Anatomy of Racism*, edited by David T. Goldberg. Minneapolis: University of Minnesota Press.

Hart, Janet. 1992. "Cracking the Code: Narrative and Political Mobilization in the Greek Resistance." *Social Science History* 16:631–68.

Hasselbach, Ingo, with Tom Reiss. 1996. *Führer-ex: Memoirs of a Former Neo-Nazi*. New York: Random House.

Hofstadter, Richard. 1965. *The Paranoid Style in American Politics and Other Essays.* New York: Alfred A. Knopf.

Koonz, Claudia. 1984. "The Competition for Women's *Lebensraum, 1928–1934.*" In *When Biology Became Destiny: Women in Weimar and Nazi Germany,* edited by Renate Bridethal, Atina Grossmann, and Marion Kaplan. New York: Monthly Review.

Luchterhand, Elmer and Nobert Wieland. 1981. "The Focused Life History in Studying Involvement in a Genocidal Situation in Nazi Germany." In *Biography and Society: The Life History Approach in the Social Sciences,* edited by Daniel Bertaux. Beverly Hills, CA: Sage.

Peukert, Detlev J. K. 1982. *Inside Nazi Germany: Conformity, Opposition and Racism in Everyday Life.* New Haven, CT: Yale University Press.

Ridgeway, James. 1990. *Blood in the Face: The Ku Klux Klan, Aryan Nations, Nazi Skinheads, and the Rise of a New White Culture.* New York: Thunder's Mouth.

Rose, Douglas, ed. 1992. *The Emergence of David Duke and the Politics of Race.* Chapel Hill: University of North Carolina Press.

Rosenthal, Gabriele. 1991. "German War Memories: Narrative and the Biographical and Social Functions of Remembering." *Oral History* 19:34–41.

Southern Poverty Law Center. 1985–95. *Intelligence Report.* Published bimonthly by the Southern Poverty Law Center.

———1990–95. *SPLC Report.* Periodical published by Klanwatch and Teaching Tolerance. Montgomery, AL.

Yohn, Susan M. 1994. "Will the Real Conservative Please Stand Up? Or, the Pitfalls Involved in Examining Ideological Sympathies." *American Historical Review* 99: 430–37.

18

DESCENT INTO MADNESS
The New Mexico State Prison Riot

MARK COLVIN

Prisons are another type of social structure often studied by sociologists. This selection by Mark Colvin, a professor of sociology in the Department of Justice Studies at Kent State University, is written as the introduction to the 1997 book *Descent into Madness: An Inmate's Experience of the New Mexico State Prison Riot* by Mike Rolland. Colvin was hired by New Mexico's Office of the Attorney General to help with the investigation into the events and causes of the 1980 riot at the Penitentiary of New Mexico. In the excerpt that follows, Colvin provides important insights into the history and social structure of the prison and how the breakdown in that social structure enabled violence and disorganization to occur.

T he riot at the Penitentiary of New Mexico (PNM) on February 2 and 3, 1980, is without parallel for its violence, destruction, and disorganization. During the 36 hours of the riot, 33 inmates were killed by other inmates; many of the victims were tortured and mutilated. (A 34th inmate died several months later from injuries he received during the riot.) As many as 200 inmates were severely injured from beatings, stabbings, and rapes. Many more suffered less serious injuries. In addition, scores of inmates were treated for overdoses of drugs taken from the prison's pharmacy during the riot. That more inmates did not die can be attributed to the dedicated work of medical personnel and emergency crews who treated the injured and transported them to local hospitals. In fact, many inmates were later surprised to learn of riot survivors whom they thought had certainly died during the event.

Seven of the 12 correctional officers who were taken hostage were beaten, stabbed, or sodomized. None of the hostages were killed. Some of the guard hostages were protected by small groups of inmates during the riot. A few hostages were even assisted in leaving the prison during the riot by sympathetic inmates.

Correctional officers and many more inmates would have certainly died in the riot had it not been for heroic efforts of some prisoners who risked their lives to save others from harm. Indeed, this prison riot brought out not only the evil potential of human beings (upon which we tend to focus after such an event) but also the potential for virtue. We are quick to condemn the evil acts and use these as an excuse to label all prisoners as "animals." But to do so is to ignore the acts of kindness and courage displayed by many inmates; to ignore the fact that the overwhelming majority of inmates only wanted to escape the mayhem, the violence, and the fear; and to ignore the essential humanity of the great majority of the people we lock up in prisons. Focusing on the evil acts of those few prisoners who engaged in them also distracts us from the evil of a taxpayer-supported prison system that produces events like the New Mexico State Prison riot.

The riot caused $20 million in physical damage to the institution. Fires were started throughout the prison, and water flooded the prison water mains. More than $200 million in riot-related expenses were incurred by the state for medical, police, fire, and national guard response, lawsuits for injuries and wrongful death, transportation of inmates to federal and other state prison systems, prosecutions of crimes committed during the riot, and official investigations of the events and causes of the riot.

The official investigation of the riot was headed by then-Attorney General of New Mexico Jeff Bingaman. I was hired by the Attorney General as a principal researcher for the riot investigation. In that role, I, along with the riot investigation team, conducted more than 300 in-depth interviews with former and then-current prisoners, correctional officers, and corrections officials in an attempt to reconstruct the events of the riot and understand its long-term causes and effects. The riot investigation presented its findings and conclusions in a two-part report (Office of the Attorney General 1980a,b). More recently, I published a book that presents a detailed social and organizational history of the Penitentiary of New Mexico State Prison leading up to this riot (Colvin 1992). . . .

In this introduction, I hope to provide the reader with a context for understanding . . . the New Mexico State Prison riot. It is important to understand the history of this prison, since it was not always a violent and disorderly institution. It was only in the three to four years preceding the riot that the prison had moved toward becoming the type of violent and disorganized organization that could produce an event as brutal as the 1980 riot. . . .

Background of the Riot

The 1980 New Mexico State Prison riot stands in stark contrast to the 1971 Attica prison riot. At Attica, after a few hours of chaos and destruction in which three inmates were killed by other inmates, inmate leaders were able to take command of rioting inmates and turn the event into an organized protest about prison conditions; after that point, no other deaths occurred until state authorities violently retook the prison, killing 29 inmates and 10 guard hostages in the process (Wicker 1975). At New Mexico, inmate leaders, to the extent that there were any, were unable to organize inmates or stop the inmate-on-inmate violence. All inmates were killed by other inmates. No one was killed when state authorities retook the prison. The disorganization of the riot and the inmate-on-inmate killings, and the brutality of many of these killings, are what distinguish the New Mexico State Prison riot.

As stated, the Penitentiary of New Mexico (PNM) was not always a violent, disorganized prison. In fact, on July 14, 1976, inmates at this prison staged a well-organized, peaceful protest of prison conditions. In the previous six months, a new prison administration had begun dismantling prison programs and reducing inmate privileges. The curtailment of programs and special privileges soon led to an open confrontation between the new prison administration and inmates. Prisoners organized a massive sit-down strike in which nearly 800 of the prison's 912 inmates refused to leave their living quarters for work or meals. The level of participation in this 1976 strike demonstrated a high degree of solidarity and cooperation among inmates. There was no violence among inmates during this event. (In fact, no inmate had been killed by another inmate at this prison since before 1970.) The prison administration's response to this June 1976 inmate strike inaugurated a new era in staff and inmate relations and in relations among inmates. It was a new era characterized by coercion and violence.

The strike was broken by the staff with violence. Housing units were teargassed and many inmates were forced to run a gauntlet of prison staff members who were armed with ax handles (Office of the Attorney General 1980b; Colvin 1992). Leaders of the strike were identified and segregated or transferred out of state. The stable inmate leadership, which had been the impetus for inmate social cohesion, was thus systematically eliminated. The prison staff, after this point, began to rely increasingly on coercion to maintain control of the institution. The "hole," which had been closed since 1968, was reopened and used frequently; the number of inmates in disciplinary segregation grew substantially (from less than 5 percent of the inmate population before June 1976 to as much as 25 percent of the inmate population after June 1976).

As this crackdown on organized inmate activity continued at the prison, the corrections department was undergoing rapid and confusing organizational changes. Turnover in the state's top corrections post occurred repeatedly, with five different heads of the corrections department between 1975 and 1980. A similar turnover in the warden's position took place, with five penitentiary wardens between 1975 and 1980. This administrative confusion resulted in inconsistent policy directives from the top of the organization and in the emergency of a middle-level clique of administrators who were virtually unaccountable to anyone in authority. This clique of administrators, by the middle of 1978, had been left to run the prison in any fashion they saw fit.

Under this middle-level clique, there were growing inconsistencies in both security procedures and discipline of inmates. Some shift supervisors followed very closely the proper security procedures; others did not follow them at all. Lax security had long been a problem at PNM, but the tendency toward inconsistency in security operations worsened after 1978 when various shift supervisors ran the prison at their own discretion. Similar problems of inconsistency in discipline were also evident. Some shift captains would enforce rules, at times inappropriately placing inmates in the "hole" for minor violations, while other shift captains would fail to punish some major violations of rules. Consistency in operation and a set routine provides stability for an institution. At PNM, it was difficult for inmates to calculate which behaviors would be punished or when they would be punished. Inmates were thus kept off balance.

This inconsistency by the prison staff was often interpreted by inmates as blatant harassment. In some cases, correctional officers, including some lieutenants and captains, were caught up in a game of mutual harassment with inmates. The game proceeded through interactions in which an officer would verbally humiliate an inmate and the inmate would respond in kind. Often this led to confrontations in which the inmate was led off to disciplinary segregation. The minority of prison officers who engaged in these activities poisoned relations between the staff and inmates and created enormous hostility.

As the middle-level administrators gained dominance after 1978, a new coercive "snitch system" emerged. This system had its roots in the aftermath of the June 1976 inmate strike when staff members attempted to identify the strike leaders. Inmates were threatened with disciplinary lockup if they did not identify strike participants and leaders. By 1978, these tactics had become a key aspect of the institution's inmate control system. Since inmates were not forthcoming with voluntary information, many members of the correctional staff began soliciting information through threats and promises. Inmates were promised early parole consideration, protection, and transfer to minimum-security institutions. They were also threatened with being locked up in disciplinary segregation or, in other cases, were refused protective custody if they did not inform. Another coercive tactic was to intimidate an inmate by threatening to "hang a snitch jacket" on him. This tactic, which involved the threat of labeling an inmate a "snitch" (or informant) was used to solicit information, gain control over an inmate, and, in some instances, retaliate against an inmate.

This came to be known as the "snitch game." The "snitch game" had the effect of breaking apart any sense of inmate solidarity. As the official report (Office of the Attorney General 1980b:24–25) on the riot maintained:

> The "snitch game" . . . create[d] suspicion and antagonism among inmates. "You can't even trust your old friends," was a sentiment voiced by several inmates. Inmate opinions of "snitches" included this often-repeated characterization, "It's just like in a war. You're all on the same side. It's us (inmates) against them (guards). And it's the same mentality. If you cross to the other side, you're no more, no less than a traitor and a spy." In the late '70s, correctional staff's increased use of the "snitch game" for information promoted enmity among inmates. In fact, some prison staff attempted to use the hatred which the snitch game created in the inmate society as a means of controlling inmates. In order to coerce particular information from an inmate, some staff members threatened to tell other inmates that he was a snitch. The inmate would usually capitulate, knowing the consequences of wearing a "snitch jacket." The consequences could be severe. First, snitches became more easily identifiable because a few guards were reckless or careless about protecting the identify of inmates who provided information. . . . Inmates also knew that the prison increasingly used Cellblock 4 as a place to house and to protect "snitches" after they were "used up." Second, inmates and staff attributed some of the increase in violence during the late '70s to the motivation for revenge against "snitches." This vengeful violence reached its horrible climax in the 1980 riot.

Some inmates labeled as "snitches" may not have been informants at all. Correctional officers discussed with Attorney General investigators the labeling of inmates as "snitches" as a coercive tactic (quoted in Colvin 1992:154).

> *Correctional Officer: If I was a guard and he was an inmate and I didn't like him, I'd punch him around and say, "Hey, man, let's put a snitch jacket on this guy." And another inmate come up behind me and I'd say, "Hey man, this dude dropped a dime on this guy over here." They'll put a "jacket" on you and life expectancy with a "jacket" on you isn't too long. And that's what [gives names of several PNM administrators, captains, and lieutenants] all of them would do. If they didn't like you, they'd put a jacket on you, plain and simple. . . . I caught [name of correctional officer] lying about another inmate to four or five inmates and the other inmates turned around and looked at him and said, "We'll take care of this."*
>
> *Interviewer:* What was the purpose of doing this?
>
> *Correctional Officer: To get even . . . If I was to walk up to an inmate and just started kicking the hell out of him, I would have a lawsuit on me, but what goes on behind closed doors, only the inmates know.*

Whether an inmate had actually been an informant or not, the label of "snitch" could have deadly consequences, a fact that was used to intimidate inmates and create friction among prisoners. After inmate solidarity displayed during the June 1976 strike moved the prison administration to smash inmate organization and leadership, the inmate society became more fragmented and violent. From 1969 through July 1976 there were no killings at PNM, no prison officers were attacked, and inmate fights and sexual assaults were rare. From August 1976 to January 1980, six inmates were killed by other inmates, several attacks on prison officers occurred, and fighting among inmates became routine. And sexual assaults, by the late 1970s, had become so routine that there was "at least one reported case a day [and] 10 to 15 more nonreported cases daily" (*Albuquerque Journal*, 9/16/79:B1).

The administration's tactics for breaking up inmate solidarity led to a series of changes within the inmate society that spawned violence and disorder. As inmate groups broke down into small, self-protective cliques, forces within the inmate society that formerly were capable of holding back disorder and violence among inmates diminished. The lack of inmate leaders in the late 1970s meant that new inmates entering PNM were no longer under the restraints of an established order among inmates. Inmates could no longer socialize new arrivals to the increasingly unstable environment. Some of the new inmates directly challenged the power and control exercised by older inmates who had not already been removed by the administration.

While many observers relate the growing inmate violence to newly arriving inmates, it does not appear that the violent behavior was being imported from outside. Rather, new inmates, as never before, were entering a disorganized social situation with undefined roles and lack of leadership. As they confronted, and were confronted by, this increasingly chaotic situation, many of the new inmates resorted to violence. That the violence was not imported from outside is supported by data on inmates' convictions. In 1970, 45 percent of all crimes for which New Mexico prisoners were convicted were violent crimes. By 1975, the figure had dropped to 38 percent, and by 1979 it was 33 percent (Department of Corrections 1971, 1976, 1980). Also, a profile of PNM inmates compiled in 1977 (when the inmate violence began increasing dramatically) by consultants for the New Mexico Corrections Master Plan indicated that in comparison to national averages, PNM inmates were relatively nonviolent and unsophisticated in the criminal activity that led to their convictions (Governor's Council on Criminal Justice Planning 1978).

Rather than importing the violence, inmates were becoming more violent in reaction to a prison social structure that elicited such a response. With a paucity of inmate leaders to guide and ease the transition to prison life for younger inmates, these new inmates were left to their own devices to deal with the fear of assault. By 1978, the fear of being assaulted, especially of being sexually attacked, had become a prevalent feature of inmate life, especially for younger inmates. These new inmates were faced with a deadly dilemma that increasingly set the tone of inmate relations in the late 1970s. The fear created by violent confrontations, or by the mere anticipation of them, produced inmates who either submitted to the exploitation of other inmates (became "punks"), sought protection from officials (became "snitches"), or fought (to prove themselves as "good people" to other inmates by developing a reputation as violent). Most inmates agreed that the only rational choice when faced with the irrational confrontation of a sexual assault was to fight viciously and develop a reputation as someone who others "did not mess with." The other choices, submission or official protection, would lead to a prison experience of perpetual victimization.

In the late 1970s, confrontational situations among inmates sharply increased, forcing more inmates into the deadly dilemma of choosing a course of action against assaults. Some submitted and were marked as punks or homosexuals. This submission did not label them necessarily as sexual deviants but, more importantly, as "morally weak" individuals who would not stand up for themselves. Inmates who chose to seek protective custody, who in the inmates' vocabulary "pc'd up," were also seen as "weak" inmates who could not withstand the pressures of prison life. Added to being marked as weak was the stigma of being a snitch, since it was widely believed among inmates (though by no means always true) that protective custody was a payoff for informing. For "regular" inmates who were "on line" standing up for themselves in the daily battles with other inmates and the prison staff, an inmate who gives in to pressure from other inmates by not standing up for himself, and then gives in to pressure from the administration by informing, was truly a person of "weak moral character." A snitch label (whether deserved or not) thus implies the weakest of inmates who were so low as to sell out their fellow inmates because of fear and intimidation. These inmates were allowing both other inmates *and* the administration to humiliate them. Succumbing to other people's attempts at humiliation is the worst possible fate for a convict (Abbott 1981). Fear of humiliation drove much of the violence in the inmate society. Violent confrontations were events in which inmates' characters ("weak" or "strong") were being tested. They were also situations in which reputations for violence were being built.

Developing a reputation for violence became a full-time activity as a growing number of inmates were confronted by the prison's deadly dilemma. As inmates vied for violent reputations, the number of confrontational incidents between inmates increased. This competition for violent reputations accelerated the cycle of confrontations and produced a growing number of both violence-prone inmates and those who were perceived as weak. Under these circumstances, the struggle involved in relegating inmates to the roles of victims or victimizers became a monotonous, horrifying, daily occurrence.

The violence led to further fragmentation of the inmate society. Inmates increasingly formed into small cliques for self-protection. These cliques did not constitute the types of gang structures witnessed in other prisons (Irwin 1980; Jacobs 1977). For the most part, these cliques were very loosely organized groupings that provided inmates small, often temporary, "ecological niches" (Hagel-Seymour 1988) relatively free from the violence of the prison.

Some inmate groups began to emerge as influential in 1978. The ACLU lawsuit against PNM (*Duran v. Apodaca*) gave a few Chicano inmates a limited leadership role within some inmate factions. These inmates were directly involved in negotiations for settlement of the lawsuit. But this leadership role was diminishing by late 1979 as the negotiations in the lawsuit bogged down because of disagreements among state officials over issues involved in the lawsuit. Inmates, generally, began to perceive little gain from the lawsuit and the inmates involved in it began to lose influence.

Other inmate cliques gained power by 1978 because of their violent reputations. In 1976 and 1977, Anglo convicts were very disorganized and were regularly attacked by Chicano inmates. Then, some strong Anglo cliques began to surface in 1977. One of the more notorious cliques was associated with three Anglo inmates who, on April 16, 1978, beat another Anglo inmate to death with a baseball bat for allegedly being a snitch. This clique emerged as an important power that struggled with other inmate cliques for dominance.

The inmates caught up in the competition for dominance and violent reputations composed PNM's hardcore cliques. While the total number of inmates involved in these hardcore cliques was about 150 of the more than 1,000 inmates in the prison, their behavior and disruptiveness set the tone for inmate social relations. In stark contrast to the early 1970s, when inmate leaders helped keep the lid on violence among inmates, inmate leadership, to the extent that it existed at all, fell by 1979 to these small, hardcore cliques of inmates who actively engaged in violence and disruption. These hardcore cliques, produced inadvertently by the administration's coercive tactics used to break up inmate solidarity, were leading the inmate society toward an implosion of violence. Inmate solidarity had indeed been eliminated by 1980. But the administration's control of the prison was now more precarious than ever. Their coercive tactics, including use of the "snitch game," produced a fragmented inmate society that promoted inmate-on-inmate violence. The riot that exploded at 1:40 a.m. on February 2, 1980, would reflect this fragmented inmate society and the coercive tactics of control that produced an inmate society.

Overview of the 1980 Riot at the Penitentiary of New Mexico

There were a number of forewarnings that a major disturbance was imminent, yet no decisive actions were taken. Forewarnings included a mix of rumors and intelligence, none of which could be confirmed. Officials had no way to distinguish reliable from unreliable information, a legacy of the coercive snitch system which often resulted in inmates telling officials anything (whether true or not) to escape punishment or receive protection. As it turned out, among the many rumors was one specific bit of information, concerning a possible hostage-taking, that was an accurate forewarning.

Shortly after midnight, on February 2, 1980, the evening and morning shifts completed a count of inmates in the institution, which held 1,157 inmates that night, including 34 in a modular unit outside the main penitentiary building. All inmates were accounted for at the time of the count. About 1 A.M., two groups composed of four correctional officers each began a routine check of all cellhouses and dormitories in the south wing of the prison. At 1:40 A.M., one group, which included the shift captain, entered Dorm E-2, the upstairs dormitory in the E-wing.

Inmates in Dorm E-2 had been drinking "home brew" made of yeast and raisins smuggled in from the prison's kitchen. The inmates, sometime between 12:30 A.M. and 1:15 A.M., had hastily agreed upon a plan to jump the guards during their routine check of the dorm. It was not clear whether the plan included an attempt to exit the dormitory. Hostages would be taken in the dormitory; and if the entry door could be successfully jumped, additional hostages would be taken in the south wing of the prison. Beyond the plan to take some guards hostage, the inmates had no idea of what they would do next.

At 1:40 A.M., the dormitory door and the three officers who had just entered Dorm E-2 were jumped simultaneously. Inmates quickly overpowered the officer at the door and the other officers inside the dormitory. The guard at the door had the keys to other dormitories. Four hostages were then under the control of these inmates, who now had access to the main corridor.

At 1:45 A.M., inmates from Dorm E-2 jumped the officer outside Dorm F-2, seized the keys he held to other dormitories, and captured two other guards who were just entering Dorm F-2. A third guard, who had just entered the dorm, ran into the dayroom at the opposite end of the dorm; he was protected by some sympathetic Dorm F-2 inmates, who later helped him escape the prison. Total hostages were now eight, including the protected guard in the Dorm F-2 dayroom.

By 1:50 A.M., hundreds of inmates were milling around the main corridor in the south wing of the prison. At 1:57 A.M., two guards leaving the officers' mess hall, located in the central area of the institution, saw inmates beating and dragging a naked man (later identified as a hostage guard) up the south corridor toward the grill that separated the south wing from the central area of the prison. They also noticed that this corridor grill, contrary to prison policy, was open. Inmates were about to come through the opened grill. The two guards then raced north up the main corridor, passing the control center and entering the north wing of the prison, closing the corridor grill to the north wing behind them. Soon, scores of inmates were in front of the control center, which was separated from the rioters by what was supposed to be "shatterproof" glass. Inmates used a metal-canister fire extinguisher, pulled from the wall in the main corridor, to break the control center glass. The control center officers ran toward the front entrance of the prison and to the safety of the Tower 1 gatehouse. The inmates entered the control center through the smashed window and trashed its interior, sending keys flying in all directions from the key PegBoards.

By 2:02 A.M., inmates had gained access to the north wing and to the administration wing, since the grills to these areas were opened electronically from the control center. It took the inmates time to find keys to specific cellblocks since keys were scattered by those inmates who first breached the control center, which indicates the unplanned nature of the takeover. But by 3 A.M., inmates had found the key to the disciplinary unit, Cellblock 3. Here they captured three more correctional officers, bringing the total to 11 hostages. (By this point, two guards had hidden themselves in the crawl space in the basement of Cellblock 5, where they remained undetected by rioters throughout the riot. And the hospital technician locked himself and seven inmate-patients into the upstairs floor of the Hospital Unit, where they also remained undetected until the riot was over.)

The first inmate killings during the riot occurred in Cellblock 3 at about 3:15 A.M. An inmate, shouting in Spanish, "No era yo. No lo hice." ("It wasn't me. I didn't do it.") was beaten, tortured, and mutilated. This inmate was assumed to have informed on other inmates who were also locked in the disciplinary unit. Another inmate, who was mentally disturbed and apparently had kept other Cellblock 3 inmates awake at night with his screams, was shot in the head at close range with a canister fired from a teargas launcher taken from the control center.

At about the same time, another group of inmates had found keys to the prison pharmacy, located on the first floor of the Hospital Unit. The pharmacy contained narcotics, barbiturates, and sedatives, which were ingested in massive doses by inmates throughout the riot.

Other inmates in the early morning hours of the first day of the riot found keys to the basement area of the prison, below the kitchen. Here they retrieved an acetylene blowtorch that was used at about 3:15 A.M. to open the far south corridor grill, leading to the Educational Unit and Dorm D-1, which contained the twelfth (and last) guard to be taken hostage. This blowtorch was later taken to the other end of the prison to open the far north corridor grill and Cellblock 5. Cellblock 5 was vacant due to renovation. But construction crews had left in the Cellhouse 2 additional acetylene torches. Later, these blowtorches would be used to open Cellblock 4, the Protective Custody unit.

The period between 3 A.M. and 7 A.M. was characterized by chaos, infighting, and violence. There was no leadership throughout the riot. Inmates' actions were completely uncoordinated. Some inmates were setting fires in the administrative offices, others in the Psychological Unit. At certain points, inmates manning walkie-talkies radioed for firefighting crews to come into the prison; when firefighters approached the prison they were driven back by other inmates who threw debris at them. Other inmates were fighting, forming into groups for self-protection, or hiding in fear.

While all these uncoordinated activities and fighting were going on during the early hours of the riot, a few inmates who had been released from Cellblock 3 and Cellhouse 6 discussed organizing the riot into a protest against the administration. These inmates included those involved in the ACLU lawsuit (*Duran v. Apodaca*). They managed in the early hours of the riot to get control of the three hostages captured in Cellblock 3. However, they were able to gain control of only one of the other nine hostages. The other hostages were being held by various groups in the south wing of the institution. A few were held by sympathetic inmates who protected them. The shift captain was moved frequently and may have been under the control of different groups throughout the riot, some of whom beat him mercilessly, others of whom tended to his wounds and protected him. Unlike the three hostages who were captured in Cellblock 3, who were treated relatively well for the remainder of the riot, many of the hostages held in the south wing of the prison were beaten, stabbed, and sodomized.

The Cellblock 3 and Cellhouse 6 inmates who were attempting to organize the riot into a protest had little influence on the behavior of the rioting inmates. One inmate, who identified himself as a leader in this attempt to turn the riot into a protest, said:

> *There were a few of us in here that were trying to freeze that [inmate-to-inmate violence] because it was wrong, it was dead wrong. Three hours after the riot started there was no stopping it. But there were a few of us that were saying,*

"Hey, if you want to burn it down, burn it down or tear it up or whatever you want, but quit killing people and don't turn this thing against ourselves. If you got to fight somebody now, fight the Man, fight the administration." (Quoted in Colvin 1992:183–84)

But his and the other inmates' efforts to turn the riot into a protest were futile.

As fights began to break out in the south wing of the prison, injuries to inmates and killings began to increase. Many of the deaths that occurred in the south wing were the result of fights between small groups of inmates and between individuals. Fights over hostages held in the south wing occurred. Many inmates, perceived as weak or defenseless, were attacked and raped; those offering resistance were beaten severely, a few were killed. Some assaults in the south wing appeared to be random. Inmates suffered injuries when they were hacked with meat cleavers, stabbed, or hit with pipes for no reasons apparent to the victims. A few of the killings in the south wing also appear to have been random. Of the 33 killings during the riot, 17 occurred in the south wing, many in the early morning hours of the first day. Of the approximately 400 injuries and rapes, the vast majority also occurred in the south wing.

More inmates would have been killed had Dorm E-1 been entered by the rioters. This semi-protection unit's inmates successfully fought off attempts by rioters to enter this dorm. A sympathetic inmate, who had some friends in the unit, tossed a three-foot long wrench through a hole in the wire mesh above the dorm entrance. This inmate was immediately jumped by other inmates in the main corridor who had observed this action; he was beaten to death. But because he had tossed them this heavy wrench the Dorm E-1 inmates were able to knock bars out of a window at the rear of the dormitory and make it to the perimeter fence and surrender to authorities for safety. Up to 80 inmates housed in the semi-protection unit were saved by this inmate's action.

The most horrific killings of the riot occurred in the north wing of the penitentiary, specifically in Cellblock 4, the Protective Custody unit. By 7 A.M., small groups of inmates entered Cellblock 4 after burning through its entrance grills with blowtorches. As these inmates entered the cellblock, they began shouting the names of intended victims. As rioting inmates operated the control panels that gang locked and unlocked cell doors, many Cellblock 4 inmates were able to leave their cells, blend in with the rioters, and escape the carnage. Other Cellblock 4 inmates were not so fortunate. On tiers where inmates had jammed the locks to their cell grills, the gang locking and unlocking mechanisms would not operate. These inmates were trapped in their cells. Using blowtorches, rioting inmates cut through the bars of entrance grills to the individual cells containing inmates. As the intended victims suffered through the agonizing wait while their cells were entered, they were taunted and told in vivid detail exactly how they would be tortured and killed.

These protective custody inmates were apparently killed by four or five small groups, containing three to five inmates each. The groups appeared to have acted independently in choosing victims. Inmates were tortured, stabbed, mutilated, burned, bludgeoned, hanged, and thrown off upper-tier catwalks into the basement. One Cellblock 4 inmate, a 36-year-old African American, was killed and decapitated. Whether this occurred in the cellblock or elsewhere in the prison could not be established by investigators. His head was reportedly placed on a pole, paraded through the main corridor, and shown to the guards captured in Cellblock 3. This inmate's body was later deposited outside the prison's front entrance with the head stuffed between the legs. Another inmate, while reportedly still alive, had a steel rod hammered completely through his head. One inmate victim was drenched with glue and set on fire. Other atrocities were also reported to investigators.

There was an apparent competition between the groups in both the quantity and "quality" of their killings. There does not appear to have been any motive, such as personal revenge, to account for these killings. No particular inmate killer among the suspects, for example, had apparently been "snitched off" by any of the victims. In fact, only a few of the inmates killed in Cellblock 4 were later identified by staff and inmates as suspected informants. These inmate victims were viewed as "weak" inmates and thus vulnerable targets of violence, whose deaths would not be avenged by other inmates. The fact that the victims were trapped in protective isolation not only increased the killers' sense of total domination but demonstrated the killers' "superiority" since they outsmarted the state authorities who were charged with protecting these inmate victims. In addition, a group dynamic of proving one's commitment to deviance was amplified in Cellblock 4 since small groups of inmates were competing for images as dominatingly "awesome" deviants. (See Jack Katz [1988] for a discussion of the dynamics involved in cold-blooded killings.) Each group felt compelled to outdo the other in its acts of violence. These brutal acts marked their victims as "morally weak" and their perpetrators as "morally superior" in the upside-down world that the inmate society had become. Inmates involved in these killings could count on gaining reputations as the most violent and feared inmates in the prison.

Most of the Cellblock 4 killings were apparently over by 10 A.M. on the first morning of the riot. More inmates would have undoubtedly died had they not been able to escape Cellblock 4. Besides those inmates who left their cells and escaped the protective custody unit when it was opened, other inmates living in this unit were rescued by sympathetic inmates. Some individual inmates entered Cellblock 4, found specific inmate friends, and sneaked them out of the unit. One contingent of about 20 African American inmates from Cellhouse 6 converged on Cellblock 4 about 7:30 A.M. to rescue one of their leaders, a Black Muslim minister, who had been locked in the protection unit. Upon his release, the Muslim minister told his followers to get as many protective custody inmates out of Cellblock 4 as possible. This group saved many of the intended victims (Anglo, Hispanic, and African American) from certain death. They brought these inmates to Cellhouse 6 where they combined forces for self-protection. At about noon, on the first day of the riot, they were able to fight their way to Dorm E-1 and leave the prison through the rear window that had been broken open earlier.

By noon on the first day, many inmates had managed to find routes from which to exit the prison and surrender to authorities who controlled the perimeter fence. By 5 P.M., more than 350 inmates had left the prison. They would continue to stream out of the prison for the rest of the riot. By 1 P.M. on the second (and final) day of the riot, only 100 of the prison's 1,157 inmates remained inside.

The final morning of the riot saw the setting of more fires, an increasingly larger stream of inmates leaving the prison to surrender to authorities, inmates being rushed to hospitals for injuries and pharmacy-drug overdoses, and bodies of inmates being deposited in the yard in front of the prison. Intermittent negotiations between state authorities and some prisoners continued and seemed to reach a climax by the final morning of the riot.

Throughout the riot, sporadic attempts at negotiating the release of hostages were made by state authorities. Negotiations were complicated by the fact that more than one group controlled hostages, and some of these groups had no interest in negotiating release. Three hostages were released at different times either in anticipation of or in response to talking to the news media. At one point, an NBC cameraman entered the prison's entrance lobby and recorded inmates' grievances. The lobby was filled with smoke as inmates presented their grievances about poor food, nepotism, harassment, overcrowding, idleness, inadequate recreation facilities, and arbitrary discipline practices by the administration. At another point, two inmates met with two news reporters just outside the entrance of the prison building. Beyond the release of these three hostages, however, negotiations with inmates had very little to do with the release of hostages or ending the riot.

Two hostages managed, with the help of sympathetic inmates, to leave the prison disguised as inmates. Other hostages were released by inmates because these inmates feared these hostages might die from injuries, which they thought would provoke an immediate retaking of the prison. One other hostage was released after an apparent agreement emerged from negotiations.

At about 8:30 A.M. on February 3, the second (and last) day of the riot, three Hispanic inmates (Lonnie Duran, Vincent Candelaria, and Kendrick Duran), who were among the few inmates attempting, unsuccessfully, to organize the riot into a protest over prison conditions, ironed out an agreement for ending the riot with prison authorities during a meeting in the gatehouse beneath Tower 1. The agreement had five points: (1) no retaliation against rioting inmates; (2) segregation policies be reviewed; (3) inmates be permitted to meet with the press; (4) no double-bunking of inmates in Cellblock 3; and (5) inmates be given water hoses to douse fires inside the prison. The Durans and Candelaria returned to the prison to seek approval from other inmates. They re-emerged from the prison shortly before noon for continued negotiations. By noon, only two hostages remained in the prison.

The final hour of negotiations leading up to the end of the riot was witnessed by reporter Peter Katel who later, with co-author Michael Serrill, gave the following account:

> The two Durans and Candelaria emerged from the prison and announced that they had approval from other inmates to sign the agreement negotiated [earlier that morning]. . . . Then negotiations became more complicated. Other inmates joined the Durans and Candelaria at the negotiating table. They haggled over exactly how the agreement was to be implemented by prison officials. . . . Officials were particularly worried about the presence of three new inmates, William Jack Stephens, Michael Colby and Michael Price, at the negotiations. Colby and Stephens escaped on Dec. 9 and were recaptured. . . . In 1978, they, together with Price, beat another inmate to death with baseball bats. . . . Their commitment to a peaceful resolution of the riot was considered dubious. Later, they were identified as prime suspects in some of the [riot] killings. . . . At about 12:30 P.M., Colby, Stephens and other inmates rejoined the talks and started making new demands. . . . [Deputy Corrections Director Felix] Rodriguez says that at this point he began to worry that the Durans and Candelaria were losing control. He also began to wonder whether the majority of inmates inside were really aware of and had agreed to the five rather mild demands. (Serrill and Katel 1980:21)

Rodriguez, fearing that Colby and Stephens were gaining control of the situation, made a deal with them. He promised to transport them immediately to another prison out of state and told them to go back inside the prison to get their belongings. As soon as Colby and Stephens left, Rodriguez ordered Vincent Candelaria and Lonnie and Kendrick Duran (the inmates with whom he had been negotiating) to get the remaining two hostages, who were now seated blindfolded on the grass outside the main entrance. A few minutes later, at about 1:30 P.M., these last hostages were brought to Rodriguez. Immediately, police, National Guardsmen, and prison employees rushed the prison to retake it from the approximately 100 inmates still within. Authorities encountered no resistance from inmates during the retaking of the prison. No shots were fired. The riot was over.

Summary

The 1980 riot was a dramatic and explosive episode in a continuing pattern of disorder that had its roots several years earlier. Two things stand out as characteristics of the 1980 riot at PNM: the almost total lack of organization by inmates and the inmate-to-inmate violence that punctuated the event. The extreme violence was caused by a small number of inmates who belonged to some particularly violent inmate cliques. The emergence of these violent inmate cliques was largely an organizational phenomenon. They had their origin in the 1976 shift in tactics of inmate control, when measures, including the coercive snitch system, were used to undermine inmate solidarity. As inmate solidarity disintegrated, young prisoners began entering a social situation that elicited violence from a growing number of inmates. These social dynamics came together in the early morning hours of February 2, 1980, to produce the most horrific prison riot in history.

REFERENCES

Abbott, Jack Henry. 1981. *In the Belly of the Beast.* New York: Vintage.

Albuquerque Journal. 1979. "Prison Sexual Brutality Changes Inmate." Sept. 16, Sec. B, p. 1.

Colvin, Mark. 1992. *The Penitentiary in Crisis: From Accommodation to Riot in New Mexico.* Albany, NY: SUNY Press.

Department of Corrections. 1980. *Annual Report.* Santa Fe, NM: State of New Mexico.

———. 1976. *Annual Report.* Santa Fe, NM: State of New Mexico.

———. 1971. *Annual Report.* Santa Fe, NM: State of New Mexico.

Governor's Council on Criminal Justice Planning. 1978. "Technical Report 6: Inmate Profile." *Sourcebook for New Mexico Corrections Planning.* Santa Fe, NM: State of New Mexico.

Hagel-Seymour, John. 1988. "Environmental Sanctuaries for Susceptible Prisoners." Pp. 267–84 in *The Pains of Imprisonment,* edited by Robert Johnson and Hans Toch. Prospect Hills, IL: Waveland Press.

Irwin, John. 1980. *Prisons in Turmoil.* Boston, MA: Little, Brown.

Jacobs, James B. 1977. *Stateville: The Penitentiary in Mass Society.* Chicago, IL: University of Chicago Press.

Katz, Jack. 1988. *Seductions of Crime.* New York: Basic Books.

Office of the Attorney General. 1980a. *Report of the Attorney General on the February 2 and 3, 1980 Riot at the Penitentiary of New Mexico, Part I.* Santa Fe, NM: State of New Mexico.

———. 1980b. *Report of the Attorney General on the February 2 and 3 Riot at the Penitentiary of New Mexico, Part II.* Santa Fe, NM: State of New Mexico.

Serrill, Michael S. and Peter Katel. 1980. "New Mexico: The Anatomy of a Riot." *Corrections Magazine* 6(April):6–24.

Wicker, Tom. 1975. *A Time to Die.* New York: Ballantine.

19

ON BEING SANE IN INSANE PLACES

DAVID L. ROSENHAN

Sociologists have a long-standing interest in the study of social deviance, which is explored in the next four readings. *Deviance* is the recognized violation of social norms. As norms cover a wide range of human behavior, deviant acts are plentiful in any given society. Moreover, whether a person is labeled deviant depends on how others perceive, define, and respond to that person's behavior. In this selection, originally published in 1973, David L. Rosenhan explores the social deviance of mental illness and the consequences of labeling people "sane" or "insane." Rosenhan is currently professor emeritus of psychology and law at Stanford University.

If sanity and insanity exist . . . how shall we know them? The question is neither capricious nor itself insane. However much we may be personally convinced that we can tell the normal from the abnormal, the evidence is simply not compelling. It is commonplace, for example, to read about murder trials wherein eminent psychiatrists for the defense are contradicted by equally eminent psychiatrists for the prosecution on the matter of the defendant's sanity. More generally, there is a great deal of conflicting data on the reliability, utility, and meaning of such terms as *sanity, insanity, mental illness,* and *schizophrenia.*[1] Finally, as early as 1934, Benedict suggested that normality and abnormality are not universal.[2] What is viewed as normal in one culture may be seen as quite aberrant in another. Thus, notions of normality and abnormality may not be quite as accurate as people believe they are.

To raise questions regarding normality and abnormality is in no way to question the fact that some behaviors are deviant or odd. Murder is deviant. So, too, are hallucinations. Nor does raising such questions deny the existence of the personal anguish that is often associated with "mental illness."

Reading 19: Reprinted with permission from *Science,* 179: 250–58 (1973). Copyright © 1973 by the American Association for the Advancement of Science

Anxiety and depression exist. Psychological suffering exists. But normality and abnormality, sanity and insanity, and the diagnoses that flow from them may be less substantive than many believe them to be.

At its heart, the question of whether the sane can be distinguished from the insane (and whether degrees of insanity can be distinguished from each other) is a simple matter: Do the salient characteristics that lead to diagnoses reside in the patients themselves or in the environments and contexts in which observers find them? From Bleuler, through Kretchmer, through the formulations of the recently revised [1968] *Diagnostic and Statistical Manual* of the American Psychiatric Association, the belief has been strong that patients present symptoms, that those symptoms can be categorized, and, implicitly, that the sane are distinguishable from the insane. More recently, however, this belief has been questioned. Based in part on theoretical and anthropological considerations, but also on philosophical, legal, and therapeutic ones, the view has grown that psychological categorization of mental illness is useless at best and downright harmful, misleading, and pejorative at worst. Psychiatric diagnoses, in this view, are in the minds of the observers and are not valid summaries of characteristics displayed by the observed.[3, 4, 5]

Gains can be made in deciding which of these is more nearly accurate by getting normal people (that is, people who do not have, and have never suffered, symptoms of serious psychiatric disorders) admitted to psychiatric hospitals and then determining whether they were discovered to be sane and, if so, how. If the sanity of such pseudopatients were always detected, there would be *prima facie* evidence that a sane individual can be distinguished from the insane context in which he is found. Normality (and presumably abnormality) is distinct enough that it can be recognized wherever it occurs, for it is carried within the person. If, on the other hand, the sanity of the pseudopatients were never discovered, serious difficulties would arise for those who support traditional modes of psychiatric diagnosis. Given that the hospital staff was not incompetent, that the pseudopatient had been behaving as sanely as he had been outside of the hospital, and that it had never been previously suggested that he belonged in a psychiatric hospital, such an unlikely outcome would support the view that psychiatric diagnosis betrays little about the patient but much about the environment in which an observer finds him.

This article describes such an experiment. Eight sane people gained secret admission to twelve different hospitals.[6] Their diagnostic experiences constitute the data of the first part of this article; the remainder is devoted to a description of their experiences in psychiatric institutions. Too few psychiatrists and psychologists, even those who have worked in such hospitals, know what the experience is like. They rarely talk about it with former patients, perhaps because they distrust information coming from the previously insane. Those who have worked in psychiatric hospitals are likely to have adapted so thoroughly to the settings that they are insensitive to the impact of that experience. And while there have been occasional reports of researchers who submitted themselves to psychiatric hospitalization,[7] these researchers have commonly remained in the hospitals for short periods of time, often with the knowledge of the hospital staff. It is difficult to know the extent to which they were treated like patients or like research colleagues. Nevertheless, their reports about the inside of the psychiatric hospital have been valuable. This article extends those efforts.

Pseudopatients and Their Settings

The eight pseudopatients were a varied group. One was a psychology graduate student in his 20s. The remaining seven were older and "established." Among them were three psychologists, a pediatrician, a psychiatrist, a painter, and a housewife. Three pseudopatients were women, five were men. All of them employed pseudonyms, lest their alleged diagnoses embarrass them later. Those who were in mental health professions alleged another occupation in order to avoid the special attentions that might be accorded by staff, as a matter of courtesy or caution, to ailing colleagues.[8] With the exception of myself (I was the first pseudopatient and my presence was known to the hospital administrator and chief psychologist and, so far as I can tell, to them alone), the presence of pseudopatients and the nature of the research program were not known to the hospital staffs.[9]

The settings were similarly varied. In order to generalize the findings, admission into a variety of hospitals was sought. The 12 hospitals in the sample were located in five different states on the East and West coasts. Some were old and shabby, some were quite new. Some were research-oriented, others not. Some had good staff-patient ratios, others were quite understaffed. Only one was a strictly private hospital. All of the others were supported by state or federal funds or, in one instance, by university funds.

After calling the hospital for an appointment, the pseudopatient arrived at the admissions office complaining that he had been hearing voices. Asked what the voices said, he replied that they were often unclear, but as far as he could tell they said "empty," "hollow," and "thud." The voices were unfamiliar and were of the same sex as the pseudopatient. The choice of these symptoms was occasioned by their apparent similarity to existential symptoms. Such symptoms are alleged to arise from painful concerns about the perceived meaninglessness of one's life. It is as if the hallucinating person were saying, "My life is empty and hollow." The choice of these symptoms was also determined by the *absence* of a single report of existential psychoses in the literature.

Beyond alleging the symptoms and falsifying name, vocation, and employment, no further alterations of person, history, or circumstances were made. The significant events of the pseudopatient's life history were presented as they had actually occurred. Relationships with parents and siblings, with spouse and children, with people at work and in school, consistent with the aforementioned exceptions, were described as they were or had been. Frustrations and upsets were described along with joys and satisfactions. These facts are important to remember. If anything, they strongly biased the subsequent results in favor of detecting sanity, since none of their histories or current behaviors were seriously pathological in any way.

Immediately upon admission to the psychiatric ward, the pseudopatient ceased simulating *any* symptoms of abnormality. In some cases, there was a brief period of mild nervousness and anxiety, since none of the pseudopatients really believed that they would be admitted so easily. Indeed, their shared fear was that they would be immediately exposed as frauds and greatly embarrassed. Moreover, many of them had never visited a psychiatric ward; even those who had, nevertheless had some genuine fears about what might happen to them. Their nervousness, then, was quite appropriate to the novelty of the hospital setting, and it abated rapidly.

Apart from that short-lived nervousness, the pseudopatient behaved on the ward as he "normally" behaved. The pseudopatient spoke to patients and staff as he might ordinarily. Because there is uncommonly little to do on a psychiatric ward, he attempted to engage others in conversation. When asked by the staff how he was feeling, he indicated that he was fine, that he no longer experienced symptoms. He responded to instructions from attendants, to calls for medication (which was not swallowed), and to dining-hall instructions. Beyond such activities as were available to him on the admissions ward, he spent his time writing down his observations about the ward, its patients, and the staff. Initially these notes were written "secretly," but as it soon became clear that no one much cared, they were subsequently written on standard tablets of paper in such public places as the dayroom. No secret was made of these activities.

The pseudopatient, very much as a true psychiatric patient, entered a hospital with no foreknowledge of when he would be discharged. Each was told that he would have to get out by his own devices, essentially by convincing the staff that he was sane. The psychological stresses associated with hospitalization were considerable, and all but one of the pseudopatients desired to be discharged almost immediately after being admitted. They were, therefore, motivated not only to behave sanely, but to be paragons of cooperation. That their behavior was in no way disruptive is confirmed by nursing reports, which have been obtained on most of the patients. These reports uniformly indicate that the patients were "friendly," "cooperative," and "exhibited no abnormal indications."

The Normal Are Not Detectably Sane

Despite their public "show" of sanity, the pseudopatients were never detected. Admitted, except in one case, with a diagnosis of schizophrenia,[10] each was discharged with a diagnosis of schizophrenia "in remission." The label "in remission" should in no way be dismissed as a formality, for at no time during any hospitalization had any question been raised about any pseudo-patient's simulation. Nor are there any indications in the hospital records that the pseudopatient's status was suspect. Rather, the evidence is strong that, once labeled schizophrenic, the pseudopatient was stuck with that label. If the pseudopatient was to be discharged, he must naturally be "in remission"; but he was not sane, nor, in the institution's view, had he ever been sane.

The uniform failure to recognize sanity cannot be attributed to the quality of the hospitals, for, although there were considerable variations among them, several are considered excellent. Nor can it be alleged that there was simply not enough time to observe the pseudopatients. Length of hospitalization ranged from 7 to 52 days, with an average of 19 days. The pseudopatients were not, in fact, carefully observed, but this failure clearly speaks more to the traditions within psychiatric hospitals than to lack of opportunity.

Finally, it cannot be said that the failure to recognize the pseudopatients' sanity was due to the fact that they were not behaving sanely. While there was clearly some tension present in all of them, their daily visitors could detect no serious behavioral consequences—nor, indeed, could other patients. It was quite common for the patients to "detect" the pseudopatients' sanity. During the first three hospitalizations, when accurate counts were kept, 35 of a total of 118 patients on the admissions ward voiced their suspicions, some vigorously. "You're not crazy. You're a journalist, or a professor [referring to the continual note-taking]. You're checking up on the hospital." While most of the patients were reassured by the pseudopatient's insistence that he had been sick before he came in but was fine now, some continued to believe that the pseudopatient was sane throughout his hospitalization.[11] The fact that the patients often recognized normality when staff did not raises important questions.

Failure to detect sanity during the course of hospitalization may be due to the fact that physicians operate with a strong bias toward what statisticians call the type 2 error.[12] This is to say that physicians are more inclined to call a healthy person sick (a false positive, type 2) than a sick person healthy (a false negative, type 1). The reasons for this are not hard to find: It is clearly more dangerous to misdiagnose illness than health. Better to err on the side of caution, to suspect illness even among the healthy.

But what holds for medicine does not hold equally well for psychiatry. Medical illnesses, while unfortunate, are not commonly pejorative. Psychiatric diagnoses, on the contrary, carry with them personal, legal, and social stigmas.[13] It was therefore important to see whether the tendency toward diagnosing the sane insane could be reversed. The following experiment was arranged at a research and teaching hospital whose staff had heard these findings but doubted that such an error could occur in their hospital. The staff was informed that at some time during the following three months, one or more pseudopatients would attempt to be admitted into the psychiatric hospital. Each staff member was asked to rate each patient who presented himself at admissions or on the ward according to the likelihood that the patient was a pseudopatient. A 10-point scale was used, with a 1 and 2 reflecting high confidence that the patient was a pseudopatient.

Judgments were obtained on 193 patients who were admitted for psychiatric treatment. All staff who had had sustained contact with or primary responsibility for the patient—attendants, nurses, psychiatrists, physicians, and psychologists—were asked to make judgments. Forty-one patients were alleged, with high confidence, to be pseudopatients by at least one member of the staff. Twenty-three were considered suspect by at least one psychiatrist. Nineteen were suspected by one psychiatrist and one other staff member. Actually, no genuine pseudopatient (at least from my group) presented himself during this period.

The experiment is instructive. It indicates that the tendency to designate sane people as insane can be reversed when the stakes (in this case, prestige and diagnostic acumen) are high. But what can be said of the 19 people who were suspected of being "sane" by one psychiatrist and another staff member? Were these people truly "sane," or was it rather the case that in the course of avoiding the type 2 error the staff tended to make more errors of the first sort—calling the crazy "sane"? There is no way of knowing. But one thing is certain: Any diagnostic process that lends itself so readily to massive errors of this sort cannot be a very reliable one.

The Stickiness of Psychodiagnostic Labels

Beyond the tendency to call the healthy sick—a tendency that accounts better for diagnostic behavior on admission than it does for such behavior after a lengthy period of exposure—the data speak to the massive role of labeling in psychiatric assessment. Having once been labeled schizophrenic, there is nothing the pseudopatient can do to overcome the tag. The tag profoundly colors others' perceptions of him and his behavior.

From one viewpoint, these data are hardly surprising, for it has long been known that elements are given meaning by the context in which they occur. Gestalt psychology made this point vigorously, and Asch[14] demonstrated that there are "central" personality traits (such as "warm" versus "cold") which are so powerful that they markedly color the meaning of other information in forming an impression of a given personality.[15] "Insane," "schizophrenic," "manic-depressive," and "crazy" are probably among the most powerful of such central traits. Once a person is designated abnormal, all of his other behaviors and characteristics are colored by that label. Indeed, that label is so powerful that many of the pseudopatients' normal behaviors were overlooked entirely or profoundly misinterpreted. Some examples may clarify this issue.

Earlier I indicated that there were no changes in the pseudopatient's personal history and current status beyond those of name, employment, and, where necessary, vocation. Otherwise, a veridical description of personal history and circumstances was offered. Those circumstances were not psychotic. How were they made consonant with the diagnosis of psychosis? Or were those diagnoses modified in such a way as to bring them into accord with the circumstances of the pseudopatient's life, as described by him?

As far as I can determine, diagnoses were in no way affected by the relative health of the circumstances of a pseudopatient's life. Rather, the reverse occurred: The perception of his circumstances was shaped entirely by the diagnosis. A clear example of such translation is found in the case of a pseudopatient who had had a close relationship with his mother but was rather remote from his father during his early childhood. During adolescence and beyond, however, his father became a close friend, while his relationship with his mother cooled. His present relationship with his wife was characteristically close and warm. Apart from occasional angry exchanges, friction was minimal. The children had rarely been spanked. Surely there is nothing especially pathological about such a history. Indeed, many readers may see a similar pattern in their own experiences, with no markedly deleterious consequences. Observe, however, how such a history was translated in the psychopathological context, this from the case summary prepared after the patient was discharged.

> This white 39-year-old male . . . manifests a long history of considerable ambivalence in close relationships, which begins in early childhood. A warm relationship with his mother cools during adolescence. A distant relationship to his father is described as becoming very intense. Affective stability is absent. His attempts to control emotionality with his wife and children are punctuated by angry outbursts and, in the case of the children, spankings. And while he says that he has several good friends, one senses considerable ambivalence embedded in those relationships also.

The facts of the case were unintentionally distorted by the staff to achieve consistency with a popular theory of the dynamics of schizophrenic reaction.[16] Nothing of an ambivalent nature had been described in relations with parents, spouse, or friends. To the extent that ambivalence could be inferred, it was probably not greater than is found in all human relationships. It is true the pseudopatient's relationships with his parents changed over time, but in the ordinary context that would hardly be remarkable—indeed, it might very well be expected. Clearly, the meaning ascribed to his verbalizations (that is, ambivalence, affective instability) was determined by the diagnosis: schizophrenia. An entirely different meaning would have been ascribed if it were known that the man was "normal."

All pseudopatients took extensive notes publicly. Under ordinary circumstances, such behavior would have raised questions in the minds of observers, as, in fact, it did among patients. Indeed, it seemed so certain that the notes would elicit suspicion that elaborate precautions were taken to remove them from the ward each day. But the precautions proved needless. The closest any staff member came to questioning these notes occurred when one pseudopatient asked his physician what kind of medication he was receiving and began to write down the response. "You needn't write it," he was told gently. "If you have trouble remembering, just ask me again."

If no questions were asked of the pseudopatients, how was their writing interpreted? Nursing records for three patients indicate that the writing was seen as an aspect of their pathological behavior. "Patient engages in writing behavior" was the daily nursing comment on one of the pseudopatients who was never questioned about his writing. Given that the patient is in the hospital, he must be psychologically disturbed. And given that he is disturbed, continuous writing must be a behavioral manifestation of that disturbance, perhaps a subset of the compulsive behaviors that are sometimes correlated with schizophrenia.

One tacit characteristic of psychiatric diagnosis is that it locates the sources of aberration within the individual and only rarely within the complex of stimuli that surrounds him. Consequently, behaviors that are stimulated by the environment are commonly misattributed to the patient's disorder. For example, one kindly nurse found a pseudopatient pacing the long hospital corridors. "Nervous, Mr. X?" she asked. "No, bored," he said.

The notes kept by pseudopatients are full of patient behaviors that were misinterpreted by well-intentioned staff. Often enough, a patient would go "berserk" because he had, wittingly or unwittingly, been mistreated by, say, an attendant. A nurse coming upon the scene would rarely inquire even cursorily into the environmental stimuli of the patient's behavior. Rather, she assumed that his upset derived from his pathology, not from his present interactions with other staff members. Occasionally, the staff might assume that the patient's family (especially when they had recently visited) or other patients had stimulated the outburst. But never were the staff found to assume that one of themselves or the structure of the hospital had anything to do with a patient's behavior. One psychiatrist pointed to a group of patients who were sitting outside the cafeteria entrance half an hour before lunchtime. To a group of young residents he indicated that such behavior was characteristic of the oral-acquisitive nature of the syndrome. It seemed not to occur to him that there were very few things to anticipate in the psychiatric hospital besides eating.

A psychiatric label has a life and an influence of its own. Once the impression has been formed that the patient is schizophrenic, the expectation is that he will continue to be schizophrenic. When a sufficient amount of time has passed, during which the patient has done nothing bizarre, he is considered to be in remission and available for discharge. But the label endures beyond discharge, with the unconfirmed expectation that he will behave as a schizophrenic again. Such labels, conferred by mental health professionals, are as influential on the patient as they are on his relatives and friends, and it should not surprise anyone that the diagnosis acts on all of them as a self-fulfilling prophecy. Eventually, the patient himself accepts the diagnosis, with all of its surplus meanings and expectations, and behaves accordingly.[17]

The inferences to be made from these matters are quite simple. Much as Zigler and Phillips have demonstrated that there is enormous overlap in the symptoms presented by patients who have been variously diagnosed,[18] so there is enormous overlap in the behaviors of the sane and the insane. The sane are not "sane" all of the time. We lose our tempers "for no good reason." We are occasionally depressed or anxious, again for no good reason. And we may find it difficult to get along with one or another person—again for no reason that we can specify. Similarly, the insane are not always insane. Indeed, it was the impression of the pseudopatients while living with them that they were sane for long periods of time—that the bizarre behaviors upon which their diagnoses were allegedly predicated constituted only a small fraction of their total behavior. If it makes no sense to label ourselves permanently depressed on the basis of an occasional depression, then it takes evidence that is presently available to label all patients insane or schizophrenic on the basis of bizarre behaviors or cognitions. It seems more useful, as Mischel[19] has pointed out, to limit our discussions to *behaviors,* the stimuli that provoke them, and their correlates.

It is not known why powerful impressions of personality traits, such as "crazy" or "insane," arise. Conceivably, when the origins of and stimuli that give rise to a behavior are remote or unknown, or when the behavior strikes us as immutable, trait labels regarding the *behavior* arise. When, on the other hand, the origins and stimuli are known and available, discourse is limited to the behavior itself. Thus, I may hallucinate because I am sleeping, or I may hallucinate because I have ingested a peculiar drug. These are termed sleep-induced hallucinations, or dreams, and drug-induced hallucinations, respectively. But when the stimuli to my hallucinations are unknown, that is called craziness, or schizophrenia—as if that inference were somehow as illuminating as the others.

The Consequences of Labeling and Depersonalization

Whenever the ratio of what is known to what needs to be known approaches zero, we tend to invent "knowledge" and assume that we understand more than we actually do. We seem unable to acknowledge that we simply don't know. The needs for diagnosis and remediation of behavioral and emotional problems are enormous. But rather than acknowledge that we are just embarking on understanding, we continue to label patients "schizophrenic," "manic-depressive," and "insane," as if in those words we had captured the essence of understanding. The facts of the matter are that we have known for a long time that diagnoses are often not useful or reliable, but we have nevertheless continued to use them. We now know that we cannot distinguish insanity from sanity. It is depressing to consider how that information will be used.

Not merely depressing, but frightening. How many people, one wonders, are sane but not recognized as such in our psychiatric institutions? How many have been needlessly stripped of their privileges of citizenship, from the right to vote and drive to that of handling their own accounts? How many have feigned insanity in order to avoid the criminal consequences of their behavior, and conversely, how many would rather stand trial than live interminably in a psychiatric hospital—but are wrongly thought to be mentally ill? How many have been stigmatized by well-intentioned, but nevertheless erroneous, diagnoses? On the last point, recall again that a "type 2 error" in psychiatric diagnosis does not have the same consequences it does in medical diagnosis. A diagnosis of cancer that has been found to be in error is cause for celebration. But psychiatric diagnoses are rarely found to be in error. The label sticks, a mark of inadequacy forever.

ENDNOTES

[1] P. Ash, *Journal of Abnormal and Social Psychology* 44 (1949): 272; A. T. Beck, *American Journal of Psychiatry* 119 (1962): 210; A. T. Boisen, *Psychiatry* 2 (1938): 233; J. Kreitman, *Journal of Mental Science* 107 (1961): 876; N. Kreitman, P. Sainsbury, J. Morrisey, J. Towers, and J. Scrivener, *Journal of Mental Science* 107 (1961): 887; H. O. Schmitt and C. P. Fonda, *Journal of Abnormal Social Psychology* 52 (1956): 262; W. Seeman, *Journal of Nervous Mental Disorders* 118 (1953): 541. For analysis of these artifacts and summaries of the disputes, see J. Zubin, *Annual Review of Psychology* 18 (1967): 373; L. Phillips and J. G. Draguns, *Annual Review of Psychology* 22 (1971): 447.

[2] R. Benedict, *Journal of General Psychology* 10 (1934): 59.

[3] See in this regard Howard Becker, *Outsiders: Studies in the Sociology of Deviance* (New York: Free Press, 1963); B. M. Braginsky, D. D. Braginsky, and K. Ring, *Methods of Madness: The Mental Hospital As a Last Resort* (New York: Holt, Rinehart and Winston, 1969); G. M. Crocetti and P. V. Lemkau, *American Sociological Review* 30 (1965): 577; Erving Goffman, *Behavior in Public Places* (New York: Free Press, 1964); R. D. Laing, *The Divided Self: A Study of Sanity and Madness* (Chicago: Quadrangle, 1960); D. L. Phillips, *American Sociological Review* 28 (1963): 963; T. R. Sarbin, *Psychology Today* 6 (1972): 18; E. Schur, *American Journal of Sociology* 75 (1969): 309; Thomas Szasz, *The Myth of Mental Illness: Foundations of a Theory of Mental Illness* (New York: Hoeber Harper, 1963). For a critique of some of these views, see W. R. Gave, *American Sociological Review* 35 (1970): 873.

[4] Erving Goffman, *Asylums* (Garden City, NY: Doubleday, 1961).

[5] T. J. Scheff, *Being Mentally Ill: A Sociological Theory* (Chicago: Aldine, 1966).

[6] Data from a ninth pseudopatient are not incorporated in this report because, although his sanity went undetected, he falsified aspects of his personal history, including his marital status and parental relationships. His experimental behaviors therefore were not identical to those of the other pseudopatients.

[7] A. Barry, *Bellevue Is a State of Mind* (New York: Harcourt Brace Jovanovich, 1971); I. Belknap, *Human Problems of a State Mental Hospital* (New York: McGraw-Hill, 1956);

W. Caudill, F. C. Redlich, H. R. Gilmore, and E. B. Brody, *American Journal of Orthopsychiatry* 22 (1952): 314; A. R. Goldman, R. H. Bohr, and T. A. Steinberg, *Professional Psychology* 1 (1970): 427; *Roche Report* 1, no. 13 (1971): 8.

[8] Beyond the personal difficulties that the pseudopatient is likely to experience in the hospital, there are legal and social ones that, combined, require considerable attention before entry. For example, once admitted to a psychiatric institution, it is difficult, if not impossible, to be discharged on short notice, state law to the contrary notwithstanding. I was not sensitive to these difficulties at the outset of the project, nor to the personal and situational emergencies that can arise, but later a writ of habeas corpus was prepared for each of the entering pseudopatients and an attorney was kept "on call" during every hospitalization. I am grateful to John Kaplan and Robert Bartels for legal advice and assistance in these matters.

[9] However distasteful such concealment is, it was a necessary first step to examining these questions. Without concealment, there would have been no way to know how valid these experiences were; nor was there any way of knowing whether whatever detections occurred were a tribute to the diagnostic acumen of the staff or to the hospital's rumor network. Obviously, since my concerns are general ones that cut across individual hospitals and staffs, I have respected their anonymity and have eliminated clues that might lead to their identification.

[10] Interestingly, of the 12 admissions, 11 were diagnosed as schizophrenic and one, with the identical symptomatology, as manic-depressive psychosis. This diagnosis has a more favorable prognosis, and it was given by the only private hospital in our sample. On the relations between social class and psychiatric diagnosis, see A. B. Hollinghead and F. C. Redlich, *Social Class and Mental Illness: A Community Study* (New York: Wiley, 1958).

[11] It is possible, of course, that patients have quite broad latitudes in diagnosis and therefore are inclined to call many people sane, even those whose behavior is patently aberrant. However, although we have no hard data on this matter, it was our distinct impression that this was not the case. In many instances, patients not only singled us out for attention, but came to imitate our behaviors and styles.

[12] Scheff, *Being Mentally Ill.*

[13] J. Cumming and E. Cumming, *Community Mental Health* 1 (1965): 135; A. Farina and K. Ring, *Journal of Abnormal Psychology* 40 (1965): 47; H. E. Freeman and O. G. Simmons, *The Mental Patient Comes Home* (New York: Wiley, 1963); W. J. Johannsen, *Mental Hygiene* 53 (1969): 218; A. S. Linsky, *Social Psychology* 5 (1970): 166.

[14] S. E. Asch, *Abnormal Social Psychology* 41 (1946): 258; S. E. Asch, *Social Psychology* (New York: Prentice-Hall, 1952).

[15] See also I. N. Mensch and J. Wishner, *Journal of Personality* 16 (1947): 188; J. Wishner, *Psychological Review* 67 (1960): 96; J. S. Bruner and K. R. Tagiuri in *Handbook of Social Psychology*, vol. 2, ed. G. Lindzey (Cambridge, MA: Addison-Wesley, 1954), pp. 634–54; J. S. Bruner, D. Shapiro, and R. Tagiuri in *Person Perception and Interpersonal Behavior*, ed. R. Tagiuri and L. Petrullo (Stanford, CA: Stanford University Press, 1958), pp. 277–88.

[16] For an example of a similar self-fulfilling prophecy, in this instance dealing with the "central" trait of intelligence, see R. Rosenthal and L. Jacobson, *Pygmalion in the Classroom* (New York: Holt, Rinehart and Winston, 1968).

[17] Scheff, *Being Mentally Ill.*

[18] E. Zigler and L. Phillips, *Journal of Abnormal and Social Psychology* 63 (1961): 69. See also R. K. Freudenberg and J. P. Robertson, *A.M.A. Archives of Neurological Psychiatry* 76 (1956): 14.

[19] W. Mischel, *Personality and Assessment* (New York: Wiley, 1968).

20

ANOREXIA NERVOSA AND BULIMIA
The Development of Deviant Identities

PENELOPE A. McLORG • DIANE E. TAUB

Symbolic interactionists claim that deviance is relative depending on the situation and who is perceiving the act of deviance. Thus, according to *labeling theory,* people label certain acts as deviant and others as normal. This reading by Penelope McLorg and Diane Taub, both professors at Southern Illinois University at Carbondale, further illustrates this subjective process of deviance identification. In the reading below, originally published in 1987, McLorg and Taub employ labeling theory to explain how eating disorders have become defined as deviant behaviors and how some young women acquire deviant identities by modifying their self-concepts to conform to the societal labels of a person with an eating disorder.

Introduction

Current appearance norms stipulate thinness for women and muscularity for men; these expectations, like any norms, entail rewards for compliance and negative sanctions for violations. Fear of being overweight—of being visually deviant—has led to a striving for thinness, especially among women. In the extreme, this avoidance of overweight engenders eating disorders, which themselves constitute deviance. Anorexia nervosa, or purposeful starvation, embodies visual as well as behavioral deviation; bulimia, binge-eating followed by vomiting and/or laxative abuse, is primarily behaviorally deviant.

Besides a fear of fatness, anorexics and bulimics exhibit distorted body images. In anorexia nervosa, a 20–25 percent loss of initial body weight occurs, resulting from self-starvation alone or in combination with excessive exercising, occasional binge-eating, vomiting and/or laxative abuse. Bulimia denotes cyclical (daily, weekly, for example) binge-eating followed by vomiting or laxative abuse; weight is normal or close to normal (Humphries, Wrobel, and Weigert 1982). Common physical manifestations of these eating disorders include menstrual cessation or irregularities and electrolyte imbalances; among behavioral traits are depression, obsessions/compulsions, and anxiety (Russell 1979; Thompson and Schwartz 1982).

Increasingly prevalent in the past two decades, anorexia nervosa and bulimia have emerged as major health and social problems. Termed an epidemic on college campuses (Brody, as quoted in Schur 1984:76), bulimia affects 13 percent of college students (Halmi, Falk, and Schwartz 1981). Less prevalent, anorexia nervosa was diagnosed in 0.6 percent of students utilizing a university health center (Stangler and Printz 1980). However, the overall mortality rate of anorexia nervosa is 6 percent (Schwartz and Thompson 1981) to 20 percent (Humphries et al. 1982); bulimia appears to be less life-threatening (Russell 1979).

Particularly affecting certain demographic groups, eating disorders are most prevalent among young, white, affluent (upper-middle to upper class) women in modern, industrialized countries (Crisp 1977; Willi and Grossman 1983). Combining all of these risk factors (female sex, youth, high socioeconomic status, and residence in an industrialized country), prevalence of anorexia nervosa in upper-class English girls' schools is reported at 1 in 100 (Crisp, Palmer, and Kalucy 1976). The age of onset for anorexia nervosa is bimodal at 14.5 and 18 years (Humphries et al. 1982); the most frequent age of onset for bulimia is 18 (Russell 1979).

Eating disorders have primarily been studied from psychological and medical perspectives.[1] Theories of etiology have generally fallen into three categories: the ego psychological (involving an impaired child-maternal environment); the family systems (implicating enmeshed, rigid families); and the endocrinological (involving a precipitating hormonal defect). Although relatively ignored in previous studies, the sociocultural components of anorexia nervosa and bulimia (the slimness norm and its agents of reinforcement, such as role models) have been postulated as accounting for the recent, dramatic increases in these disorders (Boskind-White 1985; Schwartz, Thompson, and Johnson 1982).[2]

Medical and psychological approaches to anorexia nervosa and bulimia obscure the social facets of the disorders and neglect the individuals' own definitions of their situations. Among the social processes involved in the development of an eating disorder is the sequence of conforming behavior, primary deviance, and secondary deviance. Societal reaction is the critical mediator affecting the movement through the deviant career (Becker 1973). Within a framework of labeling theory, this study focuses on the emergence of anorexic and bulimic identities, as well as on the consequences of being career deviants.

Methodology

Sampling and Procedures

Most research on eating disorders has utilized clinical subjects or nonclinical respondents completing questionnaires. Such studies can be criticized for simply counting and describing behaviors and/or neglecting the social construction of the disorders. Moreover, the work of clinicians is often limited by therapeutic orientation. Previous research may also have included individuals who were not in therapy on their own volition and who resisted admitting that they had an eating disorder.

Past studies thus disregard the intersubjective meanings respondents attach to their behavior and emphasize researchers' criteria for definition as anorexic or bulimic. In order to supplement these sampling and procedural designs, the present study utilizes participant observation of a group of self-defined anorexics and bulimics.[3] As the individuals had acknowledged their eating disorders, frank discussion and disclosure were facilitated.

Data are derived from a self-help group, BANISH, Bulimics/Anorexics in Self-Help, which met at a university in an urban center of the mid-South. Founded by one of the researchers (D.E.T.), BANISH was advertised in local newspapers as offering a group experience for individuals who were anorexic or bulimic. Despite the local advertisements, the campus location of the meeting may have selectively encouraged university students to attend. Nonetheless, in view of the modal age of onset and socioeconomic status of individuals with eating disorders, college students have been considered target populations (Crisp et al. 1976; Halmi et al. 1981).

The group's weekly two-hour meetings were observed for two years. During the course of this study, 30 individuals attended at least one of the meetings. Attendance at meetings was varied: Ten individuals came nearly every Sunday; five attended approximately twice a month; and the remaining 15 participated once a month or less frequently, often when their eating problems were "more severe" or "bizarre." The modal number of members at meetings was 12. The diversity in attendance was to be expected in self-help groups of anorexics and bulimics:

> Most people's involvement will not be forever or even a long time. Most people get the support they need and drop out. Some take the time to help others after they themselves have been helped but even they may withdraw after a time. It is a natural and in many cases *necessary* process (emphasis in original). (American Anorexia and Bulimia Association 1983)

Modeled after Alcoholics Anonymous, BANISH allowed participants to discuss their backgrounds and experiences with others who empathized. For many members, the group constituted their only source of help; these respondents were reluctant to contact health professionals because of shame, embarrassment, or financial difficulties.

In addition to field notes from group meetings, records of other encounters with all members were maintained. Participants visited the office of one of the researchers (D.E.T.), called both researchers by phone, and invited them to their homes or out for a cup of coffee. Such interaction facilitated genuine communication and mutual trust. Even among the 15 individuals who did not attend the meetings regularly, contact was maintained with 10 members on a monthly basis.

Supplementing field notes were informal interviews with 15 group members, lasting from two to four hours. Because they appeared to represent more extensive experience with eating disorders, these interviewees were chosen to amplify their comments about the labeling process, made during group meetings. Conducted near the end of the two-year observation period, the interviews focused on what the respondents thought antedated and maintained their eating disorders. In addition, participants described others' reactions to their behaviors as well as their own interpretations of these reactions. To protect the confidentiality of individuals quoted in the study, pseudonyms are employed.

Description of Members

The demographic composite of the sample typifies what has been found in other studies (Crisp 1977; Fox and James 1976; Herzog 1982; Schlesier-Stropp 1984). Group members' ages ranged from 19 to 36, with the modal age being 21. The respondents were white, and all but one were female. The sole male and three of the females were anorexic; the remaining females were bulimic.[4]

Primarily composed of college students, the group included four nonstudents, three of whom had college degrees. Nearly all members derived from upper-middle- or lower-upper-class households. Eighteen students and two nonstudents were never married and uninvolved in serious relationships; two nonstudents were married (one with two children); two students were divorced (one with two children); and six students were involved in serious relationships. The duration of eating disorders ranged from 3 to 15 years.

Conforming Behavior

In the backgrounds of most anorexics and bulimics, dieting figures prominently, beginning in the teen years (Crisp 1977; Johnson, Stuckey, Lewis, and Schwartz 1982; Lacey, Coker, and Birtchnell 1986). As dieters, these individuals are conformist in their adherence to the cultural norms emphasizing thinness (Garner, Garfinkel, Schwartz, and Thompson 1980; Schwartz, Thompson, and Johnson 1982). In our society, slim bodies are regarded as the most worthy and attractive; overweight is viewed as physically and morally unhealthy—"obscene," "lazy," "slothful," and "gluttonous" (DeJong 1980; Ritenbaugh 1982; Schwartz et al. 1982).

Among the agents of socialization promoting the slimness norm is advertising. Female models in newspaper, magazine, and television advertisements are uniformly slender. In addition, product names and slogans exploit the thin orientation; examples include "Ultra Slim Lipstick," "Miller Lite," and "Virginia Slims." While retaining pressures toward thinness, an Ayds commercial attempts a compromise for those wanting to savor food: "Ayds . . . so you can taste, chew, and enjoy, while you lose weight." Appealing particularly to women, a nationwide fast-food restaurant chain offers low-calorie selections, so individuals can have a "license to eat." In the latter two examples, the notion of enjoying food is combined with the message to be slim. Food and restaurant advertisements overall convey the pleasures of eating, whereas advertisements for other products, such as fashions and diet aids, reinforce the idea that fatness is undesirable.

Emphasis on being slim affects everyone in our culture, but it influences women especially because of society's traditional emphasis on women's appearance. The slimness norm and its concomitant narrow beauty standards exacerbate the objectification of women (Schur 1984). Women view themselves as visual entities and recognize that conforming to appearance expectations and "becoming attractive object[s] [are] role obligation[s]" (Laws, as quoted in Schur 1984:66). Demonstrating the beauty motivation behind dieting, a Nielson survey indicated that of the 56 percent of all women aged 24 to 54 who dieted during the previous year, 76 percent did so for cosmetic, rather than health, reasons (Schwartz et al. 1982). For most female group members, dieting was viewed as a means of gaining attractiveness and appeal to the opposite sex. The male respondent, as well, indicated that "when I was fat, girls didn't look at me, but when I got thinner, I was suddenly popular."

In addition to responding to the specter of obesity, individuals who develop anorexia nervosa and bulimia are conformist in their strong commitment to other conventional norms and goals. They consistently excel at school and work (Bruch 1981; Humphries et al. 1982; Russell 1979), maintaining high aspirations in both areas (Lacey et al. 1986; Theander 1970). Group members generally completed college-preparatory courses in high school, aware from an early age that they would strive for a college degree. Also, in college as well as high school, respondents joined honor societies and academic clubs.

Moreover, pre-anorexics and -bulimics display notable conventionality as "model children" (Humphries et al. 1982:199), "the pride and joy" of their parents (Bruch 1981:215), accommodating themselves to the wishes of others. Parents of these individuals emphasize conformity and value achievement (Bruch 1981). Respondents felt that perfect or near-perfect grades were expected of them; however, good grades were not rewarded by parents, because "A's" were common for these children. In addition, their parents suppressed conflicts, to preserve the image of the "all-American family" (Humphries et al. 1982). Group members reported that they seldom, if ever, heard their parents argue or raise their voices.

Also conformist in their affective ties, individuals who develop anorexia nervosa and bulimia are strongly, even excessively, attached to their parents. Respondents' families appeared close-knit, demonstrating palpable emotional ties. Several group members, for example, reported habitually calling home at prescribed times, whether or not they had any news. Such families have been termed "enmeshed" and "overprotective," displaying intense interaction and concern for members' welfare (Minuchin, Rosman, and Baker 1978; Selvini-Palazzoli 1978). These qualities could be viewed as marked conformity to the norm of familial closeness.[5]

Another element of notable conformity in the family milieu of pre-anorexics and -bulimics concerns eating, body weight and shape, and exercising (Humphries et al. 1982; Kalucy, Crisp, and Harding 1977). Respondents reported their fathers' preoccupation with exercising and their mothers' engrossment in food preparation. When group members dieted and lost weight, they received an extraordinary amount of approval. Among the family, body size became a matter of "friendly rivalry." One bulimic informant recalled that she, her mother, and her coed sister all strived to wear a size 5, regardless of their heights and body frames. Subsequent to this study, the researchers learned that both the mother and sister had become bulimic.

As pre-anorexics and -bulimics, group members thus exhibited marked conformity to cultural norms of thinness, achievement, compliance, and parental attachment. Their families reinforced their conformity by adherence to norms of family closeness and weight and body shape consciousness.

Primary Deviance

Even with familial encouragement, respondents, like nearly all dieters (Chernin 1981), failed to maintain their lowered weights. Many cited their lack of willpower to eat only restricted foods. For the emerging anorexics and bulimics, extremes such as purposeful starvation or binging accompanied by vomiting and/or laxative abuse appeared as "obvious solutions" to the problem of retaining weight loss. Associated with these behaviors was a regained feeling of control in lives that had been disrupted by a major crisis. Group members' extreme weight-loss efforts operated as coping mechanisms for entering college, leaving home, or feeling rejected by the opposite sex.

The primary inducement for both eating adaptations was the drive for slimness: With slimness came more self-respect and a feeling of superiority over "unsuccessful dieters." Brian, for example, experienced a "power trip" upon consistent weight loss through starvation. Binges allowed the purging respondents to cope with stress through eating while maintaining a slim appearance. As former strict dieters, Teresa and Jennifer used binging and purging as an alternative to the constant self-denial of starvation. Acknowledging their parents' desires for them to be slim, most respondents still felt it was a conscious choice on their part to continue extreme weight-loss efforts. Being thin became the "most important thing" in their lives—their "greatest ambition."

In explaining the development of an anorexic or bulimic identity, Lemert's (1951, 1967) concept of primary deviance is salient. Primary deviance refers to a transitory period of norm violations which do not affect an individual's self-concept or performance of social roles. Although respondents were exhibiting anorexic or bulimic behavior, they did not consider themselves to be anorexic or bulimic.

At first, anorexics' significant others complimented their weight loss, expounding on their new "sleekness" and "good looks." Branch and Eurman (1980) also found anorexics' families and friends describing them as "well groomed," "neat," "fashionable," and "victorious" (p. 631). Not until the respondents approached emaciation did some parents or friends become concerned and withdraw their praise. Significant others also became increasingly aware of the anorexics' compulsive exercising, preoccupation with food preparation (but not consumption), and ritualistic eating patterns (such as cutting food into minute pieces and eating only certain foods at prescribed times).

For bulimics, friends or family members began to question how the respondents could eat such large amounts of food (often in excess of 10,000 calories a day) and stay slim. Significant others also noticed calluses across the bulimics' hands, which were caused by repeated inducement of vomiting. Several bulimics were "caught in the act," bent over commodes. Generally, friends and family required substantial evidence before believing that the respondents' binging or purging was no longer sporadic.

Secondary Deviance

Heightened awareness of group members' eating behavior ultimately led others to label the respondents "anorexic" or "bulimic." Respondents differed in their histories of being labeled and accepting the labels. Generally first termed anorexic by friends, family, or medical personnel, the anorexics initially vigorously denied the label. They felt they were not "anorexic enough," not skinny enough; Robin did not regard herself as having the "skeletal" appearance she associated with anorexia nervosa. These group members found it difficult to differentiate between socially approved modes of weight loss—eating less and exercising more—and the extremes of those behaviors. In fact, many of their activities—cheerleading, modeling, gymnastics, aerobics—reinforced their pursuit of thinness. Like other anorexics, Chris felt she was being "ultra-healthy," with "total control" over her body.

For several respondents, admitting they were anorexic followed the realization that their lives were disrupted by their eating disorder. Anorexics' inflexible eating patterns unsettled family meals and holiday gatherings.

Their regimented lifestyle of compulsively scheduled activities—exercising, school, and meals—precluded any spontaneous social interactions. Realization of their adverse behaviors preceded the anorexics' acknowledgment of their subnormal body weight and size.

Contrasting with anorexics, the binge/purgers, when confronted, more readily admitted that they were bulimic and that their means of weight loss was "abnormal." Teresa, for example, knew "very well" that her bulimic behavior was "wrong and unhealthy," although "worth the physical risks." While the bulimics initially maintained that their purging was only a temporary weight-loss method, they eventually realized that their disorder represented a "loss of control." Although these respondents regretted the self-indulgence, "shame," and "wasted time," they acknowledged their growing dependence on binging and purging for weight management and stress regulation.

The application of anorexic or bulimic labels precipitated secondary deviance, wherein group members internalized these identities. Secondary deviance refers to norm violations which are a response to society's labeling: "Secondary deviation . . . becomes a means of social defense, attack or adaptation to the overt and covert problems created by the societal reaction to primary deviance" (Lemert 1967:17). In contrast to primary deviance, secondary deviance is generally prolonged, alters the individual's self-concept, and affects the performance of his/her social roles.

As secondary deviants, respondents felt that their disorders "gave a purpose" to their lives. Nicole resisted attaining a normal weight because it was not "her"—she accepted her anorexic weight as her "true" weight. For Teresa, bulimia became a "companion"; and Julie felt "every aspect of her life," including time management and social activities, was affected by her bulimia. Group members' eating disorders became the salient element of their self-concepts so that they related to familiar people and new acquaintances as anorexics or bulimics. For example, respondents regularly compared their body shapes and sizes with those of others. They also became sensitized to comments about their appearance, whether or not the remarks were made by someone aware of their eating disorder.

With their behavior increasingly attuned to their eating disorders, group members exhibited role engulfment (Schur 1971). Through accepting anorexic or bulimic identities, individuals centered activities around their deviant role, downgrading other social roles. Their obligations as students, family members, and friends became subordinate to their eating and exercising rituals. Socializing, for example, was gradually curtailed because it interfered with compulsive exercising, binging, or purging.

Labeled anorexic or bulimic, respondents were ascribed a new status with a different set of role expectations. Regardless of other positions the individuals occupied, their deviant status, or master status (Becker 1973; Hughes 1958), was identified before all others. Among group members, Nicole, who was known as the "school's brain," became known as the "school's anorexic."

No longer viewed as conforming model individuals, some respondents were termed "starving waifs" or "pigs."

Because of their identities as deviants, anorexics' and bulimics' interactions with others were altered. Group members' eating habits were scrutinized by friends and family and used as a "catchall" for everything negative that happened to them. Respondents felt self-conscious around individuals who knew of their disorders; for example, Robin imagined people "watching and whispering" behind her. In addition, group members believed others expected them to "act" anorexic or bulimic. Friends of some anorexic group members never offered them food or drink, assuming continued disinterest on the respondents' part. While being hospitalized, Denise felt she had to prove to others she was not still vomiting, by keeping her bathroom door open. Other bulimics, who lived in dormitories, were hesitant to use the restroom for normal purposes lest several friends be huddling at the door, listening for vomiting. In general, individuals interacted with the respondents largely on the basis of their eating disorder; in doing so, they reinforced anorexic and bulimic behaviors.

Bulimic respondents, whose weight-loss behavior was not generally detectable from their appearance, tried earnestly to hide their bulimia by binging and purging in secret. Their main purpose in concealment was to avoid the negative consequences of being known as a bulimic. For these individuals, bulimia connoted a "cop-out": Like "weak anorexics," bulimics pursued thinness but yielded to urges to eat. Respondents felt other people regarded bulimia as "gross" and had little sympathy for the sufferer. To avoid these stigmas or "spoiled identities," the bulimics shrouded their behaviors.

Distinguishing types of stigma, Goffman (1963) describes discredited (visible) stigmas and discreditable (invisible) stigmas. Bulimics, whose weight was approximately normal or even slightly elevated, harbored discreditable stigmas. Anorexics, on the other hand, suffered both discreditable and discredited stigmas—the latter due to their emaciated appearance. Certain anorexics were more reconciled than the bulimics to their stigmas: For Brian, the "stigma of anorexia was better than being fat." Common to the stigmatized individuals was an inability to interact spontaneously with others. Respondents were constantly on guard against topics of eating and body size.

Both anorexics and bulimics were held responsible by others for their behavior and presumed able to "get out of it if they tried." Many anorexics reported being told to "just eat more," while bulimics were enjoined to simply "stop eating so much." Such appeals were made without regard for the complexities of the problem. Ostracized by certain friends and family members, anorexics and bulimics felt increasingly isolated. For respondents, the self-help group presented a nonthreatening forum for discussing their disorders. Here, they found mutual understanding, empathy, and support. Many participants viewed BANISH as a haven from stigmatization by "others."

Group members, as secondary deviants, thus endured negative consequences, such as stigmatization, from being labeled. As they internalized the labels anorexic or bulimic, individuals' self-concepts were significantly influenced. When others interacted with the respondents on the basis of their eating disorders, anorexic or bulimic identities were encouraged. Moreover, group members' efforts to counteract the deviant labels were thwarted by their master status.

Discussion

Previous research on eating disorders has dwelt almost exclusively on medical and psychological facets. Although necessary for a comprehensive understanding of anorexia nervosa and bulimia, these approaches neglect the social processes involved. The phenomena of eating disorders transcend concrete disease entities and clinical diagnoses. Multifaceted and complex, anorexia nervosa and bulimia require a holistic research design, in which sociological insights must be included.

A limitation of medical and psychiatric studies, in particular, is researchers' use of a priori criteria in establishing salient variables. Rather than utilizing predetermined standards of inclusion, the present study allows respondents to construct their own reality. Concomitant to this innovative approach to eating disorders is the selection of a sample of self-admitted anorexics and bulimics. Individuals' perceptions of what it means to become anorexic or bulimic are explored. Although based on a small sample, findings can be used to guide researchers in other settings.

With only 5 to 10 percent of reported cases appearing in males (Crisp 1977; Stangler and Printz 1980), eating disorders are primarily a women's aberrance. The deviance of anorexia nervosa and bulimia is rooted in the visual objectification of women and attendant slimness norm. Indeed, purposeful starvation and binging and purging reinforce the notion that "a society gets the deviance it deserves" (Schur 1979:71). As noted (Schur 1984), the sociology of deviance has generally bypassed systematic studies of women's norm violations. Like male deviants, females endure label applications, internalizations, and fulfillments.

The social processes involved in developing anorexic or bulimic identities comprise the sequence of conforming behavior, primary deviance, and secondary deviance. With a background of exceptional adherence to conventional norms, especially the striving for thinness, respondents subsequently exhibit the primary deviance of starving or binging and purging. Societal reaction to these behaviors leads to secondary deviance, wherein respondents' self-concepts and master statuses become anorexic or bulimic. Within this framework of labeling theory, the persistence of eating disorders, as well as the effects of stigmatization, are elucidated.

Although during the course of this research some respondents alleviated their symptoms through psychiatric help or hospital treatment programs, no one was labeled "cured." An anorexic is considered recovered when weight is normal for two years; a bulimic is termed recovered after being symptom-free for one and one-half years (American Anorexia and Bulimia Association Newsletter 1985). Thus deviance disavowal (Schur 1971), or efforts after normalization to counteract deviant labels, remains a topic for future exploration.

ENDNOTES

[1] Although instructive, an integration of the medical, psychological, and socio-cultural perspectives on eating disorders is beyond the scope of this paper.

[2] Exceptions to the neglect of sociocultural factors are discussions of sex-role socialization in the development of eating disorders. Anorexics' girlish appearance has been interpreted as a rejection of femininity and womanhood (Bruch 1981; Orbach 1979, 1985). In contrast, bulimics have been characterized as overconforming to traditional female sex roles (Boskind-Lodahl 1976).

[3] Although a group experience for self-defined bulimics has been reported (Boskind-Lodahl 1976), the researcher, from the outset, focused on Gestalt and behaviorist techniques within a feminist orientation.

[4] One explanation for fewer anorexics than bulimics in the sample is that, in the general population, anorexics are outnumbered by bulimics at 8 or 10 to 1 (Lawson, as reprinted in American Anorexia and Bulimia Association Newsletter 1985:1). The proportion of bulimics to anorexics in the sample is 6.5 to 1. In addition, compared to bulimics, anorexics may be less likely to attend a self-help group as they have a greater tendency to deny the existence of an eating problem (Humphries et al. 1982). However, the four anorexics in the present study were among the members who attended the meetings most often.

[5] Interactions in the families of anorexics and bulimics might seem deviant in being inordinately close. However, in the larger societal context, the family members epitomize the norms of family cohesiveness. Perhaps unusual in their occurrence, these families are still within the realm of conformity. Humphries and colleagues (1982) refer to the "highly enmeshed and protective" family as part of the "idealized family myth" (p. 202).

REFERENCES

American Anorexia / Bulimia Association. 1983, April. Correspondence.
American Anorexia / Bulimia Association Newsletter. 1985. 8(3).
Becker, Howard S. 1973. *Outsiders.* New York: Free Press.
Boskind-Lodahl, Marlene. 1976. "Cinderella's Stepsisters: A Feminist Perspective on Anorexia Nervosa and Bulimia." *Signs, Journal of Women in Culture and Society* 2:342–56.
Boskind-White, Marlene. 1985. "Bulimarexia: A Sociocultural Perspective." Pp. 113–26 in *Theory and Treatment of Anorexia Nervosa and Bulimia: Biomedical, Sociocultural and Psychological Perspectives,* edited by S. W. Emmett. New York: Brunner / Mazel.
Branch, C. H. Hardin and Linda J. Eurman. 1980. "Social Attitudes toward Patients with Anorexia Nervosa." *American Journal of Psychiatry* 137:631–32.
Bruch, Hilda. 1981. "Developmental Considerations of Anorexia Nervosa and Obesity." *Canadian Journal of Psychiatry* 26:212–16.
Chernin, Kim. 1981. *The Obsession: Reflections on the Tyranny of Slenderness.* New York: Harper & Row.
Crisp, A. H. 1977. "The Prevalence of Anorexia Nervosa and Some of Its Associations in the General Population." *Advances in Psychosomatic Medicine* 9:38–47.

Crisp, A. H., R. L. Palmer, and R. S. Kalucy. 1976. "How Common Is Anorexia Nervosa? A Prevalence Study." *British Journal of Psychiatry* 128:549–54.

DeJong, William. 1980. "The Stigma of Obesity: The Consequences of Naive Assumptions Concerning the Causes of Physical Deviance." *Journal of Health and Social Behavior* 21:75–87.

Fox, K. C. and N. McI. James. 1976. "Anorexia Nervosa: A Study of 44 Strictly Defined Cases." *New Zealand Medical Journal* 84:309–12.

Garner, David M., Paul E. Garfinkel, Donald Schwartz, and Michael Thompson. 1980. "Cultural Expectations of Thinness in Women." *Psychological Reports* 47:483–91.

Goffman, Erving. 1963. *Stigma.* Englewood Cliffs, NJ: Prentice-Hall.

Halmi, Katherine A., James R. Falk, and Estelle Schwartz. 1981. "Binge-Eating and Vomiting: A Survey of a College Population." *Psychological Medicine* 11:697–706.

Herzog, David B. 1982. "Bulimia: The Secretive Syndrome." *Psychosomatics* 23:481–83.

Hughes, Everett C. 1958. *Men and Their Work.* New York: Free Press.

Humphries, Laurie L., Sylvia Wrobel, and H. Thomas Wiegert. 1982. "Anorexia Nervosa." *American Family Physician* 26:199–204.

Johnson, Craig L., Marilyn K. Stuckey, Linda D. Lewis, and Donald M. Schwartz. 1982. "Bulimia: A Descriptive Survey of 316 Cases." *International Journal of Eating Disorders* 2(1):3–16.

Kalucy, R. S., A. H. Crisp, and Britta Harding. 1977. "A Study of 56 Families with Anorexia Nervosa." *British Journal of Medical Psychology* 50:381–95.

Lacey, Hubert J., Sian Coker, and S. A. Birtchnell. 1986. "Bulimia: Factors Associated with Its Etiology and Maintenance." *International Journal of Eating Disorders* 5:475–87.

Lemert, Edwin M. 1951. *Social Pathology.* New York: McGraw-Hill.

———. 1967. *Human Deviance, Social Problems and Social Control.* Englewood Cliffs, NJ: Prentice-Hall.

Minuchin, Salvador, Bernice L. Rosman, and Lester Baker. 1978. *Psychosomatic Families: Anorexia Nervosa in Context.* Cambridge, MA: Harvard University Press.

Orbach, Susie. 1979. *Fat Is a Feminist Issue.* New York: Berkeley.

———. 1985. "Visibility/Invisibility: Social Considerations in Anorexia Nervosa—a Feminist Perspective." Pp. 127–38 in *Theory and Treatment of Anorexia Nervosa and Bulimia: Biomedical, Sociocultural and Psychological Perspectives,* edited by S. W. Emmett. New York: Brunner/Mazel.

Ritenbaugh, Cheryl. 1982. "Obesity As a Culture-Bound Syndrome." *Culture, Medicine and Psychiatry* 6:347–61.

Russell, Gerald. 1979. "Bulimia Nervosa: An Ominous Variant of Anorexia Nervosa." *Psychological Medicine* 9:429–48.

Schlesier-Stropp, Barbara. 1984. "Bulimia: A Review of the Literature." *Psychological Bulletin* 95:247–57.

Schur, Edwin M. 1971. *Labeling Deviant Behavior.* New York: Harper & Row.

———. 1979. *Interpreting Deviance: A Sociological Introduction.* New York: Harper & Row.

———. 1984. *Labeling Women Deviant: Gender, Stigma, and Social Control.* New York: Random House.

Schwartz, Donald M. and Michael G. Thompson. 1981. "Do Anorectics Get Well? Current Research and Future Needs." *American Journal of Psychiatry* 138:319–23.

Schwartz, Donald M., Michael G. Thompson, and Craig L. Johnson. 1982. "Anorexia Nervosa and Bulimia: The Socio-Cultural Context." *International Journal of Eating Disorders* 1(3):20–36.

Selvini-Palazzoli, Mara. 1978. *Self-Starvation: From Individual to Family Therapy in the Treatment of Anorexia Nervosa.* New York: Jason Aronson.

Stangler, Ronnie S. and Adolph M. Printz. 1980. "DSM-III: Psychiatric Diagnosis in a University Population." *American Journal of Psychiatry* 137:937–40.

Theander, Sten. 1970. "Anorexia Nervosa." *Acta Psychiatrica Scandinavica Supplement* 214:24–31.

Thompson, Michael G. and Donald M. Schwartz. 1982. "Life Adjustment of Women with Anorexia Nervosa and Anorexic-like Behavior." *International Journal of Eating Disorders* 1(2):47–60.

Willi, Jurg and Samuel Grossman. 1983. "Epidemiology of Anorexia Nervosa in a Defined Region of Switzerland." *American Journal of Psychiatry* 140:564–67.

21

IN SEARCH OF RESPECT
Selling Crack in El Barrio

PHILIPPE BOURGOIS

One type of social deviance, according to sociologists, is crime. If deviance is the violation of a social norm, then a *crime* is the violation of social norms that have been made into laws. One type of crime that sociologists have long studied is illegal drug use. Why do segments of the population use and abuse illegal drugs? How can we explain the growing underground economy of illegal drugs? In this selection, taken from *In Search of Respect: Selling Crack in El Barrio* (1995), Philippe Bourgois takes us inside the crack economy in East Harlem, New York City. Bourgois, professor and chair of anthropology at the San Francisco Urban Institute, spent three and a half years living in "El Barrio," where he came to know the residents and their day-to-day struggles for economic survival. Bourgois' ethnographic account of life and social marginalization in this inner-city neighborhood reveals that many social factors lead people to deal illegal drugs and that other social barriers prevent them from reentering the legal economy.

I was forced into crack against my will. When I first moved to East Harlem—"El Barrio"—as a newlywed in the spring of 1985, I was looking for an inexpensive New York City apartment from which I could write about the experience of poverty and ethnic segregation in the heart of one of the most expensive cities in the world. I was interested in the political economy of inner-city street culture. I wanted to probe the Achilles' heel of the richest industrialized nation in the world by documenting how it imposes racial segregation and economic marginalization on so many of its Latino/a and African American citizens.

My original subject was the entire underground (untaxed) economy, from curbside car repairing and baby-sitting to unlicensed off-track betting and drug dealing. I had never even heard of crack when I first arrived in the neighborhood—no one knew about this particular substance yet, because this brittle compound of cocaine and baking soda processed into efficiently smokable pellets was not yet available as a mass-marketed product. By the end of the year, however, most of my friends, neighbors and acquaintances had been swept into the multibillion-dollar crack cyclone: selling it, smoking it, fretting over it. I followed them, and I watched the murder rate in the projects opposite my crumbling tenement apartment spiral into one of the highest in Manhattan.

But this essay is not about crack, or drugs, per se. Substance abuse in the inner city is merely a symptom—and a vivid symbol—of deeper dynamics of social marginalization and alienation. Of course, on an immediately visible personal level, addiction and substance abuse are among the most immediate, brutal facts shaping daily life on the street. Most important, however, the two dozen street dealers and their families that I befriended were not interested in talking primarily about drugs. On the contrary, they wanted me to learn all about their daily struggles for subsistence and dignity at the poverty line.

Through the 1980s and 1990s, slightly more than one in three families in El Barrio have received public assistance. Female heads of these impoverished households have to supplement their meager checks in order to keep their children alive. Many are mothers who make extra money by baby-sitting their neighbors' children, or by housekeeping for a paying boarder. Others may bartend at one of the half-dozen social clubs and after-hours dancing spots scattered throughout the neighborhood. Some work "off the books" in their living rooms as seamstresses for garment contractors. Finally, many also find themselves obliged to establish amorous relationships with men who are willing to make cash contributions to their household expenses.

Male income-generating strategies in the underground economy are more publicly visible. Some men repair cars on the curb; others wait on stoops for unlicensed construction subcontractors to pick them up for fly-by-night demolition jobs or window renovation projects. Many sell "numbers"—the street's version of off-track betting. The most visible cohorts hawk "nickels and dimes" of one illegal drug or another. They are part of the most robust, multibillion-dollar sector of the booming underground economy. Cocaine and crack, in particular during the mid-1980s and through the early 1990s, followed by heroin in the mid-1990s, have become the fastest-growing—if not the only—equal-opportunity employers of men in Harlem. Retail drug sales easily outcompete other income-generating opportunities, whether legal or illegal.

Why should these young men and women take the subway to work minimum-wage jobs—or even double-minimum-wage jobs—in downtown offices when they can usually earn more, at least in the short run, by selling drugs on the street corner in front of their apartment or schoolyard? In fact, I am always surprised that so many inner-city men and women remain in the legal economy and work nine-to-five plus overtime, barely making ends meet. According to the 1990 Census of East Harlem, 48 percent of all males and 35 percent of females over 16 were employed in officially reported jobs, compared with a citywide average of 64 percent for men and 49 percent for women. In the census tracts surrounding my apartment, 53 percent of all men over 16 years of age (1,923 out of 3,647) and 28 percent of all women over 16 (1,307 out of 4,626) were working legally in officially censused jobs. An additional 17 percent of the civilian labor force was unemployed but actively looking for work, compared with 16 percent for El Barrio as a whole, and 9 percent for all of New York City.

"If I Was Working Legal . . ."

Street dealers tend to brag to outsiders and to themselves about how much money they make each night. In fact, their income is almost never as consistently high as they report it to be. Most street sellers, like my friend Primo (who, along with other friends and co-workers, allowed me to tape hundreds of hours of conversation with him over five years), are paid on a piece-rate commission basis. When converted into an hourly wage, this is often a relatively paltry sum. According to my calculations, the workers in the Game Room crackhouse, for example, averaged slightly less than double the legal minimum wage—between seven and eight dollars an hour. There were plenty of exceptional nights, however, when they made up to ten times minimum wage—and these are the nights they remember when they reminisce. They forget about all the other shifts when they were unable to work because of police raids, and they certainly do not count as forfeited working hours the nights they spent in jail.

This was brought home to me symbolically one night as Primo and his co-worker Caesar were shutting down the Game Room. Caesar unscrewed the fuses in the electrical box to disconnect the video games. Primo had finished stashing the leftover bundles of crack vials inside a hollowed-out live electrical socket and was counting the night's thick wad of receipts. I was struck by how thin the handful of bills was that he separated out and folded neatly into his personal billfold. Primo and Caesar then eagerly lowered the iron riot gates over the Game Room's windows and snapped shut the heavy Yale padlocks. They were moving with the smooth, hurried gestures of workers preparing to go home after an honest day's hard labor. Marveling at the universality in the body language of workers rushing at closing time, I felt an urge to compare the wages paid by this alternative economy. I grabbed Primo's wallet out of his back pocket, carefully giving a wide berth to the fatter wad in his front pocket that represented Ray's share of the night's income—and that could cost Primo his life if it were waylaid. Unexpectedly, I pulled out fifteen dollars' worth of food stamps along with two $20 bills. After an embarrassed giggle, Primo stammered that his mother had added him to her food-stamp allotment.

> Primo: *I gave my girl, Maria, half of it. I said, "Here take it, use it if you need it for whatever." And then the other half I still got it in my wallet for emergencies.*
>
> *Like that, we always got a couple of dollars here and there, to survive with. Because tonight, straight cash, I only got garbage. Forty dollars! Do you believe that?*

At the same time that wages can be relatively low in the crack economy, working conditions are often inferior to those in the legal economy. Aside from the obvious dangers of being shot, or of going to prison, the physical work space of most crackhouses is usually unpleasant. The infrastructure of the Game Room, for example, was much worse than that of any legal retail outfit in East Harlem: There was no bathroom, no running water, no telephone, no heat in the winter and no air conditioning in the summer. Primo occasionally complained:

> *Everything that you see here* [sweeping his arm at the scratched and dented video games, the walls with peeling paint, the floor slippery with litter, the filthy windows pasted over with ripped movie posters] *is fucked up. It sucks, man* [pointing at the red 40-watt bare bulb hanging from an exposed fixture in the middle of the room and exuding a sickly twilight].

Indeed, the only furnishings besides the video games were a few grimy milk crates and bent aluminum stools. Worse yet, a smell of urine and vomit usually permeated the locale. For a few months Primo was able to maintain a rudimentary sound system, but it was eventually beaten to a pulp during one of Caesar's drunken rages. Of course, the deficient infrastructure was only one part of the depressing working conditions.

> Primo: *Plus I don't like to see people fucked up* [handing over three vials to a nervously pacing customer]. *This is fucked-up shit. I don't like this crack dealing. Word up.*
>
> [gunshots in the distance] *Hear that?*

In private, especially in the last few years of my residence, Primo admitted that he wanted to go back to the legal economy.

Primo: I just fuck up the money here. I rather be legal.

Philippe: But you wouldn't be the head man on the block with so many girlfriends.

Primo: I might have women on my dick right now but I would be much cooler if I was working legal. I wouldn't be drinking and the coke wouldn't be there every night.

  Plus if I was working legally I would have women on my dick too, because I would have money.

Philippe: But you make more money here than you could ever make working legit.

Primo: O.K. So you want the money but you really don't want to do the job.

  I really hate it, man. Hate it! I hate the people! I hate the environment! I hate the whole shit, man! But it's like you get caught up with it. You do it, and you say, "Ay, fuck it today!" Another day, another dollar. [pointing at an emaciated customer who was just entering] *But I don't really, really think that I would have hoped that I can say I'm gonna be richer one day. I can't say that. I think about it, but I'm just living day to day.*

  If I was working legal, I wouldn't be hanging out so much. I wouldn't be treating you. [pointing to the 16-ounce can of Colt 45 in my hand] *In a job, you know, my environment would change . . . totally. 'Cause I'd have different friends. Right after work I'd go out with a co-worker, for lunch, for dinner. After work I may go home; I'm too tired for hanging out—I know I gotta work tomorrow.*

  After working a legal job, I'm pretty sure I'd be good.

Burned in the FIRE Economy

The problem is that Primo's good intentions do not lead anywhere when the only legal jobs he can compete for fail to provide him with a livable wage. None of the crack dealers were explicitly conscious of the links between their limited options in the legal economy, their addiction to drugs, and their dependence on the crack economy for economic survival and personal dignity. Nevertheless, all of Primo's colleagues and employees told stories of rejecting what they considered to be intolerable working conditions at entry-level jobs.

Most entered the legal labor market at exceptionally young ages. By the time they were 12, they were bagging and delivering groceries at the supermarket for tips, stocking beer off the books in local bodegas, or running errands. Before reaching 21, however, virtually none had fulfilled their early childhood dreams of finding stable, well-paid legal work.

The problem is structural: From the 1950s through the 1980s, second-generation inner-city Puerto Ricans were trapped in the most vulnerable niche of a factory-based economy that was rapidly being replaced by service industries. Between 1950 and 1990, the proportion of factory jobs in New York City decreased approximately threefold at the same time that service-sector jobs doubled. The Department of City Planning calculates that more than 800,000 industrial jobs were lost from the 1960s through the early 1990s, while the total number of jobs in all categories remained more or less constant at 3.5 million.

Few scholars have noted the cultural dislocations of the new service economy. These cultural clashes have been most pronounced in the office-work service jobs that have multiplied because of the dramatic expansion of the finance, insurance and real estate (FIRE) sector in New York City. Service work in professional offices is the most dynamic place for ambitious inner-city youths to find entry-level jobs if they aspire to upward mobility. Employment as mailroom clerks, photocopiers, and messengers in the high-rise office corridors of the financial district propels many into a wrenching cultural confrontation with the upper-middle-class white world. Obedience to the norms of high-rise, office-corridor culture is in direct contradiction to street culture's definitions of personal dignity, especially for males who are socialized not to accept public subordination.

Most of the dealers have not completely withdrawn from the legal economy. On the contrary—they are precariously perched on its edge. Their poverty remains their only constant as they alternate between street-level crack dealing and just-above-minimum-wage legal employment. The working-class jobs they manage to find are objectively recognized to be among the least desirable in U.S. society; hence the following list of just a few of the jobs held by some of the Game Room regulars during the years I knew them: unlicensed asbestos remover, home attendant, street-corner flier distributor, deep-fat fry cook, and night-shift security guard on the violent ward at the municipal hospital for the criminally insane.

The stable factory-worker incomes that might have allowed Caesar and Primo to support families have largely disappeared from the inner city. Perhaps if their social network had not been confined to the weakest sector of manufacturing in a period of rapid job loss, their teenage working-class dreams might have stabilized them long enough to enable them to adapt to the restructuring of the local economy. Instead, they find themselves propelled headlong into an explosive confrontation between their sense of cultural dignity versus the humiliating interpersonal subordination of service work.

Workers like Caesar and Primo appear inarticulate to their professional supervisors when they try to imitate the language of power in the workplace; they stumble pathetically over the enunciation of unfamiliar words. They cannot decipher the hastily scribbled instructions—rife with mysterious abbreviations—that are left for them by harried office managers on diminutive Post-its. The "common sense" of white-collar work is foreign to them; they do not, for example, understand the logic in filing triplicate copies of memos or for postdating invoices. When they attempt to improvise or show initiative, they fail miserably and instead appear inefficient—or even hostile—for failing to follow "clearly specified" instructions.

In the high-rise office buildings of midtown Manhattan or Wall Street, newly employed inner-city high school dropouts suddenly realize they look like idiotic buffoons to the men and women for whom they work. But people like Primo and Caesar have not passively accepted their structural victimization. On the contrary, by embroiling themselves in the underground economy and proudly embracing street culture, they are seeking an alternative to their social marginalization. In the process, on a daily level, they become the actual agents administering their own destruction and their community's suffering.

Both Primo and Caesar experienced deep humiliation and insecurity in their attempts to penetrate the foreign, hostile world of high-rise office corridors. Primo had bitter memories of being the mailroom clerk and errand boy at a now-defunct professional trade magazine. The only time he explicitly admitted to having experienced racism was when he described how he was treated at that particular work setting.

> *Primo: I had a prejudiced boss. . . . When she was talking to people she would say, "He's illiterate," as if I was really that stupid that I couldn't understand what she was talking about.*
>
> *So what I did one day—you see they had this big dictionary right there on the desk, a big heavy motherfucker—so what I just did was open up the dictionary, and I just looked up the word, "illiterate." And that's when I saw what she was calling me.*
>
> *So she's saying that I'm stupid or something. I'm stupid!* [pointing to himself with both thumbs and making a hulking face] *"She doesn't know shit."*

In contrast, in the underground economy Primo never had to risk this kind of threat to his self-worth.

> *Primo: Ray would never disrespect me that way; he wouldn't tell me that because he's illiterate too, plus I've got more education than him. I almost got a G.E.D.*

The contemporary street sensitivity to being dissed immediately emerges in these memories of office humiliation. The machismo of street culture exacerbates the sense of insult experienced by men because the majority of office supervisors at the entry level are women. In the lowest recesses of

New York City's FIRE sector, tens of thousands of messengers, photocopy machine operators, and security guards serving the Fortune 500 companies are brusquely ordered about by young white executives—often female—who sometimes make bimonthly salaries superior to their underlings' yearly wages. The extraordinary wealth of Manhattan's financial district exacerbates the sense of sexist-racist insult associated with performing just-above-minimum-wage labor.

"I Don't Even Got a Dress Shirt"

Several months earlier, I had watched Primo drop out of a "motivational training" employment program in the basement of his mother's housing project, run by former heroin addicts who had just received a multimillion-dollar private sector grant for their innovative approach to training the "unemployable." Primo felt profoundly disrespected by the program, and he focused his discontent on the humiliation he faced because of his inappropriate wardrobe. The fundamental philosophy of such motivational job-training programs is that "these people have an attitude problem." They take a boot-camp approach to their unemployed clients, ripping their self-esteem apart during the first week in order to build them back up with an epiphanic realization that they want to find jobs as security guards, messengers, and data-input clerks in just-above-minimum-wage service-sector positions. The program's highest success rate had been with middle-aged African American women who wanted to terminate their relationship to welfare once their children leave home.

I originally had a "bad attitude" toward the premise of psychologically motivating and manipulating people to accept boring, poorly paid jobs. At the same time, however, the violence and self-destruction I was witnessing at the Game Room were convincing me that it is better to be exploited at work than to be outside the legal labor market. In any case, I persuaded Primo and a half-dozen of his Game Room associates to sign up for the program. Even Caesar was tempted to join.

None of the crack dealers lasted for more than three sessions. Primo was the first to drop out, after the first day. For several weeks he avoided talking about the experience. I repeatedly pressed him to explain why he "just didn't show up" at the sessions. Only after repeated badgering on my part did he finally express the deep sense of shame and vulnerability he experienced whenever he attempted to venture into the legal labor market.

Philippe: Yo, Primo, listen to me. I worry that there's something taking place that you're not aware of, in terms of yourself. Like the coke that you be sniffing all the time; it's like every night.

Primo: What do you mean?

Philippe: Like not showing up at the job training. You say it's just procrastination, but I'm scared it's something deeper that you're not dealing with. Like wanting to be partying all night, and sniffing. Maybe that's why you never went back.

Primo: The truth though—listen, Felipe—my biggest worry was the dress code, 'cause my gear is limited. I don't even got a dress shirt, I only got one pair of shoes, and you can't wear sneakers at that program. They wear ties too—don't they? Well, I ain't even got ties—I only got the one you lent me.

I would've been there three weeks in the same gear. T-shirt and jeans. Estoy jodido como un bón! *[I'm all fucked up like a bum!]*

Philippe: What the fuck kinda bullshit excuse are you talking about? Don't tell me you were thinking that shit. No one notices how people are dressed.

Primo: Yo, Felipe, this is for real! Listen to me! I was thinking about that shit hard. Hell yeah!

Hell yes they would notice, because I would notice if somebody's wearing a fucked-up tie and shirt.

I don't want to be in a program all abochornado *[bumlike]*. I probably won't even concentrate, getting dissed, like . . . and being looked at like a sucker. Dirty jeans . . . or like old jeans, because I would have to wear jeans, 'cause I only got one slack. Word though! I only got two dress shirts and one of them is missing buttons.

I didn't want to tell you about that because it's like a poor excuse, but that was the only shit I was really thinking about. At the time I just said, "Well, I just don't show up."

And Felipe, I'm a stupid *[very]* skinny nigga'. So I have to be careful how I dress, otherwise people will think I be on the stem *[a crack addict who smokes out of a glass-stem pipe]*.

Philippe: [nervously] Oh shit. I'm even skinnier than you. People must think I'm a total drug addict.

Primo: Don't worry. You're white.

Obviously, the problem is deeper than not having enough money to buy straight-world clothes. Racism and the other subtle badges of symbolic power are expressed through wardrobes and body language. Ultimately, Primo's biggest problem was that he had no idea of what clothes might be appropriate in the professional, service sector context. Like Caesar, he feared he might appear to be a buffoon on parade on the days when he was trying to dress up. He admitted that the precipitating factor in his decision not to go back to the job training program was when he overheard someone accusing Candy of "looking tacky" after she proudly inaugurated her new fancy clothes at the first class. As a matter of fact, Primo had thought she had looked elegant in her skintight, yellow jumpsuit when she came over to his apartment to display her new outfit proudly to him and his mother before going to class.

Isolating oneself in inner-city street culture removes any danger of having to face the humiliations Candy, Caesar, or Primo inevitably confront when they venture out of their social circle to try to find legal employment. . . .

Conclusion

Ooh, Felipe! You make us sound like such sensitive crack dealers.

—CAESAR [COMMENTING ON THE MANUSCRIPT]

There is no panacea for the suffering and self-destruction of the protagonists in these pages. Solutions to inner-city poverty and substance abuse framed in terms of public policy often appear naive or hopelessly idealistic. Given the dimensions of structural oppression in the United States, it is atheoretical to expect isolated policy initiatives, or even short-term political reforms, to remedy the plight of the poor in U.S. urban centers in the short or medium term. Racism and class segregation in the United States are shaped in too complex a mesh of political-economic structural forces, historical legacies, cultural imperatives, and individual actions to be susceptible to simple solutions.

There are also the inevitable limits of political feasibility. For a number of complicated historical and ideological reasons, the United States simply lacks the political will to address poverty in any concerted manner. Nevertheless, I hope my presentation of the experience of social marginalization in El Barrio, as seen through the struggles for dignity and survival of Ray's crack dealers and their families, contributes on a concrete practical level to calling attention to the tragedy of persistent poverty and racial segregation in the urban United States. I cannot resign myself to the terrible irony that the richest industrialized nation on earth, and the greatest world power in history, confines so many of its citizens to poverty and to prison. . . .

The increasing material and political powerlessness of the working poor in the United States needs to become a central concern. The concentration of poverty, substance abuse, and criminality within inner-city enclaves such as East Harlem is the product of state policy and free market forces that have inscribed spatially the rising levels of social inequality discussed earlier. More subtly, this urban decay expresses itself in the growing polarization around street culture in North America, giving rise to what some observers call a "crisis in U.S. race relations." Middle-class society and its elites increasingly have been able to disassociate themselves from the ethnically distinct, urban-based working poor and unemployed who inhabit the inner city. Budget cuts and fiscal austerity have accelerated the trend toward public sector breakdown in impoverished urban neighborhoods, while services improve, or at least stay the same, in Anglo-dominated, wealthy suburban communities.

The psychological-reductionist and cultural-essentialist analyses of social marginalization that pass for common sense in the United States frame solutions to racism and poverty around short-term interventions that target the "bad attitude" of individuals. The biggest sociological unit for most poverty policy intervention, for example, is the nuclear family. Job training programs emphasize attitude and personal empowerment. Seminars designed to promote multicultural sensitivity are fashionable in both public and private sector institutions. While these initiatives are not harmful, and might even help superficially on the margins, it is the institutionalized expression of racism—America's de facto apartheid and inner-city public sector breakdown—that government policy and private sector philanthropy need to address if anything is ever to change significantly in the long run.

In other words, to draw on a classic metaphor from sports, the United States needs to level its playing field. Concretely, this means that the garbage needs to be picked up, schools have to teach, and laws must be enforced, as effectively in Latino/a, African American, Asian, and Native American communities as they are in white, middle-class suburbs. There is nothing particularly complicated or subtle about remedying the unequal provision of public funds and services across class and ethnic lines. Hundreds of short-term policy and legal reforms immediately jump to mind: from tax reform— namely, taxing the home mortgages of the upper middle class and exempting the federal and state transfer benefits of the poor—to streamlining access to social welfare benefits and democratizing educational institutions—namely, universal affordable health care coverage, free day care, equalizing per capita funding for schools and universities, and so on.

One message the crack dealers communicated clearly to me is that they are not driven solely by simple economic exigency. Like most humans on earth, in addition to material subsistence, they are also searching for dignity and fulfillment. In the Puerto Rican context, this incorporates cultural definitions of *respeto* built around a personal concern for autonomy, self-assertion, and community within constantly changing social hierarchies of statuses based on kinship, age, and gender. Complex cultural and social dimensions that extend far beyond material and logistical requirements have to be addressed by poverty policies if the socially marginal in the United States are ever going to be able to demand, and earn, the respect that mainstream society needs to share with them for its own good. Specifically, this means evaluating how public policy initiatives and the more impersonal political economy forces of the larger society interact with rapidly changing cultural definitions of gender and family. Women, children, and the elderly constitute most of the poor in the United States. Public policy intervention consequently should prioritize the needs of women and children instead of marginalizing them. Most important, poor women should not be forced to seek desperate alliances with men in order to stay sheltered, fed, clothed, and healthy. Current welfare policy explicitly encourages mothers to seek men with unreported illegal income. . . .

The painful symptoms of inner-city apartheid will continue to produce record numbers of substance abusers, violent criminals, and emotionally disabled and angry youths if nothing is done to reverse the trends in the United

States since the late 1960s around rising relative poverty rates and escalating ethnic and class segregation.

Given the bleak perspectives for policy reform at the federal level, on the one hand, or for political mobilization in the U.S. inner city, on the other, my most immediate goal in this research is to humanize the public enemies of the United States without sanitizing or glamorizing them. In documenting the depths of personal pain that are inherent to the experience of persistent poverty and institutional racism, I hope to contribute to our understanding of the fundamental processes and dynamics of oppression in the United States. More subtly, I also want to place drug dealers and street-level criminals into their rightful position within the mainstream of U.S. society. They are not "exotic others" operating in an irrational netherworld. On the contrary, they are "made in America." Highly motivated, ambitious inner-city youths have been attracted to the rapidly expanding, multibillion-dollar drug economy during the 1980s and 1990s precisely because they believe in Horatio Alger's version of the American Dream.

Like most other people in the United States, drug dealers and street criminals are scrambling to obtain their piece of the pie as fast as possible. In fact, in their pursuit of success they are even following the minute details of the classical Yankee model for upward mobility. They are aggressively pursuing careers as private entrepreneurs; they take risks, work hard, and pray for good luck. They are the ultimate rugged individualists braving an unpredictable frontier where fortune, fame, and destruction are all just around the corner, and where the enemy is ruthlessly hunted down and shot. In the specifically Puerto Rican context, resistance to mainstream society's domination and pride in street culture identity resonates with a reinvented vision of the defiant *jíbaro* who refused to succumb to elite society's denigration under Spanish and U.S. colonialism. The hyper-urban reconstruction of a hip-hop version of the rural *jíbaro* represents the triumph of a newly constituted Puerto Rican cultural assertion among the most marginalized members of the Puerto Rican diaspora. The tragedy is that the material base for this determined search for cultural respect is confined to the street economy.

At the same time, there is nothing exotically Puerto Rican about the triumphs and failures of the protagonists of this study. On the contrary, "mainstream America" should be able to see itself in the characters presented on these pages and recognize the linkages. The inner city represents the United States' greatest domestic failing, hanging like a Damocles sword over the larger society. Ironically, the only force preventing this suspended sword from falling is that drug dealers, addicts, and street criminals internalize their rage and desperation. They direct their brutality against themselves and their immediate community rather than against their structural oppressors. From a comparative perspective, and in a historical context, the painful and prolonged self-destruction of people like Primo, Caesar, Candy, and their children is cruel and unnecessary. There is no technocratic solution. Any long-term paths out of the quagmire will have to address the structural and political economic roots, as well as the ideological and cultural roots, of social marginalization. The first step out of the impasse, however, requires a fundamental ethical and political reevaluation of basic socioeconomic models and human values.

22

FRATERNITIES AND COLLEGIATE RAPE CULTURE
Why Are Some Fraternities More Dangerous Places for Women?

A. AYRES BOSWELL • JOAN Z. SPADE

Conflict theory suggests that, in our society, who and what the label "deviant" is placed on is based primarily on relative power. Those who have more authority and control define what is "normal" and what is deviant. Moreover, conflict theorists argue that social norms, including laws, generally reflect the interests of the rich and powerful. Thus, historically, we have property laws to protect against the theft of property of the landowning classes and domestic laws that protect the status of men, as patriarchs, within the family. This reading by A. Ayres Boswell and Joan Z. Spade, originally published in 1996, exemplifies this process, in which the privileged attempt to socially construct deviance and crime to their advantage. In particular, Boswell and Spade analyze the social contexts of and gendered relations in male fraternities that contribute to the high incidence of violence against women on many college campuses. Joan Z. Spade is a professor of sociology at the State University of New York, Brockport.

Date rape and acquaintance rape on college campuses are topics of concern to both researchers and college administrators. Some estimate that 60 to 80 percent of rapes are date or acquaintance rape (Koss, Dinero, Seibel, and Cox 1988). Further, 1 out of 4 college women say they were raped or experienced an attempted rape, and 1 out of 12 college men say they forced a woman to have sexual intercourse against her will (Koss, Gidycz, and Wisniewski 1985).

From *Gender & Society,* Vol. 10, no. 2, 1996, pp. 133–47. Reprinted by permission from Sage Publications, Inc. Copyright © 1996 by Sage Publications, Inc.

Although considerable attention focuses on the incidence of rape, we know relatively little about the context or the *rape culture* surrounding date and acquaintance rape. Rape culture is a set of values and beliefs that provide an environment conducive to rape (Buchwald, Fletcher, and Roth 1993; Herman 1984). The term applies to a generic culture surrounding and promoting rape, not the specific settings in which rape is likely to occur. We believe that the specific settings also are important in defining relationships between men and women.

Some have argued that fraternities are places where rape is likely to occur on college campuses (Martin and Hummer 1989; O'Sullivan 1993; Sanday 1990) and that the students most likely to accept rape myths and be more sexually aggressive are more likely to live in fraternities and sororities, consume higher doses of alcohol and drugs, and place a higher value on social life at college (Gwartney-Gibbs and Stockard 1989; Kalof and Cargill 1991). Others suggest that sexual aggression is learned in settings such as fraternities and is not part of predispositions or preexisting attitudes (Boeringer, Shehan, and Akers 1991). To prevent further incidences of rape on college campuses, we need to understand what it is about fraternities in particular and college life in general that may contribute to the maintenance of a rape culture on college campuses.

Our approach is to identify the social contexts that link fraternities to campus rape and promote a rape culture. Instead of assuming that all fraternities provide an environment conducive to rape, we compare the interactions of men and women at fraternities identified on campus as being especially *dangerous* places for women, where the likelihood of rape is high, to those seen as *safer* places, where the perceived probability of rape occurring is lower. Prior to collecting data for our study, we found that most women students identified some fraternities as having more sexually aggressive members and a higher probability of rape. These women also considered other fraternities as relatively safe houses, where a woman could go and get drunk if she wanted to and feel secure that the fraternity men would not take advantage of her. We compared parties at houses identified as high-risk and low-risk houses as well as at two local bars frequented by college students. Our analysis provides an opportunity to examine situations and contexts that hinder or facilitate positive social relations between undergraduate men and women.

The abusive attitudes toward women that some fraternities perpetuate exist within a general culture where rape is intertwined in traditional gender scripts. Men are viewed as initiators of sex and women as either passive partners or active resisters, preventing men from touching their bodies (LaPlante, McCormick, and Brannigan 1980). Rape culture is based on the assumptions that men are aggressive and dominant whereas women are passive and acquiescent (Buchwald, Fletcher, and Roth 1993; Herman 1984). What occurs on college campuses is an extension of the portrayal of domination and aggression of men over women that exemplifies the double standard of sexual behavior in U.S. society (Barthel 1988; Kimmel 1993).

Sexually active men are positively reinforced by being referred to as "studs," whereas women who are sexually active or report enjoying sex are derogatorily labeled as "sluts" (Herman 1984; O'Sullivan 1993). These gender scripts are embodied in rape myths and stereotypes such as "She really wanted it; she just said no because she didn't want me to think she was a bad girl" (Burke, Stets, and Pirog-Good 1989; Jenkins and Dambrot 1987; Lisak and Roth 1988; Malamuth 1986; Muehlenhard and Linton 1987; Peterson and Franzese 1987). Because men's sexuality is seen as more natural, acceptable, and uncontrollable than women's sexuality, many men and women excuse acquaintance rape by affirming that men cannot control their natural urges (Miller and Marshall 1987).

Whereas some researchers explain these attitudes toward sexuality and rape using an individual or a psychological interpretation, we argue that rape has a social basis, one in which both men and women create and recreate masculine and feminine identities and relations. Based on the assumption that rape is part of the social construction of gender, we examine how men and women "do gender" on a college campus (West and Zimmerman 1987). We focus on fraternities because they have been identified as settings that encourage rape (Sanday 1990). By comparing fraternities that are viewed by women as places where there is a high risk of rape to those where women believe there is a low risk of rape as well as two local commercial bars, we seek to identify characteristics that make some social settings more likely places for the occurrence of rape.

Results

The Settings

Fraternity Parties   We observed several differences in the quality of the interaction of men and women at parties at high-risk fraternities compared to those at low-risk houses. A typical party at a low-risk house included an equal number of women and men. The social atmosphere was friendly, with considerable interaction between women and men. Men and women danced in groups and in couples, with many of the couples kissing and displaying affection toward each other. Brothers explained that, because many of the men in these house had girlfriends, it was normal to see couples kissing on the dance floor. Coed groups engaged in conversations at many of these houses, with women and men engaging in friendly exchanges, giving the impression that they knew each other well. Almost no cursing and yelling was observed at parties in low-risk houses; when pushing occurred, the participants apologized. Respect for women extended to the women's bathrooms, which were clean and well supplied.

At high-risk houses, parties typically had skewed gender ratios, sometimes involving more men and other times involving more women. Gender segregation also was evident at these parties, with the men on one side of a room or in the bar drinking while women gathered in another area. Men treated women differently in the high-risk houses. The women's bathrooms in the high-risk houses were filthy, including clogged toilets and vomit in the sinks. When a brother was told of the mess in the bathroom at a high-risk house, he replied, "Good, maybe some of these beer wenches will leave so there will be more beer for us."

Men attending parties at high-risk houses treated women less respectfully, engaging in jokes, conversations, and behaviors that degraded women. Men made a display of assessing women's bodies and rated them with thumbs up or thumbs down for the other men in the sight of the women. One man attending a party at a high-risk fraternity said to another, "Did you know that this week is Women's Awareness Week? I guess that means we get to abuse them more this week." Men behaved more crudely at parties at high-risk houses. At one party, a brother dropped his pants, including his underwear, while dancing in front of several women. Another brother slid across the dance floor completely naked.

The atmosphere at parties in high-risk fraternities was less friendly over all. With the exception of greetings, men and women rarely smiled or laughed and spoke to each other less often than was the case at parties in low-risk houses. The few one-on-one conversations between women and men appeared to be strictly flirtatious (lots of eye contact, touching, and very close talking). It was rare to see a group of men and women together talking. Men were openly hostile, which made the high-risk parties seem almost threatening at times. For example, there was a lot of touching, pushing, profanity, and name calling, some done by women.

Students at parties at the high-risk houses seemed self-conscious and aware of the presence of members of the opposite sex, an awareness that was sexually charged. Dancing early in the evening was usually between women. Close to midnight, the sex ratio began to balance out with the arrival of more men or more women. Couples began to dance together but in a sexual way (close dancing with lots of pelvic thrusts). Men tried to pick up women using lines such as "Want to see my fish tank?" and "Let's go upstairs so that we can talk; I can't hear what you're saying in here."

Although many of the same people who attended high-risk parties also attended low-risk parties, their behavior changed as they moved from setting to setting. Group norms differed across contexts as well. At a party that was held jointly at a low-risk house with a high-risk fraternity, the ambience was that of a party at a high-risk fraternity with heavier drinking, less dancing, and fewer conversations between women and men. The men from both high- and low-risk fraternities were very aggressive; a fight broke out, and there was pushing and shoving on the dance floor and in general.

As others have found, fraternity brothers at high-risk houses on this campus told about routinely discussing their sexual exploits at breakfast the morning after parties and sometimes at house meetings (cf. Martin and

Hummer 1989; O'Sullivan 1993; Sanday 1990). During these sessions, the brothers we interviewed said that men bragged about what they did the night before with stories of sexual conquests often told by the same men, usually sophomores. The women involved in these exploits were women they did not know or knew but did not respect, or *faceless victims*. Men usually treated girlfriends with respect and did not talk about them in these storytelling sessions. Men from low-risk houses, however, did not describe similar sessions in their houses.

The Bar Scene   The bar atmosphere and social context differed from those of fraternity parties. The music was not as loud, and both bars had places to sit and have conversations. At all fraternity parties, it was difficult to maintain conversations with loud music playing and no place to sit. The volume of music at parties at high-risk fraternities was even louder than it was at low-risk houses, making it virtually impossible to have conversations. In general, students in the local bars behaved in the same way that students did at parties in low-risk houses with conversations typical, most occurring between men and women.

The first bar, frequented by older students, had live entertainment every night of the week. Some nights were more crowded than others, and the atmosphere was friendly, relaxed, and conducive to conversation. People laughed and smiled and behaved politely toward each other. The ratio of men to women was fairly equal, with students congregating in mostly coed groups. Conversation flowed freely and people listened to each other.

Although the women and men at the first bar also were at parties at low- and high-risk fraternities, their behavior at the bar included none of the blatant sexual or intoxicated behaviors observed at some of these parties. As the evenings wore on, the number of one-on-one conversations between men and women increased and conversations shifted from small talk to topics such as war and AIDS. Conversations did not revolve around picking up another person, and most people left the bar with same-sex friends or in coed groups.

The second bar was less popular with older students. Younger students, often under the legal drinking age, went there to drink, sometimes after leaving campus parties. This bar was much smaller and usually not as crowded as the first bar. The atmosphere was more mellow and relaxed than it was at the fraternity parties. People went there to hang out and talk to each other.

On a couple of occasions, however, the atmosphere at the second bar became similar to that of a party at a high-risk fraternity. As the number of people in the bar increased, they removed chairs and tables, leaving no place to sit and talk. The music also was turned up louder, drowning out conversation. With no place to dance or sit, most people stood around but could not maintain conversations because of the noise and crowds. Interactions between women and men consisted mostly of flirting. Alcohol consumption also was greater than it was on the less crowded nights, and the number of visibly drunk people increased. The more people drank, the more conversation and socializing broke down. The only differences between this setting and that of a party at a high-risk house were that brothers no longer controlled the territory and bedrooms were not available upstairs.

Gender Relations

Relations between women and men are shaped by the contexts in which they meet and interact. As is the case on other college campuses, *hooking up* has replaced dating on this campus, and fraternities are places where many students hook up. Hooking up is a loosely applied term on college campuses that had different meanings for men and women on this campus.

Most men defined hooking up similarly. One man said it was something that happens

> *when you're really drunk and meet up with a woman you sort of know, or possibly don't know at all and don't care about. You go home with her with the intention of getting as much sexual, physical pleasure as she'll give you, which can range anywhere from kissing to intercourse, without any strings attached.*

The exception to this rule is when men hook up with women they admire. Men said they are less likely to press for sexual activity with someone they know and like because they want the relationship to continue and be based on respect.

Women's version of hooking up differed. Women said they hook up only with men they cared about and described hooking up as kissing and petting but not sexual intercourse. Many women said that hooking up was disappointing because they wanted longer-term relationships. First-year women students realized quickly that hook-ups were usually one-night stands with no strings attached, but many continued to hook up because they had few opportunities to develop relationships with men on campus. One first-year woman said that *"70 percent of hook-ups never talk again and try to avoid one another; 26 percent may actually hear from them or talk to them again, and 4 percent may actually go on a date, which can lead to a relationship."* Another first-year woman said, *"It was fun in the beginning. You get a lot of attention and kiss a lot of boys and think this is what college is about, but it gets tiresome fast."*

Whereas first-year women get tired of the hook-up scene early on, many men do not become bored with it until their junior or senior year. As one upperclassman said, *"The whole game of hooking up became really meaningless and tiresome for me during my second semester of my sophomore year, but most of my friends didn't get bored with it until the following year."*

In contrast to hooking up, students also described monogamous relationships with steady partners. Some type of commitment was expected, but most people did not anticipate marriage. The term *seeing each other* was applied when people were sexually involved but free to date other people. This type of relationship involved less commitment than did one of boyfriend/ girlfriend but was not considered to be a hook-up.

The general consensus of women and men interviewed on this campus was that the Greek system, called "the hill," set the scene for gender relations. The predominance of Greek membership and subsequent living arrangements segregated men and women. During the week, little interaction occurred between women and men after their first year in college because students in fraternities or sororities live and dine in separate quarters. In addition, many non-Greek upper-class students move off campus into apartments. Therefore, students see each other in classes or in the library, but there is no place where students can just hang out together.

Both men and women said that fraternities dominate campus social life, a situation that everyone felt limited opportunities for meaningful interactions. One senior Greek man said,

> *This environment is horrible and so unhealthy for good male and female relationships and interactions to occur. It is so segregated and male dominated. . . . It is our party, with our rules and our beer. We are allowing these women and other men to come to our party. Men can feel superior in their domain.*

Comments from a senior woman reinforced his views: "*Men are dominant; they are the kings of the campus. It is their environment that they allow us to enter; therefore, we have to abide by their rules.*" A junior woman described fraternity parties as

> *good for meeting acquaintances but almost impossible to really get to know anyone. The environment is so superficial, probably because there are so many social cliques due to the Greek system. Also, the music is too loud and the people are too drunk to attempt to have a real conversation, anyway.*

Some students claim that fraternities even control the dating relationships of their members. One senior woman said, "*Guys dictate how dating occurs on this campus, whether it's cool, who it's with, how much time can be spent with the girlfriend and with the brothers.*" Couples either left campus for an evening or hung out separately with their own same-gender friends at fraternity parties, finally getting together with each other at about 2 A.M. Couples rarely went together to fraternity parties. Some men felt that a girlfriend was just a replacement for a hook-up. According to one junior man, "*Basically a girlfriend is someone you go to at 2 A.M. after you've hung out with the guys. She is the sexual outlet that the guys can't provide you with.*"

Some fraternity brothers pressure each other to limit their time with and commitment to their girlfriends. One senior man said, "*The hill [fraternities] and girlfriends don't mix.*" A brother described a constant battle between girlfriends and brothers over who the guy is going out with for the night, with the brothers usually winning. Brothers teased men with girlfriends with remarks such as "whipped" or "where's the ball and chain?" A brother from a high-risk house said that few brothers at his house had girlfriends; some did, but it was uncommon. One man said that from the minute he was a pledge he knew he would probably never have a girlfriend on this campus because *"it was just not the norm in my house. No one has girlfriends; the guys have too much fun with [each other]."*

The pressure on men to limit their commitment to girlfriends, however, was not true of all fraternities or of all men on campus. Couples attended low-risk fraternity parties together, and men in the low-risk houses went out on dates more often. A man in one low-risk house said that about 70 percent of the members of his house were involved in relationships with women, including the pledges (who were sophomores).

Treatment of Women

Not all men held negative attitudes toward women that are typical of a rape culture, and not all social contexts promoted the negative treatment of women. When men were asked whether they treated the women on campus with respect, the most common response was "On an individual basis, yes, but when you have a group of men together, no." Men said that, when together in groups with other men, they sensed a pressure to be disrespectful toward women. A first-year man's perception of the treatment of women was that *"they are treated with more respect to their faces, but behind closed doors, with a group of men present, respect for women is not an issue."* One senior man stated, *"In general, college-aged men don't treat women their age with respect because 90 percent of them think of women as merely a means to sex."* Women reinforced this perception. A first-year woman stated, *"Men here are more interested in hooking up and drinking beer than they are in getting to know women as real people."* Another woman said, *"Men here use and abuse women."*

Characteristic of rape culture, a double standard of sexual behavior for men versus women was prevalent on this campus. As one Greek senior man stated, "Women who sleep around are sluts and get bad reputations; men who do are champions and get a pat on the back from their brothers." Women also supported a double standard for sexual behavior by criticizing sexually active women. A first-year woman spoke out against women who are sexually active: *"I think some girls here make it difficult for the men to respect women as a whole."*

One concrete example of demeaning sexually active women on this campus is the "walk of shame." Fraternity brothers come out on the porches of their houses the night after parties and heckle women walking by. It is assumed that these women spent the night at fraternity houses and that the men they were with did not care enough about them to drive them home. Although sororities now reside in former fraternity houses, this practice continues and sometimes the victims of hecklings are sorority women on their way to study in the library.

A junior man in a high-risk fraternity described another ritual of disrespect toward women called "chatter." When an unknown woman sleeps over at the house, the brothers yell degrading remarks out the window at her as she leaves the next morning such as "Fuck that bitch" and "Who is that slut?" He said that sometimes brothers harass the brothers whose girlfriends stay over instead of heckling those women.

Fraternity men most often mistreated women they did not know personally. Men and women alike reported incidents in which brothers observed other brothers having sex with unknown women or women they knew only casually. A sophomore woman's experience exemplifies this anonymous state: *"I don't mind if 10 guys were watching or it was videotaped. That's expected on this campus. It's the fact that he didn't apologize or even offer to drive me home that really upset me."* Descriptions of sexual encounters involved the satisfaction of men by nameless women. A brother in a high-risk fraternity described a similar occurrence:

> *A brother of mine was hooking up upstairs with an unattractive woman who had been pursuing him all night. He told some brothers to go outside the window and watch. Well, one thing led to another and they were almost completely naked when the woman noticed the brothers outside. She was then unwilling to go any further, so the brother went outside and yelled at the other brothers and then closed the shades. I don't know if he scored or not, because the woman was pretty upset. But he did win the award for hooking up with the ugliest chick that weekend.*

Attitudes toward Rape

The sexually charged environment of college campuses raises many questions about cultures that facilitate the rape of women. How women and men define their sexual behavior is important legally as well as interpersonally. We asked students how they defined rape and had them compare it to the following legal definition: the perpetration of an act of sexual intercourse with a female against her will and consent, whether her will is overcome by force or fear resulting from the threat of force, or by drugs or intoxicants; or when, because of mental deficiency, she is incapable of exercising rational judgment. (Brownmiller 1975:368)

When presented with this legal definition, most women interviewed recognized it as well as the complexities involved in applying it. A first-year woman said, *"If a girl is drunk and the guy knows it and the girl says, 'Yes, I want to have sex,' and they do, that is still rape because the girl can't make a conscious, rational decision under the influence of alcohol."* Some women disagreed. Another first-year woman stated, *"I don't think it is fair that the guy gets blamed when both people involved are drunk."*

The typical definition men gave for rape was "when a guy jumps out of the bushes and forces himself sexually onto a girl." When asked what date rape was, the most common answer was "when one person has sex with another person who did not consent." Many men said, however, that "date rape is when a woman wakes up the next morning and regrets having sex." Some men said that date rape was too gray an area to define. *"Consent is a fine line,"* said a Greek senior man student. For the most part, the men we spoke with argued that rape did not occur on this campus. One Greek sophomore man said, *"I think it is ridiculous that someone here would rape someone."* A first-year man stated, *"I have a problem with the word rape. It sounds so criminal, and we are not criminals; we are sane people."*

Whether aware of the legal definitions of rape, most men resisted the idea that a woman who is intoxicated is unable to consent to sex. A Greek junior man said, *"Men should not be responsible for women's drunkenness."* One first-year man said, *"If that is the legal definition of rape, then it happens all the time on this campus."* A senior man said, *"I don't care whether alcohol is involved or not; that is not rape. Rapists are people that have something seriously wrong with them."* A first-year man even claimed that when women get drunk, they invite sex. He said, *"Girls get so drunk here and then come on to us. What are we supposed to do? We are only human."*

Discussion and Conclusion

These findings describe the physical and normative aspects of one college campus as they relate to attitudes about and relations between men and women. Our findings suggest that an explanation emphasizing rape culture also must focus on those characteristics of the social setting that play a role in defining heterosexual relationships on college campuses (Kalof and Cargill 1991). The degradation of women as portrayed in rape culture was not found in all fraternities on this campus. Both group norms and individual behavior changed as students went from one place to another. Although individual men are the ones who rape, we found that some settings are more likely places for rape than are others. Our findings suggest that rape cannot be seen only as an isolated act and blamed on individual behavior and proclivities, whether it be alcohol consumption or attitudes. We also must consider characteristics of the settings that promote the behaviors that reinforce a rape culture.

Relations between women and men at parties in low-risk fraternities varied considerably from those in high-risk houses. Peer pressure and situational norms influenced women as well as men. Although many men in high- and low-risk houses shared similar views and attitudes about the Greek system, women on this campus, and date rape, their behaviors at fraternity parties were quite different.

Women who are at highest risk of rape are women whom fraternity brothers did not know. These women are faceless victims, nameless acquaintances—not friends. Men said their responsibility to such persons and the level of guilt they feel later if the hook-ups end in sexual intercourse are much lower if they hook up with women they do not know. In high-risk houses, brothers treated women as subordinates and kept them at a distance. Men in high-risk houses actively discouraged ongoing heterosexual relationships, routinely degraded women, and participated more fully in the hook-up scene; thus, the probability that women would become faceless victims was higher in these houses. The flirtatious nature of the parties indicated that women go to these parties looking for available men, but finding boyfriends or relationships was difficult at parties in high-risk houses. However, in the low-risk houses, where more men had long-term relationships, the women were not strangers and were less likely to become faceless victims.

The social scene on this campus, and on most others, offers women and men few other options to socialize. Although there may be no such thing as a completely safe fraternity party for women, parties at low-risk houses and commercial bars encouraged men and women to get to know each other better and decreased the probability that women would become faceless victims. Although both men and women found the social scene on this campus demeaning, neither demanded different settings for socializing, and attendance at fraternity parties is a common form of entertainment.

These findings suggest that a more conducive environment for conversation can promote more positive interactions between men and women. Simple changes would provide the opportunity for men and women to interact in meaningful ways such as adding places to sit and lowering the volume of music at fraternity parties or having parties in neutral locations, where men are not in control. The typical party room in fraternity houses includes a place to dance but not to sit and talk. The music often is loud, making it difficult, if not impossible, to carry on conversations; however, there were more conversations at the low-risk parties, where there also was more respect shown toward women. Although the number of brothers who had steady girlfriends in the low-risk houses as compared to those in the high-risk houses may explain the differences, we found that commercial bars also provided a context for interaction between men and women. At the bars, students sat and talked and conversations between men and women flowed freely, resulting in deep discussions and fewer hook-ups.

Alcohol consumption was a major focus of social events here and intensified attitudes and orientations of a rape culture. Although pressure to drink was evident at all fraternity parties and at both bars, drinking dominated high-risk fraternity parties, at which nonalcoholic beverages usually were not available and people chugged beers and became visibly drunk. A rape culture is strengthened by rules that permit alcohol only at fraternity parties. Under this system, men control the parties and dominate the men as well as the women who attend. As college administrators crack down on fraternities and alcohol on campus, however, the same behaviors and norms may transfer to other places such as parties in apartments or private homes where administrators have much less control. At commercial bars, interaction and socialization with others were as important as drinking, with the exception of the nights when the bar frequented by under-class students became crowded. Although one solution is to offer nonalcoholic social activities, such events receive little support on this campus. Either these alternative events lacked the prestige of the fraternity parties or the alcohol was seen as necessary to unwind, or both.

In many ways, the fraternities on this campus determined the settings in which men and women interacted. As others before us have found, pressures for conformity to the norms and values exist at both high-risk and low-risk houses (Kalof and Cargill 1991; Martin and Hummer 1989; Sanday 1990). The desire to be accepted is not unique to this campus or the Greek system (Holland and Eisenhart 1990; Horowitz 1988; Moffat 1989). The degree of conformity required by Greeks may be greater than that required in most social groups, with considerable pressure to adopt and maintain the image of their houses. The fraternity system intensifies the "groupthink syndrome" (Janis 1972) by solidifying the identity of the in-group and creating an us/them atmosphere. Within the fraternity culture, brothers are highly regarded and women are viewed as outsiders. For men in high-risk fraternities, women threatened their brotherhood; therefore, brothers discouraged relationships and harassed those who treated women as equals or with respect. The pressure to be one of the guys and hang out with the guys strengthens a rape culture on college campus by demeaning women and encouraging the segregation of men and women.

Students on this campus were aware of the contexts in which they operated and the choices available to them. They recognized that, in their interactions, they created differences between men and women that are not natural, essential, or biological (West and Zimmerman 1987). Not all men and women accepted the demeaning treatment of women, but they continued to participate in behaviors that supported aspects of a rape culture. Many women participated in the hook-up scene even after they had been humiliated and hurt because they had few other means of initiating contact with men on campus. Men and women alike played out this scene, recognizing its injustices in many cases but being unable to change the course of their behaviors.

Although this research provides some clues to gender relations on college campuses, it raises many questions. Why do men and women participate in activities that support a rape culture when they see its injustices? What would happen if alcohol were not controlled by groups of men who admit that they disrespect women when they get together? What can be done to give men and women on college campuses more opportunities to interact responsibly and get to know each other better? These questions should be studied on other campuses with a focus on the social settings in which the incidence of rape and the attitudes that support a rape culture exist. Fraternities are social contexts that may or may not foster a rape culture.

Our findings indicate that a rape culture exists in some fraternities, especially those we identified as high-risk houses. College administrators are responding to this situation by providing counseling and educational programs that increase awareness of date rape, including campaigns such as "No means no." These strategies are important in changing attitudes, values, and behaviors; however, changing individuals is not enough. The structure of campus life and the impact of that structure on gender relations on campus are highly determinative. To eliminate campus rape culture, student leaders and administrators must examine the situations in which women and men meet and restructure these settings to provide opportunities for respectful interaction. Change may not require abolishing fraternities; rather, it may require promoting settings that facilitate positive gender relations.

REFERENCES

Barthel, D. 1988. *Putting on Appearances: Gender and Advertising.* Philadelphia: Temple University Press.

Boeringer, S. B., C. L. Shehan, and R. L. Akers. 1991. "Social Contexts and Social Learning in Sexual Coercion and Aggression: Assessing the Contribution of Fraternity Membership." *Family Relations* 40:58–64.

Brownmiller, S. 1975. *Against Our Will: Men, Women and Rape.* New York: Simon & Schuster.

Buchwald, E., P. R. Fletcher, and M. Roth, eds. 1993. *Transforming a Rape Culture.* Minneapolis, MN: Milkweed Editions.

Burke, P., J. E. Stets, and M. A. Pirog-Good. 1989. "Gender Identity, Self-esteem, Physical Abuse and Sexual Abuse in Dating Relationships." In *Violence in Dating Relationships: Emerging Social Issues,* edited by M. A. Pirog-Good and J. E. Stets. New York: Praeger.

Gwartney-Gibbs, P. and J. Stockard. 1989. "Courtship Aggression and Mixed-Sex Peer Groups." In *Violence in Dating Relationships: Emerging Social Issues,* edited by M. A. Pirog-Good and J. E. Stets. New York: Praeger.

Herman, D. 1984. "The Rape Culture." In *Women: A Feminist Perspective,* edited by J. Freeman. Mountain View, CA: Mayfield.

Holland, D. C. and M. A. Eisenhart. 1990. *Educated in Romance: Women, Achievement, and College Culture.* Chicago: University of Chicago Press.

Horowitz, H. I. 1988. *Campus Life: Undergraduate Cultures from the End of the 18th Century to the Present.* Chicago: University of Chicago Press.

Janis, I. L. 1972. *Victims of Groupthink.* Boston: Houghton Mifflin.

Jenkins, M. J. and F. H. Dambrot. 1987. "The Attribution of Date Rape: Observer's Attitudes and Sexual Experiences and the Dating Situation." *Journal of Applied Social Psychology* 17:875–95.

Kalof, I. and T. Cargill. 1991. "Fraternity and Sorority Membership and Gender Dominance Attitudes." *Sex Roles* 25:417–23.

Kimmel, M. S. 1993. "Clarence, William, Iron Mike, Tailhook, Senator Packwood, Spur Posse, Magic . . . and Us. In *Transforming a Rape Culture,* edited by E. Buchwald, P. R. Fletcher, and M. Roth. Minneapolis, MN: Milkweed Editions.

Koss, M. P., T. E. Dinero, C. A. Seibel, and S. L. Cox. 1988. "Stranger and Acquaintance Rape: Are There Differences in the Victim's Experience?" *Psychology of Women Quarterly* 12:1–24.

Koss, M. P., C. A. Gidycz, and N. Wisniewski. 1985. "The Scope of Rape: Incidence and Prevalence of Sexual Aggression and Victimization in a National Sample of Higher Education Students." *Journal of Consulting and Clinical Psychology* 55:162–70.

LaPlante, M. N., N. McCormick, and G. G. Brannigan. 1980. "Living the Sexual Script: College Students' Views of Influence in Sexual Encounters." *Journal of Sex Research* 16:338–55.

Lisak, D. and S. Roth. 1988. "Motivational Factors in Nonincarcerated Sexually Aggressive Men." *Journal of Personality and Social Psychology* 55:795–802.

Malamuth, N. 1986. "Predictors of Naturalistic Sexual Aggression." *Journal of Personality and Social Psychology* 50:953–62.

Martin, P. Y. and R. Hummer. 1989. "Fraternities and Rape on Campus." *Gender & Society* 3:457–73.

Miller, B. and J. C. Marshall. 1987. "Coercive Sex on the University Campus." *Journal of College Student Personnel* 28:38–47.

Moffat, M. 1989. *Coming of Age in New Jersey: College Life in American Culture.* New Brunswick, NJ: Rutgers University Press.

Muchlenhard, C. L. and M. A. Linton. 1987. "Data Rape and Sexual Aggression in Dating Situations: Incidence and Risk Factors." *Journal of Counseling Psychology* 34:186–96.

O'Sullivan, C. 1993. "Fraternities and the Rape Culture." In *Transforming a Rape Culture,* edited by E. Buchwald, P. R. Fletcher, and M. Roth. Minneapolis, MN: Milkweed Editions.

Peterson, S. A. and B. Franzese. 1987. "Correlates of College Men's Sexual Abuse of Women." *Journal of College Student Personnel* 28:223–28.

Sanday, P. R. 1990. *Fraternity Gang Rape: Sex, Brotherhood, and Privilege on Campus.* New York: New York University Press.

West, C. and D. Zimmerman. 1987. "Doing Gender." *Gender & Society* 1:125–51.

23

SOME PRINCIPLES OF STRATIFICATION

KINGSLEY DAVIS • WILBERT E. MOORE
WITH A RESPONSE BY MELVIN TUMIN

In the following four selections, we investigate social inequality that results from social class membership. *Social class* refers to categories of people who share common economic interests in a stratification system. The first selection is a classic piece excerpted from a 1945 article by sociologists Kingsley Davis and Wilbert E. Moore. Davis and Moore argue that not only are all societies stratified, but that stratification is a functional necessity. Davis and Moore also argue that stratification occurs because some social positions are more important to the social system than others, and as such, social positions are valued and rewarded differently. In 1953, sociologist Melvin Tumin published a response to Davis and Moore's classic article, which suggests that social stratification may be dysfunctional for society.

S tarting from the proposition that no society is "classless," or unstratified, an effort is made to explain, in functional terms, the universal necessity which calls forth stratification in any social system. Next, an attempt is made to explain the roughly uniform distribution of prestige as between the major types of positions in every society. Since, however, there occur between one society and another great differences in the degree and kind of stratification, some attention is also given to the varieties of social inequality and the variable factors that give rise to them. . . .

Throughout, it will be necessary to keep in mind one thing—namely, that the discussion relates to the system of positions, not to the individuals occupying those positions. It is one thing to ask why different positions carry

Sources: "Some Principles of Stratification," by Kingsley Davis and Wilbert E. Moore, in *American Sociological Review,* vol. 10, no. 2 (April, 1945), pp. 242–44. "Some Principles of Stratification: A Critical Analysis," by Melvin Tumin, in *American Sociological Review,* vol. 18, no. 4 (Aug., 1953), pp. 387–93. Reprinted with permission.

different degrees of prestige, and quite another to ask how certain individuals get into those positions. Although, as the argument will try to show, both questions are related, it is essential to keep them separate in our thinking. Most of the literature on stratification has tried to answer the second question (particularly with regard to the ease or difficulty of mobility between strata) without tackling the first. The first question, however, is logically prior and, in the case of any particular individual or group, factually prior.

The Functional Necessity of Stratification

Curiously, however, the main functional necessity explaining the universal presence of stratification is precisely the requirement faced by any society of placing and motivating individuals in the social structure. As a functioning mechanism a society must somehow distribute its members in social positions and induce them to perform the duties of these positions. It must thus concern itself with motivation at two different levels: to instill in the proper individuals the desire to fill certain positions, and, once in these positions, the desire to perform the duties attached to them. Even though the social order may be relatively static in form, there is a continuous process of metabolism as new individuals are born into it, shift with age, and die off. Their absorption into the positional system must somehow be arranged and motivated. This is true whether the system is competitive or noncompetitive. A competitive system gives greater importance to the motivation to achieve positions, whereas a noncompetitive system gives perhaps greater importance to the motivation to perform the duties of the positions; but in any system both types of motivation are required.

If the duties associated with the various positions were all equally pleasant to the human organism, all equally important to societal survival, and all equally in need of the same ability or talent, it would make no difference who got into which positions, and the problem of social placement would be greatly reduced. But actually it does make a great deal of difference who gets into which positions, not only because some positions are inherently more agreeable than others, but also because some require special talents or training and some are functionally more important than others. Also, it is essential that the duties of the positions be performed with the diligence that their importance requires. Inevitably, then, a society must have, first, some kind of rewards that it can use as inducements, and, second, some way of distributing these rewards differentially according to positions. The rewards and their distribution become a part of the social order, and thus give rise to stratification.

One may ask what kind of rewards a society has at its disposal in distributing its personnel and securing essential services. It has, first of all, the things that contribute to sustenance and comfort. It has, second, the things that contribute to humor and diversion. And it has, finally, the things that contribute to self-respect and ego expansion. The last, because of the peculiarly social character of the self, is largely a function of the opinion of others, but it nonetheless ranks in importance with the first two. In any social system all three kinds of rewards must be dispensed differentially according to positions.

In a sense the rewards are "built into" the position. They consist in the "rights" associated with the position, plus what may be called its accompaniments or perquisites. Often the rights, and sometimes the accompaniments, are functionally related to the duties of the position. (Rights as viewed by the incumbent are usually duties as viewed by other members of the community.) However, there may be a host of subsidiary rights and perquisites that are not essential to the function of the position and have only an indirect and symbolic connection with its duties, but which still may be of considerable importance in inducing people to seek the positions and fulfill the essential duties.

If the rights and perquisites of different positions in a society must be unequal, then the society must be stratified, because that is precisely what stratification means. Social inequality is thus an unconsciously evolved device by which societies insure that the most important positions are conscientiously filled by the most qualified persons. Hence every society, no matter how simple or complex, must differentiate persons in terms of both prestige and esteem, and must therefore possess a certain amount of institutionalized inequality.

It does not follow that the amount or type of inequality need be the same in all societies. This is largely a function of factors that will be discussed presently.

The Two Determinants of Positional Rank

Granting the general function that inequality subserves, one can specify the two factors that determine the relative rank of different positions. In general those positions convey the best reward, and hence have the highest rank, which (a) have the greatest importance for the society and (b) require the greatest training or talent. The first factor concerns function and is a matter of relative significance; the second concerns means and is a matter of scarcity.

Differential Functional Importance

Actually a society does not need to reward positions in proportion to their functional importance. It merely needs to give sufficient reward to them to ensure that they will be filled competently. In other words, it must see that less essential positions do not compete successfully with more essential ones. If a position is easily filled, it need not be heavily rewarded, even though important. On the other hand, if it is important but hard to fill, the reward must be high enough to get it filled anyway. Functional importance is therefore a necessary but not a sufficient cause of high rank being assigned to a position.[1]

Differential Scarcity of Personnel

Practically all positions, no matter how acquired, require some form of skill or capacity for performance. This is implicit in the very notion of position, which implies that the incumbent must, by virtue of his incumbency, accomplish certain things.

There are, ultimately, only two ways in which a person's qualifications come about: through inherent capacity or through training. Obviously, in concrete activities both are always necessary, but from a practical standpoint the scarcity may lie primarily in one or the other, as well as in both. Some positions require innate talents of such high degree that the persons who fill them are bound to be rare. In many cases, however, talent is fairly abundant in the population but the training process is so long, costly, and elaborate that relatively few can qualify. Modern medicine, for example, is within the mental capacity of most individuals, but a medical education is so burdensome and expensive that virtually none would undertake it if the position of the M.D. did not carry a reward commensurate with the sacrifice.

If the talents required for a position are abundant and the training easy, the method of acquiring the position may have little to do with its duties. There may be, in fact, a virtually accidental relationship. But if the skills required are scarce by reason of the rarity of talent or the costliness of training, the position, if functionally important, must have an attractive power that will draw the necessary skills in competition with other positions. This means, in effect, that the position must be high in the social scale—must command great prestige, high salary, ample leisure, and the like.

How Variations Are to Be Understood

Insofar as there is a difference between one system of stratification and another, it is attributable to whatever factors affect the two determinants of differential reward—namely, functional importance and scarcity of personnel. Positions important in one society may not be important in another, because the conditions faced by the societies, or their degree of internal development, may be different. The same conditions, in turn, may affect the question of scarcity; for in some societies the stage of development, or the external situation, may wholly obviate the necessity of certain kinds of skill or talent. Any particular system of stratification, then, can be understood as a product of the special conditions affecting the two aforementioned grounds of differential reward.

Critical Response by Melvin Tumin

The fact of social inequality in human society is marked by its ubiquity and its antiquity. Every known society, past and present, distributes its scarce and demanded goods and services unequally. And there are attached to the positions which command unequal amounts of such goods and services certain highly morally-toned evaluations of their importance for the society.

The ubiquity and the antiquity of such inequality has given rise to the assumption that there must be something both inevitable and positively functional about such social arrangements. . . . Clearly, the truth or falsity of such an assumption is a strategic question for any general theory of social organization. It is therefore most curious that the basic premises and implications of the assumption have only been most casually explored by American sociologists. . . .

Let us take [the Davis and Moore] propositions and examine them *seriatim.*

(1) *Certain positions in any society are more functionally important than others and require special skills for their performance.*

The key term here is "functionally important." The functionalist theory of social organization is by no means clear and explicit about this term. The minimum common referent is to something known as the "survival value" of a social structure. This concept immediately involves a number of perplexing questions. Among these are (a) the issue of minimum versus maximum survival, and the possible empirical referents which can be given to those terms; (b) whether such a proposition is a useless tautology since any *status quo* at any given moment is nothing more and nothing less than everything present in the *status quo.* In these terms, all acts and structures must be judged positively functional in that they constitute essential portions of the *status quo;* (c) what kind of calculus of functionality exists which will enable us, at this point in our development, to add and subtract long- and short-range consequences, with their mixed qualities, and arrive at some summative judgment regarding the rating an act or structure should receive on a scale of greater or lesser functionality? At best, we tend to make primarily intuitive judgments. Often enough, these judgments involve the use of value-laden criteria, or, at least, criteria which are chosen in preference to others not for any sociologically systematic reasons but by reason of certain implicit value preferences. . . .

A generalized theory of social stratification must recognize that the prevailing system of inducements and rewards is only one of many variants in the whole range of possible systems of motivation which, at least theoretically, are capable of working in human society. It is quite conceivable, of course, that a system of norms could be institutionalized in which the idea of threatened withdrawal of services, except under the most extreme circumstances, would be considered as absolute moral anathema. In such a case, the whole notion of relative functionality, as advanced by Davis and Moore, would have to be radically revised.

(2) *Only a limited number of individuals in any society have the talents which can be trained into the skills appropriate to these positions (i.e., the more functionally important positions).*

The truth of this proposition depends at least in part on the truth of proposition 1 above. It is, therefore, subject to all the limitations indicated above. But for the moment, let us assume the validity of the first proposition and concentrate on the question of the rarity of appropriate talent.

If all that is meant is that in every society there is a *range* of talent, and that some members of any society are by nature more talented than others, no sensible contradiction can be offered, but a question must be raised here regarding the amount of sound knowledge present in any society concerning the presence of talent in the population.

For, in every society there is some demonstrable ignorance regarding the amount of talent present in the population. *And the more rigidly stratified a society is, the less chance does that society have of discovering any new facts about the talents of its members.* Smoothly working and stable systems of stratification, wherever found, tend to build in obstacles to the further exploration of the range of available talent. This is especially true in those societies where the opportunity to discover talent in any one generation varies with the differential resources of the parent generation. Where, for instance, access to education depends upon the wealth of one's parents, and where wealth is differentially distributed, large segments of the population are likely to be deprived of the chance even to *discover* what are their talents.

Whether or not differential rewards and opportunities are functional in any one generation, it is clear that if those differentials are allowed to be socially inherited by the next generation, then the stratification system is specifically dysfunctional for the discovery of talents in the next generation. In this fashion, systems of social stratification tend to limit the chances available to maximize the efficiency of discovery, recruitment and training of "functionally important talent."

. . . In this context, it may be asserted that there is some noticeable tendency for elites to restrict further access to their privileged positions, once they have sufficient power to enforce such restrictions. This is especially true in a culture where it is possible for an elite to contrive a high demand and a proportionately higher reward for its work by restricting the numbers of the elite available to do the work. The recruitment and training of doctors in modern United States is at least partly a case in point. . . .

(3) *The conversion of talents into skills involves a training period during which sacrifices of one kind or another are made by those undergoing the training.*

Davis and Moore introduce here a concept, "sacrifice," which comes closer than any of the rest of their vocabulary of analysis to being a direct reflection of the rationalizations, offered by the more fortunate members of a society, of the rightness of their occupancy of privileged positions. It is the least critically thought-out concept in the repertoire, and can also be shown to be least supported by the actual facts.

In our present society, for example, what are the sacrifices which talented persons undergo in the training period? The possibly serious losses involve the surrender of earning power and the cost of the training. The latter is generally borne by the parents of the talented youth undergoing training, and not by the trainees themselves. But this cost tends to be paid out of income which the parents were able to earn generally by virtue of *their* privileged positions in the hierarchy of stratification. That is to say, the parents' ability to pay for the training of their children is part of the differential *reward* they, the parents, received for their privileged positions in the society. And to charge this sum up against sacrifices made by the youth is falsely to perpetuate a bill or a debt already paid by the society to the parents. . . .

What tends to be completely overlooked, in addition, are the psychic and spiritual rewards which are available to the elite trainees by comparison with their age peers in the labor force. There is, first, the much higher prestige enjoyed by the college student and the professional-school student as compared with persons in shops and offices. There is, second, the extremely highly valued privilege of having greater opportunity for self-development. There is, third, all the psychic gain involved in being allowed to delay the assumption of adult responsibilities such as earning a living and supporting a family. There is, fourth, the access to leisure and freedom of a kind not likely to be experienced by the persons already at work.

If these are never taken into account as rewards of the training period it is not because they are not concretely present, but because the emphasis in American concepts of reward is almost exclusively placed on the material returns of positions. The emphases on enjoyment, entertainment, ego enhancement, prestige and esteem are introduced only when the differentials in these which accrue to the skilled positions need to be justified. If these other rewards were taken into account, it would be much more difficult to demonstrate that the training period, as presently operative, is really sacrificial. Indeed, it might turn out to be the case that even at this point in their careers, the elite trainees were being differentially rewarded relative to their age peers in the labor force. . . .

(4) *In order to induce the talented persons to undergo these sacrifices and acquire the training, their future positions must carry an inducement value in the form of differential, i.e., privileged and disproportionate access to the scarce and desired rewards which the society has to offer.*

Let us assume, for the purposes of the discussion, that the training period is sacrificial and the talent is rare in every conceivable human society. There is still the basic problem as to whether the allocation of differential rewards in scarce and desired goods and services is the only or the most efficient way of recruiting the appropriate talent to these positions.

For there are a number of alternative motivational schemes whose efficiency and adequacy ought at least to be considered in this context. What can be said, for instance, on behalf of the motivation which De Man called "joy in work," Veblen termed "instinct for workmanship" and which we latterly have come to identify as "intrinsic work satisfaction"? Or, to what extent could the motivation of "social duty" be institutionalized in such a fashion that self-interest and social interest come closely to coincide? Or, how much prospective confidence can be placed in the possibilities of institution-alizing "social service" as a widespread motivation for seeking one's appropriate position and fulfilling it conscientiously?

Are not these types of motivations, we may ask, likely to prove most appropriate for precisely the "most functionally important positions"? Especially in a mass industrial society, where the vast majority of positions become standardized and routinized, it is the skilled jobs which are likely to retain most of the quality of "intrinsic job satisfaction" and be most readily identifiable as socially serviceable. Is it indeed impossible then to build these motivations into the socialization pattern to which we expose our talented youth? . . .

(5) *These scarce and desired goods consist of rights and perquisites attached to, or built into, the positions and can be classified into those things which contribute to (a) sustenance and comfort; (b) humor and diversion; (c) self-respect and ego expansion.*

(6) *This differential access to the basic rewards of the society has as a consequence the differentiation of the prestige and esteem which various strata acquire. This may be said, along with the rights and perquisites, to constitute institutionalized social inequality, i.e., stratification.*

With the classification of the rewards offered by Davis and Moore there need be little argument. Some question must be raised, however, as to whether any reward system, built into a general stratification system, must allocate equal amounts of all three types of reward in order to function effectively, or whether one type of reward may be emphasized to the virtual neglect of others. This raises the further question regarding which type of emphasis is likely to prove most effective as a differential inducer. Nothing in the known facts about human motivation impels us to favor one type of reward over the other, or to insist that all three types of reward must be built into the positions in comparable amounts if the position is to have an inducement value.

It is well known, of course, that societies differ considerably in the kinds of rewards they emphasize in their efforts to maintain a reasonable balance between responsibility and reward. There are, for instance, numerous societies in which the conspicuous display of differential economic advantage is considered extremely bad taste. In short, our present knowledge commends to us the possibility of considerable plasticity in the way in which different types of rewards can be structured into a functioning society. This is to say, it cannot yet be demonstrated that it is *unavoidable* that differential prestige and esteem shall accrue to positions which command differential rewards in power and property.

What does seem to be unavoidable is that differential prestige shall be given to those in any society who conform to the normative order as against those who deviate from that order in a way judged immoral and detrimental. On the assumption that the continuity of a society depends on the continuity and stability of its normative order, some such distinction between conformists and deviants seems inescapable.

It also seems to be unavoidable that in any society, no matter how literate its tradition, the older, wiser, and more experienced individuals who are charged with the enculturation and socialization of the young must have more power than the young, on the assumption that the task of effective socialization demands such differential power.

But this differentiation in prestige between the conformist and the deviant is by no means the same distinction as that between strata of individuals each of which operates *within* the normative order, and is composed of adults. . . .

(7) *Therefore, social inequality among different strata in the amounts of scarce and desired goods, and the amounts of prestige and esteem which they receive, is both positively functional and inevitable in any society.*

If the objections which have heretofore been raised are taken as reasonable, then it may be stated that the only items which any society *must* distribute unequally are the power and property necessary for the performance of different tasks. If such differential power and property are viewed by all as commensurate with the differential responsibilities, and if they are culturally defined as *resources* and not as rewards, then no differentials in prestige and esteem need follow.

Historically, the evidence seems to be that every time power and property are distributed unequally, no matter what the cultural definition, prestige and esteem differentiations have tended to result as well. Historically, however, no systematic effort has ever been made, under propitious circumstances, to develop the tradition that each man is as socially worthy as all other men so long as he performs his appropriate tasks conscientiously. While such a tradition seems utterly utopian, no known facts in psychological or social science have yet demonstrated its impossibility or its dysfunctionality for the continuity of a society. The achievement of a full institutionalization of such a tradition seems far too remote to contemplate. Some successive approximations at such a tradition, however, are not out of the range of prospective social innovation.

What, then, of the "positive functionality" of social stratification? Are there other, negative, functions of institutionalized social inequality which can be identified, if only tentatively? Some such dysfunctions of stratification have already been suggested in the body of this paper. Along with others they may now be stated, in the form of provisional assertions, as follows:

1. Social stratification systems function to limit the possibility of discovery of the full range of talent available in a society. This results from the fact of unequal access to appropriate motivation, channels of recruitment, and centers of training.

2. In foreshortening the range of available talent, social stratification systems function to set limits upon the possibility of expanding the productive resources of the society, at least relative to what might be the case under conditions of greater equality of opportunity.

3. Social stratification systems function to provide the elite with the political power necessary to procure acceptance and dominance of an ideology which rationalizes the *status quo,* whatever it may be, as "logical," "natural" and "morally right." In this manner, social stratification systems function as essentially conservative influences in the societies in which they are found.

4. Social stratification systems function to distribute favorable self-images unequally throughout a population. To the extent that such favorable self-images are requisite to the development of the creative potential inherent in men, to that extent stratification systems function to limit the development of this creative potential.

5. To the extent that inequalities in social rewards cannot be made fully acceptable to the less privileged in a society, social stratification systems function to encourage hostility, suspicion, and distrust among the various segments of a society and thus to limit the possibilities of extensive social integration.

6. To the extent that the sense of significant membership in a society depends on one's place on the prestige ladder of the society, social stratification systems function to distribute unequally the sense of significant membership in the population.

7. To the extent that loyalty to a society depends on a sense of significant membership in the society, social stratification systems function to distribute loyalty unequally in the population.

8. To the extent that participation and apathy depend upon the sense of significant membership in the society, social stratification systems function to distribute the motivation to participate unequally in a population.

Each of the eight foregoing propositions contains implicit hypotheses regarding the consequences of unequal distribution of rewards in a society in accordance with some notion of the functional importance of various positions. These are empirical hypotheses, subject to test. They are offered here only as exemplary of the kinds of consequences of social stratification which are not often taken into account in dealing with the problem. They should also serve to reinforce the doubt that social inequality is a device which is uniformly functional for the role of guaranteeing that the most important tasks in a society will be performed conscientiously by the most competent persons.

The obviously mixed character of the functions of social inequality should come as no surprise to anyone. If sociology is sophisticated in any sense, it is certainly with regard to its awareness of the mixed nature of any social arrangement, when the observer takes into account long- as well as short-range consequences and latent as well as manifest dimensions.

ENDNOTE

[1] Unfortunately, functional importance is difficult to establish. To use the position's prestige to establish it, as is often unconsciously done, constitutes circular reasoning from our point of view. There are, however, two independent clues: (a) the degree to which a position is functionally unique, there being no other positions that can per-

form the same function satisfactorily; and (b) the degree to which other positions are dependent on the one in question. Both clues are best exemplified in organized systems of positions built around one major function. Thus in most complex societies the religious, political, economic, and educational functions are handled by distinct structures not easily interchangeable. In addition, each structure possesses many different positions, some clearly dependent on, if not subordinate to, others. In sum, when an institutional nucleus becomes differentiated around one main function, and at the same time organizes a large portion of the population into its relationships, *key* positions in it are of the highest functional importance. The absence of such specialization does not prove functional unimportance, for the whole society may be relatively unspecialized; but it is safe to assume that the more important functions receive the first and clearest structural differentiation.

24

WHO RULES AMERICA?
The Corporate Community and the Upper Class

G. WILLIAM DOMHOFF

Sociologists utilize various indicators to measure social class. For example, *socioeconomic status* (SES) is calculated using income, educational attainment, and occupational status. Sociologists also employ subjective indicators of social class, such as attitudes and values, class identification, and consumption patterns. This selection is by G. William Domhoff, a professor emeritus of psychology at the University of California, Santa Cruz, and it is taken from his 1998 book, *Who Rules America Now? Power and Politics in the Year 2000.* Using both objective and subjective indicators of social class status, Domhoff finds that in addition to wealth, the upper class shares a distinctive lifestyle through participation in various social institutions. Domhoff argues not only that there is a cohesive upper class in the United States, but also that the upper class has a disproportionate share of power through its control over economic and political decision making in this country.

Most Americans do not like the idea that there are social classes. Classes imply that people have relatively fixed stations in life. They fly in the face of beliefs about equality of opportunity and seem to ignore the evidence of upward social mobility. Even more, Americans tend to deny that social classes are based in wealth and occupational roles but then belie that denial through a fascination with rags-to-riches stories and the trappings of wealth. . . .

If there is an American upper class, it must exist not merely as a collection of families who feel comfortable with each other and tend to exclude outsiders from their social activities. It must exist as a set of interrelated social institutions. That is, there must be patterned ways of organizing the lives of its members from infancy to old age that create a relatively unique style of life, and there must be mechanisms for socializing both the younger generation and new adult members who have risen from lower social levels. If the class is a reality, the names and faces may change somewhat over the years, but the social institutions that underlie the upper class must persist with remarkably little change over several generations. This emphasis on the institutionalized nature of the upper class, which reflects a long-standing empirical tradition in studies of it, is compatible with the theoretical focus of the "new institutionalists" within sociology and political science.

Four different types of empirical studies establish the existence of an interrelated set of social institutions, organizations, and social activities. They are historical case studies, quantitative studies of biographical directories, open-ended surveys of knowledgeable observers, and interview studies with members of the upper-middle and upper classes. . . .

Prepping for Power

From infancy through young adulthood, members of the upper class receive a distinctive education. This education begins early in life in preschools that frequently are attached to a neighborhood church of high social status. Schooling continues during the elementary years at a local private school called a day school. During the adolescent years the student may remain at day school, but there is a strong chance that at least one or two years will be spent away from home at a boarding school in a quiet rural setting. Higher education will take place at one of a small number of heavily endowed private colleges and universities. Large and well-known Ivy League schools in the East and Stanford in the West head the list, followed by smaller Ivy League schools in the East and a handful of other small private schools in other parts of the country. Although some upper-class children may attend public high school if they live in a secluded suburban setting, or go to a state university if there is one of great esteem and tradition in their home state, the system of formal schooling is so insulated that many upper-class students never see the inside of a public school in all their years of education.

This separate educational system is important evidence for the distinctiveness of the mentality and lifestyle that exists within the upper class because schools play a large role in transmitting the class structure to their students. Surveying and summarizing a great many studies on schools in general, sociologist Randall Collins concludes: "Schools primarily teach vocabulary and inflection, styles of dress, aesthetic tastes, values and manners."[1] His statement takes on greater significance for studies of the upper class when it is added that only 1 percent of American teenagers attend independent private high schools of an upper-class nature.[2]

The training of upper-class children is not restricted to the formal school setting, however. Special classes, and even tutors, are a regular part of their extracurricular education. This informal education usually begins with dancing classes in the elementary years, which are seen as important for learning proper manners and the social graces. Tutoring in a foreign language may begin in the elementary years, and there are often lessons in horseback riding and music as well. The teen years find the children of the upper class in summer camps or on special travel tours, broadening their perspectives and polishing their social skills.

The linchpins in the upper-class educational system are the dozens of boarding schools founded in the last half of the nineteenth and the early part of the twentieth centuries. Baltzell concludes that these schools became "surrogate families" that played a major role "in creating an upper-class subculture on almost a national scale in America."[3] The role of boarding schools in providing connections to other upper-class social institutions is also important. As one informant explained to Ostrander in her interview study of upper-class women: "Where I went to boarding school, there were girls from all over the country, so I know people from all over. It's helpful when you move to a new city and want to get invited into the local social club."[4]

It is within these few hundred schools that are consciously modeled after their older and more austere British counterparts that a distinctive style of life is inculcated through such traditions as the initiatory hazing of beginning students, the wearing of school blazers or ties, compulsory attendance at chapel services, and participation in esoteric sports such as squash and crew. Even a different terminology is adopted to distinguish these schools from public schools. The principal is a headmaster or rector, the teachers are sometimes called masters, and the students are in forms, not grades. Great emphasis is placed on the building of "character." The role of the school in preparing the future leaders of America is emphasized through the speeches of the headmaster and the frequent mention of successful alumni. Thus, boarding schools are in many ways the kind of highly effective socializing agent that sociologist Erving Goffman calls "total institutions," isolating their members from the outside world and providing them with a set of routines and traditions that encompass most of their waking hours.[5] The end result is a feeling of separateness and superiority that comes from having survived a rigorous education. As a retired business leader told one of my research assistants: "At school we were made to feel somewhat better [than other people] because of our class. That existed, and I've always disliked it intensely. Unfortunately, I'm afraid some of these things rub off on one."[6]

Almost all graduates of private secondary schools go on to college, and almost all do so at prestigious universities. Graduates of the New England boarding schools, for example, historically found themselves at one of four large Ivy League universities: Harvard, Yale, Princeton, and Columbia. . . . Now many upper-class students attend a select handful of smaller private liberal arts colleges, most of which are in the East, but there are a few in the South and West as well.

Graduates of private schools outside of New England most frequently attend a prominent state university in their area, but a significant minority go to Eastern Ivy League and top private universities in other parts of the country. . . . A majority of private-school graduates pursue careers in business, finance, or corporate law. For example, a classification of the occupations of a sample of the graduates of four private schools—St. Mark's, Groton, Hotchkiss, and Andover—showed that the most frequent occupation for all but the Andover graduates was some facet of finance and banking. Others became presidents of medium-size businesses or were partners in large corporate law firms. A small handful went to work as executives for major national corporations.[7] . . .

Although finance, business, and law are the most typical occupations of upper-class males, there is no absence of physicians, architects, museum officials, and other professional occupations. This fact is demonstrated most systematically in Baltzell's study of Philadelphia: 39 percent of the Philadelphia architects and physicians listed in *Who's Who* for the early 1940s were also listed in the *Social Register,* as were 35 percent of the museum officials. These figures are close to the 51 percent for lawyers and the 42 percent for businessmen, although they are far below the 75 percent for bankers—clearly the most prestigious profession in Philadelphia at that time.[8] . . .

From kindergarten through college, then, schooling is very different for members of the upper class and it teaches them to be distinctive in many ways. In a country where education is highly valued and nearly everyone attends public schools, this private system benefits primarily members of the upper class and provides one of the foundations for the old-boy and old-girl networks that will be with them throughout their lives.

Social Clubs

Just as private schools are a pervasive feature in the lives of upper-class children, so, too, are private social clubs a major point of orientation in the lives of upper-class adults. These clubs also play a role in differentiating members of the upper class from other members of society. According to Baltzell, "the club serves to place the adult members of society and their families within the social hierarchy." He quotes with approval the suggestion by historian Crane Brinton that the club "may perhaps be regarded as taking the place of those extensions of the family, such as the clan and the brotherhood, which have disappeared from advanced societies."[9] Conclusions similar to Baltzell's resulted from an interview study in Kansas City: "Ultimately, say upper-class Kansas Citians, social standing in their world reduces to one issue: where does an individual or family rank on the scale of private club memberships and informal cliques?"[10]

The clubs of the upper class are many and varied, ranging from family-oriented country clubs and downtown men's and women's clubs to highly specialized clubs for yacht owners, gardening enthusiasts, and fox hunters. Many families have memberships in several different types of clubs, but the days when most of the men by themselves were in a half dozen or more clubs faded before World War II. Downtown men's clubs originally were places for having lunch and dinner, and occasionally for attending an evening performance or a weekend party. But as upper-class families deserted the city for large suburban estates, a new kind of club, the country club, gradually took over some of these functions. The downtown club became almost entirely a luncheon club, a site to hold meetings, or a place to relax on a free afternoon. The country club, by contrast, became a haven for all members of the family. It offered social and sporting activities ranging from dances, parties, and banquets to golf, swimming, and tennis. Special group dinners were often arranged for all members on Thursday night—the traditional maid's night off across the United States.

Sporting activities are the basis for most of the specialized clubs of the upper class. The most visible are the yachting and sailing clubs, followed by the clubs for lawn tennis or squash. The most exotic are the several dozen fox hunting clubs. They have their primary strongholds in rolling countrysides from southern Pennsylvania down into Virginia, but they exist in other parts of the country as well. Riding to hounds in scarlet jackets and black boots, members of the upper class sustain over 130 hunts under the banner of the Masters of Fox Hounds Association. The intricate rituals and grand feasts accompanying the event, including the Blessing of the Hounds by an Episcopal bishop in the Eastern hunts, go back to the eighteenth century in the United States.[11]

Initiation fees, annual dues, and expenses vary from a few thousand dollars in downtown clubs to tens of thousands of dollars in some country clubs, but money is not the primary barrier in gaining membership to a club. Each club has a very rigorous screening process before accepting new members. Most require nomination by one or more active members, letters of recommendation from three to six members, and interviews with at least some members of the membership committee. Names of prospective members are sometimes posted in the clubhouse, so all members have an opportunity to make their feelings known to the membership committee. Negative votes by two or three members of what is typically a ten- to twenty-person committee often are enough to deny admission to the candidate. The carefulness with which new members are selected extends to a guarding of club membership lists, which are usually available only to club members. Older membership lists are sometimes given to libraries by members or their surviving spouses, but for most clubs there are no membership lists in the public domain.

Not every club member is an enthusiastic participant in the life of the club. Some belong out of tradition or a feeling of social necessity. One woman told Ostrander the following about her country club: "We don't feel we should withdraw our support even though we don't go much." Others mentioned a feeling of social pressure: "I've only been to [the club] once this year. I'm really a loner, but I feel I have to go and be pleasant even though I don't want to." Another volunteered: "I think half the members go because they like it and half because they think it's a social necessity." [12]

People of the upper class often belong to clubs in several cities, creating a nationwide pattern of overlapping memberships. These overlaps provide evidence for social cohesion within the upper class. An indication of the nature and extent of this overlapping is revealed by sociologist Philip Bonacich's study of membership lists for twenty clubs in several major cities across the country, including the Links in New York, the Century Association in New York, the Duquesne in Pittsburgh, the Chicago in Chicago, the Pacific Union in San Francisco, and the California in Los Angeles. Using his own original clustering technique based on Boolean algebra, his study revealed there was sufficient overlap among eighteen of the twenty clubs to form three regional groupings and a fourth group that provided a bridge between the two largest regional groups. The several dozen men who were in three or more of the clubs—most of them very wealthy people who also sat on several corporate boards—were especially important in creating the overall pattern. At the same time, the fact that these clubs often have from 1,000 to 2,000 members makes the percentage of overlap within this small number of clubs relatively small, ranging from as high as 20 to 30 percent between clubs in the same city to as low as 1 or 2 percent in clubs at opposite ends of the country. [13]

The overlap of this club network with corporate boards of directors provides evidence for the intertwining of the upper class and corporate community. In one study, the club memberships of the chairs and outside directors of the twenty largest industrial corporations were counted. The overlaps with upper-class clubs in general were ubiquitous, but the concentration of directors in a few clubs was especially notable. At least one director from twelve of the twenty corporations was a member of the Links Club, which Baltzell calls "the New York rendezvous of the national corporate establishment." [14] Seven of General Electric's directors were members, as were four from Chrysler, four from Westinghouse, three from IBM, and two from U.S. Steel. In addition to the Links, several other clubs had directors from four or more corporations. A study I did using membership lists from eleven prestigious clubs in different parts of the country confirmed and extended these findings. A majority of the top twenty-five corporations in every major sector of the economy had directors in at least one of these clubs, and several had many more. . . .

There seems to be a great deal of truth to the earlier-cited suggestion by Crane Brinton that clubs may function within the upper class the way that the clan or brotherhood does in tribal societies. With their restrictive membership policies, initiatory rituals, private ceremonials, and great emphasis on tradition, clubs carry on the heritage of primitive secret societies. They create among their members an attitude of prideful exclusiveness that contributes greatly to an in-group feeling and a sense of fraternity within the upper class.

In concluding this discussion of . . . [social clubs and] the intersection of the upper class and corporate community, it needs to be stressed that the [social club] is not a place of power. No conspiracies are hatched there, nor anywhere else. Instead, it is a place where powerful people relax, make new acquaintances, and enjoy themselves. It is primarily a place of social bonding. The main sociological function of . . . [social] clubs is stated by sociologist Thomas Powell, based on his own interview study of members in upper-class clubs:

> The clubs are a repository of the values held by the upper-level prestige groups in the community and are a means by which these values are transferred to the business environment. The clubs are places in which the beliefs, problems, and values of the industrial organization are discussed and related to the other elements in the larger community. Clubs, therefore, are not only effective vehicles of informal communication, but also valuable centers where views are presented, ideas are modified, and new ideas emerge. Those in the interview sample were appreciative of this asset; in addition, they considered the club as a valuable place to combine social and business contacts.[15]

The Female Half of the Upper Class

During the late nineteenth and early twentieth centuries, women of the upper class carved out their own distinct roles within the context of male domination in business, finance, and law. They went to separate private schools, founded their own social clubs, and belonged to their own volunteer associations. As young women and party goers, they set the fashions for society. As older women and activists, they took charge of the nonprofit social welfare and cultural institutions of the society, serving as fund-raisers, philanthropists, and directors in a manner parallel to what their male counterparts did in business and politics. To prepare themselves for their leadership roles, in 1901 they created the Junior League to provide internships, role models, mutual support, and training in the management of meetings.

Due to the general social changes of the 1960s—and in particular the revival of the feminist movement—the socialization of wealthy young women has changed somewhat in recent decades. Many private schools are now coeducational. Their women graduates are encouraged to go to major four-year colleges rather than finishing schools. Women of the upper class are more likely to have careers; there are already two or three examples of women who have risen to the top of their family's business. They are also more likely to serve on corporate boards. Still, due to its emphasis on tradition, there may be even less gender equality in the upper class than there is in the professional stratum; it is not clear how much more equality will be attained.

The female half of the upper class has been studied by several sociologists. Their work provides an important window into the upper class and class consciousness in general as well as a portrait of the socialization of well-born women. But before focusing on their work, it is worthwhile to examine one unique institution of the upper class that has not changed very much in its long history—the debutante party that announces a young woman's coming of age and eligibility for marriage. It contains general lessons on class consciousness and the difficulties of maintaining traditional socializing institutions in a time of social unrest.

The Debutante Season

The debutante season is a series of parties, teas, and dances that culminates in one or more grand balls. It announces the arrival of young women of the upper class into adult society with the utmost of formality and elegance. These highly expensive rituals—in which great attention is lavished on every detail of the food, decorations, and entertainment—have a long history in the upper class. They made their first appearance in Philadelphia in 1748 and Charleston, South Carolina, in 1762, and they vary only slightly from city to city across the country. They are a central focus of the Christmas social season just about everywhere, but in some cities debutante balls are held in the spring as well.

Dozens of people are involved in planning the private parties that most debutantes have before the grand ball. Parents, with the help of upper-class women who work as social secretaries and social consultants, spend many hours with dress designers, caterers, florists, decorators, bandleaders, and champagne importers, deciding on just the right motif for their daughter's coming out. Most parties probably cost between $25,000 and $75,000, but sometimes the occasion is so extraordinary that it draws newspaper attention. Henry Ford II spent $250,000 on a debutante party for one of his daughters, hiring a Paris designer to redo the Country Club of Detroit in an eighteenth-century chateau motif and flying in 2 million magnolia boughs from Mississippi to cover the walls of the corridor leading to the reception room. A Texas oil and real estate family chartered a commercial jet airliner for a party that began in Dallas and ended with an all-night visit to the clubs in the French Quarter of New Orleans.[16]

The debutante balls themselves are usually sponsored by local social clubs. Sometimes there is an organization whose primary purpose is the selection of debutantes and the staging of the ball, such as the Saint Cecilia Society in Charleston, South Carolina, or the Allegro Club in Houston, Texas. Adding to the solemnity of the occasion, the selection of the season's debutantes is often made by the most prominent upper-class males in the city, often through such secret societies as the Veiled Prophet in St. Louis or the Mardi Gras krewes in New Orleans.

Proceeds from the balls are usually given to a prominent local charity sponsored by members of the upper class. "Doing something for charity makes the participants feel better about spending," explains Mrs. Stephen Van Rensselear Strong, a social press agent in New York and herself a member of the upper class.[17] It also makes at least part of the expense of the occasion tax deductible.

Evidence for the great traditional importance attached to the debut is to be found in the comments Ostrander received from women who thought the whole process unimportant but made their daughters go through it anyhow: "I think it's passé, and I don't care about it, but it's just something that's done," explained one woman. Another commented: "Her father wanted her to do it. We do have a family image to maintain. It was important to the grandparents, and I felt it was an obligation to her family to do it." When people begin to talk about doing something out of tradition or to uphold an image, Ostrander suggests, then the unspoken rules that dictate class-oriented behavior are being revealed through ritual behavior.[18]

Despite the great importance placed on the debut by upper-class parents, the debutante season came into considerable disfavor among young women as the social upheavals of the late 1960s and early 1970s reached their climax. This decline reveals that the reproduction of the upper class as a social class is an effort that must be made with each new generation. Although enough young women participated to keep the tradition alive, a significant minority refused to participate, which led to the cancellation of some balls and the curtailment of many others. Stories appeared on the women's pages across the country telling of debutantes who thought the whole process was "silly" or that the money should be given to a good cause. By 1973, however, the situation began to change again, and by the mid-1970s things were back to normal.[19]

The decline of the debutante season and its subsequent resurgence in times of domestic tranquility reveal very clearly that one of its latent functions is to help perpetuate the upper class from generation to generation. When the underlying values of the class were questioned by a few of its younger members, the institution went into decline. Attitudes toward such social institutions as the debutante ball are one indicator of whether adult members of the upper class have succeeded in insulating their children from the rest of society.

The Role of Volunteer

The most informative and intimate look at the adult lives of traditional upper-class women is provided in three different interview and observation studies, one on the East Coast, one in the Midwest, and one on the West

Coast. They reveal the women to be both powerful and subservient, playing decision-making roles in numerous cultural and civic organizations but also accepting traditional roles at home vis-à-vis their husbands and children. By asking the women to describe a typical day and to explain which activities were most important to them, sociologists Arlene Daniels, Margot McLeod, and Susan Ostrander found that the role of community volunteer is a central preoccupation of upper-class women, having significance as a family tradition and as an opportunity to fulfill an obligation to the community. One elderly woman involved for several decades in both the arts and human services told Ostrander: "If you're privileged, you have a certain responsibility. This was part of my upbringing; it's a tradition, a pattern of life that my brothers and sisters do too." [20]

This volunteer role is institutionalized in the training programs and activities of a variety of service organizations, especially the Junior League, which is meant for women between 20 and 40 years of age, including some upwardly mobile professional women. "Volunteerism is crucial and the Junior League is the quintessence of volunteer work," said one woman. "Everything the League does improves the situation but doesn't rock the boat. It fits into existing institutions." [21]

Quite unexpectedly, Ostrander found that many of the women serving as volunteers, fund-raisers, and board members for charitable and civic organizations viewed their work as a protection of the American way of life against the further encroachment of government into areas of social welfare. Some even saw themselves as bulwarks against socialism. "There must always be people to do volunteer work," one said. "If you have a society where no one is willing, then you may as well have communism where it's all done by the government." Another commented: "It would mean that the government would take over, and it would all be regimented. If there are no volunteers, we would live in a completely managed society which is quite the opposite to our history of freedom." Another equated government support with socialism: "You'd have to go into government funds. That's socialism. The more we can keep independent and under private control, the better it is." [22]

Despite this emphasis on volunteer work, the women placed high value on family life. They arranged their schedules to be home when children came home from school (thirty of the thirty-eight in Ostrander's study had three or more children), and they emphasized that their primary concern was to provide a good home for their husbands. Several wanted to have greater decision-making power over their inherited wealth, but almost all wanted to take on the traditional roles of wife and mother, at least until their children were grown.

In recent years, thanks to the pressures on corporations from the women's movement, upper-class women have expanded their roles to include corporate directorships. A study of women in the corporate community by former sociologist Beth Ghiloni, now a corporate executive, found that 26 percent of all women directors had upper-class backgrounds, a figure very similar to overall findings for samples of predominantly male directors. The figure was even higher, about 71 percent, for the one-fifth of directors who described themselves as volunteers before joining corporate boards. Many of these women told Ghiloni that their contacts with male corporate leaders on the boards of women's colleges and cultural organizations led to their selection as corporate directors.[23]

Women of the upper class are in a paradoxical position. They are subordinate to male members of their class, but they nonetheless exercise important class power in some institutional arenas. They may or may not be fully satisfied with their ambiguous power status, but they bring an upper-class, antigovernment perspective to their exercise of power. There is thus class solidarity between men and women toward the rest of society. Commenting on the complex role of upper-class women, feminist scholar Catherine Stimson draws the following stark picture: "First they must do to class what gender has done to their work—render it invisible. Next, they must maintain the same class structure they have struggled to veil."[24]

Marriage and Family Continuity

The institution of marriage is as important in the upper class as it is in any level of American society, and it does not differ greatly from other levels in its patterns and rituals. Only the exclusive site of the occasion and the lavishness of the reception distinguish upper-class marriages. The prevailing wisdom within the upper class is that children should marry someone of their own social class. The women interviewed by Ostrander, for example, felt that marriage was difficult enough without differences in "interests" and "background," which seemed to be the code words for class in discussions of marriage. Marriages outside the class were seen as likely to end in divorce.[25]

The original purpose of the debutante season was to introduce the highly sheltered young women of the upper class to eligible marriage partners. It was an attempt to corral what Baltzell calls "the democratic whims of romantic love," which "often play havoc with class solidarity."[26] But the day when the debut could play such a role was long past, even by the 1940s. The function of directing romantic love into acceptable channels was taken over by fraternities and sororities, singles-only clubs, and exclusive summer resorts.

However, in spite of parental concerns and institutionalized efforts to provide proper marriage partners, some upper-class people marry members of the upper-middle and middle classes. Although there are no completely satisfactory studies, and none that are very recent, what information is available suggests that members of the upper class are no more likely to marry within their class than people of other social levels. The most frequently cited evidence on upper-class marriage patterns appears as part of biographical studies of prominent families. Though these studies demonstrate that a great many marriages take place within the class—and often between scions of very large fortunes—they also show that some marriages are to sons and daughters of middle-class professionals and managers. No systematic conclusions can be drawn from these examples.

Wedding announcements that appear in major newspapers provide another source of evidence on this question. In a study covering prominent wedding stories on the society pages on Sundays in June for two different years one decade apart, it was found that 70 percent of the grooms and 84 percent of the brides had attended a private secondary school. Two-thirds of the weddings involved at least one participant who was listed in the *Social Register,* with both bride and groom listed in the *Social Register* in 24 percent of the cases.[27] However, those who marry far below their station may be less likely to have wedding announcements prominently displayed, so such studies must be interpreted with caution.

A study that used the *Social Register* as its starting point may be indicative of rates of intermarriage within the upper class, but it is very limited in its scope and therefore can only be considered suggestive. It began with a compilation of all the marriages listed in the Philadelphia *Social Register* for 1940 and 1960. Since the decision to list these announcements may be a voluntary one, a check of the marriage announcements in the *Philadelphia Bulletin* for those years was made to see if there were any marriages involving listees in the *Social Register* that had not been included, but none was found. One in every three marriages for 1940 and one in five for 1961 involved partners who were both listed in the *Social Register.* When private-school attendance and social club membership as well as the *Social Register* were used as evidence for upper-class standing, the rate of intermarriage averaged 50 percent for the two years. This figure is very similar to that for other social levels.[28]

The general picture for social class and marriage in the United States is suggested in a statistical study of neighborhoods and marriage patterns in the San Francisco area. Its results are very similar to those of the Philadelphia study using the *Social Register.* Of eighty grooms randomly selected from the highest-level neighborhoods, court records showed that 51 percent married brides of a comparable level. The rest married women from middle-level neighborhoods; only one or two married women from lower-level residential areas. Conversely, 63 percent of eighty-one grooms from the lowest-level neighborhoods married women from comparable areas, with under 3 percent having brides from even the lower end of the group of top neighborhoods. Completing the picture, most of the eighty-two men from middle-level areas married women from the same types of neighborhoods, but about 10 percent married into higher-level neighborhoods. Patterns of intermarriage, then, suggest both stability and some upward mobility through marriage into the upper class.[29]

Turning now to the continuity of the upper class, there is evidence that it is very great from generation to generation. This finding conflicts with the oft-repeated folk wisdom that there is a large turnover at the top of the American social ladder. Once in the upper class, families tend to stay there even as they are joined in each generation by new families and by middle-class brides and grooms who marry into their families. One study demonstrating this point began with a list of twelve families who were among the top wealthholders in Detroit for 1860, 1892, and 1902. After demonstrating their high social standing as well as their wealth, it traced their Detroit-based descendants to 1970. Nine of the twelve families still had members in the Detroit upper class; members from six of the families were directors of top corporations in the city. The study cast light on some of the reasons why the continuity is not even greater. One of the top wealthholders of 1860 had only one child, who in turn had no children. Another family dropped out of sight after the six children of the original 1860 wealthholder's only child went to court to divide the dwindling estate of $250,000 into six equal parts. A third family persisted into a fourth generation of four great-granddaughters, all of whom married outside of Detroit.[30] . . .

Tracing the families of the steel executives into the twentieth century, John Ingham determined that most were listed in the *Social Register*, were members of the most exclusive social clubs, lived in expensive neighborhoods, and sent their children to Ivy League universities. He concludes that "there has been more continuity than change among the business elites and upper classes in America," and he contrasts his results with the claims made by several generations of impressionistic historians that there has been a decline of aristocracy, the rise of a new plutocracy, or a passing of the old order.[31] . . .

It seems likely, then, that the American upper class is a mixture of old and new members. There is both continuity and social mobility, with the newer members being assimilated into the lifestyle of the class through participation in the schools, clubs, and other social institutions described [here]. There may be some tensions between those newly arrived and those of established status—as novelists and journalists love to point out—but what they have in common soon outweighs their differences.[32]

ENDNOTES

[1] Randall Collins, "Functional and Conflict Theories of Educational Stratification," *American Sociological Review* 36 (1971): 1010.

[2] "Private Schools Search for a New Role," *National Observer* (August 26, 1968), p. 5. For an excellent account of major boarding schools, see Peter Cookson and Caroline Hodge Persell, *Preparing for Power: America's Elite Boarding Schools* (New York: Basic Books, 1985).

[3] E. Digby Baltzell, *Philadelphia Gentlemen: The Making of a National Upper Class* (Glencoe, IL: Free Press, 1958), p. 339.

[4] Susan Ostrander, *Women of the Upper Class* (Philadelphia: Temple University Press, 1984), p. 85.

[5] Erving Goffman, *Asylums* (Chicago: Aldine, 1961).

[6] Interview conducted for G. William Domhoff by research assistant Deborah Samuels, February 1975; see also Gary Tamkins, "Being Special: A Study of the Upper Class" (Ph.D. Dissertation, Northwestern University, 1974).

[7] Steven Levine, "The Rise of the American Boarding Schools" (Senior Honors Thesis, Harvard University, 1975), pp. 128–30.

[8] Baltzell, *Philadelphia Gentlemen,* pp. 51–65.

[9] Baltzell, *Philadelphia Gentlemen,* p. 373.

[10] Richard P. Coleman and Lee Rainwater, *Social Standing in America* (New York: Basic Books, 1978), p. 144.

[11] Sophy Burnham, *The Landed Gentry* (New York: G. P. Putnam's Sons, 1978).

[12] Ostrander, *Women of the Upper Class,* p. 104.

[13] Philip Bonacich and G. William Domhoff, "Latent Classes and Group Membership," *Social Networks* 3 (1981).

[14] G. William Domhoff, *Who Rules America?* (Englewood Cliffs, NJ: Prentice-Hall, 1967), p. 26; E. Digby Baltzell, *The Protestant Establishment,* op. cit., p. 371.

[15] Thomas Powell, *Race, Religion, and the Promotion of the American Executive* (Columbus: Ohio State University Press, 1969), p. 50.

[16] Gay Pauley, "Coming-Out Party: It's Back in Style," *Los Angeles Times,* March 13, 1977, section 4, p. 22; "Debs Put Party on Jet," *San Francisco Chronicle,* December 18, 1965, p. 2.

[17] Pauley, "Coming-Out Party."

[18] Ostrander, "Upper-Class Women: Class Consciousness As Conduct and Meaning," *Women of the Upper Class,* pp. 93–94; Ostrander, *Women of the Upper Class,* pp. 89–90.

[19] "The Debut Tradition: A Subjective View of What It's All About," *New Orleans Times-Picayune,* August 29, 1976, section 4, p. 13; Tia Gidnick, "On Being 18 in '78: Deb Balls Back in Fashion," *Los Angeles Times,* November 24, 1978, part 4, p. 1; Virginia Lee Warren, "Many Young Socialites Want Simpler Debutante Party, or None," *New York Times,* July 2, 1972, p. 34; Mary Lou Loper, "The Society Ball: Tradition in an Era of Change," *Los Angeles Times,* October 28, 1973, part 4, p. 1.

[20] Ostrander, *Women of the Upper Class,* pp. 128–29. For three other fine accounts of the volunteer work of upper-class women, see Arlene Daniels, *Invisible Careers* (Chicago: University of Chicago Press, 1988); Margot MacLeod, "Influential Women Volunteers" (paper presented to the meetings of the American Sociological Association, San Antonio, August 1984); and Margot MacLeod, "Older Generation, Younger Generation: Transition in Women Volunteers' Lives" (unpublished manuscript, 1987). For women's involvement in philanthropy and on the boards of nonprofit organizations, see Teresa Odendahl, *Charity Begins at Home: Generosity and Self-Interest among the Philanthropic Elite* (New York: Basic Books, 1990), and Teresa Odendahl and Michael O'Neill, eds., *Women and Power in the Nonprofit Sector* (San Francisco: Jossey-Bass, 1994). For in-depth interviews of both women and men philanthropists, see Francie Ostrower, *Why the Wealthy Give: The Culture of Elite Philanthropy* (Princeton, NJ: Princeton University Press, 1995).

[21] Ostrander, *Women of the Upper Class,* pp. 113, 115.

[22] Ostrander, "Upper-Class Women," p. 84; Ostrander, *Women of the Upper Class,* pp. 132–37.

[23] Beth Ghiloni, "New Women of Power" (Ph.D. Dissertation, University of California, Santa Cruz, 1986), pp. 122, 159.

[24] Daniels, *Invisible Careers,* p. x.

[25] Ostrander, *Women of the Upper Class,* pp. 85–88.

[26] Baltzell, *Philadelphia Gentlemen*, p. 26.

[27] Paul M. Blumberg and P. W. Paul, "Continuities and Discontinuities in Upper-Class Marriages," *Journal of Marriage and the Family*, vol. 37, no. 1 (February 1975): 63–77; David L. Hatch and Mary A. Hatch, "Criteria of Social Status As Derived from Marriage Announcements in the *New York Times*," *American Sociological Review* 12 (August 1947): 396–403.

[28] Lawrence Rosen and Robert R. Bell, "Mate Selection in the Upper Class," *Sociological Quarterly* 7 (Spring 1966): 157–66. I supplemented the original study by adding the information on schools and clubs.

[29] Robert C. Tryon, "Identification of Social Areas by Cluster Analysis: A General Method with an Application to the San Francisco Bay Area," *University of California Publications in Psychology* 8 (1955); Robert C. Tryon, "Predicting Group Differences in Cluster Analysis: The Social Areas Problem," *Multivariate Behavioral Research* 2 (1967):4 53–75.

[30] T. D. Schuby, "Class Power, Kinship, and Social Cohesion: A Case Study of a Local Elite," *Sociological Focus* 8, no. 3 (August 1975): 243–55; Donald Davis, "The Price of Conspicuous Production: The Detroit Elite and the Automobile Industry, 1900–1933," *Journal of Social History* 16 (1982): 21–46.

[31] John Ingham, *The Iron Barons* (Westport, CT: Greenwood Press, 1978), pp. 230–31. For the continuity of a more general sample of wealthy families, see Michael Allen, *The Founding Fortunes* (New York: Truman Talley Books, 1987).

[32] For further evidence of the assimilation of new members into the upper class, see the study of the social affiliations and attitudes of the successful Jewish business owners who become part of the upper class by Richard L. Zweigenhaft and G. William Domhoff, *Jews in the Protestant Establishment* (New York: Praeger, 1982).

25

BLACK WEALTH/WHITE WEALTH
A New Perspective on Racial Inequality

MELVIN L. OLIVER • THOMAS M. SHAPIRO

As G. William Domhoff argues in the previous selection, social classes do exist in America, and class distinctions can be observed through a variety of objective and subjective indicators. To understand social class relationships fully, however, sociologists also must examine racial-ethnic differences in the indicators of socioeconomic status. For example, data show persistent wealth discrepancies between African Americans and European Americans with similar achievements and credentials. Sociologists Melvin L. Oliver and Thomas M. Shapiro examine this racial inequality in wealth in their book *Black Wealth/White Wealth: A New Perspective on Racial Inequality* (1995). In the excerpt that follows, Oliver and Shapiro analyze state policies that currently and historically have curtailed opportunities for wealth accumulation among African Americans.

A frican Americans are vastly overrepresented among those Americans whose lives are the most economically and socially distressed. As William Julius Wilson has argued in *The Truly Disadvantaged*, "the most disadvantaged segments of the black urban community" have come to make up the majority of "that heterogeneous grouping of families and individuals who are outside the mainstream of the American occupational system," and who are euphemistically called the underclass.[1] With little or no access to jobs, trapped in poor areas with bad schools and little social and economic opportunity, members of the underclass resort to crime, drugs, and other forms of aberrant behavior to make a living and eke some degree of meaning out of their materially impoverished existence. Douglas Massey and Nancy Denton's *American Apartheid* has reinforced in our minds the crucial significance of racial segregation, which Lawrence Bobo calls the veritable "structural linchpin" of American racial inequality.[2]

These facts should not be in dispute. What is in dispute is our understanding of the source of such resounding levels of racial inequality. What factors were responsible for their creation and what are the sources of their continuation? Sociologists and social scientists have focused on either race or class or on some combination or interaction of the two as overriding factors responsible for racial inequality.

A focus on race suggests that race has had a unique cultural meaning in American society wherein blacks have been oppressed in such a way as to perpetuate their inferiority and second-class citizenship. Race in this context has a socially constructed meaning that is acted on by whites to purposefully limit and constrain the black population. The foundation of this social construction is the ideology of racism. Racism is a belief in the inherent inferiority of one race in relation to another. Racism both justifies and dictates the actions and institutional decisions that adversely affect the target group.[3]

Class explanations emphasize the relational positioning of blacks and whites in society and the differential access to power that accrues to the status of each group. Those classes with access to resources through the ownership or control of capital (in the Marxian variant) or through the occupational hierarchy (in the Weberian variant) are able to translate these resources into policies and structures through their access to power. In some cases this can be seen in the way in which those who control the economy also control the polity. In other cases it can be observed in the way in which institutional elites control institutions. In any case the class perspective emphasizes the relative positions of blacks and whites with respect to the ownership and control of the means of production and to access to valued occupational niches, both historically and contemporaneously. Because blacks have traditionally had access to few of these types of valued resources, they share an interest with the other have-nots. As Raymond Franklin notes in *Shadows of Race and Class*, "Ownership carries with it domination; its absence leads to subordination." [4] The subordinated and unequal status of African Americans, in the class perspective, grows out of the structured class divisions between blacks and a small minority of resource-rich and powerful whites.

Each of these perspectives has been successfully applied to understanding racial inequality. However, each also has major failings. The emphasis on race creates problems of evidence. Especially in the contemporary period, as William Wilson notes in *The Declining Significance of Race*, it is difficult to trace the enduring existence of racial inequality to an articulated ideology of racism. The trail of historical evidence proudly left in previous periods is made less evident by heightened sensitivity to legal sanctions and racial civility in language. Thus those who still emphasize race in the modern era speak of covert racism and use as evidence racial disparities in income, jobs, and housing. In fact, however, impersonal structural forces whose racial motivation cannot be ascertained are often the cause of the black disadvantage that observers identify. Likewise, class perspectives usually wash away any reference to race.[5] Moreover, the class-based analysis that blacks united with low-income white workers and other disadvantaged groups would be the most likely source of collective opposition to current social economic arrangements has given way to continued estrangement between these groups.[6] The materialist perspective that policy should address broad class groups as opposed to specific racial groups leaves the unique historical legacy of race untouched.

Despite these weaknesses it is imperative that race and class factors be taken into consideration in any attempt to understand contemporary racial inequality. It is clear, however, that a singular focus on one as opposed to another is counterproductive. Take, for example, earnings inequality. As economists assert, earnings are affected today more by class than by racial factors. Human capital attributes (such as education, experience, skills, etc.) that may result from historical disadvantages play an important role in the earnings gap between blacks and whites. But because of the unique position of black Americans, earnings must be viewed in relation to joblessness. If you do not have a job, you have no earnings. Here it is clear that race and class are important. As structural changes in the economy have occurred, blacks have been disproportionately disadvantaged. Such structural changes as the movement of entry-level jobs outside of the central city, the change in the economy from goods to service production, and the shift to higher skill levels have created a jobless black population.[7] Furthermore, increasing numbers of new entrants into the labor market find low-skill jobs below poverty wages that do not support a family. Nevertheless, race is important as well. Evidence from employers shows that negative racial attitudes about black workers are still motivating their hiring practices, particularly in reference to central-city blacks and in the service economy. In service jobs nonblacks are preferred over blacks, particularly black men, a preference that contributes to the low wages blacks earn, to high rates of joblessness, and thus to earnings inequality.[8]

Because of the way in which they reveal the effect of historical factors on contemporary processes, racial differences in wealth provide an important means of combining race and class arguments about racial inequality. We therefore turn to a theoretical discussion of wealth and race that develops aspects of traditional race and class arguments in an attempt to illuminate the processes that have led to wealth disparities between black and white Americans.

Toward a Sociology of Race and Wealth

A sociology of race and wealth must go beyond the traditional analysis of wealth that economists have elaborated. Economists begin with the assumption that wealth is a combination of inheritance, earnings, and savings and is enhanced by prudent consumption and investment patterns over a person's lifetime. Of course, individual variability in any of these factors depends on a whole set of other relationships that are sociologically relevant. Obviously, one's inheritance depends on the family into which one is born. If one's family of origin is wealthy, one's chances of accumulating more wealth in a lifetime are greater. Earnings, the economists tell us, are a function of the productivity of our human capital: our education, experience, and skills. Since these are, at least in part, dependent on an investment in training activities, they can be acquired by means of inherited resources. Savings are a function of both our earning power and our consumption patterns. Spendthrifts will have little or no disposable income to save, while those who are frugal can find ways to put money aside. Those with high levels of human capital, who socially interact in the right circles, and who have knowledge of investment opportunities, will increase their wealth substantially more during their lifetime, than will those who are only thrifty. And since money usually grows over time, the earlier one starts and the longer one's money is invested, the more wealth one will be able to amass. Economists therefore explain differences in wealth accumulation by pointing to the lack of resources that blacks inherit compared to whites, their low investment in human capital, and their extravagant patterns of consumption.

Sociologists do not so much disagree with the economists' emphasis on these three factors and their relationship to human capital in explaining black-white differences in wealth; rather, they are concerned that economists have not properly appreciated the social context in which the processes in question take place. Quite likely, formal models would accurately predict wealth differences. However, in the real world, an emphasis on these factors isolated from the social context misses the underlying reasons for why whites and blacks have displayed such strong differences in their ability to generate wealth. The major reason that blacks and whites differ in their ability to accumulate wealth is not only that they come from different class backgrounds or that their consumption patterns are different or that they fail to save at the same rate but that the structure of investment opportunity that blacks and whites face has been dramatically different. Work and wages play a smaller role in the accumulation of wealth than the prevailing discourse admits.

Blacks and whites have faced an opportunity to create wealth that has been structured by the intersection of class and race. Economists rightly note that blacks' lack of desirable human capital attributes places them at a disadvantage in the wealth accumulation process. However, those human capital deficiencies can be traced, in part, to barriers that denied blacks access to quality education, job training opportunities, jobs, and other work-related factors. Below we develop three concepts—the racialization of the state, the economic detour, and the sedimentation of racial inequality—to help us situate the distinct structures of investment opportunity that blacks and whites have faced in their attempts to generate wealth.

Racialization of the State

The context of one's opportunity to acquire land, build community, and generate wealth has been structured particularly by state policy. Slavery itself, the most constricting of social systems, was a result of state policy that gave blacks severely limited economic rights. Slaves were by law not able to own property or accumulate assets.[9] In contrast, no matter how poor whites were, they had the right—if they were males, that is—if not the ability, to buy land, enter into contracts, own businesses, and develop wealth assets that could build equity and economic self-sufficiency for themselves and their families. Some argue that it was the inability to participate in and develop a habit of savings during slavery that directly accounts for low wealth development among blacks today. Using a cultural argument, they assert that slaves developed a habit of excessive consumerism and not one of savings and thrift. This distorts the historical reality, however. While slaves were legally not able to amass wealth they did, in large numbers, acquire assets through thrift, intelligence, industry, and their owners' liberal paternalism. These assets were used to buy their own and their loved ones' freedom, however, and thus did not form the core of a material legacy that could be passed from generation to generation. Whites could use their wealth for the future; black slaves' savings could only buy the freedom that whites took for granted.

Slavery was only one of the racialized state policies that have inhibited the acquisition of assets for African Americans. . . . The homestead laws that opened up the East during colonial times and West during the nineteenth century created vastly different opportunities for black and white settlers. One commentator even suggests land grants "allowed three-fourths of America's colonial families to own their own farms."[10] Black settlers in California, the "Golden State," found that their claims for homestead status were not legally enforceable. Thus African Americans were largely barred from taking advantage of the nineteenth-century federal land-grant program.[11]

A centerpiece of the New Deal social legislation and a cornerstone of the modern welfare state, the old-age insurance program of the Social Security Act of 1935 virtually excluded African Americans and Latinos, for it exempted agricultural and domestic workers from coverage and marginalized low-wage workers.[12] As Gwendolyn Mink shows in "The Lady and the Tramp," men's benefits were tied to wages, military service, and unionism rather than to need or any notion of equality. Thus blacks were disadvantaged in New Deal legislation because they were historically less well paid, less fully employed, disproportionately ineligible for military service, and less fully unionized than white men. Minority workers were covered by social security and New Deal labor policies if employed in eligible occupations and if they earned the minimum amount required. Because minority wages were so low, minority workers fell disproportionately below the threshold for coverage in comparison to whites. In 1935, for example, 42 percent of black workers in occupations covered by social insurance did not earn enough to qualify for benefits compared to 22 percent for whites.[13]

Not only were blacks initially disadvantaged in their eligibility for social security, but they have disproportionately paid more into the system and received less. Because social security contributions are made on a flat rate and black workers earn less, as Jill Quadagno explains in *The Color of Welfare,* "black men were taxed on 100 percent of their income, on average, while white men earned a considerable amount of untaxed income." Black workers also earn lower retirement benefits. And benefits do not extend as long as for whites because their life span is shorter. Furthermore, since more black women are single, divorced, or separated, they cannot look forward to sharing a spouse's benefit. As Quadagno notes, again, the tax contributions of black working women "subsidize the benefits of white housewives."[14] In many ways, social security is a model state program that allows families to preserve assets built over a lifetime. For African Americans, however, it is a different kind of model of state bias. Initially built on concessions made to white racial privilege in the South, the social security program today is a system in which blacks pay more to receive less. It is a prime example of how the political process and state policy build opportunities for asset accumulation sharply skewed along racial lines.

We now turn to three other instruments of state policy that we feel have been central to creating structured opportunities for whites to build assets while significantly curtailing access to those same opportunities among blacks. Sometimes the aim was blatantly racial; sometimes the racial intention was not clear. In both instances, however, the results have been explicitly racial. They are the Federal Housing Authority; the Supplementary Social Security Act, which laid the foundation for . . . Aid to Families with Dependent Children (AFDC); and the United States tax code. In each case, state policies have created differential opportunities for blacks and whites to develop disposable income and to generate wealth.

FHA

As noted in earlier research, the development of low-interest, long-term mortgages backed by the federal government marked the appearance of a crucial opportunity for the average American family to generate a wealth stake. The purchase of a home has now become the primary mechanism for generating wealth. However, the FHA's conscious decision to channel loans away from the central city and to the suburbs has had a powerful effect on the creation of segregated housing in post–World War II America. George Lipsitz reports in "The Possessive Investment in Whiteness" that in the Los Angeles area of Boyle Heights, FHA appraisers denied home loans to prospective buyers because the neighborhood was "a melting pot area literally honeycombed with diverse and subversive elements." [15] Official government policy supported the prejudiced attitudes of private finance companies, realtors, appraisers, and a white public resistant to sharing social space with blacks.

The FHA's official handbook even went so far as to provide a model "restrictive covenant" that would pass court scrutiny to prospective white homebuyers. Such policies gave support to white neighborhoods like those in East Detroit in 1940. Concerned that blacks would move in, the Eastern Detroit Realty Association sponsored a luncheon on "the benefits of an improvement association" where the speaker, a lawyer, lectured on how "to effect legal restrictions against the influx of colored residents into white communities." [16] He went on to present the elements needed to institute a legally enforceable restrictive covenant for "a district of two miles square." Such a task was too much for one man and would require an "organization" that could mobilize and gain the cooperation of "everyone in a subdivision." Imagine the hurdles that are placed in the path of blacks' attempts to move into white neighborhoods when communities, realtors, lawyers, and the federal government are all wholly united behind such restrictions!

Restrictive covenants and other "segregation markers" have been ruled unconstitutional in a number of important court cases. But the legacy of the FHA's contribution to racial residential segregation lives on in the inability of blacks to incorporate themselves into integrated neighborhoods in which the equity and demand for their homes is maintained. This is seen most clearly in the fact that black middle-class homeowners end up with less valuable homes even when their incomes are similar to those of whites. When black middle-class families pursue the American Dream in white neighborhoods adjacent to existing black communities, a familiar process occurs. As one study explains it:

> White households will begin to move out and those neighborhoods will tend to undergo complete racial transition or to "tip." Typically, when the percentage of blacks in a neighborhood increases to a relatively small amount, 10 to 20 percent, white demand for housing in the neighborhood will fall off and the neighborhood will tip toward segregation.[17]

Even though the neighborhood initially has high market value generated by the black demand for houses, as the segregation process kicks in, housing values rise at a slower rate. By the end of the racial transition, housing prices have declined as white homeowners flee. Thus middle-class blacks encounter lower rates of home appreciation than do similar middle-class whites in all-white communities. As Raymond Franklin notes in *Shadows of Race and Class,* this is an example of how race and class considerations are involved in producing black-white wealth differentials. The "shadow" of class creates a situation of race. To quote Franklin:

> In sum, because there is a white fear of being inundated with lower-class black "hordes" who lack market capacities, it becomes necessary to prevent the entry of middle-class black families who have market capacities. In this way, middle-class blacks are discriminated against for purely racial reasons. . . . Given the "uncertainty inherent in racial integration and racial transition," white families—unwilling to risk falling property values—leave the area. This, of course, leads to falling prices, enabling poorer blacks' to enter the neighborhood "until segregation becomes complete."[18]

The impact of race and class is also channeled through institutional mechanisms that help to destabilize black communities. Insurance redlining begins to make it difficult and/or expensive for homes and businesses to secure coverage. City services begin to decline, contributing to blight. As the community declines, it becomes the center for antisocial activities: drug dealing, hanging out, and robbery and violence.[19] In this context the initial investment that the middle-class black family makes either stops growing or grows at a rate that is substantially lower than the rate at which a comparable investment made by a similarly well-off, middle-class white in an all-white community would gain in value. Racialized state policy contributed to this pattern, and the pattern continues unabated today.

AFDC

Within the public mind and according to [recent] political debate, AFDC [became] synonymous with "welfare," even though it represents less than 10 percent of all assistance for the poor.[20] The small sums paid to women and their children are designed not to provide families a springboard for their future but to help them survive in a minimal way from day to day. When the initial legislation for AFDC was passed, few of its supporters envisioned a program that would serve large numbers of African American women and their children; the ideal recipient, according to Michael Katz in *In the Shadow of the Poor House,* "was a white widow and her young children." Until the mid-1960s, states enforced this perception through the establishment of eligibility requirements that disproportionately excluded black women and their children. Southern states routinely deemed black women and their children as "unsuitable" for welfare by way of demeaning home inspections and searches. Northern states likewise created barriers that were directly targeted at black-female-headed families. They participated in "midnight raids" to discover whether a "man was in the house" or recomputed budgets to find clients ineligible and keep them off the rolls. Nonetheless, by the mid-1960s minorities were disproportionately beneficiaries of AFDC, despite intentions to the contrary. In 1988 while blacks and Hispanics made up only 44 percent of all women who headed households, they constituted 55 percent of all AFDC recipients.[21]

In exchange for modest and sometimes niggardly levels of income support, women must go through an "assets test" before they are eligible. Michael Sherraden describes it this way in his *Assets and the Poor:*

> The assets test requires that recipients have no more than minimal assets (usually $1,500, with home equity excluded) in order to become or remain eligible for the program. The asset test effectively prohibits recipients from accumulating savings.[22]

As a consequence, women enter welfare on the economic edge. They deplete almost all of their savings in order to become eligible for a program that will not provide more than a subsistence living. What little savings remain are usually drawn down to meet routine shortfalls and emergencies. The result is that AFDC [became] for many women, especially African American women, a state-sponsored policy to encourage and maintain asset poverty.

To underscore the impact of AFDC's strictures, let us draw the distinction between this program and Supplementary Security Income (SSI), a program that provides benefits for women and children whose spouses have died or become disabled after paying into social security. In contrast to AFDC benefits, SSI payments are generous. More important perhaps, eligibility for SSI does not require drawing down a family's assets as part of a "means test." The result, which is built into the structure of American welfare policy, is that "means tested" programs like AFDC and "non-means tested" social insurance programs like social security and SSI, in Michael Katz's words, have "preserved class distinctions" and "in no way redistribute income."[23] It is also an example of how the racialization of the state preserves and broadens the already deep wealth divisions between black and white.

The Internal Revenue Code

A substantial portion of state expenditures take the form of tax benefits, or "fiscal welfare." These benefits are hidden in the tax code as taxes individuals do not have to pay because the government has decided to encourage certain types of activity and behavior and not others. In *America: Who Really Pays the Taxes?* Donald Barlett and James Steele write that one of the most cherished privileges of the very rich and powerful resides in their ability to influence the tax code for their own benefit by protecting capital assets. Tax advantages may come in the form of different rates on certain types of income, tax deferral, or deductions, exclusions, and credits. Many are asset-based: if you own certain assets, you receive a tax break. In turn, these tax breaks directly help people accumulate financial and real assets. They benefit not only the wealthy but the broad middle class of homeowners and pension holders as well. More important, since blacks have fewer assets to begin with, the effect of the tax code's "fiscal welfare" is to limit the flow of tax relief to blacks and to redirect it to those who already have assets. The seemingly race-neutral tax code thus generates a racial effect that deepens rather than equalizes the economic gulf between blacks and whites.

Two examples will illustrate how the current functioning of the tax code represents yet another form of the "racialization of state policy." The *lower tax rates on capital gains* and the *deduction for home mortgages and real estate taxes,* we argue, flow differentially to blacks and whites because of the fact that blacks generally have fewer and different types of assets than whites with similar incomes.

For most of our nation's tax history, the Internal Revenue Code has encouraged private investment by offering lower tax rates for income gained through "capital assets." This policy exists to encourage investment and further asset accumulation, not to provide more spendable income. In 1994, earned income in the top bracket was taxed at 39.6 percent, for example, while capital gains were taxed at 24 percent, a figure that can go as low as 14 percent. One has to be networked with accountants, tax advisers, investors, partners, and friends knowledgeable about where to channel money to take advantage of these breaks. Capital gains may be derived from the sale of stocks, bonds, commodities, and other assets. In 1989 the IRS reported that $150.2 billion in capital gains income was reported by taxpayers.[24] While this sounds like a lot of capital gains for everyone to divvy up, the lion's share (72 percent) went to individuals and families earning more than $100,000 yearly. These families represented only 1 percent of all tax filers. The remaining $42 billion in capital gains income was reported by only 7.2 million people with incomes of under $100,000 per year. This group represented only 6 percent of tax filers. Thus for more than nine of every ten tax filers (93 percent) no capital gains income was reported. Clearly then, the tax-reduction benefits on capital gains income are highly concentrated among the nation's wealthiest individuals and families. Thus it would follow that blacks, given their lower incomes and fewer assets, would be much less likely than whites to gain the tax advantage associated with capital gains. The black disadvantage becomes most obvious when one compares middle-class and higher-income blacks to whites at a similar level of earnings. Despite comparable incomes, middle-class blacks have fewer of their wealth holdings in capital-producing assets than similarly situated whites. Our data show that among high-earning families ($50,000 a year or more) 17 percent of whites' assets are in stocks, bonds, and mortgages versus 5.4 percent for blacks. Thus, while race-neutral in intent, the current tax policy on capital gains provides disproportionate benefits to high-income whites, while limiting a major tax benefit to practically all African Americans.

Accessible to a larger group of Americans are those tax deductions, exclusions, and deferrals that the IRS provides to homeowners. Four IRS-mandated benefits can flow from home ownership: (1) the home mortgage interest deduction; (2) the deduction for local real estate taxes; (3) the avoidance of taxes on the sale of a home when it is "rolled over" into another residence; and (4) the one-time permanent exclusion of up to $125,000 of profit on the sale of a home after the age of fifty-five. Put quite simply, since blacks are less likely to own homes, they are less likely to be able to take advantage of these benefits. Furthermore, since black homes are on average less expensive than white homes, blacks derive less benefit than whites when they do utilize these tax provisions. And finally, since most of the benefits in question here are available only when taxpayers itemize their deductions, there is a great deal of concern that many black taxpayers may not take advantage of the tax breaks they are eligible for because they file the short tax form. The stakes here are very high. The subsidy that goes to homeowners in the form of tax deductions for mortgage interest and property taxes alone comes to $54 billion, about $20 billion of which goes to the top 5 percent of taxpayers.[25]

These examples illustrate how the U.S. tax code channels benefits and encourages property and capital asset accumulation differentially by race. They are but a few of several examples that could have been used. Tax provisions pertaining to inheritance, gift income, alimony payments, pensions and Keogh accounts, and property appreciation, along with the marriage tax and the child-care credit, on their face are not color coded, yet they carry with them the potential to channel benefits away from most blacks and toward some whites. State policy has racialized the opportunities for the development of wealth, creating and sustaining the existing patterns of wealth inequality and extending them into the future. . . .

The Sedimentation of Racial Inequality

The disadvantaged status of contemporary African Americans cannot be divorced from the historical processes that undergird racial inequality. The past has a living effect on the present. We argue that the best indicator of this sedimentation of racial inequality is wealth. Wealth is one indicator of material disparity that captures the historical legacy of low wages, personal and organizational discrimination, and institutionalized racism. The low levels of wealth accumulation evidenced by current generations of black Americans best represent the position of blacks in the stratificational order of American society.

Each generation of blacks generally began life with few material assets and confronted a world that systematically thwarted any attempts to economically better their lives. In addition to the barriers that we have just described in connection with the racialization of state policy and the economic detour, blacks also faced other major obstacles in their quest for economic security. In the South, for example, as W. E. B. Du Bois notes in *Black Reconstruction in America,* blacks were tied to a system of peonage that kept them in debt virtually from cradle to grave. Schooling was segregated and unequally funded. Blacks in the smokestack industries of the North and the South were paid less and assigned to unskilled and dirty jobs.[26] The result was that generation after generation of blacks remained anchored to the lowest economic status in American society. The effect of this "generation after generation" of poverty and economic scarcity for the accumulation of wealth has been to "sediment" this kind of inequality into the social structure.

The sedimentation of inequality occurred because blacks had barriers thrown up against them in their quest for material self-sufficiency. Whites in general, but well-off whites in particular, were able to amass assets and use their secure economic status to pass their wealth from generation to generation. What is often not acknowledged is that the accumulation of wealth for some whites is ultimately tied to the poverty of wealth for most blacks.[27] Just as blacks have had "cumulative disadvantages," whites have had "cumulative advantages." Practically, every circumstance of bias and discrimination against blacks has produced a circumstance and opportunity of positive gain for whites. When black workers were paid less than white workers, white workers gained a benefit; when black businesses were confined to the segregated black market, white businesses received the benefit of diminished competition; when FHA policies denied loans to blacks, whites were the beneficiaries of the spectacular growth of good housing and housing equity in the suburbs. The cumulative effect of such a process has been to sediment blacks at the bottom of the social hierarchy and to artificially raise the relative position of some whites in society.

To understand the sedimentation of racial inequality, particularly with respect to wealth, is to acknowledge the way in which structural disadvantages have been layered one upon the other to produce black disadvantage and white privilege. Returning again to the Federal Housing Act of 1934, we may recall that the federal government placed its credit behind private loans to homebuyers, thus putting home ownership within the reach of millions of citizens for the first time. White homeowners who had taken advantage of FHA financing policies saw the value of their homes increase dramatically, especially during the 1970s when housing prices tripled.[28] As previously noted, the same FHA policies excluded blacks and segregated them into all-black areas that either were destroyed during urban renewal in the sixties or benefited only marginally from the inflation of the 1970s. Those who were locked out of the housing market by FHA policies and who later sought to become first-time homebuyers faced rising housing costs that curtailed their ability to purchase the kind of home they desired. The postwar generation of whites whose parents gained a foothold in the housing market through the FHA will harvest a bounteous inheritance in the years to come.[29] Thus the process of asset accumulation that began in the 1930s has become layered over and over by social and economic trends that magnify inequality over time and across generations.

ENDNOTES

[1] Wilson (1987:8).

[2] Bobo (1989:307).

[3] See Omi and Winant (1986).

[4] Franklin (1991:xviii).

[5] See Baran and Sweezy (1966) and Cox (1948).

[6] See Hill (1977) and Jacobson (1968).

[7] See Johnson and Oliver (1992); Kasarda (1988); and Wilson (1987).

[8] See Kirschenman and Neckerman (1991).

[9] See Butler (1991); Light (1972); and Myrdal (1944).

[10] Anderson (1994:123).

[11] See Beasley (1919).

[12] See Quadagno (1994:20–24).

[13] Quadagno (1994:161).

[14] Ibid., p. 162.

[15] Lipsitz (1995).

[16] Thomas (1992:140).

[17] Mieszkowski and Syron (1979:35).

[18] Franklin (1991:126).

[19] See Skogan (1990).

[20] See Rank (1994) and Stack (1974).

[21] Sherraden (1991:63).

[22] Ibid., p. 64.

[23] See Katz (1986:247).

[24] See Barlett and Steele (1992).

[25] See Jackman and Jackman (1980); Ong and Grigsby (1988); and Horton and Thomas (1993).

[26] See Jaynes (1986) and Lieberson (1980); Bloch (1969) and Bonacich (1976).

[27] See Blauner (1972); Lipsitz (1995); and Thurow (1975).

[28] See Adams (1988) and Stutz and Kartman (1982).

[29] See Levy and Michel (1996).

REFERENCES

Adams, John. 1988. "Growth of U.S. Cities and Recent Trends in Urban Real Estate Values." Pp. 108–45 in *Cities and Their Vital Systems,* edited by J. H. Ausubel and R. Herman. Washington, DC: National Academy Press.

Anderson, Claud. 1994. *Black Labor, White Wealth: The Search for Power and Economic Justice.* Edgewood, MD: Duncan and Duncan.

Baran, Paul A. and Paul M. Sweezy. 1966. *Monopoly Capital.* New York: Monthly Review Press.

Barlett, Donald L. and James B. Steele. 1992. *America: What Went Wrong?* Kansas City: Andrews and McMeel.

———. 1994. *America: Who Really Pays the Taxes?* New York: Touchstone.

Beasley, Delilah. 1919. *Negro Trail Blazers of California.* Los Angeles: Times Mirror Print and Binding House.

Blauner, Bob. 1972. *Racial Oppression in America.* New York: Harper.

Bloch, Herman David. 1969. *The Circle of Discrimination: An Economic and Social Study of the Black Man in New York.* New York: New York University Press.

Bobo, Lawrence. 1989. "Keeping the Linchpin in Place: Testing the Multiple Sources of Opposition to Residential Integration." *Revue Internationale de Psychologie Sociale* 2:306–23.

Bonacich, Edna. 1976. "Advanced Capitalism and Black-White Relations in the United States: A Split Labor Market Interpretation." *American Sociological Review* 37:547–59.

Butler, John Sibley. 1991. *Entrepreneurship and Self-Help among Black Americans: A Reconsideration of Race and Economics.* Albany: State University of New York Press.

Cox, Oliver C. 1948. *Caste, Race, and Class.* New York: Modern Reader Paperback.

Du Bois, W. E. B. 1935. *Black Reconstruction in America.* New York: Harcourt, Brace.

Franklin, Raymond S. 1991. *Shadows of Race and Class.* Minneapolis: University of Minnesota Press.

Hill, Herbert. 1977. *Black Labor and the American Legal System: Race, Work, and the Law.* Madison: University of Wisconsin Press.

Horton, Hayward Derrick and Melvin E. Thomas. 1993. "Race, Class, and Family Structure: Differences in Housing Values for Black and White Homeowners." Unpublished manuscript.

Jackman, Mary R. and Robert W. Jackman. 1980. "Racial Inequalities in Home Ownership." *Social Forces* 58:1221–33.

Jacobson, Julius, ed. 1968. *The Negro and the American Labor Movement.* New York: Anchor.

Jaynes, Gerald D. 1986. *Branches without Roots: Genesis of the Black Working Class in the American South, 1862–1882.* New York: Oxford University Press.

Johnson, James H. and Melvin L. Oliver. 1992. "Structural Changes in the U.S. Economy and Black Male Joblessness: A Reassessment." Pp. 113–47 in *Urban Labor Markets and Job Opportunity,* edited by George Peterson and Wayne Vroman. Washington, DC: Urban Institute Press.

Kasarda, John D. 1988. "Jobs, Migration, and Emerging Urban Mismatches." Pp. 148–98 in *Urban Change and Poverty,* edited by M. G. H. McGeary and L. E. Lynn, Jr. Washington, DC: National Academy Press.

Katz, Michael. 1986. *In the Shadow of the Poor House: A Social History of Welfare in America.* New York: Basic Books.

Kirschenman, Joleen and Katherine Neckerman. 1991. "'We'd Love to Hire Them But': The Meaning of Race for Employers." Pp. 203–32 in *The Urban Underclass,* edited by Christopher Jencks and Paul Peterson. Washington, DC: Brookings Institution.

Levy, Frank S. and Richard Michel. 1996. "An Economic Bust for the Baby Boom." *Challenge,* March/April: 33–39.

Lieberson, Stanley. 1980. *A Piece of the Pie.* Berkeley: University of California Press.

Light, Ivan. 1972. *Ethnic Enterprise in America.* Berkeley: University of California Press.

Lipsitz, George. 1995. "The Possessive Investment in Whiteness: The 'White' Problem in American Studies." *American Quarterly,* Fall.

Massey, Douglas S. and Nancy A. Denton. 1993. *American Apartheid: Segregation and the Making of the Underclass.* Cambridge, MA: Harvard University Press.

Mieszkowski, Peter and Richard F. Syron. 1979. "Economic Explanations for Housing Segregation." *New England Economic Review,* November/December: 33–34.

Mink, Gwendolyn. 1990. "The Lady and the Tramp: Gender, Race, and the Origins of the American Welfare State." Pp. 92–122 in *Women, the State, and Welfare,* edited by Linda Gordon. Madison: University of Wisconsin Press.

Myrdal, Gunnar. 1944. *An American Dilemma.* New York: Harper.

Omi, Michael and Howard Winant. 1986. *Racial Formation in the United States: From the 1960s to the 1980s.* New York: Routledge.

Ong, Paul and Eugene Grigsby, III. 1988. "Race and Life Cycle Effects on Home Ownership in Los Angeles, 1970 to 1980." *Urban Affairs Quarterly* 23:601–15.

Quadagno, Jill. 1994. *The Color of Welfare.* New York: Oxford University Press.

Rank, Mark R. 1994. *Living on the Edge: The Realities of Welfare in America.* New York: Columbia University Press.

Sherraden, Michael. 1991. *Assets and the Poor: A New American Welfare Policy.* New York: Sharpe.

Skogan, Wesley G. 1990. *Disorder and Decline: Crime and the Spiral of Decay in American Neighborhoods.* New York: Free Press.

Stack, Carol. 1974. *All Our Kin.* New York: Harper.

Stutz, Fred and A. E. Kartman. 1982. "Housing Affordability and Spatial Price Variation in the United States." *Economic Geography* 58:221–35.

Thomas, Richard Walter. 1992. *Life for Us Is What We Make It: Building Black Community in Detroit, 1915–1945.* Bloomington: Indiana University Press.

Thurow, Lester C. 1975. *Generating Inequality: Mechanisms of Distribution in the U.S. Economy.* New York: Basic Books.

Wilson, William J. 1978. *The Declining Significance of Race.* Chicago: University of Chicago Press.

———. 1987. *The Truly Disadvantaged.* Chicago: University of Chicago Press.

26

NICKEL-AND-DIMED
on (Not) Getting By in America

BARBARA EHRENREICH

As the previous reading by Oliver and Shapiro demonstrated, the American Dream and accumulation of wealth have been difficult to obtain for African Americans. They also have been impossible goals for the working poor. Instead, many working-class people struggle to meet the economic requirements of everyday survival. In the excerpt below, Barbara Ehrenreich describes what it is like to try to work and survive on the wages most unskilled workers receive in America. Ehrenreich began her field research in 1998 to find out whether welfare reform's back-to-work programs really have the ability to lift poor women out of poverty and provide them a future in the labor market. The results of Ehrenreich's research are published in her 2001 book, *Nickel and Dimed: On (Not) Getting By in America.*

At the beginning of June 1998 I leave behind everything that normally soothes the ego and sustains the body—home, career, companion, reputation, ATM card—for a plunge into the low-wage workforce. There, I become another, occupationally much diminished "Barbara Ehrenreich"—depicted on job-application forms as a divorced homemaker whose sole work experience consists of housekeeping in a few private homes. I am terrified, at the beginning, of being unmasked for what I am: a middle-class journalist setting out to explore the world that welfare mothers are entering, at the rate of approximately 50,000 a month, as welfare reform kicks in. Happily, though, my fears turn out to be entirely unwarranted: during a month of poverty and toil, my name goes unnoticed and for the most part unuttered. In this parallel universe where my father never got out of the mines and I never got through college, I am "baby," "honey," "blondie," and, most commonly, "girl."

My first task is to find a place to live. I figure that if I can earn $7 an hour—which, from the want ads, seems doable—I can afford to spend $500 on rent, or maybe, with severe economies, $600. In the Key West area, where I live, this pretty much confines me to flophouses and trailer homes—like the one, a pleasing fifteen-minute drive from town, that has no air-conditioning, no screens, no fans, no television, and, by way of diversion, only the challenge of evading the landlord's Doberman pinscher. The big problem with this place, though, is the rent, which at $675 a month is well beyond my reach. All right, Key West is expensive. But so is New York City, or the Bay Area, or Jackson Hole, or Telluride, or Boston, or any other place where tourists and the wealthy compete for living space with the people who clean their toilets and fry their hash browns.[1] Still, it is a shock to realize that "trailer trash" has become, for me, a demographic category to aspire to.

So I decide to make the common trade-off between affordability and convenience, and go for a $500-a-month efficiency thirty miles up a two-lane highway from the employment opportunities of Key West, meaning forty-five minutes if there's no road construction and I don't get caught behind some sun-dazed Canadian tourists. I hate the drive, along a roadside studded with white crosses commemorating the more effective head-on collisions, but it's a sweet little place—a cabin, more or less, set in the swampy back yard of the converted mobile home where my landlord, an affable TV repairman, lives with his bartender girlfriend. Anthropologically speaking, a bustling trailer park would be preferable, but here I have a gleaming white floor and a firm mattress, and the few resident bugs are easily vanquished.

Besides, I am not doing this for the anthropology. My aim is nothing so mistily subjective as to "experience poverty" or find out how it "really feels" to be a long-term low-wage worker. I've had enough unchosen encounters with poverty and the world of low-wage work to know it's not a place you want to visit for touristic purposes; it just smells too much like fear. And with all my real-life assets—bank account, IRA, health insurance, multiroom home—waiting indulgently in the background, I am, of course, thoroughly insulated from the terrors that afflict the genuinely poor.

No, this is a purely objective, scientific sort of mission. The humanitarian rationale for welfare reform—as opposed to the more punitive and stingy impulses that may actually have motivated it—is that work will lift poor women out of poverty while simultaneously inflating their self-esteem and hence their future value in the labor market. Thus, whatever the hassles involved in finding child care, transportation, etc., the transition from welfare to work will end happily, in greater prosperity for all. Now there are many problems with this comforting prediction, such as the fact that the economy will inevitably undergo a downturn, eliminating many jobs. Even without a downturn, the influx of a million former welfare recipients into the low-wage labor market could depress wages by as much as 11.9 percent, according to the Economic Policy Institute (EPI) in Washington, D.C.

But is it really possible to make a living on the kinds of jobs currently available to unskilled people? Mathematically, the answer is no, as can be shown by taking $6 to $7 an hour, perhaps subtracting a dollar or two an hour for child care, multiplying by 160 hours a month, and comparing the result to the prevailing rents. According to the National Coalition for the Homeless, for example, in 1998 it took, on average nationwide, an hourly wage of $8.89 to afford a one-bedroom apartment, and the Preamble Center for Public Policy estimates that the odds against a typical welfare recipient's landing a job at such a "living wage" are about 97 to 1. If these numbers are right, low-wage work is not a solution to poverty and possibly not even to homelessness.

It may seem excessive to put this proposition to an experimental test. As certain family members keep unhelpfully reminding me, the viability of low-wage work could be tested, after a fashion, without ever leaving my study. I could just pay myself $7 an hour for eight hours a day, charge myself for room and board, and total up the numbers after a month. Why leave the people and work that I love? But I am an experimental scientist by training. In that business, you don't just sit at a desk and theorize; you plunge into the everyday chaos of nature, where surprises lurk in the most mundane measurements. Maybe, when I got into it, I would discover some hidden economies in the world of the low-wage worker. After all, if 30 percent of the workforce toils for less than $8 an hour, according to the EPI, they may have found some tricks as yet unknown to me. Maybe—who knows?—I would even be able to detect in myself the bracing psychological effects of getting out of the house, as promised by the welfare wonks at places like the Heritage Foundation. Or, on the other hand, maybe there would be unexpected costs—physical, mental, or financial—to throw off all my calculations. Ideally, I should do this with two small children in tow, that being the welfare average, but mine are grown and no one is willing to lend me theirs for a month-long vacation in penury. So this is not the perfect experiment, just a test of the best possible case: an unencumbered woman, smart and even strong, attempting to live more or less off the land.

On the morning of my first full day of job searching, I take a red pen to the want ads, which are auspiciously numerous. Everyone in Key West's booming "hospitality industry" seems to be looking for someone like me—trainable, flexible, and with suitably humble expectations as to pay. . . .

Most of the big hotels run ads almost continually, just to build a supply of applicants to replace the current workers as they drift away or are fired, so finding a job is just a matter of being at the right place at the right time and flexible enough to take whatever is being offered that day. This finally happens to me at a one of the big discount hotel chains, where I go, as usual, for housekeeping and am sent, instead, to try out as a waitress at the attached "family restaurant," a dismal spot with a counter and about thirty tables that looks out on a parking garage and features such tempting fare as "Polish [sic] sausage and BBQ sauce" on 95-degree days. Phillip, the dapper young West Indian who introduces himself as the manager, interviews me with about as much enthusiasm as if he were a clerk processing me for Medicare, the principal questions being what shifts can I work and when can I start. I mutter something about being woefully out of practice as a waitress, but he's already on to the uniform: I'm to show up tomorrow wearing black slacks and black shoes; he'll provide the rust-colored polo shirt with HEARTHSIDE embroidered on it, though I might want to wear my own shirt to get to work, ha ha. At the word "tomorrow," something between fear and indignation rises in my chest. I want to say, "Thank you for your time, sir, but this is just an ex-periment, you know, not my actual life."

So begins my career at the Hearthside, I shall call it, one small profit cen-ter within a global discount hotel chain, where for two weeks I work from 2:00 till 10:00 P.M. for $2.43 an hour plus tips.[2] In some futile bid for gentility, the management has barred employees from using the front door, so my first day I enter through the kitchen, where a red-faced man with shoulder-length blond hair is throwing frozen steaks against the wall and yelling, "Fuck this shit!" "That's just Jack," explains Gail, the wiry middle-aged waitress who is assigned to train me. "He's on the rag again"—a condition occasioned, in this instance, by the fact that the cook on the morning shift had forgotten to thaw out the steaks. For the next eight hours, I run after the agile Gail, absorbing bits of instruction along with fragments of personal tragedy. All food must be trayed, and the reason she's so tired today is that she woke up in a cold sweat thinking of her boyfriend, who killed himself recently in an upstate prison. No refills on lemonade. And the reason he was in prison is that a few DUIs caught up with him, that's all, could have happened to anyone. Carry the creamers to the table in a monkey bowl, never in your hand. And after he was gone she spent several months living in her truck, peeing in a plastic pee bot-tle and reading by candlelight at night, but you can't live in a truck in the summer, since you need to have the windows down, which means anything can get in, from mosquitoes on up.

At least Gail puts to rest any fears I had of appearing overqualified. From the first day on, I find that of all the things I have left behind, such as home and identity, what I miss the most is competence. Not that I have ever felt ut-terly competent in the writing business, in which one day's success augurs nothing at all for the next. But in my writing life, I at least have some notion of procedure: do the research, make the outline, rough out a draft, etc. As a server, though I am beset by requests like bees: more iced tea here, ketchup over there, a to-go box for table fourteen, and where are the high chairs, any-way? Of the twenty-seven tables, up to six are usually mine at any time, though on slow afternoons or if Gail is off, I sometimes have the whole place to myself. There is the touch-screen computer-ordering system to master, which is, I suppose, meant to minimize server-cook contact, but in practice requires constant verbal fine-tuning: "That's gravy on the mashed, okay? None on the meatloaf," and so forth—while the cook scowls as if I were in-venting these refinements just to torment him. Plus, something I had forgot-ten in the years since I was eighteen: about a third of a server's job is "side work" that's invisible to customers—sweeping, scrubbing, slicing, refilling, and restocking. If it isn't all done, every little bit of it, you're going to face the 6:00 P.M. dinner rush defenseless and probably go down in flames. I screw up dozens of times at the beginning, sustained in my shame entirely by Gail's support—"It's okay, baby, everyone does that sometime"—because, to my total surprise and despite the scientific detachment I am doing my best to maintain, I care. . . .

On my first Friday at the Hearthside there is a "mandatory meeting for all restaurant employees," which I attend, eager for insight into our overall marketing strategy and the niche (your basic Ohio cuisine with a tropical twist?) we aim to inhabit. But there is no "we" at this meeting. Phillip, our top manager except for an occasional "consultant" sent out by corporate headquarters, opens it with a sneer: "The break room—it's disgusting. Butts in the ashtrays, newspapers lying around, crumbs." This windowless little room, which also houses the time clock for the entire hotel, is where we stash our bags and civilian clothes and take our half-hour meal breaks. But a break room is not a right, he tells us. It can be taken away. We should also know that the lockers in the break room and whatever is in them can be searched at any time. Then comes gossip; there has been gossip; gossip (which seems to mean employees talking among themselves) must stop. Off-duty employees are henceforth barred from eating at the restaurant, because "other servers gather around them and gossip." When Phillip has exhausted his agenda of rebukes, Joan complains about the condition of the ladies' room and I throw in my two bits about the vacuum cleaner. But I don't see any backup coming from my fellow servers, each of whom has subsided into her own personal funk; Gail, my role model, stares sorrowfully at a point six inches from her nose. The meeting ends when Andy, one of the cooks, gets up, muttering about breaking up his day off for this almighty bullshit.

Just four days later we are suddenly summoned into the kitchen at 3:30 P.M., even though there are live tables on the floor. We all—about ten of us—stand around Phillip, who announces grimly that there has been a report of some "drug activity" on the night shift and that, as a result, we are now to be a "drug-free" workplace, meaning that all new hires will be tested, as will possibly current employees on a random basis. I am glad that this part of the kitchen is so dark, because I find myself blushing as hard as if I had been caught toking up in the ladies' room myself: I haven't been treated this way—lined up in the corridor, threatened with locker searches, peppered with carelessly aimed accusations—since junior high school. Back on the floor, Joan cracks, "Next they'll be telling us we can't have sex on the job." When I ask Stu what happened to inspire the crackdown, he just mutters about "management decisions" and takes the opportunity to upbraid Gail and me for being too generous, with the rolls. From now on there's to be only one per customer, and it goes out with the dinner, not with the salad. He's also been riding the cooks, prompting Andy to come out of the kitchen and observe—with the serenity of a man whose customary implement is a butcher knife—that "Stu has a death wish today."

The other problem, in addition to the less-than-nurturing management style, is that this job shows no sign of being financially viable. You might imagine, from a comfortable distance, that people who live, year in and year out, on $6 to $10 an hour have discovered some survival stratagems unknown to the middle class. But no. It's not hard to get my co-workers to talk about their living situations, because housing, in almost every case, is the principal source of disruption in their lives, the first thing they fill you in on when they arrive for their shifts. After a week, I have compiled the following survey:

- ▾ Gail is sharing a room in a well-known downtown flophouse for which she and a roommate pay about $250 a week. Her roommate, a male friend, has begun hitting on her, driving her nuts, but the rent would be impossible alone.
- ▾ Claude, the Haitian cook, is desperate to get out of the two-room apartment he shares with his girlfriend and two other, unrelated, people. As far as I can determine, the other Haitian men (most of whom only speak Creole) live in similarly crowded situations.
- ▾ Annette, a twenty-year-old server who is six months pregnant and has been abandoned by her boyfriend, lives with her mother, a postal clerk.
- ▾ Marianne and her boyfriend are paying $170 a week for a one-person trailer.
- ▾ Jack, who is, at $10 an hour, the wealthiest of us, lives in the trailer he owns, paying only the $400-a-month lot fee.
- ▾ The other white cook, Andy, lives on his dry-docked boat, which, as far as I can tell from his loving descriptions, can't be more than twenty feet long. He offers to take me out on it, once it's repaired, but the offer comes with inquiries as to my marital status, so I do not follow up on it.
- ▾ Tina and her husband are paying $60 a night for a double room in a Days Inn. This is because they have no car and the Days Inn is within walking distance of the Hearthside. When Marianne, one of the breakfast servers, is tossed out of her trailer for subletting (which is against the trailer-park rules), she leaves her boyfriend and moves in with Tina and her husband.
- ▾ Joan, who had fooled me with her numerous and tasteful outfits (hostesses wear their own clothes), lives in a van she parks behind a shopping center at night and showers in Tina's motel room. The clothes are from thrift shops.[3]

It strikes me, in my middle-class solipsism, that there is gross improvidence in some of these arrangements. When Gail and I are wrapping silverware in napkins—the only task for which we are permitted to sit—she tells me she is thinking of escaping from her roommate by moving into the Days Inn herself. I am astounded: How can she even think of paying between $40 and $60 a day? But if I was afraid of sounding like a social worker, I come out just sounding like a fool. She squints at me in disbelief, "And where am I supposed to get a month's rent and a month's deposit for an apartment?" I'd been feeling pretty smug about my $500 efficiency, but of course it was made possible only by the $1,300 I had allotted myself for start-up costs when I began my low-wage life: $1,000 for the first month's rent and deposit, $100 for initial groceries and cash in my pocket, $200 stuffed away for emergencies. In poverty, as in certain propositions in physics, starting conditions are everything.

There are no secret economies that nourish the poor; on the contrary, there are a host of special costs. If you can't put up the two months' rent you need to secure an apartment, you end up paying through the nose for a room by the week. If you have only a room, with a hot plate at best, you can't save by cooking up huge lentil stews that can be frozen for the week ahead. You eat fast food, or the hot dogs and styrofoam cups of soup that can be microwaved in a convenience store. If you have no money for health insurance—and the Hearthside's niggardly plan kicks in only after three months—you go without routine care or prescription drugs and end up paying the price. Gail, for example, was fine until she ran out of money for estrogen pills. She is supposed to be on the company plan by now, but they claim to have lost her application form and need to begin the paperwork all over again. So she spends $9 per migraine pill to control the headaches she wouldn't have, she insists, if her estrogen supplements were covered. Similarly, Marianne's boyfriend lost his job as a roofer because he missed so much time after getting a cut on his foot for which he couldn't afford the prescribed antibiotic.

My own situation, when I sit down to assess it after two weeks of work, would not be much better if this were my actual life. The seductive thing about waitressing is that you don't have to wait for payday to feel a few bills in your pocket, and my tips usually cover meals and gas, plus something left over to stuff into the kitchen drawer I use as a bank. But as the tourist business slows in the summer heat, I sometimes leave work with only $20 in tips (the gross is higher, but servers share about 15 percent of their tips with the busboys and bartenders). With wages included, this amounts to about the minimum wage of $5.15 an hour. Although the sum in the drawer is piling up, at the present rate of accumulation it will be more than a hundred dollars short of my rent when the end of the month comes around. Nor can I see any expenses to cut. True, I haven't gone the lentil-stew route yet, but that's because I don't have a large cooking pot, pot holders, or a ladle to stir with (which cost about $30 at Kmart, less at thrift stores), not to mention onions, carrots, and the indispensable bay leaf. I do make my lunch almost every day—usually some slow-burning, high-protein combo like frozen chicken patties with melted cheese on top and canned pinto beans on the side. Dinner is at the Hearthside, which offers its employees a choice of BLT, fish sandwich, or hamburger for only $2. The burger lasts longest, especially if it's heaped with gut-puckering jalapenos, but by midnight my stomach is growling again.

So unless I want to start using my car as a residence, I have to find a second, or alternative, job. I call all the hotels where I filled out housekeeping applications weeks ago—the Hyatt, Holiday Inn, Econo Lodge, Hojo's, Best Western, plus a half dozen or so locally run guesthouses. Nothing. Then I start making the rounds again, wasting whole mornings waiting for some assistant manager to show up, even dipping into places so creepy that the front-desk clerk greets you from behind bulletproof glass and sells pints of liquor over the counter. But either someone has exposed my real-life housekeeping habits—which are, shall we say, mellow—or I am at the wrong end of some infallible ethnic equation: most, but by no means all, of the working house-keepers I see on my job searches are African Americans, Spanish-speaking, or immigrants from the Central European post-Communist world, whereas servers are almost invariably white and monolingually English-speaking. When I finally get a positive response, I have been identified once again as server material. Jerry's, which is part of a well-known national family restaurant chain and physically attached here to another budget hotel chain, is ready to use me at once. The prospect is both exciting and terrifying, because, with about the same number of tables and counter seats, Jerry's attracts three or four times the volume of customers as the gloomy old Hearthside. . . .

I start out with the beautiful, heroic idea of handling the two jobs at once, and for two days I almost do it: the breakfast/lunch shift at Jerry's, which goes till 2:00, arriving at the Hearthside at 2:10, and attempting to hold out until 10:00. In the ten minutes between jobs, I pick up a spicy chicken sandwich at the Wendy's drive-through window, gobble it down in the car, and change from khaki slacks to black, from Hawaiian to rust polo. There is a problem, though. When during the 3:00 to 4:00 P.M. dead time I finally sit down to wrap silver, my flesh seems to bond to the seat. I try to refuel with a purloined cup of soup, as I've seen Gail and Joan do dozens of times, but a manager catches me and hisses "No eating!" though there's not a customer around to be offended by the sight of food making contact with a server's lips. So I tell Gail I'm going to quit, and she hugs me and says she might just follow me to Jerry's herself.

But the chances of this are minuscule. She has left the flophouse and her annoying roommate and is back to living in her beat-up old truck. But guess what? she reports to me excitedly later that evening: Phillip has given her permission to park overnight in the hotel parking lot, as long as she keeps out of sight, and the parking lot should be totally safe, since it's patrolled by a hotel security guard! With the Hearthside offering benefits like that, how could anyone think of leaving? . . .

Management at Jerry's is generally calmer and more "professional" than at the Hearthside, with two exceptions. One is Joy, a plump, blowsy woman in her early thirties, who once kindly devoted several minutes to instructing me in the correct one-handed method of carrying trays but whose moods change disconcertingly from shift to shift and even within one. Then there's B.J., a.k.a. B.J.-the-bitch, whose contribution is to stand by the kitchen counter and yell, "Nita, your order's up, move it!" or, "Barbara, didn't you see you've got another table out there? Come on, girl!" Among other things, she is hated for having replaced the whipped-cream squirt cans with big plastic whipped-cream-filled baggies that have to be squeezed with both hands— because, reportedly, she saw or thought she saw employees trying to inhale the propellant gas from the squirt cans, in the hope that it might be nitrous oxide. On my third night, she pulls me aside abruptly and brings her face so close that it looks as if she's planning to butt me with her forehead. But instead of saying, "You're fired," she says, "You're doing fine." The only trouble is I'm spending time chatting with customers: "That's how they're getting you." Furthermore I am letting them "run me," which means harassment by sequential demands: you bring the ketchup and they decide they want extra Thousand Island; you bring that and they announce they now need a side of fries; and so on into distraction. Finally she tells me not to take her wrong. She tries to say things in a nice way, but you get into a mode, you know, because everything has to move so fast. . . .[4]

I make the decision to move closer to Key West. First, because of the drive. Second and third, also because of the drive: gas is eating up $4 to $5 a day, and although Jerry's is as high-volume as you can get, the tips average only 10 percent, and not just for a newbie like me. Between the base pay of $2.15 an hour and the obligation to share tips with the busboys and dishwashers, we're averaging only about $7.50 an hour. Then there is the $30 I had to spend on the regulation tan slacks worn by Jerry's servers—a setback it could take weeks to absorb. (I had combed the town's two downscale department stores hoping for something cheaper but decided in the end that these marked-down Dockers, originally $49, were more likely to survive a daily washing.) Of my fellow servers, everyone who lacks a working husband or boyfriend seems to have a second job: Nita does something at a computer eight hours a day; another welds. Without the forty-five-minute commute, I can picture myself working two jobs and having the time to shower between them.

So I take the $500 deposit I have coming from my landlord, the $400 I have earned toward the next month's rent, plus the $200 reserved for emergencies, and use the $1,100 to pay the rent and deposit on trailer number 46 in the Overseas Trailer Park, a mile from the cluster of budget hotels that constitute Key West's version of an industrial park. Number 46 is about eight feet in width and shaped like a barbell inside, with a narrow region—because of the sink and the stove—separating the bedroom from what might optimistically be called the "living" area, with its two-person table and half-sized couch. The bathroom is so small my knees rub against the shower stall when I sit on the toilet, and you can't just leap out of the bed; you have to climb down to the foot of it in order to find a patch of floor space to stand on. Outside, I am within a few yards of a liquor store, a bar that advertises "free beer tomorrow," a convenience store, and a Burger King—but no supermarket or, alas, laundromat. By reputation, the Overseas park is a nest of crime and crack, and I am hoping at least for some vibrant, multicultural street life. But desolation rules night and day, except for a thin stream of pedestrian traffic heading for their jobs at the Sheraton or 7-Eleven. There are not exactly people here but what amounts to canned labor, being preserved from the heat between shifts.

In line with my reduced living conditions, a new form of ugliness arises at Jerry's. First we are confronted—via an announcement on the computers through which we input orders—with the new rule that the hotel bar is henceforth off-limits to restaurant employees. The culprit, I learn through the grapevine, is the ultra-efficient gal who trained me—another trailer-home dweller and a mother of three. Something had set her off one morning, so she slipped out for a nip and returned to the floor impaired. This mostly hurts Ellen, whose habit it is to free her hair from its rubber band and drop by the bar for a couple of Zins before heading home at the end of the shift, but all of us feel the chill. Then the next day, when I go for straws, for the first time I find the dry-storage room locked. Ted, the portly assistant manager who opens it for me, explains that he caught one of the dishwashers attempting to steal something, and, unfortunately, the miscreant will be with us until a re-placement can be found—hence the locked door. I neglect to ask what he had been trying to steal, but Ted tells me who he is—the kid with the buzz cut and the earring. You know, he's back there right now.

I wish I could say I rushed back and confronted George to get his side of the story. I wish I could say I stood up to Ted and insisted that George be given a translator and allowed to defend himself, or announced that I'd find a lawyer who'd handle the case pro bono. The mystery to me is that there's not much worth stealing in the dry-storage room, at least not in any fenceable quantity: "Is Gyorgi here, and am having 200—maybe 250—ketchup pack-ets. What do you say?" My guess is that he had taken—if he had taken any-thing at all—some Saltines or a can of cherry-pie mix, and that the motive for taking it was hunger.

So why didn't I intervene? Certainly not because I was held back by the kind of moral paralysis that can pass as journalistic objectivity. On the con-trary, something new—something loathsome and servile—had infected me, along with the kitchen odors that I could still sniff on my bra when I finally undressed at night. In real life I am moderately brave, but plenty of brave people shed their courage in concentration camps, and maybe something similar goes on in the infinitely more congenial milieu of the low-wage American workplace. Maybe, in a month or two more at Jerry's, I might have regained my crusading spirit. Then again, in a month or two I might have turned into a different person altogether—say, the kind of person who would have turned George in.

But this is not something I am slated to find out. When my month-long plunge into poverty is almost over, I finally land my dream job—housekeep-ing. I do this by walking into the personnel office of the only place I figure I might have some credibility, the hotel attached to Jerry's, and confiding urgently that I have to have a second job if I am to pay my rent and, no, it couldn't be front-desk clerk. "All right," the personnel lady fairly spits, "so it's housekeeping," and she marches me back to meet Maria, the housekeeping manager, a tiny, frenetic Hispanic woman who greets me as "babe" and hands me a pamphlet emphasizing the need for a positive attitude. The hours are nine in the morning till whenever, the pay is $6.10 an hour, and there's one week of vacation a year. I don't have to ask about health insurance once I meet

Carlotta, the middle-aged African American woman who will be training me. Carla, as she tells me to call her, is missing all of her top front teeth.

On that first day of housekeeping and last day of my entire project— although I don't yet know it's the last—Carla is in a foul mood. We have been given nineteen rooms to clean, most of them "checkouts," as opposed to "stay-overs," that require the whole enchilada of bed-stripping, vacuuming, and bathroom-scrubbing. When one of the rooms that had been listed as a stay-over turns out to be a checkout, Carla calls Maria to complain, but of course to no avail. "So make up the motherfucker," Carla orders me, and I do the beds while she sloshes around the bathroom. For four hours without a break I strip and remake beds, taking about four and a half minutes per queen-sized bed, which I could get down to three if there were any reason to. We try to avoid vacuuming by picking up the larger specks by hand, but often there is nothing to do but drag the monstrous vacuum cleaner—it weighs about thirty pounds—off our cart and try to wrestle it around the floor. Sometimes Carla hands me the squirt bottle of "BAM" (an acronym for something that begins, ominously, with "butyric"; the rest has been worn off the label) and lets me do the bathrooms. No service ethic challenges me here to new heights of performance. I just concentrate on removing the pubic hairs from the bathtubs, or at least the dark ones that I can see. . . .

When I request permission to leave at about 3:30, another housekeeper warns me that no one has so far succeeded in combining housekeeping at the hotel with serving at Jerry's: "Some kid did it once for five days, and you're no kid." With that helpful information in mind, I rush back to number 46, down four Advils (the name brand this time), shower, stooping to fit into the stall, and attempt to compose myself for the oncoming shift. So much for what Marx termed the "reproduction of labor power," meaning the things a worker has to do just so she'll be ready to work again. The only unforeseen obstacle to the smooth transition from job to job is that my tan Jerry's slacks, which had looked reasonably clean by 40-watt bulb last night when I hand-washed my Hawaiian shirt, prove by daylight to be mottled with ketchup and ranch-dressing stains. I spend most of my hour-long break between jobs attempting to remove the edible portions with a sponge and then drying the slacks over the hood of my car in the sun.

I can do this two-job thing, is my theory, if I can drink enough caffeine and avoid getting distracted by George's ever more obvious suffering.[5] The first few days after being caught he seemed not to understand the trouble he was in, and our chirpy little conversations had continued. But the last couple of shifts he's been listless and unshaven, and tonight he looks like the ghost we all know him to be, with dark half-moons hanging from his eyes. At one point, when I am briefly immobilized by the task of filling little paper cups with sour cream for baked potatoes, he comes over and looks as if he'd like to explore the limits of our shared vocabulary, but I am called to the floor for a table. I resolve to give him all my tips that night and to hell with the experiment in low-wage money management. At eight, Ellen and I grab a snack together standing at the mephitic end of the kitchen counter, but I can only manage two or three mozzarella sticks and lunch had been a mere handful of McNuggets. I am not tired at all, I assure myself, though it may be that there is simply no more "I" left to do the tiredness monitoring. What I would see, if I were more alert to the situation, is that the forces of destruction are already massing against me. There is only one cook on duty, a young man named Jesus ("Hay-Sue," that is) and he is new to the job. And there is Joy, who shows up to take over in the middle of the shift, wearing high heels and a long, clingy white dress and fuming as if she'd just been stood up in some cocktail bar.

Then it comes, the perfect storm. Four of my tables fill up at once. Four tables is nothing for me now, but only so long as they are obligingly staggered. As I bev table 27, tables 25, 28, and 24 are watching enviously. As I bev 25, 24 glowers because their bevs haven't even been ordered. Twenty-eight is four yuppyish types, meaning everything on the side and agonizing instructions as to the chicken Caesars. Twenty-five is a middle-aged black couple, who complain, with some justice, that the iced tea isn't fresh and the tabletop is sticky. But table 24 is the meteorological event of the century: ten British tourists who seem to have made the decision to absorb the American experience entirely by mouth. Here everyone has at least two drinks—iced tea and milk shake, Michelob and water (with lemon slice, please)—and a huge promiscuous orgy of breakfast specials, mozz sticks, chicken strips, quesadillas, burgers with cheese and without, sides of hash browns with cheddar, with onions, with gravy, seasoned fries, plain fries, banana splits. Poor Jesus! Poor me! Because when I arrive with their first tray of food—after three prior trips just to refill bevs—Princess Di refuses to eat her chicken strips with her pancake-and-sausage special, since, as she now reveals, the strips were meant to be an appetizer. Maybe the others would have accepted their meals, but Di, who is deep into her third Michelob, insists that everything else go back while they work on their "starters." Meanwhile, the yuppies are waving me down for more decaf and the black couple looks ready to summon the NAACP.

Much of what happened next is lost in the fog of war. Jesus starts going under. The little printer on the counter in front of him is spewing out orders faster than he can rip them off, much less produce the meals. Even the invincible Ellen is ashen from stress. I bring table 24 their reheated main courses, which they immediately reject as either too cold or fossilized by the microwave. When I return to the kitchen with their trays (three trays in three trips), Joy confronts me with arms akimbo: "What is this?" She means the food—the plates of rejected pancakes, hash browns in assorted flavors, toasts, burgers, sausages, eggs. "Uh, scrambled with cheddar," I try, "and that's . . ." "NO," she screams in my face. "Is it a traditional, a super-scramble, an eye-opener?" I pretend to study my check for a clue, but entropy has been up to its tricks, not only on the plates but in my head, and I have to admit that the original order is beyond reconstruction. "You don't know an eye-opener from a traditional?" she demands in outrage. All I know, in fact, is that my legs have lost interest in the current venture and have announced their intention to fold. I am saved by a yuppie (mercifully not one of mine) who chooses this moment to charge into the kitchen to bellow that his food is twenty-five minutes late. Joy screams at him to get the hell out of her kitchen, please, and then turns on Jesus in a fury, hurling an empty tray across the room for emphasis.

I leave. I don't walk out; I just leave. I don't finish my side work or pick up my credit-card tips, if any, at the cash register or, of course, ask Joy's permission to go. And the surprising thing is that you can walk out without permission, that the door opens, that the thick tropical night air parts to let me pass, that my car is still parked where I left it. There is no vindication in this exit, no fuck-you surge of relief, just an overwhelming, dank sense of failure pressing down on me and the entire parking lot. I had gone into this venture in the spirit of science, to test a mathematical proposition, but somewhere along the line, in the tunnel vision imposed by long shifts and relentless concentration, it became a test of myself, and clearly I have failed. Not only had I flamed out as a housekeeper/server, I had even forgotten to give George my tips, and, for reasons perhaps best known to hardworking, generous people like Gail and Ellen, this hurts. I don't cry, but I am in a position to realize, for the first time in many years, that the tear ducts are still there, and still capable of doing their job.

When I moved out of the trailer park, I gave the key to number 46 to Gail and arranged for my deposit to be transferred to her. She told me that Joan is still living in her van and that Stu had been fired from the Hearthside. I never found out what happened to George.

In one month, I had earned approximately $1,040 and spent $517 on food, gas, toiletries, laundry, phone, and utilities. If I had remained in my $500 efficiency, I would have been able to pay the rent and have $22 left over (which is $78 less than the cash I had in my pocket at the start of the month). During this time I bought no clothing except for the required slacks and no prescription drugs or medical care (I did finally buy some vitamin B to compensate for the lack of vegetables in my diet). Perhaps I could have saved a little on food if I had gotten to a supermarket more often, instead of convenience stores, but it should be noted that I lost almost four pounds in four weeks, on a diet weighted heavily toward burgers and fries.

How former welfare recipients and single mothers will (and do) survive in the low-wage workforce, I cannot imagine. Maybe they will figure out how to condense their lives—including child-raising, laundry, romance, and meals—into the couple of hours between full-time jobs. Maybe they will take up residence in their vehicles, if they have one. All I know is that I couldn't hold two jobs and I couldn't make enough money to live on with one. And I had advantages unthinkable to many of the long-term poor—health, stamina, a working car, and no children to care for and support. Certainly nothing in my experience contradicts the conclusion of Kathryn Edin and Laura

Lein, in their [1997] book *Making Ends Meet: How Single Mothers Survive Welfare and Low-Wage Work,* that low-wage work actually involves more hardship and deprivation than life at the mercy of the welfare state. In the coming months and years, economic conditions for the working poor are bound to worsen, even without the almost inevitable recession. As mentioned earlier, the influx of former welfare recipients into the low-skilled workforce will have a depressing effect on both wages and the number of jobs available. A general economic downturn will only enhance these effects, and the working poor will of course be facing it without the slight, but nonetheless often saving, protection of welfare as a backup.

The thinking behind welfare reform was that even the humblest jobs are morally uplifting and psychologically buoying. In reality they are likely to be fraught with insult and stress. But I did discover one redeeming feature of the most abject low-wage work—the camaraderie of people who are, in almost all cases, far too smart and funny and caring for the work they do and the wages they're paid. The hope, of course, is that someday these people will come to know what they're worth, and take appropriate action.

ENDNOTES

[1] According to the Department of Housing and Urban Development, the "fair-market rent" for an efficiency is $551 here in Monroe County, Florida. A comparable rent in the five boroughs of New York City is $704; in San Francisco, $713; and in the heart of Silicon Valley, $808. The fair-market rent for an area is defined as the amount that would be needed to pay rent plus utilities for "privately owned, decent, safe, and sanitary rental housing of a modest (non-luxury) nature with suitable amenities."

[2] According to the Fair Labor Standards Act, employers are not required to pay "tipped employees," such as restaurant servers, more than $2.13 an hour in direct wages. However, if the sum of tips plus $2.13 an hour falls below the minimum wage, or $5.15 an hour, the employer is required to make up the difference. This fact was not mentioned by managers or otherwise publicized at either of the restaurants where I worked.

[3] I could find no statistics on the number of employed people living in cars or vans, but according to the National Coalition for the Homeless's 1997 report "Myths and Facts about Homelessness," nearly one in five homeless people (in twenty-nine cities across the nation) is employed in a full- or part-time job.

[4] In *Workers in a Lean World: Unions in the International Economy* (Verso, 1997), Kim Moody cites studies finding an increase in stress-related workplace injuries and illness between the mid-1980s and the early 1990s. He argues that rising stress levels reflect a new system of "management by stress," in which workers in a variety of industries are being squeezed to extract maximum productivity, to the detriment of their health.

[5] In 1996, the number of persons holding two or more jobs averaged 7.8 million, or 6.2 percent of the workforce. It was about the same rate for men and for women (6.1 versus 6.2), though the kinds of jobs differ by gender. About two thirds of multiple jobholders work one job full-time and the other part-time. Only a heroic minority—4 percent of men and 2 percent of women—work two full-time jobs simultaneously. (From John F. Stinson Jr., "New Data on Multiple Jobholding Available from the CPS," in the *Monthly Labor Review,* March 1997.)

GENDER

27

GENDER AS STRUCTURE

BARBARA RISMAN

Gender stratification, examined in the next four selections, refers to those social systems in which socioeconomic resources and political power are distributed on the basis of one's sex and gender. In any social system, we can measure the gendered distribution of resources and rewards to see whether men or women have a higher social status. Objective indices of gender inequality include income, educational attainment, wealth, occupational status, mortality rates, and access to social institutions. In the selection that follows, Barbara Risman, a professor of sociology at North Carolina State University, examines four theories that attempt to explain why gender stratification exists.

There are three distinct theoretical traditions that help us to understand sex and gender, and a fourth is now taking shape. The first tradition focuses on gendered selves, whether sex differences are biological or social in origin. The second tradition . . . focuses on how the social structure (as opposed to biology or individual learning) creates gendered behavior. The third tradition . . . emphasizes contextual issues and how doing gender re-creates inequality during interaction. The fourth, multilevel approach treats gender itself as built in to social life via socialization, interaction, and institutional organization. This new perspective integrates the previous ones; it is formed on the assumption that each viewpoint sheds different light on the same question. . . .

Gendered Selves

There are numerous theoretical perspectives within this tradition, but all share the assumption that maleness and femaleness are, or become, properties of individuals. . . . Research questions in this tradition focus on the development of sex differences and their relative importance for behavior. . . .

Sociobiologists have argued that such behaviors as male aggressiveness and female nurturance result from natural selection. Biosociologists stress the infant care skills in which females appear to excel. Their perspective has been criticized for its ethnocentrism and its selective use of biological species as evidence. . . .

More recent biosocial theories have posited complex interactions between environment and biological predispositions, with attention to explaining intrasex differences. This new version of biosociology may eventually help to identify the biological parameters that, in interaction with environmental stimuli, affect human behavior. . . .

Sex-role theory suggests that early childhood socialization is an influential determinant of later behavior, and research has focused on how societies create feminine women and masculine men. There is an impressive variety of sex-role explanations for gender-differentiated behavior in families. Perhaps the most commonly accepted explanation is reinforcement theory (e.g., Bandura and Walters 1963, Mischel 1966, and Weitzman 1979). Reinforcement theory suggests, for example, that girls develop nurturant personalities because they are given praise and attention for their interest in dolls and babies, and that boys develop competitive selves because they are positively reinforced for winning, whether at checkers or football. Although much literature suggests that the socialization experiences of boys and girls continue to differ dramatically, it is clearly the case that most girls raised in the 1990s have received ambiguous gender socialization: they have been taught to desire domesticity (dolls remain a popular toy for girls), as well as to pursue careers. For generations, African American girls have been socialized for both motherhood and paid work (Collins 1990).

Nancy Chodorow's (1978, 1989) feminist psychoanalytic analysis approach has also been influential, particularly in feminist scholarship. Chodorow develops an object-relations psychoanalytic perspective to explain how gendered personalities develop as a result of exclusively female mothering. . . . Chodorow notices . . . that mothers are responsible for young children almost universally. She argues that mothers relate to their boy and girl infants differently, fusing identities with their daughters while relating to their sons as separate and distinct. As a result, according to this feminist version of psychoanalysis, girls develop selves based on connectedness and relationships while boys develop selves based on independence and autonomy. In addition, boys must reject their first love-object (mother) in order to adopt masculinity, and they do this by rejecting and devaluing what is feminine in themselves and in society. Thus, we get nurturant women and independent men in a society dominated by men and which values independence. Many feminist studies have incorporated this psychoanalytic view of gender as an underlying assumption (Keller 1985; L. Rubin 1982; Williams 1989). . . .

Other feminist theorists, such as Ruddick (1989, 1992) and Aptheker (1989), build on the notion that the constant nature of mothering creates a certain kind of thinking, what Ruddick calls "maternal thinking." The logic of this argument does not depend on a psychoanalytic framework, but it implicitly uses one: through nurturing their children, women develop psychological frameworks that value peace and justice. Therefore, if women (or men who mothered children) were powerful political actors, governments would use more peaceful conflict resolution strategies and value social justice more highly.

All individualist theories, including sex-role socialization and psychoanalytic thought, posit that by adulthood most men and women have developed very different personalities. Women have become nurturant, person oriented, and child centered. Men have become competitive and work oriented. According to individualist theorists, there are limits to flexibility. Intensely held emotions, values, and inclinations developed during childhood coalesce into a person's self-identity. Although these theorists do not deny that social structures influence family patterns, nor that notions of gender meaning are always evolving . . . they focus on how culturally determined family patterns and sex-role socialization create gendered selves, which then provide the motivations for individuals to fill their socially appropriate roles.

Historically, sex-role theorists have assumed that men and women behave differently because gender resides primarily in personality. This approach has several serious conceptual weaknesses. . . . First, such theories usually presume behavioral continuity throughout the life course. In fact, women socialized for nurturance are capable of competitive and aggressive behavior, and men raised without any expectation of taking on primary responsibility can "mother" when they need to (Bielby and Bielby 1984; Gerson 1985, 1993; Risman 1987). Another weakness of these individualist-oriented theories is their oversocialized conception of human behavior—that once we know how an individual has been raised, the training is contained primarily inside his or her head (cf. Wrong 1961). Such theories might suggest, for example, that women do not revolt and are not necessarily unhappy with their subordinate status because they have been so well trained for femininity. . . .

This overdependence on internalization of culture and socialization leads to the most serious problem with sex-role theory: its depoliticization of gender inequality. Although sex-role socialization and revisionist psychoanalytic theorists often have explicitly feminist goals, their focus on sex differences has legitimated a dualistic conception of gender that relies on a reified male/female dichotomy. The very notion of comparing all men to all women without regard for diversity within groups presumes that gender is primarily about individual differences between biological males and biological females, downplaying the role of interactional expectations and the social structure.

The sex-role socialization theory is an application of a normative role theory for human behavior. It assumes that social stability is motivated primarily by beliefs and values acquired during socialization. Individuals are assumed to use whatever resources are available to realize these values and to maintain their identities. As Stokes and Hewitt (1976) have argued, socialization cannot serve as the fundamental link between culture and action. Indeed, studies of intergenerational shifts in values suggest that economic and political conditions produce beliefs, attitudes, and preferences for action that overcome those acquired during childhood (Inglehart 1977, 1981; Lesthaeghe 1980). We cannot assume that internalization of norms—through psychoanalytic processes or sex-role socialization—is the primary means by which society organizes human conduct. . . .

Structure vs. Personality

The overreliance on gendered selves as the primary explanation for sexual stratification led many feminist sociologists—myself included—to argue that what appear to be sex differences are really, in Epstein's terms, "deceptive distinctions" (Epstein 1988; Kanter 1977; Risman and Schwartz 1989). Although empirically documented sex differences do occur, structuralists like me have argued that men and women behave differently because they fill different positions in institutional settings, work organizations, or families. That is, the previous structural perspectives on gender assume that work and family structures create empirically distinct male and female behavior. . . . Within this perspective, men and women in the same structural slots are expected to behave identically. Epstein's (1988) voluminous review of the multidisciplinary research on gender and sex differences is perhaps the strongest and most explicit support for a social-structural explanation of gendered behavior. She suggests that there are perhaps no empirically documented differences that can be traced to the predispositions of males and females. Instead, the deceptive differences reflect women's lack of opportunity in a male-dominated society.

Gender relations in the labor force have received far more of this sort of structural analysis than have gender relations in intimate settings. Kanter's classic work *Men and Women of the Corporation* (1977) introduced this kind of structural perspective on gender in the workplace. Kanter showed that when women had access to powerful mentors, interactions with people like themselves, and the possibility for upward mobility, they behaved like others—regardless of sex—with similar advantages. These social network variables could explain success at work far better than could assumptions of masculine versus feminine work styles. Women were less often successful because they were more often blocked from network advantages, not because they feared success or had never developed competitive strategies. Men who lacked such opportunities did not advance, and they behaved with stereotypical feminine work styles. Kanter argued persuasively that structural system properties better explain sex differences in workplace behavior than does sex-role socialization. . . .

The application of a structural perspective to gender within personal relationships has been less frequent. . . . In a series of studies (Risman 1986, 1987, 1988), I tested whether apparent sex differences in parenting styles are better attributed to sex-role socialization or to the structural contingencies of adult life. The question I asked was "Can men mother?" The answer is yes, but only if they do not have women to do it for them. The lack of sex-role socialization for nurturance did not inhibit the development of male mothering when structural contingencies demanded it. This is an important part of the story, but not all of it. . . .

While applications of structural perspectives both to workplaces and to intimate relationships have furthered the sociological understanding of gender, there is a fundamental flaw in the logic of these arguments. . . .

Several studies (Williams 1992; Yoder 1991; Zimmer 1988) found that Kanter's hypotheses about the explanatory power of social structural variables such as relative numbers, access to mentors, and upward mobility are not, in fact, gender neutral. That is, Kanter's hypotheses are supported empirically only when societally devalued groups enter traditionally white male work environments. When white males enter traditionally female work environments, they do not hit the glass ceiling, they ride glass elevators. Reskin (1988) has suggested that we have so accepted these "structural" arguments that we sometimes forget that sexism itself stratifies our labor force. Evidence similarly points to continued existence of gendered behavior in family settings. Hertz reported that in her 1986 study of couples in which husbands and wives held equivalent, high-status corporate jobs and brought similar resources to their marriages, the wives continued to shoulder more responsibility for family work (even if that means hiring and supervising help). Despite the importance of structural variables in explaining behavior in families, the sex category itself remains a powerful predictor of who does what kind of family work (Brines 1994; South and Spitz 1994). Gender stratification remains even when other structural aspects of work or of family life are divorced from sex category. The interactionist theory discussed below helps us to understand why.

Doing Gender

This approach to gender was best articulated by West and Zimmerman in their 1987 article "Doing Gender." . . . West and Zimmerman suggest that once a person is labeled a member of a sex category, she or he is morally accountable for behaving as persons in that category do. That is, the person is expected to "do gender"; the ease of interaction depends on it. One of the groundbreaking aspects in this argument is that doing gender implies legitimating inequality. The authors suggest that, by definition, what is female in a patriarchal society is devalued. Within this theoretical framework, the very belief that biological males and females are essentially different (apart from their reproductive capabilities) exists to justify male dominance.

The tradition of doing gender has been well accepted in feminist sociology (West and Zimmerman's article was cited in journals more than one hundred times by 1995). West and Zimmerman articulated an insight whose time had come—that gender is not what we are but something that we do. Psychologists Deaux and Major (1990) . . . argue that interactional contexts take priority over individual traits and personality differences; others' expectations create the self-fulfilling prophecies that lead all of us to do gender. . . . They suggest that actual behavior depends on the interaction of participants' self-definitions, the expectations of others, and the cultural expectations attached to the context itself. I agree. The weakness in the doing-gender approach is that it undertheorizes the pervasiveness of gender inequality in organizations and gendered identities.

Although gender is always present in our interaction, it is not present only in interaction. We must have a theoretical link from material constraints to what we do now, to who we think we are. I suggest that the doing-gender perspective is incomplete because it slights the institutional level of analysis and the links among institutional gender stratification, situational expectations, and gendered selves.

West and Fenstermaker (1995) have extended the argument from doing gender to "doing difference." They suggest that just as we create inequality when we create gender during interaction, so we create race and class inequalities when we interact in daily life. Race does not generally hold the biologically based assumption of dichotomy (as sex category does), yet in American society we constantly use race categories to guide our interactional encounters. This extension of theoretical ideas from gender to the analysis of inequalities is perhaps the most important direction gender theorizing has taken in the past decade. . . .

Gender as Social Structure

The sex-differences literature, the doing-gender contextual analyses, and the structural perspectives are not necessarily incompatible, although I, as well as others, have portrayed them as alternatives (e.g., Epstein 1988, Ferree 1990, Kanter 1977, Risman 1987, Risman and Schwartz 1989). . . . My view of gender as a social structure incorporates each level of analysis. . . .

Lorber (1994) argues that gender is an entity in and of itself that establishes patterns of expectations for individuals, orders social processes of everyday life, and is built into all other major social organizations of society. She goes further, however, to argue that gender difference is *primarily* a means to justify sexual stratification. Gender is so ubiquitous because unless we see difference, we cannot justify inequality. Lorber provides much cross-cultural, literary, and scientific evidence to show that gender difference is socially constructed and yet is universally used to justify stratification. She writes that "the continuing purpose of gender as a modern social institution is to construct women as a group to be subordinate to men as a group" (p. 33).

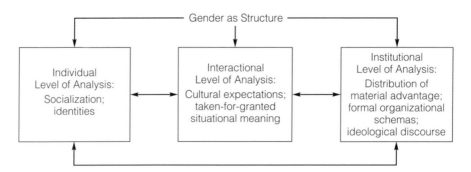

FIGURE 1   **Gender as Structure**

I build on this notion that gender is an entity in and of itself and has consequences at every level of analysis. And I share the concern that the very creation of difference is the foundation on which inequality rests. In my view, it
is most useful to conceptualize gender as a structure that has consequences
for every aspect of society. . . .

Gender itself must be considered a structural property of society. It is not
manifested just in our personalities, our cultural rules, or other institutions.
Gender is deeply embedded as a basis for stratification, differentiating opportunities and constraints. This differentiation has consequences on three
levels: (1) at the individual level, for the development of gendered selves;
(2) at the interactional level, for men and women face different expectations
even when they fill the identical structural position; and (3) at the institutional level, for rarely will women and men be given identical positions. Differentiation at the institutional level is based on explicit regulations or laws
regarding resource distribution, whether resources be defined as access to
opportunities or actual material goods. (See Figure 1 for a schematic summary of the argument thus far.)

While the *gender structure* clearly affects selves, cultural rules, and institutions, far too much explanatory power is presumed to rest in the motivation of gendered selves. We live in a very individualistic society that teaches
us to make our own choices and take responsibility for our own actions.
What this has meant for theories about gender is that a tremendous amount
of energy is spent on trying to understand why women and men "choose" to
devote their life energies to such different enterprises. The distinctly sociological contribution to the explanation hasn't had enough attention: even
when individual women and men do *not* desire to live gendered lives or to
support male dominance, they often find themselves compelled to do so by
the logic of gendered choices. That is, interactional pressures and institutional design create gender and the resultant inequality, even in the absence
of individual desires. . . .

Choices often assumed to be based on personalities and individual preferences (e.g., consequences of the gender structure at the individual level) are better understood as social constructions based on institutionally constrained opportunities and the limited availability of nongendered cognitive images. . . .

Even if individuals are capable of change and wish to eradicate male dominance from their personal lives, the influence of gendered institutions and interactional contexts persists. These contexts are organized by gender stratification at the institutional level, which includes the distribution of material resources organized by gender, the ways by which formal organizations and institutions themselves are gendered, and gendered ideological discourse. For example, in a society in which girls are not taught to read, we could never find a young woman who would be considered a potential international leader. Nor would men denied access to jobs with "family wages" be seen by middle-class American women as good catches for husbands.

At this moment in American society, cultural rules and cognitive images that operate at the interactional level are particularly important in the persistence of gender stratification in families. It is not that sex-role socialization or early childhood experience is trivial; gender structure creates gendered selves. But, at this point in history, sex-role socialization itself is ambivalent. In addition, it is clear that even women with feminist worldviews and substantial incomes are constrained by gender structures.

In spite of the removal of some gender discrimination in both law and organizations, gender stratification remains. That is, formal access to opportunities may be gender neutral, yet equality of results may not ensue. Therefore, neither the individual-level explanations nor those based solely on institutional discrimination can explain continued gender stratification in families. Instead, the cognitive images to which we must respond during interaction are the engines that drive continued gender stratification when individuals desire egalitarian relationships and the law allows them (cf. Ridgeway 1997). . . .

The social structure clearly constrains gendered action even as it makes it possible. Wives, even those who have no motivation to provide domestic service to their husbands, are constrained to do so by social expectations. A husband who has a disheveled appearance reflects poorly on his wife's domestic abilities (in real life as well as "ring around the collar'" commercials). A wife will be sanctioned by friends and family for keeping a cluttered and dusty home; a husband will not be. Husbands' behaviors are constrained as well. A husband who is content with a relatively low-wage, low-stress occupation may be pressured (by his wife, among others) to provide more for his family. Few wives, however, are pressured into higher-stress, higher-wage occupations by their families. The expectations we face during ongoing interaction often push us to behave as others want us to (Heiss 1981).

Cultural images within marriage also make gendered action possible. Husbands are not free to work long hours in order to climb the career ladder or increase income unless they are superordinate partners in a system in which wives provide them the "leisure" (i.e., freedom from responsibility for self-care or family care) to do so. Some married women may leave jobs they dislike because the position of domestic wife is open to them. A husband and father unable to keep a job has few other options for gaining self-esteem and identity.

Individuals often act in a structurally patterned fashion, without much thought. Routine is taken for granted even when the action re-creates the inequitable social structure. A woman may choose to change her name upon marriage simply because it seems easier. (Some women may not even know they are making a choice, as name change is so routine in their social circle.) Yet by changing her name a woman implicitly supports and re-creates a reflective definition of wifehood. She does gender. Similarly, when a woman assents to her children carrying her husband's surname (even when she herself has retained her own), she is re-creating a patrilineal system by which family identity is traced primarily through the male line. In both these examples, a couple's intention may be to create a nuclear family identity and to avoid the awkwardness of hyphenated names for children. Whatever the intention, the structure has constrained the possible choices available to them. Their purposive actions may provide them with both the desired consequences (one family name) *and* the unintended consequence of re-creating a gender structure based on reflective female identity and patrilineal family names.

REFERENCES

Aptheker, Bettina. 1989. *Tapestries of Life: Women's Work, Women's Consciousness, and the Meaning of Daily Experience.* Amherst: University of Massachusetts Press.

Bandura, Albert and Richard H. Walters. 1963. *Social Learning and Personality.* New York: Holt, Rinehart and Winston.

Bielby, Denise D. and William T Bielby. 1984. "Work Commitment and Sex-Role Attitudes." *American Sociological Review* 49:234–47.

Brines, Julie. 1994. "Economic Dependency and the Division of Labor." *American Journal of Sociology* 100(3):652–88.

Chodorow, Nancy. 1978. *The Reproduction of Mothering.* Berkeley: University of California Press.

———. 1989. *Feminism and Psychoanalytic Theory.* New Haven, CT: Yale University Press.

Collins, Patricia Hill. 1990. *Black Feminist Thought: Knowledge, Consciousness, and the Politics of Empowerment.* Boston: Unwin, Hyman.

Deaux, Kay and Brenda Major. 1990. "A Social–Psychological Model of Gender." In *Theoretical Perspectives on Sexual Difference,* edited by Deborah Rhode. New Haven, CT: Yale University Press.

Epstein, Cynthia Fuchs. 1988. *Deceptive Distinctions: Sex, Gender, and the Social Order.* New Haven, CT: Yale University Press.

Ferree, Myra Marx. 1990. "Beyond Separate Spheres: Feminism and Family Research." *Journal of Marriage and the Family* 53(4):866–84.

Gerson, Kathleen. 1985. *Hard Choices.* Berkeley: University of California Press.

————. 1993. *No Man's Land*. New York: Basic Books.

Heiss, Jerold. 1981. "Social Rules." In *Social Psychology: Sociological Perspectives*, edited by Morris Rosenberg and Ralph H. Turner. New York: Basic Books.

Hertz, Rosanna. 1986. *More Equal Than Others: Women and Men in Dual-Career Marriages*. Berkeley: University of California Press.

Inglehart, Ronald. 1977. *The Silent Revolution: Changing Values and Political Styles among Western Publics*. Princeton, NJ: Princeton University Press.

————. 1981. "Post-Materialism in an Environment of Insecurity." *American Political Science Review* 75:880–900.

Kanter, Rosabeth. 1977. *Men and Women of the Corporation*. New York: Harper and Row.

Keller, Evelyn Fox. 1985. *Reflections on Gender and Science*. New Haven, CT: Yale University Press.

Lesthaeghe, Ron. 1980. "On the Social Control of Human Reproduction." *Population and Development Review* 4:427–548.

Lorber, Judith. 1994. *Paradoxes of Gender*. New Haven, CT: Yale University Press.

Mischel, Walter. 1966. "A Social Learning View of Sex Differences in Behavior." Pp. 56–81 in *The Development of Sex Differences*, edited by Eleanor Maccoby. Stanford, CA: Stanford University Press.

Reskin, Barbara. 1988. "Bringing the Men Back In: Sex Differentiation and the Devaluation of Women's Work." *Gender and Society* 2:58–81.

Ridgeway, Cecilia. 1997. "Interaction and the Conservation of Gender Inequality: Considering Employment." *American Sociological Review* 62:218–35.

Risman, Barbara. 1986. "Can Men 'Mother'?: Life as a Single Father." *Family Relations* 35:95–102.

————. 1987. "Intimate Relationships from a Microstructural Perspective: Mothering Men." *Gender and Society* 1:6–32.

————. 1988. "Just the Two of Us: Parent–Child Relationships in Single Parent Homes." *Journal of Marriage and the Family* 50:1049–62.

Risman, Barbara and Pepper Schwartz. 1989. *Gender in Intimate Relationships*. Belmont, CA: Wadsworth.

Rubin, Lillian. 1982. *Intimate Strangers*. New York: Harper and Row.

Ruddick, Sara. 1989. *Maternal Thinking*. Boston: Beacon Press.

————. 1992. "Thinking About Fathers." In *Rethinking the Family: Some Feminist Questions*, edited by Barrie Thorne. Boston: Northeastern University Press.

South, Scott J. and Glenna Spitz. 1994. "Housework in Marital and Nonmarital Households." *American Sociological Review* 59:327–47.

Stokes, Randall and John Hewitt. 1976. "Aligning Actions." *American Sociological Review* 41:838–49.

Weitzman, Lenore Jacqueline. 1979. *Sex Role Socialization: A Focus on Women*. Palo Alto, CA: Mayfield.

West, Candace and Sarah Fenstermaker. 1995. "Doing Difference." *Gender and Society* 9:8–37.

West, Candace and Don H. Zimmerman. 1987. "Doing Gender." *Gender and Society* 1(2):125–51.

Williams, Christine. 1989. *Gender Differences at Work*. Berkeley: University of California Press.

————. 1992. "The Glass Escalator: Hidden Advantages for Men in the 'Female' Professions." *Social Problems* 39:253–67.

Wrong, Dennis H. 1961. "The Oversocialized Conception of Man in Modern Sociology." *American Sociological Review* 26:183–93.

Yoder, Janice. 1991. "Rethinking Tokenism: Looking Beyond Numbers." *Social Problems* 5:178–92.

Zimmer, Lynn. 1988. "Tokenism and Women in the Workplace: The Limits of Gender-Neutral Theory." *Social Problems* 35:64–77.

28

THE GLASS ESCALATOR
Hidden Advantages for Men
in the "Female" Professions

CHRISTINE L. WILLIAMS

Sociologists argue that individuals learn gender roles and gender stereotyping through socialization. Gender role socialization often reinforces gender inequality because men and women are expected to fulfill different family and occupation roles. Thus, in U.S. society, women traditionally are assigned the roles of homemaker, nurse, teacher, and secretary, which typically have less social status and lower salaries than male occupational roles. This 1992 article by Christine L. Williams is an analysis of what happens when men enter traditionally defined "female" occupations. Williams, a professor of sociology at the University of Texas at Austin, has researched gender issues for a number of years, especially society's treatment of men and the changing cultural definitions of masculinity. The study excerpted here utilizes in-depth interviews to reveal the advantages and disadvantages experienced by male nurses, teachers, librarians, and social workers.

The sex segregation of the U.S. labor force is one of the most perplexing and tenacious problems in our society. Even though the proportion of men and women in the labor force is approaching parity (particularly for younger cohorts of workers) (U.S. Department of Labor 1991:18), men and women are still generally confined to predominantly single-sex occupations. Forty percent of men or women would have to change major occupational categories to achieve equal representation of men and women in all jobs (Reskin and Roos 1990:6), but even this figure underestimates the true degree of sex segregation. It is extremely rare to find specific jobs where equal numbers of men and women are engaged in the same activities in the same industries (Bielby and Baron 1984).

Most studies of sex segregation in the workforce have focused on women's experiences in male-dominated occupations. Both researchers and advocates for social change have focused on the barriers faced by women who try to integrate predominantly male fields. Few have looked at the "flip

From *Social Problems* 39, no. 3 (August 1992):253–67. © 1992 by The Society for the Study of Social Problems. Reprinted by permission from University of California Press.

side" of occupational sex segregation: the exclusion of men from predominantly female occupations (exceptions include Schreiber 1979; Williams 1989; Zimmer 1988). But the fact is that men are less likely to enter female sex-typed occupations than women are to enter male-dominated jobs (Jacobs 1989). Reskin and Roos, for example, were able to identify 33 occupations in which female representation increased by more than nine percentage points between 1970 and 1980, but only three occupations in which the proportion of men increased as radically (1990: 20–21).

In this paper, I examine men's underrepresentation in four predominantly female occupations—nursing, librarianship, elementary school teaching, and social work. Throughout the twentieth century, these occupations have been identified with "women's work"—even though prior to the Civil War, men were more likely to be employed in these areas. These four occupations, often called the female "semi-professions" (Hodson and Sullivan 1990), today range from 5.5 percent male (in nursing) to 32 percent male (in social work). These percentages have not changed substantially in decades. In fact, two of these professions—librarianship and social work—have experienced declines in the proportions of men since 1975. Nursing is the only one of the four experiencing noticeable changes in sex composition, with the proportion of men increasing 80 percent between 1975 and 1990. Even so, men continue to be a tiny minority of all nurses. . . .

Methods

I conducted in-depth interviews with 76 men and 23 women in four occupations from 1985 to 1991. Interviews were conducted in four metropolitan areas: San Francisco/Oakland, California; Austin, Texas; Boston, Massachusetts; and Phoenix, Arizona. These four areas were selected because they show considerable variation in the proportions of men in the four professions. For example, Austin has one of the highest percentages of men in nursing (7.7 percent), whereas Phoenix's percentage is one of the lowest (2.7 percent) (U.S. Bureau of the Census 1980). The sample was generated using "snowballing" techniques. Women were included in the sample to gauge their feelings and responses to men who enter "their" professions. . . .

Discrimination in Hiring

Contrary to the experience of many women in the male-dominated professions, many of the men and women I spoke to indicated that there is a *preference* for hiring men in these four occupations. A Texas librarian at a junior high school said that his school district "would hire a male over a female."

I: Why do you think that is?

R: *Because there are so few, and the . . . ones that they do have, the library directors seem to really . . . think they're doing great jobs. I don't know, maybe they just feel they're being progressive or something, [but] I have had a real sense that they really appreciate having a male, particularly at the junior high. . . . As I said, when seven of us lost our jobs from the high schools and were redistributed, there were only four positions at junior high, and I got one of them. Three of the librarians, some who had been here longer than I had with the school district, were put down in elementary school as librarians. And I definitely think that being male made a difference in my being moved to the junior high rather than an elementary school.*

Many of the men perceived their token status as males in predominantly female occupations as an *advantage* in hiring and promotions. I asked an Arizona teacher whether his specialty (elementary special education) was an unusual area for men compared to other areas within education. He said,

Much more so. I am extremely marketable in special education. That's not why I got into the field. But I am extremely marketable because I am a man.

In several cases, the more female-dominated the specialty, the greater the apparent preference for men. For example, when asked if he encountered any problem getting a job in pediatrics, a Massachusetts nurse said,

No, no, none. . . . I've heard this from managers and supervisory-type people with men in pediatrics: "It's nice to have a man because it's such a female-dominated profession."

However, there were some exceptions to this preference for men in the most female-dominated specialties. In some cases, formal policies actually barred men from certain jobs. This was the case in some rural Texas school districts, which refused to hire men in the youngest grades (K–3). Some nurses also reported being excluded from positions in obstetrics and gynecology wards, a policy encountered more frequently in private Catholic hospitals.

But often the pressures keeping men out of certain specialties were more subtle than this. Some men described being "tracked" into practice areas within their professions which were considered more legitimate for men. For example, one Texas man described how he was pushed into administration and planning in social work, even though "I'm not interested in writing policy; I'm much more interested in research and clinical stuff." A nurse who is interested in pursuing graduate study in family and child health in Boston said he was dissuaded from entering the program specialty in favor of a concentration in "adult nursing." A kindergarten teacher described the difficulty of finding a job in his specialty after graduation: "I was recruited immediately to start getting into a track to become an administrator. And it was men who recruited me. It was men that ran the system at that time, especially in Los Angeles."

This tracking may bar men from the most female-identified specialties within these professions. But men are effectively being "kicked upstairs" in the process. Those specialties considered more legitimate practice areas for men also tend to be the most prestigious, better-paying ones. A distinguished kindergarten teacher, who had been voted citywide "Teacher of the Year," told me that even though people were pleased to see him in the classroom, "there's been some encouragement to think about administration, and there's been some encouragement to think about teaching at the university level or something like that, or supervisory-type position." That is, despite his aptitude and interest in staying in the classroom, he felt pushed in the direction of administration.

The effect of this "tracking" is the opposite of that experienced by women in male-dominated occupations. Researchers have reported that many women encounter a "glass ceiling" in their efforts to scale organizational and professional hierarchies. That is, they are constrained by invisible barriers to promotion in their careers, caused mainly by sexist attitudes of men in the highest positions (Freeman 1990). In contrast to the "glass ceiling," many of the men I interviewed seem to encounter a "glass escalator." Often, despite their intentions, they face invisible pressures to move up in their professions. As if on a moving escalator, they must work to stay in place.

A public librarian specializing in children's collections (a heavily female-dominated concentration) described an encounter with this "escalator" in his very first job out of library school. In his first six-months' evaluation, his supervisors commended him for his good work in storytelling and related activities, but they criticized him for "not shooting high enough."

> *Seriously. That's literally what they were telling me. They assumed that because I was a male—and they told me this—and that I was being hired right out of graduate school, that somehow I wasn't doing the kind of management-oriented work that they thought I should be doing. And as a result, really they had a lot of bad marks, as it were, against me on my evaluation. And I said I couldn't believe this!*

Throughout his 10-year career, he has had to struggle to remain in children's collections.

The glass escalator does not operate at all levels. In particular, men in academia reported some gender-based discrimination in the highest positions due to their universities' commitment to affirmative action. Two nursing professors reported that they felt their own chances of promotion to deanships were nil because their universities viewed the position of nursing dean as a guaranteed female appointment in an otherwise heavily male-dominated administration. One California social work professor reported his university canceled its search for a dean because no minority male or female candidates had been placed on their short list. It was rumored that other schools on campus were permitted to go forward with their searches—even though they also failed to put forward names of minority candidates—because the higher administration perceived it to be "easier" to fulfill affirmative action goals in the social work school. The interviews provide greater evidence of the "glass escalator" at work in the lower levels of these professions.

Of course, men's motivations also play a role in their advancement to higher professional positions. I do not mean to suggest that the men I talked to all resented the informal tracking they experienced. For many men, leaving the most female-identified areas of their professions helped them resolve internal conflicts involving their masculinity. One man left his job as a school social worker to work in a methadone drug treatment program not because he was encouraged to leave by his colleagues, but because "I think there was some macho shit there, to tell you the truth, because I remember feeling a little uncomfortable there . . . ; it didn't feel right to me." Another social worker, employed in the mental health services department of a large urban area in California, reflected on his move into administration:

> The more I think about it, through our discussion, I'm sure that's a large part of why I wound up in administration. It's okay for a man to do the administration. In fact, I don't know if I fully answered a question that you asked a little while ago about how did being male contribute to my advancing in the field. I was saying it wasn't because I got any special favoritism as a man, but . . . I think . . . because I'm a man, I felt a need to get into this kind of position. I may have worked harder toward it, may have competed harder for it, than most women would do, even women who think about doing administrative work.

Elsewhere I have speculated on the origins of men's tendency to define masculinity through single-sex work environments (Williams 1989). Clearly, personal ambition does play a role in accounting for men's movement into more "male-defined" arenas within these professions. But these occupations also structure opportunities for males independent of their individual desires or motives.

The interviews suggest that men's underrepresentation in these professions cannot be attributed to discrimination in hiring or promotions. Many of the men indicated that they received preferential treatment because they were men. Although men mentioned gender discrimination in the hiring process, for the most part they were channeled into the more "masculine" specialties within these professions, which ironically meant being "tracked" into better-paying and more prestigious specialties.

Supervisors and Colleagues: The Working Environment

Researchers claim that subtle forms of workplace discrimination push women out of male-dominated occupations (Jacobs 1989; Reskin and Hartmann 1986). In particular, women report feeling excluded from informal leadership and decision-making networks, and they sense hostility from their male co-workers, which makes them feel uncomfortable and unwanted (Carothers and Crull 1984). Respondents in this study were asked about their relationships with supervisors and female colleagues to ascertain whether men also experienced "poisoned" work environments when entering gender atypical occupations.

A major difference in the experience of men and women in nontraditional occupations is that men in these situations are far more likely to be supervised by a member of their own sex. In each of the four professions I studied, men are overrepresented in administrative and managerial capacities, or, as is the case of nursing, their positions in the organizational hierarchy are governed by men (Grimm and Stern 1974; Phenix 1987; Schmuck 1987; Williams 1989; York, Henley, and Gamble 1987). Thus, unlike women who enter "male fields," the men in these professions often work under the direct supervision of other men.

Many of the men interviewed reported that they had good rapport with their male supervisors. Even in professional school, some men reported extremely close relationships with their male professors. For example, a Texas librarian described an unusually intimate association with two male professors in graduate school:

> I can remember a lot of times in the classroom there would be discussions about a particular topic or issue, and the conversation would spill over into their office hours, after the class was over. And even though there were . . . a couple of the other women that had been in on the discussion, they weren't there. And I don't know if that was preferential or not. . . . It certainly carried over into personal life as well. Not just at the school and that sort of thing. I mean, we would get together for dinner. . . .

Other men reported similar closeness with their professors. A Texas psychotherapist recalled his relationships with his male professors in social work school:

> I made it a point to make a golfing buddy with one of the guys that was in administration. He and I played golf a lot. He was the guy who kind of ran the research training, the research part of the master's program. Then there was a sociologist who ran the other part of the research program. He and I developed a good friendship.

This close mentoring by male professors contrasts with the reported experience of women in nontraditional occupations. Others have noted a lack of solidarity among women in nontraditional occupations. Writing about military academies, for example, Yoder (1989) describes the failure of token women to mentor succeeding generations of female cadets. She argues that women attempt to play down their gender difference from men because it is the source of scorn and derision.

Because women felt unaccepted by their male colleagues, one of the last things they wanted to do was to emphasize their gender. Some women thought that, if they kept company with other women, this would highlight their gender and would further isolate them from male cadets. These women desperately wanted to be accepted as cadets, not as *women* cadets. Therefore, they did everything from not wearing skirts as an option with their uniforms to avoiding being a part of a group of women. (P. 532)

Men in nontraditional occupations face a different scenario—their gender is construed as a *positive* difference. Therefore, they have an incentive to bond together and emphasize their distinctiveness from the female majority. . . .

Openly gay men may encounter less favorable treatment at the hands of their supervisors. For example, a nurse in Texas stated that one of the physicians he worked with preferred to staff the operating room with male nurses exclusively—as long as they weren't gay. Stigma associated with homosexuality leads some men to enhance, or even exaggerate, their "masculine" qualities and may be another factor pushing men into more "acceptable" specialties for men.

Not all men who work in these occupations are supervised by men. Many of the men interviewed who had female bosses also reported high levels of acceptance—although levels of intimacy with women seemed lower than with other men. In some cases, however, men reported feeling shut out from decision making when the higher administration was constituted entirely by women. I asked an Arizona librarian whether men in the library profession were discriminated against in hiring because of their sex:

> *Professionally speaking, people go to considerable lengths to keep that kind of thing out of their [hiring] deliberations. Personally, is another matter. It's pretty common around here to talk about the "old girl network." This is one of the few libraries that I've had any intimate knowledge of which is actually controlled by women. . . . Most of the department heads and upper-level administrators are women. And there's an "old girl network" that works just like the "old boy network," except that the important conferences take place in the women's room rather than on the golf course. But the political mechanism is the same, the exclusion of the other sex from decision making is the same. The reasons are the same. It's somewhat discouraging. . . .*

Although I did not interview many supervisors, I did include 23 women in my sample to ascertain their perspectives about the presence of men in their professions. All of the women I interviewed claimed to be supportive of their male colleagues, but some conveyed ambivalence. For example, a social work professor said she would like to see more men enter the social work profession, particularly in the clinical specialty (where they are underrepresented). Indeed, she favored affirmative action hiring guidelines for men in the profession. Yet, she resented the fact that her department hired "another white male" during a recent search. . . .

Even outside work, most of the men interviewed said they felt fully accepted by their female colleagues. They were usually included in informal socializing occasions with the women—even though this frequently meant attending baby showers or Tupperware parties. Many said that they declined offers to attend these events because they were not interested in "women's things," although several others claimed to attend everything: The minority men I interviewed seemed to feel the least comfortable in these informal contexts. One social worker in Arizona was asked about socializing with his female colleagues:

> *I:* So in general, for example, if all the employees were going to get together to have a party, or celebrate a bridal shower or whatever, would you be invited along with the rest of the group?
>
> *R:* *They would invite me, I would say, somewhat reluctantly. Being a black male, working with all white females, it did cause some outside problems. So I didn't go to a lot of functions with them. . . .*
>
> *I:* You felt that there was some tension there on the level of your acceptance . . . ?
>
> *R:* *Yeah. It was OK working, but on the outside, personally, there was some tension there. It never came out, that they said, "Because of who you are we can't invite you" [laughs], and I wouldn't have done anything anyway. I would have probably respected them more for saying what was on their minds. But I never felt completely in with the group.*

Some single men also said they felt uncomfortable socializing with married female colleagues because it gave the "wrong impression." But in general, the men said that they felt very comfortable around their colleagues and described their workplaces as very congenial for men. It appears unlikely, therefore, that men's underrepresentation in these professions is due to hostility toward men on the part of supervisors or women workers.

Discrimination from "Outsiders"

The most compelling evidence of discrimination against men in these professions is related to their dealings with the public. Men often encounter negative stereotypes when they come into contact with clients or "outsiders"—people they meet outside of work. For instance, it is popularly assumed that male nurses are gay. Librarians encounter images of themselves as "wimpy" and asexual. Male social workers describe being typecast as "feminine" and "passive." Elementary school teachers are often confronted by suspicions that they are pedophiles. One kindergarten teacher described an experience that occurred early in his career, which was related to him years afterward by his principal:

> *He indicated to me that parents had come to him and indicated to him that they had a problem with the fact that I was a male. . . . I recall almost exactly what he said. There were three specific concerns that the parents had: One parent said, "How can he love my child; he's a man." The second thing that I recall, he said the parent said, "He has a beard." And the third thing was, "Aren't you concerned about homosexuality?"*

Such suspicions often cause men in all four professions to alter their work behavior to guard against sexual abuse charges, particularly in those specialties requiring intimate contact with women and children.

Men are very distressed by these negative stereotypes, which tend to undermine their self-esteem and to cause them to second-guess their motivations for entering these fields. A California teacher said,

> *If I tell men that I don't know, that I'm meeting for the first time, that that's what I do, . . . sometimes there's a look on their faces that, you know, "Oh, couldn't get a real job?"*

When asked if his wife, who is also an elementary school teacher, encounters the same kind of prejudice, he said,

> *No, it's accepted because she's a woman. . . . I think people would see that as a . . . step up, you know. "Oh, you're not a housewife, you've got a career. That's great . . . that you're out there working. And you have a daughter, but you're still out there working. You decided not to stay home, and you went out there and got a job." Whereas for me, it's more like I'm supposed to be out working anyway, even though I'd rather be home with [my daughter].*

Unlike women who enter traditionally male professions, men's movement into these jobs is perceived by the "outside world" as a step down in status. This particular form of discrimination may be most significant in explaining why men are underrepresented in these professions. Men who otherwise might show interest in and aptitudes for such careers are probably discouraged from pursuing them because of the negative popular stereotypes associated with the men who work in them. This is a crucial difference from the experience of women in nontraditional professions: "My daughter, the physician," resonates far more favorably in most people's ears than "my son, the nurse."

Many of the men in my sample identified the stigma of working in a female-identified occupation as the major barrier to more men entering their professions. However, for the most part, they claimed that these negative stereotypes were not a factor in their own decisions to join these occupations. Most respondents didn't consider entering these fields until well into adulthood, after working in some related occupation. Several social workers and librarians even claimed they were not aware that men were a minority in their chosen professions. Either they had no well-defined image or stereotype, or their contacts and mentors were predominantly men. For example, prior to entering library school, many librarians held part-time jobs in university libraries, where there are proportionally more men than in the profession generally. Nurses and elementary school teachers were more aware that mostly women worked in these jobs, and this was often a matter of some concern to them. However, their choices were ultimately legitimized by mentors, or by encouraging friends or family members who implicitly reassured them that entering these occupations would not typecast them as feminine. In some cases, men were told by recruiters there were special advancement opportunities for men in these fields, and they entered them expecting rapid promotion to administrative positions.

> *I:*   Did it ever concern you when you were making the decision to enter nursing school, the fact that it is a female-dominated profession?
>
> *R:*   *Not really. I never saw myself working on the floor. I saw myself pretty much going into administration, just getting the background and then getting a job someplace as a supervisor and then working, getting up into administration.*

Because of the unique circumstances of their recruitment, many of the respondents did not view their occupational choices as inconsistent with a male gender role, and they generally avoided the negative stereotypes directed against men in these fields.

Indeed, many of the men I interviewed claimed that they did not encounter negative professional stereotypes until they had worked in these fields for several years. Popular prejudices can be damaging to self-esteem and probably push some men out of these professions altogether. Yet, ironically, they sometimes contribute to the "glass escalator" effect I have been describing. Men seem to encounter the most vituperative criticism from the public when they are in the most female-identified specialties. Public concerns sometimes result in their being shunted into more "legitimate" positions for men. A librarian formerly in charge of a branch library's children's collection, who now works in the reference department of the city's main library, describes his experience:

> *R:*   *Some of the people [who frequented the branch library] complained that they didn't want to have a man doing the storytelling scenario. And I got transferred here to the central library in an equivalent job. . . . I thought that I did a good job. And I had been told by my supervisor that I was doing a good job.*
>
> *I:*   Have you ever considered filing some sort of lawsuit to get that other job back?
>
> *R:*   *Well, actually, the job I've gotten now . . . well, it's a reference librarian; it's what I wanted in the first place. I've got a whole lot more authority here. I'm also in charge of the circulation desk. And I've recently been promoted*

because of my new stature, so . . . no, I'm not considering trying to get that other job back.

The negative stereotypes about men who do "women's work" can push men out of specific jobs. However, to the extent that they channel men into more "legitimate" practice areas, their effects can actually be positive. Instead of being a source of discrimination, these prejudices can add to the "glass escalator effect" by pressuring men to move *out* of the most female-identified areas and *up* to those regarded more legitimate and prestigious for men.

Author's Note: This research was funded in part by a faculty grant from the University of Texas at Austin. I also acknowledge the support of the sociology departments of the University of California, Berkeley; Harvard University; and Arizona State University. I would like to thank Judy Auerbach, Martin Button, Robert Nye, Teresa Sullivan, Debra Umberson, Mary Waters, and the reviewers at *Social Problems* for their comments on earlier versions of this paper.

REFERENCES

Bielby, William T. and James N. Baron. 1984. "A Woman's Place Is with Other Women: Sex Segregation within Organizations." Pp. 27–55 in *Sex Segregation in the Workplace: Trends, Explanations, Remedies,* edited by Barbara Reskin. Washington, DC: National Academy Press.

Carothers, Suzanne C. and Peggy Crull. 1984. "Contrasting Sexual Harassment in Female-Dominated and Male-Dominated Occupations." Pp. 220–27 in *My Troubles Are Going to Have Trouble with Me: Everyday Trials and Triumphs of Women Workers,* edited by Karen B. Sacks and Dorothy Remy. New Brunswick, NJ: Rutgers University Press.

Freeman, Sue J. M. 1990. *Managing Lives: Corporate Women and Social Change.* Amherst: University of Massachusetts Press.

Grimm, James W. and Robert N. Stern. 1974. "Sex Roles and Internal Labor Market Structures: The Female Semi-Professions." *Social Problems* 21:690–705.

Hodson, Randy and Teresa Sullivan. 1990. *The Social Organization of Work.* Belmont, CA: Wadsworth Publishing Co.

Jacobs, Jerry. 1989. *Revolving Doors: Sex Segregation and Women's Careers.* Stanford, CA: Stanford University Press.

Phenix, Katherine. 1987. "The Status of Women Librarians." *Frontiers* 9:36–40.

Reskin, Barbara and Heidi Hartmann. 1986. *Women's Work, Men's Work: Sex Segregation on the Job.* Washington, DC: National Academy Press.

Reskin, Barbara and Patricia Roos. 1990. *Job Queues, Gender Queues: Explaining Women's Inroads into Male Occupations.* Philadelphia: Temple University Press.

Schmuck, Patricia A. 1987. "Women School Employees in the United States." Pp. 75–97 in *Women Educators: Employees of Schools in Western Counties,* edited by Patricia A. Schmuck. Albany: State University of New York Press.

Schreiber, Carol. 1979. *Men and Women in Transitional Occupations.* Cambridge, MA: MIT Press.

U.S. Bureau of the Census. 1980. *Detailed Population Characteristics,* vol. 1, chap. D. Washington, DC: Government Printing Office.

U.S. Department of Labor. Bureau of Labor Statistics. 1991. *Employment and Earnings.* Washington, DC: Government Printing Office.

Williams, Christine L. 1989. *Gender Differences at Work: Women and Men in Nontraditional Occupations.* Berkeley: University of California Press.

Yoder, Janice D. 1989. "Women at West Point: Lessons for Token Women in Male-Dominated Occupations." Pp. 523–37 in *Women: A Feminist Perspective,* edited by Jo Freeman. Mountain View, CA: Mayfield Publishing Company.

York, Reginald O., H. Carl Henley, and Dorothy N. Gamble. 1987. "Sexual Discrimination in Social Work: Is It Salary or Advancement?" *Social Work* 32:336–40.

Zimmer, Lynn. 1988. "Tokenism and Women in the Workplace." *Social Problems* 35: 64–77.

29

THE RACIAL CONSTRUCTION OF ASIAN AMERICAN WOMEN AND MEN

YEN LE ESPIRITU

Gender inequality has enormous consequences for women, men, and society. Gender inequality reinforces and perpetuates *sexism,* which is prejudice and discrimination against a person on the basis of his or her sex. The costs and consequences of sexism are extensive and include the wage gap, the feminization of poverty, high rates of female victimization as a result of male violence, and psychological and physical health problems in both women and men. This selection by Yen Le Espiritu, taken from *Asian American Women and Men: Labor, Laws, and Love* (1997), reveals the rampant sexism and racism within the institution of the media, both historically and currently. Specifically, Espiritu, a professor of ethnic studies at the University of California, San Diego, examines the interaction between race, social class, and gender in the treatment of Asian American women and men by the media and by the dominant culture. She finds that the cultural images of Asian Americans often contain sexual stereotypes, which are both racist and sexist, and that they reinforce racial, patriarchal, and social class domination.

The slit-eyed, bucktooth Jap thrusting his bayonet, thirsty for blood. The inscrutable, wily Chinese detective with his taped eyelids and wispy moustache. The childlike, indolent Filipino houseboy. Always giggling. Bowing and scraping. Eager to please, but untrustworthy. The sexless, hairless Asian male. The servile, oversexed Asian female. The Geisha. The sultry, sarong-clad, South Seas maiden. The serpentine, cunning Dragon Lady. Mysterious and evil, eager to please. Effeminate. Untrustworthy. Yellow Peril. Fortune Cookie Psychic. Savage. Dogeater. Invisible. Mute. Faceless peasants breeding too many children. Gooks. Passive Japanese Americans obediently marching off to "relocation camps" during the Second World War.

—JESSICA HAGEDORN (1993:XXII)

Focusing on the material lives of Asian Americans, . . . [earlier research explored] . . . how racist and gendered immigration policies and labor conditions have worked in tandem to keep Asian Americans in an assigned, subordinate place. But as is evident from the stereotypes listed above, besides structural discrimination, Asian American men and women have been subject to ideological assaults. Focusing on the ideological dimension of Asian American oppression, this [article] examines the cultural symbols—or what Patricia Hill Collins (1991) called "controlling images" (pp. 67–68)—generated by the dominant group to help justify the economic exploitation and social oppression of Asian American men and women over time. Writing on the objectification of black women, Collins (1991) observed that the exercise of political-economic domination by racial elites "always involves attempts to objectify the subordinate group" (p. 69). Transmitted through cultural institutions owned, controlled, or supported by various elites, these "controlling images" naturalize racism, sexism, and poverty by branding subordinate groups as alternatively inferior, threatening, or praiseworthy. These controlling images form part of a larger system of what Donald G. Baker (1983) referred to as "psychosocial dominance" (p. 37). Along with the threat and occasional use of violence, the psychosocial form of control conditions the subject minority to become the stereotype, to "live it, talk it, embrace it, measure group and individual worth in its terms, and believe it" (Chin and Chan 1972:66–67). In so doing, minority members reject their own individual and group identity and accept in its stead "a white supremacist complex that establishes the primacy of Euro-American cultural practices and social institutions" (Hamamoto 1994:2). But the objectification of Asian Americans as the exotic and inferior "other" has never been absolute. Asian Americans have always, but particularly since the 1960s, resisted race, class, and gender exploitation not only through political and economic struggles but also through cultural activism. My goal is to understand how the internalization and renunciation of these stereotypes have shaped sexual and gender politics within Asian America. In particular, I explore the conflicting politics of gender between Asian American men and women as they negotiate the difficult terrain of cultural nationalism—the construction of an antiassimilationist, native Asian American subject—and gender identities.

Yellow Peril, Charlie Chan, and Suzie Wong

A central aspect of racial exploitation centers on defining people of color as "the other" (Said 1979). The social construction of Asian American "otherness"—through such controlling images as the Yellow Peril, the model minority, the Dragon Lady, and the China Doll—is "the precondition for their cultural marginalization, political impotence, and psychic alienation from mainstream American society" (Hamamoto 1994:5). As indicated by these stereotypes, representations of gender and sexuality figure strongly in the articulation of racism. These racist stereotypes collapse gender and sexuality: Asian men have been constructed as hypermasculine, in the image of the "Yellow Peril," but also as effeminate, in the image of the "model minority," and Asian women have been depicted as superfeminine, in the image of the "China Doll," but also as castrating, in the image of the "Dragon Lady" (Mullings 1994:279–80; Okihiro 1995). As Mary Ann Doane (1991) suggested, sexuality is "indissociable from the effects of polarization and differentiation, often linking them to structures of power and domination" (p. 217). In the Asian American case, the gendering of ethnicity—the process whereby white ideology assigns selected gender characteristics to various ethnic "others"—cast Asian American men and women as simultaneously masculine and feminine but also as neither masculine nor feminine. On the one hand, as part of the Yellow Peril, Asian American men and women have been depicted as a *masculine* threat that needs to be contained. On the other hand, both sexes have been skewed toward the female side: an indication of the group's marginalization in U.S. society and its role as the compliant "model minority" in contemporary U.S. cultural ideology. Although an apparent disjunction, both the feminization and masculinization of Asian men and women exist to define and confirm the white man's superiority (Kim 1990). . . .

The Racial Construction of Asian American Manhood

Like other men of color, Asian American men have been excluded from white-based cultural notions of the masculine. Whereas white men are depicted both as virile and as protectors of women, Asian men have been characterized both as asexual *and* as threats to white women. It is important to note the historical contexts of these seemingly divergent representations of Asian American manhood. The racist depictions of Asian men as "lascivious and predatory" were especially pronounced during the nativist movement against Asians at the turn of the century (Frankenberg 1993:75–76). The exclusion of Asian women from the United States and the subsequent establishment of bachelor societies eventually reversed the construction of Asian masculinity from "hypersexual" to "asexual" and even "homosexual." The contemporary model-minority stereotype further emasculates Asian American men as passive and malleable. Disseminated and perpetuated through the popular media, these stereotypes of the emasculated Asian male construct a reality in which social and economic discrimination against these men appears defensible. As an example, the desexualization of Asian men naturalized their inability to establish conjugal families in pre–World War II United States. Gliding over race-based exclusion laws that banned the immigration of most Asian women and antimiscegenation laws that prohibited men of color from marrying white women, these dual images of the eunuch and the rapist attributed the "womanless households" characteristic of pre-war Asian America to Asian men's lack of sexual prowess and desirability.

A popular controlling image applied to Asian American men is that of the sinister Oriental—a brilliant, powerful villain who plots the destruction of Western civilization. Personified by the movie character of Dr. Fu Manchu, this Oriental mastermind combines Western science with Eastern magic and commands an army of devoted assassins (Hoppenstand 1983: 178). Though ruthless, Fu Manchu lacks masculine heterosexual prowess (Wang 1988:19), thus privileging heterosexuality. Frank Chin and Jeffrey Chan (1972), in a critique of the desexualization of Asian men in Western culture, described how the Fu Manchu character undermines Chinese American virility:

> Dr. Fu, a man wearing a long dress, batting his eyelashes, surrounded by muscular black servants in loin cloths, and with his habit of caressingly touching white men on the leg, wrist, and face with his long fingernails is not so much a threat as he is a frivolous offense to white manhood. (P. 60)

In another critique that glorifies male aggression, Frank Chin (1972) contrasted the neuterlike characteristics assigned to Asian men to the sexually aggressive images associated with other men of color: "Unlike the white stereotype of the evil black stud, Indian rapist, Mexican macho, the evil of the evil Dr. Fu Manchu was not sexual, but homosexual" (p. 66). However, Chin failed to note that as a homosexual, Dr. Fu (and, by extension, Asian men) threatens and offends white masculinity—and therefore needs to be contained ideologically and destroyed physically.[1]

Whereas the evil Oriental stereotype marks Asian American men as the white man's enemy, the stereotype of the sexless Asian sidekick—Charlie Chan, the Chinese laundryman, the Filipino houseboy—depicts Asian men as devoted and impotent, eager to please. William Wu (1982) reported that the Chinese servant "is the most important single image of the Chinese immigrants" in American fiction about Chinese Americans between 1850 and 1940 (p. 60). More recently, such diverse television programs as *Bachelor Father* (1957–1962), *Bonanza* (1959–1973), *Star Trek* (1966–1969), and *Falcon Crest* (1981–1990) all featured the stock Chinese bachelor domestic who dispenses sage advice to his superiors in addition to performing traditional female functions within the household (Hamamoto 1994:7). By trapping Chinese men (and, by extension, Asian men) in the stereotypical "feminine" tasks of serving white men, American society erases the figure of the Asian "masculine" plantation worker in Hawaii or railroad construction worker in the western United States, thus perpetuating the myth of the androgynous and effeminate Asian man (Goellnicht 1992:198). This feminization, in turn, confines Asian immigrant men to the segment of the labor force that performs women's work.

The motion picture industry has been key in the construction of Asian men as sexual deviants. In a study of Asians in the U.S. motion pictures, Eugene Franklin Wong maintained that the movie industry filmically castrates Asian males to magnify the superior sexual status of white males (1978:27). As on-screen sexual rivals of whites, Asian males are neutralized, unable to sexually engage Asian women and prohibited from sexually engaging white women. By saving the white woman from sexual contact with the racial "other," the motion picture industry protects the Anglo-American, bourgeois male establishment from any challenges to its hegemony (Marchetti 1993:218). At the other extreme, the industry has exploited one of the most potent aspects of the Yellow Peril discourses—the sexual danger of contact between the races—by concocting a sexually threatening portrayal of the licentious and aggressive Yellow Man lusting after the White Woman (Marchetti 1993:3). Heedful of the larger society's taboos against Asian male-white female sexual union, white male actors donning "yellowface"—instead of Asian male actors—are used in these "love scenes." Nevertheless, the message of the perverse and animalistic Asian male attacking helpless white women is clear (Wong 1978). Though depicting sexual aggression, this image of the rapist, like that of the eunuch, casts Asian men as sexually undesirable. As Wong (1978) succinctly stated, in Asian male-white female relations, "There can be rape, but there cannot be romance" (p. 25). Thus, Asian males yield to the sexual superiority of the white males who are permitted filmically to maintain their sexual dominance over both white women and women of color. A young Vietnamese American man describes the damaging effect of these stereotypes on his self-image:

> Every day I was forced to look into a mirror created by white society and its media. As a young Asian man, I shrank before white eyes. I wasn't tall, I wasn't fair, I wasn't muscular, and so on. Combine that with the enormous insecurities any pubescent teenager feels, and I have no difficulty in knowing now why I felt naked before a mass of white people. (Nguyen 1990:23)

White cultural and institutional racism against Asian males is also reflected in the motion picture industry's preoccupation with the death of Asians—a filmic solution to the threats of the Yellow Peril. In a perceptive analysis of Hollywood's view of Asians in films made from the 1930s to the 1960s, Tom Engelhardt (1976) described how Asians, like Native Americans, are seen by the movie industry as inhuman invaders, ripe for extermination.

He argued that the theme of the nonhumanness of Asians prepares the audience to accept, without flinching, "the levelling and near-obliteration of three Asian areas in the course of three decades" (Engelhardt 1976:273). The industry's death theme, though applying to all Asians, is mainly focused on Asian males, with Asian females reserved for sexual purposes (Wong 1978:35). Especially in war films, Asian males, however advantageous their initial position, inevitably perish at the hands of the superior white males (Wong 1978:34).

The Racial Construction of Asian American Womanhood

Like Asian men, Asian women have been reduced to one-dimensional caricatures in Western representation. The condensation of Asian women's multiple differences into gross character types—mysterious, feminine, and nonwhite—obscures the social injustice of racial, class, and gender oppression (Marchetti 1993:71). Both Western film and literature promote dichotomous stereotypes of the Asian woman: She is either the cunning Dragon Lady or the servile Lotus Blossom Baby (Tong 1994:197). Though connoting two extremes, these stereotypes are interrelated: Both eroticize Asian women as exotic "others"—sensuous, promiscuous, but untrustworthy. Whereas American popular culture denies "manhood" to Asian men, it endows Asian women with an excess of "womanhood," sexualizing them but also impugning their sexuality. In this process, both sexism and racism have been blended together to produce the sexualization of white racism (Wong 1978:260). Linking the controlling images of Asian men and women, Elaine Kim (1990) suggested that Asian women are portrayed as sexual for the same reason that men are asexual: "Both exist to define the white man's virility and the white man's superiority" (p. 70).

As the racialized exotic "others," Asian American women do not fit the white-constructed notions of the feminine. Whereas white women have been depicted as chaste and dependable, Asian women have been represented as promiscuous and untrustworthy. In a mirror image of the evil Fu Manchu, the Asian woman was portrayed as the castrating Dragon Lady who, while puffing on her foot-long cigarette holder, could poison a man as easily as she could seduce him. "With her talon-like six-inch fingernails, her skin-tight satin dress slit to the thigh," the Dragon Lady is desirable, deceitful, and dangerous (Ling 1990:11). In the 1924 film *The Thief of Baghdad,* Anna May Wong, a pioneer Chinese American actress, played a handmaid who employed treachery to help an evil Mongol prince attempt to win the hand of the Princess of Baghdad (Tajima 1989:309). In so doing, Wong unwittingly popularized a common Dragon Lady social type: treacherous women who are partners in crime with men of their own kind. The publication of *Daughter of Fu Manchu* (1931) firmly entrenched the Dragon Lady image in white consciousness. Carrying on her father's work as the champion of Asian hegemony over the white race, Fah Lo Sue exhibited, in the words of American studies scholar William F. Wu, "exotic sensuality, sexual availability to a white man, and a treacherous nature" (cited in Tong 1994:197). A few years later, in 1934, Milton Caniff inserted into his adventure comic strip *Terry and the Pirates* another version of the Dragon Lady who "combines all the best features of past moustache twirlers with the lure of the handsome wench" (Hoppenstand 1983:178). As such, Caniff's Dragon Lady fuses the image of the evil male Oriental mastermind with that of the Oriental prostitute first introduced some 50 years earlier in the dime novels.

At the opposite end of the spectrum is the Lotus Blossom stereotype, reincarnated throughout the years as the China Doll, the Geisha Girl, the War Bride, or the Vietnamese prostitute—many of whom are the spoils of the last three wars fought in Asia (Tajima 1989:309). Demure, diminutive, and deferential, the Lotus Blossom Baby is "modest, tittering behind her delicate ivory hand, eyes downcast, always walking ten steps behind her man, and, best of all, devot[ing] body and soul to serving him" (Ling 1990:11). Interchangeable in appearance and name, these women have no voice; their "nonlanguage" includes uninterpretable chattering, pidgin English, giggling, or silence (Tajima 1989). These stereotypes of Asian women as submissive and dainty sex objects not only have impeded women's economic mobility but also have fostered an enormous demand for X-rated films and pornographic materials featuring Asian women in bondage, for "Oriental" bathhouse workers in U.S. cities, and for Asian mail-order brides (Kim 1984:64).

Sexism, Racism, and Love

The racialization of Asian manhood and womanhood upholds white masculine hegemony. Cast as sexually available, Asian women become yet another possession of the white man. In motion pictures and network television programs, interracial sexuality, though rare, occurs principally between a white male and an Asian female. A combination of sexism and racism makes this form of miscegenation more acceptable: Race mixing between an Asian male and a white female would upset not only racial taboos but those that attend patriarchal authority as well (Hamamoto 1994:39). Whereas Asian men are depicted as either the threatening rapist or the impotent eunuch, white men are endowed with the masculine attributes with which to sexually attract the Asian women. Such popular television shows as *Gunsmoke* (1955–1975) and *How the West Was Won* (1978–1979) clearly articulate the theme of Asian female sexual possession by the white male. In these shows, only white males have the prerogative to cross racial boundaries and to choose freely from among women of color as sex partners. Within a system of racial and gender oppression, the sexual possession of women and men of color by white men becomes yet another means of enforcing unequal power relations (Hamamoto 1994:46).

The preference for white male–Asian female is also prevalent in contemporary television news broadcasting, most recently in the 1993–1995 pairing

of Dan Rather and Connie Chung as co-anchors of the *CBS Evening News.*
Today, virtually every major metropolitan market across the United States
has at least one Asian American female newscaster (Hamamoto 1994:245).
While female Asian American anchorpersons—Connie Chung, Tritia Toyota,
Wendy Tokuda, and Emerald Yeh—are popular television news figures,
there is a nearly total absence of Asian American men. Critics argue that this
is so because the white male hiring establishment, and presumably the larger
American public, feels more comfortable (i.e., less threatened) seeing a white
male sitting next to a minority female at the anchor desk than the reverse.
Stephen Tschida of WDBJ-TV (Roanoke, Virginia), one of only a handful of
male Asian American television news anchors, was informed early in his
career that he did not have the proper "look" to qualify for the anchor-
person position. Other male broadcast news veterans have reported being
passed over for younger, more beauteous, female Asian Americans (Hamamoto 1994:245). This gender imbalance sustains the construction of Asian
American women as more successful, assimilated, attractive, and desirable
than their male counterparts.

To win the love of white men, Asian women must reject not only Asian
men but their entire culture. Many Hollywood narratives featuring romances
between Anglo American men and Asian women follow the popular Pocahontas mythos: The Asian woman, out of devotion for her white American
lover, betrays her own people and commits herself to the dominant white
culture by dying, longing for, or going to live with her white husband in his
country. For example, in the various versions of *Miss Saigon,* the contemporary version of *Madame Butterfly,* the tragic Vietnamese prostitute eternally
longs for the white boy soldier who has long abandoned her and their son
(Hagedorn 1993:xxii). These tales of interracial romance inevitably have a
tragic ending. The Asian partner usually dies, thus providing a cinematic resolution to the moral lapse of the Westerner. The Pocahontas paradigm can be
read as a narrative of salvation; the Asian woman is saved either spiritually
or morally from the excesses of her own culture, just as she physically saves
her Western lover from the moral degeneracy of her own people (Marchetti
1993:218). For Asian women, who are marginalized not only by gender
but also by class, race, or ethnicity, the interracial romance narratives promise "the American Dream of abundance, protection, individual choice, and
freedom from the strictures of a traditional society in the paternalistic name
of heterosexual romance" (Marchetti 1993:91). These narratives also carry a
covert political message, legitimizing a masculinized Anglo American rule
over a submissive, feminized Asia. The motion picture *China Gate* (1957) by
Samuel Fuller and the network television program *The Lady from Yesterday*
(1985), for example, promote an image of Vietnam that legitimizes American
rule. Seduced by images of U.S. abundance, a feminized Vietnam sacrifices
herself for the possibility of future incorporation into America, the land of
individual freedom and economic opportunities. Thus, the interracial tales

function not only as a romantic defense of traditional female roles within the patriarchy but also as a political justification of American hegemony in Asia (Marchetti 1993:108).

Fetishized as the embodiment of perfect womanhood and genuine exotic femininity, Asian women are pitted against their more modern, emancipated Western sisters (Tajima 1989). In two popular motion pictures, *Love Is a Many-Splendored Thing* (1955) and *The World of Suzie Wong* (1960), the white women remain independent and potentially threatening, whereas both Suyin and Suzie give up their independence in the name of love. Thus, the white female characters are cast as calculating, suffocating, and thoroughly undesirable, whereas the Asian female characters are depicted as truly "feminine"—passive, subservient, dependent, and domestic. Implicitly, these films warn white women to embrace the socially constructed passive Asian beauty as the feminine ideal if they want to attract and keep a man. In pitting white women against Asian women, Hollywood affirms white male identity against the threat of emerging feminism and the concomitant changes in gender relations (Marchetti 1993:115–16). As Robyn Wiegman (1991) observed, the absorption of women of color into gender categories traditionally reserved for white women is "part of a broader program of hegemonic recuperation, a program that has as its main focus the reconstruction of white masculine power" (p. 320). It is also important to note that as the racialized exotic "other," Asian women do not replace but merely substitute for white women, and thus will be readily dismissed once the "real" mistress returns.

The controlling images of Asian men and Asian women, exaggerated out of all proportion in Western representation, have created resentment and tension between Asian American men and women. Given this cultural milieu, many American-born Asians do not think of other Asians in sexual terms (Fung 1994:163). In particular, due to the persistent desexualization of the Asian male, many Asian females do not perceive their ethnic counterparts as desirable marriage partners (Hamamoto 1992:42). In so doing, these women unwittingly enforce the Eurocentric gender ideology that objectifies both sexes and racializes all Asians (see Collins 1990:185–86). In a column to *Asian Week,* a weekly Asian American newspaper, Daniel Yoon (1993) reported that at a recent dinner discussion hosted by the Asian American Students Association at his college, the Asian American women in the room proceeded, one after another, to describe how "Asian American men were too passive, too weak, too boring, too traditional, too abusive, too domineering, too ugly, too greasy, too short, too . . . Asian. Several described how they preferred white men, and how they never had and never would date an Asian man" (p. 16). Partly as a result of the racist constructions of Asian American womanhood and manhood and their acceptance by Asian Americans, intermarriage patterns are high, with Asian American women intermarrying at a much higher rate than Asian American men.[2] Moreover, Asian women involved in intermarriage have usually married white partners

(Agbayani-Siewert and Revilla 1995:156; Min 1995:22; Nishi 1995:128). In part, these intermarriage patterns reflect the sexualization of white racism that constructs white men as the most desirable sexual partners, frowns on Asian male-white women relations, and fetishizes Asian women as the embodiment of perfect womanhood. Viewed in this light, the high rate of outmarriage for Asian American women is the "material outcome of an interlocking system of sexism and racism" (Hamamoto 1992:42).[3]

Cultural Resistance: Reconstructing Our Own Images

"One day/I going to write/about you," wrote Lois-Ann Yamanaka (1993) in "Empty Heart" (p. 548). And Asian Americans did write—"to inscribe our faces on the blank pages and screens of America's hegemonic culture" (Kim 1993:xii). As a result, Asian Americans' objectification as the exotic aliens who are different from, and other than, Euro-Americans has never been absolute. Within the confines of race, class, and gender oppression, Asian Americans have maintained independent self-definitions, challenging controlling images and replacing them with Asian American standpoints. The civil rights and ethnic studies movements of the late 1960s were training grounds for Asian American cultural workers and the development of oppositional projects. Grounded in the U.S. black power movement and in anticolonial struggles of Third World countries, Asian American antihegemonic projects have been unified by a common goal of articulating cultural resistance. Given the historical distortions and misrepresentations of Asian Americans in mainstream media, most cultural projects produced by Asian American men and women perform the important tasks of correcting histories, shaping legacies, creating new cultures, constructing a politics of resistance, and opening spaces for the forcibly excluded (Fung 1994:165; Kim 1993:xiii).

Fighting the exoticization of Asian Americans has been central in the ongoing work of cultural resistance. As discussed above, Asian Americans, however rooted in this country, are represented as recent transplants from Asia or as bearers of an exotic culture. . . . Asian American cultural workers simply do not accept the exotic, one-dimensional caricatures of themselves in U.S. mass media. . . . Asian American cultural projects also deconstruct the myth of the benevolent United States promised to women and men from Asia. . . . To reject the myth of a benevolent United States is also to refute ideological racism: the justification of inequalities through a set of controlling images that attribute physical and intellectual traits to racially defined groups (Hamamoto 1994:3). . . . Finally, Asian American cultural workers reject the narrative of salvation: the myth that Asian women (and a feminized Asia) are saved, through sexual relations with white men (and a masculinized United States), from the excesses of their own culture. Instead, they underscore the considerable potential for abuse in these inherently unequal relationships. . . .

Conclusion

Ideological representations of gender and sexuality are central in the exercise and maintenance of racial, patriarchal, and class domination. In the Asian American case, this ideological racism has taken seemingly contrasting forms: Asian men have been cast as both hypersexual and asexual, and Asian women have been rendered both superfeminine and masculine. Although in apparent disjunction, both forms exist to define, maintain, and justify white male supremacy. The racialization of Asian American manhood and womanhood underscores the interconnections of race, gender, and class. As categories of difference, race and gender relations do not parallel but intersect and confirm each other, and it is the complicity among these categories of difference that enables U.S. elites to justify and maintain their cultural, social, and economic power. Responding to the ideological assaults on their gender identities, Asian American cultural workers have engaged in a wide range of oppositional projects to defend Asian American manhood and womanhood. In the process, some have embraced a masculinist cultural nationalism, a stance that marginalizes Asian American women and their needs. Though sensitive to the emasculation of Asian American men, Asian American feminists have pointed out that Asian American nationalism insists on a fixed masculinist identity, thus obscuring gender differences. Though divergent, both the nationalist and feminist positions advance the dichotomous stance of man or woman, gender or race or class, without recognizing the complex relationality of these categories of oppression. It is only when Asian Americans recognize the intersections of race, gender, and class that we can transform the existing hierarchical structure.

ENDNOTES

[1] I thank Mary Romero for pointing this out to me.

[2] Filipino Americans provide an exception in that Filipino American men tend to intermarry as frequently as Filipina American women. This is partly so because they are more Americanized and have a relatively more egalitarian gender-role orientation than other Asian American men (Agbayani-Siewert and Revilla 1995:156).

[3] In recent years, Asian Americans' rising consciousness, coupled with their phenomenal growth in certain regions of the United States, has led to a significant increase in inter-Asian marriages (e.g., Chinese Americans to Korean Americans). In a comparative analysis of the 1980 and 1990 Decennial Census, Larry Hajimi Shinagawa and Gin Yong Pang [1993] found a dramatic decrease of interracial marriages and a significant rise of inter-Asian marriages. In California (where 39% of all Asian Pacific Americans reside), inter-Asian marriages increased from 21.1% in 1980 to 64% in

1990 of all intermarriages for Asian American husbands, and from 10.8% to 45% for Asian American wives during the same time period.

REFERENCES

Agbayani-Siewart, Pauline and Linda Revilla. 1995. "Filipino Americans." Pp. 134–68 in *Asian Americans: Contemporary Trends and Issues,* edited by P. G. Min. Thousand Oaks, CA: Sage.

Baker, Donald G. 1983. *Race, Ethnicity, and Power: A Comparative Study.* New York: Routledge.

Chin, Frank. 1972. "Confessions of the Chinatown Cowboy." *Bulletin of Concerned Asian Scholars* 4(3):66.

Chin, Frank and Jeffrey P. Chan. 1972. "Racist Love." Pp. 65–79 in *Seeing through Shuck,* edited by R. Kostelanetz. New York: Ballantine.

Collins, Patricia Hill. 1990. *Black Feminist Thought: Knowledge, Consciousness, and the Politics of Empowerment.* New York: Routledge.

Doane, Mary Ann. 1991. *Femme Fatales: Feminism, Film Theory, Psychoanalysis.* New York: Routledge.

Engelhardt, Tom. 1976. "Ambush at Kamikaze Pass." Pp. 270–79 in *Counterpoint: Perspectives on Asian America,* edited by E. Gee. Los Angeles: University of California at Los Angeles, Asian American Studies Center.

Frankenberg, Ruth. 1993. *White Women, Race Matters: The Social Construction of Whiteness.* Minneapolis: University of Minnesota Press.

Fung, R. 1994. "Seeing Yellow: Asian Identities in Film and Video." Pp. 161–71 in *The State of Asian America,* edited by K. Aguilar-San Juan. Boston: South End Press.

Goellnicht, D. C. 1992. "Tang Ao in America: Male Subject Positions in *China Men.*" Pp. 191–212 in *Reading the Literatures of Asian America,* edited by S. G. Lim and A. Ling. Philadelphia: Temple University Press.

Hagedorn, J. 1993. "Introduction: 'Role of Dead Man Requires Very Little Acting.'" Pp. xxi–xxx in *Charlie Chan Is Dead: An Anthology of Contemporary Asian American Fiction,* edited by J. Hagedorn. New York: Penguin.

Hamamoto, D. Y. 1992. "Kindred Spirits: The Contemporary Asian American Family on Television." *Amerasia Journal* 18(2):35–53.

———. 1994. *Monitored Peril: Asian Americans and the Politics of Representation.* Minneapolis: University of Minnesota Press.

Hoppenstand, G. 1983. "Yellow Devil Doctors and Opium Dens: A Survey of the Yellow Peril Stereotypes in Mass Media Entertainment." Pp. 171–85 in *The Popular Culture Reader,* edited by C. D. Geist and J. Nachbar. Bowling Green, OH: Bowling Green University Press.

Kim, E. 1984. "Asian American Writers: A Bibliographical Review." *American Studies International* 22:2.

———. 1990. "'Such Opposite Creatures': Men and Women in Asian American Literature." *Michigan Quarterly Review* 29:68–93.

———. 1993. "Preface." Pp. vii–xiv in *Charlie Chan Is Dead: An Anthology of Contemporary Asian American Fiction,* edited by J. Hagedorn. New York: Penguin.

Ling, A. 1990. *Between Worlds: Women Writers of Chinese Ancestry.* New York: Pergamon.

Marchetti, G. 1993. *Romance and the "Yellow Peril": Race, Sex, and Discursive Strategies in Hollywood Fiction.* Berkeley: University of California Press.

Min, P. G. 1995. "Korean Americans." Pp. 199–231 in *Asian Americans: Contemporary Trends and Issues,* edited by P. G. Min. Thousand Oaks, CA: Sage.

Mullings, L. 1994. "Images, Ideology, and Women of Color." Pp. 265–89 in *Women of*

Color in U.S. Society, edited by M. B. Zinn and B. T. Dill. Philadelphia: Temple University Press.

Nguyen, V. 1990. "Growing Up in White America." *Asian Week,* December 7, p. 23.

Nishi, S. M. 1995. "Japanese Americans." Pp. 95–133 in *Asian Americans: Contemporary Trends and Issues,* edited by P. G. Min. Thousand Oaks, CA: Sage.

Okihiro, G. Y. 1995. "Reading Asian Bodies, Reading Anxieties." Paper presented at the University of California, San Diego Ethnic Studies Colloquium, La Jolla, CA. November.

Said, E. 1979. *Orientalism.* New York: Random House.

Shinagawa, Larry Hajimi and Gin Yong Pang. 1999. *Asian American Intermarriage.* Boston: Beacon Press.

Tajima, R. 1989. "Lotus Blossoms Don't Bleed: Images of Asian Women." Pp. 308–17 in *Making Waves: An Anthology of Writings by and about Asian American Women,* edited by Asian Women United of California. Boston: Beacon.

Tong, B. 1994. *Unsubmissive Women: Chinese Prostitutes in Nineteenth-Century San Francisco.* Norman: University of Oklahoma Press.

Wang, A. 1988. "Maxine Hong Kingston's Reclaiming of America: The Birthright of the Chinese American Male." *South Dakota Review* 26:18–29.

Wiegman, Robin. 1991. "Black Bodies/American Commodities: Gender, Race, and the Bourgeois Ideal in Contemporary Film." Pp. 308–28 in *Unspeakable Images: Ethnicity and the American Cinema,* edited by L. D. Friedman. Urbana: University of Illinois Press.

Wong, Eugene Franklin. 1978. *On Visual Media Racism: Asians in the American Motion Pictures.* New York: Arno.

Wu, William F. 1982. *The Yellow Peril: Chinese Americans in American Fiction, 1850–1940.* Hamden, CT: Archon.

Yamanaka, Lois-Ann. 1993. "Empty Heart." Pp. 544–50 in *Charlie Chan Is Dead: An Anthology of Contemporary Asian American Fiction,* edited by J. Hagedorn. New York: Penguin.

Yoon, D. D. 1993. "Asian American Male: Wimp or What?" *Asian Week,* November 26, p. 16.

30

FAILING AT FAIRNESS
Hidden Lessons

MYRA SADKER • DAVID SADKER

Few social institutions mold the social environment as faithfully as schools do. The institution of education reinforces social inequality by teaching the dominant culture's values and biases. The following reading by Myra Sadker and David Sadker, professors of education at The American University, examines how the social institution of education has replicated social hierarchies that perpetuate gender inequality. In this excerpt, taken from their 1994 book, *Failing at Fairness: How America's Schools Cheat Girls,* they illustrate the gender biases that permeate the institution of education.

S itting in the same classroom, reading the same textbook, listening to the same teacher, boys and girls receive very different educations. From grade school through graduate school, female students are more likely to be invisible members of classrooms. Teachers interact with males more frequently, ask them better questions, and give them more precise and helpful feedback. Over the course of years the uneven distribution of teacher time, energy, attention, and talent, with boys getting the lion's share, takes its toll on girls. Since gender bias is not a noisy problem, most people are unaware of the secret sexist lessons and the quiet losses they engender.

Girls are the majority of our nation's schoolchildren, yet they are second-class educational citizens. The problems they face—loss of self-esteem, decline in achievement, and elimination of career options—are at the heart of the educational process. Until educational sexism is eradicated, more than half our children will be shortchanged and their gifts lost to society.

Award-winning author Susan Faludi discovered that backlash "is most powerful when it goes private, when it lodges inside a woman's mind and turns her vision inward, until she imagines the pressure is all in her head, until she begins to enforce the backlash too—on herself."[1] Psychological backlash internalized by adult women is a frightening concept, but what is even more terrifying is a curriculum of sexist school lessons becoming secret mind games played against female children, our daughters, tomorrow's women.

After almost two decades of research grants and thousands of hours of classroom observation, we remain amazed at the stubborn persistence of these hidden sexist lessons. When we began our investigation of gender bias, we looked first in the classrooms of one of Washington, D.C.'s elite and expensive private schools. Uncertain of exactly what to look for, we wrote nothing down; we just observed. The classroom was a whirlwind of activity, so fast paced we could easily miss the quick but vital phrase or gesture, the insidious incident, the tiny inequity that held a world of meaning. As we watched, we had to push ourselves beyond the blind spots of socialization and gradually focus on the nature of the interaction between teacher and student. On the second day we saw our first example of sexism, a quick, jarring flash within the hectic pace of the school day:

Two second-graders are kneeling beside a large box. They whisper excitedly to each other as they pull out wooden blocks, colored balls, counting sticks. So absorbed are these two small children in examining and sorting the materials, they are visibly startled by the teacher's impatient voice as she hovers over them. "Ann! Julia! Get your cotton-pickin' hands out of the math box. Move over so the boys can get in there and do their work."

Isolated here on the page of a book, this incident is not difficult to interpret. It becomes even more disturbing if you think of it with the teacher making a racial distinction. Picture Ann and Julia as African American children moved away so white children can gain access to the math materials. If Ann and Julia's parents had observed this exchange, they might justifiably wonder whether their tuition dollars were well spent. But few parents actually watch teachers in action, and fewer still have learned to interpret the meaning behind fast-paced classroom events.

The incident unsettles, but it must be considered within the context of numerous interactions this harried teacher had that day. While she talked to the two girls, she was also keeping a wary eye on fourteen other active children. Unless you actually shadowed the teacher, stood right next to her as we did, you might not have seen or heard the event. After all, it lasted only a few seconds.

It took us almost a year to develop an observation system that would register the hundreds of daily classroom interactions, teasing out the gender bias embedded in them. Trained raters coded classrooms in math, reading, English, and social studies. They observed students from different racial and ethnic backgrounds. They saw lessons taught by women and by men, by teachers of different races. In short, they analyzed America's classrooms. By the end of the year we had thousands of observation sheets, and after another year of statistical analysis, we discovered a syntax of sexism so elusive that most teachers and students were completely unaware of its influence.[2]

Recently a producer of NBC's "Dateline" contacted us to learn more about our discovery that girls don't receive their fair share of education. Jane Pauley, the show's anchorwoman, wanted to visit classrooms, capture these covert sexist lessons on videotape, and expose them before a television audience. The task was to extricate sound bites of sexism from a fifth-grade classroom where the teacher, chosen to be the subject of the exposé, was aware she was being scrutinized for sex bias.

"Dateline" had been taping in her class for two days when we received a concerned phone call. "This is a fair teacher," the producer said. "How can we show sexism on our show when there's no gender bias in this teacher's class?" We drove to the NBC studio in Washington, D.C., and found two "Dateline" staffers, intelligent women concerned about fair treatment in school, sitting on the floor in a darkened room staring at the videotape of a fifth-grade class. "We've been playing this over and over. The teacher is terrific. There's no bias in her teaching. Come watch."

After about twenty minutes of viewing, we realized it was a case of déjà vu: The episodal sexist themes and recurring incidents were all too familiar. The teacher was terrific, but she was more effective for half of the students than she was for the other. She was, in fact, a classic example of the hundreds of skillful well-intentioned professionals we have seen who inadvertently teach boys better than girls.

We had forgotten how difficult it was to recognize subtle sexism before you learn how to look. It was as if the "Dateline" staff members were wearing blinders. We halted the tape, pointed out the sexist behaviors, related them to incidents in our research, and played the tape again. There is a classic "aha!" effect in education when people finally "get it." Once the hidden lessons of unconscious bias are understood, classrooms never look the same again to the trained observer.

Much of the unintentional gender bias in that fifth-grade class could not be shown in the short time allowed by television, but the sound bites of sexism were also there. "Dateline" chose to show a segregated math group: boys sitting on the teacher's right side and girls on her left. After giving the math book to a girl to hold open at the page of examples, the teacher turned her back to the girls and focused on the boys, teaching them actively and directly. Occasionally she turned to the girls' side, but only to read the examples in the book. This teacher, although aware that she was being observed for sexism, had unwittingly transformed the girls into passive spectators, an audience for the boys. All but one, that is: The girl holding the math book had become a prop.

"Dateline" also showed a lively discussion in the school library. With both girls' hands and boys' hands waving for attention, the librarian chose boy after boy to speak. In one interaction she peered through the forest of girls' hands waving directly in front of her to acknowledge the raised hand of a boy in the back of the room. Startled by the teacher's attention, the boy muttered, "I was just stretching."

The next day we discussed the show with future teachers, our students at The American University. They were bewildered. "Those teachers really were sexist. They didn't mean to be, but they were. How could that happen—with the cameras and everyone watching?" When we took those students into classrooms to discover the hidden lessons for themselves, they began to understand. It is difficult to detect sexism unless you know precisely how to observe. And if a lifetime of socialization makes it difficult to spot gender bias even when you're looking for it, how much harder it is to avoid the traps when you are the one doing the teaching.

Among Schoolchildren

Subtle sexism is visible to only the most astute readers of *Among Schoolchildren*, Tracy Kidder's chronicle of real-life educator Chris Zajac. A thirty-four-year-old teacher in Mt. Holyoke, Massachusetts, Mrs. Zajac is a no-nonsense veteran of the classroom. She does not allow her fifth-grade students to misbehave, forget to do their homework, or give up without trying their hardest. Underlying her strict exterior is a woman who cares about schoolchildren. Our students admired her dedication and respected her as a good human being, and it took several readings and discussions before they discovered her inadvertent gender bias. Then came the questions: Does Mrs. Zajac work harder teaching boys than girls? Does she know there is sex bias in her classroom?

These questions probably do not occur to most readers of *Among Schoolchildren* and might jolt both Chris Zajac and the author who so meticulously described the classroom. Here's how Tracy Kidder begins the story of a year in the life of this New England teacher:

> Mrs. Zajac wasn't born yesterday. She knows you didn't do your best work on this paper, Clarence. Don't you remember Mrs. Zajac saying that if you didn't do your best, she'd make you do it over? As for you, Claude, God forbid that you should ever need brain surgery. But Mrs. Zajac hopes that if you do, the doctor won't open up your head and walk off saying he's almost done, as you said when Mrs. Zajac asked you for your penmanship, which, by the way, looks like you did it and ran. Felipe, the reason you have hiccups is, your mouth is always open and the wind rushes in. You're in fifth grade now. So, Felipe, put a lock on it. Zip it up. Then go get a drink of water. Mrs. Zajac means business, Robert. The sooner you realize she never said everybody in the room has to do the work except for Robert, the sooner you'll get along with her. And . . . Clarence. Mrs. Zajac knows you didn't try. You don't just hand in junk to Mrs. Zajac. She's been teaching an awful lot of years. She didn't fall off the turnip cart yesterday. She told you she was an old-lady teacher."[3]

Swiftly, adroitly, Kidder introduces the main characters in the classroom—Clarence, Claude, Felipe, Robert, and back to Clarence, the boy in whom Mrs. Zajac invests most. But where are the girls?

As our students analyzed the book and actually examined who Mrs. Zajac was speaking to, they saw that page after page she spent time with the boys—disciplining them, struggling to help them understand, teaching them with all the energy and talent she could muster. In contrast, the pages that showed Mrs. Zajac working with girls were few and far between.

When we ask teachers at our workshops why they spend more time helping boys, they say, "Because boys need it more" or "Boys have trouble reading, writing, doing math. They can't even sit still. They need me more." In *Among Schoolchildren*, Chris Zajac feels that way, too. Kidder describes how she allows boys to take her over because she thinks they need her.

So teachers of good intention, such as Chris Zajac, respond to boys and teach them more actively, but their time and attention are not limitless. While the teachers are spending time with boys, the girls are being ignored and shortchanged. The only girl clearly realized in *Among Schoolchildren* is Judith, a child who is so alert that she has a vast English vocabulary even though her parents speak only Spanish. But while Judith is a girl of brilliant potential, she rarely reaps the benefit of Mrs. Zajac's active teaching attention. In fact, rather than trouble her teacher and claim time and attention for herself, Judith helps Mrs. Zajac, freeing her to work with the more demanding boys. Mrs. Zajac knows she isn't giving this talented girl what she needs and deserves: "If only I had more time," she thinks as she looks at Judith.

On a field trip to old Sturbridge Village, the children have segregated themselves by sex on the bus, with the boys claiming the back. In a moment of quiet reflection, Chris realizes that in her classroom "the boys rarely give her a chance to spend much time with her girls." She changes her seat, joins the girls, and sings jump rope songs with them for the remainder of the trip.[4]

But her time spent with the girls is short-lived—the length of the day-long field trip—and her recognition of the gender gap in time and attention is brief: a paragraph-long flash of understanding in a book of more than three hundred pages. On the whole, Chris Zajac does not invest her talent in girls. But nurturing children is not unlike tending a garden: Neglect, even when benign, is withering; time and attention bear fruit. Mrs. Zajac and other caring teachers across the country are unaware of the full impact of uneven treatment. They do not realize the high academic and emotional price many girls pay for being too good. Drawn from years of research, the episodes that follow demonstrate the sexist lessons taught daily in America's classrooms.[5] Pulled out of the numerous incidents in a school day, these inequities become enlarged, as if observed through a magnifying glass, so we can see clearly how they extinguish learning and shatter self-esteem. Imagine yourself in a sixth-grade science class like the one we observed in Maryland.

The teacher is writing a list of inventors and their discoveries on the board:

Elias Howe	sewing machine
Robert Fulton	steamboat
Thomas A. Edison	light bulb
James Otis	elevator

Alexander Graham Bell	telephone
Cyrus McCormick	reaper
Eli Whitney	cotton gin
Orville and Wilbur Wright	airplane

A girl raises her hand and asks, "It looks like all the inventors were men. Didn't women invent anything?" The teacher does not add any female inventors to the list, nor does he discuss new scholarship recognizing the involvement of women in inventions such as the cotton gin. He does not explain how hard it was in times past for women to obtain patents in their own names, and therefore we may never know how many female inventors are excluded from the pages of our history books. Instead he grins, winks, and says, "Sweetheart, don't worry about it. It's the same with famous writers and painters. It's the man's job to create things and the woman's job to look beautiful so she can inspire him." Several boys laugh. A few clown around by flexing their muscles as they exclaim, "Yes!" One girl rolls her eyes toward the ceiling and shakes her head in disgust. The incident lasts less than a minute, and the discussion of male inventors continues.

We sometimes ask our students at The American University to list twenty famous women from American history. There are only a few restrictions. They cannot include figures from sports or entertainment. Presidents' wives are not allowed unless they are clearly famous in their own right. Most students cannot do it. The seeds of their ignorance were sown in their earliest years of schooling.

In the 1970s, analyses of best-selling history books showed a biological oddity, a nation with only founding fathers.[6] More space was given to the six-shooter than to the women's suffrage movement. In fact, the typical history text gave only two sentences to enfranchising half the population. Science texts continued the picture of a one-gender world, with the exception of Marie Curie who was permitted to stand behind her husband and peer over his shoulder as he looked into a microscope. Today's history and science texts are better—but not much.[7]

At our workshops we ask teachers and parents to tell or write about any sexism they have seen in their schools. We have been collecting their stories for years.[8] A Utah teacher told us: "Last year I had my U.S. history class write biographies about famous Americans. When I collected all one hundred and fifty, I was dismayed to find only five on women. When I asked my kids why, they said they didn't know any famous women. When I examined their textbook more closely, I saw there were few females in it. And there were even fewer books on famous American women in our school library."

Teachers add to textbook bias when they produce sexist materials of their own. One parent described her efforts to stop a teacher-made worksheet that perpetuated stereotypes of yesteryear:

A few years ago my daughter came home upset over her grade. When I looked at her paper, I got more angry than she was. At the top of the worksheet were the faces of a man and a woman. At the bottom were different objects—nails, a saw, a sewing needle, thread, a hammer, a screwdriver, a broom. The directions said to draw a line from the woman to the objects that go with her. In our house my husband does the cooking and I do the repair work, so you can imagine what the lines on my daughter's paper looked like. There was a huge red F in the middle of her worksheet. I called the teacher right away. She was very understanding and assured me the F wouldn't count. A small victory, I thought, and forgot about it.

This year my son is in her class. Guess what he brought home last week. Same worksheet—same F. Nothing had changed at all.

When girls do not see themselves in the pages of textbooks, when teachers do not point out or confront the omissions, our daughters learn that to be female is to be an absent partner in the development of our nation. And when teachers add their stereotypes to the curriculum bias in books, the message becomes even more damaging.

In a 1992 survey in *Glamour*, 74 percent of those responding said that they had "a teacher who was biased against females or paid more attention to the boys." Math class was selected as the place where inequities were most likely to occur. Fifty-eight percent picked it as their most sexist subject. Physical education was second, and science came in third, selected by 47 percent of the respondents.[9] Women at our workshops recall remarks made by math and science teachers that years later still leave them upset and angry:

In my A.P. physics class in high school in 1984 there were only three girls and twenty-seven boys. The three girls, myself included, consistently scored at the top end of the scale. On one test I earned a 98. The next closest boy earned an 88. The teacher handed the tests back saying, "Boys, you are failing. These three pretty cookies are outscoring you guys on every test." He told the boys it was embarrassing for them to be beaten by a girl. He always referred to us (the girls) as "Cookie" or made our names sound very cutesy!

Sometimes the humiliating lessons come not from school policies, teachers, or books but from boys, the very individuals that adolescent girls most want to impress:

The New England high school was having an assembly during the last period on Friday, and the auditorium was packed with more than a thousand students, who were restless as they listened to announcements. A heavy, awkward tenth-grader made her way across the stage to reach the microphone located in the center. As she walked, several male students made loud barking noises to signify she was a dog. Others oinked like pigs. Later a slender long-haired senior walked to the mike; she was greeted by catcalls and whistles. Nobody attempted to stop the demeaning and hurtful public evaluation of the appearance of these teenage girls.

Tolerated under the assumption that "boys will be boys" and hormone levels are high in high school, sexual harassment is a way of life in America's schools. While teachers and administrators look the other way, sexually denigrating comments, pinching, touching, and propositioning happen daily. Sensitive and insecure about their appearance, some girls are so intimidated they suffer in silence. Others fight back only to find this heightens the harassment. Many girls don't even realize they have a right to protest. And when they do come forward, bringing school sexual harassment into the open, it is often dealt with quickly and nervously; it is swept under the rug, turned aside, or even turned against the girl who had the courage to complain. A teacher at a workshop in Indiana told us: "In our school a girl was pinched on the derriere by two boys and verbally harassed. When she reported the incident to the principal, she was told that her dress was inappropriate and that she had asked for it."

Intimidating comments and offensive sexual jokes are even more common in college and sometimes are even made public as part of a classroom lecture and discussion. A female faculty member, teaching at a university that was historically all male, told us about one of the most popular teachers on campus, an economics professor:

> *He would show slides illustrating an economic theory and insert women in bikinis in the middle "to keep students interested." He illustrated different phases of the economic cycle by showing a slide of a woman's breast and pointed out how far away from the nipple each phase was. When a number of female students complained, the local newspaper supported the professor and criticized the "ultrasensitive coeds." That semester the university gave the professor the Teacher of the Year award.*

Although sexually harassing remarks, stories, and jokes occur only occasionally in classrooms, female silence is the norm. During our two-year study of colleges, our raters found that girls grow quieter as they grow older. In coeducational classes, college women are even less likely to participate in discussions than elementary and secondary school girls. In the typical college classroom, 45 percent of students do not speak; the majority of these voiceless students are women.[10]

Breaking the Sound Barrier

Women who have spent years learning the silence in elementary, secondary, and college classrooms have trouble regaining their voices. In our workshops we often set up a role play to demonstrate classroom sex bias. Four volunteers, two women and two men, are asked to pretend to be students in a middle school social studies lesson. They have no script; their only direction is to take a piece of paper with them as David, playing the part of the social studies teacher, ushers them to four chairs in front of the room. He tells the audience that he will condense all the research on sexism in the classroom into a ten-minute lesson, so the bias will look blatant, even overwhelming. The job of the parents and teachers in the audience is to detect the different forms of egregious sexism. He begins the lesson.

"Today we're going to discuss the chapter in your book, 'The Gathering Clouds of War,' about the American Revolution. But first I'd like you to take out your homework so I can check it." David walks over to Sarah, the first student in the line of four. (In real life she is an English teacher at the local high school.)

"Let's see your paper, Sarah." He pauses to look it over. "Questions three and seven are not correct." Sarah looks concerned.

David moves to Peggy (who is a communications professor at a state college). "Oh, Peggy, Peggy, Peggy!" She looks up as everyone stares. David holds up Peggy's paper. "Would you all look at this. It is sooo neat. You print just like a typewriter. This is the kind of paper I like to put on the bulletin board for open school night." Peggy looks down, smiles, blushes, looks up wide-eyed, and bats her eyelashes. She is not faking or exaggerating these behaviors. Before our eyes she has returned to childhood as the stereotypical good girl with pretty penmanship. The lessons have been well learned.

Next, David stops by Tony (who is a vocational education teacher) and looks at the blank paper he is holding. "Tony, you've missed questions three, seven, and eleven. I think you would do better on your assignments if you used the bold headings to guide your reading. I know you can get this if you try harder." Tony nods earnestly as David moves to Roy. Sarah, who missed questions three and seven, looks perplexed.

David scans Roy's paper and hands it back. "Roy, where's your homework?"

Roy (a college physics teacher) stammers, "Here it is," and again offers the blank paper that served as homework for the others in the role play.

"Roy, that's not your history homework. That's science." Roy still looks puzzled. "Trust me, Roy," David says. "No matter what you come up with, it won't be history homework. Now, where is it?"

"The dog ate it," Roy mutters, getting the picture and falling into the bad boy role.

Next, David discusses revolutionary battles, military tactics, and male leaders—George Washington, John and Samuel Adams, Paul Revere, Benjamin Franklin, Thomas Jefferson, and more. He calls on Roy and Tony more than twenty times each. When they don't know the answer, he probes, jokes, challenges, offers hints. He calls on Sarah only twice. She misses both her questions because David gives her less than half a second to speak. After effusively praising Peggy's pretty paper, David never calls on her again. As the lesson progresses, Sarah's face takes on a sad, almost vacant expression. Peggy keeps on smiling.

When the scene of blatant sexism is over, many in the audience want to know how the two women felt.

"That was me all through school," Peggy blurts out. "I did very well. My work was neat. I was always prepared. I would have had the right answer if someone had called on me. But they never did."

"Why did you watch the two males get all the attention?" we ask. "If you weren't called on, why didn't you call out?"

"I tried. I just couldn't do it."

"Why? You weren't wearing a muzzle. The men were calling out."

"I know. I felt terrible. It reminded me of all those years in school when I wanted to say something but couldn't."

"What about you, Sarah?" we ask. "Why didn't you just shout out an answer?"

"It never occurred to me to do it," Sarah says, then pauses. "No, that's not true. I thought about it, but I didn't want to be out there where I might get laughed at or ridiculed."

David has taught this role play class hundreds and hundreds of times in workshops in big cities and small towns all across the United States. Each time he demonstrates sex bias by blatantly and offensively ignoring female students, and almost always the adult women, put back into the role of twelve-year-olds, sit and say nothing; once again they become the nice girls watching the boys in action. Inside they may feel sad or furious or relieved, but like Sarah and Peggy, they remain silent.

When women try to get into classroom interaction, they rarely act directly. Instead they doodle, write letters, pass notes, and wait for the teacher to notice them. In a California workshop, one parent who was playing the part of a student developed an elaborate pantomime. She reached into her large purse, pulled out a file, and began to do her nails. When that failed to attract David's attention, she brought out a brush, makeup, and a mirror. But David continued to ignore her, talking only with the two males.

"I was so mad I wanted to hit you," the woman fumed at the end of the role play when she was invited to express her feelings.

"What did you do to show your anger?" David asked.

"I didn't do anything." Then she paused, realizing the passive-aggressive but ultimately powerless strategy she had pursued. "No, I did do something—my nails," she said sadly.

After hundreds of these role plays, we are still astonished at how quickly the veneer of adulthood melts away. Grown women and men replay behavior they learned as children at school. The role plays are always revealing—funny, sad, and sometimes they even have a troubling twist.

At a workshop for college students at a large university in the Midwest, one of the young women ignored in the role play did not exhibit the usual behavior of silence or passive hostility. Instead, in the middle of the workshop in front of her classmates, she began to sob. She explained later in private that as one of only a few girls in the university's agricultural program, she had been either ignored or harassed. That week in an overenrolled course an instructor had announced, "There are too many students in this class. Everyone with ovaries—out!"

"What did you do?"

"What could I do? I left. Later I told my adviser about it. He was sympathetic but said if there was no room, I should consider another major."

Silent Losses

Each time a girl opens a book and reads a womanless history, she learns she is worth less. Each time the teacher passes over a girl to elicit the ideas and opinions of boys, that girl is conditioned to be silent and to defer. As teachers use their expertise to question, praise, probe, clarify, and correct boys, they help these male students sharpen ideas, refine their thinking, gain their voice, and achieve more. When female students are offered the leftovers of teacher time and attention, morsels of amorphous feedback, they achieve less.

Then girls and women learn to speak softly or not at all; to submerge honest feelings, withhold opinions, and defer to boys; to avoid math and science as male domains; to value neatness and quiet more than assertiveness and creativity; to emphasize appearance and hide intelligence. Through this curriculum in sexism they are turned into educational spectators instead of players; but education is not a spectator sport.

When blatantly sexual or sexist remarks become an accepted part of classroom conversation, female students are degraded. Sexual harassment in business and the military now causes shock waves and legal suits. Sexual harassment in schools is dismissed as normal and unavoidable "boys will be boys" behavior; but by being targeted, girls are being intimidated and caused to feel like members of an inferior class.

Like a thief in school, sexist lessons subvert education, twisting it into a system of socialization that robs potential. Consider this record of silent, devastating losses.[11]

- ▼ In the early grades, girls are ahead of or equal to boys on almost every standardized measure of achievement and psychological well-being. By the time they graduate from high school or college, they have fallen back. Girls enter school ahead but leave behind.[12]

- ▼ In high school, girls score lower on the SAT and ACT tests, which are critical for college admission. The greatest gender gap is in the crucial areas of science and math.

- ▼ Girls score far lower on College Board Achievement tests, which are required by most of the highly selective colleges.

- Boys are much more likely to be awarded state and national college scholarships.

- The gap does not narrow in college. Women score lower on all sections of the Graduate Record Exam, which is necessary to enter many graduate programs.

- Women also trail on most tests needed to enter professional schools: the GMAT for business school, the LSAT for law school, and the MCAT for medical school.

- From elementary school through higher education, female students receive less active instruction, both in the quantity and in the quality of teacher time and attention.[13]

In addition to the loss of academic achievement, girls suffer other difficulties:

- Eating disorders among girls in middle and secondary schools and in college are rampant and increasing.[14]

- Incidents of school-based sexual harassment are now reported with alarming frequency.[15]

- One in ten teenage girls becomes pregnant each year. Unlike boys, when girls drop out, they usually stay out.[16]

- As girls go through school, their self-esteem plummets, and the danger of depression increases.[17]

- Economic penalties follow women after graduation. Careers that have a high percentage of female workers, such as teaching and nursing, are poorly paid. And even when women work in the same jobs as men, they earn less money. Most of America's poor live in households that are headed by women.

If the cure for cancer is forming in the mind of one of our daughters, it is less likely to become a reality than if it is forming in the mind of one of our sons. Until this changes, everybody loses.

ENDNOTES

[1]Susan Faludi, *Backlash: The Undeclared War against American Women* (New York: Crown, 1991), p. xxii.

[2]Our first study, which analyzed gender bias in elementary and secondary classrooms, lasted more than three years and was funded by the National Institute of Education. The report submitted to the government was Myra Sadker and David Sadker, *Year 3: Final Report: Promoting Effectiveness in Classroom Instruction* (Washington, DC: National Institute of Education, 1984); Myra Sadker and David Sadker, "Sexism in the Schoolroom of the Eighties," *Psychology Today,* March 1985, pp. 54–57; Myra Sadker and David Sadker, "Sexism in the Classroom: From Grade School to Graduate School," *Phi Delta Kappan* 67, no. 7 (March 1986): 512–15. We also reported this study as one of the contributing authors to Wellesley College Center for Research on

Women, *How Schools Shortchange Girls: The AAUW Report* (Washington, DC: American Association of University Women Educational Foundation), 1992.

[3] Tracy Kidder, *Among Schoolchildren* (Boston: Houghton Mifflin, 1989), p. 3.

[4] Kidder, *Among Schoolchildren,* p. 262.

[5] These episodes are drawn primarily from our three-year study of sex bias in elementary and secondary classrooms. They are also taken from classroom observations conducted as we supervised student teachers at The American University and as we consulted with schools around the country and assessed their classrooms for gender bias.

[6] Janice Law Trecker, "Women in U.S. History High School Textbooks," *Social Education* 35 (1971): 249–60.

[7] Lenore Weitzman and Diane Rizzo, *Biased Textbooks: Images of Males and Females in Elementary School Textbooks* (Washington, DC: Resource Center on Sex Roles in Education, 1976); Terry Saario, Carol Jacklin, and Carol Tittle, "Sex Role Stereotyping in the Public Schools," *Harvard Educational Review* 43:386–416; Women on Words and Images, *Dick and Jane As Victims: Sex Stereotyping in Children's Readers* (Princeton, NJ: Carolingian Press, 1972).

[8] For more than a decade we have offered workshops on gender bias for educators and parents around the country. At these workshops we have collected anecdotes and stories from students, teachers, and parents about sex bias that they faced at school.

[9] "This Is What You Thought: Were Any of Your Teachers Biased against Females?" *Glamour,* August 1992, p. 157.

[10] Following our three-year study of elementary and secondary classrooms, we conducted a two-year study of college classrooms and were sponsored by the Fund for the Improvement of Postsecondary Education. The project report submitted to the government was Myra Sadker and David Sadker, *Final Report: Project Effect (Effectiveness and Equity in College Teaching),* Washington, DC: Fund for the Improvement of Postsecondary Education, 1986; Myra Sadker and David Sadker, "Confronting Sexism in the College Classroom," in Susan Gabriel and Isaiah Smithson (eds.), *Gender in the Classroom: Power and Pedagogy* (Urbana: University of Illinois Press, 1990), pp. 176–87.

[11] Myra Sadker, David Sadker, and Susan Klein, "The Issue of Gender in Elementary and Secondary Education," in Gerald Grant (ed.), *Review of Research in Education,* vol. 17. (Washington, DC: American Educational Research Association, 1991); Wellesley College Center for Research on Women, *How Schools Shortchange Girls: The AAUW Report.*

[12] Data documenting the loss of academic achievement were obtained from reports, tables, news releases, and studies issued by test publishers. The Educational Testing Service in Princeton, New Jersey, provided several reports and statistics related to the Preliminary Scholastic Aptitude Test, the Scholastic Aptitude Test, the Achievement tests, the Graduate Record Exam, and the Graduate Management Admissions Test. While the Graduate Record Exam data were from 1987–1988 (the most recently published), all other data reflected 1991 and 1992 test administrations. The American College Testing Program data were derived from a variety of profile and normative reports for 1990 and 1991 issued by American College Testing in Iowa City, Iowa.

Professional organizations and schools often contract with testing services to develop and administer their admissions tests. For example, the Medical College Admission Test (MCAT) is developed by ACT in Iowa City. For each of these admission tests the professional association responsible was contacted first, and it provided the requisite information. These organizations included the Association of American

Medical Colleges, the Graduate Management Admissions Council, and the Law School Data Assembly Service.

[13] Sadker and Sadker, *Year 3: Final Report;* Sadker and Sadker, *Final Report: Project Effect.*

[14] K. L. Nagel and Karen H. Jones, "Sociological Factors in the Development of Eating Disorders," *Adolescence* 27 (Spring 1992): 107–13; Claire Wiseman, James Gray, James Mosimann, and Anthony Ahrens, "Cultural Expectations of Thinness in Women: An Update," *International Journal of Eating Disorders* 11, no. 1 (1992): 85–89; Eric Button, "Self-Esteem in Girls Aged 11–12. Baseline Findings from a Planned Prospective Study of Vulnerability to Eating Disorders," *Journal of Adolescence* 13 (December 7, 1990): 407–13.

[15] Jean O'Gorman Hughes and Bernice Sandler, *Peer Harassment: Hassles for Women on Campus* (Washington, DC: Project on the Status and Education of Women, Association of American Colleges, 1988); Nan Stein, "Sexual Harassment in Schools," *The School Administrator,* January 1993, pp. 14–21.

[16] Janice Earle, *Counselor/Advocates: Keeping Pregnant and Parenting Teens in School* (Alexandria, VA: National Association of State Boards of Education, 1990).

[17] A vast body of research documents girls' declining self-esteem at adolescence: Betty Allgood-Merten, Peter Lewinsohn, and Hyman Hops, "Sex Differences and Adolescent Depression," *Journal of Abnormal Psychology* 99, no. 1 (February 1990): 55–63; Herman Brutsaert, "Changing Sources of Self-Esteem among Girls and Boys in Secondary Schools," *Urban Education* 24, no. 4 (January 1990): 432–39; Kevin Kelly and LaVerne Jordan, "Effects of Academic Achievement and Gender on Academic and Social Self-Concept: A Replication Study," *Journal of Counseling and Development* 69 (November–December 1990): 173–77; Keith Widaman, et al. "Differences in Adolescents' Self-Concept As a Function of Academic Level, Ethnicity, and Gender," *American Journal of Mental Retardation* 96, no. 4 (1992): 387–404; Sheila Williams and Rob McGee, "Adolescents' Self-Perceptions of Their Strengths," *Journal of Youth and Adolescence* 20, no. 3 (June 1991): 325–37.

RACE AND ETHNICITY

31

RACIAL FORMATIONS IN THE UNITED STATES

MICHAEL OMI • HOWARD WINANT

Race and ethnicity are the topics explored in the next four selections. *Race* is a creation of culture that reflects social distinctions and power. To say that race is a social construction, however, does not mean that race is not real. Many people believe in the existence of discrete biological racial categories. The first reading, by Michael Omi, associate professor of ethnic studies at the University of California at Berkeley, and Howard Winant, professor at the University of California at Santa Barbara, examines the social construction of race. In this now-classic selection, excerpted from their 1994 book, *Racial Formations in the United States,* Omi and Winant investigate how race has been defined in different social and historical contexts in the United States.

In 1982–83, Susie Guillory Phipps unsuccessfully sued the Louisiana Bureau of Vital Records to change her racial classification from black to white. The descendant of an eighteenth-century white planter and a black slave, Phipps was designated "black" in her birth certificate in accordance with a 1970 state law which declared anyone with at least one-thirty-second "Negro blood" to be black. The legal battle raised intriguing questions about the concept of race, its meaning in contemporary society, and its use (and abuse) in public policy. Assistant Attorney General Ron Davis defended the law by pointing out that some type of racial classification was necessary to comply with federal record-keeping requirements and to facilitate programs for the prevention of genetic diseases. Phipps' attorney, Brian Begue, argued that the assignment of racial categories on birth certificates was unconstitutional and that the one-thirty-second designation was inaccurate. He called on a retired Tulane University professor who cited research indicating that most whites have one-twentieth "Negro" ancestry. In the end, Phipps lost. The court upheld a state law which quantified racial identity, and in so doing affirmed the legality of assigning individuals to specific racial groupings.[1]

The Phipps case illustrates the continuing dilemma of defining race and establishing its meaning in institutional life. Today, to assert that variations in human physiognomy are racially based is to enter a constant and intense debate. *Scientific* interpretations of race have not been alone in sparking heated controversy; *religious* perspectives have done so as well.[2] Most centrally, of course, race has been a matter of *political* contention. This has been particularly true in the United States, where the concept of race has varied enormously over time without ever leaving the center stage of U.S. history.

What Is Race?

Race consciousness, and its articulation in theories of race, is largely a modern phenomenon. When European explorers in the New World "discovered" people who looked different than themselves, these "natives" challenged then existing conceptions of the origins of the human species, and raised disturbing questions as to whether *all* could be considered in the same "family of man."[3] Religious debates flared over the attempt to reconcile the Bible with the existence of "racially distinct" people. Arguments took place over creation itself, as theories of polygenesis questioned whether God had made only one species of humanity ("monogenesis"). Europeans wondered if the natives of the New World were indeed human beings with redeemable souls. At stake were not only the prospects for conversion, but the types of treatment to be accorded them. The expropriation of property, the denial of political rights, the introduction of slavery and other forms of coercive labor, as well as outright extermination, all presupposed a worldview which distinguished Europeans—children of God, human beings, etc.—from "others." Such a worldview was needed to explain why some should be "free" and others enslaved, why some had rights to land and property while others did not. Race, and the interpretation of racial differences, was a central factor in that worldview.

In the colonial epoch, science was no less a field of controversy than religion in attempts to comprehend the concept of race and its meaning. Spurred on by the classificatory scheme of living organisms devised by Linnaeus in *Systema Naturae,* many scholars in the eighteenth and nineteenth centuries dedicated themselves to the identification and ranking of variations in humankind. Race was thought of as a *biological* concept, yet its precise definition was the subject of debates which, as we have noted, continue to rage today. Despite efforts ranging from Dr. Samuel Morton's studies of cranial capacity[4] to contemporary attempts to base racial classification on shared gene pools,[5] the concept of race has defied biological definition. . . .

Attempts to discern the *scientific meaning* of race continue to the present day. Although most physical anthropologists and biologists have abandoned the quest for a scientific basis to determine racial categories, controversies have recently flared in the area of genetics and educational psychology. For instance, an essay by Arthur Jensen which argued that hereditary factors shape intelligence not only revived the "nature or nurture" controversy, but raised highly volatile questions about racial equality itself.[6] Clearly the attempt to establish a *biological* basis of race has not been swept into the dustbin of history, but is being resurrected in various scientific arenas. All such attempts seek to remove the concept of race from fundamental social, political, or economic determination. They suggest instead that the truth of race lies in the terrain of innate characteristics, of which skin color and other physical attributes provide only the most obvious, and in some respects most superficial, indicators.

Race as a Social Concept

The social sciences have come to reject biologistic notions of race in favor of an approach which regards race as a *social* concept. Beginning in the eighteenth century, this trend has been slow and uneven, but its direction clear. In the nineteenth century, Max Weber discounted biological explanations for racial conflict and instead highlighted the social and political factors which engendered such conflict.[7] The work of pioneering cultural anthropologist Franz Boas was crucial in refuting the scientific racism of the early twentieth century by rejecting the connection between race and culture, and the assumption of a continuum of "higher" and "lower" cultural groups. Within the contemporary social science literature, race is assumed to be a variable which is shaped by broader societal forces.

Race is indeed a pre-eminently *sociohistorical* concept. Racial categories and the meaning of race are given concrete expression by the specific social relations and historical context in which they are embedded. Racial meanings have varied tremendously over time and between different societies.

In the United States, the black/white color line has historically been rigidly defined and enforced. White is seen as a "pure" category. Any racial intermixture makes one "nonwhite." In the movie *Raintree County*, Elizabeth Taylor describes the worst of fates to befall whites as "havin' a little Negra blood in ya'—just one little teeny drop and a person's all Negra."[8] This thinking flows from what Marvin Harris has characterized as the principle of *hypo-descent:*

> By what ingenious computation is the genetic tracery of a million years of evolution unraveled and each man [sic] assigned his proper social box? In the United States, the mechanism employed is the rule of hypo-descent. This descent rule requires Americans to believe that anyone who is known to have had a Negro ancestor is a Negro. We admit nothing in between. . . . "Hypo-descent" means affiliation with the subordinate rather than the superordinate group in order to avoid the ambiguity of intermediate identity. . . . The rule of hypo-descent is, therefore, an in-

vention, which we in the United States have made in order to keep biological facts from intruding into our collective racist fantasies.[9]

The Susie Guillory Phipps case merely represents the contemporary expression of this racial logic.

By contrast, a striking feature of race relations in the lowland areas of Latin America since the abolition of slavery has been the relative absence of sharply defined racial groupings. No such rigid descent rule characterizes racial identity in many Latin American societies. Brazil, for example, has historically had less rigid conceptions of race, and thus a variety of "intermediate" racial categories exist. Indeed, as Harris notes, "One of the most striking consequences of the Brazilian system of racial identification is that parents and children and even brothers and sisters are frequently accepted as representatives of quite opposite racial types."[10] Such a possibility is incomprehensible within the logic of racial categories in the United States.

To suggest another example: the notion of "passing" takes on new meaning if we compare various American cultures' means of assigning racial identity. In the United States, individuals who are actually "black" by the logic of hypo-descent have attempted to skirt the discriminatory barriers imposed by law and custom by attempting to "pass" for white.[11] Ironically, these same individuals would not be able to pass for "black" in many Latin American societies.

Consideration of the term "black" illustrates the diversity of racial meanings which can be found among different societies and historically within a given society. In contemporary British politics the term "black" is used to refer to all nonwhites. Interestingly this designation has not arisen through the racist discourse of groups such as the National Front. Rather, in political and cultural movements, Asian as well as Afro-Caribbean youth are adopting the term as an expression of self-identity.[12] The wide-ranging meanings of "black" illustrate the manner in which racial categories are shaped politically.[13]

The meaning of race is defined and contested throughout society, in both collective action and personal practice. In the process, racial categories themselves are formed, transformed, destroyed, and re-formed. We use the term *racial formation* to refer to the process by which social, economic, and political forces determine the content and importance of racial categories, and by which they are in turn shaped by racial meanings. Crucial to this formulation is the treatment of race as a *central axis* of social relations which cannot be subsumed under or reduced to some broader category or conception.

Racial Ideology and Racial Identity

The seemingly obvious "natural" and "common sense" qualities which the existing racial order exhibits themselves testify to the effectiveness of the racial formation process in constructing racial meanings and racial identities.

One of the first things we notice about people when we meet them (along with their sex) is their race. We utilize race to provide clues about *who* a person is. This fact is made painfully obvious when we encounter someone whom we cannot conveniently racially categorize—someone who is, for example, racially "mixed" or of an ethnic/racial group with which we are not familiar. Such an encounter becomes a source of discomfort and momentarily a crisis of racial meaning. Without a racial identity, one is in danger of having no identity.

Our compass for navigating race relations depends on preconceived notions of what each specific racial group looks like. Comments such as, "Funny, you don't look black," betray an underlying image of what black should be. We also become disoriented when people do not act "black," "Latino," or indeed "white." The content of such stereotypes reveals a series of unsubstantiated beliefs about who these groups are and what "they" are like.[14]

In U.S. society, then, a kind of "racial etiquette" exists, a set of interpretive codes and racial meanings which operate in the interactions of daily life. Rules shaped by our perception of race in a comprehensively racial society determine the "presentation of self,"[15] distinctions of status, and appropriate modes of conduct. "Etiquette" is not mere universal adherence to the dominant group's rules, but a more dynamic combination of these rules with the values and beliefs of subordinated groupings. This racial "subjection" is quintessentially ideological. Everybody learns some combination, some version, of the rules of racial classification, and of their own racial identity, often without obvious teaching or conscious inculcation. Race becomes "common sense"—a way of comprehending, explaining, and acting in the world.

Racial beliefs operate as an "amateur biology," a way of explaining the variations in "human nature."[16] Differences in skin color and other obvious physical characteristics supposedly provide visible clues to differences lurking underneath. Temperament, sexuality, intelligence, athletic ability, aesthetic preferences, and so on are presumed to be fixed and discernible from the palpable mark of race. Such diverse questions as our confidence and trust in others (for example, clerks or salespeople, media figures, neighbors), our sexual preferences and romantic images, our tastes in music, films, dance, or sports, and our very ways of talking, walking, eating, and dreaming are ineluctably shaped by notions of race. Skin color "differences" are thought to explain perceived differences in intellectual, physical, and artistic temperaments, and to justify distinct treatment of racially identified individuals and groups.

The continuing persistence of racial ideology suggests that these racial myths and stereotypes cannot be exposed as such in the popular imagination. They are, we think, too essential, too integral, to the maintenance of the U.S. social order. Of course, particular meanings, stereotypes, and myths can change, but the presence of a *system* of racial meanings and stereotypes, of racial ideology, seems to be a permanent feature of U.S. culture.

Film and television, for example, have been notorious in disseminating images of racial minorities which establish for audiences what people from these groups look like, how they behave, and "who they are." [17] The power of the media lies not only in their ability to reflect the dominant racial ideology, but in their capacity to shape that ideology in the first place. D. W. Griffith's epic *Birth of a Nation*, a sympathetic treatment of the rise of the Ku Klux Klan during Reconstruction, helped to generate, consolidate, and "nationalize" images of blacks which had been more disparate (more regionally specific, for example) prior to the film's appearance.[18] In U.S. television, the necessity to define characters in the briefest and most condensed manner has led to the perpetuation of racial caricatures, as racial stereotypes serve as shorthand for scriptwriters, directors and actors, in commercials, etc. Television's tendency to address the "lowest common denominator" in order to render programs "familiar" to an enormous and diverse audience leads it regularly to assign and reassign racial characteristics to particular groups, both minority and majority.

These and innumerable other examples show that we tend to view race as something fixed and immutable—something rooted in "nature." Thus we mask the historical construction of racial categories, the shifting meaning of race, and the crucial role of politics and ideology in shaping race relations. Races do not emerge full-blown. They are the results of diverse historical practices and are continually subject to challenge over their definition and meaning.

Racialization: The Historical Development of Race

In the United States, the racial category of "black" evolved with the consolidation of racial slavery. By the end of the seventeenth century, Africans whose specific identity was Ibo, Yoruba, Fulani, etc., were rendered "black" by an ideology of exploitation based on racial logic—the establishment and maintenance of a "color line." This of course did not occur overnight. A period of indentured servitude which was not rooted in racial logic preceded the consolidation of racial slavery. With slavery, however, a racially based understanding of society was set in motion which resulted in the shaping of a specific *racial* identity not only for the slaves but for the European settlers as well. Winthrop Jordan has observed: "From the initially common term *Christian*, at mid-century there was a marked shift toward the terms *English* and *free*. After about 1680, taking the colonies as a whole, a new term of self-identification appeared—*white*." [19]

We employ the term *racialization* to signify the extension of racial meaning to a previously racially unclassified relationship, social practice, or group. Racialization is an ideological process, a historically specific one. Racial ideology is constructed from pre-existing conceptual (or, if one prefers, "discursive") elements and emerges from the struggles of competing political projects and ideas seeking to articulate similar elements differently. An account of racialization processes that avoids the pitfalls of U.S. ethnic history[20] remains to be written.

Particularly during the nineteenth century, the category of "white" was subject to challenges brought about by the influx of diverse groups who were not of the same Anglo-Saxon stock as the founding immigrants. In the nineteenth century, political and ideological struggles emerged over the classification of Southern Europeans, the Irish, and Jews, among other "non-white" categories.[21] Nativism was only effectively curbed by the institutionalization of a racial order that drew the color line *around*, rather than *within*, Europe.

By stopping short of racializing immigrants from Europe after the Civil War, and by subsequently allowing their assimilation, the American racial order was reconsolidated in the wake of the tremendous challenge placed before it by the abolition of racial slavery[22] With the end of Reconstruction in 1877, an effective program for limiting the emergent class struggles of the later nineteenth century was forged: the definition of the working class *in racial terms*—as "white." This was not accomplished by any legislative decree or capitalist maneuvering to divide the working class, but rather by white workers themselves. Many of them were recent immigrants, who organized on racial lines as much as on traditionally defined class lines.[23] The Irish on the West Coast, for example, engaged in vicious anti-Chinese race-baiting and committed many pogrom-type assaults on Chinese in the course of consolidating the trade union movement in California.

Thus the very political organization of the working class was in important ways a racial project. The legacy of racial conflicts and arrangements shaped the definition of interests and in turn led to the consolidation of institutional patterns (e.g., segregated unions, dual labor markets, exclusionary legislation) which perpetuated the color line *within* the working class. Selig Perlman, whose study of the development of the labor movement is fairly sympathetic to this process, notes that:

> The political issue after 1877 was racial, not financial, and the weapon was not merely the ballot, but also "direct action"—violence. The anti-Chinese agitation in California, culminating as it did in the Exclusion Law passed by Congress in 1882, was doubtless the most important single factor in the history of American labor, for without it the entire country might have been overrun by Mongolian [sic] labor and *the labor movement might have become a conflict of races instead of one of classes.*[24]

More recent economic transformations in the U.S. have also altered interpretations of racial identities and meanings. The automation of southern agriculture and the augmented labor demand of the postwar boom transformed blacks from a largely rural, impoverished labor force to a largely urban, working-class group by 1970.[25] When boom became bust and liberal welfare statism moved rightwards, the majority of blacks came to be seen, increasingly, as part of the "underclass," as state "dependents." Thus the particularly deleterious effects on blacks of global and national economic shifts (generally rising unemployment rates, changes in the employment structure away from reliance on labor intensive work, etc.) were explained once again in the late 1970s and 1980s (as they had been in the 1940s and mid-1960s) as the result of defective black cultural norms, of familial disorganization, etc.[26] In this way new racial attributions, new racial myths, are affixed to "blacks."[27] Similar changes in racial identity are presently affecting Asians and Latinos, as such economic forces as increasing Third World impoverishment and indebtedness fuel immigration and high interest rates, Japanese competition spurs resentments, and U.S. jobs seem to fly away to Korea and Singapore.[28] . . .

Once we understand that race overflows the boundaries of skin color, superexploitation, social stratification, discrimination and prejudice, cultural domination and cultural resistance, state policy (or of any other particular social relationship we list), once we recognize the racial dimension present to some degree in every identity, institution, and social practice in the United States—once we have done this, it becomes possible to speak of *racial formation*. This recognition is hard-won; there is a continuous temptation to think of race as an *essence*, as something fixed, concrete and objective, as (for example) one of the categories just enumerated. And there is also an opposite temptation: to see it as a mere illusion, which an ideal social order would eliminate.

In our view it is crucial to break with these habits of thought. The effort must be made to understand race as *an unstable and "decentered" complex of social meanings constantly being transformed by political struggle.* . . .

ENDNOTES

[1] *San Francisco Chronicle,* 14 September 1982, 19 May 1983. Ironically, the 1970 Louisiana law was enacted to supersede an old Jim Crow statute which relied on the idea of "common report" in determining an infant's race. Following Phipps' unsuccessful attempt to change her classification and have the law declared unconstitutional, a legislative effort arose which culminated in the repeal of the law. See *San Francisco Chronicle,* June 23, 1983.

[2] The Mormon church, for example, has been heavily criticized for its doctrine of black inferiority.

[3] Thomas F. Gossett notes:

Race theory . . . had up until fairly modern times no firm hold on European thought. On the other hand, race theory and race prejudice were by no means unknown at the time when the English colonists came to North America. Undoubtedly, the age of exploration led many to speculate on race differences at a period when neither Europeans nor Englishmen were prepared to make allowances for vast cultural diversities. Even though race theories had not then secured wide acceptance or even sophisticated formulation, the first contacts of the Spanish with the Indians in the Americas can now be recognized as the beginning of a struggle between conceptions of the nature of primitive peoples which has not yet been wholly settled. (Thomas F. Gossett, *Race: The History of an Idea in America* (New York: Schocken Books, 1965), p. 16.)

Winthrop Jordan provides a detailed account of early European colonialists' attitudes about color and race in *White Over Black: American Attitudes Toward the Negro, 1550–1812* (New York: Norton, 1977 [1968]), pp. 3–43.

[4] Pro-slavery physician Samuel George Morton (1799–1851) compiled a collection of 800 crania from all parts of the world which formed the sample for his studies of race. Assuming that the larger the size of the cranium translated into greater intelligence, Morton established a relationship between race and skull capacity. Gossett reports that

> In 1849, one of his studies included the following results: The English skulls in his collection proved to be the largest, with an average cranial capacity of 96 cubic inches. The Americans and Germans were rather poor seconds, both with cranial capacities of 90 cubic inches. At the bottom of the list were the Negroes with 83 cubic inches, the Chinese with 82, and the Indians with 79. (Ibid., p. 74.)

On Morton's methods, see Stephen J. Gould, "The Finagle Factor," *Human Nature* (July 1978).

[5] Definitions of race founded upon a common pool of genes have not held up when confronted by scientific research which suggests that the differences *within* a given human population are greater than those *between* populations. See L. L. Cavalli-Sforza, "The Genetics of Human Populations," *Scientific American* (September 1974), pp. 81–89.

[6] Arthur Jensen, "How Much Can We Boost IQ and Scholastic Achievement?" *Harvard Educational Review,* vol. 39 (1969), pp. 1–123.

[7] Ernst Moritz Manasse, "Max Weber on Race," *Social Research,* vol. 14 (1947), pp. 191–221.

[8] Quoted in Edward D. C. Campbell, Jr., *The Celluloid South: Hollywood and the Southern Myth* (Knoxville: University of Tennessee Press, 1981), pp. 168–70.

[9] Marvin Harris, *Patterns of Race in the Americas* (New York: Norton, 1964), p. 56.

[10] Ibid., p. 57.

[11] After James Meredith had been admitted as the first black student at the University of Mississippi, Harry S. Murphy announced that he, and not Meredith, was the first black student to attend "Ole Miss." Murphy described himself as black but was able to pass for white and spent nine months at the institution without attracting any notice (ibid., p. 56).

[12] A. Sivanandan, "From Resistance to Rebellion: Asian and Afro-Caribbean Struggles in Britain," *Race and Class,* vol. 23, nos. 2–3 (Autumn–Winter 1981).

[13] Consider the contradictions in racial status which abound in the country with the most rigidly defined racial categories—South Africa. There a race classification agency is employed to adjudicate claims for upgrading of official racial identity. This is particularly necessary for the "coloured" category. The apartheid system considers Chinese as "Asians" while the Japanese are accorded the status of "honorary whites." This logic nearly detaches race from any grounding in skin color and other physical attributes and nakedly exposes race as a juridical category subject to economic, social, and political influences. (We are indebted to Steve Talbot for clarification of some of these points.)

[14] Gordon W. Allport, *The Nature of Prejudice* (Garden City, New York: Doubleday, 1958), pp. 184–200.

[15] We wish to use this phrase loosely, without committing ourselves to a particular position on such social psychological approaches as symbolic interactionism, which

are outside the scope of this study. An interesting study on this subject is S. M. Lyman and W. A. Douglass, "Ethnicity: Strategies of Individual and Collective Impression Management," *Social Research,* vol. 40, no. 2 (1973).

[16] Michael Billig, "Patterns of Racism: Interviews with National Front Members," *Race and Class,* vol. 20, no. 2 (Autumn 1978), pp. 161–79.

[17] "Miss San Antonio USA Lisa Fernandez and other Hispanics auditioning for a role in a television soap opera did not fit the Hollywood image of real Mexicans and had to darken their faces before filming." Model Aurora Garza said that their faces were bronzed with powder because they looked too white. "I'm a real Mexican [Garza said] and very dark anyway. I'm even darker right now because I have a tan. But they kept wanting me to make my face darker and darker" (*San Francisco Chronicle,* September 21, 1984). A similar dilemma faces Asian American actors who feel that Asian character lead roles inevitably go to white actors who make themselves up to be Asian. Scores of Charlie Chan films, for example, have been made with white leads (the last one was the 1981 *Charlie Chan and the Curse of the Dragon Queen*). Roland Winters, who played in six Chan features, was asked by playwright Frank Chin to explain the logic of casting a white man in the role of Charlie Chan: "The only thing I can think of is, if you want to cast a homosexual in a show, and you get a homosexual, it'll be awful. It won't be funny . . . and maybe there's something there . . ." (Frank Chin, "Confessions of the Chinatown Cowboy," *Bulletin of Concerned Asian Scholars,* vol. 4, no. 3 [Fall 1972]).

[18] Melanie Martindale-Sikes, "Nationalizing 'Nigger' Imagery Through 'Birth of a Nation,'" paper prepared for the 73rd Annual Meeting of the American Sociological Association, 4–8 September 1978 in San Francisco.

[19] Winthrop D. Jordan, op. cit., p. 95; emphasis added.

[20] Historical focus has been placed either on particular racially defined groups or on immigration and the "incorporation" of ethnic groups. In the former case the characteristic ethnicity theory pitfalls and apologetics such as functionalism and cultural pluralism may be avoided, but only by sacrificing much of the focus on race. In the latter case, race is considered a manifestation of ethnicity.

[21] The degree of antipathy for these groups should not be minimized. A northern commentator observed in the 1850s: "An Irish Catholic seldom attempts to rise to a higher condition than that in which he is placed, while the Negro often makes the attempt with success." Quoted in Gossett, op. cit., p. 288.

[22] This analysis, as will perhaps be obvious, is essentially DuBoisian. Its main source will be found in the monumental (and still largely unappreciated) *Black Reconstruction in the United States 1860–1880* (New York: Atheneum, 1977 [1935]).

[23] Alexander Saxton argues that

> North Americans of European background have experienced three great racial confrontations: with the Indian, with the African, and with the Oriental. Central to each transaction has been a totally one-sided preponderance of power, exerted for the exploitation of nonwhites by the dominant white society. In each case (but especially in the two that began with systems of enforced labor), white workingmen have played a crucial, yet ambivalent role. They have been both exploited and exploiters. On the one hand, thrown into competition with nonwhites as enslaved or "cheap" labor, they suffered economically; on the other hand, being white, they benefited by that very exploitation which was compelling the nonwhites to work for low wages or for nothing. Ideologically they were drawn in opposite directions. *Racial identification cut at right angles to class consciousness.* (Alexander Saxton, *The Indispensable Enemy: Labor and the Anti-Chinese Movement in California* (Berkeley and Los Angeles: University of California Press, 1971), p. 1, emphasis added.)

[24]Selig Perlman, *The History of Trade Unionism in the United States* (New York: Augustus Kelley, 1950), p. 52; emphasis added.

[25]Whether Southern blacks were "peasants" or rural workers is unimportant in this context. Some time during the 1960s blacks attained a higher degree of urbanization than whites. Before World War II, most blacks had been rural dwellers and nearly 80 percent lived in the South.

[26]See George Gilder, *Wealth and Poverty* (New York: Basic Books, 1981); Charles Murray, *Losing Ground* (New York: Basic Books, 1984).

[27]A brilliant study of the racialization process in Britain, focused on the rise of "mugging" as a popular fear in the 1970s, is Stuart Hall et al., *Policing the Crisis* (London: Macmillan, 1978).

[28]The case of Vincent Chin, a Chinese American man beaten to death in 1982 by a laid-off Detroit auto worker and his stepson who mistook him for Japanese and blamed him for the loss of their jobs, has been widely publicized in Asian American communities. On immigration conflicts and pressures, see Michael Omi, "New Wave Dread: Immigration and Intra-Third World Conflict," *Socialist Review*, no. 60 (November–December 1981).

32

BEYOND BLACK AND WHITE
Remaking Race in America

JENNIFER LEE • FRANK D. BEAN

Sociologists are concerned not only with how race and ethnicity are defined but also with the consequences of those distinctions. One important aspect in the social construction of race and ethnicity is how the U.S. government defines and measures both of these concepts. Until recently, many government documents simply measured race as "white, black, or other." Think how difficult it would be to answer this question on racial identification if one had a parent who was African American and another parent who was Latina. Thus, in 2000, the U.S. Census began allowing Americans to identify more than one racial group on the U.S. Census forms. In the selection that follows, Jennifer Lee, an associate professor of sociology at the University of California at Irvine, and Frank D. Bean, a professor of sociology at the University of California, examine the consequences of this measurement change and the growing numbers of multiracial people in the United States.

S tarting with the 2000 census, Americans could officially label themselves and their children as members of more than one race. Nearly 7 million Americans, 2.4 percent of the nation's population, were recorded as being multiracial. This option and these numbers signal a profound loosening of the rigid racial and ethnic boundaries that have so long divided the country. The immigration patterns behind these changes also point to potentially important realignments in America's color lines.

How might a black father and a white mother fill out official government documents, like U.S. Census forms, requiring them to designate the race of their child? Before 2000, such an intermarried couple had no alternative but to list their child as either black or white. Similarly, a child born to a white father and an Asian mother had to be listed as either Asian or white, but not Asian and white. Not any more. Americans can now officially identify themselves and their children as black and white, or white and Asian. Indeed, respondents can now choose a combination of up to six different categories of races, including "Other." The 2000 Census reported one in every forty Americans was registered as belonging to two or more racial groups. Many sociologists think this ratio could soar to one in five Americans by the year 2050.

Why does this checking of additional boxes matter? For one thing, how people report themselves racially provides information needed to implement and enforce important legislation, such as the Voting Rights Act. The Department of Justice uses the statistics to identify places where substantial minority populations exist and may be subject to disenfranchisement. For another, the counts document social and economic disparities among racial groups in America. Countries like France that do not collect data on race cannot verify the existence and effects of racial discrimination even when other evidence suggests such discrimination is a major problem. These data also signal the official recognition and hence the influence of groups that define themselves on the basis of common national origin, skin color, or ancestry. Americans of Pacific Islander origin, for example, recently asked to be separately classified. On the other hand, critics worry that official data on race perpetuate rather than eliminate racial identities and divisions. A ballot initiative being circulated in California, for example, would largely ban the state's collection of racial information.

But the new opportunity to mark more than one race is also important because it indicates that people can now officially recognize the mixing of racial backgrounds in American society. If the United States was once thought of as a black-and-white society, this is certainly no longer so. Continued immigration from Latin America and Asia, the rise in intermarriage over the past 30 years, and the formal recognition of the multiracial population are moving America far beyond black and white. Yet, while America's increasing diversity implies that racial divisions may be weakening, it does not mean that race has become irrelevant. Instead, new kinds of color lines may be emerging. For now, however, the rearrangement seems to leave African Americans facing a new black-nonblack, instead of the old black-white, racial divide.

Why There Are More Multiracial Americans

The growth of the multiracial population is a result both of increasing intermarriage between whites and nonwhites and of peoples' increasing willingness to report their multiracial backgrounds. The number of racial intermarriages in the United States grew from 150,000 in 1960 to 1.6 million in 1990—a tenfold increase over three decades. It is still the exception rather than the rule for whites and blacks in this country, however. Just 6 percent of whites and 10 percent of blacks marry someone of a different race. By contrast, more than one-quarter of all native-born Asians and Latinos marry someone of a different race. (For this discussion, we will speak of Latinos as if they were a "race," although government forms count Hispanic background separately, so that people who say they are Latino can report themselves as belonging to any racial group, such as white, black, or Asian.) Even more striking is that two of every five young Latinos and two of every three young Asians born in the United States marry someone of a different race, and the majority marry whites. Asians and Latinos—many of whom are either immigrants or the children of immigrants—are three times as likely to marry whites as blacks are to marry whites.

Coinciding with the rise in intermarriage has been the growth of a new immigrant stream from Latin America and Asia. Today, immigrants and their children total more than 60 million people, approximately 22 percent of the U.S. population. The increase in immigration from non-European countries over the past 35 years has converted the United States from a largely white and black society into one that is comprised of numerous racial and ethnic groups. This, plus increasing intermarriage, and the increasing willingness of Americans to call themselves multiracial has changed the way race is measured in America.

The Origin of "Mark One or More Races"

Since its inception in 1790, the decennial U.S. Census has determined taxation, the numbers of representatives from each state, and the boundaries of Congressional districts. And it has always counted the U.S. population by race. The way that race is measured and even the racial categories themselves, however, have changed considerably. For example, in 1850, the Census added the category "mulatto," and in 1890, it added the categories "quadroon" and "octoroon" in an effort to more precisely measure the representation of black mixtures in the population. ("Mulatto" refers to people of mixed black and white "blood," "quadroon" to people with one-fourth black blood, and "octoroon" to those with one-eighth black blood). However, "quadroon" and "octoroon" were promptly removed in 1900 because they caused countless statistical inaccuracies. The Census Board determined that the "mulatto" category provided clearer data on the U.S. population with mixed blood, but eventually dropped this category in 1930. By that time, the law of the country, with the census following suit, had adopted the "one-drop rule" of hypodescent (by which all persons with any trace of black ancestry were labeled racially black) as an appropriate criterion by which to attempt to measure race. Importantly, census enumerators classified the people they interviewed by race.

In the 1960s, racial categories came under scrutiny once again, and the Civil Rights Movement prompted one of the most significant changes in the political context and purpose of racial categorization. The argument spread that Americans should be able to mark their own race to identify themselves and their children rather than leaving this to enumerators. Some politicians and experts asserted that the racial categories should more accurately reflect America's diversity and lobbied for new categories, distinguishing among categories of whites, and substituting the term "ethnic" in place of "race." Changes in the 1970 Census reflected some of these currents, with self-identification replacing enumerator identification in order to satisfy public sentiments. By the mid-1970s, groups wanting to be recognized as racial minorities organized advisory committees to seek official statistical representation so that they could participate in federal programs designed to assist racial "minorities." These advisory committees lobbied for the adoption of five racial categories—white, black, Asian, Native American, and other—by the Census and all federal agencies. In 1980, the Census categories changed yet again, this time including the category of Hispanic origin separately from race, and modifying one of the racial categories to Asian-Pacific Islander.

During the early 1990s, new advocacy groups arose with a different agenda. These groups criticized the government standards for not accurately reflecting the diversity in the country brought about by increases in immigration and interracial marriage. In particular, advocates from groups such as the Association for Multi-Ethnic Americans (AMEA) and Project RACE (Reclassify All Children Equally) lobbied the Census Bureau to adopt a "multiracial" category. Advocates argued that it was an affront to force them or their children into a single racial category. Furthermore, they argued that forced mono-racial identification was inaccurate because it denies the existence of interracial marriages, and is ultimately discriminatory. A year later in 1994, the Office of Management and Budget (OMB), which managed this issue, acknowledged that the racial categories were of decreasing value and considered an alternate strategy: allowing respondents to identify with as many races as they wished. While the spokespeople for the multiracial movement were not entirely satisfied with this option, they conceded that it was an improvement over forced mono-racial identification.

Not everyone favored adding a multiracial category or allowing Americans to mark more than one race. Civil rights groups—and in particular, black civil rights groups such as the NAACP—strongly objected. They feared that those who would otherwise be counted as black or Hispanic would now choose to identify as multiracial and, depending on how such persons were counted, diminish their official counts. This, in turn, could undermine enforcement of the Voting Rights Act and potentially reduce the size and effectiveness of government programs aimed at helping minorities.

On October 30, 1997, the Census Bureau announced its final decision that all persons would have the option to identify with two or more races, starting with the 2000 Census and extending to all federal data systems by the year 2003. The racial options on the 2000 Census included "White," "Black," "Asian," "Native Hawaiian or Other Pacific Islander," "American Indian and Alaska Native," and "Other." While "Latino" or "Hispanic" was not a racial category on the 2000 Census, OMB mandated two distinct questions: one on race and a second asking whether a person is "Spanish/Hispanic/Latino." Because those who classify themselves as "Spanish/Hispanic/Latino" can be of any race, the Census asks both questions in order to identify the Latino population in the United States.

The Census Bureau's decision to allow Americans to "mark one or more races" is a landmark change in the way the U.S. government collects data on race. Perhaps even more importantly, it gives official status and recognition to individuals who see themselves or their children as having mixed racial heritage—an acknowledgement that speaks volumes about how far the country has come since the days when the "one-drop rule" enjoyed legal legitimacy. Moreover, such changes may mean that old racial divides are beginning to fade. Multiracial reporting, however, has not been equally distributed across all racial and ethnic groups. Rather, those who choose to mark two or more races are distinctive.

Who Are the Multiracials?

As we noted, in 2000, 6.8 million people, or 2.4 percent of the population, were reported as multiracial. While these figures may not appear large, a recent National Academy of Science study estimated that the multiracial population could rise to 21 percent by the year 2050 because of rising intermarriage, when as many as 35 percent of Asians and 45 percent of Hispanics could claim a multiracial background. Of the multiracial population in 2000, 93 percent reported two races, 6 percent reported three races, and 1 percent reported four or more races.

As Table 32.1 illustrates, the groups with high percentages of multiracial persons include "Native Hawaiian or Other Pacific Islander," "American Indian and Alaska Native," "Other," and "Asian." The categories with the low-

TABLE 32.1   Multiracial Identification by Race: People Recorded as One Race
Who Are Also Recorded as One or More Other Races

	Racial Identification (millions)	Multiracial Identification (millions)	Percent Multiracial
White	216.5	5.1	2.3%
Black	36.2	1.5	4.2
Asian	11.7	1.4	12.4
Other	18.4	3.0	16.4
American Indian and Alaska Native	3.9	1.4	36.4
Native Hawaiian or Other Pacific Islander	0.7	0.3	44.8

Source: U.S. Census 2000.

est proportion of persons who claim a multiracial background are "White" and "Black."

The proportion of blacks who identify as multiracial is quite small, accounting for just 4.2 percent of the total black population. These figures stand in sharp contrast to those among American Indian/Alaska Natives and Native Hawaiian or other Pacific Islanders, who have the highest percentage of multiracials as a proportion of their populations at 36.4 and 44.8 percent, respectively. The particular combinations are of interest. Among those identified as black, Asian, or Latino, 2 percent, 7 percent, and 5 percent, respectively, also claim a white identity. Among Asians, the Asian-white multiracial combination is about three and a half times more likely to occur, and among Latinos, the Latino-white combination is more than two and a half times more likely to occur, as the black-white combination occurs among blacks. Why this is so is particularly perplexing when we consider that the Census Bureau has estimated that at least three-quarters of black Americans have some white ancestry and thus could claim a multiracial identity on this basis alone.

The tendency of black Americans not to report multiracial identifications undoubtedly owes in part to the legacy of slavery, lasting discrimination, and both the legal and de facto invocation of the "one-drop rule." For no other racial or ethnic group in the United States does the one-drop rule limit identity choices and options. Recent sociological studies find that about 50 percent of American Indian-white and Asian-white intermarried couples report a white racial identity for their children. In a study of multiracial Hispanic students, we found that 44 percent chose a Hispanic identity. Without the imposition of the "one-drop rule" that historically imposed a black racial identity on multiracial black Americans, multiracial Asians, Latinos, and

American Indians appear to have much more leeway to choose among different racial options.

In addition, because a significant proportion of Latinos and Asians in the United States are either immigrants or the children of immigrants, their understanding of race, racial boundaries, and the black-white color divide is shaped by a different set of circumstances than those of African Americans. Most importantly, Latinos' and Asians' experiences are not rooted in the same legacy of slavery with its systematic and persistent patterns of legal and institutional discrimination and inequality through which the tenacious black-white divide was formed and cemented. For these reasons, racial and ethnic boundaries appear more fluid for the newest immigrants than for native-born blacks, providing multiracial Asians and Latinos more racial options than their black counterparts.

Remaking Race and Redrawing the Color Line

What do current trends and patterns in immigration, intermarriage, and multiracial identification tell us about the remaking of race in America? It appears that increases in intermarriage and the growth of the multiracial population reflect a blending of races and the shifting of color lines. Because interracial marriage and multiracial identification indicate a reduction in social distance and racial prejudice, these phenomena provide evidence of loosening racial boundaries. At first glance, these patterns offer an optimistic portrait of the weakening of color lines. For instance, interracial marriage was illegal in 16 states as recently as 1967, but today, about 13 percent of American marriages involve persons of different races. If we go back even further to 1880, the rates of intermarriage among Asians and Latinos in this country were close to zero, but now, more than a quarter of all native-born Asians and Latinos marry someone of a different racial background, mostly whites.

Yet, upon closer examination, we find that patterns of intermarriage and multiracial identification are not similar across all groups. Not only are Latinos and Asians more likely to intermarry than blacks, they are also more likely to report a multiracial identification. These different rates suggest that while racial boundaries may be fading, they are not disappearing at the same pace for all groups.

What is crucial here is how we interpret the intermarriage and multiracial identification rates for Latinos and Asians. If we consider Latinos and Asians as discriminated-against racial minorities, closer to blacks than whites in their social disadvantages, then their high levels of multiracial identification suggest that racial border lines might be fading for all nonwhite groups. Latinos and Asians look more, however, like immigrant groups whose disadvantages derive from their not having had time to join the economic mainstream, but who soon will. Their high levels of intermarriage and multiracial reporting therefore signal an experience and trajectory different from that of blacks. Their situations do not necessarily indicate that similar assimilation can be expected among blacks.

Based on the patterns of intermarriage and multiracial identification noted above, the color line appears less rigid for Latinos and Asians than blacks. Asians and Latinos have high rates of intermarriage and multiracial reporting because they were not and are not treated as blacks have been. While the color line may also be shifting for blacks, this shift is occurring more slowly, leaving Asians and Latinos socially nearer to whites. Much of America's racial history has revolved around who was white and who was not; the next phase may revolve instead around who is black and who is not.

The emergence of a black-nonblack divide in a context where diversity is increasing and other racial and ethnic boundaries are diminishing represents a good news–bad news outcome for America. That a white-nonwhite color line does not seem to be enduring is the good news. But that newer nonwhite immigrant groups appear to be jumping ahead of African Americans in a hierarchy still divided by race is the bad news. Based on immigration, intermarriage, and multiracial identification, it appears that Latinos and Asians are closer to whites than to blacks, and consequently may be participants in a new color line that continues to disadvantage blacks.

As a final matter, one might ask: What does all of this imply for the future of measuring race in the census? Critics of racial labels argue that if racial and ethnic boundaries are loosening, we should abandon the use of racial categories in the census altogether and learn to get along without them in our policy making. They argue that if racial labels could be eliminated, racial discrimination itself would be eradicated. However, in the United States today, because the practice of discrimination based on physical characteristics such as skin color continues to persist, at least for African Americans, eradicating racial labels would simply put us in a position where we know less about the disadvantages experienced by blacks and can do less about it.

RECOMMENDED RESOURCES

Bean, Frank D. and Gillian Stevens. 2003. *America's Newcomers and the Dynamics of Diversity.* New York: Russell Sage Foundation. This book explores the significance of immigration for America, including its implications for loosening racial and ethnic boundaries.

Davis, F. James. 1991. *Who Is Black? One Nation's Definition.* University Park, PA: Pennsylvania State University Press. Davis details the history of the "one-drop rule" in the United States.

Gerstle, Gary. 1991. "Liberty, Coercion, and the Making of Americans." In *The Handbook of International Migration,* edited by Charles Hirschman, Philip Kasinitz, and Josh DeWind. New York: Russell Sage Foundation. A history of racial categories and how they have changed.

Loewen, James. 1971. *The Mississippi Chinese: Between Black and White.* Cambridge, MA: Harvard University Press. Loewen shows how Chinese immigrants changed their racial classification from almost black to almost white.

Nobles, Melissa. 2000. *Shades of Citizenship: Race and the Census in Modern Politics.* Stanford, CA: Stanford University Press. A history of racial categories in the Census in the United States.

Perlmann, Joel and Mary C. Waters, eds. 2002. *The New Race Question: How the Census Counts Multiracial Individuals.* New York: Russell Sage Foundation. This anthology examines the history of racial enumeration, the likely effects of the Census change in the race question, and possible policy implications for the future.

Qian, Zhenchao. 1997. "Breaking the Racial Barriers: Variations in Interracial Marriage between 1980 and 1990." *Demography* 34(2):263–76. This study illustrates the growing trends in interracial marriage.

Waters, Mary C. 2000. "Multiple Ethnicities and Identity in the United States." In *We Are a People: Narrative and Multiplicity in Constructing Identity,* edited by Paul Spikard and W. Jeffrey Burroughs. Philadelphia: Temple University Press. Waters examines the different ways interracial couples identify their children.

33

"IS THIS A WHITE COUNTRY, OR WHAT?"

LILLIAN B. RUBIN

In this reading, Lillian B. Rubin presents her findings of racial hostility among working-class white ethnics. Rubin, a senior research fellow at the Institute for the Study of Social Change at the University of California, Berkeley, finds that the "color line" has been redefined to include immigrants and all people of color. Using interviews and document analysis, Rubin compares the anti-immigrant, racist beliefs of her respondents with actual demographic data on immigration and social opportunities in the United States. This excerpt is taken from Rubin's 1994 book, *Families on the Fault Line: America's Working Class Speaks about the Family, the Economy, Race, and Ethnicity.*

They're letting all these coloreds come in and soon there won't be any place left for white people," broods Tim Walsh, a 33-year-old white construction worker. "It makes you wonder: Is this a white country, or what?"

It's a question that nags at white America, one perhaps that's articulated most often and most clearly by the men and women of the working class. For it's they who feel most vulnerable, who have suffered the economic con-

---

tractions of recent decades most keenly, who see the new immigrants most clearly as direct competitors for their jobs.

It's not whites alone who stew about immigrants. Native-born blacks, too, fear the newcomers nearly as much as whites—and for the same economic reasons. But for whites the issue is compounded by race, by the fact that the newcomers are primarily people of color. For them, therefore, their economic anxieties have combined with the changing face of America to create a profound uneasiness about immigration—a theme that was sounded by nearly 90 percent of the whites I met, even by those who are themselves first-generation, albeit well-assimilated, immigrants.

Sometimes they spoke about this in response to my questions; equally often the subject of immigration arose spontaneously as people gave voice to their concerns. But because the new immigrants are predominantly people of color, the discourse was almost always cast in terms of race as well as immigration, with the talk slipping from immigration to race and back again as if these are not two separate phenomena. "If we keep letting all them foreigners in, pretty soon there'll be more of them than us and then what will this country be like?" Tim's wife, Mary Anne, frets. "I mean, this is *our* country, but the way things are going, white people will be the minority in our own country. Now, does that make any sense?"

Such fears are not new. Americans have always worried about the strangers who came to our shores, fearing that they would corrupt our society, dilute our culture, debase our values. So I remind Mary Anne, "When your ancestors came here, people also thought we were allowing too many foreigners into the country. Yet those earlier immigrants were successfully integrated into the American society. What's different now?"

"Oh, it's different, all right," she replies without hesitation. "When my people came, the immigrants were all white. That makes a big difference."

"Why do you think that's so?"

"I don't know; it just is, that's all. Look at the black people; they've been here a long time, and they still don't live like us—stealing and drugs and having all those babies."

"But you were talking about immigrants. Now you're talking about blacks, and they're not immigrants."

"Yeah, I know," she replies with a shrug. "But they're different, and there's enough problems with them, so we don't need any more. With all these other people coming here now, we just have more trouble. They don't talk English; and they think different from us, things like that."

Listening to Mary Anne's words, I was reminded again how little we Americans look to history for its lessons, how impoverished is our historical memory. For, in fact, being white didn't make "a big difference" for many of those earlier immigrants. The dark-skinned Italians and the eastern European Jews who came in the late nineteenth and early twentieth centuries didn't look very white to the fair-skinned Americans who were here then. Indeed, the same people we now call white—Italians, Jews, Irish—were seen as another race at that time. Not black or Asian, it's true, but an alien other, a race apart, although one that didn't have a clearly defined name. Moreover, the racist fears and fantasies of native-born Americans were far less contained then than they are now, largely because there were few social constraints on their expression.

When, during the nineteenth century, for example, some Italians were taken for blacks and lynched in the South, the incidents passed virtually unnoticed. And if Mary Anne and Tim Walsh, both of Irish ancestry, had come to this country during the great Irish immigration of that period, they would have found themselves defined as an inferior race and described with the same language that was used to characterize blacks: "low-browed and savage, grovelling and bestial, lazy and wild, simian and sensual."[1] Not only during that period but for a long time afterward as well, the U.S. Census Bureau counted the Irish as a distinct and separate group, much as it does today with the category it labels "Hispanic."

But there are two important differences between then and now, differences that can be summed up in a few words: the economy and race. Then, a growing industrial economy meant that there were plenty of jobs for both immigrant and native workers, something that can't be said for the contracting economy in which we live today. True, the arrival of the immigrants, who were more readily exploitable than native workers, put Americans at a disadvantage and created discord between the two groups. Nevertheless, work was available for both.

Then, too, the immigrants—no matter how they were labeled, no matter how reviled they may have been—were ultimately assimilable, if for no other reason than that they were white. As they began to lose their alien ways, it became possible for native Americans to see in the white ethnics of yesteryear a reflection of themselves. Once this shift in perception occurred, it was possible for the nation to incorporate them, to take them in, chew them up, digest them, and spit them out as Americans—with subcultural variations not always to the liking of those who hoped to control the manners and mores of the day, to be sure, but still recognizably white Americans.

Today's immigrants, however, are the racial other in a deep and profound way. It's true that race is not a fixed category, that it's no less an *idea* today than it was yesterday. And it's also possible, as I have already suggested, that we may be witness to social transformation from race to ethnicity among some of the most assimilated—read: middle-class—Asians and Latinos. But even if so, there's a long way to go before that metamorphosis is realized. Meanwhile, the immigrants of this era not only bring their own language and culture, they are also people of color—men, women, and children whose skin tones are different and whose characteristic features set them apart and justify the racial categories we lock them into.[2] And integrating masses of people of color into a society where race consciousness lies at the very heart of our central nervous system raises a whole new set of anxieties and tensions.

It's not surprising, therefore, that racial dissension has increased so sharply in recent years. What is surprising, however, is the passion for ethnicity and the preoccupation with ethnic identification among whites that seems suddenly to have burst upon the public scene. . . .

What does being German, Irish, French, Russian, Polish mean to someone who is an American? It's undoubtedly different for recent immigrants than for those who have been here for generations. But even for a relative newcomer, the inexorable process of becoming an American changes the meaning of ethnic identification and its hold on the internal life of the individual. Nowhere have I seen this shift more eloquently described than in a recent op-ed piece published in the *New York Times*. The author, a Vietnamese refugee writing on the day when Vietnamese either celebrate or mourn the fall of Saigon, depending on which side of the conflict they were on, writes:

> Although I sometimes mourn the loss of home and land, it's the American landscape and what it offers that solidify my hyphenated identity. . . . Assimilation, education, the English language, the American 'I'—these have carried me and many others further from that beloved tropical country than the C-130 ever could. . . . When did this happen? Who knows? One night, America quietly seeps in and takes hold of one's mind and body, and the Vietnamese soul of sorrows slowly fades away. In the morning, the Vietnamese American speaks a new language of materialism: his vocabulary includes terms like career choices, down payment, escrow, overtime.[3]

A new language emerges, but it lives, at least for another generation, alongside the old one; Vietnamese, yes, but also American, with a newly developed sense of self and possibility—an identity that continues to grow stronger with each succeeding generation. It's a process we have seen repeated throughout the history of American immigration. The American world reaches into the immigrant communities and shapes and changes the people who live in them.[4] By the second generation, ethnic identity already is attenuated; by the third, it usually has receded as a deeply meaningful part of life.

[Residential segregation, occupational concentration, and a common language and culture—these historically have been the basis for ethnic solidarity and identification. As strangers in a new land, immigrants banded together, bound by their native tongue and shared culture.] The sense of affinity they felt in these urban communities was natural; they were a touch of home, of the old country, of ways they understood. Once within their boundaries, they could feel whole again, sheltered from the ridicule and revulsion with which they were greeted by those who came before them. For whatever the myth about America's welcoming arms, nativist sentiment has nearly always been high and the anti-immigrant segment of the population large and noisy.

Ethnic solidarity and identity in America, then, were the consequence of the shared history each group brought with it, combined with the social and psychological experience of establishing themselves in the new land. But powerful as these were, the connections among the members of the group

were heightened and sustained by the occupational concentration that followed—the Irish in the police departments of cities like Boston and San
Francisco, for example, the Jews in New York City's garment industry, the
east central Europeans in the mills and mines of western Pennsylvania.[5]

As each ethnic group moved into the labor force, its members often
became concentrated in a particular occupation, largely because they were
helped to find jobs there by those who went before them. For employers, this
ethnic homogeneity made sense. They didn't have to cope with a babel of different languages, and they could count on the older workers to train the newcomers and keep them in line. For workers, there were advantages as well. It
meant that they not only had compatible workmates, but that they weren't
alone as they faced the jeers and contempt of their American-born counterparts. And perhaps most important, as more and more ethnic peers filled the
available jobs, they began to develop some small measure of control in the
workplace.

The same pattern of occupational concentration that was characteristic of
yesterday's immigrant groups exists among the new immigrants today, and
for the same reasons. The Cubans in Florida and the Dominicans in New
York,[6] the various Asian groups in San Francisco, the Koreans in Los Angeles
and New York—all continue to live in ethnic neighborhoods; all use the networks established there to find their way into the American labor force.[7]

For the white working-class ethnics whose immigrant past is little more
than part of family lore, the occupational, residential, and linguistic chain has
been broken. This is not to say that white ethnicity has ceased to be an ob-
servable phenomenon in American life. Cities like New York, Chicago, and
San Francisco still have white ethnic districts that influence their culture, especially around food preferences and eating habits. But as in San Francisco's
North Beach or New York's Little Italy, the people who once created vibrant
neighborhoods, where a distinct subculture and language remained vividly
alive, long ago moved out and left behind only the remnants of the commercial life of the old community. As such transformations took place, ethnicity
became largely a private matter, a distant part of the family heritage that had
little to do with the ongoing life of the family or community.

What, then, are we to make of the claims to ethnic identity that have become so prominent in recent years? Herbert Gans has called this identification "symbolic ethnicity"—that is, ethnicity that's invoked or not as the
individual chooses.[8] Symbolic ethnicity, according to Gans, has little impact
on a person's daily life and, because it is not connected to ethnic structures or
activities—except for something like the wearing of the green on St. Patrick's
Day—it makes no real contribution to ethnic solidarity or community.

The description is accurate. But it's a mistake to dismiss ethnic identification, even if only symbolic, as relatively meaningless. Symbols, after all, become symbolic precisely because they have meaning. In this case, the symbol
has meaning at two levels: One is the personal and psychological, the other
is the social and political.

At the personal level, in a nation as large and diverse as ours—a nation that defines itself by its immigrant past, where the metaphor for our national identity has been the melting pot—defining oneself in the context of an ethnic group is comforting. It provides a sense of belonging to some recognizable and manageable collectivity—an affiliation that has meaning because it's connected to the family where, when we were small children, we first learned about our relationship to the group. As Vilma Janowski, a 24-year-old first-generation Polish American who came here as a child put it: "Knowing there's other people like you is really nice. It's like having a big family, even if you don't ever really see them. It's just nice to know they're there. Besides, if I said I was American, what would it mean? Nobody's just American."

Which is true. Being an American is different from being French or Dutch or any number of other nationalities because, except for Native Americans, there's no such thing as an American without a hyphen somewhere in the past. To identify with the front end of that hyphen is to maintain a connection—however tenuous, illusory, or sentimentalized—with our roots. It sets us apart from others, allows us the fantasy of uniqueness—a quest given particular urgency by a psychological culture that increasingly emphasizes the development of the self and personal history. Paradoxically, however, it also gives us a sense of belonging—of being one with others like ourselves—that helps to overcome some of the isolation of modern life.

But these psychological meanings have developed renewed force in recent years because of two significant sociopolitical events. The first was the civil rights movement with its call for racial equality. The second was the change in the immigration laws, which, for the first time in nearly half a century, allowed masses of immigrants to enter the country.

It was easy for northern whites to support the early demands of the civil rights movement when blacks were asking for the desegregation of buses and drinking fountains in the South. But supporting the black drive to end discrimination in jobs, housing, and education in the urban North was quite another matter—especially among those white ethnics whose hold on the ladder of mobility was tenuous at best and with whom blacks would be most likely to compete, whether in the job market, the neighborhood, or the classroom. As the courts and legislatures around the country began to honor some black claims for redress of past injustices, white hackles began to rise.

It wasn't black demands alone that fed the apprehensions of whites, however. In the background of the black civil rights drive, there stood a growing chorus of voices, as other racial groups—Asian Americans, Latinos, and Native Americans—joined the public fray to seek remedy for their own grievances. At the same time that these home-grown groups were making their voices heard and, not incidentally, affirming their distinctive cultural heritages and calling for public acknowledgment of them, the second great wave of immigration in this century washed across our shores.

After having closed the gates to mass immigration with the National Origins Act of 1924, Congress opened them again when it passed the

Immigration Act of 1965.[9] This act, which was a series of amendments to the McCarran-Walter Act of 1952, essentially jettisoned the national origins provisions of earlier law and substituted overall hemisphere caps. The bill, according to immigration historian Roger Daniels, "changed the whole course of American immigration history" and left the door open for a vast increase in the numbers of immigrants.[10]

More striking than the increase in numbers has been the character of the new immigrants. Instead of the large numbers of western Europeans whom the sponsors had expected to take advantage of the new policy, it has been the people of Asia, Latin America, and the Caribbean who rushed to the boats. "It is doubtful if any drafter or supporter of the 1965 act envisaged this result," writes Daniels.[11] In fact, when members of Lyndon Johnson's administration, under whose tenure the bill became law, testified before Congress, they assured the legislators and the nation that few Asians would come in under the new law.[12]

This is a fascinating example of the unintended consequences of a political act. The change in the law was sponsored by northern Democrats who sought to appeal to their white ethnic constituencies by opening the gates to their countrymen once again—that is, to the people of eastern and southern Europe whom the 1924 law had kept out for nearly half a century. But those same white ethnics punished the Democratic Party by defecting to the Republicans during the Reagan-Bush years, a defection that was at least partly related to their anger about the new immigrants and the changing racial balance of urban America.

During the decade of the 1980s, 2.5 million immigrants from Asian countries were admitted to the United States, an increase of more than 450 percent over the years between 1961 and 1970, when the number was slightly less than half a million. In 1990 alone, nearly as many Asian immigrants—one-third of a million—entered the country as came during the entire decade of the 1960s. Other groups show similarly noteworthy increases. Close to three-quarters of a million documented Mexicans crossed the border in the single year of 1990, compared to less than half a million during all of the 1960s. Central American immigration, too, climbed from just under one hundred thousand between 1961 and 1970 to more than triple that number during the 1980s. And immigrants from the Caribbean, who numbered a little more than half a million during the 1960s, increased to over three-quarters of a million in the years between 1981 and 1989.[13]

Despite these large increases and the perception that we are awash with new immigrants, it's worth noting that they are a much smaller proportion of the total population today, 6.2 percent, than they were in 1920, when they were a hefty 13.2 percent of all U.S. residents.[14] But the fact that most immigrants today are people of color gives them greater visibility than ever before.

Suddenly, the nation's urban landscape has been colored in ways unknown before. In 1970, the California cities that were the site of the original research for *Worlds of Pain* were almost exclusively white. Twenty years later, the 1990 census reports that their minority populations range from 54 to 69 percent. In the nation at large, the same census shows nearly one in four Americans with African, Asian, Latino, or Native American ancestry, up from one in five in 1980.[15] So dramatic is this shift that whites of European descent now make up just over two-thirds of the population in New York State, while in California they number only 57 percent. In cities like New York, San Francisco, and Los Angeles whites are a minority—accounting for 38, 47, and 37 percent of residents, respectively. Twenty years ago the white population in all these cities was over 75 percent.[16]

The increased visibility of other racial groups has focused whites more self-consciously than ever on their own racial identification. Until the new immigration shifted the complexion of the land so perceptibly, whites didn't think of themselves as white in the same way that Chinese know they're Chinese and African Americans know they're black. Being white was simply a fact of life, one that didn't require any public statement, since it was the definitive social value against which all others were measured. "It's like everything's changed and I don't know what happened," complains Marianne Bardolino. "All of a sudden you have to be thinking all the time about these race things. I don't remember growing up thinking about being white like I think about it now. I'm not saying I didn't know there was coloreds and whites; it's just that I didn't go along thinking, *Gee, I'm a white person.* I never thought about it at all. But now with all the different colored people around, you have to think about it because they're thinking about it all the time."

"You say you feel pushed now to think about being white, but I'm not sure I understand why. What's changed?" I ask.

"I told you," she replies quickly, a small smile covering her impatience with my question. "It's because they think about what they are, and they want things their way, so now I have to think about what I am and what's good for me and my kids." She pauses briefly to let her thoughts catch up with her tongue, then continues. "I mean, if somebody's always yelling at you about being black or Asian or something, then it makes you think about being white. Like, they want the kids in school to learn about their culture, so then I think about being white and being Italian and say: What about my culture? If they're going to teach about theirs, what about mine?"

To which America's racial minorities respond with bewilderment. "I don't understand what white people want," says Gwen Tomalson. "They say if black kids are going to learn about black culture in school, then white people want their kids to learn about white culture. I don't get it. What do they think kids have been learning about all these years? It's all about white people and how they live and what they accomplished. When I was in school you wouldn't have thought black people existed for all our books ever said about us."

As for the charge that they're "thinking about race all the time," as Marianne Bardolino complains, people of color insist that they're forced into it by a white world that never lets them forget. "If you're Chinese, you can't forget it, even if you want to, because there's always something that reminds you," Carol Kwan's husband, Andrew, remarks tartly. "I mean, if Chinese kids get good grades and get into the university, everybody's worried and you read about it in the papers."

While there's little doubt that racial anxieties are at the center of white concerns, our historic nativism also plays a part in escalating white alarm. The new immigrants bring with them a language and an ethnic culture that's vividly expressed wherever they congregate. And it's this also, the constant reminder of an alien presence from which whites are excluded, that's so troublesome to them.

The nativist impulse isn't, of course, given to the white working class alone. But for those in the upper reaches of the class and status hierarchy— those whose children go to private schools, whose closest contact with public transportation is the taxicab—the immigrant population supplies a source of cheap labor, whether as nannies for their children, maids in their households, or workers in their businesses. They may grouse and complain that "nobody speaks English anymore," just as working-class people do. But for the people who use immigrant labor, legal or illegal, there's a payoff for the inconvenience—a payoff that doesn't exist for the families in this study but that sometimes costs them dearly.[17] For while it may be true that American workers aren't eager for many of the jobs immigrants are willing to take, it's also true that the presence of a large immigrant population—especially those who come from developing countries where living standards are far below our own—helps to make these jobs undesirable by keeping wages depressed well below what most American workers are willing to accept.[18]

Indeed, the economic basis of our immigration policies too often gets lost in the lore that we are a land that says to the world, "Give me your tired, your poor, your huddled masses, yearning to breathe free."[19] I don't mean to suggest that our humane impulses are a fiction, only that the reality is far more complex than Emma Lazarus' poem suggests. The massive immigration of the nineteenth and early twentieth centuries didn't just happen spontaneously. America may have been known as the land of opportunity to the Europeans who dreamed of coming here—a country where, as my parents once believed, the streets were lined with gold. But they believed these things because that's how America was sold by the agents who spread out across the face of Europe to recruit workers—men and women who were needed to keep the machines of our developing industrial society running and who, at the same time, gave the new industries a steady supply of hungry workers willing to work for wages well below those of native-born Americans.

The enormous number of immigrants who arrived during that period accomplished both those ends. In doing so, they set the stage for a long history of antipathy to foreign workers. For today, also, one function of the new immigrants is to keep our industries competitive in a global economy. Which simply is another way of saying that they serve to depress the wages of native American workers.

It's not surprising, therefore, that working-class women and men speak so angrily about the recent influx of immigrants. They not only see their jobs and their way of life threatened, they feel bruised and assaulted by an environment that seems suddenly to have turned color and in which they feel like strangers in their own land. So they chafe and complain: "They come here to take advantage of us, but they don't really want to learn our ways," Beverly Sowell, a 33-year-old white electronics assembler, grumbles irritably. "They live different than us; it's like another world how they live. And they're so clannish. They keep to themselves, and they don't even *try* to learn English. You go on the bus these days and you might as well be in a foreign country; everybody's talking some other language, you know, Chinese or Spanish or something. Lots of them have been here a long time, too, but they don't care; they just want to take what they can get."

But their complaints reveal an interesting paradox, an illuminating glimpse into the contradictions that beset native-born Americans in their relations with those who seek refuge here. On the one hand, they scorn the immigrants; on the other, they protest because they "keep to themselves." It's the same contradiction that dominates black–white relations. Whites refuse to integrate blacks but are outraged when they stop knocking at the door, when they move to sustain the separation on their own terms—in black theme houses on campuses, for example, or in the newly developing black middle-class suburbs.

I wondered, as I listened to Beverly Sowell and others like her, why the same people who find the lifeways and languages of our foreign-born population offensive also care whether they "keep to themselves."

"Because like I said, they just shouldn't, that's all," Beverly says stubbornly. "If they're going to come here, they should be willing to learn our ways—you know what I mean, be real Americans. That's what my grandparents did, and that's what they should do."

"But your grandparents probably lived in an immigrant neighborhood when they first came here, too," I remind her.

"It was different," she insists. "I don't know why; it was. They wanted to be Americans; these here people now, I don't think they do. They just want to take advantage of this country."

She stops, thinks for a moment, then continues, "Right now it's awful in this country. Their kids come into the schools, and it's a big mess. There's not enough money for our kids to get a decent education, and we have to spend money to teach their kids English. It makes me mad. I went to public school, but I have to send my kids to Catholic school because now on top of the black kids, there's all these foreign kids who don't speak English. What kind of an education can kids get in a school like that? Something's wrong when plain old American kids can't go to their own schools.

"Everything's changed, and it doesn't make sense. Maybe you get it, but I don't. We can't take care of our own people and we keep bringing more and more foreigners in. Look at all the homeless. Why do we need more people here when our own people haven't got a place to sleep?"

"Why do we need more people here?"—a question Americans have asked for two centuries now. Historically, efforts to curb immigration have come during economic downturns, which suggests that when times are good, when American workers feel confident about their future, they're likely to be more generous in sharing their good fortune with foreigners. But when the economy falters, as it did in the 1990s, and workers worry about having to compete for jobs with people whose standard of living is well below their own, resistance to immigration rises. "Don't get me wrong; I've got nothing against these people," Tim Walsh demurs. "But they don't talk English, and they're used to a lot less, so they can work for less money than guys like me can. I see it all the time; they get hired and some white guy gets left out."

It's this confluence of forces—the racial and cultural diversity of our new immigrant population; the claims on the resources of the nation now being made by those minorities who, for generations, have called America their home; the failure of some of our basic institutions to serve the needs of our people; the contracting economy, which threatens the mobility aspirations of working-class families—all these have come together to leave white workers feeling as if everyone else is getting a piece of the action while they get nothing. "I feel like white people are left out in the cold," protests Diane Johnson, a 28-year-old white single mother who believes she lost a job as a bus driver to a black woman. "First it's the blacks; now it's all those other colored people, and it's like everything always goes their way. It seems like a white person doesn't have a chance anymore. It's like the squeaky wheel gets the grease, and they've been squeaking and we haven't," she concludes angrily.

Until recently, whites didn't need to think about having to "squeak"—at least not specifically as whites. They have, of course, organized and squeaked at various times in the past—sometimes as ethnic groups, sometimes as workers. But not as whites. As whites they have been the dominant group, the favored ones, the ones who could count on getting the job when people of color could not. Now suddenly there are others—not just individual others but identifiable groups, people who share a history, a language, a culture, even a color—who lay claim to some of the rights and privileges that formerly had been labeled "for whites only." And whites react as if they've been betrayed, as if a sacred promise has been broken. They're white, aren't they? They're *real* Americans, aren't they? This is their country, isn't it?

ENDNOTES

[1] David R. Roediger, *The Wages of Whiteness* (New York: Verso, 1991), p. 133.
[2] I'm aware that many Americans who have none of the characteristic features associated with their African heritage are still defined as black. This is one reason why I characterize race as an idea, not a fact. Nevertheless, the main point I am making here

still holds—that is, the visible racial character of a people makes a difference in whether white Americans see them as assimilable or not.

[3] *New York Times*, April 30, 1993.

[4] For an excellent historical portrayal of the formation of ethnic communities among the east central European immigrants in Pennsylvania, the development of ethnic identity, and the process of Americanization, see Ewa Morawska, *For Bread with Butter* (New York: Cambridge University Press, 1985).

[5] Ibid.

[6] Alejandro Portes and Ruben G. Rumbaut, *Immigrant America* (Berkeley: University of California Press, 1990).

[7] One need only walk the streets of New York to see the concentration of Koreans in the corner markets and the nail care salons that dot the city's landscape.

In San Francisco the Cambodians now own most of the donut shops in the city. It all started when, after working in such a shop, an enterprising young Cambodian combined the family resources and opened his own store and bakery. He now has 20 shops and has been instrumental in helping his countrymen open more, all of them buying their donuts from his bakery.

[8] Herbert Gans, "Symbolic Ethnicity: The Future of Ethnic Groups and Cultures in America," *Ethnic and Racial Studies* 2 (1979): 1–18.

[9] Despite nativist protests, immigration had proceeded unchecked by government regulation until the end of the nineteenth century. The first serious attempt to restrict immigration came in 1882 when, responding to the clamor about the growing immigration of Chinese laborers to California and other western states, Congress passed the Chinese Exclusion Act. But European immigration remained unimpeded. In the years between 1880 and 1924, twenty-four million newcomers arrived on these shores, most of them eastern and southern Europeans, all bringing their own language and culture, and all the target of pervasive bigotry and exploitation by native-born Americans. By the early part of the twentieth century, anti-immigration sentiments grew strong enough to gain congressional attention once again. The result was the National Origins Act of 1924, which established the quota system that sharply limited immigration, especially from the countries of southern and eastern Europe.

[10] Roger Daniels, *Coming to America: A History of Immigration and Ethnicity in American Life* (New York: HarperCollins, 1990), pp. 338–44.

[11] Daniels, *Coming to America*, p. 341, writes further, "In his Liberty Island speech Lyndon Johnson stressed the fact that he was redressing the wrong done [by the McCarran-Walter Act] to those 'from southern or eastern Europe,' and although he did mention 'developing continents,' there was no other reference to Asian or Third World immigration."

[12] For a further review of the Immigration Act of 1965, see chapter 13 (pp. 328–49) of *Coming to America*.

[13] *Statistical Abstract*, U.S. Bureau of the Census (1992), Table 8, p. 11.

[14] *Statistical Abstract*, U.S. Bureau of the Census (1992), Table 45, p. 42.

[15] *Statistical Abstract*, U.S. Bureau of the Census (1992), Table 18, p. 18, and Table 26, p. 24.

[16] U.S. Bureau of the Census, *Population Reports*, 1970 and 1990. Cited in Mike Davis, "The Body Count," *Crossroads* (June 1993). The difference in the racial composition of New York and San Francisco explains, at least in part, why black–white tensions are so much higher in New York City than they are in San Francisco. In New York, 38 percent of the population is now white, 30 percent black, 25 percent Hispanic,

and 7 percent Asian. In San Francisco, whites make up 47 percent of the residents, blacks 11 percent, Hispanics 14 percent, and Asians 29 percent. Thus, blacks in New York reflect the kind of critical mass that generally sparks racial prejudices, fears, and conflicts. True, San Francisco's Asian population—three in ten of the city's residents—also form that kind of critical and noticeable mass. But whatever the American prejudice against Asians, and however much it has been acted out in the past, Asians do not stir the same kind of fear and hatred in white hearts as do blacks.

[17] Zoë Baird, the first woman ever to be nominated to be attorney general of the United States, was forced to withdraw when it became known that she and her husband had hired an illegal immigrant as a nanny for their three-year-old child. The public indignation that followed the revelation came largely from people who were furious that, in a time of high unemployment, American workers were bypassed in favor of cheaper foreign labor.

[18] This is now beginning to happen in more skilled jobs as well. In California's Silicon Valley, for example, software programmers and others are being displaced by Indian workers, people who are trained in India and recruited to work here because they are willing to do so for lower wages than similarly skilled Americans (*San Francisco Examiner*, February 14, 1993).

[19] From Emma Lazarus' "The New Colossus," inscribed at the base of the Statue of Liberty in New York's harbor, the gateway through which most of the immigrants from Europe passed as they came in search of a new life.

34

AT A SLAUGHTERHOUSE, SOME THINGS NEVER DIE

CHARLIE LeDUFF

⌈*Racism* is any prejudice or discrimination against an individual or a group based on their race, ethnicity, or some other perceived difference.⌉ The following reading by Charlie LeDuff, a reporter for the *New York Times*, takes us inside one workplace site to examine the everyday reality of racial interactions among one group of employees. In the slaughterhouse in Tar Heel, North Carolina, racism occurs on many levels, including racial stereotyping, verbal harassment, and even the threat of physical violence and death. The employers also effectively use racist strategies, such as enforcing a racial hierarchy among workers and exploiting racial tensions among their workers, to maintain an economic advantage and social control over their employees.⌋

Tar Heel, North Carolina

It must have been 1 o'clock. That's when the white man usually comes out of his glass office and stands on the scaffolding above the factory floor. He stood with his palms on the rails, his elbows out. He looked like a tower guard up there or a border patrol agent. He stood with his head cocked.

One o'clock means it is getting near the end of the workday. Quota has to be met and the workload doubles. The conveyor belt always overflows with meat around 1 o'clock. So the workers double their pace, hacking pork from shoulder bones with a driven single-mindedness. They stare blankly, like mules in wooden blinders, as the butchered slabs pass by.

It is called the picnic line: eighteen workers lined up on both sides of a belt, carving meat from bone. Up to 16 million shoulders a year come down that line here at the Smithfield Packing Company, the largest pork production plant in the world. That works out to about 32,000 a shift, sixty-three a minute, one every seventeen seconds for each worker for eight and a half hours a day. The first time you stare down at that belt you know your body is going to give in way before the machine ever will.

On this day the boss saw something he didn't like. He climbed down and approached the picnic line from behind. He leaned into the ear of a broad-shouldered black man. He had been riding him all day, and the day before. The boss bawled him out good this time, but no one heard what was said. The roar of the machinery was too ferocious for that. Still, everyone knew what was expected. They worked harder.

The white man stood and watched for the next two hours as the blacks worked in their groups and the Mexicans in theirs. He stood there with his head cocked.

At shift change the black man walked away, hosed himself down and turned in his knives. Then he let go. He threatened to murder the boss. He promised to quit. He said he was losing his mind, which made for good comedy since he was standing near a conveyor chain of severed hogs' heads, their mouths yoked open.

"Who that cracker think he is?" the black man wanted to know. There were enough hogs, he said, "not to worry about no fleck of meat being left on the bone. Keep treating me like a Mexican and I'll beat him."

The boss walked by just then and the black man lowered his head.

Who Gets the Dirty Jobs

The first thing you learn in the hog plant is the value of a sharp knife. The second thing you learn is that you don't want to work with a knife. Finally you learn that not everyone has to work with a knife. Whites, blacks, American Indians, and Mexicans, they all have their separate stations.

The few whites on the payroll tend to be mechanics or supervisors. As for the Indians, a handful are supervisors; others tend to get clean menial jobs like warehouse work. With few exceptions, that leaves the blacks and Mexicans with the dirty jobs at the factory, one of the only places within a fifty-mile radius in this muddy corner of North Carolina where a person might make more than $8 an hour.

While Smithfield's profits nearly doubled in the past year, wages have remained flat. So a lot of Americans here have quit and a lot of Mexicans have been hired to take their places. But more than management, the workers see one another as the problem, and they see the competition in skin tones.

The locker rooms are self-segregated and so is the cafeteria. The enmity spills out into the towns. The races generally keep to themselves. Along Interstate 95 there are four tumbledown bars, one for each color: white, black, red, and brown.

Language is also a divider. There are English and Spanish lines at the Social Security office and in the waiting rooms of the county health clinics. This means different groups don't really understand one another and tend to be suspicious of what they do know.

You begin to understand these things the minute you apply for the job.

Blood and Burnout

"Treat the meat like you going to eat it yourself," the hiring manager told the thirty applicants, most of them down on their luck and hungry for work. The Smithfield plant will take just about any man or woman with a pulse and a sparkling urine sample, with few questions asked. This reporter was hired using his own name and acknowledged that he was currently employed, but was not asked where and did not say.

Slaughtering swine is repetitive, brutish work, so grueling that three weeks on the factory floor leave no doubt in your mind about why the turnover is 100 percent. Five thousand quit and five thousand are hired every year. You hear people say, They don't kill pigs in the plant, they kill people. So desperate is the company for workers, its recruiters comb the streets of New York's immigrant communities, personnel staff members say, and word of mouth has reached Mexico and beyond.

The company even procures criminals. Several at the morning orientation were inmates on work release in green uniforms, bused in from the county prison.

The new workers were given a safety speech and tax papers, shown a promotional video and informed that there was enough methane, ammonia, and chlorine at the plant to kill every living thing here in Bladen County. Of the thirty new employees, the black women were assigned to the chitterlings room, where they would scrape feces and worms from intestines. The black men were sent to the butchering floor. Two free white men and the Indian were given jobs making boxes. This reporter declined a box job and ended up with most of the Mexicans, doing knife work, cutting sides of pork into smaller and smaller products.

Standing in the hiring hall that morning, two women chatted in Spanish about their pregnancies. A young black man had heard enough. His small town the next county over was crowded with Mexicans. They just started showing up three years ago—drawn to rural Robeson County by the plant—and never left. They stood in groups on the street corners, and the young black man never knew what they were saying. They took the jobs and did them for less. Some had houses in Mexico, while he lived in a trailer with his mother.

Now here he was, trying for the only job around, and he had to listen to Spanish, had to compete with peasants. The world was going to hell.

"This is America and I want to start hearing some English, now!" he screamed.

One of the women told him where to stick his head and listen for the echo. "Then you'll hear some English," she said.

An old white man with a face as pinched and lined as a pot roast complained, "The tacos are worse than the niggers," and the Indian leaned against the wall and laughed. In the doorway, the prisoners shifted from foot to foot, watching the spectacle unfold from behind a cloud of cigarette smoke.

The hiring manager came out of his office and broke it up just before things degenerated into a brawl. Then he handed out the employment stubs. "I don't want no problems," he warned. He told them to report to the plant on Monday morning to collect their carving knives.

$7.70 an Hour, Pain All Day

Monday. The mist rose from the swamps and by 4:45 A.M. thousands of headlamps snaked along the old country roads. Cars carried people from the backwoods, from the single and double-wide trailers, from the cinder-block houses and wooden shacks: whites from Lumberton and Elizabethtown; blacks from Fairmont and Fayetteville; Indians from Pembroke; the Mexicans from Red Springs and St. Pauls.

They converge at the Smithfield plant, a 973,000-square-foot leviathan of pipe and steel near the Cape Fear River. The factory towers over the tobacco and cotton fields, surrounded by pine trees and a few of the old whitewashed plantation houses. Built seven years ago, it is by far the biggest employer in this region, seventy-five miles west of the Atlantic and ninety miles south of the booming Research Triangle around Chapel Hill.

The workers filed in, their faces stiffened by sleep and the cold, like saucers of milk gone hard. They punched the clock at 5 A.M., waiting for the knives to be handed out, the chlorine freshly applied by the cleaning crew burning their eyes and throats. Nobody spoke.

The hallway was a river of brown-skinned Mexicans. The six prisoners who were starting that day looked confused.

"What the hell's going on?" the only white inmate, Billy Harwood, asked an older black worker named Wade Baker.

"Oh," Baker said, seeing that the prisoner was talking about the Mexicans. "I see you been away for a while."

Billy Harwood had been away—nearly seven years, for writing phony payroll checks from the family pizza business to buy crack. He was Rip Van Winkle standing there. Everywhere he looked there were Mexicans. What he didn't know was that one out of three newborns at the nearby Robeson County health clinic was a Latino; that the county's Roman Catholic church had a special Sunday Mass for Mexicans said by a Honduran priest; that the schools needed Spanish speakers to teach English.

With less than a month to go on his sentence, Harwood took the pork job to save a few dollars. The word in jail was that the job was a cakewalk for a white man.

But this wasn't looking like any cakewalk. He wasn't going to get a boxing job like a lot of other whites. Apparently inmates were on the bottom rung, just like Mexicans.

Billy Harwood and the other prisoners were put on the picnic line. Knife work pays $7.70 an hour to start. It is money unimaginable in Mexico, where the average wage is $4 a day. But the American money comes at a price. The work burns your muscles and dulls your mind. Staring down into the meat for hours strains your neck. After thousands of cuts a day your fingers no longer open freely. Standing in the damp 42-degree air causes your knees to lock, your nose to run, your teeth to throb.

The whistle blows at three, you get home by four, pour peroxide on your nicks by five. You take pills for your pains and stand in a hot shower trying to wash it all away. You hurt. And by eight o'clock you're in bed, exhausted, thinking of work.

The convict said he felt cheated. He wasn't supposed to be doing Mexican work. After his second day he was already talking of quitting. "Man, this can't be for real," he said, rubbing his wrists as if they'd been in handcuffs. "This job's for an ass. They treat you like an animal."

He just might have quit after the third day had it not been for Mercedes Fernández, a Mexican. He took a place next to her by the conveyor belt. She smiled at him, showed him how to make incisions. That was the extent of his on-the-job training. He was peep-eyed, missing a tooth and squat from the starchy prison food, but he acted as if this tiny woman had taken a fancy to him. In truth, she was more fascinated than infatuated, she later confided. In her year at the plant, he was the first white person she had ever worked with.

The other workers noticed her helping the white man, so unusual was it for a Mexican and a white to work shoulder to shoulder, to try to talk or even to make eye contact.

As for blacks, she avoided them. She was scared of them. "Blacks don't want to work," Fernández said when the new batch of prisoners came to work on the line. "They're lazy."

Everything about the factory cuts people off from one another. If it's not the language barrier, it's the noise—the hammering of compressors, the screeching of pulleys, the grinding of the lines. You can hardly make your voice heard. To get another's attention on the cut line, you bang the butt of your knife on the steel railings, or you lob a chunk of meat. Fernández would sometimes throw a piece of shoulder at a friend across the conveyor and wave good morning.

The Kill Floor

The kill floor sets the pace of the work, and for those jobs they pick strong men and pay a top wage, as high as $12 an hour. If the men fail to make quota, plenty of others are willing to try. It is mostly the blacks who work the kill floor, the stone-hearted jobs that pay more and appear out of bounds for all but a few Mexicans. Plant workers gave various reasons for this: the Mexicans are too small; they don't like blood; they don't like heavy lifting; or just plain "We built this country and we ain't going to hand them everything," as one black man put it.

Kill-floor work is hot, quick, and bloody. The hog is herded in from the stockyard, then stunned with an electric gun. It is lifted onto a conveyor belt, dazed but not dead, and passed to a waiting group of men wearing blood-stained smocks and blank faces. They slit the neck, shackle the hind legs and watch a machine lift the carcass into the air, letting its life flow out in a purple gush, into a steaming collection trough.

The carcass is run through a scalding bath, trolleyed over the factory floor, and then dumped onto a table with all the force of a quarter-ton water balloon. In the misty-red room, men slit along its hind tendons and skewer the beast with hooks. It is again lifted and shot across the room on a pulley and bar, where it hangs with hundreds of others as if in some kind of horrific dry-cleaning shop. It is then pulled through a wall of flames and met on the other side by more black men who, stripped to the waist beneath their smocks, scrape away any straggling bristles.

The place reeks of sweat and scared animal, steam and blood. Nothing is wasted from these beasts, not the plasma, not the glands, not the bones. Everything is used, and the kill men, repeating slaughterhouse lore, say that even the squeal is sold.

The carcasses sit in the freezer overnight and are then rolled out to the cut floor. The cut floor is opposite to the kill floor in nearly every way. The workers are mostly brown—Mexicans—not black; the lighting yellow, not red. The vapor comes from cold breath, not hot water. It is here that the hog is quartered. The pieces are parceled out and sent along the disassembly lines to be cut into ribs, hams, bellies, loins, and chops.

People on the cut lines work with a mindless fury. There is tremendous pressure to keep the conveyor belts moving, to pack orders, to put bacon and ham and sausage on the public's breakfast table. There is no clock, no window, no fragment of the world outside. Everything is pork. If the line fails to keep pace, the kill men must slow down, backing up the slaughter. The boxing line will have little to do, costing the company payroll hours. The blacks who kill will become angry with the Mexicans who cut, who in turn will become angry with the white superintendents who push them.

10,000 Unwelcome Mexicans

The Mexicans never push back. They cannot. Some have legitimate work papers, but more, like Mercedes Fernández, do not.

Even worse, Fernández was several thousand dollars in debt to the smugglers who had sneaked her and her family into the United States and owed a thousand more for the authentic-looking birth certificate and Social Security card that are needed to get hired. She and her husband, Armando, expected to be in debt for years. They had mouths to feed back home.

The Mexicans are so frightened about being singled out that they do not even tell one another their real names. They have their given names, their work-paper names, and "Hey you," as their American supervisors call them. In the telling of their stories, Mercedes and Armando Fernández insisted that their real names be used, to protect their identities. It was their work names they did not want used, names bought in a back alley in Barstow, Texas.

Rarely are the newcomers welcomed with open arms. Long before the Mexicans arrived, Robeson County, one of the poorest in North Carolina, was an uneasy racial mix. In the 1990 census, of the 100,000 people living in Robeson, nearly 40 percent were Lumbee Indian, 35 percent white, and 25 percent black. Until a dozen years ago the county schools were de facto segregated, and no person of color held any meaningful county job from sheriff to court clerk to judge.

At one point in 1988, two armed Indian men occupied the local newspaper office, taking hostages and demanding that the sheriff's department be investigated for corruption and its treatment of minorities. A prominent Indian lawyer, Julian Pierce, was killed that same year, and the suspect turned up dead in a broom closet before he could be charged. The hierarchy of power was summed up on a plaque that hangs in the courthouse commemorating the dead of World War I. It lists the veterans by color: "white" on top, "Indian" in the middle, and "colored" on the bottom.

That hierarchy mirrors the pecking order at the hog plant. The Lumbees— who have fought their way up in the county apparatus and have built their own construction businesses—are fond of saying they are too smart to work in the factory. And the few who do work there seem to end up with the cleaner jobs.

But as reds and blacks began to make progress in the 1990s—for the first time an Indian sheriff was elected, and a black man is now the public defender—the Latinos began arriving. The United States Census Bureau estimated that one thousand Latinos were living in Robeson County in 1999. People only laugh at that number.

"A thousand? Hell, there's more than that in the Wal-Mart on a Saturday afternoon," said Bill Smith, director of county health services. He and other officials guess that there are at least 10,000 Latinos in Robeson, most having arrived since 1997.

"When they built that factory in Bladen, they promised a trickle-down effect," Smith said. "But the money ain't trickling down this way. Bladen got the money and Robeson got the social problems."

In Robeson there is the strain on public resources. There is the substandard housing. There is the violence. In 1999 twenty-seven killings were committed in Robeson, mostly in the countryside, giving it a higher murder rate than Detroit or Newark. Three Mexicans were robbed and killed that fall. Latinos have also been the victims of highway stickups.

In the yellow-walled break room at the plant, Mexicans talked among themselves about their three slain men, about the midnight visitors with obscured faces and guns, men who knew that the illegal workers used mattresses rather than banks. Mercedes Fernández, like many Mexicans, would not venture out at night. "Blacks have a problem," she said. "They live in the past. They are angry about slavery, so instead of working, they steal from us."

She and her husband never lingered in the parking lot at shift change. That is when the anger of a long day comes seeping out. Cars get kicked and faces slapped over parking spots or fender benders. The traffic is a serpent. Cars jockey for a spot in line to make the quarter-mile crawl along the plant's one-lane exit road to the highway. Usually no one will let you in. A lot of the scuffling is between black and Mexican. . . .

Living It, Hating It

Billy Harwood had been working at the plant ten days when he was released from the Robeson County Correctional Facility. He stood at the prison gates in his work clothes with his belongings in a plastic bag, waiting. A friend dropped him at the Salvation Army shelter, but he decided it was too much like prison. Full of black people. No leaving after 10 P.M. No smoking indoors. "What you doing here, white boy?" they asked him.

He fumbled with a cigarette outside the shelter. He wanted to quit the plant. The work stinks, he said, "but at least I ain't a nigger. I'll find other work soon. I'm a white man." He had hopes of landing a roofing job through a friend. The way he saw it, white society looks out for itself.

On the cut line he worked slowly and allowed Mercedes Fernández and the others to pick up his slack. He would cut only the left shoulders; it was easier on his hands. Sometimes it would be three minutes before a left shoulder came down the line. When he did cut, he didn't clean the bone; he left chunks of meat on it.

Fernández was disappointed by her first experience with a white person. After a week she tried to avoid standing by Billy Harwood. She decided it wasn't just the blacks who were lazy, she said.

Even so, the supervisor came by one morning, took a look at one of Harwood's badly cut shoulders and threw it at Fernández, blaming her. He said obscene things about her family. She didn't understand exactly what he said, but it scared her. She couldn't wipe the tears from her eyes because her gloves were covered with greasy shreds of swine. The other cutters kept their heads down, embarrassed.

Her life was falling apart. She and her husband both worked the cut floor. They never saw their daughter. They were twenty-six but rarely made love anymore. All they wanted was to save enough money to put plumbing in their house in Mexico and start a business there. They come from the town of Tehuacán, in a rural area about 150 miles southeast of Mexico City. His mother owns a bar there and a home but gives nothing to them. Mother must look out for her old age.

"We came here to work so we have a chance to grow old in Mexico," Fernández said one evening while cooking pork and potatoes. Now they were into a smuggler for thousands. Her hands swelled into claws in the evenings and stung while she worked. She felt trapped. But she kept at it for the money, for the $9.60 an hour. The smuggler still had to be paid.

They explained their story this way: The coyote drove her and her family from Barstow a year ago and left them in Robeson. They knew no one. They did not even know they were in the state of North Carolina. They found shelter in a trailer park that had once been exclusively black but was rapidly filling with Mexicans. There was a lot of drug dealing there and a lot of tension. One evening, Armando Fernández said, he asked a black neighbor to move his business inside and the man pulled a pistol on him.

"I hate the blacks," he said in Spanish, sitting in the break room not ten feet from Wade Baker and his black friends. Billy Harwood was sitting two tables away with the whites and Indians.

After the gun incident, Armando Fernández packed up his family and moved out into the country, to a prefabricated number sitting on a brick foundation off in the woods alone. Their only contact with people is through the satellite dish. Except for the coyote. The coyote knows where they live and comes for his money every other month.

Their five-year-old daughter has no playmates in the back country and few at school. That is the way her parents want it. "We don't want her to be American," her mother said.

"We Need a Union"

The steel bars holding a row of hogs gave way as a woman stood below them. Hog after hog fell around her with a sickening thud, knocking her senseless, the connecting bars barely missing her face. As co-workers rushed to help the woman, the supervisor spun his hands in the air, a signal to keep working. Wade Baker saw this and shook his head in disgust. Nothing stops the disassembly lines.

"We need a union," he said later in the break room. It was payday and he stared at his check: $288. He spoke softly to the black workers sitting near him. Everyone is convinced that talk of a union will get you fired. After two years at the factory, Baker makes slightly more than $9 an hour toting meat away from the cut line, slightly less than $20,000 a year, 45 cents an hour less than Mercedes Fernández.

"I don't want to get racial about the Mexicans," he whispered to the black workers. "But they're dragging down the pay. It's pure economics. They say Americans don't want to do the job. That ain't exactly true. We don't want to do it for $8. Pay $15 and we'll do it."

These men knew that in the late seventies, when the meat-packing industry was centered in northern cities like Chicago and Omaha, people had a union getting them $18 an hour. But by the mid-eighties, to cut costs, many of the packing houses had moved to small towns where they could pay a lower, nonunion wage.

The black men sitting around the table also felt sure that the Mexicans pay almost nothing in income tax, claiming eight, nine even ten exemptions. The men believed that the illegal workers should be rooted out of the factory. "It's all about money," Baker said.

His co-workers shook their heads. "A plantation with a roof on it," one said.

For their part, many of the Mexicans in Tar Heel fear that a union would place their illegal status under scrutiny and force them out. The United Food and Commercial Workers Union last tried organizing the plant in 1997, but the idea was voted down nearly two to one.

One reason Americans refused to vote for the union was because it refuses to take a stand on illegal laborers. Another reason was the intimidation. When workers arrived at the plant the morning of the vote, they were met by Bladen County deputy sheriffs in riot gear. "Nigger Lover" had been scrawled on the union trailer.

Five years ago the work force at the plant was 50 percent black, 20 percent white and Indian, and 30 percent Latino, according to union statistics. Company officials say those numbers are about the same today. But from inside the plant, the breakdown appears to be more like 60 percent Latino, 30 percent black, 10 percent white and red.

Sherri Buffkin, a white woman and the former director of purchasing who testified before the National Labor Relations Board in an unfair-labor-practice suit brought by the union in 1998, said in an interview that the company assigns workers by race. She also said that management had kept lists of union sympathizers during the '97 election, firing blacks and replacing them with Latinos. "I know because I fired at least fifteen of them myself," she said.

The company denies those accusations. Michael H. Cole, a lawyer for Smithfield who would respond to questions about the company's labor practices only in writing, said that jobs at the Tar Heel plant were awarded through a bidding process and not assigned by race. The company also denies ever having kept lists of union sympathizers or singled out blacks to be fired.

The hog business is important to North Carolina. It is a multibillion-dollar-a-year industry in the state, with nearly two pigs for every one of its 7.5 million people. And Smithfield Foods, a publicly traded company based in Smithfield, Virginia, has become the No. 1 producer and processor of pork in the world. It slaughters more than 20 percent of the nation's swine, more than 19 million animals a year.

The company, which has acquired a network of factory farms and slaughterhouses, worries federal agriculture officials and legislators, who see it siphoning business from smaller farmers. And environmentalists contend that Smithfield's operations contaminate local water supplies. (The Environmental Protection Agency fined the company $12.6 million in 1996 after its processing plants in Virginia discharged pollutants into the Pagan River.) The chairman and chief executive, Joseph W. Luter III, declined to be interviewed.

Smithfield's employment practices have not been so closely scrutinized. And so every year, more Mexicans get hired. "An illegal alien isn't going to complain all that much," said Ed Tomlinson, acting supervisor of the Immigration and Naturalization Service bureau in Charlotte.

But the company says it does not knowingly hire illegal aliens. Smithfield's lawyer, Cole, said all new employees must present papers showing that they can legally work in the United States. "If any employee's documentation appears to be genuine and to belong to the person presenting it," he said in his written response, "Smithfield is required by law to take it at face value."

The naturalization service—which has only eighteen agents in North Carolina—has not investigated Smithfield because no one has filed a complaint, Ed Tomlinson said. "There are more jobs than people," he said, "and a lot of Americans will do the dirty work for a while and then return to their couches and eat bonbons and watch Oprah."

PART VII

Social Institutions

35

THE POWER ELITE

C. WRIGHT MILLS

Who really governs in the United States? In this selection, C. Wright Mills argues that the most important decisions in this country are made by a cohesive "power elite." This *power elite* consists of the top leaders in three areas: The corporate elite is made up of the executives from large companies; the military elite is the senior officers; and the small political elite includes the president and top officials in the executive and legislative branches. According to Mills' argument, these elite officials all know each other and act in unison when critical decisions must be made. This selection, originally published in 1956, is the first of three addressing power and politics.

The powers of ordinary men are circumscribed by the everyday worlds in which they live, yet even in these rounds of job, family, and neighborhood they often seem driven by forces they can neither understand nor govern. "Great changes" are beyond their control, but affect their conduct and outlook nonetheless. The very framework of modern society confines them to projects not their own, but from every side, such changes now press upon the men and women of the mass society, who accordingly feel that they are without purpose in an epoch in which they are without power.

But not all men are in this sense ordinary. As the means of information and of power are centralized, some men come to occupy positions in American society from which they can look down upon, so to speak, and by their decisions mightily affect, the everyday worlds of ordinary men and women. They are not made by their jobs; they set up and break down jobs for thousands of others; they are not confined by simple family responsibilities; they can escape. They may live in many hotels and houses, but they are bound by no one community. They need not merely "meet the demands of the day and hour"; in some part, they create these demands and cause others to meet them. Whether or not they profess their power, their technical and political experience of it far transcends that of the underlying population. What Jacob Burckhardt [a German historian, 1818–1897] said of "great men," most Americans might well say of their elite: "They are all that we are not."

The power elite is composed of men whose positions enable them to transcend the ordinary environments of ordinary men and women; they are in positions to make decisions having major consequences. Whether they do or do not make such decisions is less important than the fact that they do occupy such pivotal positions: Their failure to act, their failure to make decisions, is itself an act that is often of greater consequence than the decisions they do make. For they are in command of the major hierarchies and organizations of modern society. They rule the big corporations. They run the machinery of the state and claim its prerogatives. They direct the military establishment. They occupy the strategic command posts of the social structure, in which are now centered the effective means of the power and the wealth and the celebrity which they enjoy.

The power elite are not solitary rulers. Advisers and consultants, spokesmen and opinion makers are often the captains of their higher thought and decision. Immediately below the elite are the professional politicians of the middle levels of power, in the Congress and in the pressure groups, as well as among the new and old upper classes of town and city and region. Mingling with them, in curious ways which we shall explore, are those professional celebrities who live by being continually displayed but are never, so long as they remain celebrities, displayed enough. If such celebrities are not at the head of any dominating hierarchy, they do often have the power to distract the attention of the public or afford sensations to the masses, or, more directly, to gain the ear of those who do occupy positions of direct power. More or less unattached, as critics of morality and technicians of power, as spokesmen of God and creators of mass sensibility, such celebrities and consultants are part of the immediate scene in which the drama of the elite is enacted. But that drama itself is centered in the command posts of the major institutional hierarchies.

The truth about the nature and the power of the elite is not some secret which men of affairs know but will not tell. Such men hold quite various theories about their own roles in the sequence of event and decision. Often they are uncertain about their roles, and even more often they allow their fears and their hopes to affect their assessment of their own power. No matter how great their actual power, they tend to be less acutely aware of it than of the resistances of others to its use. Moreover, most American men of affairs have learned well the rhetoric of public relations, in some cases even to the point of using it when they are alone, and thus coming to believe it. The personal awareness of the actors is only one of the several sources one must examine in order to understand the higher circles. Yet many who believe that there is no elite, or at any rate none of any consequence, rest their argument upon what men of affairs believe about themselves, or at least assert in public.

There is, however, another view: Those who feel, even if vaguely, that a compact and powerful elite of great importance does now prevail in America often base that feeling upon the historical trend of our time. They have felt, for example, the domination of the military event, and from this they infer that generals and admirals, as well as other men of decision influenced by them, must be enormously powerful. They hear that the Congress has again abdicated to a handful of men decisions clearly related to the issue of war or peace. They know that the bomb was dropped over Japan in the name of the United States of America, although they were at no time consulted about the matter. They feel that they live in a time of big decisions; they know that they are not making any. Accordingly, as they consider the present as history, they infer that at its center, making decisions or failing to make them, there must be an elite of power.

On the one hand, those who share this feeling about big historical events assume that there is an elite and that its power is great. On the other hand, those who listen carefully to the reports of men apparently involved in the great decisions often do not believe that there is an elite whose powers are of decisive consequence.

Both views must be taken into account, but neither is adequate. The way to understand the power of the American elite lies neither solely in recognizing the historic scale of events nor in accepting the personal awareness reported by men of apparent decision. Behind such men and behind the events of history, linking the two, are the major institutions of modern society. These hierarchies of state and corporation and army constitute the means of power; as such they are now of a consequence not before equaled in human history—and at their summits, there are now those command posts of modern society which offer us the sociological key to an understanding of the role of the higher circles in America.

Within American society, major national power now resides in the economic, the political, and the military domains. Other institutions seem off to the side of modern history, and, on occasion, duly subordinated to these. No family is as directly powerful in national affairs as any major corporation; no church is as directly powerful in the external biographies of young men in America today as the military establishment; no college is as powerful in the shaping of momentous events as the National Security Council. Religious, educational, and family institutions are not autonomous centers of national power; on the contrary, these decentralized areas are increasingly shaped by the big three, in which developments of decisive and immediate consequence now occur.

Families and churches and schools adapt to modern life; governments and armies and corporations shape it; and, as they do so, they turn these lesser institutions into means for their ends. Religious institutions provide chaplains to the armed forces where they are used as a means of increasing the effectiveness of its morale to kill. Schools select and train men for their jobs in corporations and their specialized tasks in the armed forces. The extended family has, of course, long been broken up by the industrial revolution, and now the son and the father are removed from the family, by compulsion if need be, whenever the army of the state sends out the call. And the symbols of all these lesser institutions are used to legitimate the power and the decisions of the big three.

The life-fate of the modern individual depends not only upon the family into which he was born or which he enters by marriage, but increasingly upon the corporation in which he spends the most alert hours of his best years; not only upon the school where he is educated as a child and adolescent, but also upon the state which touches him throughout his life; not only upon the church in which on occasion he hears the word of God, but also upon the army in which he is disciplined.

If the centralized state could not rely upon the inculcation of nationalist loyalties in public and private schools, its leaders would promptly seek to modify the decentralized educational system. If the bankruptcy rate among the top 500 corporations were as high as the general divorce rate among the 37 million married couples, there would be economic catastrophe on an international scale. If members of armies gave to them no more of their lives than do believers to the churches to which they belong, there would be a military crisis.

Within each of the big three, the typical institutional unit has become enlarged, has become administrative, and, in the power of its decisions, has become centralized. Behind these developments there is a fabulous technology, for as institutions, they have incorporated this technology and guide it, even as it shapes and paces their developments.

The economy—once a great scatter of small productive units in autonomous balance—has become dominated by two or three hundred giant corporations, administratively and politically interrelated, which together hold the keys to economic decisions.

The political order, once a decentralized set of several dozen states with a weak spinal cord, has become a centralized, executive establishment which has taken up into itself many powers previously scattered, and now enters into each and every cranny of the social structure.

The military order, once a slim establishment in a context of distrust fed by state militia, has become the largest and most expensive feature of government, and, although well-versed in smiling public relations, now has all the grim and clumsy efficiency of a sprawling bureaucratic domain.

In each of these institutional areas, the means of power at the disposal of decision makers have increased enormously; their central executive powers have been enhanced; within each of them modern administrative routines have been elaborated and tightened up.

As each of these domains becomes enlarged and centralized, the consequences of its activities become greater, and its traffic with the others increases. The decisions of a handful of corporations bear upon military and political as well as upon economic developments around the world. The decisions of the military establishment rest upon and grievously affect political life as well as the very level of economic activity. The decisions made within the political domain determine economic activities and military programs. There is no longer, on the one hand, an economy, and, on the other hand, a political order containing a military establishment unimportant to politics and to money making. There is a political economy linked, in a thousand ways, with military institutions and decisions. On each side of the world-split running through central Europe and around the Asiatic rimlands, there is an ever-increasing interlocking of economic, military, and political structures. If there is government intervention in the corporate economy, so is there corporate intervention in the governmental process. In the structural sense, this triangle of power is the source of the interlocking directorate that is most important for the historical structure of the present.

The fact of the interlocking is clearly revealed at each of the points of crisis of modern capitalist society—slump, war, and boom. In each, men of decision are led to an awareness of the interdependence of the major institutional orders. In the nineteenth century, when the scale of all institutions was smaller, their liberal integration was achieved in the automatic economy, by an autonomous play of market forces, and in the automatic political domain, by the bargain and the vote. It was then assumed that out of the imbalance and friction that followed the limited decisions then possible a new equilibrium would in due course emerge. That can no longer be assumed, and it is not assumed by the men at the top of each of the three dominant hierarchies.

For given the scope of their consequences, decisions—and indecisions—in any one of these ramify into the others, and hence top decisions tend either to become coordinated or to lead to a commanding indecision. It has not always been like this. When numerous small entrepreneurs made up the economy, for example, many of them could fail and the consequences still remain local; political and military authorities did not intervene. But now, given political expectations and military commitments, can they afford to allow key units of the private corporate economy to break down in slump? Increasingly, they do intervene in economic affairs, and as they do so, the controlling decisions in each order are inspected by agents of the other two, and economic, military, and political structures are interlocked.

At the pinnacle of each of the three enlarged and centralized domains, there have arisen those higher circles which make up the economic, the political, and the military elites. At the top of the economy, among the corporate rich, there are the chief executives; at the top of the political order, the members of the political directorate; at the top of the military establishment, the elite of soldier-statesmen clustered in and around the Joint Chiefs of Staff and the upper echelon. As each of these domains has coincided with the others, as decisions tend to become total in their consequence, the leading men in each of the three domains of power—the warlords, the corporation chieftains, the political directorate—tend to come together, to form the power elite of America.

The higher circles in and around these command posts are often thought of in terms of what their members possess: They have a greater share than other people of the things and experiences that are most highly valued. From this point of view, the elite are simply those who have the most of what there is to have, which is generally held to include money, power, and prestige—as well as all the ways of life to which these lead. But the elite are not simply those who have the most, for they could not "have the most" were it not for their positions in the great institutions. For such institutions are the necessary bases of power, of wealth, and of prestige, and at the same time, the chief means of exercising power, of acquiring and retaining wealth, and of cashing in the higher claims for prestige.

By the powerful we mean, of course, those who are able to realize their will, even if others resist it. No one, accordingly, can be truly powerful unless he has access to the command of major institutions, for it is over these institutional means of power that the truly powerful are, in the first instance, powerful. Higher politicians and key officials of government command such institutional power; so do admirals and generals, and so do the major owners and executives of the larger corporations. Not all power, it is true, is anchored in and exercised by means of such institutions, but only within and through them can power be more or less continuous and important.

Wealth also is acquired and held in and through institutions. The pyramid of wealth cannot be understood merely in terms of the very rich; for the great inheriting families, as we shall see, are now supplemented by the corporate institutions of modern society: Every one of the very rich families has been and is closely connected—always legally and frequently managerially as well—with one of the multimillion-dollar corporations.

The modern corporation is the prime source of wealth, but, in latter-day capitalism, the political apparatus also opens and closes many avenues to wealth. The amount as well as the source of income, the power over consumer's goods as well as over productive capital, are determined by position within the political economy. If our interest in the very rich goes beyond their lavish or their miserly consumption, we must examine their relations to modern forms of corporate property as well as to the state; for such relations now determine the chances of men to secure big property and to receive high income.

Great prestige increasingly follows the major institutional units of the social structure. It is obvious that prestige depends, often quite decisively, upon access to the publicity machines that are now a central and normal feature of all the big institutions of modern America. Moreover, one feature of these hierarchies of corporation, state, and military establishment is that their top positions are increasingly interchangeable. One result of this is the accumulative nature of prestige. Claims for prestige, for example, may be initially based on military roles, then expressed in and augmented by an educational institution run by corporate executives, and cashed in, finally, in the political order, where, for General Eisenhower and those he represents, power and prestige finally meet at the very peak. Like wealth and power, prestige tends to be cumulative: The more of it you have, the more you can get. These values also tend to be translatable into one another: The wealthy find it easier than the poor to gain power; those with status find it easier than those without it to control opportunities for wealth.

If we took the one hundred most powerful men in America, the one hundred wealthiest, and the one hundred most celebrated away from the institutional positions they now occupy, away from their resources of men and women and money, away from the media of mass communication that are now focused upon them—then they would be powerless and poor and uncelebrated. For power is not of a man. Wealth does not center in the person of the wealthy. Celebrity is not inherent in any personality. To be celebrated, to be wealthy, to have power requires access to major institutions, for the institutional positions men occupy determine in large part their chances to have and to hold these valued experiences.

The people of the higher circles may also be conceived as members of a top social stratum, as a set of groups whose members know one another, see one another socially and at business, and so, in making decisions, take one another into account. The elite, according to this conception, feel themselves to be, and are felt by others to be, the inner circle of "the upper social classes." They form a more or less compact social and psychological entity; they have become self-conscious members of a social class. People are either accepted into this class or they are not, and there is a qualitative split, rather than merely a numerical scale, separating them from those who are not elite. They are more or less aware of themselves as a social class, and they behave toward one another differently from the way they do toward members of other classes. They accept one another, understand one another, marry one another, tend to work and to think if not together at least alike.

Now, we do not want by our definition to prejudge whether the elite of the command posts are conscious members of such a socially recognized class, or whether considerable proportions of the elite derive from such a clear and distinct class. These are matters to be investigated. Yet in order to be able to recognize what we intend to investigate, we must note something that all biographies and memoirs of the wealthy and the powerful and the eminent make clear: No matter what else they may be, the people of these higher circles are involved in a set of overlapping "crowds" and intricately connected "cliques." There is a kind of mutual attraction among those who "sit on the same terrace"—although this often becomes clear to them, as well as to others, only at the point at which they feel the need to draw the line; only when, in their common defense, they come to understand what they have in common, and so close their ranks against outsiders.

The idea of such ruling stratum implies that most of its members have similar social origins, that throughout their lives they maintain a network of informal connections, and that to some degree there is an interchangeability of position between the various hierarchies of money and power and celebrity. We must, of course, note at once that if such an elite stratum does exist, its social visibility and its form, for very solid historical reasons, are quite different from those of the noble cousinhoods that once ruled various European nations.

That American society has never passed through a feudal epoch is of decisive importance to the nature of the American elite, as well as to American society as a historic whole. For it means that no nobility or aristocracy, established before the capitalist era, has stood in tense opposition to the higher bourgeoisie. It means that this bourgeoisie has monopolized not only wealth but prestige and power as well. It means that no set of noble families has commanded the top positions and monopolized the values that are generally held in high esteem; and certainly that no set has done so explicitly by inherited right. It means that no high church dignitaries or court nobilities, no entrenched landlords with honorific accouterments, no monopolists of high army posts have opposed the enriched bourgeoisie and in the name of birth and prerogative successfully resisted its self-making.

But this does *not* mean that there are no upper strata in the United States. That they emerged from a "middle class" that had no recognized aristocratic superiors does not mean they remained middle class when enormous increases in wealth made their own superiority possible. Their origins and their newness may have made the upper strata less visible in America than elsewhere. But in America today there are in fact tiers and ranges of wealth and power of which people in the middle and lower ranks know very little and may not even dream. There are families who, in their well-being, are quite insulated from the economic jolts and lurches felt by the merely prosperous and those farther down the scale. There are also men of power who in quite small groups make decisions of enormous consequence for the underlying population.

36

DOLLARS AND VOTES
How Business Campaign
Contributions Subvert Democracy

DAN CLAWSON • ALAN NEUSTADTL • MARK WELLER

Sociological research supports the thesis that a power elite exists in this country. A point of debate is the degree of interconnection among the three groups—the corporate, military, and political elite. Nonetheless, current social research still indicates that power is concentrated among a few social groups and institutions, as shown in a 1998 study discussed in this selection by Dan Clawson, Alan Neustadtl, and Mark Weller. After investigating 309 corporate political action committees (PACs), the authors conclude that PACs, which represent corporate interests, ensure that the concerns of Big Business are heard on Capitol Hill.

The Money Primary

Imagine the November election is just a few weeks away, and your friend Sally Robeson is seriously considering running for Congress two years from now. This year the incumbent in your district, E. Chauncey DeWitt III, will (again!) be reelected by a substantial margin, but you and Sally hate Chauncey's positions on the issues and are convinced that with the right campaign he can be beaten. Sally is capable, articulate, well informed, respected in the community, politically and socially connected, charming, good at talking to many kinds of people, and highly telegenic. She has invited you and several other politically active friends to meet with her immediately after the election to determine what she would need to do to become a viable candidate.

The meeting that takes place covers a host of topics: What are the key issues? On which of these are Sally's stands popular, and on which unpopular? What attacks, and from what quarters, will be launched against her? What individuals or groups can she count on for support? How, why, and where is the incumbent vulnerable? But lurking in the background is the question that cannot be ignored: *Can Sally (with the help of her friends and backers) raise enough money to be a contender?*

This is the *money primary, the first, and, in many instances, the most important round of the contest.* It eliminates more candidates than any other hurdle. Because it eliminates them so early and so quietly, its impact is often unobserved. To make it through, candidates don't have to come in first, but they do need to raise enough money to be credible contenders. Although having the most money is no guarantee of victory, candidates who don't do well in the money primary are no longer serious contenders. Certainly, plenty of well-funded candidates lose—Michael Huffington spent $25 million of his own money in an unsuccessful 1994 race for the Senate. But in order to be viable, a candidate needs to raise a substantial minimum.

How much is needed? If Sally hopes to win, rather than just put up a good fight, she, you, and the rest of her supporters will need to raise staggering amounts. (At least they are staggering from the perspective of most Americans; Ross Perot, Steve Forbes, or Michael Huffington may view the matter differently.) In order to accumulate the *average* amount for major-party congressional candidates in the general election, you will collectively need to raise $4,800 next week. And the week after. And *every* week for the next two years.

But even that is not enough. The average amount includes many candidates who were never "serious"; that is, they didn't raise enough to have a realistic hope of winning. If you and your friends want to raise the average amount spent by a *winning* candidate for the House, you'll have to come up with $6,730 next week and every single week until the election, two years away.

Well, you say, your candidate is hardly average. She is stronger, smarter, more politically appealing, and more viable than the "average" challenger. You think she can win even if she doesn't raise $6,730 a week. Let's use past experience—the results of the 1996 elections—to consider the likelihood of winning for challengers, based on how much money they raised. In 1996 more than 360 House incumbents were running for reelection; only 23 of them were beaten by their challengers. The average successful challenger spent $1,045,361—that is, he or she raised an average of over $10,000 every week for two years. What were the chances of winning without big money? Only one winning challenger spent less than $500,000, 12 spent between a half-a-million and a million dollars, and 10 spent more than a million dollars. Furthermore, 13 of the 23 winning challengers outspent the incumbent. A House challenger who can't raise at least a half-million dollars doesn't have a one percent chance of winning; the key primary is the money primary. The *Boston Globe* reported that "House candidates who headed into the final three weeks with the most in combined spending and cash on hand won 93 percent of the time."[1] What about that one low-spending winner? She is Carolyn Cheeks Kilpatrick, who won election by beating an incumbent in the primary and then having a walkover in the general election; the district, in Detroit, is the fourth poorest in the nation and consistently votes more than 80 percent Democratic. Although Kilpatrick spent only $174,457, few other districts make possible a similar election strategy.

In the Senate, even more money is needed. Suppose your candidate were going to run for the Senate, and started fundraising immediately after an election, giving her six years to prepare for the next election. How much money would she need to raise each and every week for those *six* years? The average winning Senate candidate raised approximately $15,000 per week.

For presidential candidates, the stakes are, of course, much higher: "The prevailing view is that for a politician to be considered legitimate, he or she must collect at least $20 million by the first of January 2000."[2] Presumably any candidate who does not do so is "illegitimate" and does not belong in the race. . . .

Coming up with the money is a major hassle; even for incumbents, it requires constant effort. *National Journal,* probably the single most authoritative source on the Washington scene, reports that "there is widespread agreement that the congressional money chase has become an unending marathon, as wearying to participants as it is disturbing to spectators," and quoted an aide to a Democratic senator as observing, "During hearings of Senate committees, you can watch senators go to phone booths in the committee rooms to dial for dollars." Just a few years ago—in 1990, the date of this statement—soliciting funds from federal property, whether Congress or the White House, was routine, openly discussed, and not regarded as problematic. The activity had always been technically illegal, but only in 1997 did it become an issue, with President Clinton and (especially) Vice President Gore singled out as if they were the only offenders. . . .

Not only is it necessary to raise lots of money; it is important—for both incumbents and challengers—to raise it early. Senator Rudy Boschwitz, Republican of Minnesota, was clear about this as a strategy. He spent $6 million getting reelected in 1984 and had raised $1.5 million of it by the beginning of the year, effectively discouraging the most promising Democratic challengers. After the election he wrote, and typed up himself, a secret evaluation of his campaign strategy:

> "Nobody in politics (except me!) likes to raise money, so I thought the best way of discouraging the toughest opponents from running was to have a few dollars in the sock. *I believe it worked. . . . From all forms of fundraising I raised $6 million plus and got 3 or 4 (maybe even 5) stories and cartoons* that irked me," he said. "In retrospect, I'm glad I had the money."[3]

Similarly, in March 1996 Bill Paxon, chair of the House Republican campaign committee, said, "We've been pounding on members to raise more money by the filing deadline; if they show a good balance, that could ward off opponents."[4]

The Contributors' Perspective

Candidates need money, lots of it, if they are to have any chance of winning. The obvious next question, and in some sense the focus of [our research], is who gives, why, and what they expect for it.

Contributions are made for many different reasons. The candidate's family and friends chip in out of loyalty and affection. Others contribute because they are asked to do so by someone who has done favors for them. People give because they agree with the candidate's stand on the issues, either on a broad ideological basis or on a specific issue. Sometimes these donations are portrayed as a form of voting—people show that they care by putting their money where their mouth is, anyone can contribute, and the money raised reflects the wishes of the people. Even for these contributions, however, if voting with dollars replaces voting at the ballot box, then the votes will be very unequally distributed: the top 1 percent of the population by wealth will have more "votes" than the bottom 90 percent of the population. In the 1996 elections, less than one-fourth of one percent of the population gave contributions of $200 or more to a federal candidate.[5] PACs and large contributors provide most of the money, however; small contributors accounted for under one-third of candidate receipts.[6]

It is not just that contributions come from the well-to-do. Most contributors have a direct material interest in what the government does or does not do. Their contributions, most of them made directly or indirectly by business, provide certain people a form of leverage and "access" not available to the rest of us. The chair of the political action committee at one of the twenty-five largest manufacturing companies in the United States explained to us why his corporation has a PAC:

> The PAC gives you access. It makes you a player. These congressmen, in particular, are constantly fundraising. Their elections are very expensive, and getting increasingly expensive each year. So they have an ongoing need for funds.
>
> It profits us in a sense to be able to provide some funds because in the provision of it you get to know people, you help them out. There's no real quid pro quo. There is nobody whose vote you can count on, not with the kind of money we are talking about here. But the PAC gives you access. Puts you in the game.
>
> You know, some congressman has got X number of ergs of energy and here's a person or a company who wants to come see him and give him a thousand dollars, and here's another one who wants to just stop by and say hello. And he only has time to see one. Which one? So the PAC's an attention getter.

So-called soft money, where the amount of the contribution is unlimited, might appear to be an exception: Isn't $100,000 enough to buy a guaranteed outcome? We will argue that it is *not*, at least not in any simple and straightforward way. PAC contributions are primarily for members of Congress; they are for comparatively small amounts, but enough to gain access to individual members of Congress. The individual member, however, has limited power. Soft money donations are best thought of as a way of gaining access to the president, top party leaders, and the executive branch. These individuals are more powerful than ordinary members of Congress, so access to them comes at a higher price. That privileged access is invaluable, but, as we will try to show, it does not—and is not expected to—*guarantee* a quid pro quo. The following example illustrates how corporations benefit from this "access" and how they use it to manipulate the system.

Why Does the Air Stink?

Everybody wants clean air. Who could oppose it? "I spent seven years of my life trying to stop the Clean Air Act," explained the vice president of a major corporation that is a heavy-duty polluter. Nonetheless, he was perfectly willing to make campaign contributions to members who voted for the act:

> How a person votes on the final piece of legislation often is not representative of what they have done. Somebody will do a lot of things during the process. How many guys voted against the Clean Air Act? But during the process some of them were very sympathetic to some of our concerns.

In the world of Congress and political action committees things, are not always what they seem. Members of Congress all want to vote for clean air, but they also want to get campaign contributions from corporations, and they want to pass a law that business will accept as "reasonable." The compromise solution is to gut the bill by crafting dozens of loopholes. These are inserted in private meetings or in subcommittee hearings that don't get much (if any) attention in the press. Then the public vote on the final bill can be nearly unanimous. Members of Congress can reassure both their constituents and their corporate contributors: constituents, that they voted for the final bill; corporations, that they helped weaken it in private. [Our research] analyzes how this happens; clean air, and especially the Clean Air Act of 1990, can serve as an introduction to the kind of process we try to expose.

The public strongly supports clean air and is unimpressed when corporate officials and apologists trot out their normal arguments—"corporations are already doing all they reasonably can to improve environmental quality," "we need to balance the costs against the benefits," "people will lose their jobs if we make controls any stricter." The original Clean Air Act was passed in 1970, revised in 1977, and not revised again until 1990. Although the initial goal was to have us breathing clean air by 1975, the deadline has been repeatedly extended—and the 1990 legislation provides a new set of deadlines to be reached sometime in the distant future.

Corporations control the production process unless the government specifically intervenes. Therefore, any delay in government action leaves corporations free to do as they choose; business often prefers a weak, ineffective, and unenforceable law. The laws have not only been slow to come, but corporations have also fought to delay or subvert implementation. The 1970 law ordered the Environmental Protection Agency (EPA) to regulate the hundreds of poisonous chemicals that are emitted by corporations, but, as William Greider notes, "In twenty years of stalling, dodging, and fighting off court orders, the EPA has managed to issue regulatory standards for a total of seven toxics."[7]

Corporations have done exceptionally well politically, given the problem they face: The interests of business are diametrically opposed to those of the public. Clean-air laws and amendments have been few and far between, enforcement is ineffective, and the penalties minimal. On the one hand, corporations *have* had to pay *billions* for cleanups; on the other, the costs to date are a small fraction of what would be needed to actually clean up the environment.

This corporate struggle for the right to pollute has taken place on many fronts. The most visible is public relations: the Chemical Manufacturers Association took out a two-page Earth Day ad in the *Washington Post* to demonstrate its concern; coincidentally, the names of many of the corporate signers of this ad appear on the EPA's list of high-risk producers.[8] Another front is expert studies that delay action while more information is gathered. The federally funded National Acid Precipitation Assessment Program took ten years and $600 million to figure out whether acid rain was in fact a problem. Both business and the Reagan administration argued that nothing should be done until the study was completed.[9] Ultimately, the study was discredited: The "summary of findings" minimized the impact of acid rain, even though this did not accurately represent the expert research in the report. But the key site of struggle was Congress. For years, corporations successfully defeated legislation. In 1987 utility companies were offered a compromise bill on acid rain, but they "were very adamant that they had beat the thing since 1981 and they could always beat it," according to Representative Edward Madigan (Republican–Illinois).[10] The utilities beat back all efforts at reform through the 1980s, but their intransigence probably hurt them when revisions finally came to be made.

The stage was set for a revision of the Clean Air Act when George Bush, "the environmental president," was elected, and George Mitchell, a strong supporter of environmentalism, became the Senate majority leader. But what sort of clean air bill would it be? "What we wanted," said Richard Ayres, head of the environmentalists' Clean Air Coalition, "is a health based standard—one-in-1-million cancer risk," a standard that would require corporations to clean up their plants until the cancer risk from their operations was reduced to 1 in a million. "The Senate bill still has the requirement," Ayres said, "but there are forty pages of extensions and exceptions and qualifications and loopholes that largely render the health standard a nullity."[11] Greider reports, for example, "According to the EPA, there are now twenty-six coke ovens that pose a cancer risk greater than 1 in 1000 and six where the risk is greater than 1 in 100. Yet the new clean-air bill will give the steel industry another thirty years to deal with the problem." [12]

This change from what the bill was supposed to do to what it did do came about through what corporate executives like to call the "access" process. The principal aim of most corporate campaign contributions is to help corporate executives gain "access" to key members of Congress and their staffs. In these meetings, corporate executives (and corporate PAC money) work to persuade the member of Congress to accept a predesigned loophole that will sound innocent but effectively undercut the stated intention of the bill. Representative John D. Dingell (Democrat–Michigan), who was chair of the House committee, is a strong industry supporter; one of the people we interviewed called him "the point man for the Business Roundtable on clean air." Representative Henry A. Waxman (Democrat–California), chair of the subcommittee, is an environmentalist. Observers had expected a confrontation and contested votes on the floor of the Congress.

The problem for corporations was that, as one Republican staff aide said, "If any bill has the blessing of Waxman and the environmental groups, unless it is totally in outer space, who's going to vote against it?" [13] But corporations successfully minimized public votes. Somehow, Waxman was persuaded to make behind-the-scenes compromises with Dingell so members, during an election year, didn't have to side publicly with business against the environment. Often the access process leads to loopholes that protect a single corporation, but for "clean" air most of the special deals targeted not specific companies but entire industries. The initial bill, for example, required cars to be able to use carefully specified, cleaner fuels. But the auto industry wanted the rules loosened, and Congress eventually incorporated a variant of a formula suggested by the head of General Motors' fuels and lubricants department.

Nor did corporations stop fighting even after they gutted the bill through amendments. Business pressed the EPA for favorable regulations to implement the law: "The cost of this legislation could vary dramatically, depending on how EPA interprets it," said William D. Fay, vice president of the National Coal Association, who headed the hilariously misnamed Clean Air Working Group, an industry coalition that fought to weaken the legislation. [14] As one EPA aide working on acid rain regulations reported, "We're having a hard time getting our work done because of the number of phone calls we're getting" from corporations and their lawyers.

Corporations trying to get federal regulators to adopt the "right" regulations don't rely exclusively on the cogency of their arguments. They often exert pressure on a member of Congress to intervene for them at the EPA or other agency. Senators and representatives regularly intervene on behalf of constituents and contributors by doing everything from straightening out a social security problem to asking a regulatory agency to explain why it is pressuring a company. This process—like campaign finance—usually follows rules of etiquette. In addressing a regulatory agency, the senator does not say: "Lay off my campaign contributors or I'll cut your budget." One standard phrasing for letters asks regulators to resolve the problem "as quickly as possible within applicable rules and regulations."[15] No matter how mild and careful the inquiry, the agency receiving the request is certain to give it extra attention; only after careful consideration will they refuse to make any accommodation.

Soft money—unregulated megabuck contributions—also shaped what happened to air quality. Archer Daniels Midland argued that increased use of ethanol would reduce pollution from gasoline; coincidentally, ADM controls a majority of the ethanol market. To reinforce its arguments, in the 1992 election ADM gave $90,000 to Democrats and $600,000 to Republicans, the latter supplemented with an additional $200,000 as an individual contribution from the company head, Dwayne Andreas. Many environmentalists were skeptical about ethanol's value in a clean-air strategy, but President Bush issued regulations promoting wider use of ethanol; we presume he was impressed by the force of ADM's 800,000 Republican arguments. Bob Dole, the 1996 Republican presidential candidate, helped pass and defend special breaks for the ethanol industry; he not only appreciated ADM's Republican contributions, but presumably approved of the more than $1 million they gave to the American Red Cross during the period when it was headed by his wife, Elizabeth Dole.[16] What about the post-1994 Republican-controlled Congress, defenders of the free market and opponents of government giveaways? Were they ready to end this subsidy program, cracking down on corporate welfare as they did on people welfare? Not a chance. In 1997, the Republican chair of the House Ways and Means Committee actually attempted to eliminate the special tax breaks for ethanol. Needless to say, he was immediately put in his place by other members of the Republican leadership, including Speaker Newt Gingrich and most of the Senate, with the subsidy locked in place for years to come,[17] in spite of a General Accounting Office report that "found that the ethanol subsidy justifies none of its political boasts."[18] The Center for Responsive Politics calculated that ADM, its executives and PAC, made more than $1 million in campaign contributions of various types; the only thing that had changed was that in 1996, with a Democratic president, this money was "divided more or less evenly between Republicans and Democrats."[19]

The disparity in power between business and environmentalists looms large during the legislative process, but it is enormous afterward. When the Clean Air Act passed, corporations and industry groups offered positions, typically with large pay increases, to congressional staff members who wrote the law. The former congressional staff members who now work for corporations both know how to evade the law and can persuasively claim to EPA that they know what Congress intended. Environmental organizations pay substantially less than Congress and can't afford large staffs. They are seldom able to become involved in the details of the administrative process or to influence implementation and enforcement.[20]

Having pushed Congress and the Environmental Protection Agency to allow as much pollution as possible, business then went to the Quayle council for rules allowing even more pollution. Vice President J. Danforth Quayle's council, technically known as the "Council on Competitiveness," was created by President Bush specifically to help reduce regulations on business. Quayle told the *Boston Globe* "that his council has an 'open door' to business groups and that he has a bias against regulations."[21] During the Bush administration, this council reviewed, and could override, all regulations, including those by the EPA setting the limits at which a chemical was subject to regulation. The council also recommended that corporations be allowed to increase their polluting emissions if a state did not object within seven days of the proposed increase. Corporations thus have multiple opportunities to win. If they lose in Congress, they can win at the regulatory agency; if they lose there, they can try again at the Quayle council (or later equivalent). If they lose there, they can try to reduce the money available to enforce regulations, or tie the issue up in the courts, or plan on accepting a minimal fine.

The operation of the Quayle council would probably have received little publicity, but reporters discovered that the executive director of the council, Allan Hubbard, had a clear conflict of interest. Hubbard chaired the biweekly White House meetings on the Clean Air Act. He owned half of World Wide Chemical, received an average of more than $1 million a year in profits from it while directing the Quayle council, and continued to attend quarterly stockholder meetings. According to the *Boston Globe,* "Records on file with the Indianapolis Air Pollution Control Board show that World Wide Chemical emitted 17,000 to 19,000 pounds of chemicals into the air" in 1991.[22] At that time, the company did "not have the permit required to release the emissions," was "putting out nearly four times the allowable emissions without a permit, and could be subject to a $2,500-a-day penalty" according to David Jordan, director of the Indianapolis Air Pollution Board.[23]

This does not, however, mean that business always gets exactly what it wants. In 1997, the Environmental Protection Agency proposed tough new rules for soot and smog. Business fought hard to weaken or eliminate the rules: hiring experts (from pro-business think tanks) to attack the scientific studies supporting the regulations and putting a raft of lobbyists ("many of them former congressional staffers," the *Washington Post* reported[24]) to work securing the signatures of 250 members of Congress questioning the standards. But the late 1990s version of these industry mobilizations adds a new twist—creating a pseudo-grassroots campaign. For example, business, operating under a suitably disguised name (Foundation for Clean Air Progress), paid for television ads telling farmers that the EPA rules would prohibit them from plowing on dry windy days, with other ads predicting the EPA rules "would lead to forced carpooling or bans on outdoor barbecues—claims the

EPA dismisses as ridiculous." [25] Along with the ads, industry worked to mobilize local politicians and business executives in what business groups called a "grass tops" campaign.

Despite a massive industry campaign, EPA head Carol Browner remained firm, and President Clinton was persuaded to go along. Of course, industry immediately began working on ways to undercut the regulations with congressional loopholes and exceptions—but business had suffered a defeat, and proponents of clean air (that is, most of the rest of us) had won at least a temporary and partial victory. And who leads the struggles to overturn or uphold these regulations? Just as before, Dingell and Waxman; Republicans "are skittish about challenging" the rules publicly, "so they gladly defer to Dingell as their surrogate." [26] Dingell's forces have more than 130 cosponsors (about one-third of them Democrats) for a bill to, in effect, override the EPA standards.

In business–government relations, most attention becomes focused on instances of scandal. The real issue, however, is not one or another scandal or conflict of interest, but rather the *system* of business–government relations, and especially of campaign finance, that offers business so many opportunities to craft loopholes, undermine regulations, and subvert enforcement. Still worse, many of these actions take place beyond public scrutiny. . . . [Our research] focuses on business and the way it uses money and power to subvert the democratic process. . . .

What Is Power?

Our analysis is based on an understanding of power that differs from that usually articulated by both business and politicians. The corporate PAC directors we interviewed insisted that they have no power.

> *If you were to ask me what kind of access and influence do we have, being roughly the 150th largest PAC, I would have to tell you that on the basis of our money we have zero. . . . If you look at the level of our contributions, we know we're not going to buy anybody's vote, we're not going to rent anybody, or whatever the clichés have been over the years. We know that.*

The executives who expressed these views clearly meant these words sincerely. Their statements are based on roughly the same understanding of "power" that is current within political science, which is also the way the term was defined by Max Weber, the classical sociological theorist. Power, in this common conception, is the ability to make someone do something against their will. If that is what power means, then corporations rarely have any in relation to members of Congress, nor does soft money give the donor power over presidents. As one senior vice president said to us: "You certainly aren't going to be able to buy anybody for $500 or $1,000 or $10,000—it's a joke." . . . In this regard we agree with the corporate officials we interviewed:

A corporation is not in a position to say to a member of Congress, "Either you vote for this bill or we will defeat your bid for reelection." Rarely do they even say: "You vote for this bill or you won't get any money from us."

The definition of power as the ability to make someone do something against their will is what Steven Lukes calls a "one-dimensional" view of power.[27] A two-dimensional view recognizes the existence of nondecisions: A potential issue never gets articulated or, if articulated by someone somewhere, never receives serious consideration. For example, in 1989 and 1990 one of the major political battles, and a focus of great effort by corporate PACs, was the Clean Air Act. Yet twenty or thirty years earlier, before the rise of the environmental movement, pollution was a nonissue: it simply was not considered, although its effects were, in retrospect, of great importance. In one of the Sherlock Holmes stories, the key clue is that the dog didn't bark.[28] A two-dimensional view of power makes the same point: The most important clue in some situation may be that no one noticed power was exercised—because there was no overt conflict.

Even this model of power is too restrictive, however, because it still focuses on discrete decisions and nondecisions. Tom Wartenberg . . . argues, instead, for a "field theory" of power that analyzes social power as a force similar to a magnetic field. A magnetic field alters the motion of objects susceptible to magnetism. Similarly, the mere presence of a powerful social agent alters the social space for others and causes them to orient themselves toward the powerful agent.[29] For example, one of the executives we interviewed took it for granted that "if we go see the congressman who represents [a city where the company has a major plant], where 10,000 of our employees are also his constituents, we don't need a PAC to go see him." The corporation is so important in that area that the member has to orient himself in relation to the corporation and its concerns. In a different sense, the very act of accepting a campaign contribution changes the way a member relates to a PAC, creating a sense of obligation, a need to reciprocate. The PAC contribution has altered the member's social space, his or her awareness of the company and wish to help it, even if no explicit commitments have been made.

Business Is Different

Power, we would argue, is not just the ability to force someone to do something against their will; it is most effective (and least recognized) when it shapes the field of action. Moreover, business's vast resources, influence on the economy, and general legitimacy place it on a different footing from other campaign contributors. Every day, a member of Congress accepts a $1,000 donation from a corporate PAC, goes to a committee hearing, proposes "minor" changes in a bill's wording, and has those changes accepted without discussion or examination. The changes "clarify" the language of the bill, legalizing higher levels of pollution for a specific pollutant, or exempting the company from some tax. The media do not report this change and no one speaks against it. . . .

Even groups with great social legitimacy encounter more opposition and controversy than business faces for proposals that are virtually without public support. One example is the contrast between the largely unopposed commitment of tens or hundreds of billions of dollars for the savings and loan bailout, compared to the sharp debate, close votes, and defeats for the rights of men and women to take *unpaid* parental leaves. The classic term for something noncontroversial that everyone must support is "a motherhood issue," and while it costs little to guarantee every woman the right to an *un*paid parental leave, this measure nonetheless generated intense scrutiny and controversy—going down to defeat under President Bush, passing under President Clinton, and then again becoming a focus of attack after the 1994 Republican takeover of Congress. Few indeed are the people publicly prepared to defend pollution or tax evasion. Nonetheless, business is routinely able to win pollution exemptions and tax loopholes. Although cumulatively some vague awareness of these provisions may trouble people, most are allowed individually to pass without scrutiny. *No* analysis of corporate political activity makes sense unless it begins with a recognition of this absolutely vital point. The PAC is a vital element of corporate power, but it does not operate by itself. The PAC donation is always backed by the wider power and influence of business.

Corporations are unlike other "special interest" groups not only because business has far more resources, but also because of its acceptance and legitimacy. When people feel that "the system" is screwing them, they tend to blame politicians, the government, the media—but rarely business. In terms of campaign finance, while much of the public is outraged at the way money influences elections and public policy, the issue is almost always posed in terms of politicians, what they do or don't do. This is part of a pervasive double standard that largely exempts business from criticism. We, however, believe it is vital to scrutinize business as well. . . .

The Limits to Business Power

We have argued that power is more than winning an open conflict and that business is different from other groups because its pervasive influence on our society shapes the social space for all other actors. These two arguments, however, are joined with a third: a recognition—in fact an insistence—on the limits to business power. Though we stress the power of business, business does not feel powerful. As one executive said to us:

> *I really wish that our PAC in particular, and our lobbyists, had the influence that is generally perceived by the general population. If you see it written in the press,*

and you talk to people, they tell you about all that influence that you've got, and frankly I think that's far overplayed, as far as the influence goes. Certainly you can get access to a candidate, and certainly you can get your position known; but as far as influencing that decision, the only way you influence it is by the providing of information.

Executives believe that corporations are constantly under attack, primarily because government simply doesn't understand that business is crucial to everything the society does, but can easily be crippled by well-intentioned but unrealistic government policies. A widespread view among the people we interviewed is, "Far and away the vast majority of things that we do are literally to protect ourselves from public policy that is poorly crafted and nonresponsive to the needs and realities and circumstances of our company." These misguided policies, they feel, can come from many sources: labor unions, environmentalists, the pressure of unrealistic public interest groups, the government's constant need for money or the weight of its oppressive bureaucracy. Therefore, simply to stay even requires a pervasive effort. If attention slips for even a minute, an onerous regulation will be imposed or a precious resource taken away. To some extent such a view is an obvious consequence of the position of the people we interviewed: If business could be sure of always winning, the government relations unit (and thus the jobs of its members) would be unnecessary; if it is easy to win, PAC directors deserve little credit for company victories and much blame for defeats. But evidently the corporation agrees with them, since it devotes significant resources to political action of many kinds, including the awareness and involvement of top officials. Chief executive officers and members of the board of directors repeatedly express similar views. . . .

. . . Once upon a time, perhaps, business could simply make its wishes known and receive what it wanted; today, corporations must form PACs, give soft money, actively lobby, make their case to the public, run advocacy ads, and engage in a whole range of costly and degrading activities that they wish were unnecessary. From the outside, we are impressed with their high success rates over a wide range of issues and with the absence of a credible challenge to the general authority of business. From the inside, corporations are impressed with the serious consequences of their occasional losses and with the unremitting effort needed to maintain their privileged position.

ENDNOTES

[1] *Boston Globe,* November 8, 1996, p. A26.

[2] *New York Times,* September 3, 1997, p. A18.

[3] Boschwitz, quoted in Brooks Jackson, *Honest Graft: Big Money and the American Political Process* (New York: Knopf, 1988), pp. 251–52. Emphasis in book. (Obviously, the secret memo didn't stay secret.) Boschwitz's 1990 strategy backfired. He discouraged the most "promising" Democratic candidates, but Paul Wellstone—a true long shot by all accounts—beat him, despite Boschwitz's 4 to 1 spending advantage. In the

1996 rematch between the two candidates, Wellstone outspent Boschwitz and won handily.

[4] Quoted in Elizabeth Drew, *Whatever It Takes: The Real Struggle for Political Power in America* (New York: Viking, 1997), pp. 19–20.

[5] David Donnelly, Janice Fine, and Ellen S. Miller, "Going Public," *Boston Review,* April–May 1997. Larry Makinson, "The Big Picture: Money Follows Power Shift on Capitol Hill" (Washington, DC: Center for Responsive Politics, 1997, www.crp.org).

[6] www.fec.gov.

[7] William Greider, "Whitewash: Is Congress Conning Us on Clean Air?" *Rolling Stone,* June 14, 1990, p. 40.

[8] Greider, "Whitewash,"p. 40.

[9] Margaret E. Kriz, "Dunning the Midwest," *National Journal,* April 14, 1990, p. 895.

[10] Kriz, "Dunning the Midwest," p. 895.

[11] Quoted in Greider, "Whitewash," p. 40.

[12] Greider, "Whitewash," p. 41.

[13] Margaret E. Kriz, "Politics at the Pump," *National Journal,* June 2, 1990, p. 1328.

[14] Why can't industry just come out and name its groups "Polluters for Profit" or the "Coalition for Acid Rain Preservation" (CARP)? All quotes in this paragraph are from Carol Matlack, "It's Round Two in Clean Air Fight," *National Journal,* January 26, 1991, p. 226.

[15] *Washington Post,* January 16, 1991, p. A17.

[16] *New York Times,* April 16, 1996, p. A16.

[17] *New York Times,* June 22, 1997, p. 17.

[18] *Wall Street Journal,* June 6, 1997.

[19] *New York Times,* June 22, 1997, p. 17.

[20] Matlack, "It's Round Two," p. 227.

[21] *Boston Globe,* November 21, 1991, p. 17.

[22] *Boston Globe,* November 21, 1991, p. 17.

[23] *Boston Globe,* November 20, 1991, p. 4.

[24] *Washington Post,* June 17, 1997, p. A1.

[25] *Washington Post,* June 17, 1997, p. A1.

[26] Richard E. Cohen, "Two Dems Are on Familiar Battlefield," *National Journal,* September 6, 1997, p. 1742.

[27] Steven Lukes, *Power: A Radical View* (New York: Macmillan, 1974).

[28] Theodore J. Eismeier and Philip H. Pollock III, "The Retreat from Partisanship: Why the Dog Didn't Bark in the 1984 Election." In *Business Strategy and Public Policy,* ed. Alfred A. Marcus, Allen M. Kaufman, and David R. Beam (Westport, Conn.: Quorum Books, 1987), pp. 137–47.

[29] Thomas Wartenberg, *The Forms of Power: From Domination to Transformation* (Philadelphia: Temple University Press, 1990), p. 74.

37

PLAYING THE POLITICAL SLOTS
American Indians and Casinos

DONALD L. BARLETT • JAMES B. STEELE

C. Wright Mills' notion of the *power elite* can be seen in many social contexts in the United States, including the recent political and economic maneuvering related to American Indian reservations and gambling. The following excerpt, by investigative journalists Donald L. Barlett and James B. Steele, examines the complicated relationship between the U.S. government and American Indian tribes who have established casinos. Sadly, the reality of gambling on Indian reservations reflects power inequalities in the larger society. While a few tribes have become wealthy by exploiting gambling loopholes on reservations, most American Indians continue to live in poverty. Moreover, most of the gaming-management companies who oversee the casinos on the reservations are run by wealthy non-Native American men.

If it were a public company, the Mississippi band of Choctaw Indians would be the envy of corporate America. With a return on revenue of 41%, the tribe's Silver Star Resort & Casino would top the Fortune 500 profitability list, dwarfing even money spinners like Microsoft, whose 29% return last year seems modest by comparison. The Choctaw Tribe has proved even more productive by another crucial yardstick: influence peddling in Washington. How successful is it? In 1997 the tribe secured its very own special-interest provision hidden in a massive federal-spending bill. And it taps the government for tens of millions of dollars in federal aid every year, even though the Silver Star rakes in annual profits of about $100 million.

Indian gaming interests have come up with a one-two punch that is helping them get their way with politicians. Indian constituents, acknowledged as long-suffering victims of ill-conceived government policies, often succeed at requesting political favors. Meanwhile, they or their wealthy backers are dumping money—staggering amounts of it—into political campaigns, lobbying, and state ballot initiatives. This combination has helped create the out-of-control world of Indian gaming, a world where the leaders of newly wealthy tribes have so much political power that they can flout the rights of neighboring communities, poorer tribes, and even some of their own members. Their political clout also helps them protect a chaotic gaming system

From *Time Magazine,* December 23, 2002, Volume 160, No. 26, pp. 52–63. Copyright © 2002 Time, Inc. Reprinted by permission.

that has served them well, one that is characterized by overburdened and underfunded watchdog agencies, a mishmash of regulations and a lack of financial accountability. As a result, Washington often ignores the needs of Native Americans in distress while assisting those who least need help.

As recently as a decade ago, Indian tribes were barely a blip on the special-interest radar screen. But since 1993, they have contributed $8.6 million to federal candidates. In the Clinton years, most of the money went to Democrats. During his second run for office, in 1996, tribes handed out a total of $1.9 million, 86% of it to Democrats. But with a Republican in the White House, Indian tribes have shifted the target of their largesse. [In 2002], 56% of the $1.4 million they have donated to federal campaigns has gone to the G.O.P. The tribes have invested even more heavily in lobbying Congress. In 2000–01 they spent $20 million lobbying on such issues as preserving the tax-free status of casinos, expanding gaming operations, and protecting Indian sovereign immunity, which allows them to avoid regulations imposed on other businesses.

No tribe spends more—or more effectively—than Mississippi's Choctaw. Since 1997 the 8,800-member tribe has distributed some $11 million to Washington lobbying firms. Most of the money has gone to one of the capital's premier lobbyists, Jack Abramoff, a top Republican Party fund raiser. It was money well spent. In the 1997 legislative caper, Thad Cochran, Mississippi's five-term Republican Senator, slipped into a 40,000-word appropriations bill a 19-word sentence that exempts the tribe from oversight by the National Indian Gaming Commission (NIGC), the regulatory body created by Congress to oversee Indian gambling. The sentence also excuses the Choctaw from paying the fees levied on all other Indian gaming establishments, which are the NIGC's sole source of revenue. The savings for the tribe amount to about $180,000 a year. Cochran's provision argues that the tribe was self-regulating effectively.

Meanwhile, government audit reports show that over the past five years, federal agencies have lavished $245 million in aid on the Choctaw. In 2001 alone—the same year the tribe bought a $4.5 million corporate plane—the Choctaw collected $50.4 million from nearly 70 government programs, including $14.9 million to run their tribal government, $1.3 million for law enforcement and almost $371,000 for food distribution. It adds up to an average of $5,700 for each member. In contrast, federal aid for the Navajo Nation, the poorest tribe in America, averaged $900 for each of its 260,000 members. The Navajo have no casino.

None of this is to begrudge the Mississippi Choctaw their newfound gaming wealth. Unlike tribes that are content to rely on a casino to support themselves without looking to the future, the Choctaw have plowed their profits into new businesses, from a car dealership to an electronics plant. Nor is this to begrudge the Choctaw their ability to extract aid from Washington. What is awry is a political system that consigns the majority of Native Americans to a life of poverty while rewarding the few who have casino riches with full membership in the system.

Money Talks

These days some of the highest-stakes lobbying in the nation goes on about two miles west of Capitol Hill at the Bureau of Indian Affairs (BIA). The agency, which oversees Native American affairs, decides, among other things, which tribes qualify for federal recognition—and are thus entitled to build a casino and receive federal benefits. Not surprisingly, as Indian gaming has evolved from bingo halls to a multi-billion-dollar industry, the number of tribes clamoring for recognition has soared: there are now 337 tribes in the lower 48 states—up almost 25% since 1979.

But since 1993, while the volume and complexity of the petitions have grown, Congress has slashed the BIA's budget, forcing the agency to shrink its staff for handling petitions 35%, to just 11. The agency's Branch of Acknowledgment and Research (BAR) staff, which evaluates applicants on a complex range of factors, including genealogy, culture, and continuous existence, is overwhelmed. The result: a November 2001 report by the General Accounting Office (GAO), the investigative arm of Congress, paints the picture of a process in disarray, calling the BIA under staffed, lacking coherent guidelines, and having no clear sense of mission.

It's a situation ripe for manipulation. In the last two years of the Clinton Administration, despite a recommendation by BAR staff to deny recognition to six tribal groups, Assistant Secretary for Indian Affairs Kevin Gover, a former Clinton fund raiser appointed to the post by the President, recognized four of the tribes before he left office on Jan. 3, 2001. His successor, Michael Anderson, another Clinton appointee, then pressured the BAR staff to change its recommendation on the two other tribes. In an atmosphere so tense that a staff member later described it to the Interior Department's Inspector General as "pure hell," BAR was pushed to complete the documentation recognizing the tribes by Jan. 19, the Administration's last day in office. Three days later, on the first working day of the Bush Administration, the BAR staff discovered that Anderson had failed to sign all the documents necessary to recognize one tribe, the Duwamish of Washington State. Alerted to the omission, Anderson drove to the BIA, where an employee took the papers out to his car to be signed. The staff member, according to the Interior Department's report, then backdated the documents to Jan. 19. Anderson says politics played no role in his decision. "These tribes were well qualified to be recognized," he says. Incoming Bush BIA appointees put a hold on Anderson's two 11th-hour approvals. Neither has been recognized so far.

It didn't take the Bush Administration long to pick up where the Clintonites had left off. Last June, Bush appointees in the BIA recognized the

Eastern Pequot, and amalgamation of two Connecticut tribes with casino plans that had received preliminary approval under Clinton. In the past four years, spanning both Administrations, the tribe and its investors paid $525,000 to Ronald Kaufman—a well-connected Republican lobbyist, White House political director for the first President Bush, and a brother-in-law of current White House chief of staff Andrew Card—to press their case. The BIA's recognition came amid widespread opposition by Connecticut politicians and community groups and questions about the tribe's authenticity.

Sometimes having a sympathetic Administration in power isn't even necessary. When their agenda bogs down, well-connected tribes can go to friends in Congress, skirting the BIA and the regulatory process altogether. Congress recognized the Pokagon Band of Potawatomi Indians of Indiana and Michigan in 1994. With help from a financial backer, Lyle Berman's Lakes Entertainment Inc., the tribe is on the verge of building a casino about 70 miles east of Chicago, in New Buffalo, Mich. Meanwhile, in the Senate, Virginia Republicans George Allen and John Warner have introduced a package deal for six Virginia tribes—despite the opposition of the BIA, which says the bill would permit the tribes to bypass regular channels and allow them "to avoid the scrutiny to which other groups have been subjected."

Tax Dollars at Work

Even as they reap ever larger profits from slot machines and gaming tables, tribes with successful casinos continue to collect federal taxpayer dollars. An Office of Management and Budget report shows that from 1993 to 2001, overall federal funding for key Native American programs climbed from $5.3 billion to $9.4 billion—a 77% increase. Government and congressional officials say they have no idea how much of that went to tribes with successful casinos. But data *Time* has analyzed suggest that Washington often rewards rich tribes and penalizes poor ones by distributing funds based on historical practices rather than need. A tribe with a profitable casino often gets more money per capita than a tribe without one.

Consider the BIA's distribution of tribal-priority-allocation (TPA) funds to tribes. Each year, the BIA hands out about $800 million for basic programs such as general assistance to individual Indians and families, vocational training, and child welfare. While TPA funding is a small fraction of the BIA's total spending on Native Americans, it underscores how awry the system has gone. In President Bush's 2003 budget proposal, the 28,000 Turtle Mountain Chippewa in North Dakota, 68% of whom are unemployed, will receive the equivalent of an average $154 each. But the 400 members of the Miccosukee Tribe in Florida, whose Miccosukee Resort and Gaming Center rakes in an estimated $75 million a year, will collect $2,858 per person—almost 19 times as much. In South Dakota the 41,000 Oglala Sioux, with unemployment at 88%, will receive $168 per person. But California's Rumsey Band of Wintun Indians, whose casino takes in an estimated $150 million a year, will collect an average of $4,457 for each of its 44 members.

The GAO has twice criticized the BIA's distribution system, pointing out that "tribes with the highest reported revenues can receive more TPA base funds than other tribes with no revenues or with losses." Congress directed the BIA to report by April 1, 1999, "on alternative methods for distributing TPA funds, taking into account tribal revenues and the relative needs of tribes and tribal members." While acknowledging funding inequities, the BIA will not change the system. One reason: the tribes view such government funding as an entitlement. As an official of the Mille Lacs Band of Ojibwe Indians—a tribe in Minnesota with two casinos, which take in an estimated $200 million a year in revenue—once told a congressional committee, "The United States has a moral and legal obligation to provide TPA funding to tribal governments. . . . The facts of the inequities are not that some tribes have been given too much but rather that other tribes have been given too little."

Such inequities occur not only with BIA funds. A *Time* examination of spending by the Department of Housing and Urban Development (HUD) shows that tribes with casinos often pull in more HUD money per capita than casino-less, poor tribes. Over the past four years, while HUD has handed the Florida Seminoles housing funds averaging $2,800 per member, the tribe's five casinos have generated nearly $1 billion in revenue. The Mississippi Choctaw tribe, with its lucrative Silver Star Resort & Casino, pocketed an average of $5,900 in HUD funds per person. By contrast, the Navajo, the country's largest tribe, has a 52% unemployment rate but has received only $1,500 per member.

California Scheming

Tribes may be wielding increased political influence in Washington, but at the state level, small Indian tribes with immensely profitable casinos are exerting even more disproportionate clout. Nowhere is it greater than in California, where combined Indian gaming revenue, at $4 billion and growing, is set to surpass that of all the casinos in Las Vegas.

How much are tribes spending? To win passage of the two ballot initiatives in 1998 and 2000 that legalized Indian gaming in the state, several small tribes spent a total of nearly $100 million. The San Manuel Band of Serrano Mission Indians, which owns a casino in San Bernardino County, spent a staggering $34.7 million—an average of almost $520,000 for each of the tribe's 67 adult members. Both initiatives passed.

It's not only the size of the political expenditures that is causing concern. Some tribes have violated campaign-finance laws. Earlier this year, California's Fair Political Practices Commission, which monitors the state's elections, charged that since 1998 one tribe—the 232-member Agua Caliente Band of Cahuilla Indians, which has a pair of money-churning casinos near Palm Springs—had failed to promptly report multiple contributions totaling $8.5 million. When the commission tried to work out a settlement, the Agua Caliente would not negotiate, contending that because the tribe is a sovereign nation, California campaign-finance laws do not apply. Like all federally recognized tribes, the Agua Caliente is a self-governing entity and thus generally exempt from state and local laws.

Despite that, the commission filed a lawsuit, assuming that California's attorney general, Bill Lockyer—the state's top law-enforcement officer—would represent the agency. But he declined. Lockyer, by the way, has accepted substantial campaign contributions from Indian tribes—some $800,000 in the past four years, including $175,000 from the Agua Caliente Band. As a consequence, the commission has had to hire an outside lawyer, a move that will cost unnecessary tax dollars. Jim Knox, California Common Cause's executive director, believes that actions against the Agua Caliente and other tribes must be pursued. "If they are sovereign nations, they shouldn't be able to contribute to candidates or ballot measures," says Knox, pointing out that it's illegal for a foreign state or business to pump money into U.S. elections. "And if they aren't, they should be subject to the state's election and campaign-finance laws. The tribes are trying to have it both ways."

And so far, that has worked. Tribes have become California's largest special-interest donors. In his [2002] reelection campaign, Governor Gray Davis picked up $1.8 million from them, and he, more than anyone else, is responsible for the face of California gaming. The compacts he signed with the tribes in 1999 paved the way for the explosion in the state's Indian casinos, which number 48 and may climb to 70.

Because tribes pay no state or local taxes, the compacts Davis negotiated provide for tribal contributions to a special impact fund. The money will go to local communities overburdened by booming casinos and help defray the increased costs of local government services. California officials estimate that the tribes will pay about $100 million a year into the fund. By contrast, Connecticut collected $332 million last year from its two Indian casinos, Foxwoods and the Mohegan Sun. If California tribes were paying at the same rate—25% of slot revenue—the state would collect up to $1 billion.

Nightmare Neighbors

As the profitability and size of Indian casinos have grown, so has friction between the gaming ventures and surrounding communities. Last summer, tensions between the Rumsey Band of Wintun Indians and its neighbors in the rural Northern California Capay Valley erupted into a bitter war of words when the tribe announced plans to double the size of its hillside gaming business. Highway 16, the narrow, serpentine road that winds past the Cache Creek Indian Bingo and Casino on its way into the tiny hamlet of Brooks, is already congested from round-the-clock traffic to the casino. In 2001, traffic to Cache Creek, with its estimated $150 million annual revenue, was up 87% from the year before, according to a California department of transportation study.

Indian casinos are overloading other communities across the country. One exacerbating factor: because of tribal sovereignty, if a casino overwhelms local emergency services, draws down the local water supply or pollutes the environment, local authorities have no recourse. Tom Frederick, who owns a small vineyard north of the casino, found that out the hard way. For years, as sewage from the casino seeped onto his property, he tried to get the Rumsey Indians to deal with the problem. Recently the waste-water drainage slowed when the tribe relined a sewage-holding pond, but tribal officials will not talk to him about any damage to his property. "They use sovereignty as a shield," he says.

After protracted negotiations, the Rumsey Band and Yolo County officials reached a tentative accord on the casino expansion. The tribe, which views the deal as a concession, since it is a partial surrender of its sovereignty, agreed to slightly reduce the size of the expansion and pay the county more than $5 million a year for 18 years to deal with traffic, environmental, and other problems. But relations remain strained. Bulldozers moved onto the Rumsey reservation and began clearing land even before the county board had approved the agreement.

A Tale of Two Tribes

After the Supreme Court gave the green light to gaming on Indian reservations, Congress set up a regulatory scheme that is contradictory, inconsistent, and shielded from public scrutiny. How arbitrary is it? The National Indian Gaming Commission can levy fines but has no power to collect them. Each tribe has its own gaming commission, but that's like Enron's auditors auditing themselves. States monitor casinos in some situations but not in others. Federal prosecutors may go after one casino for a gaming violation while ignoring the same violation by a wealthy and powerful tribe.

Few tribes are more powerful than Florida's Seminoles, who pioneered high-stakes bingo and won Supreme Court approval for Indian gaming everywhere. James E. Billie, the Seminoles' alligator-wrestling, folk-singing chief from 1979 to 2001, is the person most responsible for creating the tribe's gambling wealth and also personifies its flamboyant excesses. In a power struggle last year, the tribal council suspended Billie pending resolution of a sexual-harassment lawsuit (it was recently dropped) and an audit of questionable tribal financial dealings, which is still going on. At the time, he was the highest-paid elected official in Florida, with an annual salary of $330,000. He was responsible as tribal head for the purchase of a corporate jet and a minifleet of helicopters.

But Billie also shared his wealth with tribe members, who last year received individual dividend checks of $36,000 from casino profits. And he took care of other Seminole leaders. Under his reign, each councilman had a discretionary fund of at least $5 million; Billie's was $15 million. More was available if needed, and it often was. One councilman ran through $57 million in less than four years.

Ordinarily states have no jurisdiction over sovereign Indian reservations. But if an Indian casino wants to offer Las Vegas–style games—like roulette, baccarat, and blackjack—or slot machines in a state where such gambling is illegal, it must make a regulatory compact with the state. The Seminoles have 3,160 machines that look and perform like slots. Florida, which doesn't allow such high-stakes professional gambling, also known as Class III gaming, says the machines are illegal without a compact and wants the casinos closed down. The Seminoles claim the machines are not slots but "electronic terminals," so the tribe needs no compact. The Clinton Administration, in one of the decisions made as it was turning out the lights on Jan. 19, 2001, issued an order approving the Seminole operation. The incoming Bush Administration promptly rescinded the order pending further study.

But the Seminoles aren't waiting for the Federal Government's go-ahead. They have broken ground for a casino-hotel-entertainment complex with a new partner, Hard Rock Cafe International. The casino-resort, which will also have convention facilities, a beach club, and a spa, will add to the Seminoles' lucrative gaming business. Last year the tribe's two casinos, in Hollywood and Tampa, made a combined profit of $216 million on revenue of $254 million—a return of 85%. By comparison, General Electric, often described by the media as America's best-managed company, reported net income of $13.7 billion for 2001, an 11% return on revenue.

The Santee Sioux casino is a more modest affair. Set on a 200 square mile reservation along the Missouri River in northeast Nebraska, the gambling hall was set up in a converted café and has 60 slot machines. But soon after the casino opened in 1996, federal authorities sought to close it. The issue: the tribe, like the Seminoles, has no compact with the state, though it wasn't for lack of trying.

In the early 1990s the 2,700-member tribe sought a compact with Nebraska to open a casino on the reservation where some 1,000 members still live. Nebraska refused to negotiate. In February 1996, when the only private employer on the reservation, a pharmaceutical company, closed its small plant, the tribe, with 59% of its members living below the poverty line, went ahead anyway, opening the Ohiya Casino and installing Las Vegas–style slot machines. Thelma Thomas, a Santee Sioux who managed the casino, recalls that the tribe thought it had "the inherent sovereign right and legal right" to offer Class III gaming because, she says, "Nebraska would not negotiate a tribal gaming compact after six years of negotiations."

The Indian Gaming Regulatory Act (IGRA), the law governing Indian gambling, seems to support the Santees' decision. The act says, "It is the committee's intent that the compact requirement for Class III not be used as a justification by a state for excluding Indian tribes from such gaming." No matter. The NIGC ordered the tribe to close the casino by May 1996. It did, with the understanding the state would work with the tribe on other economic development ventures.

When the state failed to deliver, the tribe reopened the casino in June. Enter the Department of Justice, which sued to close the operation down. The tribe, reluctant to end its one moneymaking venture, refused. A federal judge imposed a $3,000-a-day levy, then upped it to $6,000. In no time, the tribe owed more than $1 million. Meanwhile, the Justice Department began seizing the tribe's bank accounts, including those containing funds earmarked for child safety seats and nutrition programs for the elderly. It even took money out of individual Indians' accounts. Says Thomas: "They've virtually moved to shut this tribe down—the United States."

The uproar of negative publicity forced the government to return some of the money, but it is still holding most of it. And there is still $4 million in unpaid fines, according to the tribe's attorney, Conly J. Schulte. "The tribe to this day can't use bank accounts for fear that the Federal Government is just going to seize any money," says Schulte. That thwarts the tribe's attempts to invest in any business, even one having nothing to do with gambling.

Casting about for a way out of the dilemma, Schulte and Santee Sioux representatives traveled to Washington in February 2001 to seek the NIGC's guidance. Commission officials advised the tribe to install pseudo slot machines—like those used by the Seminoles—to get around the Class III controversy. The tribe complied—at a substantial economic cost. With the switch to the pseudo slots, Thomas says, revenue has fallen by two-thirds. The casino employs only 15 people, and the income barely covers operating costs. There is no longer any money for tribal programs.

But that's the least of the tribe's worries. The Justice Department sued the tribe again, charging that the machines the NIGC had recommended were actually illegal. A federal judge in Omaha, Neb., disagreed and sided with the Indians and the NIGC. But the Justice Department appealed the ruling and dispatched a squad of high-powered litigators who prosecute organized-crime kingpins to argue the case. Commenting on the Justice Department's actions, Thomas says, "They have done everything they could to make this tribe out to be criminals when all we are is struggling to survive."

Note: With reporting by Laura Karmatz in New York and research by Joan Levinstein, Mitch Frank, and Nadia Mustafa.

MASS MEDIA

38

THE MASS MEDIA
AS A POWER INSTITUTION

MARTIN N. MARGER

This selection by Martin N. Marger is the first of three readings to examine the institution of the mass media. Marger, an adjunct professor of sociology at the University of Windsor, Ontario, Canada, utilizes C. Wright Mills' notion of the power elite in his analysis of the mass media. As Marger argues, even though Mills recognized 50 years ago that the mass media could be an effective tool of manipulation, Mills could not have imagined how powerful the institution of the mass media would become. In fact, Marger situates the media alongside the government and economy as one of the most dominant institutions in society. Marger explains the magnitude of the mass media's authority by analyzing the ownership and control of medical industries, the content of media information, and the effects the mass media have on public opinion and political awareness.

In contemporary societies, the two major institutions of power—government and economy—must be joined by a third—the mass media—to complete any scheme of societal power. Although not formally a part of either government or the economy, the mass media are integrally tied to both, and both rely on the mass media to function as they do. Moreover, the mass media have substantial independent resources that make them a formidable institution of power in their own right.

The Societal Role of the Mass Media

The mass media are of two types: print and electronic. Print media are books, magazines, and newspapers; electronic media are television, radio, and films. To refer to them as *mass* media implies that their communicative realm is extremely broad, often encompassing the entire society. In modern societies, the mass media serve several vital functions. They are agents of socialization, instructing people in the norms and values of their society and generally transmitting the society's culture. They are sources of information, supplying citizens with knowledge about their society and especially about the political economy. They function as propaganda mechanisms through which powerful units of the government and economy seek to persuade the public either to support their policies (government) or to buy their consumer products (corporations). Finally, they serve as agents of legitimacy, generating mass belief in (and acceptance of) dominant political and economic institutions.

Given these vital functions, three queries are of fundamental importance in examining the mass media's power in modern societies. The first concerns their control and accessibility: Who owns or controls the mass media, and how much access to them is afforded individuals and groups in the society? The second question pertains to their content: What do the media present to the public, and who makes decisions regarding that content? The third question concerns the effects of mass media on public opinion and political awareness: To what extent do the mass media shape people's views of events and personalities in their society and the world, and how do the media transmit ideology?

Most media research during the past several decades has focused on the United States. The following discussion, therefore, pertains to the power of the mass media primarily in American society. Most of the patterns and tendencies apparent in the United States, however, are increasingly characteristic of the mass media in other industrial societies.

Media Control and Accessibility

Control and accessibility of the mass media in the United States and increasingly in other industrial societies are determined primarily by the economic context within which the media function and by their place in the political economy.

[In the United States, the mass media operate almost entirely as privately owned enterprises.] In most other industrial societies, newspapers are privately owned but television and radio are at least partially public corporations that compete within a mixed public-private system. Television and radio in Canada, for example, are dominated by the state-run Canadian Broadcasting Corporation (CBC), although there are also several privately owned television and radio networks. A similar system exists in Britain, where the electronic media are a mixture of public and commercial corporations. Only in autocratic societies like China are the media fully state controlled; in these societies, the media are organized and operated to implement the government's social and political policies (Wright 1986). In recent years, there has been a movement in most societies toward the dominance of privately owned and operated electronic media, although the United States remains unique in the extent of private ownership and control. Moreover, although the electronic media are nominally regulated by government, they operate with far fewer restrictions in the United States than in other societies. Meanwhile, a global trend toward convergence of national networks and companies into transnational units is increasingly evident (Schiller 1989).

[The mass media are huge corporations (or parts of corporate conglomerates) whose primary objective, like all enterprises in a capitalist economy, is to maximize their profits.] Like most industries in the American political economy, the mass media are concentrated in a few giant corporate units and thus constitute an oligopoly. Vast multifaceted companies composed of newspaper chains, radio and television stations, and recording, motion-picture, and publishing units dominate the media industry. Among the 1,600 United States daily newspapers, about a dozen corporations control more than half the circulation. The Knight-Ridder chain, for example, owns newspapers throughout the United States with three million in daily circulation, including the *Detroit Free Press,* the *Miami Herald,* the *Philadelphia Inquirer,* and numerous smaller dailies. Gannett owns *USA Today* as well as 88 other dailies with six million in circulation. Although 11,000 individual magazine titles are published in the United States, a handful of corporations derive most of the magazine revenue (Time-Warner alone controls more than 40 percent of magazine business), and among more than 2,500 book publishing companies, a half-dozen corporations sell most books. Three major studios control most of the movie business, and three corporations draw most of the audience and revenue of the television industry (Bagdikian 1989). Edward Herman and Noam Chomsky have identified 24 media giants that basically control the industry. Twenty-three of these companies had assets in excess of $1 billion in 1986, and three-quarters of them earned after-tax profits of over $100 million (Herman and Chomsky 1988).

One must also consider the scope and diversity of these companies' media holdings and activities. Time-Warner, for example, is made up of Warner Brothers Pictures (movies), dozens of popular mass circulation magazines (including *Time* and *Life*), cable television companies, and book companies. NBC is part of the RCA Corporation, which, in turn, is part of General Electric. CBS and Capital Cities/ABC are massive media conglomerates that own numerous television and radio stations, cable television networks, and magazine, recording, book publishing, and motion-picture companies.

Topping off this narrow media concentration are the wire service companies, which accumulate news stories. A large proportion of the items appearing in every mass circulation newspaper in the United States comes from the wires of the Associated Press (AP) or United Press International (UPI). Newspapers subscribe to these services, which become the major source of stories. A few of the larger newspaper companies operate their own wire services and also supply other smaller papers. Thus, in the coverage of national or international news, the difference from one newspaper to another is ordinarily slight. Radio and television news, to a lesser degree, also rely on these wire services.

It is apparent, then, that in the United States, as in most industrial societies, ownership and control of the mass media are extremely concentrated. This concentration parallels the tendency of all political and economic institutions in modern societies to converge into fewer and more powerful units. All other aspects of media power, including their content and effects, are colored by this fact.

In modern societies, to publicly communicate views or ideas requires use of the media. A critical concern, therefore, is not only who owns or controls the media but also who has access to them. In modern societies, only government and big business have the resources—money, authority, and influence—to employ the media regularly and effectively.

As privately owned enterprises, the major goal of the various media is to generate revenue. This objective requires that the media cater primarily to those who can pay to put their views on the air or into print: the major corporations, which use the media primarily to create demand for their products and services through advertising. Consider that a 30-second television commercial on Super Bowl Sunday in 1992 cost $850,000; or that Procter and Gamble spends almost $1.5 billion each year on media advertising. Advertising not only serves to create demand but also provides corporations with a means of creating a positive public image. General Electric, for example, tells the public that "we bring good things to life." Most corporations convey similar messages in which they are portrayed not as profit-seeking enterprises but as compassionate, publicly responsible citizens.

Government access to the media is founded not on financial power but on the fact that the media are closely interwoven with government, particularly at the national level. Put simply, the relationship between government and media is symbiotic; neither can function effectively without the other. As a regulated industry in the United States, the media must take into account the interests of government elites. More importantly, however, the media are heavily dependent on government elites as their major source of political information, which is the core of news. In fact, it is the actions of government elites that dominate news as presented by both print and electronic media. Moreover, much of the news transmitted by the mass media is prepared by government agencies. Studies have indicated that not only are government officials the source of most news but most news stories are drawn from situations over which newsmakers "have either complete or substantial control" (Sigal 1973).

Power elites, particularly those in the realm of government, can easily gain access to the mass media simply because they possess credibility among the public as well as among the media elite. Their accounts of events and policies are more likely to be accepted and thus become part of the news format than accounts and interpretations provided by other sources (Gans 1979). Moreover, in gathering information, the mass media ordinarily follow the path of least resistance; this means relying on official sources for information. As Herman and Chomsky (1988) have noted, "Taking information from sources that may be presumed credible reduces investigative expense, whereas material from sources that are not prima facie credible, or that will elicit criticism and threats, requires careful checking and costly research" (p. 19).

Government elites, however, are equally dependent on the mass media. This dependency stems from their need to employ the media to convey their messages to the public and thus shape and influence public opinion. Political leaders today rarely engage in face-to-face communication with the masses. Instead, they speak primarily through the electronic media in sound bites and project their images through photo opportunities. Political dialogue, particularly at the national level, is increasingly reduced to creating impressions (Postman 1985). This process reaches a high point in the orchestration of pseudo-events, that is, carefully scripted and staged events that are designed to create favorable public images but that have little basis in reality (Boorstin 1961).

Mass Media Content

The mass media exercise considerable power independently of both government and business. This power is particularly significant in their role as gatekeepers of political, economic, and social information—what is ordinarily termed "news." As information gatekeepers, it is the media who define what news is or what is socially significant. As suppliers of vital information, the mass media in modern societies are unequaled. They have become our window on the world, and it is through them that we learn about key events, personalities, and other so-called news. The media, in other words, have become a source of reality itself. As Ben Bagdikian (1971) has put it: "For most of the people of the world, for most of the events of the world, what the news systems do not transmit did not happen. To that extent, the world and its inhabitants are what the news media say they are" (pp. xii–xiii).

Given the media's strong influence on the molding of political, economic, and social reality, a key power issue concerns the decision-making process of news selection and presentation. Like critical decisions of government and the economy, this process is essentially an elite function. Events become newsworthy, and thus of importance to the society, only after they have been selected by the communications elite—editors, journalists, and media executives (Cohen and Young 1973; Epstein 1974; Gans 1979; Tuchman 1978). It is the media elite, therefore, who are largely responsible for molding the public's conception of political, economic, and social events and conditions. The media elite must therefore be added to corporate and governmental elites as top decision makers in the United States and other modern societies.

What are the consequences of this concentration of control over the shaping of sociopolitical reality? Here we must consider the political-economic context of the mass media in the United States and most other modern societies. First, because the major media operate as business enterprises, the media elite, when making content decisions, must take into account the interests of the dominant economic groups—the large corporations—that supply them with revenue. Second, given their symbiotic relationship with government, these decisions must be weighed against the interests of political elites. The result is that ideas or movements outside the political and economic mainstream receive little attention. In U.S. elections, for example, minor parties and candidates are generally treated by the mass media as curiosities, not as legitimate contenders. Hence, political debate is narrowly limited to the two major parties in the mainstream political arena, parties that rarely differ fundamentally on policy or philosophical issues. In short, ruling business and political elites are best situated to exercise influence over the content of the mass media.

With maximum access to the mass media as well as the ability to shape news, elites of the political economy are able not only to place their issues on the political agenda but also to define them in ways "likely to influence their resolution" (Bennett 1988:96). Parties, organizations, and individuals who advocate serious economic or political change but lack financial and political resources have a very difficult time communicating their messages through the mass media. It is true that challenges to established authority are often given attention by newspaper and, particularly, television journalism. But this is due primarily to the fact that "the logic of audience maintenance favors conflict between easily recognizable groups" (Epstein 1974:269). Coverage is not provided in acknowledgment of the legitimacy of challenging groups or to present the substance of their protest (Gitlin 1980).

The emphasis on official perspectives results in limited public understanding of the nature of political, economic, and social problems and how they might be resolved. Rarely do the mass media subject the dominant political economy to serious scrutiny and criticism. "The political world," Lance Bennett (1988) has explained, "becomes a caricature drawn out of unrealistic stereotypes, predictable political postures, and superficial images" (p. 96). Moreover, even when attention is drawn to societal shortcomings by public affairs or news programs or investigative journalists, it is done in the spirit of the dominant ideology. That is, problems are presented as the products of deviant individuals or groups within the context of an otherwise healthy social system. The *systemic* origins of chronic problems are rarely explained or even acknowledged. As David Paletz and Robert Entman (1981) have observed, "The mass media have never given powerless Americans the necessary information to link the ubiquitous rotten apples to the structure of the barrel" (p. 167). Questioning the structure and functioning of dominant political and economic institutions is clearly beyond the capabilities of the mass media (Gans 1979; Gitlin 1980; Parenti 1986).

The bias of mass media content toward the dominant system should not be seen, however, as the result of government and economic elites conspiring with media editors, journalists, and executives. The media elite express dominant values largely unconsciously: They see themselves as objective news commentators, not bearers of opinion. As Herbert Gans (1979) has noted, "The values in the news are rarely explicit and must be found between the lines—in what actors and activities are reported or ignored, and in how they are described" (pp. 39–40). Political objectivity, therefore, is not political neutrality. Critical information presented by the media, in the form of news and public affairs, is framed by dominant values and shaped by power elites, no matter how seemingly objective the presentation may be (Iyengar and Kinder 1987). Moreover, the very notion of objectivity among the media is illusory. As Paletz and Entman (1981) have explained, "To edit is to interpret, to speak is to define, to communicate is to structure reality" (p. 22). Hence, the media, by their very nature, cannot be objective.

The inability of the mass media to present issues to the public in a thorough and critical manner is largely a result of their commercial imperatives. News, like other aspects of mass media, must be sold as a consumer product. This requires that it be presented in an entertainment format and, as Bennett (1988) has explained, be personalized, dramatized, fragmented, and normalized. It is personalized in the sense that it "gives preference to the individual actors and human-interest angles in events while downplaying institutional and political considerations that establish the social contexts for those events" (p. 26). Similarly, the media seek out dramatic events and personalities to which viewers and readers can relate, rather than events and personalities that may be more politically significant though less glamorous and fascinating. The entertainment format of news forces it to be presented in unrelated bits and pieces rather than as a meaningful whole. As a result, news becomes a series of what Neil Postman (1985) has called "decontextualized facts," comparable to background music. Finally, information presented as news is filtered through traditional themes and images of the society, thereby assuring the viewer or reader of the merit of dominant institutions and discrediting challenges to them.

In short, although they may engage in social criticism, the mass media frame their presentations in a way that legitimizes the prevailing political economy. Although there is no blatant censorship of media content in the United States as there is in a totalitarian society, an implicit understanding exists on the part of the media elite regarding their role in upholding the status quo. Self-censorship by the media is reinforced when they anticipate the reactions of political and economic elites and alter their presentations in advance. At times, of course, more blatant attempts at censorship may arise, as when corporate advertisers exert direct pressure to influence the content of the media or when government elites pressure the media to "toe the line" (Gans 1979). Although the media elite may resist these pressures, more often their ideological perspectives are fully compatible with those of political and economic elites, and they may therefore have little inclination to follow a path not basically in line with those views. Moreover, although the media commonly present opposing sides of social and political issues, the two perspectives are only narrowly divergent and the issues are presented in ideo-logically safe stereotypes. The irony of modern communications systems is that despite the profusion of messages with which the citizenry is bom-barded daily, the absence of a thorough exploration of issues by the mass me-dia results in an increasingly uninformed public.

It is also important to consider the essentially passive role of the citizenry in the communications system of most modern societies. In essence, political communication flows only in one direction. The media are virtually unchal-lenged by consumers. There is little effective feedback from those who read newspapers and especially from those who watch television. Thus, as Mills (1956) explained [over] four decades ago, there is a growing tendency for mass media to be tools of manipulation rather than channels for the inter-change of opinion: "In the primary public the competition of opinions goes on between people holding views in the service of their interests and their reasoning. But in the mass society of media markets, competition, if any, goes on between the manipulators with their mass media on the one hand, and the people receiving their propaganda on the other" (p. 305).

[Although viewers and readers, as consumers, can choose not to buy a newspaper or watch a television program, the mass media operate in an oligopolistic market domestically and, increasingly, in an integrated inter-national market. Hence, consumer choices are limited and, in the end, it is the producers—in this case the newspapers and television networks—who make critical decisions about the product and who exercise control over its supply and demand.]

Media Effects

Concentrated media power, in the form of constricted ownership and con-trol of content, does not necessarily guarantee to the users of the media—primarily government and big business—that the effects they desire, that is, public acceptance and internalization of their messages, will be produced. To what extent are the media effective in molding public opinion and shaping people's versions of political and social reality?

Although sociologists and communications experts are not certain about the precise effects of the mass media on socialization or how the media mod-ify the influences of other socializers like the family and the school (Com-stock 1980; Gerbner 1967), it appears that the media are becoming the chief means through which people construct their versions of social reality. Well before the advent of television, Walter Lippmann (1922) explained how the mass media, by selectively reporting and interpreting events and per-sonalities, determine the pictures in our heads (stereotypes, as he referred to them) that shape our social worlds. With the predominance of television, this "reality-shaping" function of the mass media has become much more complete. Television serves increasingly in this capacity because few can escape its influence. Only sleep and work occupy more of Americans' time than television viewing. Most important, the mass media serve as the primary organs of political communication, setting the framework of public discourse, solidifying the legitimacy of powerful institutions and elites, and transmitting the society's dominant ideology.

The mediated version of social reality presented by television, newspapers, and other media is most evident in the communication of news. "News," as has been suggested, is hardly a complete or precise picture of societal or world events. Rather, it is a picture constructed by the media elite who select and interpret events, processes, and personalities. From an almost infinite number of happenings that occur each day, only a few are chosen for transmission as news. Beyond the realm of our personal lives, the issues that concern us are therefore the issues defined for us by the media elite as important and worthy of our attention.

In the early years of research on the effects of mass media on public attitudes and beliefs, the prevalent view was that media had a direct and significant influence. Starting in the 1940s, research seemed to reverse this view, concluding instead that the power of the mass media had been exaggerated. The new perspective held that viewers and readers were not to be seen as a "mass," but rather as individual consumers whose interpretations of media presentations were modified by social class, ethnicity, religion, and other social variables (Lazarsfeld, Berelson, and Gaudet 1948). People exposed themselves to the media selectively, it was suggested, so that media messages generally had the effect of simply reaffirming people's prior beliefs and views. V. O. Key (1964) warned against overestimating the effectiveness of the mass media in conveying the same messages to all people: "The flow of the messages of the mass media," he wrote, "is rather like dropping a handful of confetti from the rim of the Grand Canyon with the object of striking a man astride a burro on the canyon floor. In some measure chance determines which messages reach what targets" (p. 357). This "minimal-effects" view remains today among some media observers. Albert Gollin (1988), for example, has written that "people bring to their encounters with the mass media a formidable array of established habits, motives, social values and perceptual defenses that screen out, derail the intent or limit the force of media messages. The media certainly do affect people in obvious and subtle ways. But no simple 1:1 relationship exists between content or intent and effects" (p. 43).

More recently, researchers have pointed out that the minimal-effects view was based on perceived changes, brought about by the media, in attitudes about political issues. What was overlooked, however, was the impact of mass media on creating a public _awareness_ of issues. This has become known as the "agenda-setting function" of the mass media (McCombs and Shaw 1972). Communications researchers have explained that although television and other mass media may not be overly effective in telling us _what_ to think, they are extremely effective in telling us what and whom to think *about* (Iyengar and Kinder 1987; Shaw and McCombs 1977). Issues emphasized by the media become the issues regarded by viewers and readers as significant. As the media shift their emphasis to new issues, public perceptions change correspondingly. Moreover, Iyengar and Kinder (1987) have suggested a kind of media power that goes one step beyond agenda setting, which they call "priming." Priming refers to changes in the standards that people use in making political choices and judgments. As news, especially television news, shifts its attention from one issue to another, governments and political leaders are judged on their performance regarding those issues. Thus, by drawing attention to some aspects of political life at the expense of others, television helps bring to mind certain bits of political memory while others are ignored.

The mass media not only transmit descriptions of events and personalities but, more importantly, they convey the society's dominant ideology. It is in this sense that the media are agents of social control, used by power elites not only to communicate and legitimize their policies and actions but to stabilize the political and economic systems by generating allegiance among the public. As Todd Gitlin (1980) has explained:

> The media bring a manufactured public world into private space. From within their private crevices, people find themselves relying on the media for concepts, for images of their heroes, for guiding information, for emotional charges, for a recognition of public values, for symbols in general, even for language. Of all the institutions of daily life, the media specialize in orchestrating everyday consciousness—by virtue of their pervasiveness, their accessibility, their centralized symbolic capacity. They name the world's parts, they certify reality *as* reality—and when their certifications are doubted and opposed, as they surely are, it is those same certifications that limit the terms of effective opposition. To put it simply: the mass media have become core systems for the distribution of ideology. (Pp. 1–2)

We should not assume that the presentation of news is the mass media's only way of creating support for the society's dominant ideology and institutions. In modern societies, news and public affairs represent only a small portion of all media fare, particularly of television. The remaining entertainment, and especially the advertising that constantly accompanies it, is no less reflective and supportive of the society's prevailing value system (Bagdikian 1983; Goldsen 1977; Parenti 1986).

In recognizing the enormous power of mass media in modern societies to portray a particular version of reality, it should be understood that this is not consummate power. The ability of the media to propagate dominant values and shape political reality is by no means absolute. More specialized media (i.e., non–mass media), especially books and magazines, regularly present alternative and dissenting views. Moreover, dissident views are given coverage by the mass media once those views have gained at least some credibility. Nor can the media create problems that are nonexistent or conceal those that do exist (Iyengar and Kinder 1987).

Acknowledging the less-than-total power of mass media to influence people's social and political worlds, however, should not lead to an underestimation of the power of this institution. In all modern societies, control of information is critical: Whoever controls the means of communication has great power. Marx posited that those who control the society's means of material production are the most powerful. It might be claimed that in modern societies, great power hinges on control of the means of information—the media. This is the reason that political and economic elites make great efforts to dominate the media and to control the flow of information. Those who exert significant control over the media or who can freely gain access to them are able to exercise great influence in determining the views, images, and ideas that will become part of the public consciousness.

REFERENCES

Bagdikian, Ben. 1971. *The Information Machines.* New York: Harper & Row.
———. 1983. *The Media Monopoly.* Boston: Beacon.
———. 1989. "Missing from the News." *The Progressive* 53 (August): 32–34.
Bennett, W. Lance. 1988. *News: The Politics of Illusion.* 2d ed. New York: Longman.
Boorstin, Daniel J. 1961. *The Image: A Guide to Pseudo-Events in America.* New York: Harper & Row.
Cohen, Stanley and Jock Young, eds. 1973. *The Manufacture of News.* London: Constable.
Comstock, George. 1980. "The Impact of Television on American Institutions." Pp. 28–44 in *Readings in Mass Communication: Concepts and Issues in the Mass Media,* edited by Michael Emery and Ted Curtis Smythe. 4th ed. Dubuque, IA: Wm. C. Brown.
Epstein, Edwin Jay. 1974. *News from Nowhere.* New York: Vintage.
Gans, Herbert J. 1979. *Deciding What's News.* New York: Pantheon.
Gerbner, G. 1967. "An Institutional Approach to Mass Communications Research." Pp. 429–51 in *Communication: Theory and Research,* edited by L. Thayer. Springfield, IL: Charles C. Thomas.
Gitlin, Todd. 1980. *The Whole World Is Watching.* Berkeley: University of California Press.
Goldsen, Rose K. 1977. *The Show and Tell Machine: How Television Works and Works You Over.* New York: Dell.
Gollin, Albert E. 1988. "Media Power: On Closer Inspection, It's Not That Threatening." Pp. 41–44 in *Impacts of Mass Media,* edited by Ray Eldon Hiebert and Carol Reuss. 2d ed. New York: Longman.
Herman, Edward S. and Noam Chomsky. 1988. *Manufacturing Consent: The Political Economy of the Mass Media.* New York: Pantheon.
Iyengar, Shanto and Donald R. Kinder. 1987. *News That Matters: Television and American Opinion.* Chicago: University of Chicago Press.
Key, V. O., Jr. 1964. *Public Opinion and American Democracy.* New York: Knopf.
Lazarsfeld, Paul, Bernard Berelson, and H. Gaudet. 1948. *The People's Choice.* New York: Columbia University Press.
Lippmann, Walter. 1922. *Public Opinion.* New York: Macmillan.
McCombs, Maxwell and Donald Shaw. 1972. "The Agenda-Setting Function of Mass Media." *Public Opinion Quarterly* 36:176–87.

Mills, C. Wright. 1956. *The Power Elite*. New York: Oxford University Press.
Paletz, David L. and Robert M. Entman. 1981. *Media Power Politics*. New York: Free Press.
Parenti, Michael. 1986. *Inventing Reality: The Politics of the Mass Media*. New York: St. Martin's.
Postman, Neil. 1985. *Amusing Ourselves to Death: Public Discourse in the Age of Show Business*. New York: Penguin.
Schiller, Herbert I. 1989. *Culture, Inc.: The Corporate Takeover of Public Expression*. New York: Oxford University Press.
Shaw, Donald L. and Maxwell E. McCombs. 1977. *The Emergence of American Political Issues: The Agenda-Setting Function of the Press*. St. Paul, MN: West Publishers.
Sigal, Leon V. 1973. *Reporters and Officials: The Organization and Politics of News Reporting*. Lexington, MA: Heath.
Tuchman, Gaye. 1978. *Making News*. New York: Free Press.
Wright, Charles R. 1986. *Mass Communication: A Sociological Perspective*. 3d ed. New York: Random House.

39

MEDIA MAGIC
Making Class Invisible

GREGORY MANTSIOS

This second selection on the institution of the mass media is by Gregory Mantsios. Mantsios argues that the mass media is a powerful institution not only because it is the most influential in molding public consciousness but because the ownership and control of the mass media is highly concentrated. Think of the AOL-Time Warner merger in recent years as one example of a media giant. In addition to owning networks, publishing houses, newspapers, and so on, AOL-Time Warner also owns the CNN news affiliate. This concentration of ownership ensures little diversity in the messages that the media promotes. For example, one way the mass media shapes culture and public opinion is in the portrayals of social class. In the excerpt below, Mantsios examines the portrayals of social class in American media.

O f the various social and cultural forces in our society, the mass media is arguably the most influential in molding public consciousness. Americans spend an average twenty-eight hours per week watching television. They also spend an undetermined number of hours reading periodicals, listening to the radio, and going to the movies. Unlike other cultural

Reprinted by permission of Gregory Mantsios.

and socializing institutions, ownership and control of the mass media is highly concentrated. Twenty-three corporations own more than one-half of all the daily newspapers, magazines, movie studios, and radio and television outlets in the United States.[1] The number of media companies is shrinking and their control of the industry is expanding. And a relatively small number of media outlets is producing and packaging the majority of news and entertainment programs. For the most part, our media is national in nature and single-minded (profit-oriented) in purpose. This media plays a key role in defining our cultural tastes, helping us locate ourselves in history, establishing our national identity, and ascertaining the range of national and social possibilities. In this essay, we will examine the way the mass media shapes how people think about each other and about the nature of our society.

The United States is the most highly stratified society in the industrialized world. Class distinctions operate in virtually every aspect of our lives, determining the nature of our work, the quality of our schooling, and the health and safety of our loved ones. Yet remarkably, we, as a nation, retain illusions about living in an egalitarian society. We maintain these illusions, in large part, because the media hides gross inequities from public view. In those instances when inequities are revealed, we are provided with messages that obscure the nature of class realities and blame the victims of class-dominated society for their own plight. Let's briefly examine what the news media, in particular, tells us about class.

About the Poor

The news media provides meager coverage of poor people and poverty. The coverage it does provide is often distorted and misleading.

The Poor Do Not Exist

For the most part, the news media ignores the poor. Unnoticed are forty million poor people in the nation—a number that equals the entire population of Maine, Vermont, New Hampshire, Connecticut, Rhode Island, New Jersey, and New York combined. Perhaps even more alarming is that the rate of poverty is increasing twice as fast as the population growth in the United States. Ordinarily, even a calamity of much smaller proportion (e.g., flooding in the Midwest) would garner a great deal of coverage and hype from a media usually eager to declare a crisis, yet less than one in five hundred articles in the *New York Times* and one in one thousand articles listed in the *Reader's Guide to Periodic Literature* are on poverty. With remarkably little attention to them, the poor and their problems are hidden from most Americans.

When the media does turn its attention to the poor, it offers a series of contradictory messages and portrayals.

The Poor Are Faceless

Each year the Census Bureau releases a new report on poverty in our society and its results are duly reported in the media. At best, however, this coverage emphasizes annual fluctuations (showing how the numbers differ from previous years) and ongoing debates over the validity of the numbers (some argue the number should be lower, most that the number should be higher). Coverage like this desensitizes us to the poor by reducing poverty to a number. It ignores the human tragedy of poverty—the suffering, indignities, and misery endured by millions of children and adults. Instead, the poor become statistics rather than people.

The Poor Are Undeserving

When the media does put a face on the poor, it is not likely to be a pretty one. The media will provide us with sensational stories about welfare cheats, drug addicts, and greedy panhandlers (almost always urban and black). Compare these images and the emotions evoked by them with the media's treatment of middle-class (usually white) "tax evaders," celebrities who have a "chemical dependency," or wealthy businesspeople who use unscrupulous means to "make a profit." While the behavior of the more affluent offenders is considered an "impropriety" and a deviation from the norm, the behavior of the poor is considered repugnant, indicative of the poor in general, and worthy of our indignation and resentment.

The Poor Are an Eyesore

When the media does cover the poor, they are often presented through the eyes of the middle class. For example, sometimes the media includes a story about community resistance to a homeless shelter or storekeeper annoyance with panhandlers. Rather than focusing on the plight of the poor, these stories are about middle-class opposition to the poor. Such stories tell us that the poor are an inconvenience and an irritation.

The Poor Have Only Themselves to Blame

In another example of media coverage, we are told that the poor live in a personal and cultural cycle of poverty that hopelessly imprisons them. They routinely center on the black urban population and focus on perceived personality or cultural traits that doom the poor. While the women in these stories typically exhibit an "attitude" that leads to trouble or a promiscuity that leads to single motherhood, the men possess a need for immediate gratification that leads to drug abuse or an unquenchable greed that leads to the pursuit of fast money. The images that are seared into our mind are sexist, racist, and classist. Census figures reveal that most of the poor are white not black or Hispanic, that they live in rural or suburban areas not urban centers, and hold jobs at least part of the year.² Yet, in a fashion that is often framed in an understanding and sympathetic tone, we are told that the poor have inflicted poverty on themselves.

The Poor Are Down on Their Luck

During the Christmas season, the news media sometimes provides us with accounts of poor individuals or families (usually white) who are down on their luck. These stories are often linked to stories about soup kitchens or other charitable activities and sometimes call for charitable contributions. These "Yule time" stories are as much about the affluent as they are about the poor: they tell us that the affluent in our society are a kind, understanding, giving people—which we are not.³ The series of unfortunate circumstances that have led to impoverishment are presumed to be a temporary condition that will improve with time and a change in luck.

Despite appearances, the messages provided by the media are not entirely disparate. With each variation, the media informs us what poverty is not (i.e., systemic and indicative of American society) by informing us what it is. The media tells us that poverty is either an aberration of the American way of life (it doesn't exist, it's just another number, it's unfortunate but temporary) or an end product of the poor themselves (they are a nuisance, do not deserve better, and have brought their predicament upon themselves).

By suggesting that the poor have brought poverty upon themselves, the media is engaging in what William Ryan has called "blaming the victim."⁴ The media identifies in what ways the poor are different as a consequence of deprivation, then defines those differences as the cause of poverty itself. Whether blatantly hostile or cloaked in sympathy, the message is that there is something fundamentally wrong with the victims—their hormones, psychological makeup, family environment, community, race, or some combination of these—that accounts for their plight and their failure to lift themselves out of poverty.

But poverty in the United States is systemic. It is a direct result of economic and political policies that deprive people of jobs, adequate wages, or legitimate support. It is neither natural nor inevitable: there is enough wealth in our nation to eliminate poverty if we chose to redistribute existing wealth or income. The plight of the poor is reason enough to make the elimination of poverty the nation's first priority. But poverty also impacts dramatically on the nonpoor. It has a dampening effect on wages in general (by maintaining a reserve army of unemployed and underemployed anxious for any job at any wage) and breeds crime and violence (by maintaining conditions that invite private gain by illegal means and rebellion-like behavior, not entirely unlike the urban riots of the 1960s). Given the extent of poverty in the nation and the impact it has on us all, the media must spin considerable magic to keep the poor and the issue of poverty and its root causes out of the public consciousness.

About Everyone Else

Both the broadcast and the print news media strive to develop a strong sense of "we-ness" in their audience. They seek to speak to and for an audience that is both affluent and like-minded. The media's solidarity with affluence, that is, with the middle and upper class, varies little from one medium to another. Benjamin DeMott points out, for example, that the *New York Times* understands affluence to be intelligence, taste, public spirit, responsibility, and a readiness to rule and "conceives itself as spokesperson for a readership awash in these qualities."[5] Of course, the flip side to creating a sense of "we," or "us," is establishing a perception of the "other." The other relates back to the faceless, amoral, undeserving, and inferior "underclass." Thus, the world according to the news media is divided between the "underclass" and everyone else. Again the messages are often contradictory.

The Wealthy Are Us

Much of the information provided to us by the news media focuses attention on the concerns of a very wealthy and privileged class of people. Although the concerns of a small fraction of the populace, they are presented as though they were the concerns of everyone. For example, while relatively few people actually own stock, the news media devotes an inordinate amount of broadcast time and print space to business news and stock market quotations. Not only do business reports cater to a particular narrow clientele, so do the fashion pages (with $2,000 dresses), wedding announcements, and the obituaries. Even weather and sports news often have a class bias. An all-news radio station in New York City, for example, provides regular national ski reports. International news, trade agreements, and domestic policies issues are also reported in terms of their impact on business climate and the business community. Besides being of practical value to the wealthy, such coverage has considerable ideological value. Its message: the concerns of the wealthy are the concerns of us all.

The Wealthy (as a Class) Do Not Exist

While preoccupied with the concerns of the wealthy, the media fails to notice the way in which the rich as a class of people create and shape domestic and foreign policy. Presented as an aggregate of individuals, the wealthy appear without special interests, interconnections, or unity in purpose. Out of public view are the class interests of the wealthy, the interlocking business links, the concerted actions to preserve their class privileges and business interests (by running for public office, supporting political candidates, lobbying, etc.). Corporate lobbying is ignored, taken for granted, or assumed to be in the public interest. (Compare this with the media's portrayal of the "strong arm of labor" in attempting to defeat trade legislation that is harmful to the interests of working people.) It is estimated that two-thirds of the U.S. Senate is composed of millionaires.[6] Having such a preponderance of millionaires in the Senate, however, is perceived to be neither unusual nor anti-democratic; these millionaire senators are assumed to be serving "our" collective interests in governing.

The Wealthy Are Fascinating and Benevolent

The broadcast and print media regularly provide hype for individuals who have achieved "super" success. These stories are usually about celebrities and superstars from the sports and entertainment world. Society pages and gossip columns serve to keep the social elite informed of each others' doings, allow the rest of us to gawk at their excesses, and help to keep the American dream alive. The print media is also fond of feature stories on corporate empire builders. These stories provide an occasional "insider's" view of the private and corporate life of industrialists by suggesting a rags-to-riches account of corporate success. These stories tell us that corporate success is a series of smart moves, shrewd acquisitions, timely mergers, and well thought out executive suite shuffles. By painting the upper class in a positive light, innocent of any wrongdoing (labor leaders and union organizations usually get the opposite treatment), the media assures us that wealth and power are benevolent. One person's capital accumulation is presumed to be good for all. The elite, then, are portrayed as investment wizards, people of special talent and skill, whom even their victims (workers and consumers) can admire.

The Wealthy Include a Few Bad Apples

On rare occasions, the media will mock selected individuals for their personality flaws. Real estate investor Donald Trump and New York Yankees owner George Steinbrenner, for example, are admonished by the media for deliberately seeking publicity (a very un–upper class thing to do); hotel owner Leona Helmsley was caricatured for her personal cruelties; and junk-bond broker Michael Milkin was condemned because he had the audacity to rob the rich. Michael Parenti points out that by treating business wrongdoings as isolated deviations from the socially beneficial system of "responsible capitalism," the media overlooks the features of the system that produce such abuses and the regularity with which they occur. Rather than portraying them as predictable and frequent outcomes of corporate power and the business system, the media treats abuses as if they were isolated and atypical. Presented as an occasional aberration, these incidents serve not to challenge, but to legitimate, the system.[7]

The Middle Class Is Us

By ignoring the poor and blurring the lines between the working people and the upper class, the news media creates a universal middle class. From this perspective, the size of one's income becomes largely irrelevant: what matters is that most of "us" share an intellectual and moral superiority over the disadvantaged. As *Time* magazine once concluded, "Middle America is a state of mind."[8] "We are all middle class," we are told, "and we all share the same concerns": job security, inflation, tax burdens, world peace, the cost of food and housing, health care, clean air and water, and the safety of our streets. While the concerns of the wealthy are quite distinct from those of the middle class (e.g., the wealthy worry about investments, not jobs), the media convinces us that "we [the affluent] are all in this together."

The Middle Class Is a Victim

For the media, "we" the affluent not only stand apart from the "other"—the poor, the working class, the minorities, and their problems—"we" are also victimized by the poor (who drive up the costs of maintaining the welfare rolls), minorities (who commit crimes against us), and by workers (who are greedy and drive companies out and prices up). Ignored are the subsidies to the rich, the crimes of corporate America, and the policies that wreak havoc on the economic well-being of middle America. Media magic convinces us to fear, more than anything else, being victimized by those less affluent than ourselves.

The Middle Class Is Not a Working Class

The news media clearly distinguishes the middle class (employees) from the working class (i.e., blue-collar workers) who are portrayed, at best, as irrelevant, outmoded, and a dying breed. Furthermore, the media will tell us that the hardships faced by blue-collar workers are inevitable (due to progress), a result of bad luck (chance circumstances in a particular industry), or a product of their own doing (they priced themselves out of a job). Given the media's presentation of reality, it is hard to believe that manual, supervised, unskilled, and semiskilled workers actually represent more than 50 percent of the adult working population.[9] The working class, instead, is relegated by the media to "the other."

In short, the news media either lionizes the wealthy or treats their interests and those of the middle class as one in the same. But the upper class and the middle class do not share the same interests or worries. Members of the upper class worry about stock dividends (not employment), they profit from inflation and global militarism, their children attend exclusive private schools, they eat and live in a royal fashion, they call on (or are called upon by) personal physicians, they have few consumer problems, they can escape whenever they want from environmental pollution, and they live on streets and travel to other areas under the protection of private police forces.[10]

The wealthy are not only a class with distinct lifestyles and interests, they are a ruling class. They receive a disproportionate share of the country's yearly income, own a disproportionate amount of the country's wealth, and contribute a disproportionate number of their members to governmental bodies and decision-making groups—all traits that William Domhoff, in his classic work *Who Rules America?*, defined as characteristic of a governing class.[11]

This governing class maintains and manages our political and economic structures in such a way that these structures continue to yield an amazing proportion of our wealth to a minuscule upper class. While the media is not above referring to ruling classes in other countries (we hear, for example, references to Japan's ruling elite),[12] its treatment of the news proceeds as though there were no such ruling class in the United States.

Furthermore, the news media inverts reality so that those who are working class and middle class learn to fear, resent, and blame those below, rather than those above, them in the class structure. We learn to resent welfare, which accounts for only two cents out of every dollar in the federal budget (approximately $10 billion) and provides financial relief for the needy,[13] but learn little about the $11 billion the federal government spends on individuals with incomes in excess of $1,000,000 (not needy),[14] or the $17 billion in farm subsidies, or the $214 billion (twenty times the cost of welfare) in interest payments to financial institutions.

Middle-class whites learn to fear African Americans and Latinos, but most violent crime occurs within poor and minority communities and is neither interracial[15] nor interclass. As horrid as such crime is, it should not mask the destruction and violence perpetrated by corporate America. In spite of the fact that 14,000 innocent people are killed on the job each year, 100,000 die prematurely, 400,000 become seriously ill, and 6 million are injured from work-related accidents and diseases, most Americans fear government regulation more than they do unsafe working conditions.

Through the media, middle-class—and even working class—Americans learn to blame blue-collar workers and their unions for declining purchasing power and economic security. But while workers who managed to keep their jobs and their unions struggled to keep up with inflation, the top 1 percent of American families saw their average incomes soar 80 percent in the last decade.[16] Much of the wealth at the top was accumulated as stockholders and corporate executives moved their companies abroad to employ cheaper labor (56 cents per hour in El Salvador) and avoid paying taxes in the United States. Corporate America is a world made up of ruthless bosses, massive layoffs, favoritism and nepotism, health and safety violations, pension plan losses, union busting, tax evasions, unfair competition, and price gouging, as well as fast-buck deals, financial speculation, and corporate wheeling and dealing that serve the interests of the corporate elite, but are generally wasteful and destructive to workers and the economy in general.

It is no wonder Americans cannot think straight about class. The mass media is neither objective, balanced, independent, nor neutral. Those who own and direct the mass media are themselves part of the upper class, and neither they nor the ruling class in general have to conspire to manipulate public opinion. Their interest is in preserving the status quo, and their view of society as fair and equitable comes naturally to them. But their ideology dominates our society and justifies what is in reality a perverse social order—one that perpetuates unprecedented elite privilege and power on the one hand and widespread deprivation on the other. A mass media that did not have its own class interests in preserving the status quo would acknowledge that inordinate wealth and power undermines democracy and that a "free market" economy can ravage a people and their communities.

ENDNOTES

[1] Martin Lee and Norman Solomon, *Unreliable Sources* (New York: Lyle Stuart, 1990), p. 71. See also Ben Bagdikian, *The Media Monopoly* (Boston: Beacon Press, 1990).

[2] Department of Commerce, Bureau of the Census, "Poverty in the United States: 1992," *Current Population Reports, Consumer Income,* Series P60–185, pp. xi, xv. 1.

[3] American households with incomes of less than $10,000 give an average of 5.5 percent of their earnings to charity or to a religious organization, while those making more than $100,000 a year give only 2.9 percent. After changes in the 1986 tax code reduced the benefits of charitable giving, taxpayers earning $500,000 or more slashed their average donation by nearly one-third. Furthermore, many of these acts of benevolence do not help the needy. Rather than provide funding to social service agencies that aid the poor, the voluntary contributions of the wealthy go to places and institutions that entertain, inspire, cure, or educate wealthy Americans—art museums, opera houses, theaters, orchestras, ballet companies, private hospitals, and elite universities. (Robert Reich, "Secession of the Successful," *New York Times Magazine,* February 17, 1991, p. 43.)

[4] William Ryan, *Blaming the Victim* (New York: Vintage, 1971).

[5] Benjamin DeMott, *The Imperial Middle* (New York: William Morrow, 1990), p. 123.

[6] Fred Barnes, "The Zillionaires Club," *The New Republic,* January 29, 1990, p. 24.

[7] Michael Parenti, *Inventing Reality* (New York: St. Martin's Press, 1986), p. 109.

[8] *Time,* January 5, 1979, p. 10.

[9] Vincent Navarro, "The Middle Class—A Useful Myth," *The Nation,* March 23, 1992, p. 1.

[10] Charles Anderson, *The Political Economy of Social Class* (Englewood Cliffs, NJ: Prentice Hall, 1974), p. 137. The number of private security guards in the United States now exceeds the number of public police officers. (Robert Reich, "Secession of the Successful," *New York Times Magazine,* February 17, 1991, p. 42.)

[11] William Domhoff, *Who Rules America?* (Englewood Cliffs, NJ: Prentice Hall, 1967), p. 5.

[12] Lee and Solomon, *Unreliable Sources,* p. 179.

[13] A total of $20 billion is spent on welfare when you include all state funding. But the average state funding also comes to only two cents per state dollar.

[14] *Newsweek,* August 10, 1992, p. 57.

[15] In 92 percent of the murders nationwide, the assailant and the victim are of the same race (46 percent are white/white, 46 percent are black/black), 5.6 percent are black on white, and 2.4 percent are white on black. (FBI and Bureau of Justice Statistics, 1985–1986, quoted in Raymond S. Franklin, *Shadows of Race and Class* [Minneapolis: University of Minnesota Press, 1991], p. 108.)

[16] *Business Week,* June 8, 1992, p. 86.

40

MEDIA UNLIMITED
How the Torrent of Images and Sounds Overwhelms Our Lives

TODD GITLIN

Todd Gitlin, professor of culture, journalism, and sociology at New York University, has researched the mass media for a number of years. His most recent book, Media Unlimited: How the Torrent of Images and Sounds Overwhelms Our Lives (2001), examines how American mass media not only defines and dominates culture in the United States, but also how it defies national boundaries and overwhelms other cultures in the world. The excerpt below describes the global diaspora of American mass media and the effects it has on other cultures.

Everywhere, the media flow defies national boundaries. This is one of its obvious, but at the same time amazing, features. A global torrent is not, of course, the master metaphor to which we have grown accustomed. We're more accustomed to Marshall McLuhan's *global village.* Those who resort to this metaphor casually often forget that if the world is a global village, some live in mansions on the hill, others in huts. Some dispatch images and sounds around town at the touch of a button; others collect them at the touch of *their* buttons. Yet McLuhan's image reveals an indispensable half-truth. If there is a village, it speaks American. It wears jeans, drinks Coke, eats at the golden arches, walks on swooshed shoes, plays electric guitars, recognizes Mickey Mouse, James Dean, E.T., Bart Simpson, R2-D2, and Pamela Anderson.

At the entrance to the champagne cellar of Piper-Heidsieck in Reims, in eastern France, a plaque declares that the cellar was dedicated by Marie Antoinette. The tour is narrated in six languages, and at the end you walk back upstairs into a museum featuring photographs of famous people drinking champagne. And who are they? Perhaps members of today's royal houses, presidents or prime ministers, economic titans or Nobel Prize winners? Of course not. They are movie stars, almost all of them American—Marilyn Monroe to Clint Eastwood. The symmetry of the exhibition is obvious, the premise unmistakable: Hollywood stars, champions of consumption, are the royalty of this century, more popular by far than poor doomed Marie.

Hollywood is the global cultural capital—capital in both senses. The United States presides over a sort of World Bank of styles and symbols, an International Cultural Fund of images, sounds, and celebrities. The goods may be distributed by American-, Canadian-, European-, Japanese-, or Australian-owned multinational corporations, but their styles, themes, and images do not detectably change when a new board of directors takes over. Entertainment is one of America's top exports. In 1999, in fact, film, television, music, radio, advertising, print publishing, and computer software together *were* the top export, almost $80 billion worth, and while software alone accounted for $50 billion of the total, some of that category also qualifies as entertainment—video games and pornography, for example.[1] Hardly anyone is exempt from the force of American images and sounds. French resentment of Mickey Mouse, Bruce Willis, and the rest of American civilization is well known. Less well known, and rarely acknowledged by the French, is the fact that *Terminator 2* sold 5 million tickets in France during the month it opened—with no submachine guns at the heads of the customers. The same culture minister, Jack Lang, who in 1982 achieved a moment of predictable notoriety in the United States for declaring that *Dallas* amounted to cultural imperialism, also conferred France's highest honor in the arts on Elizabeth Taylor and Sylvester Stallone. The point is not hypocrisy pure and simple but something deeper, something obscured by a single-minded emphasis on American power: dependency. American popular culture is the nemesis that hundreds of millions—perhaps billions—of people love, and love to hate. The antagonism and the dependency are inseparable, for the media flood—essentially American in its origin, but virtually unlimited in its reach—represents, like it or not, a common imagination.

How shall we understand the Hong Kong T-shirt that says "I Feel Coke"? Or the little Japanese girl who asks an American visitor in all innocence, "Is there really a Disneyland in America?" (She knows the one in Tokyo.) Or the experience of a German television reporter sent to Siberia to film indigenous life, who after flying out of Moscow and then traveling for days by boat, bus, and jeep, arrives near the Arctic Sea where live a tribe of Tungusians known to ethnologists for their bearskin rituals. In the community store sits a grandfather with his grandchild on his knee. Grandfather is dressed in traditional Tungusian clothing. Grandson has on his head a reversed baseball cap.[2]

American popular culture is the closest approximation today to a global lingua franca, drawing the urban and young in particular into a common cultural zone where they share some dreams of freedom, wealth, comfort, innocence, and power—and perhaps most of all, youth as a state of mind. In general, despite the rhetoric of "identity," young people do not live in monocultures. They are not monocular. They are both local and cosmopolitan. Cultural bilingualism is routine. Just as their "cultures" are neither hard-wired nor uniform, so there is no simple way in which they are "Americanized," though there are American tags on their experience—low-cost links to status and fun.[3] Everywhere, fun lovers, efficiency seekers, Americaphiles, and Americaphobes alike pass through the portals of Disney and the arches of McDonald's wearing Levi's jeans and Gap jackets. Mickey Mouse and Donald Duck, John Wayne, Marilyn Monroe, James Dean, Bob Dylan, Michael Jackson, Madonna, Clint Eastwood, Bruce Willis, the multicolor chorus of Coca-Cola, and the next flavor of the month or the universe are the icons of a curious sort of one-world sensibility, a global semiculture. America's bid for global unification surpasses in reach that of the Romans, the British, the Catholic Church, or Islam; though without either an army or a God, it requires less. The Tungusian boy with the reversed cap on his head does not automatically think of it as "American," let alone side with the U.S. Army.

The misleadingly easy answer to the question of how American images and sounds became omnipresent is: American imperialism. But the images are not even faintly force-fed by American corporate, political, or military power. The empire strikes from inside the spectator as well as from outside. This is a conundrum that deserves to be approached with respect if we are to grasp the fact that Mickey Mouse and Coke are everywhere recognized and often enough *enjoyed*. In the peculiar unification at work throughout the world, there is surely a supply side, but there is not only a supply side. Some things are true even if multinational corporations claim so: there is demand.

What do American icons and styles mean to those who are not American? We can only imagine—but let us try. What young people graced with disposable income encounter in American television shows, movies, soft drinks, theme parks, and American-labeled (though not American-manufactured) running shoes, T-shirts, baggy pants, ragged jeans, and so on, is a way of being in the world, the experience of a flow of ready feelings and sensations bobbing up, disposable, dissolving, segueing to the next and the next after that—all in all, the kinetic feel that I have tried to describe in [my research]. It is a quality of immediacy and casualness not so different from what Americans desire. But what the young experience in the video-game arcade or the music megastore is more than the flux of sensation. They flirt with a loose sort of social membership that requires little but a momentary (and monetary) surrender. Sampling American goods, images, and sounds, they affiliate with an empire of informality. Consuming a commodity, wearing a slogan or a logo, you affiliate with disaffiliation. You make a limited-liability connection, a virtual one. You borrow some of the effervescence that is supposed to emanate from this American staple, and hope to be recognized as one of the elect. When you wear the Israeli version that spells *Coca-Cola* in Hebrew, you express some worldwide connection with unknown peers, or a sense of irony, or both—in any event, a marker of membership. In a world of ubiquitous images, of easy mobility and casual tourism, you get to feel not only local or national but global—without locking yourself in a box so confining as to deserve the name "identity."

We are seeing on a world scale the familiar infectious rhythm of modernity. The money economy extends its reach, bringing with it a calculating mentality. Even in the poor countries it stirs the same hunger for private feeling, the same taste for disposable labels and sensations on demand, the same attention to fashion, the new and the now, that cropped up earlier in the West. Income beckons; income rewards. The taste for the marketed spectacle and the media-soaked way of life spreads. The culture consumer may not like the American goods in particular but still acquires a taste for the media's speed, formulas, and frivolity. Indeed, the lightness of American-sponsored "identity" is central to its appeal. It imposes few burdens. Attachments and affiliations coexist, overlap, melt together, form, and re-form.

Marketers, like nationalists and fundamentalists, promote "identities," but for most people, the mélange is the message. Traditional bonds bend under pressure from imports. Media from beyond help you have your "roots" and eat them, too. You can watch Mexican television in the morning and American in the afternoon, or graze between Kurdish and English. You can consolidate family ties with joint visits to Disney World—making Orlando, Florida, the major tourist destination in the United States, and the Tokyo and Marne-la-Vallée spin-offs massive attractions in Japan and France. You can attach to your parents, or children, by playing oldie music and exchanging sports statistics. You plunge back into the media flux, looking for—what? Excitement? Some low-cost variation on known themes? Some next new thing? You don't know just what, but you will when you see it—or if not, you'll change channels. . . .

The Supply Side

About the outward thrust of the American culture industry there is no mystery. The mainspring is the classic drive to expand markets. In the latter half of the 1980s, with worldwide deregulation, export sales increased from 30 percent to 40 percent of Hollywood's total revenue for television and film. Since then, the percentages have stabilized.[4] In 2000, total foreign revenues for all film and video revenue streams averaged 37 percent—for theatrical releases, 51 percent; for television, 41 percent; and for video, 27 percent.[5]

Exporters benefit from the economies of scale afforded by serial production. American industrialists have long excelled at efficiencies, first anticipating and later developing the standardized production techniques of Henry Ford's assembly line. Early in the nineteenth century, minstrel shows were already being assembled from standardized components.[6] Such efficiencies were later applied to burlesque, melodrama, vaudeville, radio soap opera, comic books, genre literature, musical comedy, and Hollywood studio productions. Cultural formula is not unique to the United States, but Americans were particularly adept at mass-producing it, using centralized management to organize road shows and coordinate local replicas.

If the American culture industry has long depended on foreign markets, foreign markets now also depend on American formulas: Westerns, action heroes, rock music, hip-hop. Globalized distribution expedites imitation. The American way generates proven results. Little imagination is required to understand why global entertainment conglomerates copy proven recipes or why theater owners outside the United States (many of whom are themselves American) want to screen them, even if they exaggerate the degree to which formula guarantees success. In a business freighted with uncertainty, the easiest decision is to copy. Individuals making careers also want to increase their odds of success. . . .

American industrial advantages have been especially potent in movies and television, where mass promotion is linked to mass production, and language and local traditions are not as significant as in popular music. Compared with European rivals, Hollywood has the tremendous advantage of starting with a huge domestic market. Once the movie or TV show is made, each additional copy is cheap—by local standards, often ridiculously cheap. In the early 1980s, Danish television could lease a one-hour episode of *Dallas* for the cost of producing a single original *minute* of Danish drama. In television exports, Brazilian and Mexican soap operas rival American products; the Japanese remain dominant in the production and distribution of video games; and it is not inconceivable that other export powerhouses will develop. Still, for the moment, American exports predominate.

The Demand Side

But the supply-side argument won't suffice to explain global cultural dominance. American popular culture is not uniquely formulaic or transportable. . . . Moreover, availability is not popularity. No one forced Danes to watch *Dallas*, however cheaply purchased. In fact, when a new television entertainment chief took charge in 1981–82 and proceeded to cancel the show, thirty thousand protest letters poured in, and hundreds of Danes (mostly women, many rural) demonstrated in Copenhagen.[7] When the chief's superiors told him he had better rethink his decision, he passed a sleepless night, bowed, and reversed himself. The dominance of American popular culture is a soft dominance—a collaboration. In the words of media analyst James Monaco, "American movies and TV are popular because they're *popular*."[8]

That popularity has much to do with the fusion of market-mindedness and cultural diversity. The United States has the advantages of a polyglot, multirooted (or rather, uprooted) society that celebrates its compound nature and common virtues (and sins) with remarkable energy. Popular culture, by the time it ships from American shores, has already been "pretested" on a heterogeneous public—a huge internal market with variegated tastes. American popular culture is, after all, the rambunctious child of Europe and Africa. Our popular music and dance derive from the descendants of African slaves, among others. Our comic sense derives principally from the English, East European Jews, and, again, African Americans, with growing Hispanic infusions. Our stories come from everywhere; consider Ralph Waldo Ellison's *Invisible Man,* inspired jointly by Dostoyevsky, African American folktales, and jazz. American culture is spongy, or in James Monaco's happy term, *promiscuous*. He adds, "American culture simply doesn't exist without its African and European progenitors, and despite occasional outbursts of 'Americanism' it continues to accept almost any input." [9]

To expand in the United States, popular culture had a clear avenue. It did not have to squeeze up against an aristocratic model, there being no wealthy landowning class to nourish one except in the plantation South—and there, slaves were the population that produced the most influential popular culture. Outside the South, from the early nineteenth century on, the market enjoyed prestige; it was no dishonor to produce culture for popular purposes. Ecclesiastical rivals were relatively weak. From the early years of the Republic, American culture was driven by a single overriding purpose: to entertain the common man and woman. . . .

It is to America's advantage as well that commercial work emerges from Hollywood, New York, and Nashville in the principal world language. Thanks to the British Empire-cum-Commonwealth, English is the second most commonly spoken native language in the world, and the most international. . . . English is spoken and read as a second language more commonly than any other. Increasingly, the English that is taught and learned, the language in demand, is American, not British. It is the language of business and has acquired the cachet of international media. Of the major world languages, English is the most compressed; partly because of its Anglo-Saxon origins, the English version of any text is almost always shorter than translations in other languages. English is grammatically simple. American English in particular is pungent, informal, absorptive, evolving, precise when called upon to be precise, transferable between written and verbal forms, lacking in sharp distinctions between "high" and "low" forms, and all in all, well adapted for slogans, headlines, comic strips, song lyrics, jingles, slang, dubbing, and other standard features of popular culture. English is, in a word, the most torrential language. [10]

Moreover, the American language of images is even more accessible than the American language of words. The global popularity of Hollywood product often depends less on the spoken word, even when kept elementary (non-English-speakers everywhere could understand Arnold Schwarzenegger without difficulty), than on crackling edits, bright smiles, the camera tracking and swooping, the cars crashing off cliffs or smashing into other cars, the asteroids plunging dramatically toward earth. In action movies, as in the Westerns that preceded them, speech is a secondary mode of expression. European competitors cannot make this claim, though Hong Kong can.

It is also an export advantage that "American" popular culture is frequently not so American at all. "Hollywood" is an export platform that happens to be located on the Pacific coast of the United States but uses capital, hires personnel, and depicts sites from many countries. Disney casually borrows mythologies from Britain, Germany, France, Italy, Denmark, China, colonial America, the Old Testament, anywhere. Any myth can get the Disney treatment: simplified, smoothed down, prettified. Pavilions as emblems of foreign countries, sites as replicas of sites, *Fantasia, Pinocchio, Song of the South, Pocahontas, Mulan*—Disney takes material where it can, as long as it comes out Disney's industrialized fun.

Moreover, to sustain market advantages, the Hollywood multinationals, ever thirsting for novelty, eagerly import, process, and export styles and practitioners from abroad. Consider, among directors, Alfred Hitchcock, Charlie Chaplin, Douglas Sirk, Michael Curtiz, Billy Wilder, Otto Preminger, Ridley Scott, Peter Weir, Bruce Beresford, Paul Verhoeven, John Woo, Ang Lee. . . . Consider, among stars, Greta Garbo, Ingrid Bergman, Cary Grant, Anthony Quinn, Sean Connery, Arnold Schwarzenegger, Jean-Claude Van Damme, Mel Gibson, Hugh Grant, Jackie Chan, Kate Winslet, Michelle Yeoh, Chow Yun-Fat, Catherine Zeta-Jones, Antonio Banderas, Penelope Cruz. Hollywood is the global magnet—and (to mix metaphors) the acid bath into which, often enough, talent dissolves. Even the locales come from everywhere, or nowhere. It is striking how many blockbusters take place in outer space (the *Star Wars, Alien,* and *Star Trek* series), in the prenational past (the *Jurassic Park* series), in the postnational future (the *Planet of the Apes* series, the two *Terminator* films, *The Matrix*), at sea (*Titanic, The Perfect Storm*—the latter also directed by a German, Wolfgang Petersen), or on an extended hop-skip-and-jump around the world (the James Bond series, *Mission: Impossible*). . . .

No matter. Of Americanized popular culture, nothing more or less is asked but that it be *interesting,* a portal into the pleasure dome. . . .

So the disrespectful, lavish, energetic American torrent flows on and on, appealing to ideals of action and self-reinvention, extending the comforts of recognition to the uprooted. In a world of unease and uprooting, the American images, sounds, and stories overlap nations and global diasporas. Cultivating and nourishing desires, unifying but flexible, everywhere they leave behind deposits of what can only be called a civilization—not an ideology, or a system of belief, but something less resistible, a way of life soaked in feeling, seeming to absorb with equal conviction traces of every idea or, for that matter, the absence of all ideas. It has a clear field. In this time, one-world ideologies are decidedly flimsy. With socialism largely discredited, and each world religion checked by the others, the way of life with the greatest allure turns out to be this globalizing civilization of saturation and speed that enshrines individuals, links freedom to taste, tickles the senses. How odd, but inescapable, that insofar as there are unifying symbols today, they should be the undemanding ones—not the cross, the crescent, or the flag, let alone the hammer and sickle, but Coke and Mickey Mouse.

At least for now.

An End to Culture?

I have been arguing that American culture is a complex collaboration between venal, efficient suppliers and receptive, fickle consumers. The suppliers were already well understood by Alexis de Tocqueville, with his emphasis on efficiency and convenience; the consumers by Georg Simmel, with his emphasis on the hunger for feeling and the taste for the transitory. The suppliers built a machine for delivering cultural goods; the consumers acquired a taste for them. What was true when commercial American culture poured across the country in the twentieth century remains true as it pours through the world today. The preeminence of America's styles and themes is not rule from on high. To take it that way is to misunderstand its soft power.

What I have been calling the demand side is not necessarily clamor or hunger. It is more a compound of interest, liking, tolerance—and enthusiasm. There are fanatics who talk and write feverishly about the *Stars Wars* movies, auctioning and purchasing rare merchandise, going so far as to take a day off from work to buy a movie ticket to see the debut of the *trailer* for Episode I, *The Phantom Menace;* there is the wider circle of millions who look forward less passionately to the next installment; and an even wider one of more or less curious, possibly halfhearted customers keeping up with their crowds. The multiplex is filled with American films because the United States was first to produce a culture of comfort and convenience whose popularity was its primary reason for being. All in all, American popular culture is popular because (and to the extent that) its sleek, fast, fleeting styles of entertainment—its *commitment* to entertainment—dovetail with modern displacement and desire. . . .

There is no going back to the forest clan or the village. There is no repealing the technologies that spray images on our walls, graft stories onto our screens, sing songs into our headphones. There is no diversion from the seduction and clamor, the convenience and irritation of media. There is no avoiding the spread of American-style pop—its coupling of irreverence and brutality; its love of the road and its degradation of the word; its light rock and heavy metal. This amalgam flows through the world for worse and for better, inviting, in unknowable proportions, immigration, emulation, and revulsion. Where the flow goes, there follows a fear that American marketing exudes a uniform "McWorld" —and brings, in its wake, with dialectical certainty, destructive "Jihads." [11]

Yet for all the fear of standardization, American pop does not erase all the vernacular alternatives, all the local forms in which artists and writers give forth their styles and stories. The emergence of a global semiculture coexists with local sensibilities. It does not simply replace them. As the Norwegian media theorist Helge Rønning suggests, it's plausible to suppose that globalized, largely American pop has become, or is in the process of becoming, almost everyone's second culture. . . .

As for the media as a whole, what could stop the flood but a catastrophic breakdown of civilization? (In Steven Spielberg's *A.I.*, not even global warming and the total immersion of Manhattan wipe out the media.) Why would the beat not go on? Too much desire and too much convenience converge in the nonstop spectacle; too much of the human desire to play, to test and perfect oneself, to feel, to feel good, to feel with others, to feel conveniently; too much of the desire for sensory pleasure, for a refuge from calculation, for a flight from life, or from death, or from both. The media have been gathering force for centuries. Why should their songs and stories cease to generate enthusiasm and anxiety, production and consumption, celebrity and irony, fandom and boredom, criticism and jamming, paranoia and secession? Why would a society in which people have the time to indulge their fancies this way repeal these options? The media will sweep down, their flow continuous and widening, bearing banalities and mysteries, achievements and potentials, strangeness and disappointments—this would appear to be our complex fate.

I am not proposing that anyone cease trying to launch better work. Surely there will be—there *deserve* to be—fights over who gets to harness media power, over censorship, over improving contents and broadening access. Conservatives will want today's colossal controllers to keep control but clean up the sewage. Liberals will want new tributaries to flow and to bend the stream in their preferred directions. Techno-utopians will agree with the liberal law professor who writes of digital online sharing: "The result will be more music, poetry, photography, and journalism available to a far wider audience. . . . For those who worry about the cultural, economic and political power of the global media companies, the dreamed-of revolution is at hand. . . . It is we, not they, who are about to enter the promised land." [12] But these apparently different ideas share an ideal: more media, more of the time.

I cannot pretend to offer a definitive balance sheet on our odd form of life immersed in images, sounds, and stories. Nor can I suggest a ten-point program for revitalization or a list of preferable activities. I have tried to confront the media as a whole, to reconceive their onrushing immensity, and to explain how they became central to our civilization. To fans, critics, paranoids, exhibitionists, ironists, and the rest, to reformers of all stripes, I would propose taking some time to step back, forgoing the fantasies of electronic perfection, leaving behind the trend-spotting gurus and pundits who purport to interpret for us the hottest and latest. I propose that we stop—and imagine the whole phenomenon freshly, taking the media seriously not as a cornucopia of wondrous gadgets or a collection of social problems, but as a central condition of an entire way of life. Perhaps if we step away from the ripples of the moment, the week, or the season, and contemplate the torrent in its entirety, we will know what we want to do about it besides change channels.

ENDNOTES

[1] Economists Incorporated for the International Intellectual Property Alliance, Executive Summary, 2000_SIWEK_EXEC.pdf. Thanks to Siva Vaidhyanathan for his discerning analysis of these statistics.

[2] This story is told by Berndt Ostendorf in "What Makes American Popular Culture So Popular: A View from Europe" (Odense, Denmark: Oasis, 2000).

[3] I benefited from a discussion about the overuse of the term *culture* with Kevin Robins, March 2, 2001.

[4] National Technical Information Service, *Globalization of the Mass Media* (Washington, DC: Department of Commerce, 1993), pp.1–2, cited in Edward S. Herman and Robert W. McChesney, *The Global Media: The New Missionaries of Corporate Capitalism* (London: Cassell, 1997), p. 39.

[5] Calculated from *Schroder's International Media and Entertainment Report 2000*, p. 37. Courtesy of David Lieberman, media business editor of *USA Today*.

[6] Ostendorf, "What Makes American Popular Culture So Popular?" pp. 16–18, 47.

[7] Personal communications, Henrik Christiansen, former chief of entertainment for Danish television (and previously head of news), September 1998.

[8] "Images and Sounds as Cultural Commodities," p. 231, from an article I clipped a long time ago but without noting from which magazine I'd clipped it.

[9] Ibid., p. 231.

[10] Jeremy Tunstall, *Media Are American: Anglo-American Media in the World* (New York: Columbia University Press, 1977).

[11] The most impressive articulation of this position in recent years is Benjamin Barber, *Jihad vs. McWorld* (New York: Times Books, 1995). But see the critique by Fareed Zakaria, *New Republic*, January 22, 1996, pp. 27ff.

[12] Eben Moglen, "Liberation Musicology," *Nation*, March 12, 2001, p. 6.

41

MANIFESTO OF THE COMMUNIST PARTY

KARL MARX • FRIEDRICH ENGELS

The economy and work are the focus of the next three readings. The first selection in this group is an excerpt from the classic "Manifesto of the Communist Party," written by Karl Marx and Friedrich Engels in 1848. Students
often are surprised to discover the currency of many of the topics discussed
by Marx (1818–1883) and Engels (1820–1895). Specifically, Marx and Engels
foresaw the rise of global capitalism. They also accurately described ex-
ploitive industrial conditions and the oppositional interests of workers and
capitalists. Even though Marx and Engels are criticized for not foreseeing the
rise of other social agents (such as the middle class, the government, and
unions) in mediating the conflict between capitalists and workers, their theory of class struggle and revolution is still provocative and a source for
worldwide social change.

The history of all hitherto existing society is the history of class
struggles.

Freeman and slave, patrician and plebeian, lord and serf, guild-master
and journeyman, in a word, oppressor and oppressed, stood in constant opposition to one another, carried on an uninterrupted, now hidden, now open
fight, a fight that each time ended, either in a revolutionary reconstitution of
society at large, or in the common ruin of the contending classes.

In the earlier epochs of history, we find almost everywhere a complicated
arrangement of society into various orders, a manifold gradation of social
rank. In ancient Rome we have patricians, knights, plebeians, slaves; in the
Middle Ages, feudal lords, vassals, guild-masters, journeymen, apprentices,
serfs; in almost all of these classes, again, subordinate gradations.

The modern bourgeois society that has sprouted from the ruins of feudal
society has not done away with class antagonisms. It has but established new
classes, new conditions of oppression, new forms of struggle in place of the
old ones.

Our epoch, the epoch of the bourgeoisie, possesses, however, this distinctive feature: It has simplified the class antagonisms. Society as a whole is more

English translation by Friedrich Engels, 1888.

and more splitting up into two great hostile camps, into two great classes directly facing each other: Bourgeoisie and Proletariat.

From the serfs of the Middle Ages sprang the chartered burghers of the earliest towns. From these burgesses the first elements of the bourgeoisie were developed.

The discovery of America, the rounding of the Cape, opened up fresh ground for the rising bourgeoisie. The East-Indian and Chinese markets, the colonization of America, trade with the colonies, the increase in the means of exchange and in commodities generally, gave to commerce, to navigation, to industry, an impulse never before known, and thereby, to the revolutionary element in the tottering feudal society, a rapid development.

The feudal system of industry, under which industrial production was monopolized by closed guilds, now no longer sufficed for the growing wants of the new markets. The manufacturing system took its place. The guild-masters were pushed on one side by the manufacturing middle class; division of labour between the different corporate guilds vanished in the face of division of labour in each single workshop.

Meantime the markets kept ever growing, the demand ever rising. Even manufacture no longer sufficed. Thereupon, steam and machinery revolutionized industrial production. The place of manufacture was taken by the giant, Modern Industry, the place of the industrial middle class, by industrial millionaires, the leaders of whole industrial armies, the modern bourgeois.

Modern industry has established the world-market, for which the discovery of America paved the way. This market has given an immense development to commerce, to navigation, to communication by land. This development has, in its turn, reacted on the extension of industry; and in proportion as industry, commerce, navigation, railways extended, in the same proportion the bourgeoisie developed, increased its capital, and pushed into the background every class handed down from the Middle Ages.

We see, therefore, how the modern bourgeoisie is itself the product of a long course of development, of a series of revolutions in the modes of production and of exchange.

Each step in the development of the bourgeoisie was accompanied by a corresponding political advance of that class. An oppressed class under the sway of the feudal nobility, an armed and self-governing association in the mediaeval commune; here independent urban republic (as in Italy and Germany), there taxable "third estate" of the monarchy (as in France), afterwards, in the period of manufacture proper, serving either the semi-feudal or the absolute monarchy as a counterpoise against the nobility, and, in fact, corner-stone of the great monarchies in general, the bourgeoisie has at last, since the establishment of Modern Industry and of the world-market, conquered for itself, in the modern representative State, exclusive political sway. The execution of the modern State is but a committee for managing the common affairs of the whole bourgeoisie.

The bourgeoisie, historically, has played a most revolutionary part.

The bourgeoisie, wherever it has got the upper hand, has put an end to all feudal, patriarchal, idyllic relations. It has pitilessly torn asunder the motley feudal ties that bound man to his "natural superiors," and has left remaining no other nexus between man and man than naked self-interest, than callous "cash payment." It has drowned the most heavenly ecstasies of religious fervor, of chivalrous enthusiasm, of philistine sentimentalism, in the icy water of egotistical calculation. It has resolved personal worth into exchange value and, in place of the numberless indefeasible chartered freedoms, has set up that single, unconscionable freedom—Free Trade. In one word, for exploitation, veiled by religious and political illusions, it has substituted naked, shameless, direct, brutal exploitation.

The bourgeoisie has stripped of its halo every occupation hitherto honored and looked up to with reverent awe. It has converted the physician, the lawyer, the priest, the poet, the man of science, into its paid wage-labourers.

The bourgeoisie has torn away from the family its sentimental veil, and has reduced the family relation to a mere money relation.

The bourgeoisie has disclosed how it came to pass that the brutal display of vigor in the Middle Ages, which Reactionists so much admire, found its fitting complement in the most slothful indolence. It has been the first to show what man's activity can bring about. It has accomplished wonders far surpassing Egyptian pyramids, Roman aqueducts, and Gothic cathedrals; it has conducted expeditions that put in the shade all former Exoduses of nations and crusades.

The bourgeoisie cannot exist without constantly revolutionizing the instruments of production, and thereby the relations of production, and with them the whole relations of society. Conservation of the old modes of production in unaltered form, was, on the contrary, the first condition of existence for all earlier industrial classes. Constant revolutionizing of production, uninterrupted disturbance of all social conditions, everlasting uncertainty and agitation distinguish the bourgeois epoch from all earlier ones. All fixed, fast-frozen relations, with their train of ancient and venerable prejudices and opinions, are swept away, all new-formed ones become antiquated before they can ossify. All that is solid melts into air, all that is holy is profaned, and man is at last compelled to face with sober senses, his real conditions of life, and his relations with his kind.

The need of a constantly expanding market for its products chases the bourgeoisie over the whole surface of the globe. It must nestle everywhere, settle everywhere, establish connections everywhere.

The bourgeoisie has through its exploitation of the world-market given a cosmopolitan character to production and consumption in every country. To the great chagrin of Reactionists, it has drawn from under the feet of industry the national ground on which it stood. All old-established national industries have been destroyed or are daily being destroyed. They are dislodged by new industries, whose introduction becomes a life and death question for all civilized nations, by industries that no longer work up indigenous raw material, but raw material drawn from the remotest zones; industries whose products are consumed, not only at home, but in every quarter of the globe. In place of the old wants, satisfied by the productions of the country, we find new wants, requiring for their satisfaction the products of distant lands and climes. In place of the old local and national seclusion and self-sufficiency, we have intercourse in every direction, universal inter-dependence of nations. And as in material, so also in intellectual production. The intellectual creations of individual nations become common property. National one-sidedness and narrow-mindedness become more and more impossible, and from the numerous national and local literatures, there arises a world literature.

The bourgeoisie, by the rapid improvement of all instruments of production, by the immensely facilitated means of communication, draws all, even the most barbarian, nations into civilization. The cheap prices of its commodities are the heavy artillery with which it batters down all Chinese walls, with which it forces the barbarians' intensely obstinate hatred of foreigners to capitulate. It compels all nations, on pain of extinction, to adopt the bourgeois mode of production; it compels them to introduce what it calls civilization into their midst, *i.e.*, to become bourgeois themselves. In one word, it creates a world after its own image.

The bourgeoisie has subjected the country to the rule of the towns. It has created enormous cities, has greatly increased the urban population as compared with the rural, and has thus rescued a considerable part of the population from the idiocy of rural life. Just as it has made the country dependent on the towns, so it has made barbarian and semi-barbarian countries dependent on the civilized ones, nations of peasants on nations of bourgeois, the East on the West.

The bourgeoisie keeps more and more doing away with the scattered state of the population, of the means of production, and of property. It has agglomerated population, centralized means of production, and has concentrated property in a few hands. The necessary consequence of this was political centralization. Independent, or but loosely connected provinces, with separate interests, laws, governments and systems of taxation, became lumped together into one nation, with one government, one code of laws, one national class-interest, one frontier and one customs-tariff.

The bourgeoisie, during its rule of scarce one hundred years, has created more massive and more colossal productive forces than have all preceding generations together. Subjection of Nature's forces to man, machinery, application of chemistry to industry and agriculture, steam-navigation, railways, electric telegraphs, clearing of whole continents for cultivation, canalization of rivers, whole populations conjured out of the ground—what earlier century had even a presentiment that such productive forces slumbered in the lap of social labour?

We see then: the means of production and of exchange, on whose foundation the bourgeoisie built itself up, were generated in feudal society. At a certain stage in the development of these means of production and of exchange, the conditions under which feudal society produced and exchanged, the feudal organization of agriculture and manufacturing industry, in one word, the feudal relations of property became no longer compatible with the already developed productive forces; they became so many fetters. They had to be burst asunder; they were burst asunder.

Into their place stepped free competition, accompanied by a social and political constitution adapted to it, and by the economical and political sway of the bourgeois class.

A similar movement is going on before our own eyes. Modern bourgeois society with its relations of production, of exchange and of property, a society that has conjured up such gigantic means of production and of exchange, is like the sorcerer, who is no longer able to control the powers of the nether world whom he has called up by his spells. For many a decade past the history of industry and commerce is but the history of the revolt of modern productive forces against modern conditions of production, against the property relations that are the conditions for the existence of the bourgeoisie and of its rule. It is enough to mention the commercial crises that by their periodical return put on its trial, each time more threateningly, the existence of the entire bourgeois society. In these crises a great part not only of the existing products, but also of the previously created productive forces, are periodically destroyed. In these crises there breaks out an epidemic that, in all earlier epochs, would have seemed an absurdity—the epidemic of over-production. Society suddenly finds itself put back into a state of momentary barbarism; it appears as if a famine, a universal war of devastation had cut off the supply of every means of subsistence; industry and commerce seem to be destroyed; and why? Because there is too much civilization, too much means of subsistence, too much industry, too much commerce. The productive forces at the disposal of society no longer tend to further the development of the conditions of bourgeois property; on the contrary, they have become too powerful for these conditions, by which they are fettered, and so soon as they overcome these fetters, they bring disorder into the whole of bourgeois society, endanger the existence of bourgeois property. The conditions of bourgeois society are too narrow to comprise the wealth created by them. And how does the bourgeoisie get over these crises? On the one hand by enforced destruction of a mass of productive forces; on the other, by the conquest of new markets, and by the more thorough exploitation of the old ones. That is to say, by paving the way for more extensive and more destructive crises, and by diminishing the means whereby crises are prevented.

The weapons with which the bourgeoisie felled feudalism to the ground are now turned against the bourgeoisie itself.

But not only has the bourgeoisie forged the weapons that bring death to itself; it has also called into existence the men who are to wield those weapons—the modern working class—the proletarians.

In proportion as the bourgeoisie, *i.e.*, capital, is developed, in the same proportion is the proletariat, the modern working class, developed—a class of labourers, who live only so long as they find work and who find work only so long as their labour increases capital. These labourers, who must sell themselves piece-meal, are a commodity, like every other article of commerce, and are consequently exposed to all the vicissitudes of competition, to all the fluctuations of the market.

Owing to the extensive use of machinery and to division of labour, the work of the proletarians has lost all individual character and, consequently, all charm for the workman. He becomes an appendage of the machine, and it is only the most simple, most monotonous, and most easily acquired knack that is required of him. Hence, the cost of production of a workman is restricted, almost entirely, to the means of subsistence that he requires for his maintenance and for the propagation of his race. But the price of a commodity, and therefore also of labour, is equal to its cost of production. In proportion, therefore, as the repulsiveness of the work increases, the wage decreases. Nay more, in proportion as the use of machinery and division of labour increases, in the same proportion the burden of toil also increases, whether by prolongation of the working hours, by increase of the work exacted in a given time, or by increased speed of the machinery, etc.

Modern industry has converted the little workshop of the patriarchal master into the great factory of the industrial capitalist. Masses of labourers, crowded into the factory, are organised like soldiers. As privates of the industrial army they are placed under the command of a perfect hierarchy of officers and sergeants. Not only are they slaves of the bourgeois class and of the bourgeois State; they are daily and hourly enslaved by the machine, by the over-looker, and, above all, by the individual bourgeois manufacturer himself. The more openly this despotism proclaims gain to be its end and aim, the more petty, the more hateful and the more embittering it is.

The less the skill and exertion of strength implied in manual labour, in other words, the more modern industry becomes developed, the more is the labour of men superseded by that of women. Differences of age and sex have no longer any distinctive social validity for the working class. All are instruments of labour, more or less expensive to use, according to their age and sex.

No sooner is the exploitation of the labourer by the manufacturer, so far, at an end, that he receives his wages in cash, than he is set upon by the other portions of the bourgeoisie, the landlord, the shopkeeper, the pawnbroker, etc.

42

WHEN WORK DISAPPEARS
The World of the New Urban Poor

WILLIAM JULIUS WILSON

This reading is an excerpt from William Julius Wilson's 1996 book, *When Work Disappears: The World of the New Urban Poor.* Wilson, a sociologist, is the Malcolm Wiener Professor of Social Policy at the John F. Kennedy School of Government, Harvard University. Here, Wilson examines the effects joblessness and declining wages have had on inner-city neighborhoods in Chicago. Economic changes related to deindustrialization, the globalization of capitalism, and especially the decline of blue-collar jobs have contributed to the concentration of poverty in urban ghettos. In addition, Wilson analyzes other structural factors, such as residential segregation, demographic changes in the population, and local and federal policies that have contributed to the ghettoization of inner-city neighborhoods.

The disappearance of work in many inner-city neighborhoods is partly related to the nationwide decline in the fortunes of low-skilled workers. Although the growing wage inequality has hurt both low-skilled men and women, the problem of declining employment has been concentrated among low-skilled men. In 1987–89, a low-skilled male worker was jobless eight and a half weeks longer than he would have been in 1967–69. Moreover, the proportion of men who "permanently" dropped out of the labor force was more than twice as high in the late 1980s than it had been in the late 1960s. A precipitous drop in real wages—that is, wages adjusted for inflation—has accompanied the increases in joblessness among low-income workers. If you arrange all wages into five groups according to wage percentile (from highest to lowest), you see that men in the bottom fifth of this income distribution experienced more than a 30 percent drop in real wages between 1970 and 1989.

Even the low-skilled workers who are consistently employed face problems of economic advancement. Job ladders—opportunities for promotion within firms—have eroded, and many less-skilled workers stagnate in dead-end, low-paying positions. This suggests that the chances of improving one's earnings by changing jobs have declined: if jobs inside a firm have become less available to the experienced workers in that firm, they are probably even more difficult for outsiders to obtain.

But there is a paradox here. Despite the increasing economic marginality of low-wage workers, unemployment dipped below 6 percent in 1994 and early 1995, many workers are holding more than one job, and overtime work has reached a record high. Yet while tens of millions of new jobs have been created in the past two decades, men who are well below retirement age are working less than they did two decades ago—and a growing percentage are neither working nor looking for work. The proportion of male workers in the prime of their life (between the ages of 22 and 58) who worked in a given decade full-time, year-round, in at least eight out of ten years declined from 79 percent during the 1970s to 71 percent in the 1980s. While the American economy saw a rapid expansion in high technology and services, especially advanced services, growth in blue-collar factory, transportation, and construction jobs, traditionally held by men, has not kept pace with the rise in the working-age population. These men are working less as a result.

The growth of a nonworking class of prime-age males along with a larger number of those who are often unemployed, who work part-time, or who work in temporary jobs is concentrated among the poorly educated, the school dropouts, and minorities. In the 1970s, two-thirds of prime-age male workers with less than a high school education worked full-time, year-round, in eight out of ten years. During the 1980s, only half did so. Prime-age black men experienced a similar sharp decline. Seven out of ten of all black men worked full-time, year-round, in eight out of ten years in the 1970s, but only half did so in the 1980s. The figures for those who reside in the inner city are obviously even lower. . . .

Joblessness and declining wages are . . . related to the recent growth in ghetto poverty. The most dramatic increases in ghetto poverty occurred between 1970 and 1980, and they were mostly confined to the large industrial metropolises of the Northeast and Midwest, regions that experienced massive industrial restructuring and loss of blue-collar jobs during that decade. But the rise in ghetto poverty was not the only problem. Industrial restructuring had devastating effects on the social organization of many inner-city neighborhoods in these regions. The fate of the West Side black community of North Lawndale vividly exemplifies the cumulative process of economic and social dislocation that has swept through Chicago's inner city.

After more than a quarter century of continuous deterioration, North Lawndale resembles a war zone. Since 1960, nearly half of its housing stock has disappeared; the remaining units are mostly run-down or dilapidated. Two large factories anchored the economy of this West Side neighborhood in its good days—the Hawthorne plant of Western Electric, which employed over 43,000 workers; and an International Harvester plant with 14,000 workers. The world headquarters for Sears, Roebuck and Company was located there, providing another 10,000 jobs. The neighborhood also had a Copenhagen snuff plant, a Sunbeam factory, and a Zenith factory, a Dell Farm food market, an Alden's catalog store, and a U.S. Post Office bulk station. But conditions rapidly changed. Harvester closed its doors in the late 1960s. Sears moved most of its offices to the Loop in downtown Chicago in 1973; a catalog distribution center with a workforce of 3,000 initially remained in the neighborhood but was relocated outside of the state of Illinois in 1987. The Hawthorne plant gradually phased out its operations and finally shut down in 1984.

The departure of the big plants triggered the demise or exodus of the smaller stores, the banks, and other businesses that relied on the wages paid by the large employers. "To make matters worse, scores of stores were forced out of business or pushed out of the neighborhoods by insurance companies in the wake of the 1968 riots that swept through Chicago's West Side after the assassination of Dr. Martin Luther King, Jr. Others were simply burned or abandoned. It has been estimated that the community lost 75 percent of its business establishments from 1960 to 1970 alone." In 1986, North Lawndale, with a population of over 66,000, had only one bank and one supermarket; but it was also home to forty-eight state lottery agents, fifty currency exchanges, and ninety-nine licensed liquor stores and bars.

The impact of industrial restructuring on inner-city employment is clearly apparent to urban blacks. The UPFLS [Chicago Urban Poverty and Family Life Survey] survey posed the following question: "Over the past five or ten years, how many friends of yours have lost their jobs because the place where they worked shut down—would you say none, a few, some, or most?" Only 26 percent of the black residents in our sample reported that none of their friends had lost jobs because their workplace shut down. Indeed, both black men and black women were more likely to report that their friends had lost jobs because of plant closings than were the Mexicans and the other ethnic groups in our study. Moreover, nearly half of the employed black fathers and mothers in the UPFLS survey stated that they considered themselves to be at high risk of losing their jobs because of plant shutdowns. Significantly fewer Hispanic and white parents felt this way.

Some of the inner-city neighborhoods have experienced more visible job losses than others. But residents of the inner city are keenly aware of the rapid depletion of job opportunities. A 33-year-old unmarried black male of North Lawndale who is employed as a clerical worker stated: "Because of the way the economy is structured, we're losing more jobs. Chicago is losing jobs by the thousands. There just aren't any starting companies here and it's harder to find a job compared to what it was years ago."

A similar view was expressed by a 41-year-old black female, also from North Lawndale, who works as a nurse's aide:

> *Chicago is really full of peoples. Everybody can't get a good job. They don't have enough good jobs to provide for everybody. I don't think they have enough jobs period. . . . And all the factories and the places, they closed up and moved out of the city and stuff like that, you know. I guess it's one of the reasons they haven't*

got too many jobs now, 'cause a lot of the jobs now, factories and business, they're done moved out. So that way it's less jobs for lot of peoples.

Respondents from other neighborhoods also reported on the impact of industrial restructuring. According to a 33-year-old South Side janitor:

The machines are putting a lot of people out of jobs. I worked for Time *magazine for seven years on a videograph printer and they come along with the Abedic printer, it cost them half a million dollars: they did what we did in half the time, eliminated two shifts.*

"Jobs were plentiful in the past," stated a 29-year-old unemployed black male who lives in one of the poorest neighborhoods on the South Side.

You could walk out of the house and get a job. Maybe not what you want but you could get a job. Now, you can't find anything. A lot of people in this neighborhood, they want to work but they can't get work. A few, but a very few, they just don't want to work. The majority they want to work but they can't find work.

Finally, a 41-year-old hospital worker from another impoverished South Side neighborhood associated declining employment opportunities with decreasing skill levels:

Well, most of the jobs have moved out of Chicago. Factory jobs have moved out. There are no jobs here. Not like it was 20, 30 years ago. And people aren't skilled enough for the jobs that are here. You don't have enough skilled and educated people to fill them.

The increasing suburbanization of employment has accompanied industrial restructuring and has further exacerbated the problems of inner-city joblessness and restricted access to jobs. "Metropolitan areas captured nearly 90 percent of the nation's employment growth; much of this growth occurred in booming 'edge cities' at the metropolitan periphery. By 1990, many of these 'edge cities' had more office space and retail sales than the metropolitan downtowns." Over the last two decades, 60 percent of the new jobs created in the Chicago metropolitan area have been located in the northwest suburbs of Cook and Du Page counties. African Americans constitute less than 2 percent of the population in these areas.

In *The Truly Disadvantaged* (1987), I maintained that one result of these changes for many urban blacks has been a growing mismatch between the suburban location of employment and minorities' residence in the inner city. Although studies based on data collected before 1970 showed no consistent or convincing effects on black employment as a consequence of this spatial mismatch, the employment of inner-city blacks relative to suburban blacks has clearly deteriorated since then. Recent research, conducted mainly by urban and labor economists, strongly shows that the decentralization of employment is continuing and that employment in manufacturing, most of which is already suburbanized, has decreased in central cities, particularly in the Northeast and Midwest. As Farrell Bloch, an economic and statistical consultant, points out, "Not only has the number of manufacturing jobs been decreasing, but new plants now tend to locate in the suburbs to take advantage of cheap land, access to highways, and low crime rates; in addition, businesses shun urban locations to avoid buying land from several different owners, paying high demolition costs for old buildings, and arranging parking for employees and customers."

Blacks living in central cities have less access to employment, as measured by the ratio of jobs to people and the average travel time to and from work, than do central-city whites. Moreover, unlike most other groups of workers across the urban/suburban divide, less educated central-city blacks receive lower wages than suburban blacks who have similar levels of education. And the decline in earnings of central-city blacks is related to the decentralization of employment—that is, the movement of jobs from the cities to the suburbs—in metropolitan areas.

But are the differences in employment between city and suburban blacks mainly the result of changes in the location of jobs? It is possible that in recent years the migration of blacks to the suburbs has become much more selective than in earlier years, so much so that the changes attributed to job location are actually caused by this selective migration. The pattern of black migration to the suburbs in the 1970s was similar to that of whites during the 1950s and 1960s in the sense that it was concentrated among the better-educated and younger city residents. However, in the 1970s this was even more true for blacks, creating a situation in which the education and income gaps between city and suburban blacks seemed to expand at the same time that the differences between city and suburban whites seemed to contract. Accordingly, if one were to take into account differences in education, family background, and so on, how much of the employment gap between city and suburbs would remain?

This question was addressed in a study of the Gautreaux program in Chicago. The Gautreaux program was created under a 1976 court order resulting from a judicial finding of widespread discrimination in the public housing projects of Chicago. The program has relocated more than 4,000 residents from public housing into subsidized housing in neighborhoods throughout the Greater Chicago area. The design of the program permitted the researchers, James E. Rosenbaum and Susan J. Popkin, to contrast systematically the employment experiences of a group of low-income blacks who had been assigned private apartments in the suburbs with the experience of a control group with similar characteristics and histories who had been assigned private apartments in the city. Their findings support the spatial mismatch hypothesis. After taking into account the personal characteristics of the respondents (including family background, family circumstances, levels of human capital, motivation, length of time since the respondent first enrolled in the Gautreaux program), Rosenbaum and Popkin found that those who moved to apartments in the suburbs were significantly more likely to have a job after the move than those placed in the city. When asked what makes it easier to obtain employment in the suburbs, nearly all the suburban respondents mentioned the high availability of jobs.

The African Americans surveyed in the UPFLS clearly recognized a spatial mismatch of jobs. Both black men and black women saw greater job prospects outside the city. For example, only one-third of black fathers from areas with poverty rates of at least 30 percent reported that their best opportunities for employment were to be found in the city. Nearly two-thirds of whites and Puerto Ricans and over half of Mexicans living in similar neighborhoods felt this way. Getting to suburban jobs is especially problematic for the jobless individuals in the UPFLS because only 28 percent have access to an automobile. This rate falls even further to 18 percent for those living in the ghetto areas.

Among two-car middle-class and affluent families, commuting is accepted as a fact of life; but it occurs in a context of safe school environments for children, more available and accessible day care, and higher incomes to support mobile, away-from-home lifestyles. In a multitiered job market that requires substantial resources for participation, most inner-city minorities must rely on public transportation systems that rarely provide easy and quick access to suburban locations. A 32-year-old unemployed South Side welfare mother described the problem this way:

> *There's not enough jobs. I thinks Chicago's the only city that does not have a lot of opportunities opening in it. There's not enough factories, there's not enough work. Most all the good jobs are in the suburbs. Sometimes it's hard for the people in the city to get to the suburbs, because everybody don't own a car. Everybody don't drive.*

After commenting on the lack of jobs in his area, a 29-year-old unemployed South Side black male continued:

> *You gotta go out in the suburbs, but I can't get out there. The bus go out there but you don't want to catch the bus out there, going two hours each ways. If you have to be at work at eight that mean you have to leave for work at six, that mean you have to get up at five to be at work at eight. Then when wintertime come you be in trouble.*

Another unemployed South Side black male had this to say: "Most of the time . . . the places be too far and you need transportation and I don't have none right now. If I had some I'd probably be able to get one [a job]. If I had a car and went way into the suburbs, 'cause there ain't none in the city." This perception was echoed by an 18-year-old unemployed West Side black male:

> *They are most likely hiring in the suburbs. Recently, I think about two years ago, I had a job but they say that I need some transportation and they say that the bus out in the suburbs run at a certain time. So I had to pass that job up because I did not have no transport.*

An unemployed unmarried welfare mother of two from the West Side likewise stated:

> *Well, I'm goin' to tell you: most jobs, more jobs are in the suburbs. It's where the good jobs and stuff is but you gotta have transportation to get there and it's hard to be gettin' out there in the suburbs. Some people don't know where the suburbs is, some people get lost out there. It is really hard, but some make a way.*

One employed factory worker from the West Side who works a night shift described the situation this way:

> *From what I, I see, you know, it's hard to find a good job in the inner city 'cause so many people moving, you know, west to the suburbs and out of state. . . . Some people turn jobs down because they don't have no way of getting out there. . . . I just see some people just going to work—and they seem like they the type who just used to—they coming all the way from the city and go on all the way to the suburbs and, you know, you can see 'em all bundled and—catching one bus and the next bus. They just used to doing that.*

But the problem is not simply one of transportation and the length of commuting time. There is also the problem of the travel expense and of whether the long trek to the suburbs is actually worth it in terms of the income earned—after all, owning a car creates expenses far beyond the purchase price, including insurance, which is much more costly for city dwellers than it is for suburban motorists. "If you work in the suburbs you gotta have a car," stated an unmarried welfare mother of three children who lives on Chicago's West Side, "then you gotta buy gas. You spending more getting to the suburbs to work, than you is getting paid, so you still ain't getting nowhere."

Indeed, one unemployed 36-year-old black man from the West Side of Chicago actually quit his suburban job because of the transportation problem. "It was more expensive going to work in Naperville, transportation and all, and it wasn't worth it. . . . I was spending more money going to work than I earned working."

If transportation poses a problem for those who have to commute to work from the inner city to the suburbs, it can also hinder poor ghetto residents' ability to travel to the suburbs just to seek employment. For example, one unemployed man who lives on the South Side had just gone to O'Hare Airport looking for work with no luck. His complaint: "The money I spent yesterday, I coulda kept that in my pocket—I coulda kept that. 'Cause you know I musta spent $7 or somethin'. I coulda kept that."

Finally, in addition to enduring the search-and-travel costs, inner-city black workers often confront racial harassment when they enter suburban communities. A 38-year-old South Side divorced mother of two children who works as a hotel cashier described the problems experienced by her son and his co-worker in one of Chicago's suburbs:

My son, who works in Carol Stream, an all-white community, they've been stopped by a policeman two or three times asking them why they're in the community. And they're trying to go to work. They want everyone to stay in their own place. That's what society wants. And they followed them all the way to work to make sure. 'Cause it's an all-white neighborhood. But there're no jobs in the black neighborhoods. They got to go way out there to get a job.

These informal observations on the difficulties and cost of travel to suburban employment are consistent with the results of a recent study by the labor economists Harry J. Holzer, Keith R. Ihlandfeldt, and David L. Sjoquist (1994). In addition to finding that the lack of automobile ownership among inner-city blacks contributed significantly to their lower wages and lower rate of employment, these authors also reported that African Americans "spend more time traveling to work than whites," that "the time cost per mile traveled is . . . significantly higher for blacks," and that the resulting gains are relatively small. Overall, their results suggest that the amount of time and money spent in commuting, when compared with the actual income that accrues to inner-city blacks in low-skill jobs in the suburbs, acts to discourage poor people from seeking employment far from their own neighborhoods. Holzer and his colleagues concluded that it was quite rational for blacks to reject these search-and-travel choices when assessing their position in the job market.

Changes in the industrial and occupational mix, including the removal of jobs from urban centers to suburban corridors, represent external factors that have helped to elevate joblessness among inner-city blacks. But important social and demographic changes within the inner city are also associated with the escalating rates of neighborhood joblessness, and we shall consider these next.

The increase in the proportion of jobless adults in the inner city is also related to changes in the class, racial, and age composition of such neighborhoods—changes that have led to greater concentrations of poverty. Concentrated poverty is positively associated with joblessness. That is, when the former appears, the latter is found as well. As stated previously, poor people today are far more likely to be unemployed or out of the labor force than in previous years. In *The Truly Disadvantaged* (1987), I argue that in addition to the effects of joblessness, inner-city neighborhoods have experienced a growing concentration of poverty for several other reasons, including (1) the out-migration of nonpoor black families; (2) the exodus of nonpoor white and other nonblack families; and (3) the rise in the number of residents who have become poor while living in these areas. Additional research on the growth of concentrated poverty suggests another factor: the movement of poor people into a neighborhood (inmigration). And one more factor should be added to this mix: changes in the age structure of the community.

I believe that the extent to which any one factor is significant in explaining the decrease in the proportion of nonpoor individuals and families

depends on the poverty level and racial or ethnic makeup of the neighborhood at a given time. . . .

One of the important demographic shifts that had an impact on the up-
turn in the jobless rate has been the change in the age structure of inner-city
ghetto neighborhoods. Let us . . . examine the three Bronzeville neighborhoods of Douglas, Grand Boulevard, and Washington Park. . . . [T]he proportion of those in the age categories (20–64) that roughly approximate the
prime-age workforce has declined in all three neighborhoods since 1950,
whereas the proportion in the age category 65 and over has increased. Of the
adults aged 20 and over, the proportion in the prime-age categories declined
by 17 percent in Grand Boulevard, 16 percent in Douglas, and 12 percent in
Washington Park between 1950 and 1990. The smaller the percentage of
prime-age adults in a population, the lower the proportion of residents who
are likely to be employed. The proportion of residents in the age category
5–19 increased sharply in each neighborhood from 1950 to 1990, suggesting
that the growth in the proportion of teenagers also contributed to the rise in
the jobless rate. However, if we consider the fact that male employment in
these neighborhoods declined by a phenomenal 46 percent between 1950 and
1960, these demographic changes obviously can account for only a fraction,
albeit a significant fraction, of the high proportion of the area's jobless adults.

The rise in the proportion of jobless adults in the Bronzeville neighborhoods has been accompanied by an incredible depopulation—a decline of
66 percent in the three neighborhoods combined—that magnifies the problems of the new poverty neighborhoods. As the population drops and the
proportion of nonworking adults rises, basic neighborhood institutions are
more difficult to maintain: stores, banks, credit institutions, restaurants, dry
cleaners, gas stations, medical doctors, and so on lose regular and potential
patrons. Churches experience dwindling numbers of parishioners and shrinking resources; recreational facilities, block clubs, community groups, and
other informal organizations also suffer. As these organizations decline, the
means of formal and informal social control in the neighborhood become
weaker. Levels of crime and street violence increase as a result, leading to
further deterioration of the neighborhood.

The more rapid the neighborhood deterioration, the greater the institutional disinvestment. In the 1960s and 1970s, neighborhoods plagued by
heavy abandonment were frequently "redlined" (identified as areas that
should not receive or be recommended for mortgage loans or insurance); this
paralyzed the housing market, lowered property values, and further
encouraged landlord abandonment. The enactment of federal and state community reinvestment legislation in the 1970s curbed the practice of open redlining. Nonetheless, "prudent lenders will exercise increased caution in
advancing mortgages, particularly in neighborhoods marked by strong indication of owner disinvestment and early abandonment."

As the neighborhood disintegrates, those who are able to leave depart
in increasing numbers; among these are many working- and middle-class

families. The lower population density in turn creates additional problems. Abandoned buildings increase and often serve as havens for crack use and other illegal enterprises that give criminals footholds in the community. Precipitous declines in density also make it even more difficult to sustain or develop a sense of community. The feeling of safety in numbers is completely lacking in such neighborhoods.

Although changes in the economy (industrial restructuring and reorganization) and changes in the class, racial, and demographic composition of inner-city ghetto neighborhoods are important factors in the shift from institutional to jobless ghettos since 1970, we ought not to lose sight of the fact that this process actually began immediately following World War II.

The federal government contributed to the early decay of inner-city neighborhoods by withholding mortgage capital and by making it difficult for urban areas to retain or attract families able to purchase their own homes. Spurred on by massive mortgage foreclosures during the Great Depression, the federal government in the 1940s began underwriting mortgages in an effort to enable citizens to become homeowners. But the mortgage program was selectively administered by the Federal Housing Administration (FHA), and urban neighborhoods considered poor risks were redlined—an action that excluded virtually all the black neighborhoods and many neighborhoods with a considerable number of European immigrants. It was not until the 1960s that the FHA discontinued its racial restrictions on mortgages.

By manipulating market incentives, the federal government drew middle-class whites to the suburbs and, in effect, trapped blacks in the inner cities. Beginning in the 1950s, the suburbanization of the middle class was also facilitated by a federal transportation and highway policy, including the building of freeway networks through the hearts of many cities, mortgages for veterans, mortgage-interest tax exemptions, and the quick, cheap production of massive amounts of tract housing.

In the nineteenth and early twentieth centuries, with the offer of municipal services as an inducement, cities tended to annex their suburbs. But the relations between cities and suburbs in the United States began to change following a century-long influx of poor migrants who required expensive services and paid relatively little in taxes. Annexation largely ended in the mid-twentieth century as suburbs began to resist incorporation successfully. Suburban communities also drew tighter boundaries through the manipulation of zoning laws and discriminatory land-use controls and site-selection practices, making it difficult for inner-city racial minorities to penetrate.

As separate political jurisdictions, suburbs exercised a great deal of autonomy in their use of zoning, land-use policies, covenants, and deed restrictions. In the face of mounting pressures calling for integration in the 1960s, "suburbs chose to diversify by race rather than class. They retained zoning and other restrictions that allowed only affluent blacks (and, in some instances, Jews) to enter, thereby intensifying the concentration and isolation of the urban poor."

Other government policies also contributed to the growth of jobless ghettos, both directly and indirectly. Many black communities were uprooted by urban renewal and forced migration. The construction of freeway and highway networks through the hearts of many cities in the 1950s produced the most dramatic changes, as many viable low-income communities were destroyed. These networks not only encouraged relocation from the cities to the suburbs, "they also created barriers between the sections of the cities, walling off poor and minority neighborhoods from central business districts. Like urban renewal, highway and expressway construction also displaced many poor people from their homes."

Federal housing policy also contributed to the gradual shift to jobless ghettos. Indeed, the lack of federal action to fight extensive segregation against African Americans in urban housing markets and acquiescence to the opposition of organized neighborhood groups to the construction of public housing in their communities have resulted in massive segregated housing projects. The federal public housing program evolved in two policy stages that represented two distinct styles. The Wagner Housing Act of 1937 initiated the first stage. Concerned that the construction of public housing might depress private rent levels, groups such as the U.S. Building and Loan League and the National Association of Real Estate Boards successfully lobbied Congress to require, by law, that for each new unit of public housing one "unsafe or unsanitary" unit of public housing be destroyed. As Mark Condon (1991) points out, "This policy increased employment in the urban construction market while insulating private rent levels by barring the expansion of the housing stock available to low-income families."

The early years of the public housing program produced positive results. Initially, the program mainly served intact families temporarily displaced by the Depression or in need of housing after the end of World War II. For many of these families, public housing was the first step on the road toward economic recovery. Their stay in the projects was relatively brief. The economic mobility of these families "contributed to the sociological stability of the first public housing communities, and explains the program's initial success."

The passage of the Housing Act of 1949 marked the beginning of the second policy stage. It instituted and funded the urban renewal program designed to eradicate urban slums. "Public housing was now meant to collect the ghetto residents left homeless by the urban renewal bulldozers." A new, lower-income ceiling for public housing residency was established by the federal Public Housing Authority, and families with incomes above that ceiling were evicted, thereby restricting access to public housing to the most economically disadvantaged segments of the population.

This change in federal housing policy coincided with the mass migration of African Americans from the rural South to the cities of the Northeast and Midwest. Since smaller suburban communities refused to permit the construction of public housing, the units were overwhelmingly concentrated in the overcrowded and deteriorating inner city ghettos—the poorest and least socially organized sections of the city and the metropolitan area. "This growing population of politically weak urban poor was unable to counteract the desires of vocal middle- and working-class whites for segregated housing," housing that would keep blacks out of white neighborhoods. In short, public housing represents a federally funded institution that has isolated families by race and class for decades, and has therefore contributed to the growing concentration of jobless families in the inner-city ghettos in recent years.

Also, since 1980, a fundamental shift in the federal government's support for basic urban programs has aggravated the problems of joblessness and social organization in the new poverty neighborhoods. The Reagan and Bush administrations—proponents of the New Federalism—sharply cut spending on direct aid to cities, including general revenue sharing, urban mass transit, public service jobs and job training, compensatory education, social service block grants, local public works, economic development assistance, and urban development action grants. In 1980, the federal contribution to city budgets was 18 percent; by 1990 it had dropped to 6.4 percent. In addition, the economic recession which began in the Northeast in 1989 and lasted until the early 1990s sharply reduced those revenues that the cities themselves generated, thereby creating budget deficits that resulted in further cutbacks in basic services and programs along with increases in local taxes.

For many cities, especially the older cities of the East and Midwest, the combination of the New Federalism and the recession led to the worst fiscal and service crisis since the Depression. Cities have become increasingly underserviced, and many have been on the brink of bankruptcy. They have therefore not been in a position to combat effectively three unhealthy social conditions that have emerged or become prominent since 1980: (1) the prevalence of crack-cocaine addiction and the violent crime associated with it; (2) the AIDS epidemic and its escalating public health costs; and (3) the sharp rise in the homeless population not only for individuals but for whole families as well.

Although drug addiction and its attendant violence, AIDS and its toll on public health resources, and homelessness are found in many American communities, their impact on the ghetto is profound. These communities, whose residents have been pushed to the margins of society, have few resources with which to combat these social ills that arose in the 1980s. Fiscally strapped cities have watched helplessly as these problems—exacerbated by the new poverty, the decline of social organization in the jobless neighborhoods, and the reduction of social services—have made the city at large seem a dangerous and threatening place in which to live. Accordingly, working- and middle-class urban residents continue to relocate in the suburbs. Thus, while joblessness and related social problems are on the rise in inner-city neighborhoods, especially in those that represent the new poverty areas, the larger city has fewer and fewer resources with which to combat them.

Finally, policymakers indirectly contributed to the emergence of jobless ghettos by making decisions that have decreased the attractiveness of low-paying jobs and accelerated the relative decline in wages for low-income workers. In particular, in the absence of an effective labor-market policy, they have tolerated industry practices that undermine worker security, such as the reduction in benefits and the rise of involuntary part-time employment, and they have "allowed the minimum wage to erode to its second-lowest level in purchasing power in 40 years." After adjusting for inflation, "the minimum wage is 26 percent below its average level in the 1970s." Moreover, they virtually eliminated AFDC benefits for families in which a mother is employed at least half-time. In the early 1970s, a working mother with two children whose wages equaled 75 percent of the amount designated as the poverty line could receive AFDC benefits as a wage supplement in forty-nine states; in 1995 only those in three states could. . . . [E]ven with the expansion of the earned income tax credit (a wage subsidy for the working poor) such policies make it difficult for poor workers to support their families and protect their children. The erosion of wages and benefits forces many low-income workers in the inner city to move or remain on welfare.

REFERENCES

Condon, Mark. 1991. "Public Housing, Crime, and the Urban Labor Market: A Study of Black Youths in Chicago." Working paper series, Malcolm Wiener Center for Social Policy, John F. Kennedy School of Government, Harvard University, March, no. H-91-3.
Holzer, Harry J., Keith R. Ihlanfeldt, and David L. Sjoquist. 1994. "Work, Search and Travel among White and Black Youth." *Journal of Urban Economics* 35:320–45.
Wilson, William Julius. 1987. *The Truly Disadvantaged: The Inner City, the Underclass, and Public Policy.* Chicago: University of Chicago Press.

43

OVER THE COUNTER
McDonald's

ROBIN LEIDNER

Robin Leidner's 1993 case study, "Over the Counter: McDonald's," takes us inside one employment organization and reveals what it is like to work there. Leidner, an associate professor of sociology at the University of Pennsylvania, shows how McDonald's employees are intensively socialized. She also illustrates how the work is reduced to simple steps, and therefore routinized, so that managers and owners can maintain the most control over their product and over their employees. This process of increased routinization in the workplace has a long history in industrialization, especially within factory work. Many social analysts, including Karl Marx (1818–1883), have argued that the routinization of work leads to workers' feeling alienated from their products and from their sense of self.

Organizations have many ways of obtaining the cooperation of participants, ranging from persuasion and enticement to force and curtailment of options. All organizations "hope to make people want to do what the organization needs done" (Biggart 1989:128), but when they cannot count on success in manipulating people's desires they can do their best to compel people to act in the organization's interests.

Organizations choose strategies that rely on socialization and social control in varying mixtures that are determined by the aims of the organization, the constraints set by the organizational environment and the nature of the work, and the interests and resources of the parties involved. In service-providing organizations, upper-level management must concern itself with the wishes and behavior of service recipients and various groups of workers.[1] For each group, service organizations try to find the most effective and least costly ways to get people to act in the organizations' interests, proffering various carrots and sticks, making efforts to win hearts and minds, closing off choices.

Organizations that routinize work exert control primarily by closing off choices. There is much room for variation, however, in what aspects of the work organizations will choose to routinize, how they go about it, and how much freedom of decision making remains. Moreover, even when routines radically constrain choice, organizations still must socialize participants and set up systems of incentives and disincentives to ensure the compliance of workers and customers.

. . . McDonald's . . . take[s] routinization to extremes . . . includ[ing] predetermination of action and transformation of character. . . . McDonald's stresses minute specification of procedures, eliminating most decision making for most workers, although it does make some efforts to standardize operations by transforming the characters of its store-level managers. . . .

This . . . [selection] show[s] how the compan[y's] approaches to routinizing the work of those who interact with customers depend largely on the predictability of service recipients' behavior, which in turn depends on the kinds of resources the organizations have available to channel consumer behavior. . . . At McDonald's . . . the routines sharply limit the workers' autonomy without giving them much leverage over customers.

McDonald's

No one ever walks into a McDonald's and asks, "So, what's good today?" except satirically. The heart of McDonald's success is its uniformity and predictability. Not only is the food supposed to taste the same every day everywhere in the world, but McDonald's promises that every meal will be served quickly, courteously, and with a smile. Delivering on that promise over 20 million times a day in 54 countries is the company's colossal challenge (*McDonald's Annual Report* 1990:2). Its strategy for meeting that challenge draws on scientific management's most basic tenets: Find the One Best Way to do every task and see that the work is conducted accordingly.[2]

To ensure that all McDonald's restaurants serve products of uniform quality, the company uses centralized planning, centrally designed training programs, centrally approved and supervised suppliers, automated machinery and other specially designed equipment, meticulous specifications, and systematic inspections. To provide its customers with a uniformly pleasant "McDonald's experience," the company also tries to mass produce friendliness, deference, diligence, and good cheer through a variety of socialization and social control techniques. Despite sneers from those who equate uniformity with mediocrity, the success of McDonald's has been spectacular.

McFacts

By far the world's largest fast-food company, McDonald's has over 11,800 stores worldwide (*McDonald's Annual Report* 1990:1), and its 1990 international sales surpassed those of its three largest competitors combined (Berg

1991 sec. 3:6).[3] In the United States, consumer familiarity with McDonald's is virtually universal: The company estimates that 95 percent of U.S. consumers eat at a McDonald's at least once a year (Koepp 1987:58). McDonald's 1990 profits were $802.3 million, the third highest profits of any retailing company in the world (*Fortune* 1991:179). At a time when the ability of many U.S. businesses to compete on the world market is in question, McDonald's continues to expand around the globe—most recently to Morocco—everywhere remaking consumer demand in its own image.

As politicians, union leaders, and others concerned with the effects of the shift to a service economy are quick to point out, McDonald's is a major employer. McDonald's restaurants in the United States employ about half a million people (Bertagnoli 1989:33), including one out of 15 first-time job seekers (Wildavsky 1989:30). The company claims that 7 percent of all current U.S. workers have worked for McDonald's at some time (Koepp 1987:59). Not only has McDonald's directly influenced the lives of millions of workers, but its impact has also been extended by the efforts of many kinds of organizations, especially in the service sector, to imitate the organizational features they see as central to McDonald's success. . . .

The relentless standardization and infinite replication that inspire both horror and admiration are the legacy of Ray Kroc, a salesman who got into the hamburger business in 1954, when he was 52 years old, and created a worldwide phenomenon.[4] His inspiration was a phenomenally successful hamburger stand owned by the McDonald brothers of San Bernardino, California. He believed that their success could be reproduced consistently through carefully controlled franchises, and his hamburger business succeeded on an unprecedented scale. The basic idea was to serve a very few items of strictly uniform quality at low prices. Over the years, the menu has expanded somewhat and prices have risen, but the emphasis on strict, detailed standardization has never varied. . . .

Enforcement of McDonald's standards has been made easier over the years by the introduction of highly specialized equipment. Every company-owned store in the United States now has an "in-store processor," a computer system that calculates yields and food costs, keeps track of inventory and cash, schedules labor, and breaks down sales by time of day, product, and worker (*McDonald's Annual Report* 1989:29). In today's McDonald's, lights and buzzers tell workers exactly when to turn burgers or take fries out of the fat, and technologically advanced cash registers, linked to the computer system, do much of the thinking for window workers. Specially designed ketchup dispensers squirt exactly the right amount of ketchup on each burger in the approved flower pattern. The french-fry scoops let workers fill a bag and set it down in one continuous motion and help them gauge the proper serving size.

The extreme standardization of McDonald's products, and its workers, is closely tied to its marketing. The company advertises on a massive scale— in 1989, McDonald's spent $1.1 billion systemwide on advertising and promotions (*McDonald's Annual Report* 1989:32). In fact, McDonald's is the single most advertised brand in the world (*Advertising Age* 1990:6).[5] The national advertising assures the public that it will find high standards of quality, service, and cleanliness at every McDonald's store. The intent of the strict quality-control standards applied to every aspect of running a McDonald's outlet, from proper cleaning of the bathrooms to making sure the hamburgers are served hot, is to help franchise owners keep the promises made in the company's advertising.[6]

The image of McDonald's outlets promoted in the company's advertising is one of fun, wholesomeness, and family orientation. Kroc was particularly concerned that his stores not become teenage hangouts, since that would discourage families' patronage. To minimize their attractiveness to teenage loiterers, McDonald's stores do not have jukeboxes, video games, or even telephones. Kroc initially decided not to hire young women to work behind McDonald's counters for the same reason: "They attracted the wrong kind of boys" (Boas and Chain 1976:19).

You Deserve a Break Today: Conditions of Employment

Although McDonald's does not want teenagers to hang out on its premises, it certainly does want them to work in the stores. Almost half of its U.S. employees are under 20 years old (Wildavsky 1989:30). In recent years, as the McDonald's chain has grown faster than the supply of teenagers, the company has also tried to attract senior citizens and housewives as workers. What people in these groups have in common is a preference or need for part-time work, and therefore a dearth of alternative employment options. Because of this lack of good alternatives, and because they may have other means of support for themselves and their dependents, many people in these groups are willing to accept jobs that provide less than subsistence wages.

Traditionally, McDonald's has paid most of its employees the minimum wage, although labor shortages have now forced wages up in some parts of the country, raising the average hourly pay of crew people to $4.60 by 1989 (Gibson and Johnson 1989:B1). Benefits such as health insurance and sick days are entirely lacking for crew people at most franchises. In fact, when the topic of employee benefits was introduced in a class lecture at McDonald's management training center, it turned out to refer to crew meetings, individual work-evaluation sessions, and similar programs to make McDonald's management seem accessible and fair.

The lack of more tangible benefits is linked to the organization of employment at McDonald's as part-time work. According to the manager of the franchise I studied, all McDonald's hourly employees are officially part-time workers, in that no one is guaranteed a full work week. The company's labor practices are designed to make workers bear the costs of uncertainty based on fluctuation in demand. McDonald's places great emphasis on having no more crew people at work at any time than are required by customer flow at that period, as measured in half-hour increments. Most workers therefore have fluctuating schedules, and they are expected to be flexible about working late or leaving early depending on the volume of business.

Not surprisingly, McDonald's employee-turnover rates are extremely high. Turnover averaged 153 percent in 1984, and 205 percent in 1985 (training center lecture). These high rates are partly attributable to the large percentage of teenage workers, many of whom took the job with the intention of working for only a short time. However, the limited job rewards, both financial and personal, of working at McDonald's are certainly crucial contributing factors.

Some argue that the conditions of employment at McDonald's are unproblematic to the workers who take them. If we assume that most McDonald's workers are teenagers who are in school and are not responsible for supporting themselves or others, then many of the features of McDonald's work do not seem so bad. Fringe benefits and employment security are relatively unimportant to them, and the limited and irregular hours of work may actually be attractive (see Greenberger and Steinberg 1986). These arguments are less persuasive when applied to other McDonald's employees, such as mothers of young children, and retirees, although those workers might similarly appreciate the part-time hours, and access to other forms of income and benefits could make McDonald's employment conditions acceptable, if not desirable. Employment security would not be important to the many people who choose to work at McDonald's as a stopgap or for a limited period.[7] Many of the workers at the franchise I studied had taken their jobs with the intention of holding them only temporarily, and many were being supported by their parents. However, other workers there were trying to support themselves and their dependents on earnings from McDonald's, sometimes in combination with other low-paying jobs. . . .

McDonald's wants both managers and workers to dedicate themselves to the values summed up in its three-letter corporate credo, "QSC." Quality, service, and cleanliness are the ends that the company's thousands of rules and specifications are intended to achieve. Kroc promised his customers QSC,[8] and he believed firmly that if, at every level of the organization, McDonald's workers were committed to providing higher-quality food, speedier service, and cleaner surroundings than the competition, the success of the enterprise was assured. McDonald's extraordinarily elaborate training programs are designed both to teach McDonald's procedures and standards and to instill and enforce corporate values.

Kroc approached his business with a zeal and dedication that even he regarded as religious: "I've often said that *I believe in God, family, and McDonald's—and in the office that order is reversed*" (Kroc with Anderson 1977:124 [emphasis in original]). Throughout the organization, Kroc is still frequently quoted and held up as a model, and nowhere is his ongoing influence more apparent than at Hamburger University.

Taking Hamburgers Seriously: Training Managers

McDonald's main management training facility is located on 80 beautifully landscaped acres in Oak Brook, Illinois, a suburb of Chicago. Its name, Hamburger University, captures the thoroughness and intensity with which McDonald's approaches management training, and it also suggests the comic possibilities of immersion in McDonald's corporate world.[9] The company tries to produce managers "with ketchup in their veins," a common McDonald's phrase for people who love their work, take pride in it, and are extraordinarily hardworking, competitive, and loyal to McDonald's. A line I heard frequently at Hamburger U. was, "We take hamburgers very seriously here." Nothing I saw called this fixity of purpose into doubt.

Ensuring uniformity of service and products in its far-flung empire is a major challenge for McDonald's. In each McDonald's store, in regional training centers, and at Hamburger University, crew people, managers, and franchisees learn that there is a McDonald's way to handle virtually every detail of the business and that doing things differently means doing things wrong. Training begins in the stores, where crew people are instructed using materials provided by the corporation and where managers prepare for more advanced training. Management trainees and managers seeking promotion work with their store managers to learn materials in manuals and workbooks provided by the corporation. When they have completed the manual for the appropriate level, they are eligible for courses taught in regional training centers and at Hamburger University: the Basic Operations Course, the Intermediate Operations Course, the Applied Equipment Course, and, finally, the Advanced Operations Course, taught only at Hamburger University. Altogether, the full training program requires approximately six hundred to one thousand hours of work. It is required of everyone who wishes to own a McDonald's store, and it is strongly recommended for all store managers. By the time trainees get to Hamburger University for the Advanced Operations Course, they have already put in considerable time working in a McDonald's store—two to three and a half years, on average—and have acquired much detailed knowledge about McDonald's workings.

Hamburger University sometimes offers special programs and seminars in addition to the regular training courses. For example, a group of McDonald's office workers attended Hamburger University during my visit; a training manager told me that they had been brought in to get "a little shot of ketchup and mustard."[10]

The zeal and competence of franchisees and managers are of special concern to McDonald's, since they are the people responsible for daily enforcement of corporate standards. Their training therefore focuses as much on building commitment and motivation as on extending knowledge of company procedures. In teaching management skills, McDonald's also works on the personalities of its managers, encouraging both rigid adherence to routines and, somewhat paradoxically, personal flexibility. Flexibility is presented as a virtue both because the company wants to minimize resistance to adopting McDonald's ways of doing things and to frequent revision of procedures, and because managers must provide whatever responsiveness to special circumstances the system has, since crew people are allowed virtually no discretion. Hamburger University therefore provides a large dose of personal-growth cheerleading along with more prosaic skills training. . . .

The curriculum of the Advanced Operating Course includes inculcation with pride in McDonald's. Sessions are devoted to McDonald's history and McDonald's dedication to ever-improving QSC. Lectures are sprinkled with statistics attesting to McDonald's phenomenal success. Students hear the story of Ray Kroc's rise to wealth and prominence, based on his strength of character and willingness to work hard, and are assigned his autobiography, *Grinding It Out* (Kroc with Anderson 1977). Kroc is quoted frequently in lectures, and students are encouraged to model themselves on him. They are told repeatedly that they have all proven themselves "winners" by getting as far as they have at McDonald's. The theme throughout is "We're the best in the world, we know exactly what we're doing, but our success depends on the best efforts of every one of you." [11]

About 3,500 students from all over the world attend classes at Hamburger University each year, most of them taking the Advanced Operations Course (Rosenthal 1989). Those who complete the course receive diplomas proclaiming them Doctors of Hamburgerology. As late as 1978 or 1979, a training manager told me, most classes included only one or two women, but women now comprise 40–60 percent of the students, and women and minorities now make up 54 percent of McDonald's franchisees (Bertagnoli 1989:33). In my homeroom, however, the proportion of women was much smaller, and there was just a handful of minority students.

The course lasts two weeks and is extremely rigorous. Class time is about evenly divided between work in the labs and lectures on store operations and personnel management. In the labs, trainees learn the mechanics of ensuring that McDonald's food is of consistent quality and its stores in good working order. They learn to check the equipment and maintain it properly so that fries cook at precisely the right temperature, shakes are mixed to just the right consistency, and ice cubes are uniform. "Taste of Quality" labs reinforce McDonald's standards for food quality. For instance, in a Condiments Lab, trainees are taught exactly how to store vegetables and sauces, what the shelf lives of these products are, and how they should look and taste. Samples of "McDonald's quality" Big Mac Special Sauce are contrasted with samples that have been left too long unrefrigerated and should be discarded. The importance of serving only food that meets McDonald's standards is constantly emphasized and, a trainer pointed out, "McDonald's has standards for everything, down to the width of the pickle slices." . . .

The training at Hamburger University combines a sense of fun with dead seriousness about keeping McDonald's on top in the hamburger business through relentless quality control and effective management of workers and customers. It is up to the owners and managers of individual McDonald's stores to make that happen. . . .

Learning the Job

As a manager at Hamburger University explained to me, the crew training process is how McDonald's standardization is maintained, how the company ensures that Big Macs are the same everywhere in the world. The McDonald's central administration supplies franchisees with videotapes and other materials for use in training workers to meet the company's exacting specifications. The company produces a separate videotape for each job in the store, and it encourages franchisees to keep their tape libraries up-to-date as product specifications change. The Hamburger University professor who taught the Advanced Operating Course session on training said that, to keep current, franchisees should be buying 10 or 12 tapes a year. For each work station in the store, McDonald's also has a "Station Operation Checklist" (SOC), a short but highly detailed job description that lays out exactly how the job should be done: how much ketchup and mustard go on each kind of hamburger, in what sequence the products customers order are to be gathered, what arm motion is to be used in salting a batch of fries, and so on. . . .

The Routine

McDonald's had routinized the work of its crews so thoroughly that decision making had practically been eliminated from the jobs. As one window worker told me, "They've tried to break it down so that it's almost idiot-proof." Most of the workers agreed that there was little call for them to use their own judgment on the job, since there were rules about everything. If an unusual problem arose, the workers were supposed to turn it over to a manager.

Many of the noninteractive parts of the window workers' job had been made idiot-proof through automation.[12] The soda machines, for example, automatically dispensed the proper amount of beverage for regular, medium, and large cups. Computerized cash registers performed a variety of functions handled elsewhere by human waitresses, waiters, and cashiers, making some kinds of skill and knowledge unnecessary. As a customer gave an order, the window worker simply pressed the cash register button labeled with the name of the selected product. There was no need to write the orders down, because the buttons lit up to indicate which products had been selected. Nor was there any need to remember prices, because the prices were programmed into the machines. Like most new cash registers, these added the tax automatically and told workers how much change customers were owed, so the window crew did not need to know how to do those calculations. The cash registers also helped regulate some of the crew's interactive work by reminding them to try to increase the size of each sale. For example, when a customer ordered a Big Mac, large fries, and a regular Coke, the cash register buttons for cookies, hot apple pies, ice cream cones, and ice cream sundaes would light up, prompting the worker to suggest dessert. It took some skill to operate the relatively complicated cash register, as my difficulties during my first work shift made clear, but this organizationally specific skill could soon be acquired on the job.

In addition to doing much of the workers' thinking for them, the computerized cash registers made it possible for managers to monitor the crew members' work and the store's inventory very closely.[13] For example, if the number of Quarter Pounder with Cheese boxes gone did not match the number of Quarter Pounders with Cheese sold or accounted for as waste, managers might suspect that workers were giving away or taking food. Managers could easily tell which workers had brought in the most money during a given interval and who was doing the best job of persuading customers to buy a particular item. The computerized system could also complicate what would otherwise have been simple customer requests, however. For example, when a man who had not realized the benefit of ordering his son's food as a Happy Meal came back to the counter to ask whether his little boy could have one of the plastic beach pails the Happy Meals were served in, I had to ask a manager what to do, since fulfilling the request would produce a discrepancy between the inventory and the receipts.[14] Sometimes the extreme systematization can induce rather than prevent idiocy, as when a window worker says she cannot serve a cup of coffee that is half decaffeinated and half regular because she would not know how to ring up the sale.[15]

The interactive part of window work is routinized through the Six Steps of Window Service and also through rules aimed at standardizing attitudes and demeanors as well as words and actions. The window workers were taught that they represented McDonald's to the public and that their attitudes were therefore an important component of service quality. Crew people could be reprimanded for not smiling, and often were. The window workers were supposed to be cheerful and polite at all times, but they were also told to be themselves while on the job. McDonald's does not want its workers to seem like robots, so part of the emotion work asked of the window crew is that they act naturally. "Being yourself" in this situation meant behaving in a way that did not seem stilted. Although workers had some latitude to go beyond the script, the short, highly schematic routine obviously did not allow much room for genuine self-expression.

Workers were not the only ones constrained by McDonald's routines, of course. The cooperation of service recipients was crucial to the smooth functioning of the operation. In many kinds of interactive service work . . . constructing the compliance of service recipients is an important part of the service worker's job. The routines such workers use may be designed to maximize the control each worker has over customers. McDonald's window workers' routines were not intended to give them much leverage over customers' behavior, however. The window workers interacted only with people who had already decided to do business with McDonald's and who therefore did not need to be persuaded to take part in the service interaction.

Furthermore, almost all customers were familiar enough with McDonald's routines to know how they were expected to behave. For instance, I never saw a customer who did not know that she or he was supposed to come up to the counter rather than sit down and wait to be served. This customer training was accomplished through advertising, spatial design, customer experience, and the example of other customers, making it unnecessary for the window crew to put much effort into getting customers to fit into their work routines.[16]

McDonald's ubiquitous advertising trains consumers at the same time that it tries to attract them to McDonald's. Television commercials demonstrate how the service system is supposed to work and familiarize customers with new products. Additional cues about expected customer behavior are provided by the design of the restaurants. For example, the entrances usually lead to the service counter, not to the dining area, making it unlikely that customers will fail to realize that they should get in line, and the placement of waste cans makes clear that customers are expected to throw out their own trash. Most important, the majority of customers have had years of experience with McDonald's, as well as with other fast-food restaurants that have similar arrangements. The company estimates that the average customer visits a McDonald's 20 times a year (Koepp 1987:58), and it is not uncommon for a customer to come in several times per week. For many customers, then, ordering at McDonald's is as routine an interaction as it is for the window worker. Indeed, because employee turnover is so high, steady customers may be more familiar with the work routines than the workers serving them are. Customers who are new to McDonald's can take their cue from more experienced customers.[17]

Not surprisingly, then, most customers at the McDonald's I studied knew what was expected of them and tried to play their part well. They sorted themselves into lines and gazed up at the menu boards while waiting to be served. They usually gave their orders in the conventional sequence: burgers or other entrees, french fries or other side orders, drinks, and desserts. Hurried customers with savvy might order an item "only if it's in the bin," that is, ready to be served. Many customers prepared carefully so that they could give their orders promptly when they got to the counter. This preparation sometimes became apparent when a worker interrupted to ask, "What kind of dressing?" or "Cream and sugar?", flustering customers who could not deliver their orders as planned.

McDonald's routines, like those of other interactive service businesses, depend on the predictability of customers, but these businesses must not grind to a halt if customers are not completely cooperative. Some types of deviations from standard customer behavior are so common that they become routine themselves, and these can be handled through subroutines (Stinchcombe 1990:39). McDonald's routines work most efficiently when all customers accept their products exactly as they are usually prepared; indeed, the whole business is based on this premise. Since, however, some people give special instructions for customized products, such as "no onions," the routine allows for these exceptions.[18] At the franchise I studied, workers could key the special requests into their cash registers, which automatically printed out "grill slips" with the instructions for the grill workers to follow. Under this system, the customer making the special order had to wait for it to be prepared, but the smooth flow of service for other customers was not interrupted. Another type of routine difficulty was customer dissatisfaction with food quality. Whenever a customer had a complaint about the food—cold fries, dried-out burger—window workers were authorized to supply a new product immediately without consulting a supervisor.[19]

These two kinds of difficulties—special orders and complaints about food—were the only irregularities window workers were authorized to handle. The subroutines increased the flexibility of the service system, but they did not increase the workers' discretion, since procedures were in place for dealing with both situations. All other kinds of demands fell outside the window crew's purview. If they were faced with a dispute about money, an extraordinary request, or a furious customer, workers were instructed to call a manager; the crew had no authority to handle such problems.

Given the almost complete regimentation of tasks and preemption of decision making, does McDonald's need the flexibility and thoughtfulness of human workers? As the declining supply of teenagers and legislated increases in the minimum wage drive up labor costs, it is not surprising that McDonald's is experimenting with electronic replacements. So far, the only robot in use handles behind-the-scenes work rather than customer interactions. ARCH (Automated Restaurant Crew Helper) works in a Minnesota McDonald's where it does all the frying and lets workers know when to prepare sandwich buns, when supplies are running low, and when fries are no longer fresh enough to sell. Other McDonald's stores (along with Arby's and Burger King units) are experimenting with a touch-screen computer system that lets customers order their meals themselves, further curtailing the role of the window worker. Although it requires increased customer socialization and cooperation, early reports are that the system cuts service time by 30 seconds and increases sales per window worker 10–20 percent (Chaudhry 1989:F61).

Overview

McDonald's pioneered the routinization of interactive service work and remains an exemplar of extreme standardization. Innovation is not discouraged at McDonald's; the company favors experimentation, at least among managers and franchisees. Ironically, though, "the object is to look for new, innovative ways to create an experience that is exactly the same no matter what McDonald's you walk into, no matter where it is in the world"

(Rosenthal 1989:12). Thus, when someone in the field comes up with a good idea—and such McDonald's success stories as the Egg McMuffin and the Big Mac were store-level inspirations (Koepp 1987:60)—the corporation experiments, tests, and refines the idea and finally implements it in a uniform way systemwide. One distinctive feature of McDonald's-style routinization is that there, to a great extent, uniformity is a goal in itself. . . .

McDonald's . . . does promise uniform products and consistent service, and to provide them the company has broken down virtually every task required to run a store into detailed routines with clear instructions and standards. For those routines to run smoothly, conditions must be relatively predictable, so McDonald's tries to control as many contingencies as possible, including the attitudes and behavior of workers, managers, and customers. The company uses a wide array of socialization and control techniques to ensure that these people are familiar with McDonald's procedures and willing to comply with them.

Most McDonald's work is organized as low-paying, low-status, part-time jobs that give workers little autonomy. Almost every decision about how to do crew people's tasks has been made in advance by the corporation, and many of the decisions have been built into the stores' technology. Why use human workers at all, if not to take advantage of the human capacity to respond to circumstances flexibly? McDonald's does want to provide at least a simulacrum of the human attributes of warmth, friendliness, and recognition. For that reason, not only workers' movements but also their words, demeanor, and attitudes are subject to managerial control.

Although predictability is McDonald's hallmark, not all factors can be controlled by management. One of the most serious irregularities that store management must deal with is fluctuation in the flow of customers, both expected and unexpected. Since personnel costs are the most manipulable variable affecting a store's profitability, managers want to match labor power to consumer demand as exactly as possible. They do so by paying all crew people by the hour, giving them highly irregular hours based on expected sales—sometimes including split shifts—and sending workers home early or keeping them late as conditions require. In other words, the costs of uneven demand are shifted to workers whenever possible. Since most McDonald's crew people cannot count on working a particular number of hours at precisely scheduled times, it is hard for them to make plans based on how much money they will earn or exactly what times they will be free. Workers are pressured to be flexible in order to maximize the organization's own flexibility in staffing levels. In contrast, of course, flexibility in the work process itself is minimized.

Routinization has not made the crew people's work easy. Their jobs, although highly structured and repetitive, are often demanding and stressful. Under these working conditions, the organization's limited commitment to workers, as reflected in job security, wages, and benefits, makes the task of maintaining worker motivation and discipline even more challenging. A variety of factors, many orchestrated by the corporation, keeps McDonald's crew people hard at work despite the limited rewards. Socialization into McDonald's norms, extremely close supervision (both human and electronic), individual and group incentives, peer pressure, and pressure from customers all play their part in getting workers to do things the McDonald's way.

Because franchisees and store-level managers are responsible for enforcing standardization throughout the McDonald's system, their socialization includes a more intensive focus on building commitment to and pride in the organization than does crew training. In fact, it is the corporate attempt at transforming these higher-level McDonald's people by making them more loyal, confident, flexible, and sensitive to others, as well as more knowledgeable about company procedures, that makes the extreme rigidity of the crew training workable. The crew people do not have to be trusted with decision-making authority, because all unusual problems are referred to managers. Their more extensive training gives them the knowledge and attitudes to make the kinds of decisions the corporation would approve. . . . In addition to thorough socialization, McDonald's managers and franchisees are subjected to close corporate oversight. Every aspect of their stores' operations is rated by corporate staff, and they are sanctioned accordingly.

Despite elaborate socialization and social controls, McDonald's stores do not, of course, carry out every corporate directive exactly as recommended. In the store I studied, managers did not always provide their workers with the mandated support and encouragement, crew trainers did not always follow the four-step training system, and window workers did not always carry out the Six Steps of Window Service with the required eye contact and smile. There were many kinds of pressures to deviate from corporate standards. Nonetheless, the benefits of standardization should not be underestimated. As every Durkheimian knows, clear rules and shared standards provide support and coherence as well as constraint. Although some aspects of the routines did strike the participants as overly constraining, undignified, or silly, the approved routines largely worked. In all of these examples of deviation, the routines would have produced more efficient and pleasant service, and those that apply to management and training would have benefited workers as well as customers.

Obtaining the cooperation of workers and managers is not enough to ensure the smooth functioning of McDonald's relatively inflexible routines. Customers must be routinized as well. Not only do customers have to understand the service routine and accept the limited range of choices the company offers, they also must be willing to do some kinds of work that are done for them in conventional restaurants, including carrying food to the table and throwing out their trash. Experience, advertising, the example set by other customers, and clear environmental cues familiarize customers with McDonald's routines, and most want to cooperate in order to speed service. For these reasons, McDonald's interactive service workers do not have to direct most customers, and window workers' routines are therefore not designed to give them power over customers.

ENDNOTES

[1] Suppliers, competitors, and other parties outside of the organization are also relevant actors, but organizational efforts to control their behavior will not be considered here (see Prus 1989).

[2] The 1990s may bring unprecedented changes to McDonald's. Although its overseas business continues to thrive, domestic sales have been declining. To overcome the challenges to profitability presented by the economic recession, lower-priced competitors, and changes in consumer tastes, CEO Michael Quinlan has instituted experimental changes in the menu, in pricing strategy, and even in the degree of flexibility granted to franchisees (see *Advertising Age* 1991; Berg 1991; *McDonald's Annual Report* 1990; Therrien 1991).

[3] McDonald's restaurants are generally referred to as "stores" by McDonald's staff. The company's share of the domestic fast-food market has declined from 18.7 percent in 1985 to 16.6 percent in 1990 (Therrien 1991).

[4] Information about McDonald's history comes primarily from Boas and Chain 1976; Kroc with Anderson 1977; Love 1986; Luxenberg 1985; and McDonald's training materials. Reiter's (1991) description of Burger King reveals numerous parallels in the operation of the two companies, although Burger King, unlike McDonald's, is a subsidiary of a multinational conglomerate.

[5] In addition to paid advertising, McDonald's bolsters its public image with promotional and philanthropic activities such as an All-American High School Basketball Game, essay contests and scholarship programs for black and Hispanic students, and Ronald McDonald Houses where outpatient children and their families and the parents of hospitalized children can stay at minimal cost.

[6] Conversely, details of the routines are designed with marketing in mind. The bags that hold the regular-size portions of french fries are shorter than the french fries are, so that when workers fill them with their regulation french-fry scoops, the servings seem generous, overflowing the packaging. The names of the serving sizes also are intended to give customers the impression that they are getting a lot for their money: French fries come in regular and large sizes, sodas in regular, medium, and large cups. I was quickly corrected during a work shift when I inadvertently referred to an order for a "small" drink.

[7] Some commentators fall into the trap of assuming that workers' preferences are determinative of working conditions, a mistake they do not make when discussing higher-status workers such as faculty who must rely on a string of temporary appointments.

[8] Actually, Kroc usually spoke of QSCV—quality, service, cleanliness, and value (see Kroc with Anderson 1977)—but QSC was the term used in most McDonald's training and motivational materials at the time of my research. The company cannot enforce "value" because antitrust restrictions prevent McDonald's from dictating prices to its franchisees (Love 1986:145). Nevertheless, recent materials return to the original four-part pledge of QSC & V (see, e.g., *McDonald's Annual Report* 1989:i).

[9] Branches of Hamburger University now operate in London, Munich, and Tokyo (*McDonald's Annual Report* 1989:28). Burger King University is similar in many respects (Reiter 1991).

[10] The effort to involve corporate employees in the central mission of the organization extends beyond such special programs. McDonald's prides itself on keeping its corporate focus firmly on store-level operations, and it wants all its employees to have a clear idea of what it takes to make a McDonald's restaurant work. Therefore, all McDonald's employees, from attorneys to data-entry clerks, spend time working in a McDonald's restaurant.

[11] Biggart (1989:143–47) shows that both adulation of a charismatic founder and repeated characterization of participants as winners are common in direct-sales organizations. Like McDonald's, such organizations face the problem of motivating people who are widely dispersed geographically and who are not corporate employees.

[12] The in-store processors similarly affected managers' work. A disaffected McDonald's manager told Garson, "There is no such thing as a McDonald's manager. The computer manages the store" (Garson 1988:39).

[13] Garson (1988) provides an extended discussion of this point.

[14] The manager gave him the pail but had to ring it up on the machine as if he had given away a whole Happy Meal.

[15] Thanks to Charles Bosk for this story.

[16] Mills (1986) elaborates on "customer socialization." Environmental design as a factor in service provision is discussed by Wener (1985) and Normann (1984).

[17] The importance of customer socialization becomes apparent when people with very different consumer experiences are introduced to a service system. When the first McDonald's opened in the Soviet Union in 1990, Moscow's citizens did not find the system immediately comprehensible. They had to be persuaded to get on the shortest lines at the counter, since they had learned from experience that desirable goods were available only where there are long lines (Goldman 1990).

[18] Burger King's "Have it your way" campaign virtually forced McDonald's to allow such customized service.

[19] The defective food or its container was put into a special waste bin. Each shift, one worker or manager had the unenviable task of counting the items in the waste bin so that the inventory could be reconciled with the cash intake.

REFERENCES

Advertising Age. 1990. "Adman of the Decade: McDonald's Fred Turner: Making All the Right Moves," January 1, p. 6.

———. 1991. "100 Leading National Advertisers: McDonald's," September 25, pp. 49–50.

Berg, Eric N. 1991. "An American Icon Wrestles with a Troubled Future." *New York Times,* May 12, sec. 3, pp. 1, 6.

Bertagnoli, Lisa. 1989. "McDonald's: Company of the Quarter Century." *Restaurants and Institutions,* July 10, pp. 32–60.

Biggart, Nicole Woolsey. 1989. *Charismatic Capitalism: Direct Selling Organizations in America.* Chicago: University of Chicago Press. Pp. 128, 143–47.

Boas, Max and Steve Chain. 1976. *Big Mac: The Unauthorized Story of McDonald's.* New York: New American Library. P. 19.

Chaudhry, Rajan. 1989. "Burger Giants Singed by Battle." *Nation's Restaurant News,* August 7, p. F61.

"Fortune Global Service 500: The 50 Largest Retailing Companies." 1991. *Fortune,* August 26, p. 179.

Garson, Barbara. 1988. *The Electronic Sweatshop: How Computers Are Transforming the*

Office of the Future into the Factory of the Past. New York: Simon and Schuster. P. 39.

Gibson, Richard and Robert Johnson. 1989. "Big Mac Plots Strategy to Regain Sizzle." *Wall Street Journal,* September 29, p. B1.

Goldman, Marshall. 1990. Presentation at colloquium on Reforming the Soviet Economy, University of Pennsylvania, May 17.

Greenberger, Ellen and Laurence Steinberg. 1986. *When Teenagers Work: The Psychological and Social Costs of Adolescent Employment.* New York: Basic Books.

Koepp, Stephen. 1987. "Big Mac Strikes Back." *Time,* April 13, p. 60.

Kroc, Ray with Robert Anderson. 1977. *Grinding It Out: The Making of McDonald's.* Chicago: Contemporary Books. P. 124.

Love, John F. 1986. *McDonald's: Behind the Arches.* New York: Bantam Books. P. 145.

Luxenberg, Stan. 1985. *Roadside Empires: How the Chains Franchised America.* New York: Viking.

McDonald's Annual Report. 1989. Oak Brook, Illinois. Pp. i, 28, 29, 32.

———. 1990. Oak Brook, Illinois. Pp. 1–2.

Mills, Peter K. 1986. *Managing Service Industries: Organizational Practices in a Post-Industrial Economy.* Cambridge, MA: Ballinger.

Normann, Richard. 1984. *Service Management: Strategy and Leadership in Service Businesses.* Chichester, England: Wiley.

Prus, Robert. 1989. *Pursuing Customers: An Ethnography of Marketing Activities.* Newbury Park, CA: Sage.

Reiter, Ester. 1991. *Making Fast Food: From the Frying Pan into the Fryer.* Montreal: McGill-Queen's University Press.

Rosenthal, Herman M. 1989. "Inside Big Mac's World." *Newsday,* June 4, p. 12.

Stinchcombe, Arthur L. 1990. *Information and Organizations.* Berkeley: University of California Press. P. 39.

Therrien, Lois. 1991. "McRisky." *Business Week,* October 21, pp. 114–22.

Wener, Richard E. 1985. "The Environmental Psychology of Service Encounters." Pp. 101–12 in *The Service Encounter: Managing Employee/Customer Interaction in Service Businesses,* edited by John A. Czepiel, Michael R. Solomon, and Carol F. Surprenant. Lexington, MA: Lexington Books.

Wildavsky, Ben. 1989. "McJobs: Inside America's Largest Youth Training Program." *Policy Review* 49:30–37.

44

THE PROTESTANT ETHIC
AND THE SPIRIT OF CAPITALISM

MAX WEBER

The institution of religion is the topic of the following three selections. Sociologists have long studied how religion affects the social structure and the personal experience of individuals in society. Max Weber (1864–1920), for example, often placed the institution of religion at the center of his social analyses. Weber was particularly concerned with how changes in the institution of religion influenced changes in other social institutions, especially the economy. The selection excerpted here is from Weber's definitive and most famous study, *The Protestant Ethic and the Spirit of Capitalism* (1905). In his analysis of capitalism, Weber argues that the early Protestant worldviews of Calvinism and Puritanism were the primary factors in influencing the development of a capitalist economic system. Without the Protestant Reformation and a change in societal values toward rationality, capitalism would not have evolved as we know it today.

A product of modern European civilization, studying any problem of universal history, is bound to ask himself to what combination of circumstances the fact should be attributed that in Western civilization, and in Western civilization only, cultural phenomena have appeared which (as we like to think) lie in a line of development having *universal* significance and value. . . . All over the world there have been merchants, wholesale and retail, local and engaged in foreign trade. . . .

But in modern times the Occident has developed, in addition to this, a very different form of capitalism which has appeared nowhere else: the rational capitalistic organization of (formally) free labour. Only suggestions of it are found elsewhere. Even the organization of unfree labour reached a considerable degree of rationality only on plantations and to a very limited extent in the *Ergasteria* of antiquity. In the manors, manorial workshops, and domestic industries on estates with serf labour it was probably somewhat

From *The Protestant Ethic and the Spirit of Capitalism* by Max Weber, © 1958 Prentice-Hall, Inc. Reprinted by permission of Pearson Education, Upper Saddle River, NJ.

less developed. Even real domestic industries with free labour have definitely been proved to have existed in only a few isolated cases outside the Occident. . . .

Rational industrial organization, attuned to a regular market, and neither to political nor irrationally speculative opportunities for profit, is not, however, the only peculiarity of Western capitalism. The modern rational organization of the capitalistic enterprise would not have been possible without two other important factors in its development: the separation of business from the household, which completely dominates modern economic life, and closely connected with it, rational bookkeeping. . . .

Hence in a universal history of culture the central problem for us is not, in the last analysis, even from a purely economic view-point, the development of capitalistic activity as such, differing in different cultures only in form: the adventurer type, or capitalism in trade, war, politics, or administration as sources of gain. It is rather the origin of this sober bourgeois capitalism with its rational organization of free labour. Or in terms of cultural history, the problem is that of the origin of the Western bourgeois class and of its peculiarities, a problem which is certainly closely connected with that of the origin of the capitalistic organization of labour, but is not quite the same thing. For the bourgeois as a class existed prior to the development of the peculiar modern form of capitalism, though, it is true, only in the Western hemisphere.

Now the peculiar modern Western form of capitalism has been, at first sight, strongly influenced by the development of technical possibilities. Its rationality is today essentially dependent on the calculability of the most important technical factors. But this means fundamentally that it is dependent on the peculiarities of modern science, especially the natural sciences based on mathematics and exact and rational experiment. On the other hand, the development of these sciences and of the technique resting upon them now receives important stimulation from these capitalistic interests in its practical economic application. It is true that the origin of Western science cannot be attributed to such interests. Calculation, even with decimals, and algebra have been carried on in India, where the decimal system was invented. But it was only made use of by developing capitalism in the West, while in India it led to no modern arithmetic or book-keeping. Neither was the origin of mathematics and mechanics determined by capitalistic interests. But the *technical* utilization of scientific knowledge, so important for the living conditions of the mass of people, was certainly encouraged by economic considerations, which were extremely favourable to it in the Occident. But this encouragement was derived from the peculiarities of the social structure of the Occident. We must hence ask, from *what* parts of that structure was it derived, since not all of them have been of equal importance?

Among those of undoubted importance are the rational structures of law and of administration. For modern rational capitalism has need, not only of the technical means of production, but of a calculable legal system and of administration in terms of formal rules. Without it adventurous and speculative trading capitalism and all sorts of politically determined capitalisms are possible, but no rational enterprise under individual initiative, with fixed capital and certainty of calculations. Such a legal system and such administration have been available for economic activity in a comparative state of legal and formalistic perfection only in the Occident. We must hence inquire where that law came from. Among other circumstances, capitalistic interest have in turn undoubtedly also helped, but by no means alone nor even principally, to prepare the way for the predominance in law and administration of a class of jurists specially trained in rational law. But these interests did not themselves create that law. Quite different forces were at work in this development. And why did not the capitalistic interests do the same in China or India? Why did not the scientific, the artistic, the political, or the economic development there enter upon that path of rationalization which is peculiar to the Occident?

For in all the above cases it is a question of the specific and peculiar rationalism of Western culture. . . . It is hence our first concern to work out and to explain genetically the special peculiarity of Occidental rationalism, and within this field that of the modern Occidental form. Every such attempt at explanation must, recognizing the fundamental importance of the economic factor, above all take account of the economic conditions. But at the same time the opposite correlation must not be left out of consideration. For though the development of economic rationalism is partly dependent on rational technique and law, it is at the same time determined by the ability and disposition of men to adopt certain types of practical rational conduct. When these types have been obstructed by spiritual obstacles, the development of rational economic conduct has also met serious inner resistance. The magical and religious forces, and the ethical ideas of duty based upon them, have in the past always been among the most important formative influences on conduct. In the studies collected here we shall be concerned with these forces.

Two older essays have been placed at the beginning which attempt, at one important point, to approach the side of the problem which is generally most difficult to grasp: the influence of certain religious ideas on the development of an economic spirit, or the *ethos* of an economic system. In this case we are dealing with the connection of the spirit of modern economic life with the rational ethics of ascetic Protestantism. Thus we treat here only one side of the causal chain. . . .

. . . [T]hat side of English Puritanism which was derived from Calvinism gives the most consistent religious basis for the idea of the calling. . . . For the saints' everlasting rest is in the next world; on earth man must, to be certain of his state of grace, "do the works of him who sent him, as long as it is yet day." Not leisure and enjoyment, but only activity serves to increase the glory of God according to the definite manifestations of His will.

Waste of time is thus the first and in principle the deadliest of sins. The span of human life is infinitely short and precious to make sure of one's own election. Loss of time through sociability, idle talk, luxury, even more sleep than is necessary for health, six to at most eight hours, is worthy of absolute moral condemnation. It does not yet hold, with Franklin, that time is money, but the proposition is true in a certain spiritual sense. It is infinitely valuable because every hour lost is lost to labour for the glory of God. Thus inactive contemplation is also valueless, or even directly reprehensible if it is at the expense of one's daily work. . . .

[T]he same prescription is given for all sexual temptation as is used against religious doubts and a sense of moral unworthiness: "Work hard in your calling." But the most important thing was that even beyond that labour came to be considered in itself the end of life, ordained as such by God. St. Paul's "He who will not work shall not eat" holds unconditionally for everyone. Unwillingness to work is symptomatic of the lack of grace.

Here the difference from the mediæval viewpoint becomes quite evident. Thomas Aquinas also gave an interpretation of that statement of St. Paul. But for him labour is only necessary *naturali ratione* for the maintenance of individual and community. Where this end is achieved, the precept ceases to have any meaning. Moreover, it holds only for the race, not for every individual. It does not apply to anyone who can live without labour on his possessions, and of course contemplation, as a spiritual form of action in the Kingdom of God, takes precedence over the commandment in its literal sense. Moreover, for the popular theology of the time, the highest form of monastic productivity lay in the increase of the *Thesaurus ecclesliæ* through prayer and chant.

. . . For everyone without exception God's Providence has prepared a calling, which he should profess and in which he should labour. And this calling is not, as it was for the Lutheran, a fate to which he must submit and which he must make the best of, but God's commandment to the individual to work for the divine glory. This seemingly subtle difference had far-reaching psychological consequences, and became connected with a further development of the providential interpretation of the economic order which had begun in scholasticism.

It is true that the usefulness of a calling, and thus its favour in the sight of God, is measured primarily in moral terms, and thus in terms of the importance of the goods produced in it for the community. But a further, and, above all, in practice the most important, criterion is found in private profitableness. For if that God, whose hand the Puritan sees in all the occurrences of life, shows one of His elect a chance of profit, he must do it with a purpose. Hence the faithful Christian must follow the call by taking advantage of the opportunity. "If God show you a way in which you may lawfully get more than in another way (without wrong to your soul or to any other), if you refuse this, and choose the less gainful way, you cross one of the ends of your calling, and you refuse to be God's steward, and to accept His gifts and use them for Him when He requireth it: you may labour to be rich for God, though not for the flesh and sin.". . .

The superior indulgence of the *seigneur* and the parvenu ostentation of the *nouveau riche* are equally detestable to asceticism. But, on the other hand, it has the highest ethical appreciation of the sober, middle-class, self-made man. "God blesseth His trade" is a stock remark about those good men who had successfully followed the divine hints. The whole power of the God of the Old Testament, who rewards His people for their obedience in this life, necessarily exercised a similar influence on the Puritan who ... compared his own state of grace with that of the heroes of the Bible. . . .

Although we cannot here enter upon a discussion of the influence of Puritanism in all . . . directions, we should call attention to the fact that the toleration of pleasure in cultural goods, which contributed to purely aesthetic or athletic enjoyment, certainly always ran up against one characteristic limitation: They must not cost anything. Man is only a trustee of the goods which have come to him through God's grace. He must, like the servant in the parable, give an account of every penny entrusted to him, and it is at least hazardous to spend any of it for a purpose which does not serve the glory of God but only one's own enjoyment. What person, who keeps his eyes open, has not met representatives of this viewpoint even in the present? The idea of a man's duty to his possessions, to which he subordinates himself as an obedient steward, or even as an acquisitive machine, bears with chilling weight on his life. The greater the possessions the heavier, if the ascetic attitude toward life stands the test, the feeling of responsibility for them, for holding them undiminished for the glory of God and increasing them by restless effort. The origin of this type of life also extends in certain roots, like so many aspects of the spirit of capitalism, back into the Middle Ages. But it was in the ethic of ascetic Protestantism that it first found a consistent ethical foundation. Its significance for the development of capitalism is obvious.

This worldly Protestant asceticism, as we may recapitulate up to this point, acted powerfully against the spontaneous enjoyment of possessions; it restricted consumption, especially of luxuries. On the other hand, it had the psychological effect of freeing the acquisition of goods from the inhibitions of traditionalistic ethics. It broke the bonds of the impulse of acquisition in that it not only legalized it, but (in the sense discussed) looked upon it as directly willed by God. . . .

As far as the influence of the Puritan outlook extended, under all circumstances—and this is, of course, much more important than the mere encouragement of capital accumulation—it favoured the development of a rational bourgeois economic life; it was the most important, and above all the only consistent influence in the development of that life. It stood at the cradle of the modern economic man.

To be sure, these Puritanical ideals tended to give way under excessive pressure from the temptations of wealth, as the Puritans themselves knew very well. With great regularity we find the most genuine adherents of Puritanism among the classes which were rising from a lowly status, the small bourgeois and farmers while the *beati possidentes,* even among Quakers, are often found tending to repudiate the old ideals. It was the same fate which again and again befell the predecessor of this worldly asceticism, the monastic asceticism of the Middle Ages. In the latter case, when rational economic activity had worked out its full effects by strict regulation of conduct and limitation of consumption, the wealth accumulated either succumbed directly to the nobility, as in the time before the Reformation, or monastic discipline threatened to break down, and one of the numerous reformations became necessary.

In fact the whole history of monasticism is in a certain sense the history of a continual struggle with the problem of the secularizing influence of wealth. The same is true on a grand scale of the worldly asceticism of Puritanism. The great revival of Methodism, which preceded the expansion of English industry toward the end of the eighteenth century, may well be compared with such a monastic reform. We may hence quote here a passage from John Wesley himself which might well serve as a motto for everything which has been said above. For it shows that the leaders of these ascetic movements understood the seemingly paradoxical relationships which we have here analysed perfectly well, and in the same sense that we have given them. He wrote:

> I fear, wherever riches have increased, the essence of religion has decreased in the same proportion. Therefore I do not see how it is possible, in the nature of things, for any revival of true religion to continue long. For religion must necessarily produce both industry and frugality, and these cannot but produce riches. But as riches increase, so will pride, anger, and love of the world in all its branches. How then is it possible that Methodism, that is, a religion of the heart, though it flourishes now as a green bay tree, should continue in this state? For the Methodists in every place grow diligent and frugal; consequently they increase in goods. Hence they proportionately increase in pride, in anger, in the desire of the flesh, the desire of the eyes, and the pride of life. So, although the form of religion remains, the spirit is swiftly vanishing away. Is there no way to prevent this—this continual decay of pure religion? We ought not to prevent people from being diligent and frugal; *we must exhort all Christians to gain all they can, and to save all they can; that is, in effect, to grow rich.*

As Wesley here says, the full economic effect of those great religious movements, whose significance for economic development lay above all in their ascetic educative influence, generally came only after the peak of the purely religious enthusiasm was past. Then the intensity of the search for the Kingdom of God commenced gradually to pass over into sober economic virtue; the religious roots died out slowly, giving way to utilitarian worldliness. Then, as Dowden puts it, as in *Robinson Crusoe*, the isolated economic man who carries on missionary activities on the side takes the place of the lonely spiritual search for the Kingdom of Heaven of Bunyan's pilgrim, hurrying through the market-place of Vanity. . . .

A specifically bourgeois economic ethic had grown up. With the consciousness of standing in the fullness of God's grace and being visibly blessed by Him, the bourgeois business man, as long as he remained within the bounds of formal correctness, as long as his moral conduct was spotless and the use to which he put his wealth was not objectionable, could follow his pecuniary interests as he would and feel that he was fulfilling a duty in doing so. The power of religious asceticism provided him in addition with sober, conscientious, and unusually industrious workmen, who clung to their work as to a life purpose willed by God.

Finally, it gave him the comforting assurance that the unequal distribution of the goods of this world was a special dispensation of Divine Providence, which in these differences, as in particular grace, pursued secret ends unknown to men. . . .

One of the fundamental elements of the spirit of modern capitalism, and not only of that but of all modern culture: Rational conduct on the basis of the idea of the calling, was born—that is what this discussion has sought to demonstrate—from the spirit of Christian asceticism. One has only to reread the passage from Franklin, quoted at the beginning of this essay, in order to see that the essential elements of the attitude which was there called the spirit of capitalism are the same as what we have just shown to be the content of the Puritan worldly asceticism, only without the religious basis, which by Franklin's time had died away. . . .

Since asceticism undertook to remodel the world and to work out its ideals in the world, material goods have gained an increasing and finally an inexorable power over the lives of men as at no previous period in history. Today the spirit of religious asceticism—whether finally, who knows?—has escaped from the cage. But victorious capitalism, since it rests on mechanical foundations, needs its support no longer. The rosy blush of its laughing heir, the Enlightenment, seems also to be irretrievably fading, and the idea of duty in one's calling prowls about in our lives like the ghost of dead religious beliefs. Where the fulfilment of the calling cannot directly be related to the highest spiritual and cultural values, or when, on the other hand, it need not be felt simply as economic compulsion, the individual generally abandons the attempt to justify it at all. In the field of its highest development, in the United States, the pursuit of wealth, stripped of its religious and ethical meaning, tends to become associated with purely mundane passions, which often actually give it the character of sport.

No one knows who will live in this cage in the future, or whether at the end of this tremendous development entirely new prophets will arise, or there will be a great rebirth of old ideas and ideals, or, if neither, mechanized petrification, embellished with a sort of convulsive self-importance. For of the last stage of this cultural development, it might well be truly said:

"Specialists without spirit, sensualists without heart; this nullity imagines that it has attained a level of civilization never before achieved."

But this brings us to the world of judgments of value and of faith, with which this purely historical discussion need not be burdened. . . .

Here we have only attempted to trace the fact and the direction of its influence to their motives in one, though a very important point. But it would also further be necessary to investigate how Protestant Asceticism was in turn influenced in its development and its character by the totality of social conditions, especially economic. The modern man is in general, even with the best will, unable to give religious ideas a significance for culture and national character which they deserve. But it is, of course, not my aim to substitute for a one-sided materialistic an equally one-sided spiritualistic causal interpretation of culture and of history. Each is equally possible, but each, if it does not serve as the preparation, but as the conclusion of an investigation, accomplishes equally little in the interest of historical truth.

45

ABIDING FAITH

MARK CHAVES

Sociologists who study the institution of religion are documenting the changes occurring within this social institution. One current debate is whether religiosity is growing in the United States or if it is declining due to increasing secularization. In this reading, Mark Chaves, a professor of sociology at the University of Arizona, investigates this controversy and finds that contrary to popular opinion, Americans have not become more secular, but are as religious as ever. Chaves argues that organized religion occupies less of Americans' time and exerts less influence on society as a whole than it did in the past.

God is dead—or God is taking over. Depending on the headlines of the day, soothsayers pronounce the end of religion or the ascendancy of religious extremists. What is really going on?

Taking stock of religion is almost as old as religion itself. Tracking religious trends is difficult, however, when religion means so many different

Chaves, Mark. "Abiding Faith." Copyright © 2002 by American Sociological Association. Reprinted with permission from *Contexts*, Vol. 1, Number 2, Summer 2002, pp. 19–26.

things. Should we look at belief in the supernatural? Frequency of formal religious worship? The role of faith in major life decisions? The power of individual religious movements? These different dimensions of religion can change in different ways. Whether religion is declining or not depends on the definition of religion and what signifies a decline.

Perhaps the most basic manifestation of religious observance is piety: individual belief and participation in formal religious worship. Recent research on trends in American piety supports neither simple secularization nor staunch religious resilience in the face of modern life. Instead, Americans seem to believe as much but practice less.

Religious Belief

Conventional Judeo-Christian religious belief remains very high in the United States, and little evidence suggests it has declined in recent decades. Gallup polls and other surveys show that more than 90 percent of Americans believe in a higher power, and more than 60 percent are certain that God exists. Approximately 80 percent believe in miracles and in life after death, 70 percent believe in heaven, and 60 percent believe in hell. Far fewer Americans—from two in three in 1963 to one in three today—believe the Bible is the literal Word of God. The number who say the Bible is either the inerrant or the inspired Word of God is still impressively high, however—four of every five.

Religious faith in the United States is more broad than deep, and it has been for as long as it has been tracked. Of Americans who say the Bible is either the actual or the inspired Word of God, only half can name the first book in the Bible and only one-third can say who preached the Sermon on the Mount. More than 90 percent believe in a higher power, but only one-third say they rely more on that power than on themselves in overcoming adversity. People who claim to be born-again or evangelical Christians are no less likely than others to believe in ideas foreign to traditional Christianity, such as reincarnation (20 percent of all Americans), channeling (17 percent), or astrology (26 percent), and they are no less likely to have visited a fortune teller (16 percent).

Despite the superficiality of belief among many, the percentage of Americans expressing religious faith is still remarkably high. How should we understand this persistent religious belief? High levels of religious belief in the United States seem to show that, contrary to widespread expectations of many scholars, industrialization, urbanization, bureaucratization, advances in science and other developments associated with modern life do not automatically undermine religious belief. In part this is because modernization does not immunize people against the human experiences that inspire religious sentiment. As anthropologist Mary Douglas points out, scientific advances do not make us less likely to feel awe and wonder when we ponder the universe and its workings. For example, our feelings of deference to physicians, owing to their experience and somewhat mysterious scientific knowledge, may not be so different from the way other people feel about traditional healers—even if the outcomes of treatment are indeed different. Likewise, bureaucracy does not demystify our world—on the contrary, it may make us feel more helpless and confused in the face of powers beyond our control. When confronted with large and complex bureaucracies, modern people may not feel any more in control of the world around them than a South Pacific Islander confronted with the prospect of deep-sea fishing for shark. Modern people still turn to religion in part because certain experiences—anthropologist Clifford Geertz emphasizes bafflement, pain, and moral dilemmas—remain part of the human condition.

That condition cannot, however, completely explain the persistence of religious belief. It is clearly possible to respond in nonreligious ways to these universal human experiences, and many people do, suggesting that religiosity is a feature of some responses to these experiences, not an automatic consequence of the experiences themselves. From this perspective, attempting to explain religion's persistence by the persistence of bafflement, pain and moral paradox sidesteps a key question: Why do so many people continue to respond to these experiences by turning to religion?

Another, more sociological explanation of the persistence of religious belief emphasizes the fact that religion—like language and ethnicity—is one of the main ways of delineating group boundaries and collective identities. As long as who we are and how we differ from others remains a salient organizing principle for social movements and institutions, religion can be expected to thrive. Indeed, this identity-marking aspect of religion may also explain why religious belief often seems more broad than deep. If affirming that the Bible is the inerrant Word of God serves in part to identify oneself as part of the community of Bible-believing Christians, it is not so important to know in much detail what the Bible actually says.

The modern world is not inherently inhospitable to religious belief, and many kinds of belief have not declined at all over the past several decades. Certain aspects of modernity, however, do seem to reduce levels of religious observance. In a recent study of 65 countries, Ronald Inglehart and Wayne Baker find that people in industrialized and wealthy nations are typically less religious than others. That said, among advanced industrial democracies the United States still stands out for its relatively high level of religious belief. When asked to rate the importance of God in their lives on a scale of 1 to 10, 50 percent of Americans say "10," far higher than the 28 percent in Canada, 26 percent in Spain, 21 percent in Australia, 16 percent in Great Britain and Germany, and 10 percent in France. Among advanced industrial democracies, only Ireland, at 40 percent, approaches the U.S. level of religious conviction.

Religious Participation

Cross-national comparisons also show that Americans participate in organized religion more often than do people in other affluent nations. In the United States, 55 percent of those who are asked say they attend religious services at least once a month, compared with 40 percent in Canada, 38 percent in Spain, 25 percent in Australia, Great Britain, and West Germany, and 17 percent in France.

The trends over time, however, are murkier. Roger Finke and Rodney Stark have argued that religious participation has increased over the course of American history. This claim is based mainly on increasing rates of church membership. In 1789 only 10 percent of Americans belonged to churches, with church membership rising to 22 percent in 1890 and reaching 50 to 60 percent in the 1950s. Today, about two-thirds of Americans say they are members of a church or a synagogue. These rising figures should not, however, be taken at face value, because churches have become less exclusive clubs than they were earlier in our history. Fewer people attend religious services today than claim formal membership in religious congregations, but the opposite was true in earlier times. The long-term trend in religious participation is difficult to discern.

Although we have much more evidence about recent trends in religious participation, it still is difficult to say definitively whether religious-service attendance—the main way Americans participate collectively in religion—has declined or remained stable in recent decades. The available evidence is conflicting. Surveys using the traditional approach of asking people directly about their attendance mainly show stability over time, confirming the consensus that attendance has not declined much.

New evidence, however, points toward decline. Drawing on time-use records, which ask individuals to report everything they do on a given day, Stanley Presser and Linda Stinson find that weekly religious-service attendance has declined over the past 30 years from about 40 percent in 1965 to about 25 percent in 1994. Sandra Hofferth and John Sandberg also find a decline in church attendance reported in children's time-use diaries. Time-use studies mitigate the over-reporting of religious-service attendance that occurs when people are asked directly whether or not they attend. Also, these time-use studies find the same lower attendance rates found by researchers who count the number of people who actually show up at church rather than take them at their word when they say they attend.

Additional evidence of declining activity comes from political scientist Robert Putnam's book on civic engagement in the United States, *Bowling Alone*. Combining survey data from five different sources, Putnam finds some decline in religious participation. Perhaps more important, because of the context they provide, are Putnam's findings about a range of civic and voluntary association activities that are closely related to religious participation.

Virtually every type of civic engagement declined in the last third of the 20th century: voting, attending political, public, and club meetings, serving as officer or committee member in local clubs and organizations, belonging to national organizations, belonging to unions, playing sports and working on community projects. If religious participation has indeed remained constant, it would be virtually the only type of civic engagement that has not declined in recent decades. Nor did the events of September 11, 2001, alter attendance patterns. If there was a spike in religious service attendance immediately following September 11, it was short-lived.

Overall, the following picture emerges from recent research: since the 1960s, Americans have engaged less frequently in religious activities, but they have continued to believe just as much in the supernatural and to be just as interested in spirituality. This pattern characterizes many other countries around the world as well. Inglehart and Baker's data suggest that American trends are similar to those in other advanced industrialized societies: declining religious activities, stability in religious belief, and increasing interest in the meaning and purpose of life.

Important differences among subgroups remain nonetheless. Blacks are more religiously active than whites, and women are more active than men. There is little reason to think, however, that the recent declines in participation vary among subgroups.

New forms of religious participation are not replacing attendance at weekend worship services. When churchgoers are asked what day they attended a service, only 3 percent mention a day other than Sunday. Perhaps more telling, when those who say they did not attend a religious service in the past week are asked if they participated in some other type of religious event or meeting, such as a prayer or Bible study group, only 2 percent say yes (although 21 percent of non-attendees say they watched religious television or listened to religious radio). The vast majority of religious activity in the United States takes place at weekend religious services. If other forms of religious activity have increased, they have not displaced traditional weekend attendance.

Overall, the current knowledge of individual piety in the United States does not conform to expectations that modernity is fundamentally hostile to religion. Many conventional religious beliefs remain popular, showing no sign of decline. That said, research on individual piety neither points to stability on every dimension nor implies that social changes associated with modernity leave religious belief and practice unimpaired. The evidence supports neither a simple version of secularization nor a wholesale rejection of secularization. Moreover, focusing on levels of religious piety diverts attention from what may be more important: the social significance of religion.

Of course, when many people are religiously active, religion can have more social influence. A society like the United States, with more than 300,000 religious congregations, presents opportunities for political mobilization that do not exist in societies where religion is a less prominent part of society. Witness the Civil Rights movement, the Religious Right and other causes that mix religion and politics. Nonetheless, religion in the United States, as in most other advanced societies, is organizationally separate from (even if occasionally overlapping) government, the economy and other parts of civil society. This limits a religion's capacity to change the world, even if it converts millions.

The social significance of religious belief and participation depends on the institutional settings in which they occur. This is why the religious movements of our day with the greatest potential for increasing religion's influence are not those that simply seek new converts or spur belief and practice, no matter how successful they may be. The movements with the greatest such potential are those that seek to expand religion's authority or influence in other domains. In some parts of the contemporary world, this has meant religious leaders seeking and sometimes achieving the power to veto legislation, dictate university curricula, exclude girls from schooling and women from working in certain jobs, and determine the kinds of art or literature offered to the public. In the United States, the most significant contemporary movement to expand religious influence probably is the effort to shape school curricula concerning evolution and creationism. Wherever they occur, when such movements succeed they change the meaning and significance of religious piety. Efforts like these reflect and shape the abiding role of religion in a society in ways that go beyond the percentages of people who believe in God, pray, or attend religious services.

RECOMMENDED RESOURCES

Chaves, Mark. 1994. "Secularization as Declining Religious Authority." *Social Forces* 72:749–74.

Gallup, George Jr. and D. Michael Lindsay. 1999. *Surveying the Religious Landscape.* Harrisburg, PA: Morehouse Publishing.

Hofferth, Sandra L. and John F. Sandberg. 2001. "Children at the Millennium: Where Have We Come From, Where Are We Going?" In *Advances in Life Course Research,* edited by T. Owens and S. Hofferth. New York: Elsevier Science. Also available at www.ethno.isr.umich.edu/06papers/html/.

Inglehart, Ronald and Wayne E. Baker. 2000. "Modernization, Cultural Change, and the Persistence of Traditional Values." *American Sociological Review* 65:19–51.

Presser, Stanley and Linda Stinson. 1998. "Data Collection Mode and Social Desirability Bias in Self-Reported Religious Attendance." *American Sociological Review* 63: 134–45.

Putnam, Robert. 2000. "Religious Participation." In *Bowling Alone: The Collapse and Revival of American Community.* New York: Simon and Schuster.

46

BARING OUR SOULS
TV Talk Shows and the Religion of Recovery

KATHLEEN S. LOWNEY

Kathleen S. Lowney, professor of sociology, anthropology, and criminal justice at Valdosta State University in Georgia, is interested in the socio-cultural study of religion, especially the history and growth of civil religions in the popular culture of the United States. In this reading, Lowney examines how television talk shows have come to be modern forms of religious re-vivals, using the religion of recovery and the pop psychology of the self-help movement to obtain converts and spectators. What follows is a fascinating sociological analysis of television talk shows and their limited potential for social change. This excerpt is taken from Lowney's 1999 book, *Baring Our Souls: TV Talk Shows and the Religion of Recovery.*

I confess—I watch television talk shows. I can't even remember when I first watched one, which is evidence that it was quite a while ago. Over the years I have had various favorite shows, depending on which shows my local stations broadcast and on how I felt about the host or the topics being covered. Occasionally today I will intensely focus on a show, but more often it serves as background "noise" while I change clothes after work, read the mail, and begin dinner. The shows and their hosts become companions as I unwind from teaching. At times they have made me laugh out loud at the outrageousness of the stories being told, at times they have made me cry, and a few times they have made me angry. And yes, I have talked—okay, I admit it, even yelled—back at the screen, telling guests, Oprah Winfrey, Phil Don-ahue, Sally Jessy Raphael, or Montel Williams what's what. My guess is that most of us have had these same experiences—we *feel* as we watch talk shows. That is what the shows are hoping for; they want us to become caught up in the stories that are being shared that day, and the next and the next. But in the past 2 years, I have begun to contemplate talk shows and the feelings they try to evoke in their audiences even more. What kinds of emotions do they pro-duce? Do they help us search for explanations of and solutions to some of our nation's most pressing social problems? Alas, I don't think that they are as useful as they can or should be, given their popularity. This [reading] will ex-plain why I am concerned about talk shows and the kind of moral code they promote. But I want to make it clear, I am critiquing talk shows as a viewer as well as a scholar. This is a friendly critique, but a critique nonetheless.

I'm a member of the television generation. I've grown up watching it. Born in 1958, I can't remember living without at least one television set, often more. I have marked the passage of time, both in my life and in the life of our nation, with television clips. . . .

So I'm not ashamed to say that I watch television and that I watch talk shows. I am not alone. During the week of July 7–13, 1997, between 3 and 6 million households watched each of the top seven rated syndicated talk shows.[1] Why do people watch these shows? Like me, many people watch them for fun. They are recreational escapes from our often-harried lives. For others, such shows are sources of information. People see a variety of illnesses or problems on the shows and recognize parallels to their own lives or the lives of their loved ones. Important issues might be debated on these shows, such as when presidential candidates appeared on some shows during the 1996 campaign. Other episodes are a way to "see how the other half lives." We might never have experienced having "embryos . . . stolen and given to another family,"[2] or having a teenage daughter who is "in love with a 76-year-old"[3] or having "had sex with [my] husband and my ex-husband on [the] same day—result, twins with different dads,"[4] but it can be exhilarating, in a vicarious sort of way, to see what kinds of problems other people have. Sometimes watching these shows, I think what a normal life I have had, overall. My problems seem much smaller, more mundane, after an hour of Oprah, Phil, Geraldo, Sally, or Montel! . . .

Yes Virginia, There *Is* Morality on Daytime Talk Shows: Explaining the Present by Looking to the Past

In this [reading] I want to explore the normative order on talk shows by examining the shows themselves. Having just written this sentence, I took a bit of a break and watched *The Jerry Springer Show*.[5] It was wild, and on one level could be used as a perfect illustration of the immorality of talk shows. The show focused on just one family, albeit a very unusual one. Amber was introduced first; she was 12 years old and had been dating, with her parents' approval, a 24-year-old guy named Glenn, who was another one of the guests. Amber admitted that she and Glenn had sexual intercourse on their first date, but only that one time, because she "didn't want Glenn to get into trouble." Her parents knew of the sexual encounter, she said. This was confirmed during the show: both parents admitted to their knowledge of the sexual relationship between their preteen daughter and Glenn. As Jerry talked with Amber, the story grew more and more complicated: her mother, Pam (the third guest) was dating Glenn and wanted to marry him. It was obvious that Amber felt betrayed and hurt by this turn of events. About 20 minutes into the show, Amber's father, Frank, came out on the stage. He promptly threatened Glenn with bodily harm, and they both had to be restrained by well-muscled male guards who worked for Springer. As the show progressed, emotions became extremely intense. Pam told her daughter that it was time that her own needs came first and her daughter would have to cope with Glenn as her new stepfather or else Amber would just have to get lost. The mother went on to say more hurtful and embarrassing things about her daughter, such as the fact that she smelled due to poor hygiene. This was the last straw for Jerry, who launched into a vehement denunciation of Pam, chastising her over and over again for being a lousy mother. He repeatedly uttered that a "good" mother always put a child's needs over her own (selfish) ones. The audience chimed in with applause and a standing ovation when he was finished.

On the surface, this show could be an excellent typifying example of what critics mean when they say that talk shows are destroying America's moral fabric. One whole television hour was devoted to discussing the sexual appetites of a 12-year-old girl and her mother. At first glance, it is hard to see how any of the guests would feel better after appearing on the show. Glenn discovered that Pam thought that he was "stupid and slow"; Pam admitted to prostitution (she said that Frank "put her on the street" and would do the same with Amber), a drug habit, and serving time in prison; Frank sort of admitted to having a violent relationship with Pam (they have been separated for 10 years, but never divorced, although they live across the street from each other); Pam called Amber lots of names (many were bleeped out), including "slut"; and Amber in turn told Pam that she no longer thought of her as a mother, because she hated her. All this in 48 minutes of airtime! It wasn't totally clear how the audience was uplifted by such a show. I'll admit that I heard a lot more than I cared to about this family. In fact, at times the show was positively painful to watch. I felt sorry for Amber, angry with her parents, especially her mother, and frustrated with Glenn's inability to see why having sex with a preteen was wrong. Sometimes I felt all these things simultaneously. My guess is many others who watched shared my reactions.

But there was more to the show. The host, Jerry Springer, played a significant role. He was constantly interrupting the guests, especially Pam, and most interruptions communicated one of two emotions. The first was incredulity—that a mother would say such hurtful, selfish things to her daughter. The second emotion was sarcasm. Jerry made pointed comments about Pam's and Frank's parenting skills, Glenn's decision-making capabilities, and even Amber's choices (though he was careful to say repeatedly that she was a child and children make mistakes and that she shouldn't be judged too harshly). Jerry definitely was grounding his remarks in a moral code that I think Bill Bennett would have approved of: children should not be having sex and should definitely not be having sex with a 24-year-old, and parents should protect their children, even if it means putting the needs of the children above those of the parents. As Jerry frequently told Pam—"it is just what you do as a parent." Near the end of the show, a male psychologist joined the family on stage. He promptly added his critical voice by telling Glenn to leave this family alone. He told Pam to start acting like a mother to her daughter, not a rival, and told both parents to start loving their daughter more if they wanted her to have any self-esteem. All of the psychological advice centered on what was best for Amber, the most vulnerable member of this family.

Clearly there was a quite strong moral message to this show. It didn't come only at the end of the show; Springer wove it throughout the program. The morality was hard to ignore. In addition to Jerry's sarcasm and his outrage, the audience was there, booing and hissing Pam, Glenn, and even Frank. They clapped wildly when Springer moralized; when he finished a 3-minute harangue against Pam, the audience gave him a standing ovation. Jerry Springer, the audience, and the psychologist reiterated time and again a moral code that valued sexual restraint and honoring commitments to others (such as mother to daughter). Still, critics such as Bennett would probably say that this is all well and good, but why does such an upstanding moral message need to be couched in the public humiliation of a 12-year-old girl? The viewing public now knows about her promiscuity and her troubled family life, and for what? What did that show cost Amber, her family, and perhaps our nation's very soul? . . .

Secular Fun: The Circus as Entertainment

. . . The roots of the modern-day talk shows lie in the nineteenth century's carnivals and revivals. The parallels are striking. The talk show and the carnival both tempt us to watch portrayals of otherness. We see behaviors that are neither common nor publicly discussed suddenly exhibited for all to see. Just as the circus performers were displayed one dimensionally, so are talk-show guests. "What does characterize the bulk of the [talk-show participants], despite the diversity, is that some feature of their lifestyles, personalities, or life histories is considered abnormal or deviant to various degrees by society. Indeed, this atypical or deviant position was what generally earned them an invitation to appear on the show."[6] And it is the talk-show host, like the circus ringmaster of old, who identifies the guests' particular deviance for us from the outset, just in case those in the audience missed it. A person's complex life becomes summarized in a simplistic, made-for-TV label just as freaks were publicized for their unique characteristics on circus handbills. These labels are reinforced throughout the program by subtitles shown just under guests' faces. But this facile labeling distorts the guests' life histories, their social location, so that the "deviant labels come to be seen by 'normals' [the in-studio and at-home audiences] as *the* defining feature, taking precedence over the other characteristics a marginalized group member may have."[7] Just this one aspect of the guests' lives is lifted up for moral judgment.

Carnivals, circuses, and talk shows highlight behavior that falls outside the realm of normality for society. Most of us do not traipse on high wires, work with animal acts, or read the future, neither are we "mothers who covered up their daughters' pregnancies,"[8] or "high-powered women derailed by menopause,"[9] or a "father who abused all four of us sisters,"[10] and so on. It seems unlikely that any one of us can personally relate to more than a small percentage of show topics. So why then do we watch? In the circus act, the performance was fraught with risk; we knew the "definition of the situation" was tenuous. We knew that no matter how practiced a performer might be, he or she was always flirting with injury, possibly even death. Amusement was a second away from possible peril. Their risk taking was part of our vicarious thrill. Likewise, guests on talk shows take risks. They expose their lives in ways that some of us might fantasize about and others might find repellant. They can disclose—and cause—wounds. We know that secrets are a moment away from being spilled. Anxiously we watch both the carnival and the talk-show "acts," always aware of the precariousness of the situation. Talk shows become glimpses into the pain (much less often the joy) that is life. Watching deviant persons suffer can make us rejoice at the life that we have while at the same time they can remind us of the need for a morality that binds people together. These shows do, then, feature a moral discourse.

Talk shows do not just entertain us—they are also a site for American revivalism, of a novel sort. They provide an "electronic tent" under which we can gather together and watch sinners confess, sometimes receiving absolution from the people whom they have hurt, and be reinstated into the moral community. The hosts are contemporary preachers, cajoling guests, studio audiences, and those of us at home to obey the normative order. Hosts take this responsibility quite seriously; "being a talk-show host is more than a job, they suggest, it's a calling."[11] And any good preacher knows that an excellent technique to facilitate conversion is to offer oneself as an exemplar of a sinner now redeemed. Talk-show hosts make good use of this rhetorical strategy; thus audiences know about Oprah Winfrey's and Ricki Lake's weight loss, Sally Jessy Raphael's daughter's drug use and subsequent death, Oprah's shame over and healing from sexual abuse, Phil Donahue's divorce and admission of being a less-than-adequate father to his children in their early years, and Geraldo Rivera's numerous sexual dalliances. These admissions of failing are used to establish a parasocial sense of solidarity between host, guest, and even audience members.[12] This parasocial connection is exhibited when the public thinks that we "know" all about celebrities even though we haven't met them—and probably never will. And hosts manipulate this parasocial relationship.

> People feel more at ease telling secrets, and can better trust advice they hear, when talking with someone who knows what it's like. As a result, the hosts need to establish a common bond with guests and viewers. And that bond is based on mutual suffering. . . . The hosts establish a standard

of behavior that fosters the kind of disclosures that ultimately benefit their shows.[13]

The hosts' life stories, so well known to viewers due in part to repeated disclosures on the shows, invite others to share their pain. And boy, do the guests talk and talk and talk some more about their troubles. We see them shamed by the host, audience, and other guests and we are reminded of what is (considered) right and wrong in our society. The hosts are pop cultural moralists and the audience accepts them in that role.

Therefore, talk shows parallel nineteenth-century Protestant revivals. The host is the visiting preacher bent on offering salvation to all those who seek it. The guests are primarily sinners—some penitent, others petulant and unwilling to change, and the audience is the ardent congregation goading, chastising, and cajoling the sinners, and celebrating their repentance. Guests not in need of conversion are the aggrieved victims, demanding change in the sinner-guest's behavior before they even will contemplate offering forgiveness. All the televisual attention is directed toward creating a conversion experience—toward sinner-guests turning from the destructive toward the good. The music, the staging techniques, and the pace of the show all parallel the structure of revivals: longer introductory segments that build tension as the sinners testify and then culminate in a segment in which the sinner is forced to make a choice—to continue to sin or move toward the good.[14]

What mattered under the revivalist's tent is also what matters under the electronic tent of the talk shows, that people convert to a moral lifestyle. Turning away from sin is not a one-time event but something that has to happen every minute of every day. In the nineteenth century, the moral community of the local church was there for the former sinner. On talk shows, the host and the psychological expert, who appears at the end of many shows, share the conversion duties. The host and audience members diagnose and emotional experts certify the moral failings of the sinner-guests so that the audience can display a type of sympathy by the end of the show. But the sinner-guests do not automatically receive this sympathy. Sympathy is interactionally constructed on these shows: sinner-guests must earn our sympathy by admitting to sin and guilt *and* by agreeing to a process that will solidify their new status of convert. The experts show the way: therapy. Guests are chided until they agree to enter therapy or go to a 12-step program or some other support group. Like the sinners on the anxious bench, conversion on talk shows is understood as tenuous; backsliding is always a possibility. It is with the support of and the interaction with a primary group of "ex-es" that the now ex-sinners can walk the straight and narrow, the moral path. Recovery is still an individual experience, yet is shared with others who are "working the (same) program." Many talk shows now have full-time staff members whose primary responsibility is to put guests in contact with counselors in their local communities. These staff experts will "follow up" with guests to see how they are doing, etc. The audience is assured that the staff will "be there" for the guests (common terminology on these shows) long after the studio lights have dimmed.

What Kind of Morality Is the Religion of Recovery?

We have come full circle—it is inaccurate to claim that there isn't morality on talk shows. Hosts, audiences, and experts all have a moral perspective that shapes their performance. Conservative critics have missed this point. The question is not whether there ought to be a moral code on talk shows, but *whose* morality it should be. Talk shows are frequent visitors in American homes. We can be enveloped in their "electronic tents" 24 hours a day if we want to, for just about any time of the day some channel is carrying one. But when we watch, to what altar, to use revivalists' language, are the guests— and ultimately the viewers—being called? I think it is important that we understand this newest form of American civil religion.[15] What kind of moral code is being internalized by the viewers? Other analysts have already commented on this:

> Attention is paid to "therapy" not solid change. The 12-step therapeutic model permeates the popular literature on addiction "treatment." . . . It has become the ideology of the new television talk shows.[16]

> Talk shows . . . never leave things hanging. They work . . . toward hour's end to bring out, insist upon, and reinforce through "expert" testimony by therapists and authors, the ultimate solution to all personal problems: the Recovery Movement as doctrine and practice. . . . Results matter here and the preferred result is that those most confused and unstable be routed to the official place of treatment: the 12 step movement.[17]

> The growing prevalence of this kind of [therapeutic] language on talk shows is the dynamic that works most profoundly to establish the Recovery Movement as a kind of common sense religion.[18]

Earlier religious revivals persuaded converts to join or rejoin the local church and act responsibly. From that foundation of moral behavior, a significant portion of Protestant and Roman Catholic believers then chose to act in and on the world, trying to help others who were less fortunate.[19] However, this newest kind of revivalism found on television talk shows encourages people to turn inward to a psychological or pseudo-psychological belief system, expressed through attendance at therapy sessions or support groups. But such a belief system rarely encourages a turn outward to help the poor or the needy; healing one's inner child becomes more important than healing the world. Converts are

> encouraged to "come to believe," as the 12 steps put it, that their troubles are internal rather than socially determined; that their cures are to be

found in private and spiritual, not social or political arenas; and that their time, as parents, friends, wives, lovers, and even workers, is best spent in spreading the word, in sponsoring and supporting more and more hurting people in 12-step activities.[20]

Perhaps the clearest statement of this Recovery Movement theology was an exchange between Oprah Winfrey and Marianne Williamson, a "New Age guru" and author. The exchange begins with Oprah stating "that the root of all problems in mankind and womankind is that people don't feel a sense of value for themselves."[21] Several minutes later they return to the same conversational thread:

Oprah Winfrey: *So when you see a child murdered or children molested or all the other things going on in the world, because you have no real value for your own self and soul.*

Ms. Williamson: *You're desensitized.*

Oprah Winfrey: *. . . you can't extend it to other people.*

Ms. Williamson: *Right.*

Oprah Winfrey: *So you can talk about it, because intellectually you know you should care . . .*

Ms. Williamson: *Right.*

Oprah Winfrey: *. . . that children are being murdered.*

Ms. Williamson: *Right.*

Oprah Winfrey: *But you don't. There's not enough of that in you to make you get up and do something about it.*

Ms. Williamson: *Right. That's why wounded people who are not themselves healed are the most dangerous. Because they are—they are lacking sensitivity to other people's pain because they haven't addressed their own.*

Oprah Winfrey: *Mm-hmm.*

Ms. Williamson: *That's why the work of personal growth and personal recovery and spiritual work on ourselves is the most important work of all.*[22]

Think of the ethical message Williamson promulgates—care for self is the most important human task. Television talk shows' new revivalism encourages people to convert to a psychological or pseudo-psychological belief system. Such a belief system rarely encourages a person to turn outward to help the poor or the suffering. Instead, one is required to work on oneself. Healing one's inner child, sadly, becomes more important than healing even one citizen of the real world.

This is not the same morality that social conservatives like Bill Bennett want to see advocated on talk shows. But this self-absorbed morality does not seem to concern them much. They abhor the sexy and violent show topics, and miss what I feel is the more substantial moral issue, the religion of self that is sanctioned on these talk shows. I wonder why, for there are significant social and moral questions that need to be asked about a civil religion based on the Recovery Movement. What kind of a society can be constructed based on these 12-step prescriptions? Will it be one that can better tolerate others different than ourselves? Will it be a society that will create new solutions to long-term social problems such as racism, sexism, or poverty? Or will it be a society so self-focused that the only time we talk to our neighbors in need will be to invite them to the next 12-step meeting? . . .

Recovery sells. Books, tapes, and workshops are big business. In particular, the production norms of talk shows make this industry a prime location to disseminate the religion of recovery. They are cost effective for companies to produce; they focus on human interest stories, but only one set and only one paid "actor"—the host—is needed, etc. But it is time to pay attention to the message of the religion of recovery. When guests, hosts, audience members, and those of us at home worship at the altar of recovery, what are we getting in return? Recovery religion removes sociological explanations for guests' behavior from public discourse in favor of solely psychological ones. Thus, on these shows, social problems are constructed as either internal psychological weaknesses or interpersonal conflicts between individuals. Individualizing social problems becomes necessary since it is not possible to interview "institutional racism" but it is possible to have a provocative interview with a "skinhead," and so on. Even more importantly, if the causes are individualized, then so must be the solutions. Larger social forces or social facts, as sociology would say, are ignored and instead solutions focus on separate individuals. But what are the social and moral consequences of psychologizing social problems?

Talk shows offer a therapeutic solution to just about every guest: if someone in an inner-city poor neighborhood is stuck in a dead-end job with no hope for a better future, all that is needed is assertiveness training, so seek out help from such a group, and so on. [I] conclude the analysis by asking if a moral code based on recovery religion as preached by talk-show hosts is what our nation needs to solve the social problems we face. How can a normative order based on the belief system of "I'm okay, you're okay—so long as you are not in denial" address the structural issues such as the widening gap between the rich and the poor, institutional systems of stratification such as racism and sexism, or even the growing threat of domestic terrorism? We need—and deserve—a moral code more adequate than what Oprah, Phil, Geraldo, Sally, and the rest are offering.

ENDNOTES

[1]Nielsen Media Research. Week of 7/7–7/13/97. www.ultimatetv.com/news/nielsen/syndication.html. This number reflects the ratings for the Oprah Winfrey, Jenny Jones, Sally Jessy Raphael, Ricki Lake, Montel Williams, Maury Povich, and the Jerry Springer Shows.

[2]*The Phil Donahue Show.* 1995. "Their Embryos Were Stolen and Given to Another Family." November 6.

[3] *The Sally Jessy Raphael Show*. 1995. "My Daughter's In Love with a 76-Year-Old." November 17.

[4] *The Phil Donahue Show*. 1996. "Had Sex with My Husband and My Ex-Husband on the Same Day—Result, Twins with Different Dads." February 2.

[5] *The Jerry Springer Show*. July 30, 1997.

[6] Priest, Patricia. 1995. *Public Images: Talk Show Participants and Tell-all TV.* Creskill, NJ: Hampton, p. 35.

[7] Priest, p. 112.

[8] *The Montel Williams Show*. 1995. "Mothers Who Covered Up Their Daughters' Pregnancies." November 16.

[9] *The Phil Donahue Show*. 1996. "High-Powered Women Derailed by Menopause." May 3.

[10] *The Montel Williams Show*. 1996. "Our Father Abused All Four of Us Sisters." February 27.

[11] Heaton, Jeanne Albronda and Nona Leigh Wilson. 1995. *Tuning In Trouble: Talk TV's Destructive Impact on Mental Health*. San Francisco: Jossey-Bass, p. 43.

[12] See Horton, Donald and Anselm Strauss. 1957. "Interaction in Audience-Participation Shows." *American Journal of Sociology* 62:579–88; and Horton, Donald and R. Richard Wohl. 1956. "Mass Communication and Para-Social InterPaction." *Psychiatry* 19:215–29.

[13] Heaton and Wilson, p. 50.

[14] I am indebted to Donileen Loseke for calling my attention to the role of music on talk shows.

[15] See, for example, Bellah, Robert. 1974. "Civil Religion in America." Pp. 21–44 in *American Civil Religion,* edited by Russell R. Richey and Donald G. Jones. New York: Harper & Row; and Wilson, John F. 1979. *Public Religion in American Culture.* Philadelphia: Temple University Press.

[16] Abt, Vicki and Mel Seesholtz. 1994. "The Shameless World of Phil, Sally, and Oprah: Television Talk Shows and the Deconstructing of Society." *Journal of Popular Culture* 28:171–91, p. 177.

[17] Rapping, Elayne. 1996. *The Culture of Recovery: Making Sense of the Self-Help Movement in Women's Lives.* Boston: Beacon. P. 40.

[18] Rapping, p. 34.

[19] This is not, however, to deny the fact that there is a pietistic, passive element in these faiths as well.

[20] Rapping, p. 94.

[21] *The Oprah Winfrey Show*. 1994. "Marianne Williamson: What Is Going On with the World?" January 11, p.10.

[22] *The Oprah Winfrey Show*, "Marianne Williamson," p. 12.

47

THE SOCIAL STRUCTURE OF MEDICINE

TALCOTT PARSONS

Medical sociology is one of the largest and fastest growing subspecialties within the discipline of sociology. Medical sociologists are concerned with all aspects of the social institution of medicine, including the socialization of doctors, the social construction of health and illness, and the social structure of hospitals and the health care system. The following three readings illustrate different perspectives within the field of medical sociology, beginning with an excerpt from Talcott Parsons' classic 1951 book, *The Social System.* Parsons (1902–1979) was well known for his contributions to the theoretical perspective of structural functionalism. In this selection, Parsons utilizes this perspective to explain how health and illness are significant within a social system, including how they influence the complementary social roles of patients and physicians.

A little reflection will show immediately that the problem of health is intimately involved in the functional prerequisites of the social system. . . . Certainly by almost any definition health is included in the functional needs of the individual member of the society so that from the point of view of functioning of the social system, too low a general level of health, too high an incidence of illness, is dysfunctional. This is in the first instance because illness incapacitates for the effective performance of social roles. It could of course be that this incidence was completely uncontrollable by social action, an independently given condition of social life. But insofar as it is controllable, through rational action or otherwise, it is clear that there is a functional interest of the society in its control, broadly in the minimization of illness. As one special aspect of this, attention may be called to premature death. From a variety of points of view, the birth and rearing of a child constitute a "cost" to the society, through pregnancy, child care, socialization, formal training, and many other channels. Premature death, before the individual has had the opportunity to play out his full quota of social roles, means that only a partial "return" for this cost has been received.

All this would be true were illness purely a "natural phenomenon" in the sense that, like the vagaries of the weather, it was not, to our knowledge, reciprocally involved in the motivated interactions of human beings. In this case illness would be something which merely "happened to" people, which involved consequences which had to be dealt with and conditions which might or might not be controllable but was in no way an expression of motivated behavior.

This is in fact the case for a very important part of illness, but it has become increasingly clear, by no means for all. In a variety of ways, motivational factors accessible to analysis in action terms are involved in the etiology of many illnesses, and conversely, though without exact correspondence, many conditions are open to therapeutic influence through motivational channels. To take the simplest kind of case, differential exposure, to injuries or to infection, is certainly motivated, and the role of unconscious wishes to be injured or to fall ill in such cases has been clearly demonstrated. Then there is the whole range of "psychosomatic" illness about which knowledge has been rapidly accumulating in recent years. Finally, there is the field of "mental disease," the symptoms of which occur mainly on the behavioral level. . . .

Summing up, we may say that illness is a state of disturbance in the "normal" functioning of the total human individual, including both the state of the organism as a biological system and of his personal and social adjustments. It is thus partly biologically and partly socially defined. . . .

Medical practice . . . is a "mechanism" in the social system for coping with the illnesses of its members. It involves a set of institutionalized roles. . . . The immediately relevant social structures consist in the patterning of the role of the medical practitioner himself and, though to common sense it may seem superfluous to analyze it, that of the "sick person" himself. . . .

The role of the medical practitioner belongs to the general class of "professional" roles, a subclass of the larger group of occupational roles. Caring for the sick is thus not an incidental activity of other roles though, for example, mothers do a good deal of it—but has become functionally specialized as a full-time "job." This, of course, is by no means true of all societies. As an occupational role it is institutionalized about the technical content of the function which is given a high degree of primacy relative to other status-determinants. It is thus inevitable both that incumbency of the role should be achieved and that performance criteria by standards of technical competence should be prominent. Selection for it and the context of its performance are to a high degree segregated from other bases of social status and solidarities. . . . Unlike the role of the businessman, however, it is collectivity-oriented not self-oriented.

The importance of this patterning is, in one context, strongly emphasized by its relation to the cultural tradition. One basis for the division of labor is the specialization of technical competence. The role of physician is far along the continuum of increasingly high levels of technical competence required for performance. Because of the complexity and subtlety of the knowledge and skill required and the consequent length and intensity of training, it is difficult to see how the functions could, under modern conditions, be ascribed to people occupying a prior status as one of their activities in that status, following the pattern by which, to a degree, responsibility for the health of her children is ascribed to the mother-status. There is an intrinsic connection between achieved statuses and the requirements of high technical competence . . .

High technical competence also implies specificity of function. Such intensive devotion to expertness in matters of health and disease precludes comparable expertness in other fields. The physician is not, by virtue of his modern role, a generalized "wise man" or sage—though there is considerable folklore to that effect—but a specialist whose superiority to his fellows is confined to the specific sphere of his technical training and experience. For example, one does not expect the physician as such to have better judgment about foreign policy or tax legislation than any other comparably intelligent and well-educated citizen. There are of course elaborate subdivisions of specialization within the profession. . . . The physician is [also] expected to treat an objective problem in objective, scientifically justifiable terms. For example, whether he likes or dislikes the particular patient as a person is supposed to be irrelevant, as indeed it is to most purely objective problems of how to handle a particular disease.

. . . The "ideology" of the profession lays great emphasis on the obligation of the physician to put the "welfare of the patient" above his personal interests, and regards "commercialism" as the most serious and insidious evil with which it has to contend. The line, therefore, is drawn primarily vis-à-vis "business." The "profit motive" is supposed to be drastically excluded from the medical world. This attitude is, of course, shared with the other professions, but it is perhaps more pronounced in the medical case than in any single one except perhaps the clergy. . . .

An increasing proportion of medical practice is now taking place in the context of organization. To a large extent this is necessitated by the technological development of medicine itself, above all the need for technical facilities beyond the reach of the individual practitioner, and the fact that treating the same case often involves the complex cooperation of several different kinds of physicians as well as of auxiliary personnel. This greatly alters the relation of the physician to the rest of the instrumental complex. He tends to be relieved of much responsibility and hence necessarily of freedom, in relation to his patients other than in his technical role. Even if a hospital executive is a physician himself he is not in the usual sense engaged in the "practice of medicine" in performing his functions any more than the president of the Miners' Union is engaged in mining coal.

As was noted, for common sense there may be some question of whether "being sick" constitutes a social role at all—isn't it simply a state of fact, a "condition"? Things are not quite so simple as this. The test is the existence of a set of institutionalized expectations and the corresponding sentiments and sanctions.

There seem to be four aspects of the institutionalized expectation system relative to the sick role. First is the exemption from normal social role responsibilities, which of course is relative to the nature and severity of the illness. This exemption requires legitimation by and to the various alters involved and the physician often serves as a court of appeal as well as a direct legitimatizing agent. It is noteworthy that like all institutionalized patterns the legitimation of being sick enough to avoid obligations can not only be a right of the sick person but an obligation upon him. People are often resistant to admitting they are sick, and it is not uncommon for others to tell them that they *ought* to stay in bed. The word generally has a moral connotation. It goes almost without saying that this legitimation has the social function of protection against "malingering."

The second closely related aspect is the institutionalized definition that the sick person cannot be expected by "pulling himself together" to get well by an act of decision or will. In this sense also he is exempted from responsibility—he is in a condition that must "be taken care of." His "condition" must be changed, not merely his "attitude." Of course the process of recovery may be spontaneous, but while the illness lasts he can't "help it." This element in the definition of the state of illness is obviously crucial as a bridge to the acceptance of "help."

The third element is the definition of the state of being ill as itself undesirable with its obligation to want to "get well." The first two elements of legitimation of the sick role thus are conditional in a highly important sense. It is a relative legitimation so long as he is in this unfortunate state which both he and alter hope he can get out of as expeditiously as possible.

Finally, the fourth closely related element is the obligation—in proportion to the severity of the condition, of course—to seek *technically competent* help, namely, in the most usual case, that of a physician and to *cooperate* with him in the process of trying to get well. It is here, of course, that the role of the sick person as patient becomes articulated with that of the physician in a complementary role structure.

It is evident from the above that the role of motivational factors in illness immensely broadens the scope and increases the importance of the institutionalized role aspect of being sick. For then the problem of social control becomes much more than one of ascertaining facts and drawing lines. The privileges and exemptions of the sick role may become objects of a "secondary gain" which the patient is positively motivated, usually unconsciously, to secure or to retain. The problem, therefore, of the balance of motivations to recover becomes of first importance. In general motivational balances of great functional significance to the social system are institutionally controlled, and it should, therefore, not be surprising that this is no exception.

A few further points may be made about the specific patterning of the sick role and its relation to social structure. It is, in the first place, a "contingent" role into which anyone, regardless of his status in other respects, may come. It is, furthermore, in the type case temporary. One may say that it is in a certain sense a "negatively achieved" role, through failure to "keep well," though, of course, positive motivations also operate, which by that very token must be motivations to deviance. . . .

The orientation of the sick role vis-à-vis the physician is also defined as collectively-oriented. It is true that the patient has a very obvious self-interest in getting well in most cases, though this point may not always be so simple. But once he has called in a physician the attitude is clearly marked, that he has assumed the obligation to cooperate with that physician in what is regarded as a common task. The obverse of the physician's obligation to be guided by the welfare of the patient is the latter's obligation to "do his part" to the best of his ability. This point is dearly brought out, for example, in the attitudes of the profession toward what is called "shopping around." By that is meant the practice of a patient "checking" the advice of one physician against that of another without telling physician A that he intends to consult physician B, or if he comes back to A that he has done so or who B is. The medical view is that if the patient is not satisfied with the advice his physician gives him, he may properly do one of two things; first he may request a consultation, even naming the physician he wishes called in, but in that case it is physician A not the patient who must call B in, the patient may not see B independently, and above all not without A's knowledge. The other proper recourse is to terminate the relation with A and become "B's patient." The notable fact here is that a pattern of behavior on the part not only of the physician but also of the patient, is expected which is in sharp contrast to perfectly legitimate behavior in a commercial relationship. If he is buying a car there is no objection to the customer going to a number of dealers before making up his mind, and there is no obligation for him to inform any one dealer what others he is consulting, to say nothing of approaching the Chevrolet dealer only through the Ford dealer.

The doctor–patient relationship is thus focused on these pattern elements. The patient has a need for technical services because he doesn't—nor do his lay associates, family members, etc.—"know" what is the matter or what to do about it, nor does he control the necessary facilities. The physician is a technical expert who by special training and experience, and by an institutionally validated status, is qualified to "help" the patient in a situation institutionally defined as legitimate in a relative sense but as needing help. . . .

48

DEATH STALKS A CONTINENT

JOHANNA McGEARY

One important aspect of medical sociology is the study of social inequalities caused by the distribution and treatment of certain illnesses. Social inequality is particularly blatant in the distribution of HIV/AIDS among world populations and the availability of resources for treatment. Nowhere is this more evident than in Africa where millions of people have already died from AIDS and millions of children are orphaned due to the loss of their parents to this illness. In the selection below, Johanna McGeary, a reporter for *Time* magazine, describes the horrific consequences of the social inequities she saw concerning HIV/AIDS in Africa.

Imagine your life this way. You get up in the morning and breakfast with your three kids. One is already doomed to die in infancy. Your husband works 200 miles away, comes home twice a year, and sleeps around in between. You risk your life in every act of sexual intercourse. You go to work past a house where a teenager lives alone tending young siblings without any source of income. At another house, the wife was branded a whore when she asked her husband to use a condom, beaten silly, and thrown into the streets. Over there lies a man desperately sick without access to a doctor or clinic or medicine or food or blankets or even a kind word. At work you eat with colleagues, and every third one is already fatally ill. You whisper about a friend who admitted she had the plague and whose neighbors stoned her to death. Your leisure is occupied by the funerals you attend every Saturday. You go to bed fearing adults your age will not live into their 40s. You and your neighbors and your political and popular leaders act as if nothing is happening.

Across the southern quadrant of Africa, this nightmare is real. The word not spoken is AIDS, and here at ground zero of humanity's deadliest cataclysm, the ultimate tragedy is that so many people don't know—or don't want to know—what is happening.

As the HIV virus sweeps mercilessly through these lands—the fiercest trial Africa has yet endured—a few try to address the terrible depredation. The rest of society looks away. Flesh and muscle melt from the bones of the sick in packed hospital wards and lonely bush kraals. Corpses stack up in morgues until those on top crush the identity from the faces underneath. Raw earth mounds scar the landscape, grave after grave without name or number. Bereft children grieve for parents lost in their prime, for siblings scattered to the winds.

The victims don't cry out. Doctors and obituaries do not give the killer its name. Families recoil in shame. Leaders shirk responsibility. The stubborn silence heralds victory for the disease: denial cannot keep the virus at bay.

The developed world is largely silent too. AIDS in Africa has never commanded the full-bore response the West has brought to other, sometimes lesser, travails. We pay sporadic attention, turning on the spotlight when an international conference occurs, then turning it off. Good-hearted donors donate; governments acknowledge that more needs to be done. But think how different the effort would be if what is happening here were happening in the West.

By now you've seen pictures of the sick, the dead, the orphans. You've heard appalling numbers: the number of new infections, the number of the dead, the number who are sick without care, the number walking around already fated to die.

But to comprehend the full horror AIDS has visited on Africa, listen to the woman we have dubbed Laetitia Hambahlane in Durban or the boy Tsepho Phale in Francistown or the woman who calls herself Thandiwe in Bulawayo or Louis Chikoka, a long-distance trucker. You begin to understand how AIDS has struck Africa—with a biblical virulence that will claim tens of millions of lives—when you hear about shame and stigma and ignorance and poverty and sexual violence and migrant labor and promiscuity and political paralysis and the terrible silence that surrounds all this dying. It is a measure of the silence that some asked us not to print their real names to protect their privacy.

Theirs is a story about what happens when a disease leaps the confines of medicine to invade the body politic, infecting not just individuals but an entire society. As AIDS migrated to man in Africa, it mutated into a complex plague with confounding social, economic, and political mechanics that locked together to accelerate the virus' progress. The region's social dynamics colluded to spread the disease and help block effective intervention.

We have come to three countries abutting one another at the bottom of Africa—Botswana, South Africa, Zimbabwe—the heart of the heart of the epidemic. For nearly a decade, these nations suffered a hidden invasion of infection that concealed the dimension of the coming calamity. Now the omnipresent dying reveals the shocking scale of the devastation.

AIDS in Africa bears little resemblance to the American epidemic, limited to specific high-risk groups and brought under control through intensive education, vigorous political action, and expensive drug therapy. Here the disease has bred a Darwinian perversion. Society's fittest, not its frailest, are the ones who die—adults spirited away, leaving the old and the children behind. You cannot define risk groups: everyone who is sexually active is at risk. Babies too, unwittingly infected by mothers. Barely a single family remains untouched. Most do not know how or when they caught the virus, many never know they have it, many who do know don't tell anyone as they lie dying. Africa can provide no treatment for those with AIDS.

They will all die, of tuberculosis, pneumonia, meningitis, diarrhea, whatever overcomes their ruined immune systems first. And the statistics, grim as they are, may be too low. There is no broad-scale AIDS testing: infection rates are calculated mainly from the presence of HIV in pregnant women. Death certificates in these countries do not record AIDS as the cause. "Whatever stats we have are not reliable," warns Mary Crewe of the University of Pretoria's Center for the Study of AIDS. "Everybody's guessing."

The TB Patient

Case no. 309 in the Tugela Ferry Home-care program shivers violently on the wooden planks someone has knocked into a bed, a frayed blanket pulled right up to his nose. He has the flushed skin, overbright eyes, and careful breathing of the tubercular. He is alone, and it is chilly within the crumbling mud walls of his hut at Msinga Top, a windswept outcrop high above the Tugela River in South Africa's KwaZulu-Natal province. The spectacular view of hills and veld would gladden a well man, but the 22-year-old we will call Fundisi Khumalo, though he does not know it, has AIDS, and his eyes seem to focus inward on his simple fear.

Before he can speak, his throat clutches in gasping spasms. Sharp pains rack his chest; his breath comes in shallow gasps. The vomiting is better today. But constipation has doubled up his knees, and he is too weak to go outside to relieve himself. He can't remember when he last ate. He can't remember how long he's been sick—"a long time, maybe since six months ago." Khumalo knows he has TB, and he believes it is just TB. "I am only thinking of that," he answers when we ask why he is so ill.

But the fear never leaves his eyes. He worked in a hair salon in Johannesburg, lived in a men's hostel in one of the cheap townships, had "a few" girlfriends. He knew other young men in the hostel who were on-and-off sick. When they fell too ill to work anymore, like him, they straggled home to rural villages like Msinga Top. But where Khumalo would not go is the hospital. "Why?" he says. "You are sick there, you die there."

"He's right, you know," says Dr. Tony Moll, who has driven us up the dirt track from the 350-bed hospital he heads in Tugela Ferry. "We have no medicines for AIDS. So many hospitals tell them, 'You've got AIDS. We can't help you. Go home and die.'" No one wants to be tested either, he adds, unless treatment is available. "If the choice is to know and get nothing," he says, "they don't want to know."

Here and in scattered homesteads all over rural Africa, the dying people say the sickness afflicting their families and neighbors is just the familiar consequence of their eternal poverty. Or it is the work of witchcraft. You have done something bad and have been bewitched. Your neighbor's jealousy has invaded you. You have not appeased the spirits of your ancestors, and they have cursed you. Some in South Africa believe the disease was introduced by the white population as a way to control black Africans after the end of apartheid.

Ignorance about AIDS remains profound. But because of the funerals, southern Africans can't help seeing that something more systematic and sinister lurks out there. Every Saturday and often Sundays too, neighbors trudge to the cemeteries for costly burial rites for the young and the middle-aged who are suddenly dying so much faster than the old. Families say it was pneumonia, TB, malaria that killed their son, their wife, their baby. "But you starting to hear the truth," says Durban home-care volunteer Busi Magwazi. "In the church, in the graveyard, they saying, 'Yes, she died of AIDS.' Oh, people talking about it even if the families don't admit it." Ignorance is the crucial reason the epidemic has run out of control. Surveys say many Africans here are becoming aware there is a sexually transmitted disease called AIDS that is incurable. But they don't think the risk applies to them. And their vague knowledge does not translate into changes in their sexual behavior. It's easy to see why so many don't yet sense the danger when few talk openly about the disease. And Africans are beset by so plentiful a roster of perils—famine, war, the violence of desperation or ethnic hatred, the regular illnesses of poverty, the dangers inside mines or on the roads—that the delayed risk of AIDS ranks low.

The Outcast

To acknowledge AIDS in yourself is to be branded as monstrous. Laetitia Hambahlane (not her real name) is 51 and sick with AIDS. So is her brother. She admits it; he doesn't. In her mother's broken-down house in the mean streets of Umlazi township, though, Laetitia's mother hovers over her son, nursing him, protecting him, resolutely denying he has anything but TB, though his sister claims the sure symptoms of AIDS mark him. Laetitia is the outcast, first from her family, then from her society.

For years Laetitia worked as a domestic servant in Durban and dutifully sent all her wages home to her mother. She fell in love a number of times and bore four children. "I loved that last man," she recalls. "After he left, I had no one, no sex." That was 1992, but Laetitia already had HIV.

She fell sick in 1996, and her employers sent her to a private doctor who couldn't diagnose an illness. He tested her blood and found she was HIV positive. "I wish I'd died right then," she says, as tears spill down her sunken cheeks. "I asked the doctor, 'Have you got medicine?' He said no. I said, 'Can't you keep me alive?'" The doctor could do nothing and sent her away. "I couldn't face the word," she says. "I couldn't sleep at night. I sat on my bed, thinking, praying. I did not see anyone day or night. I ask God, Why?"

Laetitia's employers fired her without asking her exact diagnosis. For weeks she could not muster the courage to tell anyone. Then she told her children, and they were ashamed and frightened. Then, harder still, she told her mother. Her mother raged about the loss of money if Laetitia could not work again. She was so angry she ordered Laetitia out of the house. When her daughter wouldn't leave, the mother threatened to sell the house to get rid of her daughter. Then she walled off her daughter's room with plywood partitions, leaving the daughter a pariah, alone in a cramped, dark space without windows and only a flimsy door opening into the alley. Laetitia must earn the pennies to feed herself and her children by peddling beer, cigarettes, and candy from a shopping cart in her room, when people are brave enough to stop by her door. "Sometimes they buy, sometimes not," she says. "That is how I'm surviving."

Her mother will not talk to her. "If you are not even accepted by your own family," says Magwazi, the volunteer home-care giver from Durban's Sinoziso project who visits Laetitia, "then others will not accept you." When Laetitia ventures outdoors, neighbors snub her, tough boys snatch her purse, children taunt her. Her own kids are tired of the sickness and don't like to help her anymore. "When I can't get up, they don't bring me food," she laments. One day local youths barged into her room, cursed her as a witch and a whore and beat her. When she told the police, the youths returned, threatening to burn down the house.

But it is her mother's rejection that wounds Laetitia most. "She is hiding it about my brother," she cries. "Why will she do nothing for me?" Her hands pick restlessly at the quilt covering her paper-thin frame. "I know my mother will not bury me properly. I know she will not take care of my kids when I am gone."

Jabulani Syabusi would use his real name, but he needs to protect his brother. He teaches school in a red, dusty district of KwaZulu-Natal. People here know the disease is all around them, but no one speaks of it. He eyes the scattered huts that make up his little settlement on an arid bluff. "We can count 20 who died just here as far as we can see. I personally don't remember any family that told it was AIDS," he says. "They hide it if they do know."

Syabusi's own family is no different. His younger brother is also a teacher who has just come home from Durban too sick to work anymore. He says he has tuberculosis, but after six months the tablets he is taking have done nothing to cure him. Syabusi's wife, Nomsange, a nurse, is concerned that her 36-year-old brother-in-law may have something worse. Syabusi finally asked the doctor tending his brother what is wrong. The doctor said the information is confidential and will not tell him. Neither will his brother. "My brother is not brave enough to tell me," says Syabusi, as he stares sadly toward the house next door, where his only sibling lies ill. "And I am not brave enough to ask him."

Kennedy Fugewane, a cheerful, elderly volunteer counselor, sits in an empty U.S.-funded clinic that offers fast, pinprick blood tests in Francistown,

Botswana, pondering how to break through the silence. This city suffers one of the world's highest infection rates, but people deny the disease because HIV is linked with sex. "We don't reveal anything," he says. "But people are so stigmatized even if they walk in the door." Africans feel they must keep private anything to do with sex. "If a man comes here, people will say he is running around," says Fugewane, though he acknowledges that men never do come. "If a woman comes, people will say she is loose. If anyone says they got HIV, they will be despised."

Pretoria University's Mary Crewe says, "It is presumed if you get AIDS, you have done something wrong." HIV labels you as living an immoral life. Embarrassment about sexuality looms more important than future health risks. "We have no language to talk candidly about sex," she says, "so we have no civil language to talk about AIDS." Volunteers like Fugewane try to reach out with flyers, workshops, youth meetings, and free condoms, but they are frustrated by a culture that values its dignity over saving lives. "People here don't have the courage to come forward and say, 'Let me know my HIV status,'" he sighs, much less the courage to do something about it. "Maybe one day . . ."

Doctors bow to social pressure and legal strictures not to record AIDS on death certificates. "I write TB or meningitis or diarrhea but never AIDS," says South Africa's Dr. Moll. "It's a public document, and families would hate it if anyone knew." Several years ago, doctors were barred even from recording compromised immunity or HIV status on a medical file; now they can record the results of blood tests for AIDS on patient charts to protect other health workers. Doctors like Moll have long agitated to apply the same openness to death certificates.

The Truck Driver

Here, men have to migrate to work, inside their countries or across borders. All that mobility sows HIV far and wide, as Louis Chikoka is the first to recognize. He regularly drives the highway that is Botswana's economic lifeline and its curse. The road runs for 350 miles through desolate bush that is the Texas-size country's sole strip of habitable land, home to a large majority of its 1.5 million people. It once brought prospectors to Botswana's rich diamond reefs. Now it's the link for transcontinental truckers like Chikoka who haul goods from South Africa to markets in the continent's center. And now the road brings AIDS.

Chikoka brakes his dusty, diesel-belching Kabwe Transport 18-wheeler to a stop at the dark roadside rest on the edge of Francistown, where the international trade routes converge and at least 43% of adults are HIV-positive. He is a cheerful man even after 12 hard hours behind the wheel freighting rice from Durban. He's been on the road for two weeks and will reach his destination in Congo next Thursday. At 39, he is married, the father of three, and a long-haul trucker for 12 years. He's used to it.

Lighting up a cigarette, the jaunty driver is unusually loquacious about sex as he eyes the dim figures circling the rest stop. Chikoka has parked here for a quickie. See that one over there, he points with his cigarette. "Those local ones we call bitches. They always waiting here for short service." Short service? "It's according to how long it takes you to ejaculate," he explains. "We go to the 'bush bedroom' over there [waving at a clump of trees 100 yds. away] or sometimes in the truck. Short service, that costs you 20 rands [$2.84]. They know we drivers always got money."

Chikoka nods his head toward another woman sitting beside a stack of cardboard cartons. "We like better to go to them," he says. They are the "businesswomen," smugglers with gray-market cases of fruit and toilet paper and toys that they need to transport somewhere up the road. "They come to us, and we negotiate privately about carrying their goods." It's a no-cash deal, he says. "They pay their bodies to us." Chikoka shrugs at a suggestion that the practice may be unhealthy. "I been away two weeks, madam. I'm human. I'm a man. I have to have sex."

What he likes best is dry sex. In parts of sub-Saharan Africa, to please men, women sit in basins of bleach or saltwater or stuff astringent herbs, tobacco, or fertilizer inside their vagina. The tissue of the lining swells up and natural lubricants dry out. The resulting dry sex is painful and dangerous for women. The drying agents suppress natural bacteria, and friction easily lacerates the tender walls of the vagina. Dry sex increases the risk of HIV infection for women, already two times as likely as men to contract the virus from a single encounter. The women, adds Chikoka, can charge more for dry sex, 50 or 60 rands ($6.46 to $7.75), enough to pay a child's school fees or to eat for a week.

Chikoka knows his predilection for commercial sex spreads AIDS; he knows his promiscuity could carry the disease home to his wife; he knows people die if they get it. "Yes, HIV is terrible, madam," he says as he crooks a finger toward the businesswoman whose favors he will enjoy that night. "But, madam, sex is natural. Sex is not like beer or smoking. You can stop them. But unless you castrate the men, you can't stop sex—and then we all die anyway."

Millions of men share Chikoka's sexually active lifestyle, fostered by the region's dependence on migrant labor. Men desperate to earn a few dollars leave their women at hardscrabble rural homesteads to go where the work is: the mines, the cities, the road. They're housed together in isolated males-only hostels but have easy access to prostitutes or a "town wife" with whom they soon pick up a second family and an ordinary STD and HIV. Then they go home to wives and girlfriends a few times a year, carrying the virus they do not know they have. The pattern is so dominant that rates of infection in many rural areas across the southern cone match urban numbers.

If HIV zeros in disproportionately on poor migrants, it does not skip over the educated or the well paid. Soldiers, doctors, policemen, teachers, district administrators are also routinely separated from families by a civil-service system that sends them alone to remote rural posts, where they have money and women have no men. A regular paycheck procures more access to extra-marital sex. Result: the vital professions are being devastated.

Schoolmaster Syabusi is afraid there will soon be no more teachers in his rural zone. He has just come home from a memorial for six colleagues who died over the past few months, though no one spoke the word AIDS at the service. "The rate here—they're so many," he says, shaking his head. "They keep on passing it at school." Teachers in southern Africa have one of the highest group infection rates, but they hide their status until the telltale symptoms find them out.

Before then, the men—teachers are mostly men here—can take their pick of sexual partners. Plenty of women in bush villages need extra cash, often to pay school fees, and female students know they can profit from a teacher's favor. So the schoolmasters buy a bit of sex with lonely wives and trade a bit of sex with willing pupils for A's. Some students consider it an honor to sleep with the teacher, a badge of superiority. The girls brag about it to their peers, preening in their ability to snag an older man. "The teachers are the worst," says Jabulani Siwela, an AIDS worker in Zimbabwe who saw frequent teacher-student sex in his Bulawayo high school. They see a girl they like; they ask her to stay after class; they have a nice time. "It's dead easy," he says. "These are men who know better, but they still do it all the time."

The Prostitute

The workingwoman we meet directs our car to a reedy field fringing the gritty eastern townships of Bulawayo, Zimbabwe. She doesn't want neighbors to see her being interviewed. She is afraid her family will find out she is a prostitute, so we will call her Thandiwe. She looked quite prim and proper in her green calf-length dress as she waited for johns outside 109 Tongogaro Street in the center of downtown. So, for that matter, do the dozens of other women cruising the city's dim street corners: not a mini or bustier or bared navel in sight. Zimbabwe is in many ways a prim and proper society that frowns on commercial sex work and the public display of too much skin.

That doesn't stop Thandiwe from earning a better living turning tricks than she ever could doing honest work. Desperate for a job, she slipped illegally into South Africa in 1992. She cleaned floors in a Johannesburg restaurant, where she met a cook from back home who was also illegal. They had two daughters, and they got married; he was gunned down one night at work.

She brought his body home for burial and was sent to her in-laws to be "cleansed." This common practice gives a dead husband's brother the right, even the duty, to sleep with the widow. Thandiwe tested negative for HIV in

1998, but if she were positive, the ritual cleansing would have served only to pass on the disease. Then her in-laws wanted to keep her two daughters because their own children had died, and marry her off to an old uncle who lived far out in the bush. She fled.

Alone, Thandiwe grew desperate. "I couldn't let my babies starve." One day she met a friend from school. "She told me she was a sex worker. She said, 'Why you suffer? Let's go to a place where we can get quick bucks.'" Thandiwe hangs her head. "I went. I was afraid. But now I go every night."

She goes to Tongogaro Street, where the rich clients are, tucking a few condoms in her handbag every evening as the sun sets and returning home strictly by 10 so that she won't have to service a taxi-van driver to get a ride back. Thandiwe tells her family she works an evening shift, just not at what. "I get 200 zim [$5] for sex," she says, more for special services. She uses two condoms per client, sometimes three. "If they say no, I say no." But then sometimes resentful johns hit her. It's pay-and-go until she has pocketed 1,000 or 1,500 Zimbabwe dollars and can go home—with more cash than her impoverished neighbors ever see in their roughneck shantytown, flush enough to buy a TV and fleece jammies for her girls and meat for their supper.

"I am ashamed," she murmurs. She has stopped going to church. "Every day I ask myself, 'When will I stop this business?' The answer is, 'If I could get a job' . . .'" Her voice trails off hopelessly. "At the present moment, I have no option, no other option." As trucker Chikoka bluntly puts it, "They give sex to eat. They got no man; they got no work; but they got kids, and they got to eat." Two of Thandiwe's friends in the sex trade are dying of AIDS, but what can she do? "I just hope I won't get it."

In fact, casual sex of every kind is commonplace here. Prostitutes are just the ones who admit they do it for cash. Everywhere there's premarital sex, sex as recreation. Obligatory sex and its abusive counterpart, coercive sex. Transactional sex: sex as a gift, sugar-daddy sex. Extramarital sex, second families, multiple partners. The nature of AIDS is to feast on promiscuity.

Rare is the man who even knows his HIV status: males widely refuse testing even when they fall ill. And many men who suspect they are HIV positive embrace a flawed logic: if I'm already infected, I can sleep around because I can't get it again. But women are the ones who progress to full-blown AIDS first and die fastest, and the underlying cause is not just sex but power. Wives and girlfriends and even prostitutes in this part of the world can't easily say no to sex on a man's terms. It matters little what comes into play, whether it is culture or tradition or the pathology of violence or issues of male identity or the subservient status of women.

Beneath a translucent scalp, the plates of Gertrude Dhlamini's cranium etch a geography of pain. Her illness is obvious in the thin, stretched skin under which veins throb with the shingles that have blinded her left eye and scarred that side of her face. At 39, she looks 70. The agonizing thrush, a kind of fungus, that paralyzed her throat has ebbed enough to enable her to swallow a spoon or two of warm gruel, but most of the nourishment flows away in constant diarrhea. She struggles to keep her hand from scratching rest-lessly at the scaly rash flushing her other cheek. She is not ashamed to pro-claim her illness to the world. "It must be told," she says.

Gertrude is thrice rejected. At 19 she bore a son to a boyfriend who soon left her, taking away the child. A second boyfriend got her pregnant in 1994 but disappeared in anger when their daughter was born sickly with HIV. A doctor told Gertrude it was her fault, so she blamed herself that little No-luthando was never well in the two years she survived. Gertrude never told the doctor the baby's father had slept with other women. "I was afraid to," she says, "though I sincerely believe he gave the sickness to me." Now, she says, "I have rent him from my heart. And I will never have another man in my life."

Gertrude begged her relatives to take her in, but when she revealed the name of her illness, they berated her. They made her the household drudge, telling her never to touch their food or their cooking pots. They gave her a bowl and a spoon strictly for her own use. After a few months, they threw her out.

Gertrude sits upright on a donated bed in a cardboard shack in a rough Durban township that is now the compass of her world. Perhaps 10 ft. square, the little windowless room contains a bed, one sheet and blanket, a change of clothes and a tiny cooking ring, but she has no money for paraffin to heat the food that a home-care worker brings. She must fetch water and use a toilet down the hill. "Everything I have," she says, "is a gift." Now the school that owns the land under her hut wants to turn it into a playground and she worries about where she will go. Gertrude rubs and rubs at her raw cheek. "I pray and pray to God," she says, "not to take my soul while I am alone in this room."

Women like Gertrude were brought up to be subservient to men. Espe-cially in matters of sex, the man is always in charge. Women feel powerless to change sexual behavior. Even when a woman wants to protect herself, she usually can't: it is not uncommon for men to beat partners who refuse intercourse or request a condom. "Real men" don't use them, so women who want their partners to must fight deeply ingrained taboos. Talk to him about donning a rubber sheath and be prepared for accusations, abuse, or abandonment.

A nurse in Durban, coming home from an AIDS training class, suggested that her mate should put on a condom, as a kind of homework exercise. He grabbed a pot and banged loudly on it with a knife, calling all the neighbors into his house. He pointed the knife at his wife and demanded: "Where was she between 4 p.m. and now? Why is she suddenly suggesting this? What has changed after 20 years that she wants a condom?"

Schoolteacher Syabusi is an educated man, fully cognizant of the AIDS threat. Yet even he bristles when asked if he uses a condom. "Humph," he says with a fine snort. "That question is nonnegotiable." So despite extensive distribution of free condoms, they often go unused. Astonishing myths have sprung up. If you don one, your erection can't grow. Free condoms must be too cheap to be safe: they have been stored too long, kept too hot, kept too cold. Condoms fill up with germs, so they spread AIDS. Condoms from overseas bring the disease with them. Foreign governments that donate condoms put holes in them so that Africans will die. Education programs find it hard to compete with the power of the grapevine.

The Child in No. 17

In crib no. 17 of the spartan but crowded children's ward at the Church of Scotland Hospital in KwaZulu-Natal, a tiny, staring child lies dying. She is three and has hardly known a day of good health. Now her skin wrinkles around her body like an oversize suit, and her twig-size bones can barely hold her vertical as nurses search for a vein to take blood. In the frail arms hooked up to transfusion tubes, her veins have collapsed. The nurses palpate a threadlike vessel on the child's forehead. She mews like a wounded animal as one tightens a rubber band around her head to raise the vein. Tears pour unnoticed from her mother's eyes as she watches the needle tap-tap at her daughter's temple. Each time the whimpering child lifts a wan hand to brush away the pain, her mother gently lowers it. Drop by drop, the nurses manage to collect 1 cc of blood in five minutes.

The child in crib No. 17 has had TB, oral thrush, chronic diarrhea, malnutrition, severe vomiting. The vital of blood reveals her real ailment, AIDS, but the disease is not listed on her chart, and her mother says she has no idea why her child is so ill. She breast-fed her for two years, but once the little girl was weaned, she could not keep solid food down. For a long time, her mother thought something was wrong with the food. Now the child is afflicted with so many symptoms that her mother had to bring her to the hospital, from which sick babies rarely return.

She hopes, she prays her child will get better, and like all the mothers who stay with their children at the hospital, she tends her lovingly, constantly changing filthy diapers, smoothing sheets, pressing a little nourishment between listless lips, trying to tease a smile from the vacant, staring face. Her husband works in Johannesburg, where he lives in a men's squatter camp. He comes home twice a year. She is 25. She has heard of AIDS but does not know it is transmitted by sex, does not know if she or her husband has it. She is afraid this child will die soon, and she is afraid to have more babies. But she is afraid too to raise the subject with her husband. "He would not agree to that," she says shyly. "He would never agree to have no more babies."

Dr. Annick DeBaets, 32, is a volunteer from Belgium. In the two years she has spent here in Tugela Ferry, she has learned all about how hard it is to break the cycle of HIV transmission from mother to infant. The door to this 48-cot ward is literally a revolving one: sick babies come in, receive doses of rudimentary antibiotics, vitamins, food; go home for a week or a month; then come back as ill as ever. Most, she says, die in the first or second year. If she could just follow up with really intensive care, believes Dr. DeBaets, many of the wizened infants crowding three to a crib could live longer, healthier lives. "But it's very discouraging. We simply don't have the time, money, or facilities for anything but minimal care."

Much has been written about what South African Judge Edwin Cameron, himself HIV positive, calls his country's "grievous ineptitude" in the face of the burgeoning epidemic. Nowhere has that been more evident than in the government's failure to provide drugs that could prevent pregnant women from passing HIV to their babies. The government has said it can't afford the 300-rand-per-dose, 28-dose regimen of AZT that neighboring nations like Botswana dole out, using funds and drugs from foreign donors. The late South African presidential spokesman Parks Mankahlana even suggested publicly that it was not cost effective to save these children when their mothers were already doomed to die: "We don't want a generation of orphans."

Yet these children—70,000 are born HIV positive in South Africa alone every year—could be protected from the disease for about $4 each with another simple, cheap drug called nevirapine. Until last month, the South African government steadfastly refused to license or finance the use of nevirapine despite the manufacturer's promise to donate the drug for five years, claiming that its "toxic" side effects are not yet known. This spring, however, the drug will finally be distributed to leading public hospitals in the country, though only on a limited basis at first.

The mother at crib No. 17 is not concerned with potential side effects. She sits on the floor cradling her daughter, crooning over and over, "Get well, my child, get well." The baby stares back without blinking. "It's sad, so sad, so sad," the mother says. The child died three days later.

The children who are left when parents die only add another complex dimension to Africa's epidemic. At 17, Tsepho Phale has been head of an indigent household of three young boys in the dusty township of Monarch, outside Francistown, for two years. He never met his father, his mother died of AIDS, and the grieving children possess only a raw concrete shell of a house. The doorways have no doors; the window frames no glass. There is not a stick of furniture. The boys sleep on piled-up blankets, their few clothes dangling from nails. In the room that passes for a kitchen, two paraffin burners sit on the dirt floor alongside the month's food: four cabbages, a bag of oranges and one of potatoes, three sacks of flour, some yeast, two jars of oil, and two cartons of milk. Next to a dirty stack of plastic pans lies the mealy meal and rice that will provide their main sustenance for the month. A couple of bars of soap and two rolls of toilet paper also have to last the month. Tsepho has just brought these rations home from the social-service center where the "orphan grants" are doled out.

Tsepho has been robbed of a childhood that was grim even before his mother fell sick. She supported the family by "buying and selling things," he says, but she never earned more than a pittance. When his middle brother was knocked down by a car and left physically and mentally disabled, Tsepho's mother used the insurance money to build this house, so she would have one thing of value to leave her children. As the walls went up, she fell sick. Tsepho had to nurse her, bathe her, attend to her bodily functions, try to feed her. Her one fear as she lay dying was that her rural relatives would try to steal the house. She wrote a letter bequeathing it to her sons and bade Tsepho hide it.

As her body lay on the concrete floor awaiting burial, the relatives argued openly about how they would divide up the profits when they sold her dwelling. Tsepho gave the district commissioner's office the letter, preventing his mother's family from grabbing the house. Fine, said his relations; if you think you're a man, you look after your brothers. They have contributed nothing to the boys' welfare since. "It's as if we don't exist anymore either," says Tsepho. Now he struggles to keep house for the others, doing the cooking, cleaning, laundry, and shopping.

The boys look at the future with despair. "It is very bleak," says Tsepho, kicking aimlessly at a bare wall. He had to quit school, has no job, will probably never get one. "I've given up my dreams. I have no hope."

Orphans have traditionally been cared for the African way: relatives absorb the children of the dead into their extended families. Some still try, but communities like Tsepho's are becoming saturated with orphans, and families can't afford to take on another kid, leaving thousands alone.

Now many must fend for themselves, struggling to survive. The trauma of losing parents is compounded by the burden of becoming a breadwinner. Most orphans sink into penury, drop out of school, suffer malnutrition, ostracism, psychic distress. Their makeshift households scramble to live on pitiful handouts—from overstretched relatives, a kind neighbor, a state grant—or they beg and steal in the streets. The orphans' present desperation forecloses a brighter future. "They hardly ever succeed in having a life," says Siphelile Kaseke, 22, a counselor at an AIDS orphans' camp near Bulawayo. Without education, girls fall into prostitution, and older boys migrate illegally to South Africa, leaving the younger ones to go on the streets.

Every day spent in this part of Africa is acutely depressing: there is so little countervailing hope to all the stories of the dead and the doomed. "More than anywhere else in the world, AIDS in Africa was met with apathy," says Suzanne LeClerc-Madlala, a lecturer at the University of Natal. The consequences of the silence march on: infection soars, stigma hardens, denial hastens death, and the chasm between knowledge and behavior widens. The present disaster could be dwarfed by the woes that loom if Africa's epidemic rages on. The human losses could wreck the region's frail economies, break down civil societies, and incite political instability.

In the face of that, every day good people are doing good things. Like Dr. Moll, who uses his after-job time and his own fund raising to run an extensive volunteer home-care program in KwaZulu-Natal. And Busi Magwazi, who, along with dozens of others, tends the sick for nothing in the Durban-based Sinoziso project. And Patricia Bakwinya, who started her Shining Stars orphan-care program in Francistown with her own zeal and no money, to help youngsters like Tsepho Phale. And countless individuals who give their time and devotion to ease southern Africa's plight.

But these efforts can help only thousands; they cannot turn the tide. The region is caught in a double bind. Without treatment, those with HIV will sicken and die; without prevention, the spread of infection cannot be checked. Southern Africa has no other means available to break the vicious cycle, except to change everyone's sexual behavior—and that isn't happening.

The essential missing ingredient is leadership. Neither the countries of the region nor those of the wealthy world have been able or willing to provide it.

South Africa, comparatively well off, comparatively well educated, has blundered tragically for years. AIDS invaded just when apartheid ended, and a government absorbed in massive transition relegated the disease to a back page. An attempt at a national education campaign wasted millions on a farcical musical. The premature release of a local wonder drug ended in scandal when the drug turned out to be made of industrial solvent. Those fiascoes left the government skittish about embracing expensive programs, inspiring a 1998 decision not to provide AZT to HIV-positive pregnant women. Zimbabwe too suffers savagely from feckless leadership. Even in Botswana, where the will to act is gathering strength, the resources to follow through have to come from foreign hands.

AIDS' grip here is so pervasive and so complex that all societies—theirs and ours—must rally round to break it. These countries are too poor to doctor themselves. The drugs that could begin to break the cycle will not be available here until global pharmaceutical companies find ways to provide them inexpensively. The health-care systems required to prescribe and monitor complicated triple-cocktail regimens won't exist unless rich countries help foot the bill. If there is ever to be a vaccine, the West will have to finance its discovery and provide it to the poor. The cure for this epidemic is not national but international.

The deep silence that makes African leaders and societies want to deny the problem, the corruption and incompetence that render them helpless is something the West cannot fix. But the fact that they are poor is not. The wealthy world must help with its zeal and its cash if southern Africa is ever to be freed of the AIDS plague.

49

ILLNESS AND IDENTITY

DAVID A. KARP

How should a society treat the mentally ill? For decades, sociologists have researched this question concerning the treatment of the mentally ill, resulting in such classic studies as Erving Goffman's *Asylums* (1961) and David L. Rosenhan's "On Being Sane in Insane Places" (Reading 19). Today, the deinstitutionalization movement has meant that fewer mentally ill people are hospitalized; instead, they are more likely to be treated with psychotropic drugs on an outpatient basis. The patient's experience of mental illness is the focus of this reading, taken from David Karp's award-winning book, *Speaking of Sadness: Depression, Disconnection, and the Meanings of Illness* (1996). Here, Karp, a professor of sociology at Boston College, examines how clinically depressed people experience and interpret their illnesses and their altered senses of self.

You know, I was a mental patient. That was my identity. . . . Depression is very private. Then all of a sudden it becomes public and I was a mental patient. . . . It's no longer just my own pain. I am a mental patient. I am a depressive. I am a depressive (said slowly and with intensity). This is my identity. I can't separate myself from that. When people know me they'll have to know about my psychiatric history, because that's who I am.

—FEMALE GRADUATE STUDENT, AGED 24

At the time we spoke, Karen, whose words open this chapter, had been doing well for more than two years, but described being badly frightened by a recent two-week period during which the all-too-familiar feelings of depression had begun to reappear. Aside from the terror she felt at the prospect of becoming sick, Karen realized that if depression returned, it would mean recasting her identity yet again. After two years with nothing but the "normal" ups and downs of life, she had started to feel that it might be possible to leave behind the mental patient identity she earlier thought she never could shed. By the time of our interview, only her family and a few old friends knew of her several hospitalizations. Her current roommates thought of her simply as Karen, one of about eight students in the large house they shared. She told me, "No one in my life right now knows . . . I'm so eager to talk to you about it [in this interview] because I can't talk about it with people." I said, "It must be hurtful not to be able to talk about so critical a part of your biography," and Karen responded, "Yes, but I don't want to test it with people. . . . [If I told them] they might not say anything, but their perception of me would change."

Karen was willing to be interviewed because I was one of those who knew about her history with depression. Years previously, while taking one of my undergraduate courses, she had confided that she was having a terrible time completing her course work. After much tentative discussion, the word depression finally entered the conversation. She seemed embarrassed by the admission until I opened my desk drawer and showed her a bottle of pills *I* was taking for depression. With this, we began to trade depression experiences and thereby formed the kind of bond felt by those who go through a common difficulty. As her undergraduate years passed, Karen came to my office periodically and during these visits we often spoke about depression. Our shared identity as depressed persons blurred the age and status distinctions that otherwise might have prevented our friendship. . . .

Like nearly everyone whom I talked with, Karen could pinpoint the beginning of her depression career. Although she described a "home filled with feelings of sadness" for as long as she could remember, it was, she said, "the beginning of the ninth grade that touched off . . . ten years of depression." She elaborated with the observation, "I was always sad or upset, but I was so busy and social [that the feelings were muted]. You know, things were not doing so well at home, but at school no one knew how much of a hellhole I lived in." She described a home life that was fairly stable until her father became ill when she was a sixth grader. "When he came back from the hospital," she said, "he was very different, unstable [and] extremely violent." Till then Karen had been able to keep the misery of her home life apart from her school world, which served as a refuge. By the ninth grade, however, she "could no longer keep the two worlds separate" and in both places the same intrusive questions, feelings, and ruminations colonized her mind. Now she didn't feel safe anywhere in the world and had these relentless thoughts: "I'm miserable. [There is] such a feeling of emptiness. What the hell am I doing? What is my life all about? What is the point?" "And that," she said, "basically started it."

In the ninth grade Karen had no word for the "it" that had started. When I asked whether she recognized her pain as depression then, she replied, "Did I say this was depression [then]? Did I know [what it was]? It was pain, but I don't think I would have called it depression. I think I would have called it *my* pain." There was another factor that contributed to the anonymity of her misery and kept her pain from having a name—Karen was determined to keep her torment hidden. She said, "I lived with that for . . . a couple of years, from the ninth grade until the eleventh grade. [I lived] with that feeling. . . . But it was all very private. I kept it quiet. It was something inside. I didn't really talk about it. I might have talked about it with some of my friends, but no one understood."

During this time, though, a subtle transformation was taking place in her thinking about "it." Previously, Karen felt that her pain came exclusively from her difficulties at home, but by the eleventh grade she was beginning to suspect that its locus might be elsewhere. She told me, "My family life might have been hell, but it was always, 'Oh [I feel this way] because my father is crazy. It's because of something outside of me.' But it was the first time I'm feeling awful about myself." By the eleventh grade Karen's new conscious-ness was that there was something really wrong with *her*. Now, her feelings about the pain took a critical turn when she began to say to herself, "I can't live like this. I will not survive. I will not be here. I can't live with the pain. If I have to live with the pain I will eventually kill myself." Despite such a shift in thinking, Karen still succeeded in keeping things private until she experi-enced a very public crisis. It was, moreover, a "crash" that she understood as a major "turning point" in her identity. Here's what she said:

> *My whole family life just fell apart. There was no anchor. There was no anchor. . . . [Now] I was able to label it and say it was depression when I crashed in the eleventh grade and was hospitalized. You know, in ninth grade I told you about an experience where I was conscious of feeling pain, or whatever, but no one else knew about it. . . . It is sort of like what my life is like now. I couldn't tell people about it. How can you tell people about it? What do you say? . . .*

Then the interview turned to a lengthy discussion about psychiatric hospitals, doctors, and power—all of it negative. She expressed hostility to-ward doctors who wanted her to "open up" and toward institutional rules that seemed authoritarian and arbitrary. She said, "Psychiatrists and mental health workers have the power to decide when you are going to leave, if you're going to leave, if you can go out on a pass, if you're good, if you're not good." This first hospitalization (eventually there would be four) also started a long history with medications of all sorts. When I asked whether she was treated with medications she replied, "Yup, always medication. That's the big thing. . . . Oh my God, I've had so many. . . . I don't think they really affected me that much. By the time I left I was doing okay. Did I have these problems solved? No, [but] I had an added one. Now I felt crazy." I used Karen's ob-servation about "feeling crazy" as a cue for asking if she had a disease. I said, "Did you now think of yourself as having an illness in the medical sense?" and her answer reflected the ambivalence and confusion I would later rou-tinely hear when I asked this same question of others.

> *I think of it less as an illness and more something that society defines. That's part of it, but then, it is physical. Doesn't that make it an illness? That's a question I ask myself a lot. Depression is a special case because everyone gets depressed. . . . I think that I define it as not an illness. It's a condition. When I*

hear the term illness I think of sickness. . . . [but] the term mental illness seems
to me to be very negative, maybe because I connect it with hospitalization. . . .

Before it ended, my interview with Karen covered other difficult emotional terrain, including a major suicide attempt, additional periods of hospitalization, stays in halfway houses, a traumatic college experience, failed relationships with therapists, job interviews that required lies about health history, and a personal spiritual transformation. As indicated at the outset, things had gotten better by the time of our interview and Karen believed she was pretty much past her problem with depression. She told me, "A couple of years ago, three years ago, four years ago, I would feel a need to tell people about it because I still felt depressed, because I still felt mentally ill. But now I no longer see myself in that way. I'm other things. I'm Karen the grad student. I'm Karen the one who loves to garden, the one who's interested in a lot of things. I'm not just Karen the mentally ill person." Still, such optimism about being past depression was sometimes distressingly eroded by periods of bad feelings and the ever-present edge of fear that "it" might return in its full-blown, most grotesque form. . . .

A Career View of the Depression Experience

As in many areas of social life, the notion of career seems an extremely useful, sensitizing concept. In his voluminous and influential writings on work, Everett Hughes showed the value of conceptualizing career as "the moving perspective in which the person sees his life as a whole and interprets the meanings of his various attitudes, actions, and the things which happen to him."[1] Hughes' definition directs attention to the subjective aspects of the career process and the ways in which people attach evaluative meanings to the typical sequence of movements constituting their career path. Here I shall be concerned with describing the career features associated with an especially ambiguous illness—depression.

Hughes' definition also suggests that each stage,[2] juncture, or moment in a career requires a redefinition of self. The depression experience is a heuristically valuable instance for studying the intersection of careers and identities. The following data analysis illustrates that much of the depression career is caught up with assessing self, redefining self, reinterpreting past selves, and attempting to construct a future self that will "work" better. Although all careers require periodic reassessments of self, illness careers are especially characterized by critical "turning points" in identity. In his discussion of identity transformations, Anselm Strauss[3] comments on the intersection of career and identity turning points:

In transformations of identities a person becomes something other than he or she once was. Such shifts necessitate new evaluations of self and others, of events, acts, and objects. . . . Transformation of perception is irreversible; once having changed there is no going back. One can look back, but evaluate only from the new status. . . . Certain critical incidences occur to force a person to recognize that "I am not the same as I was, as I used to be." These critical incidents constitute turning points in the onward movement of persons' careers.

. . . While there is considerable variation in the timing of events, all the respondents in this study described a process remarkably similar to the one implicit in Karen's account. Every person I interviewed moved through these identity turning points in their view of themselves and their problem with depression:

1. A period of *inchoate feelings* during which they lacked the vocabulary to label their experience as depression.
2. A phase during which they conclude that *something is really wrong with me.*
3. A *crisis stage* that thrusts them into a world of therapeutic experts.
4. A stage of *coming to grips with an illness identity* during which they theorize about the cause(s) for their difficulty and evaluate the prospects for getting beyond depression.

Each of these career moments assumes and requires redefinitions of self.

Inchoate Feelings

. . . The ages of respondents in this study range from the early twenties to the middle sixties. All these people described a period of time during which they had no vocabulary for naming their problem. Many traced feelings of emotional discomfort to ages as young as three or four, although they could not associate their feelings with something called "depression" until years later. It was typical for respondents to go for long periods of time feeling different, uncomfortable, marginal, ill-at-ease, scared, and in pain without attaching the notion of depression to their situations. A sampling of comments indicating an inchoate, obscure experience includes these:

> *Well, I knew I was different from other children. I should say that from a very early age it felt like I had this darkness about me. Sort of shadow of myself. And I always had the sense that it wasn't going to go away so easily. And it was like my battle. . . . [female travel agent, aged 41]*

> *An awareness that was more intellectual was apparent to me about my sophomore year in high school, when I'd wake up depressed and drag myself to school. . . . I didn't know that's what it was. I just knew that I had an awful hard time getting out of bed and a hard time making my bed and a hard time, you know, getting myself to school. . . . I kind of just had the feeling that something wasn't right. . . . [It was] just like a constant knot in my stomach. But I didn't*

*think that that was anxiety. I just thought I wasn't feeling good, you know
(laughing). [unemployed disabled female, aged 39]*

*If I think about it, I really can't pinpoint a moment [when I was aware that I was
depressed]. . . . [male professor, aged 48]*

Most of those reporting bad feelings from an early age could not conclude that something was "abnormal" because they had no baseline of nor-
malcy for comparison. As might be expected, several respondents in this
sample came from what they now describe as severely dysfunctional family
circumstances, often characterized by alcoholism and both physical and
emotional abuse. These individuals described feeling unsafe at home and often devised strategies to spend as much time as they could elsewhere. . . .

For most respondents the phase of inchoate feelings was the longest in
the eventual unfolding of their illness consciousness. Particularly salient in
terms of personal identity is the fact that initial definitions of their problem
centered on the "structural conditions" of their lives instead of on the structure of their selves. The focus of interpretation was on the situation rather
than on the self. Their emerging definition was that escape from the situation
would make things right. Over and again individuals recounted fantasies of
escape from their families and often from the community in which they grew
up. However, initially at least, they felt trapped without a clear notion of how
the situation might change.

*I remember from like five, starting to subtract five from eighteen, to see how
many years I have left before I could get out [of the house]. So, I would say the
overwhelming feeling was that I felt powerless. I felt a lot of things early. And
I felt that I was stuck in this house and these people controlled me, and there
wasn't anything I could do about it, and I was stuck there. So I just started
my little chart at about four and a half or five, counting when I could get out.
[female baker, aged 41]*

. . . A decisive juncture in the evolution of a "sickness" self-definition occurs when the circumstances individuals perceive as troubling their lives
change, but mood problems persist. The persistence of problems in the absence of the putative cause requires a redefinition of what is wrong. A huge
cognitive shift occurs when people come to see that the problem may be internal instead of situational; when they conclude that something is likely
wrong with *them* in a manner that transcends their immediate situation.

Something Is Really Wrong with Me

In 1977, Robert Emerson and Sheldon Messinger published a paper entitled
"The Micro-Politics of Trouble"[4] that analyzes the regular processes through
which individuals come to see a personal difficulty as sufficiently troublesome a problem that something ought to be done about it. The materials offered in this [reading] affirm the general process they describe. The process

begins with a state of affairs initially "experienced as difficult, unpleasant, or unendurable."[5] At first, sufferers try an informal remedy, which sometimes works. If it doesn't, they seek another remedy. The decision that a consequential problem exists warranting a formal remedy typically follows a "recurring cycle of trouble, remedy, failure, more trouble, and a new remedy, until the trouble stops or the troubled person forsakes further efforts."[6] Here, then, is their description of the transformation from vague, inchoate feelings to a clearer sense that one is sufficiently troubled to seek a remedy.

> Problems originate with the recognition that something is wrong and must be remedied. Trouble, in these terms, involves both definitional and remedial components. . . . On first apprehension troubles often involve little more than vague unease. . . . An understanding of the problem's dimensions may only begin to emerge as the troubled person thinks about them, discusses the matter with others, and begins to implement remedial strategies.[7]

Despite the difficulties they have in naming their feelings as a problem, all of the respondents eventually conclude that something is *really wrong with them*. To be sure, many used identical phrases in describing their situations. The phrases "something was really wrong with me" and "I felt that I could no longer live like this" were repeated over and over. Respondents commented in nearly identical ways on the heightened feeling that "something is really wrong with me."

> *When it really became apparent that I was just a mess was in January of 1989. I made the decision really quickly at the end of 1988 to go to school at [names a four-year college] and live with my father and my stepmother and commute. And I packed up all my stuff in my car and went. I was miserable. I cried every day. Every single day I cried. I think I went to two classes [at the new school] and lasted there only a month. I was absolutely miserable. There was a lot of different factors that were involved with it [but] I just didn't feel right. There was something wrong with me, you know. [unemployed female, aged 23]*

> *I guess it's the fall of '90 when I had done the family therapy. I felt great about that. I was back at Harvard. My work was going okay. I loved myself. I loved my husband. Everything was great. [But] I wanted to die. I had no pleasure in anything. What finally got me [was that] I looked at the trees turning and I didn't care. I couldn't believe it. I'd be looking at this big flaming maple and I'd look at it and I'd think, "There it is, it's a maple tree. It's bright orange and red." And nothing in me was touched. At that point I went back to my therapist and said, "There's something really wrong here." [female software quality control manager, aged 31]*

. . . These quotes suggest a fundamental transformation in perception and identity at this point in the evolution of a depression consciousness. Respondents now located the source of their problem as somewhere within their bodies and minds, as deep within themselves. Such a belief implies a problematic identity far more basic and immutable than those associated with social statuses. If, for example, someone has a disliked occupational identity, the possibilities for occupational change exist. If the occupational identity becomes onerous enough, it is possible to quit a job. Similarly, without minimizing the difficulties of change, we can choose to become single if married, to change from one religion to another, and, these days, even to change our sex if the motivation is great enough. However, to see oneself as somehow internally flawed poses substantially greater problems for identity change or remediation because one's whole personhood is implicated. Getting rid of a sick self poses far greater problems than dropping certain social statuses. The important point here is that the rejection of situational theories for bad feelings is a critical identity turning point. Full acceptance that one has a damaged self requires acknowledgment that "I am not the same as I was, as I used to be."

Another important dimension of the career process that becomes apparent at this point is the issue of whether to keep the problem private or to make it public, especially to family and friends. The private/public distinction was a dominant theme in respondents' talk throughout the history of their experience with depression. The question of being private or public is, of course, central to one's developing self-identification. As Peter Berger and Hansfried Kellner[8] point out in describing the "social construction of marriage" and Diane Vaughan[9] indicates in analyzing the process of "uncoupling" from a relationship, the moment a new status becomes public is a definitive one in solidifying a person's new identity. In the cases of both creating and disengaging from relationships, people are normally very careful not to make public announcements until they are certain they are ready to adopt new statuses and identities. The significance attached to public announcements of even modest shifts in life style is indicated by the considerable thought people sometimes give to making public such relatively benign decisions as going on diets or quitting cigarettes.

Decisions about "going public" are, of course, greatly magnified when the information to be imparted is negative and, in the case of emotional problems, potentially stigmatizing. As Emerson and Messinger note, the search for a remedy necessarily involves sharing information with others. Still, at this early juncture of dealing with bad feelings, most respondents elected to keep silent about their pain. . . .

Whether or not they made their feelings public, this second phase of their illness career involved the recognition that they possessed a self that was working badly in *every* situation. Although everyone continued to identify the kinds of *social* situations that had caused their bad feelings in the past and precipitated them in the present, the qualitative change at this juncture was in the locus of attention from external to internal causes. At this point, respondents were struggling to live their lives in the face of debilitating pain. This stage ended, however, when efforts to control things became impossible.

At some point, everyone interviewed experienced a crisis of some sort. For the majority (29) the crisis meant hospitalization. At the point of crisis, whatever their wishes might have been, they could not prevent their situation from becoming public knowledge to family, friends, and co-workers. Whether they were hospitalized or not, everyone reached a point where they felt obliged to rely on psychiatric experts to deal with their difficulty. Receiving an "official" diagnosis of depression and consequent treatment with medications greatly accelerated the need to redefine their past, present, and future in illness terms. The crisis solidified the emerging consciousness that the problem was within themselves. More than that, it was now a problem beyond their own efforts to control.

Crisis

Nearly everyone could pinpoint the precise time, situation, or set of events that moved them from the recognition that something was wrong to the realization that they were desperately sick. They could often remember in vivid detail the moment when things absolutely got out of hand.

> *So I went to law school in the fall. I was at Columbia and in the best of times Columbia is a depressing place. I mean, it's a shithole. And you know, I was pretty messed up when I got there. . . . I remember Columbia was a nightmare. . . . So, I was getting to the point where I was paranoid about going to class and so someone talked to the dean and said, "Hey, you've got to do something about this guy, he's off the deep edge." [male administrator, aged 54]*

> *I think the significant moment was when I got stage fright in high school. There were earlier moments when I felt something was wrong. I can remember feeling real dizzy when I was on the stage in the 8th grade. But the significant moment was in high school and I was seized by just pure terror. And the fear was so horrible that I couldn't tell it to anybody. I couldn't share it. It was something beyond my ability to communicate. It was so horrible that no one could understand it. [male professor, aged 66]*

. . . At the crisis point, people fully enter a therapeutic world of hospitals, mental health experts, and medications. For many, entrance into this world is simultaneous with first receiving the "official" diagnosis of depression.[10] It is difficult to overstate the critical importance of official diagnoses and labeling. The point of diagnosis was a double-edged benchmark in the illness career. On the one hand, knowing that you "have" something that doctors regard as a specific illness imposes definitional boundaries onto an array of behaviors and feelings that previously had no name. Acquiring a clear conception of what one has and having a label to attach to confounding feelings and behaviors was especially significant to those who had gone for years without being able to name their situation. To be diagnosed also suggests the possibility that the condition can be treated and that one's suffering can be diminished. At the same time, being a "depressive" places one in the devalued category of those with mental illness. On the negative side, respondents made comments like these:

> *I kept going to doctor after doctor, getting like all these new terms put on me. . . . My family was dysfunctional and I was an alcoholic with an eating disorder and bulimia and depression and it was just all these labels. "Oh my God!" [unemployed female, aged 22]*

> *My father went to his allergy doctor who referred us to a guy who turned out to be a reasonable psychiatrist. I'll never forget. He said, "Your daughter is clinically depressed." I remember sitting in his office. He saw us on a Saturday like at six o'clock. He did us a favor. And I remember I just sat there. It was a sort of darkened office. It was the first time I ever cried in front of anybody. [female social worker, aged 38]*

And on the liberating side:

> *They gave me a blood test that measures the level of something in the blood, in the brain. And they pronounced me, they said, "Mr. Smith [a pseudonym], you're depressed." And I said, "Thank God," you know. I wasn't as batty as I thought. It was like the cat was out of the bag. You know? It was a breakthrough. . . . [Before that] depression wasn't in my vocabulary. . . . It was the beginning of being able to sort out a lifetime of feelings, events . . . my entire life. It was the chance for a new beginning. [male salesman, aged 30]*

. . . It is impossible to consider the kinds of profound identity changes occasioned by any mental illness without paying special attention to the experience of hospitalization. It is one thing to deal alone with the demons of depression, or to privately see a psychiatrist for the problem, but once a person "shuts down" altogether and seeks asylum or is involuntarily "committed," he or she adds an institutional piece to their biography that is indelible. . . .

A few interviewees described the hospital as truly an asylum that provided relief and allowed them to "crash." Being hospitalized enabled them to give up the struggle of trying to appear and act normally. One person, in fact, described the hospital as a "wonderful place" where "I was taken care of, totally taken care of." Another was relieved "to go somewhere where I won't do anything to myself, where I can get in touch with this." Someone else explained, "I was glad to be there, definitely. It was a break from everything." Sometimes people were glad to be hospitalized since it provided dramatic and definitive evidence that something was really wrong with them when family and friends had been dismissing their complaints. More usual, though, were the responses like that of the person who said that "the experience of hospitalization was devastating to me" and the several who reported that being hospitalized made them feel like "damaged goods."

Of all the tough things associated with depression, nothing would frighten me more than hospitalization. . . .

Many of the 29 people who spoke of their time in hospitals spontaneously acknowledged the extraordinary impact of the experience on the way they thought about themselves. Sometimes they were themselves shocked that they had landed in a hospital. Several mentioned that hospitalization caused them to confront for the first time just how sick they were.

> *I remember being put onto the floor that was probably for the worst people of the sickness, because it was one of those floors where everything was really locked up. So I guess I was in pretty bad shape. [male administrator, aged 54]*

> *So I went to [names hospital] and I remember praying that I would get out. To me it seemed at the time as if the door would close—it was a secure facility—and I would never leave. I know I'm a basket case at this point. . . . The experience of having that severe depression, going to the hospital, and most of all being given shock treatments. . . . It made me feel . . . like damaged goods, impaired in some way that I was just not normal. It did make me feel impaired. [male professor, part-time, aged 48]*

Among the identity-related comments about the hospitalization experience, one set of observations, although made by only a few individuals, caught my attention. Once in the hospital these persons surveyed their environment, both the oppressive physical character of the place and the sad shape of their fellow "inmates," many of whom seemed to them destined for an institutionalized life. However awful their condition, these respondents made a distinction between their trouble and patients who were overtly psychotic. Unlike those unfortunates, they had a choice to make, as they saw it. Either they would capitulate completely to their depression and possibly, therefore, to a life in the mental health system or they would do whatever necessary to leave the hospital as quickly as possible.

Giving up completely did have some appealing features. Full surrender meant relief from an exhausting battle and absolution from personal responsibility. One woman said,

> *I saw these people going back and forth [in and out of the hospital] for their whole lives [and] that I could be one [of them]. If I went in that direction, it somehow absolved me from responsibility. And I teetered on the edge for a long time. It involved a conscious decision . . . [about whether] I'm going to become a [permanent] part of the system because it's safe and where I belong. . . .*

. . . It should be noted that one outstanding uniformity in the interviews was the initially strong negative reaction people had to taking drugs. One person was "leery of it" and others variously described the idea of going on medications as "revolting," "certainly not my first choice," and "embarrassing." Others elaborated on the recommendation that they begin drug therapy in ways similar to the nurse who said: "I didn't want to be told that I had something that was going to affect the rest of my life and that could only be solved by taking pills. And there was sort of a rebellion in that: 'No, I'm not like that. I don't need you and your pills.'"... [Respondents] held the shared feeling that taking drugs was yet another distressing indication of the severity of a problem they could not control by themselves. The concurrent events of crisis, hospitalization, and beginning a drug regimen worked synergistically to concretize and dramatize respondents' status as patients with an illness that required ongoing treatment by therapeutic experts.

Coming to Grips with an Illness Identity

Whether people are hospitalized or not, involvement with psychiatric experts and medications is the transition point to a number of simultaneous processes, all with implications for the reformulation of identity. They are (1) reconstructing and reinterpreting one's past in terms of current experiences, (2) looking for causes for one's situation, (3) constructing new theories about the nature of depression, and (4) establishing modes of coping behavior. All of these activities require judgments about the appropriate metaphors for describing one's situation. Especially critical to ongoing identity construction is whether respondents approve of illness metaphors for describing their experience. A few individuals were willing clearly to define their condition as a mental illness:

I know I have a mental illness. I'm beginning to feel that. [But] actually, there is a real relief in that. It's a sense of "Whew! Okay, I don't have to masquerade." I mean, sure I'll masquerade with work, because, listen, I've got to get the bread and butter on the table. But I don't have to masquerade in other ways. . . . It's sort of like mentally ill people in some ways . . . are my people. There is a fair amount of really chronically mentally ill people at [names hospital where she works]. They're all on heavy-duty meds and I figure like "I know what it's like for you." I mean, I can imagine what it's like. I know some of that pain. I'm sure I don't know all of it, because, you know, I'm not that bad off, but there is sort of a sense like they could understand me and I could understand them in something that's really, really painful. [female physical therapist, aged 42]

. . . Most, however, wanted simultaneously to embrace the definition of their problem as biochemical in nature while rejecting the notion that they suffer from a "mental" illness.

I don't see it as an illness. To me, it seems like part of myself that evolved, part of my personality. And, I mean, it sounds crazy, but it is almost like a dual personality, the happy side of me and the sad side of me. . . . [female nanny, aged 22]

Well, do you have an illness? What do you have?

I tend to think of it as a condition. I don't think of it so much as an illness, although it feels like an illness sometimes. I think it's an unintegrated dimension of myself that's taken [on] kind of a life of its own, that has its own power. . . . [unemployed female, aged 35]

. . . Adopting the view that one is victimized by a biochemically sick self constitutes a comfortable "account" for a history of difficulties and failures and absolves one of reponsibility. On the negative side, however, acceptance of a victim role, while diminishing a sense of personal responsibility, is also enfeebling. To be a victim of biochemical forces beyond one's control gives force to others' definition of oneself as a helpless, passive object of injury. . . .

Respondents generally fall into two broad categories regarding their hopes that they can put depression behind them. First are those who view having depression as a life condition that they will never fully defeat, and second are those who believe either that they are now past the depression forever or that they can attain such a status. As might be expected, the two categories are generally formed by those who have experienced depression as an ongoing chronic thing, on the one hand, in contrast to those who have had periods of depression punctuated by wellness. The role of medications is interesting in establishing for some the idea that depression is something they can leave behind. Among the words that reappeared in comments about drugs was "miracle." Although, as noted, most of those interviewed at first took medication reluctantly, several reported that often for the first time in their lives they felt okay after a drug "kicked in." Generally, subjects were split between those who felt that while there was always the possibility of a recurrence, they essentially could get past depression and those who have surrendered to its inevitability and chronicity in their lives. The following comments summarize the two positions:

I've stopped thinking, "OK, I'm going to get over this depression. I'm going to finally, like, do this primal scream thing, or whatever. . . . [At one point] I did buy into [the idea] of the pursuit of happiness and the pursuit of fulfillment. I hate that word. And the mental health equivalent to finding fulfillment is to fill up the gaps inside of you and everything grows green. And that's what [psychiatry] is really striving for . . . and that's the standard life should be lived on. . . . But then I finally realized that well, maybe I'm in a desert. Maybe your landscape is green, but, you know, I'm in the Sahara and I've stopped trying to get out. . . . I'd rather cure it if I had my choice, but I don't think that is going to happen. My choice is to integrate it into my life. So, no, I don't see it going away. I just see myself becoming, you know, better able to cope with it, more graceful about it. [female mental health worker, aged 27]

I would say that this particular period of my life is a period where I don't have the fear or feeling [that depression will recur]. That's why, for me at least, I'm more inclined now to take the depression as an aberration and to take me in my more expansive, expressive state as the norm. For me, maybe I'm deluding myself, the way I feel now, and it's been three years since the hospitalization and I take no medications of any kind, [is] that I may be out of the woods, so to speak. . . . At the moment I don't have a fear of recurrence, but I do remember having it. [male professor, part-time, aged 48]

Unfortunately, the norm is for people to have repeated bouts with depression. In this regard, the process described here has a feedback-loop quality to it. Individuals move through a crisis with all its attendant identity-altering features, come to grips with the meaning of their experience by constructing theories about causation, and then sometimes reach the point where they feel they have gone beyond the depression experience. A new episode of depression, of course, casts doubt on all the previous interpretive work and requires people to once again move through a process of sense-making and identity construction. In this way, depression is like a virus that keeps mutating since each reliving of an experience, as the philosopher Edmund Husserl tells us, is a new experience. Chronically depressed people are constantly in the throes of an illness that is tragically familiar, but always new. As such, depression often involves a life centered on a nearly continuous process of construction, destruction, and reconstruction of identities in the face of repeated problems. . . .

ENDNOTES

[1] E. Hughes, *Men and Their Work* (New York: Free Press, 1958).

[2] Although the notion of "stage" is difficult to avoid, I want to suggest that in much social science literature the term conveys a determinism that I find unfortunate. Stages imply that, for whatever process being described, everyone must move through them in a predictably timed sequence. Hence, I often use the terms "moment," "benchmark," or "juncture" in the depression career to suggest a process that is more fluid than the stage idea.

[3] A. Strauss, "Turning Points in Identity." In C. Clark and H. Robboy (eds.), *Social Interaction* (New York: St. Martin's, 1992). The identity transitions described in the pages to follow bear an instructive resemblance to the idea of biographical "epiphanies" developed by Norman Denzin in a number of important books. See N. Denzin, *The Alcoholic Self* (Newbury Park, CA: Sage, 1987); N. Denzin, *Interpretive Interactionism* (Newbury Park, CA: Sage, 1989); N. Denzin, *Interpretive Biography* (Newbury Park, CA: Sage, 1989).

[4] R. Emerson and S. Messinger, "The Micro-Politics of Trouble," *Social Problems* 25 (1977):121–33. For another formulation of the trouble idea, see the early work of Charlotte Schwartz. Schwartz's doctoral dissertation studied how 30 people who sought help at a university psychiatric service conceptualized their problem. Her interview data suggested that informants distinguished three mutually exclusive subjective states of trouble. She calls them *exigencies of living* (or momentary difficulties), *normal trouble* (ordinary trouble), and *special trouble* (serious problems). An

elaboration of these categories can be found in her work entitled *Clients' Perspectives on Psychiatric Troubles in a College Setting* (unpublished doctoral dissertation, Brandeis University, 1976). See also her article with Merton Kahne entitled "The Social Construction of Trouble and Its Implications for Psychiatrists Working in College Settings," *Journal of the American College Health Asssociation* 25 (February, 1977): 194–97.

[5] R. Emerson and S. Messinger, op. cit., p. 122.

[6] Ibid.

[7] Ibid.

[8] P. Berger and H. Kellner, "Marriage and the Construction of Reality," *Diogenes* 46 (1964): 1–25.

[9] D. Vaughan, *Uncoupling: Turning Points in Intimate Relationships* (New York: Oxford, 1986).

[10] Social scientists have been critical of the meaning of psychiatric diagnoses and the processes through which they are established. For examples, see P. Brown, "Diagnostic Conflict and Contradiction in Psychiatry," *Journal of Health and Social Behavior* 28 (1987): 37–50 and M. Rosenberg, "A Symbolic Interactionist View of Psychosis," *Journal of Health and Social Behavior* 25 (1984): 289–302.

EDUCATION

50

CIVILIZE THEM WITH A STICK

MARY CROW DOG • RICHARD ERDOES

Few students are aware of our nation's policies toward Native Americans, which included the separation of Indian children from their families and cultures so that these children could be "civilized" into the dominant society. Consequently, beginning in 1879, thousands of Native American children were forced to leave the reservation to attend boarding schools, day schools, or schools in converted Army posts. These total institutions used tactics similar to those used by the military to resocialize the young Native Americans. The peak period for Native American boarding schools was 1879–1930, but they continue, in some places, today. In the following selection, taken from *Lakota Woman* (1990), Mary Crow Dog and Richard Erdoes reveal how the institution of education can be an agent of social control whose purpose is to assimilate racial-ethnic populations, such as Native Americans, into the dominant culture. Crow Dog is a Native American activist and Erdoes is the ghostwriter of her autography.

. . . Gathered from the cabin, the wickiup, and the tepee,
partly by cajolery and partly by threats;
partly by bribery and partly by force,
they are induced to leave their kindred
to enter these schools and take upon themselves
the outward appearance of civilized life.

—ANNUAL REPORT OF THE DEPARTMENT OF INTERIOR, 1901

It is almost impossible to explain to a sympathetic white person what a typical old Indian boarding school was like; how it affected the Indian child suddenly dumped into it like a small creature from another world, helpless, defenseless, bewildered, trying desperately and instinctively to survive and sometimes not surviving at all. I think such children were like the victims of Nazi concentration camps trying to tell average, middle-class Americans what their experience had been like. Even now, when these schools are much improved, when the buildings are new, all gleaming steel and glass, the food tolerable, the teachers well trained and well intentioned, even trained in child psychology—unfortunately the psychology of white children, which is different from ours—the shock to the child upon arrival is still tremendous. Some just seem to shrivel up, don't speak for days on end, and have an empty look in their eyes. I know of an 11-year-old on another reservation who hanged herself, and in our school, while I was there, a girl jumped out of the window, trying to kill herself to escape an unbearable situation. That first shock is always there.

Although the old tiyospaye has been destroyed, in the traditional Sioux families, especially in those where there is no drinking, the child is never left alone. It is always surrounded by relatives, carried around, enveloped in warmth. It is treated with the respect due to any human being, even a small one. It is seldom forced to do anything against its will, seldom screamed at, and never beaten. That much, at least, is left of the old family group among full-bloods. And then suddenly a bus or car arrives, full of strangers, usually white strangers, who yank the child out of the arms of those who love it, taking it screaming to the boarding school. The only word I can think of for what is done to these children is kidnapping.

Even now, in a good school, there is impersonality instead of close human contact; a sterile, cold atmosphere, an unfamiliar routine, language problems, and above all the maza-skan-skan, that damn clock—white man's time as opposed to Indian time, which is natural time. Like eating when you are hungry and sleeping when you are tired, not when that damn clock says you must. But I was not taken to one of the better, modern schools. I was taken to the old-fashioned mission school at St. Francis, run by the nuns and

Catholic fathers, built sometime around the turn of the century and not improved a bit when I arrived, not improved as far as the buildings, the food,
the teachers, or their methods were concerned.

In the old days, nature was our people's only school and they needed no
other. Girls had their toy tipis and dolls, boys their toy bows and arrows.
Both rode and swam and played the rough Indian games together. Kids
watched their peers and elders and naturally grew from children into adults.
Life in the tipi circle was harmonious—until the whiskey peddlers arrived
with their wagons and barrels of "Injun whiskey." I often wished I could have
grown up in the old, before-whiskey days.

Oddly enough, we owed our unspeakable boarding schools to the do-
gooders, the white Indian-lovers. The schools were intended as an alternative to the outright extermination seriously advocated by generals Sherman
and Sheridan, as well as by most settlers and prospectors overrunning our
land. "You don't have to kill those poor benighted heathen," the do-gooders
said, "in order to solve the Indian Problem. Just give us a chance to turn them
into useful farmhands, laborers, and chambermaids who will break their
backs for you at low wages." In that way the boarding schools were born. The
kids were taken away from their villages and pueblos, in their blankets and
moccasins, kept completely isolated from their families—sometimes for as
long as ten years—suddenly coming back, their short hair slick with po-
made, their necks raw from stiff, high collars, their thick jackets always short
in the sleeves and pinching under the arms, their tight patent leather shoes
giving them corns, the girls in starched white blouses and clumsy, high-
buttoned boots—caricatures of white people. When they found out—and
they found out quickly—that they were neither wanted by whites nor by
Indians, they got good and drunk, many of them staying drunk for the rest
of their lives. I still have a poster I found among my grandfather's stuff, given
to him by the missionaries to tack up on his wall. It reads:

1. Let Jesus save you.
2. Come out of your blanket, cut your hair, and dress like a white man.
3. Have a Christian family with one wife for life only.
4. Live in a house like your white brother. Work hard and wash often.
5. Learn the value of a hard-earned dollar. Do not waste your money on
   giveaways. Be punctual.
6. Believe that property and wealth are signs of divine approval.
7. Keep away from saloons and strong spirits.
8. Speak the language of your white brother. Send your children to
   school to do likewise.
9. Go to church often and regularly.
10. Do not go to Indian dances or to the medicine men.

The people who were stuck upon "solving the Indian Problem" by making
us into whites retreated from this position only step by step in the wake of
Indian protests.

The mission school at St. Francis was a curse for our family for generations. My grandmother went there, then my mother, then my sisters and I. At one time or other, every one of us tried to run away. Grandma told me once about the bad times she had experienced at St. Francis. In those days they let students go home only for one week every year. Two days were used up for transportation, which meant spending just five days out of 365 with her family. And that was an improvement. Before grandma's time, on many reservations they did not let the students go home at all until they had finished school. Anybody who disobeyed the nuns was severely punished. The building in which my grandmother stayed had three floors, for girls only. Way up in the attic were little cells, about five by five by ten feet. One time she was in church and instead of praying she was playing jacks. As punishment they took her to one of those little cubicles where she stayed in darkness because the windows had been boarded up. They left her there for a whole week with only bread and water for nourishment. After she came out she promptly ran away, together with three other girls. They were found and brought back. The nuns stripped them naked and whipped them. They used a horse buggy whip on my grandmother. Then she was put back into the attic—for two weeks.

My mother had much the same experiences but never wanted to talk about them, and then there I was, in the same place. The school is now run by the BIA—the Bureau of Indian Affairs—but only since about 15 years ago. When I was there, during the 1960s, it was still run by the Church. The Jesuit fathers ran the boys' wing and the Sisters of the Sacred Heart ran us—with the help of the strap. Nothing had changed since my grandmother's days. I have been told recently that even in the '70s they were still beating children at that school. All I got out of school was being taught how to pray. I learned quickly that I would be beaten if I failed in my devotions or, God forbid, prayed the wrong way, especially prayed in Indian to Wakan Tanka, the Indian Creator.

The girls' wing was built like an F and was run like a penal institution. Every morning at five o'clock the sisters would come into our large dormitory to wake us up, and immediately we had to kneel down at the sides of our beds and recite the prayers. At six o'clock we were herded into the church for more of the same. I did not take kindly to the discipline and to marching by the clock, left-right, left-right. I was never one to like being forced to do something. I do something because I feel like doing it. I felt this way always, as far as I can remember, and my sister Barbara felt the same way. An old medicine man once told me: "Us Lakotas are not like dogs who can be trained, who can be beaten and keep on wagging their tails, licking the hand that whipped them. We are like cats, little cats, big cats, wildcats, bobcats, mountain lions. It doesn't matter what kind, but cats who can't be tamed, who scratch if you step on their tails." But I was only a kitten and my claws were still small.

Barbara was still in the school when I arrived and during my first year or two she could still protect me a little bit. When Barb was a seventh grader she ran away together with five other girls, early in the morning before sunrise. They brought them back in the evening. The girls had to wait for two hours in front of the mother superior's office. They were hungry and cold, frozen through. It was wintertime and they had been running the whole day without food, trying to make good their escape. The mother superior asked each girl, "Would you do this again?" She told them that as punishment they would not be allowed to visit home for a month and that she'd keep them busy on work details until the skin on their knees and elbows had worn off. At the end of her speech she told each girl, "Get up from this chair and lean over it." She then lifted the girls' skirts and pulled down their underpants. Not little girls either, but teenagers. She had a leather strap about a foot long and four inches wide fastened to a stick, and beat the girls, one after another, until they cried. Barb did not give her that satisfaction but just clenched her teeth. There was one girl, Barb told me, the nun kept on beating and beating until her arm got tired.

I did not escape my share of the strap. Once, when I was 13 years old, I refused to go to Mass. I did not want to go to church because I did not feel well. A nun grabbed me by the hair, dragged me upstairs, made me stoop over, pulled my dress up (we were not allowed at the time to wear jeans), pulled my panties down, and gave me what they called "swats"—25 swats with a board around which Scotch tape had been wound. She hurt me badly.

My classroom was right next to the principal's office and almost every day I could hear him swatting the boys. Beating was the common punishment for not doing one's homework, or for being late to school. It had such a bad effect upon me that I hated and mistrusted every white person on sight, because I met only one kind. It was not until much later that I met sincere white people I could relate to and be friends with. Racism breeds racism in reverse.

The routine at St. Francis was dreary. Six A.M., kneeling in church for an hour or so; seven o'clock, breakfast; eight o'clock, scrub the floor, peel spuds, make classes. We had to mop the dining room twice every day and scrub the tables. If you were caught taking a rest, doodling on the bench with a fingernail or knife, or just rapping, the nun would come up with a dish towel and just slap it across your face, saying, "You're not supposed to be talking, you're supposed to be working!" Monday mornings we had cornmeal mush, Tuesday oatmeal, Wednesday rice and raisins, Thursday cornflakes, and Friday all the leftovers mixed together or sometimes fish. Frequently the food had bugs or rocks in it. We were eating hot dogs that were weeks old, while the nuns were dining on ham, whipped potatoes, sweet peas, and cranberry sauce. In winter our dorm was icy cold while the nuns' rooms were always warm.

I have seen little girls arrive at the school, first graders, just fresh from home and totally unprepared for what awaited them, little girls with pretty braids, and the first thing the nuns did was chop their hair off and tie up what was left behind their ears. Next they would dump the children into tubs of alcohol, a sort of rubbing alcohol, "to get the germs off." Many of the nuns were German immigrants, some from Bavaria, so that we sometimes speculated whether Bavaria was some sort of Dracula country inhabited by monsters. For the sake of objectivity I ought to mention that two of the German fathers were great linguists and that the only Lakota-English dictionaries and grammars which are worth anything were put together by them.

At night some of the girls would huddle in bed together for comfort and reassurance. Then the nun in charge of the dorm would come in and say, "What are the two of you doing in bed together? I smell evil in this room. You girls are evil incarnate. You are sinning. You are going to hell and burn forever. You can act that way in the devil's frying pan." She would get them out of bed in the middle of the night, making them kneel and pray until morning. We had not the slightest idea what it was all about. At home we slept two and three in a bed for animal warmth and a feeling of security.

The nuns and the girls in the two top grades were constantly battling it out physically with fists, nails, and hair-pulling. I myself was growing from a kitten into an undersized cat. My claws were getting bigger and were itching for action. About 1969 or 1970 a strange young white girl appeared on the reservation. She looked about 18 or 20 years old. She was pretty and had long, blond hair down to her waist, patched jeans, boots, and a backpack. She was different from any other white person we had met before. I think her name was Wise. I do not know how she managed to overcome our reluctance and distrust, getting us into a corner, making us listen to her, asking us how we were treated. She told us that she was from New York. She was the first real hippie or Yippie we had come across. She told us of people called the Black Panthers, Young Lords, and Weathermen. She said, "Black people are getting it on. Indians are getting it on in St. Paul and California. How about you?" She also said, "Why don't you put out an underground paper, mimeograph it. It's easy. Tell it like it is. Let it all hang out." She spoke a strange lingo but we caught on fast.

Charlene Left Hand Bull and Gina One Star were two full-blood girls I used to hang out with. We did everything together. They were willing to join me in a Sioux uprising. We put together a newspaper which we called the *Red Panther*. In it we wrote how bad the school was, what kind of slop we had to eat—slimy, rotten, blackened potatoes for two weeks—the way we were beaten. I think I was the one who wrote the worst article about our principal of the moment, Father Keeler. I put all my anger and venom into it. I called him a goddam wasičun son of a bitch. I wrote that he knew nothing about Indians and should go back to where he came from, teaching white children whom he could relate to. I wrote that we knew which priests slept with which nuns and that all they ever could think about was filling their bellies and buying a new car. It was the kind of writing which foamed at the mouth, but which also lifted a great deal of weight from one's soul.

On Saint Patrick's Day, when everybody was at the big powwow, we distributed our newspapers. We put them on windshields and bulletin boards, in desks and pews, in dorms and toilets. But someone saw us and snitched on us. The shit hit the fan. The three of us were taken before a board meeting. Our parents, in my case my mother, had to come. They were told that ours was a most serious matter, the worst thing that had ever happened in the school's long history. One of the nuns told my mother, "Your daughter really needs to be talked to." "What's wrong with my daughter?" my mother asked. She was given one of our *Red Panther* newspapers. The nun pointed out its name to her and then my piece, waiting for mom's reaction. After a while she asked, "Well, what have you got to say to this? What do you think?"

My mother said, "Well, when I went to school here, some years back, I was treated a lot worse than these kids are. I really can't see how they can have any complaints, because we was treated a lot stricter. We could not even wear skirts halfway up our knees. These girls have it made. But you should forgive them because they are young. And it's supposed to be a free country, free speech and all that. I don't believe what they done is wrong." So all I got out of it was scrubbing six flights of stairs on my hands and knees, every day. And no boy-side privileges.

The boys and girls were still pretty much separated. The only time one could meet a member of the opposite sex was during free time, between 4 and 5:30, in the study hall or on benches or the volleyball court outside, and that was strictly supervised. One day Charlene and I went over to the boys' side. We were on the ball team and they had to let us practice. We played three extra minutes, only three minutes more than we were supposed to. Here was the nuns' opportunity for revenge. We got 25 swats. I told Charlene, "We are getting too old to have our bare asses whipped that way. We are old enough to have babies. Enough of this shit. Next time we fight back." Charlene only said, "Hoka-hay!". . .

In a school like this there is always a lot of favoritism. At St. Francis it was strongly tinged with racism. Girls who were near-white, who came from what the nuns called "nice families," got preferential treatment. They waited on the faculty and got to eat ham or eggs and bacon in the morning. They got the easy jobs while the skins, who did not have the right kind of background—myself among them—always wound up in the laundry room sorting out 10-bushel baskets of dirty boys' socks every day. Or we wound up scrubbing the floors and doing all the dishes. The school therefore fostered fights and antagonism between whites and breeds, and between breeds and skins. At one time Charlene and I had to iron all the robes and vestments the priests wore when saying Mass. We had to fold them up and put them into a chest in the back of the church. In a corner, looking over our shoulders, was a statue of the crucified Savior, all bloody and beaten up. Charlene looked up and said, "Look at that poor Indian. The pigs sure worked him over." That was the closest I ever came to seeing Jesus.

I was held up as a bad example and didn't mind. I was old enough to have a boyfriend and promptly got one. At the school we had an hour and a half for ourselves. Between the boys' and the girls' wings were some benches where one could sit. My boyfriend and I used to go there just to hold hands and talk. The nuns were very uptight about any boy-girl stuff. They had an exaggerated fear of anything having even the faintest connection with sex. One day in religion class, an all-girl class, Sister Bernard singled me out for some remarks, pointing me out as a bad example, an example that should be shown. She said that I was too free with my body. That I was holding hands which meant that I was not a good example to follow. She also said that I wore unchaste dresses, skirts which were too short, too suggestive, shorter than regulations permitted, and for that I would be punished. She dressed me down before the whole class, carrying on and on about my unchastity. . . .

We got a new priest in English. During one of his first classes he asked one of the boys a certain question. The boy was shy. He spoke poor English, but he had the right answer. The priest told him, "You did not say it right. Correct yourself. Say it over again." The boy got flustered and stammered. He could hardly get out a word. But the priest kept after him: "Didn't you hear? I told you to do the whole thing over. Get it right this time." He kept on and on.

I stood up and said, "Father, don't be doing that. If you go into an Indian's home and try to talk Indian, they might laugh at you and say, 'Do it over correctly. Get it right this time!'"

He shouted at me, "Mary, you stay after class. Sit down right now!"

I stayed after class, until after the bell. He told me, "Get over here!" He grabbed me by the arm, pushing me against the blackboard, shouting, "Why are you always mocking us? You have no reason to do this."

I said, "Sure I do. You were making fun of him. You embarrassed him. He needs strengthening, not weakening. You hurt him. I did not hurt you."

He twisted my arm and pushed real hard. I turned around and hit him in the face, giving him a bloody nose. After that I ran out of the room, slamming the door behind me. He and I went to Sister Bernard's office. I told her, "Today I quit school. I'm not taking any more of this, none of this shit anymore. None of this treatment. Better give me my diploma. I can't waste any more time on you people."

Sister Bernard looked at me for a long, long time. She said, "All right, Mary Ellen, go home today. Come back in a few days and get your diploma." And that was that. Oddly enough, that priest turned out okay. He taught a class in grammar, orthography, composition, things like that. I think he wanted more respect in class. He was still young and unsure of himself. But I was in there too long. I didn't feel like hearing it. Later he became a good friend of the Indians, a personal friend of myself and my husband. He stood up for us during Wounded Knee and after. He stood up to his superiors, stuck his neck way out, became a real people's priest. He even learned our language. He died prematurely of cancer. It is not only the good Indians who die young, but the good whites, too. It is the timid ones who know how to take care of themselves who grow old. I am still grateful to that priest for what he did for us later and for the quarrel he picked with me—or did I pick it with him?—because it ended a situation which had become unendurable for me. The day of my fight with him was my last day in school.

51

PREPARING FOR POWER
Cultural Capital and Curricula in America's Elite Boarding Schools

PETER W. COOKSON, JR.

CAROLINE HODGES PERSELL

In addition to teaching individuals life skills, such as reading, writing, and critical thinking, another important function of education is to help select the future employment of students. Thus, education tracks and trains people for certain jobs. Many jobs in society are based on *credentialing,* or the requirement of certain educational degrees in order to be hired and promoted. Schools also provide the valued *cultural capital* of the middle and upper classes. This knowledge of cultural background, norms, and skills of the upper classes enables students to obtain higher socioeconomic statuses. This reading by Peter W. Cookson, Jr., and Caroline Hodges Persell is taken from their 1985 book of the same title, and it examines the cultural capital students gain in elite boarding schools.

Borrowing from the British, early American headmasters and teachers advocated a boarding school curriculum that was classical, conservative, and disciplined. It wasn't until the latter part of the nineteenth century that such "soft" subjects as English, history, and mathematics were given a place beside Latin, Greek, rhetoric, and logic in the syllabus. It was the early schoolmasters' belief that young minds, especially boys' minds, if left to their own devices, were undisciplined, even anarchic. The only reliable antidote to mental flabbiness was a rigorous, regular regime of mental calisthenics. A boy who could not flawlessly recite long Latin passages was required to increase his mental workouts. Classical languages were to the mind what cold showers were to the body: tonics against waywardness.

Girls, with some exceptions, were not thought of as needing much mental preparation for their future roles as wives and mothers. Their heads were best left uncluttered by thought; too much book learning could give a girl ideas about independence. Besides, the great majority of them were not going on to college, where even more classical languages were required.

As an intellectual status symbol, the classical curriculum helped distinguish gentlemen from virtually everyone else and thus defined the difference between an "educated" man and an untutored one, as well as the difference between high culture and popular culture. Such a division is critical to exclude nonmembers from groups seeking status. For a long time a classical curriculum was the only path to admission to a university, as Harvard and many others required candidates to demonstrate proficiency in Latin and Greek (Levine 1980). Thus, the curriculum of boarding schools has long served both social and practical functions.

Culture, much like real estate or stocks, can be considered a form of capital. As the French scholars Pierre Bourdieu and Jean-Claude Passeron (1977) have indicated, the accumulation of cultural capital can be used to reinforce class differences. Cultural capital is socially created: What constitutes the "best in Western civilization" is not arrived at by happenstance, nor was it decided upon by public election. The more deeply embedded the values, the more likely they will be perceived as value free and universal.

Thus curriculum is the nursery of culture and the classical curriculum is the cradle of high culture. The definition of what is a classical course of study has evolved, of course, since the nineteenth century. Greek and Latin are no longer required subjects in most schools—electives abound. But the disciplined and trained mind is still the major objective of the boarding-school curriculum.

> The Groton curriculum is predicated on the belief that certain qualities of mind are of major importance: precise and articulate communication; the ability to compute accurately and to reason quantitatively; a grasp of scientific approaches to problem-solving; an understanding of the cultural, social, scientific, and political background of Western civilization; and the ability to reason carefully and logically and to think imaginatively and sensitively. Consequently the School puts considerable emphasis on language, mathematics, science, history, and the arts. (*Groton School* 1981–82:15)

The contrast between the relatively lean curricula of many public schools and the abundant courses offered by boarding schools is apparent. In catalogues of the boarding school's academic requirements, courses are usually grouped by subject matter, and at the larger schools course listings and descriptions can go on for several dozen pages. Far from sounding dreary, the courses described in most catalogues are designed to whet the intellectual appetite. Elective subjects in particular have intriguing titles such as "Hemingway: The Man and His Work," "Varieties of the Poetic Experience," "Effecting Political Change," "Rendezvous with Armageddon," and for those with a scientific bent, "Vertebrate Zoology" and "Mammalian Anatomy and Physiology."

Boarding-school students are urged to read deeply and widely. A term course on modern American literature may include works from as many as 10 authors, ranging from William Faulkner to Jack Kerouac. Almost all schools offer a course in Shakespeare in which six or seven plays will be read.

In history, original works are far more likely to be assigned than excerpts from a textbook. A course on the presidency at one school included the following required readings: Rossiter, *The American Presidency;* Hofstadter, *The American Political Tradition;* Hargrove, *Presidential Leadership;* Schlesinger, *A Thousand Days;* Kearns, *Lyndon Johnson and the American Dream;* and White, *Breach of Faith.* Courses often use a college-level text, such as Garraty's *The American Nation* or Palmer's *A History of the Modern World.* Economic history is taught as well—in one school we observed a discussion of the interplay between politics and the Depression of 1837—and the idea that there are multiple viewpoints in history is stressed. It is little wonder that many prep school graduates find their first year of college relatively easy.

An advanced-placement English class uses a collection of *The Canterbury Tales* by Geoffrey Chaucer that includes the original middle English on the left page and a modern English translation on the right. An advanced third-year French course includes three or four novels as well as two books of grammar and readings. Even social science courses require a great deal of reading. In a course called "An Introduction to Human Behavior," students are assigned 11 texts including works from B. F. Skinner, Sigmund Freud, Erich Fromm, Jean Piaget, and Rollo May.

Diploma requirements usually include four years of English, three years of math, three years in one foreign language, two years of history or social science, two years of laboratory science, and one year of art. Many schools require a year of philosophy or religion and also may have such noncredit diploma requirements as four years of physical education, a library skills course, introduction to computers, and a seminar on human sexuality. On average, American public high school seniors take one year less English and math, and more than a year less foreign language than boarding-school students (Coleman, Hoffer, and Kilgore 1982:90). Moreover, in the past two decades there has been a historical decline in the number of academic subjects taken by students in the public schools (Adleman 1983).

Because success on the Scholastic Aptitude Test is so critical for admission to a selective college, it is not uncommon for schools to offer English review classes that are specifically designed to help students prepare for the tests. Most schools also offer tutorials and remedial opportunities for students who are weak in a particular subject. For foreign students there is often a course in English as a second language.

As the arts will be part of the future roles of boarding school students, the music, art, and theater programs at many schools are enriching, with special courses such as "The Sound and Sense of Music," "Advanced Drawing," and "The Creative Eye in Film." Student art work is usually on display, and almost every school will produce several full-length plays each year, for example, *Arsenic and Old Lace, A Thurber Carnival, Dracula,* and *The Mousetrap.*

Music is a cherished tradition in many boarding schools, in keeping with their British ancestry. The long-standing "Songs" at Harrow, made famous because Winston Churchill liked to return to them for solace during World War II, are a remarkable display of school solidarity. All 750 boys participate, wearing identical morning coats with tails. Every seat is filled in the circular, sharply tiered replica of Shakespeare's Globe Theater as the boys rise in unison, their voices resonating in the rotunda.

The belief that a well-rounded education includes some "hands-on" experience and travel runs deep in the prep view of learning. Virtually every boarding school provides opportunities for its students to study and work off campus. As volunteers, Taft students, for instance, can "tutor on a one-to-one basis in inner-city schools in Waterbury, act as teachers' helpers in Waterbury Public Schools and work with retarded children at Southbury Training School." They can also work in convalescent homes, hospitals, and day-care centers, and act as "apprentices to veterinarians and help with Girl Scout troops" (*Taft* 1981–82:21). At the Ethel Walker School in Connecticut, girls can go on whale watches, trips to the theater, or work in the office of a local politician. The Madeira School in Virginia has a co-curriculum program requiring students to spend every Wednesday participating in volunteer or internship situations.

Generally speaking, the schools that take the position that manual labor and firsthand experience are good for the soul as well as the mind and body, are more progressive in orientation than other schools. At the Putney School every student has to take a tour of duty at the cow barn, starting at 5:30 A.M. In their own words, "Putney's work program is ambitious. We grow much of our own food, mill our own lumber, pick up our own trash, and have a large part in building our buildings. . . . Stoves won't heat until wood is cut and split" (*The Putney School* 1982:3).

Various styles of student-built structures dot the campus of the Colorado Rocky Mountain School, and at the tiny Midland School in California, there is no service staff, except for one cook. When the water pump breaks, faculty and students fix it, and when buildings are to be built, faculty and students pitch in. "We choose to live simply, to distinguish between our needs and our wants, to do without many of the comforts which often obscure the significant things in life" (*Midland School* 1983:1). The creed of self-reliance is reenacted every day at Midland. When a trustee offered to buy the school a swimming pool, he was turned down. Lounging around a pool is not part of the Midland philosophy.

Travel is very much part of the prep way of life and is continued right through the school year. Not only are semesters or a year abroad (usually in France or Spain) offered, but at some of the smaller schools, everyone goes on an extensive field trip. Every March at the Verde Valley School in Arizona the students travel to "Hopi, Navajo and Zuni reservations, to small villages in northern Mexico, to isolated Spanish-American communities in northern New Mexico and to ethnic neighborhoods of Southwestern cities. They live with native families, attend and teach in schools, work on ranches, and participate in the lives of the host families and their communities" (*Verde Valley School* 1982–83:9). Not all boarding schools, of course, place such a high value on rubbing shoulders with the outside world. At most of the academies, entrepreneurial, schools, and girls' schools the emphasis is on service rather than sharing.

While boarding schools may vary in their general philosophy, the actual curricula do not widely differ. The pressures exerted on prep schools to get their students into good colleges mean that virtually all students must study the same core subjects. Although not quick to embrace educational innovation, many boarding schools have added computers to their curricula. This has no doubt been encouraged by announcements by a number of Ivy League and other elite colleges that they want their future applicants to be "computer literate." While people at most boarding schools, or anywhere else for that matter, are not quite sure what is meant by computer literate, they are trying to provide well-equipped computer rooms and teachers who can move their students toward computer proficiency.

For students who have particular interests that cannot be met by the formal curriculum, almost all schools offer independent study, which gives students and teachers at boarding schools a great deal of intellectual flexibility. At Groton, for example, independent study can cover a diverse set of topics including listening to the works of Wagner, conducting a scientific experiment, or studying a special aspect of history.

The boarding school curriculum offers students an abundant buffet of regular course work, electives, volunteer opportunities, travel, and independent study, from which to choose a course of study. By encouraging students to treat academic work as an exciting challenge rather than just a job to be done, the prep schools not only pass on culture but increase their students' competitive edge in the scramble for admission to selective colleges.

The Importance of Sports

Even the most diligent student cannot sit in classrooms all day, and because the prep philosophy emphasizes the whole person, boarding schools offer an impressive array of extracurricular activities, the most important of which is athletics. At progressive schools, the competitive nature of sport is deemphasized. The "afternoon out-of-door program" at Putney, for example, allows for a wide variety of outdoor activities that are noncompetitive; in fact, "skiing is the ideal sport for Putney as one may ski chiefly to enjoy himself, the air, the snow" (*The Putney School* 1982:15).

Putney's sense that sport should be part of a communion with nature is not shared by most other schools, however. At most prep schools sport is about competition and, even more important, about winning. An athletically powerful prep school will field varsity, junior varsity, and third-string teams in most major sports. A typical coed or boys' school will offer football, soccer, cross-country, water polo, ice hockey, swimming, squash, basketball, wrestling, winter track, gymnastics, tennis, golf, baseball, track, and lacrosse. For the faint-hearted there are alternative activities such as modern dance, cycling, tai chi, yoga, ballet, and for the hopelessly unathletic, a "fitness" class. A truly traditional prep school will also have crew like their English forebears at Eton and Harrow. Certain schools have retained such British games as "Fives," but most stop short of the mayhem masquerading as a game called rugby.

Prep teams compete with college freshmen teams, other prep teams, and occasionally with public schools, although public school competitors are picked with care. Not only is there the possible problem of humiliation on the field, there is the even more explosive problem of fraternization in the stands when prep meets townie. Some schools, known as "jock" schools, act essentially as farm teams for Ivy League colleges, consistently providing them with athletes who have been polished by the prep experience. Many prep schools take public high school graduates for a postgraduate year, as a way of adding some size and weight to their football teams.

Prep girls also love sports; they participate as much as the boys, often in the same sports, and with as much vigor. A girls' field hockey game between Exeter and Andover is as intense as when the varsity football teams clash. Horseback riding at girls' schools is still popular; a number of the girls go on to ride in the show or hunt circuit. Unlike many of the girls in public schools, the boarding-school girl is discouraged from being a spectator. Loafing is considered to be almost as bad for girls as it is for boys.

During the school year the halls of nearly all prep schools are decorated with either bulletins of sporting outcomes or posters urging victory in some upcoming game. Pep rallies are common, as are assemblies when awards are given and competitive spirit is eulogized. Often the whole school will be bussed to an opponent's campus if the game is considered to be crucial or if the rivalry is long-standing.

Alumni return to see games, and there are frequent contests between alumni and varsity teams. Because preps retain the love of fitness and sports, it is not uncommon for the old warriors to give the young warriors a thrashing. Similarly, the prep life also invariably includes ritual competitions between, say, the girls' field hockey team and a pick-up faculty team.

Nowhere is the spirit of victory more pronounced than on the ice of the hockey rink. Few public schools can afford a hockey rink so prep schools can attract the best players without much competition. Some prep schools import a few Canadians each year to fill out the roster. Speed, strength, endurance, and fearlessness are the qualities that produce winning hockey and more than one freshman team from an Ivy League college has found itself outskated by a prep team. Whatever else may be, in Holden Caulfield's term, "phony" about prep schools, sports are for real. This emphasis on sport is not without its critics. At the Harrow School in London, the new headmaster, who was an all-England rugby player, has begun a program to reward artistic and musical prowess as well as athletic and academic skills.

The athletic facilities at prep schools are impressive and, at the larger schools, lavish. Acres and acres of playing fields, scores of tennis courts, one or more gyms, a hockey rink, a golf course, swimming pools, squash courts, workout rooms—all can be found on many prep school campuses. Generally, the facilities are extremely well maintained. The equipment most preps use is the best, as are the uniforms. One boy described how "when your gym clothes get dirty, you simply turn them in at the locker room for a fresh set." The cost of all this, of course, is extraordinary, but considered necessary, because excellence in sport is part of the definition of a gentleman or gentlewoman.

The pressure for athletic success is intense on many campuses, and a student's, as well as a school's, social standing can ride on the narrow margin between victory and defeat. Perhaps because of this, schools generally take great pains to play schools of their own size and social eliteness. A study of who plays whom among prep schools reveals that schools will travel great distances, at considerable expense, to play other prep schools whose students and traditions are similar to their own.

Extracurriculars and Preparation for Life

Not all prep school extracurricular activities require sweating, however. Like public school students, preps can work on the school newspaper or yearbook, help to organize a dance, or be part of a blood donor drive, and are much more likely than their public school counterparts to be involved in such activities, For example, one in three boarding-school students is involved in student government compared to one in five public school students, and two in five are involved in the school newspaper or yearbook compared to one in five. This evidence is consistent with other research. Coleman, Hoffer, and Kilgore (1982) found that private school students participate more in extracurricular activities than do public school students. The fact that more boarding school students than public school students are involved in activities provides additional opportunities for them to practice their verbal, interpersonal, and leadership skills.

The catalogue of clubs at prep schools is nearly endless. The opportunity for students to develop special nonacademic interests is one of the qualities of life at prep schools that distinguishes them from many public schools. Special interest clubs for chess, sailing, bowling, or gun clubs are popular at boys' schools. One elite boys' school has a "war games" club. As the boys at this school are feverishly calculating their country's next strategic arms move, the girls in a Connecticut school are attending a meeting of Amnesty

International. Girls, in general, tend to spend their off hours studying the gentler arts such as gourmet cooking and art history. One girls' school has a club with a permanent service mission to the governor's office.

At some schools, students can learn printing, metalwork, or woodworking. The shop for the latter at Groton is amply equipped and much of the work turned out by the students is of professional quality. The less traditional schools offer clubs for vegetarian cooking, weaving, quilting, folk music, and—in subtle juxtaposition to the Connecticut girls' school—international cooking. At western schools the horse still reigns supreme, and many students spend endless hours riding, training, cleaning, and loving their own horse or a horse they have leased from the school.

With the prep emphasis on music, choirs, glee clubs, madrigals, chamber music groups, as well as informal ensembles are all given places to practice. Most schools also have individual practice rooms, and like athletic teams, many prep musicians travel to other schools for concerts and performances.

Some schools offer a five-week "Winterim," during which students and faculty propose and organize a variety of off- and on-campus activities and studies. Such a program breaks the monotony of the usual class routine in the middle of winter, a season teachers repeatedly told us was the worst time at boarding school. It also enables students and faculty to explore new areas or interests in a safe way, that is, without grades.

In prep schools there is a perceived need for students to exercise authority as apprentice leaders early in their educational careers. The tradition of delegating real authority to students has British roots, where head boys and prefects have real power within the public schools. Head boys can discipline other boys by setting punishments and are treated by headmaster and housemasters alike as a part of the administration. In the United States, student power is generally more limited, although at the progressive schools students can be quite involved in the administrative decision-making process.

Virtually all prep schools have a student government. The formal structure of government usually includes a student body president, vice president, treasurer, secretary, class presidents, and dorm prefects, representatives, or "whips," as they are called at one school. Clubs also have presidents and there are always committees to be headed. Some schools have student-faculty senates and in schools like Wooster, in Connecticut, students are expected to play a major part in the disciplinary system. An ambitious student can obtain a great deal of experience in committee work, developing transferable skills for later leadership positions in finance, law, management, or politics.

The office of student body president or head prefect is used by the administration primarily as an extension of the official school culture, and most of the students who fill these offices are quite good at advancing the school's best public relations face. A successful student body president, like a good head, is artful in developing an easy leadership style, which is useful because he or she is in a structural political dilemma. Elected by the students but responsible to the school administration, the student politician is a classic go-between, always running the danger of being seen as "selling out" by students and as "uncooperative" by the administration. Occasionally students rebel against too much pandering to the administration and elect a rebel leader, who makes it his or her business to be a thorn in the side of the administration. A number of heads and deans of students watch elections closely, because if elections go "badly" it could mean a difficult year for them.

The actual content of real power varies by school. At some, authority is more apparent than real; at others, student power can affect important school decisions. At Putney, the "Big Committee" is composed of the school director, student leaders, and teachers. The powers of the Big Committee are laid out in the school's constitution, and students at Putney have real input into the decision-making process. At the Thacher School in California, the Student Leadership Council, which is composed of the school chairman, presidents of the three lower classes, and head prefects, is not only responsible for student activities and events, but also grants funds to groups who petition for special allocations. The power of the purse is learned early in the life of a prep school student. At the Westtown School in Pennsylvania, the student council arrives at decisions not by voting yea or nay, "but by following the Quaker custom of arriving at a 'sense of the meeting'" (*Westtown School* 1982–83:25).

Not all students, of course, participate in school politics; it may well be that many of the students most admired by their peers never run, or never would run, for a political position. The guerrilla leaders who emerge and flourish in the student underlife—or counterculture—may have far greater real power than the "superschoolies" that tend to get elected to public office.

In most coeducational schools, boys tend to monopolize positions of power. The highest offices are generally held by boys; girls are found in the vice presidential and secretarial positions. Politics can be important to prep families, and we suspect that a number of prep boys arrive at boarding school with a good supply of political ambition. One of the reasons advanced in support of all-girls' schools is that girls can gain important leadership experience there.

Some schools try to capture what they see as the best aspects of single-sex and coed schools. They do this by having boys and girls elect distinct school leaders, by having certain customs, places, and events that they share only with members of their own sex, and by having classes, certain other activities, and social events be coeducational. These schools, often called coordinate schools, see themselves as offering the chance to form strong single-sex bonds, to build self-confidence in adolescents, and to provide experience in working and relating to members of both sexes. Girls at coed schools more generally are likely to say they think in 10 years they will find the social skills they learned to be the most valuable part of their boarding-school experience.

Learning by Example

Part of the social learning students obtain is exposure to significant public personalities. Virtually all the schools have guest speaker programs in which well-known people can be seen and heard. Some of the speakers that have appeared at Miss Porter's School in the last several years include Alex Haley, author; Russell Baker, humorist; Arthur Miller, playwright; and Dick Gregory, comedian. At the boys' schools there is a tendency to invite men who are successful in politics and journalism. Recent speakers at the Hill School include James A. Baker III, Secretary of the Treasury (Hill class of 1948); James Reston, columnist; Frank Borman, astronaut and president of Eastern Airlines; and William Proxmire, United States senator (Hill class of 1934).

Inviting successful alumni to return for talks is one of the ways boarding schools can pass on a sense of the school's efficacy. Throughout the year panels, assemblies, and forums are organized for these occasions. Often the alumni speakers will also have informal sessions with students, visit classrooms, and stay for lunch, tea, or supper.

In keeping with cultural environments of prep schools, especially the select 16 schools, professional musicians, actors, and dancers are regularly invited to perform. Art and sculpture exhibits are common and some schools, such as Andover and Exeter, have permanent art galleries. The art at prep schools is generally either original works by artists such as Toulouse-Lautrec, Matisse, or Daumier, or the work of established contemporary artists such as Frank Stella, who graduated from Andover. At a large school there may be so much cultural activity that it is unnecessary to leave campus for any kind of high cultural event.

Those who come to elite boarding schools to talk or perform are the makers of culture. For adolescents seeking to be the best, these successful individuals give them a sense of importance and empowerment. All around them are the symbols of their special importance—in Groton's main hallway hangs a personal letter from Ronald Reagan to the headmaster, reminding the students that Groton "boasts a former President of the United States and some of America's finest statesmen." Five or six books a year will be published by a school's alumni; Exeter in particular has many alumni authors, including James Agee, Nathaniel G. Benchley, John Knowles, Dwight Macdonald, Jr., Arthur M. Schlesinger Jr., Sloan Wilson, and Gore Vidal. Roger L. Stevens, Alan Jay Lerner, and Edward Albee are all Choate-Rosemary Hall alumni, adding luster to a theater program that trains many professional actresses and actors. A student at an elite school is part of a world where success is expected, and celebrity and power are part of the unfolding of life. Not every school is as culturally rich as the elite eastern prep schools, but in the main, most schools work hard to develop an appreciation for high culture. At the Orme School in Arizona, a week is set aside each year in which the whole school participates in looking at art, watching art being made, and making art.

Nowhere is the drive for athletic, cultural, and academic excellence more apparent than in the awards, honors, and prizes that are given to outstanding teams or students at the end of each year. Sporting trophies are often large silver cups with the names of annual champions engraved on several sides. At some schools the triumphs have come with enough regularity to warrant building several hundred yards of glass casing to hold the dozens of medals, trophies, and other mementos that are the victors' spoils. Pictures of past winning teams, looking directly into the camera, seem frozen in time.

Academic prizes tend to be slightly less flashy but no less important. Much like British schoolmasters, American schoolmasters believe in rewarding excellence, so most schools give a number of cultural, service, and academic prizes at the end of each year. There is usually at least one prize in each academic discipline, as well as prizes for overall achievement and effort. There are service prizes for dedicated volunteers, as well as debating and creative writing prizes. Almost all schools have cum laude and other honor societies.

Sitting through a graduation ceremony at a boarding school can be an endurance test—some schools give so many prizes that one could fly from New York to Boston and back in the time it takes to go from the classics prize to the prize for the best woodworking or weaving project. But of course, the greatest prize of all is graduation, and more than a few schools chisel, paint, etch, or carve the names of the graduates into wood, stone, or metal to immortalize their passage from the total institution into the world.

REFERENCES

Adleman, Clifford. 1983. "Devaluation, Diffusion and the College Connection: A Study of High School Transcripts, 1964–1981." Washington, DC: National Commission on Excellence in Education.

Bourdieu, Pierre and Jean-Claude Passeron. 1977. *Reproduction: In Education, Society, and Culture.* Beverly Hills, CA: Sage.

Coleman, James S., Thomas Hoffer, and Sally Kilgore. 1982. *High School Achievement.* New York: Basic Books, p. 90.

Levine, Steven B. 1980. "The Rise of American Boarding Schools and the Development of a National Upper Class." *Social Problems* 28:63–94.

52

BAD BOYS
Public Schools in the Making of Black Masculinity

ANN ARNETT FERGUSON

The previous selection illustrates how schools socially produce and reproduce social class distinctions in the United States. In so doing, schools are an
important agent of *social reproduction*—they socially reproduce social inequalities that maintain social stratification. Schools also produce and reproduce racial distinctions found in society. The selection that follows
examines the social reproduction of race and gender in American public
schools. In particular, this excerpt, from Ann Arnett Ferguson's 2000 book,
Bad Boys: Public Schools in the Making of Black Masculinity, examines the effects
gender and racial stereotyping has on African American school boys. Ferguson, an associate professor of African American studies and women's
studies at Smith College, explores why African American boys are more often labeled as troublemakers than other gender or racial-ethnic groups of
children.

Soon after I began fieldwork at Rosa Parks Elementary School, one of the
adults, an African American man, pointed to a black boy who walked
by us in the hallway.[1] "That one has a jail-cell with his name on it," he
told me. We were looking at a ten-year-old, barely four feet tall, whose frail
body was shrouded in baggy pants and a hooded sweatshirt. The boy, Lamar,
passed with the careful tread of someone who was in no hurry to get where
he was going. He was on his way to the Punishing Room of the school. As he
glanced quickly toward and then away from us, the image of the figure of Tu-
pac Shakur on the poster advertising the movie *Juice* flashed into my mind. I
suppose it was the combination of the hooded sweatshirt, the guarded expression in his eyes, and what my companion had just said that reminded me
of the face on the film poster that stared at me from billboards and sidings all
over town.

I was shocked that judgment and sentence had been passed on this child
so matter-of-factly by a member of the school staff. But by the end of the
school year, I had begun to suspect that a prison cell might indeed have a
place in Lamar's future. What I observed at Rosa Parks during more than

From Ferguson, Ann Arnett, *Bad Boys: Public Schools and the Making of Black Masculinity.* Copyright © 2000 by The University of Michigan Press. Reprinted by
permission.

three years of fieldwork in the school, heard from the boy himself, from his teachers, from his mother, made it clear that just as children were tracked into futures as doctors, scientists, engineers, word processors, and fast-food workers, there were also tracks for some children, predominantly African American and male, that led to prison. This [article] tells the story of the making of these bad boys, not by members of the criminal justice system on street corners, or in shopping malls, or video arcades, but in and by school, through punishment. It is an account of the power of institutions to create, shape, and regulate social identities.

Unfortunately, Lamar's journey is not an isolated event, but traces a disturbing pattern of African American male footsteps out of classrooms, down hallways, and into disciplinary spaces throughout the school day in contemporary America. Though African American boys made up only one-quarter of the student body at Rosa Parks, they accounted for nearly half the number of students sent to the Punishing Room for major and minor misdeeds in 1991–92. Three-quarters of those suspended that year were boys, and, of those, four-fifths were African American.[2] In the course of my study it became clear that school labeling practices and the exercise of rules operated as part of a hidden curriculum to marginalize and isolate black male youth in disciplinary spaces and brand them as criminally inclined.

But trouble is not only a site of regulation and stigmatization. Under certain conditions it can also be a powerful occasion for identification and recognition. This study investigates this aspect of punishment through an exploration of the meaning of school rules and the interpretation of trouble from the youth's perspective. What does it mean to hear adults say that you are bound for jail and to understand that the future predicted for you is "doing time" inside prison walls? What does school trouble mean under such deleterious circumstances? How does a ten-year-old black boy fashion a sense of self within this context? Children like Lamar are not just innocent victims of arbitrary acts; like other kids, he probably talks out of turn, argues with teachers, uses profanities, brings contraband to school. However, I will argue, the meaning and consequences of these acts for young black males like himself are different, highly charged with racial and gender significance with scarring effects on adult life chances.

The pattern of punishment that emerges from the Rosa Parks data is not unique. Recent studies in Michigan, Minnesota, California, and Ohio reveal a similar pattern.[3] In the public schools of Oakland, California, for example, suspensions disproportionately involved African American males, while in Michigan schools, where corporal punishment is still permitted, blacks were more than five times more likely to be hit by school adults than were whites. In the Cincinnati schools, black students were twice as likely to end up in the in-house suspension room—popularly known as the "dungeon"—and an overwhelming proportion of them were male.[4] In an ominous parallel to Cincinnati's dungeon, disciplinary space at Rosa Parks is designated the "Jailhouse." . . .

Dreams

This [article] began with an anecdote about the school's vice principal identi-fying a small boy as someone who had a jail-cell with his name on it. I started with this story to illustrate how school personnel made predictive decisions about a child's future based on a whole ensemble of negative assumptions about African American males and their life-chances. The kids, however, imagined their future in a more positive light. They neither saw themselves as being "on the fast track to prison," as predicted by school personnel, nor did they see themselves as working at low-level service jobs as adults. The boys, in fact, had a decidedly optimistic view about their future.

This scenario, at such variance with that of the administrator's, became clear to me in my final semester at Rosa Parks, when the sixth-graders wrote an essay on the jobs they would like to have as adults. As I scanned these written accounts of students' dreams, I became conscious of a striking pat-tern. The overwhelming majority of the boys aspired to be professional ath-letes—playing basketball, baseball, or football—when they grew up. The reasons they gave for this choice were remarkably similar: the sport was something they were good at; it was work they would enjoy doing; and they would make a lot of money.[5] They acknowledged it would be extremely difficult to have such a career, but, they argued, if you worked hard and had the talent, you could make it.

These youthful essays confirmed what the boys had told me in inter-views about the adult occupations they imagined for themselves. While a few had mentioned other options such as becoming a stand-up comedian, a Supreme Court justice, or a rap musician, almost all expressed the desire to play on an NBA or NFL team. This was not just an empty fantasy. Most of the boys with whom I had contact in my research were actively and diligently in-volved in after-school sports, not just as play, but in the serious business of preparing themselves for adult careers. This dream was supported in tangi-ble ways by parents who boasted about their sons' prowess, found time to take them to practice, and cheered their teams on at games. I had assumed initially that these after-school sports activities were primarily a way of par-ents keeping kids busy to guard against their getting into drugs and sex. However, after talking to parents and kids I realized that what I observed was not just about keeping boys out of trouble but was preparation for future careers.

The occupational dreams of these boys are not at all unique. A survey by Northeastern University's Center for the Study of Sport in Society found that two-thirds of African American males between the ages of thirteen and eigh-teen believe they can earn a living playing professional sports.[6] Nor is this na-tional pattern for black youth really surprising. For African American males, disengagement from the school's agenda for approval and success is a psy-chic survival mechanism; so imagining a future occupation for which school-ing seems irrelevant is eminently rational. A career as a professional athlete represents the possibility of attaining success in terms of the dominant society via a path that makes schooling seem immaterial, while at the same time affirming central aspects of identification.

I have argued that the boys distance themselves from the school's agenda to avoid capitulating to its strategies for fashioning a self for upward mobility—strategies requiring black youth to distance themselves from family and neighborhood, to reject the language, the style of social interaction, the connections in which identities are grounded. From the highly idealized viewpoint of youth, a career in sports does not appear to require these strategic detachments. Their heroes—players like Michael Jordan, Scottie Pippen, Dennis Rodman, Rickey Henderson, to name just a few—have achieved the highest reaches of success without disguising or eradicating their Blackness.

But these are only dreams, for the chances of getting drafted by professional teams are slim to nonexistent. The probability has been calculated as somewhere in the region of one in ten thousand that a youth will end up in pro football or basketball.[7] Based on these facts, a plethora of popular and scholarly literature, as well as fiction and documentary films, have underscored how unrealistic such ambitions are, making the point that few youths who pour their hearts, energy, and schooling into sports will actually make it to the professional teams where the glory lies and the money is made.[8] They point out this discouraging scenario in order to persuade young black males to rechannel their energies and ambitions into conventional school learning that allows for more "realistic" career options.

Yet, in reality, for these youth efforts to attain high-status occupations through academic channels are just as likely to fail, given the conditions of their schooling and the unequal distribution of resources across school systems.[9] Children attending inner-city public schools are more likely to end up in dead-end, minimum-wage, service sector jobs because they do not have the quality of education available in the suburban public or elite private schools. Today's dreams will be transformed into tomorrow's nightmares.

Nightmares

While I rejected the labeling practices of the school vice principal, in my opening [paragraph], I also reluctantly admitted that by the end of the school year I, too, had come to suspect that a prison cell might have a place in the future of many Rosa Parks students. In contrast to the vice principal, this foreboding was not by any means rooted in a conclusion I had come to about individual children's proclivity for a life of crime, nor was it grounded in any evidence that, as some labeling theories hold, individuals stigmatized as deviant come to internalize this identity and adopt delinquent behaviors at rates higher than other youth. Rather, it emanated from my increased awareness of the way that racial bias in institutions external to school, such as the media and criminal justice system, mirrored and converged with that of the educational system. This convergence intensifies and weights the odds heavily in favor of a young black male ending up in jail. School seems to feed into the prison system, but what exactly is the connection between the two? What are the practical links between the punishing rooms, jailhouses, and dungeons of educational institutions and the cells of local, state, and federal prison systems? There are both long-term causal links as well as visible, immediate connections.

There are serious, long-term effects of being labeled a Troublemaker that substantially increase one's chances of ending up in jail. In the daily experience of being so named, regulated, and surveilled, access to the full resources of the school are increasingly denied as the boys are isolated in nonacademic spaces in school or banished to lounging at home or loitering on the streets. Time in the school dungeon means time lost from classroom learning; suspension, at school or at home, has a direct and lasting negative effect on the continuing growth of a child. When removal from classroom life begins at an early age, it is even more devastating, as human possibilities are stunted at a crucial formative period of life. Each year the gap in skills grows wider and more handicapping, while the overall process of disidentification that I have described encourages those who have problems to leave school rather than resolve them in an educational setting.

There is a direct relationship between dropping out of school and doing time in jail: the majority of black inmates in local, state, and federal penal systems are high school dropouts.[10] Therefore, if we want to begin to break the ties between school and jail, we must first create educational systems that foster kids' identification with school and encourage them not to abandon it.

One significant but relatively small step that could be taken to foster this attachment would be to reduce the painful, inhospitable climate of school for African American children through the validation and affirmation of Black English, the language form that many of the children bring from home/ neighborhood. As I pointed out earlier, the denigration of this form and the assumptions made about the academic potential of speakers of Ebonics pose severe dilemmas of identification for black students—especially for males. The legitimation of Black English in the world of the school would not only enrich the curriculum but would undoubtedly provide valuable lessons to all students about sociolinguistics and the contexts in which standard and nonstandard forms are appropriate. The necessary prerequisite for this inclusion would be a mandatory program for teachers and school administrators to educate them about the nature and history of Ebonics. This was of course the very change called for by the Oakland School Board in 1996. However, it is clear from the controversy that ensued and the highly racialized and obfuscatory nature of the national media's coverage of the Oakland Resolution that there is serious opposition to any innovations that appear to challenge the supremacy of English.[11]

There is also an immediate, ongoing connection between school and jail. Schools mirror and reinforce the practices and ideological systems of other institutions in the society. The racial bias in the punishing systems of the school reflects the practices of the criminal justice system. Black youth are caught up in the net of the juvenile justice system at a rate of two to four times that of white youth.[12] Does this mean that African American boys are more prone to criminal activity than white boys? There is evidence that this is not the case. A study by Huizinga and Elliot demonstrates that the contrast in incarceration statistics is the result of a different *institutional response* to the race of the youth rather than the difference in actual behavior. Drawing on a representative sample of youth between the ages of eleven and seventeen, they compare the delinquent acts individual youth admit to committing in annual self-report interviews with actual police records of delinquency in the areas in which the boys live. Based on the self-reports, they conclude that there were few, if any, differences in the number or type of delinquent acts perpetrated by the two racial groups. What they did find, however, was that there was a substantially and significantly higher risk that the minority youth would be apprehended and charged for these acts by police than the whites who reported committing the same kind of offenses. They conclude that "minorities appear to be at greater risk for being charged with more serious offenses than whites involved in comparable levels of delinquent behavior, a factor which may eventually result in higher incarceration rates among minorities."[13]

Images of black male criminality and the demonization of black children play a significant role in framing actions and events in the justice system in a way that is similar to how these images are used in school to interpret the behavior of individual miscreants. In both settings, the images result in differential treatment based on race. Jerome G. Miller, who has directed juvenile justice detention systems in Massachusetts and Illinois, describes how this works:

> I learned very early on that when we got a black youth, virtually everything—from arrest summaries, to family history, to rap sheets, to psychiatric exams, to "waiver" hearings as to whether or not he would be tried as an adult, to final sentencing—was skewed. If a middle-class white youth was sent to us as "dangerous," he was more likely actually to be so than the black teenager given the same label. The white teenager was more likely to have been afforded competent legal counsel and appropriate psychiatric and psychological testing, tried in a variety of privately funded options, and dealt with more sensitively and individually at every stage of the juvenile justice processing. For him to be labeled "dangerous," he had to have done something very serious indeed. By contrast, the black teenager was more likely to be dealt with as a stereotype from the moment the handcuffs were first put on—easily and quickly relegated to the "more dangerous" end of the "violent-nonviolent" spectrum, albeit accompanied by an official record meant to validate each of a biased series of decisions.[14]

Miller indicates that racial disparities are most obvious at the very earliest and the latest stages of processing of youth through the juvenile justice system, and African American male youth are more likely to be apprehended and caught up in the system in the very beginning. They are also more likely "to be waived to adult court, and to be adjudicated delinquent. If removed from their homes by the court, they were less likely to be placed in the better-staffed and better-run private-group home facilities and more likely to be sent into state reform schools."[15]

Given the poisonous mix of stereotyping and profiling of black males, their chances of ending up in the penal system as a juvenile is extremely high. Even if a boy manages to avoid getting caught within the juvenile justice system through luck or the constant vigilance of parents, his chances of being arrested and jailed are staggeringly high as an adult. A 1995 report by the Sentencing Project finds that nearly one in three African Americans in his twenties is in prison or jail, on probation or parole, on any given day.[16]

The school experience of African American boys is simultaneously replicated in the penal system through processes of surveillance, policing, charges, and penalties. The kids recognize this; the names they give to disciplinary spaces are not just coincidence. They are referencing the chilling parallels between the two.

A systematic racial bias is exercised in the regulation, control, and discipline of children in the United States today. African American males are apprehended and punished for misbehavior and delinquent acts that are overlooked in other children. The punishment that is meted out is usually more severe than that for other children. This racism that systematically extinguishes the potential and constrains the world of possibilities for black males would be brutal enough if it were restricted to school, but it is replicated in other disciplinary systems of the society, the most obvious parallel being the juvenile justice system.

Open Endings

Whenever I give a talk about my research, I am inevitably asked what ideas or recommendations I have for addressing the conditions that I describe. What do I think should be done, listeners want to know? The first few times this happened I felt resentful partly because I knew my colleagues who did research on subjects other than schooling were rarely asked to come up with policy recommendations to address the problems they had uncovered. This request for solutions is made on the assumption that schools, unlike the family and workplace, are basically sound albeit with flaws that need adjusting.

My hesitation to propose solutions comes from a conviction that minor inputs, temporary interventions, individual prescriptions into schools are vastly inadequate to remedy an institution that is fundamentally flawed and whose goal for urban black children seems to be the creation of "a citizenry which will simply obey the rules of society." I stand convinced that a re-structuring of the entire educational system is what is urgently required if we are to produce the thoughtful, actively questioning citizens that Baldwin de-scribes in the epigraph to this chapter. To make the point, however, that small programs at Rosa Parks school such as PALS [Partners at Learning Skills]—always underfunded, always dependent on grants of "soft" money that required big promises of quick fixes—served always too few and would in-evitably disappear entirely or be co-opted by the institution, was so dis-heartening, so paralyzing that I am forced to rethink my reply. Is it all or nothing? Can we eradicate forms of institutional racism in school without eliminating racism in the society at large? Are the alternatives either quick hopeless fixes or paralysis because small changes cannot make a difference in the long run? How can the proliferation of local initiatives that spring up, in hope and with enthusiasm, be sustained without taking on institutional goals and attitudes? How can emergent forms appear alongside and out of the old? Most important of all, will attention be paid to the counterdiscourse of the Troublemakers themselves?

When I asked the kids, Schoolboys and Troublemakers, how they thought schooling might be improved, they looked at me blankly. I think they shared my sense of despair. The responses that I wrung out of them seemed trivial, even frivolous. It was all about play, about recreation: a longer recess, bigger play areas, playgrounds with grass not asphalt—and so on. The list that I had dreamed up was the opposite of frivolous. It was all about curriculum: smaller classes, Saturday tutoring, year-round school, antiracist training for student teachers, mutual respect between adults and youth. One thing I am convinced of is that more punitive measures, tighter discipline, greater surveillance, more prisons—the very path that our society seems to be determined to pursue—is not the approach to take. Perhaps, allowing ourselves to imagine the possibilities—what could, should, and must be—is an indispensable first step.

ENDNOTES

[1] This research was assisted by an award from the Social Science Research Council through funding provided by the Rockefeller Foundation. The names of the city, school, and individuals in this ethnography are fictitious in order to preserve the anonymity of participants.

[2] Punishment resulted in suspension 20 percent of the time. Records show that in 1991–92, 250 students, or almost half of the children at Rosa Parks School, were sent to the Punishing Room by adults for breaking school rules, for a total of 1,252 journeys. This figure is based on my count of referral forms kept on file in the Punishing Room. However, it by no means represents the total number of students referred by teachers for discipline. I observed a number of instances where children came into the Punishing Room but the problem was settled by the student specialist on the spot and no paperwork was generated. This seemed especially likely to occur when the adult referring the child had written an informal note rather than on the official referral form, when a parent did not have to be called, or when the infraction was

judged by the student specialist to be insignificant. So it is likely that a much larger number of children were sent to the Punishing Room over the year but no record was made as a result of the visit.

3 "Survey: Schools Suspend Blacks More," *Detroit Free Press,* December 14, 1988, 4A; Joan Richardson, "Study Puts Michigan 6th in Student Suspensions," *Detroit Free Press,* August 21, 1990, p. 1A; Minnesota Department of Children, Families and Learning, *Student Suspension and Expulsion: Report to the Legislature* (St. Paul: Minnesota Department of Children, Families and Learning, 1996); Commission for Positive Change in the Oakland Public Schools, *Keeping Children in Schools: Sounding the Alarm on Suspensions* (Oakland, CA: The Commission, 1992), p. 1; and John D. Hull, "Do Teachers Punish According to Race?" *Time,* April 4, 1994, pp. 30–31.

4 In Oakland, while 28 percent of students in the system were African American males, they accounted for 53 percent of the suspensions. See note 3 for racial imbalance in corporal punishment in Michigan schools ("Survey: Schools Suspend Blacks More") and the racial discipline gap in Cincinnati (Hull, "Do Teachers Punish?").

5 It is interesting to note that the girls in the class all responded in a stereotypical way. The vast majority wanted to have "helping" careers in traditional female occupations: teachers, nurses, psychologists. None of the girls gave money as a reason for their choice.

6 Survey reported in *U.S. News and World Report,* March 24, 1997, p. 46.

7 Raymie E. McKerrow and Norinne H. Daly, "The Student Athlete," *National Forum* 71, no. 4 (1990): 44.

8 For examples see Gary A. Sailes, "The Exploitation of the Black Athlete: Some Alternative Solutions," *Journal of Negro Education* 55, no. 4 (1986); Robert M. Sellers and Gabriel P. Kuperminc, "Goal Discrepancy in African-American Male Student-Athletes' Unrealistic Expectations for Careers in Professional Sports," *Journal of Black Psychology* 23, no. 1 (1997); Alexander Wolf, "Impossible Dream," *Sports Illustrated,* June 2, 1997; and John Hoberman, *Darwin's Athletes: How Sport Has Damaged Black America and Preserved the Myth of Race* (Boston: Houghton Mifflin, 1997).

9 For a shocking demonstration of the difference between schools see Jonathan Kozol, *Savage Inequalities: Children in America's Schools* (New York: Crown Publishing, 1991).

10 United States Department of Justice, Profile of Jail Inmates (Washington, DC: US Government Printing Office, 1980). Two-thirds of the black inmates have less than a twelfth-grade education, while the rate of incarceration drops significantly for those who have twelve or more years of schooling.

11 For an excellent overview of the debate that ensued over the Oakland School Board's resolution and a discussion of Ebonics, see Theresa Perry and Lisa Delpit, eds., *The Real Ebonics Debate: Power, Language, and the Education of African American Children* (Boston: Beacon Press, 1998).

12 Jerome G. Miller, *Search and Destroy: African-American Males in the Criminal Justice System* (New York: Cambridge University Press, 1996), p. 73.

13 David Huizinga and Delbert Elliot, "Juvenile Offenders: Prevalence, Offender Incidence, and Arrest Rates by Race," paper presented at "Race and the Incarceration of Juveniles," Racine, Wisconsin, December 1986, quoted in ibid., p. 72.

14 Ibid., p. 78.

15 Ibid., p. 73.

16 Sentencing Project, *Young Black Americans and the Criminal Justice System: Five Years Later* (Washington, DC: Sentencing Project, 1995). This unprecedented figure reflects an increase from the 1990 Sentencing Project findings that one in four black males in their twenties was under the supervision of the criminal justice system.

THE FAMILY

53

GAY AND LESBIAN FAMILIES ARE HERE

JUDITH STACEY

This is the first of three readings that examine the social institution of the family. Some scholars argue that to understand completely the current debate about family, we need to examine the changing definitions of family. For example, many people define *family* only in terms of heterosexual marriage and blood ties. If we delineate family based on only these two criteria, think of all the people this definition leaves out, including adopted and foster children, cohabiting couples, gay and lesbian couples, and friends who are often closer than blood relatives. In the following selection, taken from *In the Name of the Family: Rethinking Family Values in the Postmodern Age* (1996), Judith Stacey challenges us to examine our heterosexist and narrow definitions of family. Stacey, a professor of sociology at the University of Southern California, argues that gay and lesbian families already exist in large numbers; they are not deviant; and many of these families are fighting for the same rights as heterosexual families, including the right to adopt children and the right to have the economic and legal benefits of marriage.

In 1992 in Houston, I talked about the cultural war going on for the soul of America. And that war is still going on! We cannot worship the false god of gay rights. To put that sort of relationship on the same level as marriage is a moral lie.

—Pat Buchanan, February 10, 1996

Homosexuality is a peculiar and rare human trait that affects only a small percentage of the population and is of little interest to the rest.

—Jonathan Rauch 1994

I came to Beijing to the Fourth World Conference of Women to speak on behalf of lesbian families. We are part of families. We are daughters, we are sisters, we are aunts, nieces, cousins. In addition, many of us are mothers and grandmoth-

ers. We share concerns for our families that are the same concerns of women around the world.

—BONNIE TINKER, *LOVE MAKES A FAMILY*, SEPTEMBER 1995

Until but a short time ago, gay and lesbian families seemed quite a queer concept, even preposterous, if not oxymoronic, not only to scholars and the general public, but even to most lesbians and gay men. The grassroots movement for gay liberation that exploded into public visibility in 1969, when gays resisted a police raid at the Stonewall bar in New York City, struggled along with the militant feminist movement of that period to liberate gays and women *from* perceived evils and injustices represented by the family, rather than *for* access to its blessings and privileges. During the early 1970s, marches for gay pride and women's liberation flaunted provocative, countercultural banners, like "Smash The Family" and "Smash Monogamy." Their legacy is a lasting public association of gay liberation and feminism with family subversion. Yet how "queer" such antifamily rhetoric sounds today, when gays and lesbians are in the thick of a vigorous profamily movement of their own.

Gay and lesbian families are indisputably here. In June of 1993, police chief Tom Potter joined his lesbian, police officer daughter in a Portland, Oregon, gay pride march for "family values." By the late 1980s an astonishing "gay-by boom" had swelled the ranks of children living with gay and lesbian parents to between six to fourteen million.[1] *Family Values* is the title of a popular 1993 book by and about a lesbian's successful struggle to become a legal second mother to one of these "turkey-baster" babies, the son she and his biological mother have co-parented since his birth.[2] In 1989 Denmark became the first nation in the world to legalize a form of gay marriage, termed "registered partnerships," and its Nordic neighbors, Norway and Sweden, soon followed suit. In 1993, thousands of gay and lesbian couples participated in a mass wedding ceremony on the Washington Mall during the largest demonstration for gay rights in U.S. history. Three years later, on March 25, 1996, Mayor of San Francisco Willie Brown proudly presided over a civic ceremony to celebrate the domestic partnerships of nearly 200 same-sex couples. "We're leading the way here in San Francisco," the mayor declared, "for the rest of the nation to fully embrace the diversity of people in love, regardless of their gender or sexual orientation."[3] By then thousands of gay and lesbian couples across the nation were eagerly awaiting the outcome of *Baehr v. Lewin,* cautiously optimistic that Hawaii's Supreme Court will soon order the state to become the first in the United States, and in the modern world, to grant full legal marriage rights to same-sex couples. As this work went to press in May 1996, the Republican party had just made gay marriage opposition a wedge issue in their presidential campaign.

Gay and lesbian families are undeniably here, yet they are not queer, if one uses the term in the sense of "odd" to signify a marginal or deviant population.[4] It is nearly impossible to define this category of families in a manner that could successfully distinguish all of its members, needs, relationships, or even their values, from those of all other families. In fact, it is almost impossible to define this category in a satisfactory, substantive way at all. What should count as a gay or lesbian family? Even if we bracket the thorny matter of how to define an individual as gay or lesbian and rely on self-identification, we still face a jesuitical challenge. Should we count only families in which every single member is gay? Clearly there are not very many, if even any, of these. Or does the presence of just one gay member color a family gay? Just as clearly, there are very many of these, including those of Ronald Reagan, Colin Powell, Phyllis Schlafly and Newt Gingrich.[5] More to the point, why would we want to designate a family type according to the sexual identity of one or more of its members? No research, as we will see, has ever shown a uniform, distinctive pattern of relationships, structure, or even of "family values," among families that include self-identified gays. Of course, most nongays restrict the term gay family to units that contain one or two gay parents and their children. However, even such families that most commonsensically qualify as gay or lesbian are as diverse as are those which do not.

Gay and lesbian families come in different sizes, shapes, ethnicities, races, religions, resources, creeds, and quirks, and even engage in diverse sexual practices. The more one attempts to arrive at a coherent, defensible sorting principle, the more evident it becomes that the category "gay and lesbian family" signals nothing so much as the consequential social fact of widespread, institutionalized homophobia.[6] The gay and lesbian family label marks the cognitive dissonance, and even emotional threat, that much of the nongay public experiences upon recognizing that gays can participate in family life at all. What unifies such families is their need to contend with the particular array of psychic, social, legal, practical, and even physical challenges to their very existence that institutionalized hostility to homosexuality produces. Paradoxically, the label "gay and lesbian family" would become irrelevant if the nongay population could only "get used to it."

In this [article] I hope to facilitate such a process of normalization, ironically, perhaps, to allow the marker "gay and lesbian" as a family category once again to seem queer—as queer, that is, as it now seems to identify a *family*, rather than an individual or a desire, as heterosexual. . . . Gay and lesbian families represent such a new, embattled, visible and necessarily self-conscious, genre of postmodern kinship, that they more readily expose the widening gap between the complex reality of postmodern family forms and the simplistic modern family ideology that still undergirds most public rhetoric, policy and law concerning families. In short, I hope to demonstrate that, contrary to Jonathan Rauch's well-meaning claim in the second epigraph above, the experience of "homosexuals"[7] should be of immense interest to everyone else. Nongay families, family scholars and policymakers alike can learn a great deal from examining the experience, struggles, conflicts, needs, and achievements of contemporary gay and lesbian families. . . .

A More, or Less, Perfect Union?

Much nearer at hand . . . than most ever dared to imagine has come the momentous prospect of legal gay marriage. The idea of same-sex marriage used to draw nearly as many jeers from gays and lesbians as from nongays. As one lesbian couple recalls, "In 1981, we were a very, very small handful of lesbians who got married. We took a lot of flak from other lesbians, as well as heterosexuals. In 1981, we didn't know any other lesbians, not a single one, who had had a ceremony in Santa Cruz, and a lot of lesbians live in that city. Everybody was on our case about it. They said, What are you doing?, How heterosexual. We really had to sell it."[8]

Less than a decade later, gay and lesbian couples could proudly announce their weddings and anniversaries, not only in the gay press, which now includes specialized magazines for gay and lesbian couples, like *Partners Magazine,* but even in such mainstream, Midwestern newspapers as the Minneapolis *Star Tribune.*[9] Jewish rabbis, Protestant ministers, Quaker meetings, and even some Catholic priests regularly perform gay and lesbian wedding or commitment ceremonies. This phenomenon is memorialized in cultural productions within the gay community, like "Chicks In White Satin," a documentary about a Jewish lesbian wedding which won prizes at recent gay film festivals, but it has also become a fashionable pop culture motif. In December 1995, the long-running TV sitcom program "Roseanne" featured a gay male wedding in a much-hyped episode called "December Bride." Even more provocative, however, was a prime-time lesbian wedding that aired one month later on "Friends," the highest rated sitcom of the 1995–1996 television season. Making a cameo appearance on the January 18, 1996 episode, Candice Gingrich, the lesbian half-sister of right-wing Speaker of the House Newt Gingrich, conducted a wedding ceremony which joined the characters who play a lesbian couple on the series "in holy matrimony" and pronounced them "wife and wife."

When the very first social science research collection about gay parents was published in 1987, not even one decade ago, its editor concluded that however desirable such unions might be, "it is highly unlikely that marriages between same-sex individuals will be legalized in any state in the foreseeable future."[10] Yet, almost immediately thereafter, precisely this specter began to exercise imaginations across the political spectrum. A national poll reported by the *San Francisco Examiner* in 1989 found that 86 percent of lesbians and gay men supported legalizing same-sex marriage.[11] However, it is the pending *Baehr v. Lewin* court decision concerning same-sex marriage rights in Hawaii that has thrust this issue into escalating levels of front-page and prime-time prominence. Amidst rampant rumors that thousands of mainland gay and lesbian couples were stocking their hope chests with Hawaiian excursion fares, poised to fly to tropical altars the instant the first gay matrimonial bans falter, right-wing Christian groups began actively mobilizing resistance. Militant antiabortion leader Randall Terry of Operation Rescue flew to Hawaii in February 1996 to fight "queer marriage," and right-wing Christian women's leader and radio broadcast personality Beverly LaHaye urged her "Godly" listeners to fight gay marriage in Hawaii.[12]

Meanwhile, fearing that Hawaii will become a gay marriage mecca, state legislators have rushed to introduce bills that exclude same-sex marriages performed in other states from being recognized in their own, because the "full faith and credit" clause of the U.S. Constitution obligates interstate recognition of legal marriages. While fourteen states had rejected such bills by May 1995, eight others had passed them, and contests were underway in numerous others, including California.[13] On May 8, 1996, gay marriage galloped onto the nation's center political stage when Republicans introduced the Defense of Marriage Act (DOMA) which defines marriage in exclusively heterosexual terms, as "a legal union between one man and one woman as husband and wife."[14] The last legislation that Republican presidential candidate Bob Dole co-sponsored before he resigned from the Senate to pursue his White House bid full throttle, DOMA exploits homophobia to defeat President Clinton and the Democrats in November 1996. With Clinton severely bruised by the political debacle incited by his support for gay rights in the military when he first took office, but still dependent upon the support of his gay constituency, the President indeed found himself "wedged" between a rock and a very hard place. Unsurprisingly, he tried to waffle. Naming this a "time when we need to do things to strengthen the American family," Clinton publicly opposed same-sex marriage at the same time that he tried to reaffirm support for gay rights and to expose the divisive Republican strategy.[15]

Polemics favoring and opposing gay marriage rights now proliferate in editorial pages and legislatures across the nation, and mainstream religious bodies find themselves compelled to confront the issue. In March 1996 the Vatican felt called upon not merely to condemn same-sex marriage as a "moral disorder," but also to warn Catholics that they would themselves risk "moral censure" if they were to support "the election of the candidate who has formally promised to translate into law the homosexual demand."[16] Just one day after the Vatican published this admonition, the Central Conference of American Rabbis, which represents the large, generally liberal wing of Judaism, took a momentous action in direct opposition. The Conference resoundingly endorsed a resolution to "support the right of gay and lesbian couples to share fully and equally in the rights of civil marriage." Unsurprisingly, Orthodox rabbis immediately condemned the action as prohibited in the Bible and "another breakdown in the family unit." [17] One week later, in another historic development, a lead editorial in the *New York Times* strongly endorsed gay marriage.[18]

As with child custody, the campaign for gay marriage clings to legal footholds carved by racial justice pioneers. It is startling to recall how recent it was that the Supreme Court finally struck down antimiscegenation laws. Not until 1967, that is only two years before Stonewall, did the high court, in *Loving v. Virginia*, find state restrictions on interracial marriages to be unconstitutional. (Twenty states still had such restrictions on the books in 1967, only one state fewer than the twenty-one which currently prohibit sodomy.) A handful of gay couples quickly sought to marry in the 1970s through appeals to this precedent, but until three lesbian and gay male couples sued Hawaii in *Baehr v. Lewin* for equal rights to choose marriage partners without restrictions on gender, all U.S. courts had dismissed the analogy. In a historic ruling in 1993, the Hawaiian state Supreme Court remanded this suit to the state, requiring it to demonstrate a "compelling state interest" in prohibiting same-sex marriage, a strict scrutiny standard that few believe the state will be able to meet. Significantly, the case was neither argued nor adjudicated as a gay rights issue. Rather, just as ERA opponents once had warned and advocates had denied, passage of an equal rights amendment to Hawaii's state constitution in 1972 paved the legal foundation for *Baehr*.[19]

Most gay activists and legal scholars anticipate a victory for gay marriage when *Baehr* is finally decided early in 1997, but they do not all look forward to this prospect with great delight. Although most of their constituents desire the right to marry, gay activists and theorists continue to vigorously debate the politics and effects of this campaign. Refining earlier feminist and socialist critiques of the gender and class inequities of marriage, an articulate, vocal minority seeks not to extend the right to marry, but to dismantle an institution they regard as inherently, and irredeemably, hierarchical, unequal, conservative, and repressive. Nancy Polikoff, one of the most articulate lesbian legal activist-scholars opposed to the marriage campaign, argues that

> Advocating lesbian and gay marriage will detract from, and even contradict, efforts to unhook economic benefits from marriage and make basic health care and other necessities available to all. It will also require a rhetorical strategy that emphasizes similarities between our relationships and heterosexual marriages, values long-term monogamous coupling above all other relationships, and denies the potential of lesbian and gay marriage to transform the gendered nature of marriage for all people. I fear that the very process of employing that rhetorical strategy for the years it will take to achieve its objective will lead our movement's public representatives, and the countless lesbians and gay men who hear us, to believe exactly what we say.[20]

A second perspective supports legal marriage as one long-term goal of the gay rights movement, but voices serious strategic objections to making this a priority before there is sufficient public support to sustain a favorable ruling in Hawaii or the nation. Such critics fear that a premature victory will prove pyrrhic, because efforts to defend it against the vehement backlash it has already begun to incite are apt to fail, after sapping resources and time better devoted to other urgent struggles for gay rights. Rather than risk a major setback for the gay movement, they advise an incremental approach to establishing legal family status for gay and lesbian kin ties through a multi-faceted struggle for family diversity.[21]

However, the largest, and most diverse, contingent of gay activist voices now supports the marriage rights campaign, perhaps because gay marriage can be read to harmonize with virtually every hue on the gay ideological spectrum. Pro-gay marriage arguments range from profoundly conservative to liberal humanist to radical and deconstructive. Conservatives, like those radicals who still oppose marriage, view it as an institution that promotes monogamy, commitment and social stability, along with interests in private property, social conformity and mainstream values. They likewise agree that legalizing gay marriage would further marginalize sexual radicals by segregating counter-cultural gays and lesbians from the "whitebread" gay couples who could then choose to marry their way into Middle America. Radicals and conservatives, in other words, envision the same prospect, but regard it with inverse sentiments.[22]

Liberal gays support legal marriage, of course, not only to affirm the legitimacy of their relationships and help sustain them in a hostile world, but as a straightforward matter of equal civil rights. As one long-coupled gay man expresses it: "I resent the fact that married people get lower taxes. But as long as there is this institution of marriage and heterosexuals have that privilege, then gay people should be able to do it too."[23] Liberals also recognize that marriage rights provide access to the social advantages of divorce law. "I used to say, 'Why do we want to get married? It doesn't work for straight people,'" one gay lawyer comments. "But now I say we should care: They have the privilege of divorce and we don't. We're left out there to twirl around in pain."[24]

Less obvious or familiar, however, are cogent arguments in favor of gay marriage that some feminist and other critical gay legal theorists have developed in response to opposition within the gay community. Nan Hunter, for example, rejects feminist legal colleague Nancy Polikoff's belief that marriage is an unalterably sexist and heterosexist institution. Building upon critical theories that reject the notion that social institutions or categories have inherent, fixed meanings apart from their social contexts, Hunter argues that legalized same-sex marriage would have "enormous potential to destabilize the gendered definition of marriage for everyone."[25]

Evan Wolfson, director of the Marriage Project of the gay legal rights organization Lambda Legal Defense, who has submitted a brief in support of

Baehr, pursues the logic of "anti-essentialism" even more consistently. The institution of marriage is neither inherently equal nor unequal, he argues, but depends upon an everchanging cultural and political context.[26] (Anyone who doubts this need only consider such examples as polygamy, arranged marriages, or the same-sex unions in early Western history documented by the late Princeton historian, John Boswell.) Hoping to use marriage precisely to change its context, gay philosopher Richard Mohr argues that access to legal marriage would provide an opportunity to reconstruct its meaning by serving "as a nurturing ground for social marriage, and not (as now) as that which legally defines and creates marriage and so precludes legal examination of it." For Mohr, social marriage represents "the fused intersection of love's sanctity and necessity's demands," and does not necessarily depend upon sexual monogamy.[27]

Support for gay marriage, not long ago anathema to radicals and conservatives, gays and nongays, alike, now issues forth from ethical and political perspectives as diverse, and even incompatible, as these. The cultural and political context has changed so dramatically since Stonewall that it now seems easier to understand why marriage has come to enjoy overwhelming support in the gay community than to grasp the depth of resistance to the institution that characterized the early movement. Still, I take seriously many of the strategic concerns about the costly political risks posed by a premature campaign. Although surveys and electoral struggles suggest a gradual growth in public support for gay rights, that support is tepid, uneven and fickle, as the debacle over Clinton's attempt to combat legal exclusion of gays from the military made distressingly clear. Thus, while 52 percent of those surveyed in a 1994 *Time* magazine/CNN poll claimed to consider gay lifestyle acceptable, 64 percent did not want to legalize gay marriages or to permit gay couples to adopt children.[28]

Gay marriage, despite its apparent compatibility with mainstream family values sentiment, raises far more threatening questions than does military service about gender relations, sexuality and family life. Few contemporary politicians, irrespective of their personal convictions, display the courage to confront this contradiction, even when urged to do so by gay conservatives. In *Virtually Normal: An Argument about Homosexuality, New Republic* editor Andrew Sullivan develops the "conservative case for gay marriage," that he earlier published as an op-ed, which stresses the contribution gay marriage could make to a conservative agenda for family and political life. A review of Sullivan's book in the *New Yorker* points out that, "here is where the advocates of gay rights can steal the conservatives' clothes."[29] The epigraph to this [article] by Jonathan Rauch about the insignificance of the homosexual minority comes from a *Wall Street Journal* op-ed he wrote to persuade Republicans that they should support legal gay marriage, not only because it is consistent with conservative values, but to guard against the possibility that gay rights advocates will exploit the party's inconsistency on this issue to political advantage.[30]

The logic behind the conservative case for gay marriage strikes me as compelling. Most importantly, gay marriage would strengthen the ranks of those endangered two-parent, "intact," married-couples families whose praises conservative, "profamily" enthusiasts never seem to tire of singing. Unsurprisingly, however, the case has won few nongay conservative converts to the cause. After all, homophobia is a matter of passion and politics, not logic. The religious right regards homosexuality as an abomination, and it has effectively consolidated its influence over the Republican Party. For example, in 1994, Republicans in the Montana state senate went so far as to pass a bill that would require anyone convicted of homosexual acts to register for life as a violent offender. They reversed their vote in response to an outpouring of public outrage.[31] It was not long afterward, however, that Republican presidential contender Robert Dole returned the thousand-dollar campaign contribution from the gay Log Cabin Republicans in the name, of course, of family values. Nor have figures prominent in the centrist, secular neo-family-values campaign or the communitarian movement, whose professed values affirm both communal support for marital commitment and for tolerance, displayed much concern for such consistency.[32] And even when, in the 1995 fall preelection season, President Clinton sought to "shore up" his standing among gays and lesbians by announcing his administration's support of a bill to outlaw employment discrimination against gays, he specifically withheld his support from gay marriage.[33] First Lady Hillary Rodham Clinton's [1996] book, *It Takes a Village*, ostensibly written to challenge "false nostalgia for family values," fails even to mention gay marriage or gay families, let alone to advocate village rights and resources for children whose parents are gay.[34]

Despite my personal political baptism in the heady, anti-family crucible of early second wave feminism, I, for one, have converted to the long-term cause. A "postmodern" ideological stew of discordant convictions enticed me to this table. Like Wolfson, Mohr, and Hunter, I have come to believe that legitimizing gay and lesbian marriages would promote a democratic, pluralistic expansion of the meaning, practice, and politics of family life in the United States. This could help to supplant the destructive sanctity of the *family* with respect for diverse and vibrant *families*.

To begin with, the liberal implications of legal gay marriage are far from trivial, as the current rush by the states and Congress to nullify them should confirm. The Supreme Court is certain to have its docket flooded far into the next century with constitutional conflicts that a favorable decision in Hawaii, or elsewhere, will unleash. Under the "full faith and credit" provision of the Constitution, which requires the 50 states to recognize each other's laws, legal gay marriage in one state could begin to threaten anti-sodomy laws in all the others. Policing marital sex would be difficult to legitimate, and differential prosecution of conjugal sex among same-sex couples could violate equal protection legislation. Likewise, if gay marriages were legalized, the myriad state barriers to child custody, adoption, fertility services, inheritance, and other family rights that lesbians and gay men currently suffer could also become subject to legal challenge. Moreover, it seems hard to overestimate the profound cultural implications for the struggle against the pernicious effects of legally condoned homophobia that would ensue were lesbian and gay relationships to be admitted into the ranks of legitimate kinship. In a society that forbids most public school teachers and counselors even the merest expression of tolerance for homosexuality, while lesbian and gay youth attempt suicide at rates three to five times greater than other youth,[35] granting full recognition to even just whitebread lesbian and gay relationships could have dramatic, and salutary, consequences.

Of course, considerations truer to some of my earlier, more visionary feminist convictions also invite me to join the gay wedding procession. For while I share some of Polikoff's disbelief that same-sex marriage can in itself dismantle the patterned gender and sexual injustices of the institution, I do believe it could make a potent contribution to those projects. . . . Moreover, as Mohr suggests, admitting gays to the wedding banquet invites gays and nongays alike to consider the kinds of place settings that could best accommodate the diverse needs of all contemporary families.

Subjecting the conjugal institution to this sort of heightened democratic scrutiny could help it to assume varied creative forms. If we begin to value the meaning and quality of intimate bonds over their customary forms, there are few limits to the kinds of marriage and kinship patterns people might wish to devise. The "companionate marriage," a much celebrated, but less often realized, ideal of modern sociological lore, could take on new life. Two friends might decide to marry without basing their bond on erotic or romantic attachment, as Dorthe, a prominent Danish lesbian activist who had initially opposed the campaign for gay marriage, fantasized after her nation's parliament approved gay registered partnerships: "If I am going to marry, it will be with one of my oldest friends in order to share pensions and things like that. But I'd never marry a lover. That is the advantage of being married to a close friend. Then, you never have to marry a lover!"[36] Or, more radical still, perhaps some might dare to question the dyadic limitations of Western marriage and seek some of the benefits of extended family life through small-group marriages arranged to share resources, nurturance and labor. After all, if it is true that "The Two-Parent Family Is Better"[37] than a single-parent family, as family-values crusaders like David Popenoe tirelessly proclaim, might not three-, four-, or more-parent families be better yet, as many utopian communards have long believed?

While conservative advocates of gay marriage surely would balk at such radical visions, they correctly realize that putative champions of committed relationships and of two-parent families who oppose gay marriage can be charged with gross hypocrisy on this score. For access to legal marriage not only would promote long-term, committed intimacy among gay couples, but also would afford invaluable protection to the children of gay parents, as well as indirect protection to closeted gay youth who reside with nongay parents. Clearly, only through a process of massive denial of the fact that millions of children living in gay and lesbian families are here, and here to stay, can anyone genuinely concerned with the best interests of children deny their parents the right to marry.

In the face of arguments for legalizing gay marriage as compelling and incongruent as these, it is hard to dispute Evan Wolfson's enthusiastic claim that "the brilliance of our movement's taking on marriage is that marriage is, at once and truly, both conservative and transformative, easily understood in basic human terms of equality and respect, and liberating in its individual and social potential." [38]

ENDNOTES

Epigraph Sources: Buchanan quoted in Susan Yoachum and David Tuller, "Right Makes Might in Iowa," *San Francisco Chronicle,* February 12, 1996: A1, 11; Rauch (see bibliographic entry); Bonnie Tinker, "Love Makes a Family," Presentation to 1995 United Nations International Women's Conference, Beijing, September 14.

[1] The estimate that at least six million children were living with a gay parent by 1985 appeared in Schulenberg, *Gay Parenting,* and has been accepted or revised upward by most scholars since then. See, for example, Bozett, *Gay and Lesbian Parents,* 39; Patterson, "Children of Lesbian and Gay Parents"; Allen and Demo, "The Families of Lesbians and Gay Men: A New Frontier in Family Research."

[2] Burke, *Family Values: A Lesbian Mother's Fight for Her Son.*

[3] Goldberg, "Virtual Marriages for Same-Sex Couples."

[4] Many gay activist groups and scholars, however, have begun to reclaim the term "queer" as a badge of pride, in much the same way that the Black power movement of the 1960s reclaimed the formerly derogatory term of blacks.

[5] Reagan and Schlafly both have gay sons, Powell has a lesbian daughter, and Gingrich has a lesbian half-sister.

[6] For a sensitive discussion of the definitional difficulties involved in research on gay and lesbian families, see Allen and Demo, "Families of Lesbians and Gay Men," 112–13.

[7] Most gay and lesbian scholars and activists reject the term "homosexual" because it originated within a medical model that classified homosexuality as a sexual perversion or disease and because the term emphasizes sexuality as at the core of the individual's identity. In this [article], I follow the generally preferred contemporary practice of using the terms "lesbians" and "gay men," but I also occasionally employ the term "gay" generically to include both women and men. I also play with the multiple, and currently shifting, meanings of the term "queer," by specifying whether I am using the term in its older pejorative sense, in its newer sense of proudly challenging fixed notions of gender and sexuality, or in its more colloquial sense of simply "odd."

[8] Quoted in Sherman, ed., *Lesbian and Gay Marriage,* 191.

[9] Ibid., 173.

[10] Bozett, epilogue to *Gay and Lesbian Parents,* 232.

[11] Cited in Sherman, *Lesbian and Gay Marriage*, 9, fn 6. A more recent poll conducted by *The Advocate* suggests that the trend of support for gay marriage is increasing. See Wolfson, "Crossing the Threshold," 583.

[12] Terry announced his plans January 24, 1996, on "Randall Terry Live," and LaHaye made her pitch the next day, January 25, 1996, on "Beverly LaHaye Live."

[13] Dunlap, "Some States Trying to Stop Gay Marriages Before They Start," A18; Dunlap, "Fearing a Toehold for Gay Marriage, Conservative Rush to Bar the Door," A7. Lockhead, "GOP Bill Targets Same-Sex Marriages," *San Francisco Chronicle*, May 9, 1996, A1, 15.

[14] Ibid., A1.

[15] Press Briefing by Mike McCurry, White House, May 14, 1996, Office of the Press Secretary.

[16] "Vatican Denounces Gay-Marriage Idea," *New York Times*, March 29, 1996, A8.

[17] Dunlap, "Reform Rabbis Vote to Back Gay Marriage," A8.

[18] "The Freedom to Marry," *New York Times*, April 7, 1996, Editorials/Letters, p. 10.

[19] The decision stated that the sexual orientation of the parties was irrelevant, because same-sex spouses could be of any sexual orientation. It was the gender discrimination involved in limiting one's choice of spouse that violated the state constitution. See Wolfson, "Crossing the Threshold," 573.

[20] Polikoff, "We Will Get What We Ask For: Why Legalizing Gay and Lesbian Marriage Will Not 'Dismantle the Legal Structure of Gender in Every Marriage.'"

[21] Law Professor Thomas Coleman, who is executive director of the "Family Diversity Project" in California, expresses these views in Sherman, 128–29.

[22] Sullivan, "A (Conservative) Case for Gay Marriage"; Rauch, "A Pro-Gay, Pro-Family Policy."

[23] Tede Matthews in Sherman, 57.

[24] Kirk Johnson quoted in Wolfson, 567.

[25] Hunter, "Marriage, Law, and Gender," 12.

[26] Wolfson, "Crossing the Threshold."

[27] Mohr, *A More Perfect Union*, 48, 41, 50.

[28] "Some Progress Found in Poll on Gay Rights," *San Francisco Chronicle*, June 20, 1994.

[29] Ryan, "No Easy Way Out," 90. Sullivan, "Here Comes the Groom."

[30] Rauch, "Pro-Gay, Pro-Family Policy."

[31] Herscher, "After Reconsidering, Montana Junks Gay Sex Bill," A2.

[32] See chap. 3, pp. 69–71, of Stacey, *In the Name of the Family: Rethinking Family Values in the Postmodern Age* (Boston: Beacon Press, 1996).

[33] Clinton, according to his senior adviser George Stephanopoulos, "thinks the proper role for the government is to work on the fight against discrimination, but he does not believe we should support (gay) marriage." Quoted in Sandalow and Tuller, "White House Tells Gays It Backs Them," A2.

[34] Clinton, *It Takes a Village*, book jacket copy.

[35] Remafedi, *Death by Denial*.

[36] Quoted in Miller, *Out in the World*, 350.

[37] This is the title and central argument of Popenoe's *New York Times* op-ed discussed above .

[38] Wolfson, "Crossing the Threshold," 599.

REFERENCES

Allen, Katherine R. and David H. Demo. 1995. "The Families of Lesbians and Gay Men: A New Frontier in Family Research." *Journal of Marriage and the Family* 57 (February): 111–27.

Bozett, Frederick W., ed. 1987. *Gay and Lesbian Parents.* New York: Praeger.

Burke, Phyllis. 1993. *Family Values: A Lesbian Mother's Fight for Her Son.* New York: Random House.

Clinton, Hillary Rodham. 1996. *It Takes a Village: And Other Lessons Children Teach Us.* New York: Simon & Schuster.

Dunlap, David W. 1995. "Some States Trying to Stop Gay Marriages Before They Start," *New York Times,* March 15, p. A18.

Goldberg, Carey. 1996. "Virtual Marriages for Same-Sex Couples." *New York Times,* March 26, p. A8.

Herscher, Elaine. 1995. "After Reconsidering, Montana Junks Gay Sex Bill," *San Francisco Chronicle,* March 24.

Hunter, Nan D. 1991. "Marriage, Law, and Gender: A Feminist Inquiry." *Law & Sexuality* 1(1):9–30.

Miller, Neil. 1992. *Out in the World: Gay and Lesbian Life from Buenos Aires to Bangkok.* New York: Random House.

Mohr, Richard. 1994. *A More Perfect Union: Why Straight America Must Stand Up for Gay Rights.* Boston: Beacon.

Patterson, Charlotte J. 1992. "Children of Lesbian and Gay Parents." *Child Development* 63:1025–42.

Polikoff, Nancy. 1993. "We Will Get What We Ask For: Why Legalizing Gay and Lesbian Marriage Will Not 'Dismantle the Legal Structure of Gender in Every Marriage,'" *Virginia Law Review* 79:1549–50.

Popenoe, David. 1992. "The Controversial Truth: The Two-Parent Family Is Better." *New York Times,* December 26, p. 13.

Rauch, Jonathan. 1994. "A Pro-Gay, Pro-Family Policy." *Wall Street Journal,* November 29, p. A22.

Remafedi, Gary. 1994. *Death by Denial.* Boston: Alyson Publications.

Ryan, Alan, ed. 1995. "No Easy Way Out." *New Yorker,* September 11, 90.

Sandalow, Marc and David Tuller. 1995. "White House Tells Gays It Backs Them." *San Francisco Chronicle,* October 21, p. A2.

Schulenberg, Joy, 1985. *Gay Parenting: A Complete Guide for Gay Men and Lesbians with Children.* New York: Anchor Books.

Sherman, Suzanne, ed. 1992. *Lesbian and Gay Marriage: Private Commitments, Public Ceremonies.* Philadelphia: Temple University Press.

Sullivan, Andrew. 1989. "Here Comes the Groom: A (Conservative) Case for Gay Marriage." *New Republic* 201(9):20–21.

Wolfson, Evan. 1994–95. "Crossing the Threshold: Equal Marriage Rights for Lesbians and Gay Men and the Intra-Community Critique." *Review of Law & Social Change* 21:3.

54

THE MOMMY TAX

ANN CRITTENDEN

In this selection, taken from *The Price of Motherhood: Why the Most Important Job in the World Is Still the Least Valued* (2001), Ann Crittenden observes how motherhood is very costly for women in the United States. Crittenden, a former reporter for the *New York Times,* states that women who decide to take time off from paid work to have and raise children pay a "mommy tax" of literally thousands of dollars every year. The amount of income women are penalized for childbearing varies by age and profession, but the overall amount working mothers are losing is staggering. Crittenden's research reveals that the institution of the family is not only gendered, but it is an institution that suffers because of economic forms of gender discrimination against women and mothers.

In the U.S. we have no way to address women's economic disadvantages except through the concept of gender. We see the problem as discrimination on the basis of gender. But what's really going on is a disadvantaging of *mothers* in the workforce.

—SUSAN PEDERSON, HISTORIAN

On April 7, 1999, the Independent Women's Forum, a conservative antifeminist organization, held a news conference at the National Press Club in Washington, D.C. Displayed in the corner of the room was a large green "check," made out to feminists, for ninety-eight cents. The point being made was that American women now make ninety-eight cents to a man's dollar and have therefore achieved complete equality in the workplace.

The sheer nerve of this little exercise in misinformation was astonishing. Upon closer examination, it turned out that the women who earn almost as much as men are a rather narrow group: those who are between the ages of twenty-seven and thirty-three and who have never had children.[1] The Independent Women's Forum was comparing young childless women to men and declaring victory for all women, glossing over the real news: that mothers are the most disadvantaged people in the workplace. One could even say that motherhood is now the single greatest obstacle left in the path to economic equality for women.

For most companies, the ideal worker is "unencumbered," that is, free of all ties other than those to his job. Anyone who can't devote all his or her energies to paid work is barred from the best jobs and has a permanently lower lifetime income. Not coincidentally, almost all the people in that category happen to be mothers.

The reduced earnings of mothers are, in effect, a heavy personal tax levied on people who care for children, or for any other dependent family members. This levy, a "mommy tax," is easily greater than $1 million in the case of a college-educated woman.[2] For working-class women, there is increasing evidence both in the United States and worldwide that mothers' differential responsibility for children, rather than classic sex discrimination, is the most important factor disposing women to poverty.[3]

"This is the issue that women's and children's advocates should be raising," argues Jane Waldfogel, a professor at Columbia University School of Social Work. "Women's equality is not about equal access to education or equal job opportunities anymore—those things are done. The part that's left is the part that has to do with family responsibilities."[4]

The much-publicized earnings gap between men and women narrowed dramatically in the 1980s and early 1990s. All a girl had to do was stay young and unencumbered. The sexual egalitarianism evident in so many television sit-coms, from *Friends* to *Seinfeld* to *Ally McBeal*, is rooted in economic reality. Young women don't need a man to pay their bills or take them out, any more than men need a woman to iron their shirts or cook their dinner. Many childless women under the age of thirty-five firmly believe that all of the feminist battles have been won, and as far as they're concerned, they're largely right.

But once a woman has a baby, the egalitarian office party is over. I ought to know.

Million-Dollar Babies

After my son was born in 1982, I decided to leave the *New York Times* in order to have more time to be a mother. I recently calculated what that decision cost me financially.

I had worked full-time for approximately twenty years, eight of those at the *Times*. When I left, I had a yearly salary of roughly $50,000, augmented by speaking fees, freelance income, and journalism awards. Had I not had a child, I probably would have worked at least another fifteen years, maybe taking early retirement to pursue other interests. Under this scenario, I would have earned a pension, which I lost by leaving the paper before I had worked the requisite ten years to become vested. (The law has since changed to allow vesting after five years with one employer.)

My annual income after leaving the paper has averaged roughly $15,000, from part-time freelance writing. Very conservatively, I lost between $600,000 and $700,000, not counting the loss of a pension. Without quite realizing what I was doing, I took what I thought would be a relatively short break, assuming it would be easy to get back into journalism after a few years, or to earn a decent income from books and other projects. I was wrong. As it turned out, I sacrificed more than half of my expected lifetime earnings. And in the boom years of the stock market, that money invested in equities would have multiplied like kudzu. As a conservative estimate, it could have generated $50,000 or $60,000 a year in income for my old age.

At the time, I never sat down and made these economic calculations. I never even thought about money in connection with motherhood, or if I did, I assumed my husband would provide all we needed. And had I been asked to weigh my son's childhood against ten or fifteen more years at the *Times,* I doubt whether the monetary loss would have tipped the scales. But still, this seems a high price to pay for doing the right thing.

The mommy tax I paid is fairly typical for an educated middle-class American woman. Economist Shirley Burggraf has calculated that a husband and wife who earn a combined income of $81,500 per year and who are equally capable will lose $1.35 million if they have a child. Most of that lost income is the wages forgone by the primary parent.[5] In a middle-income family, with one parent earning $30,000 per year as a sales representative and the other averaging $15,000 as a part-time computer consultant, the mommy tax will still be more than $600,000. Again, this seems an unreasonable penalty on the decision to raise a child, a decision that contributes to the general good by adding another productive person to the nation.

In lower-income families, the mommy tax can push a couple over the brink. Martha F. Richie, a former director of the U.S. Census Bureau, told me, "There is anecdotal evidence—no real research—that for a lower-earning married couple the decision to have a child, or a second child, throws them into poverty."[6]

Those who care for elderly relatives also discover that their altruism will be heavily penalized. A small survey of individuals who provided informal, unpaid care for family members found that it cost them an average of $659,139 in lost wages, Social Security, and pension benefits over their lifetimes. The subjects reported having to pass up promotions and training opportunities, use up their sick days and vacations, reduce their workload to part-time, and in many cases even quit their paid jobs altogether. This exorbitant "caring tax" is being paid by an increasing number of people, three-quarters of them women. A 1997 study discovered that one in four families had at least one adult who had provided care for an elderly relative or friend.[7]

The mommy tax is obviously highest for well-educated, high-income individuals and lowest for poorly educated people who have less potential income to lose. All else being equal, the younger the mother, and the more children she has, the higher her tax will be, which explains why women are having fewer children, later in life, almost everywhere.

The tax is highest in the Anglo-Saxon countries, where mothers personally bear almost all the costs of caring, and lowest in France and Scandinavia, where paid maternity leaves and public preschools make it easier for mothers to provide care without sacrificing their income. . . .

Sixty Cents to a Man's Dollar

In the Bible, in Leviticus, God instructs Moses to tell the Israelites that women, for purposes of tithing, are worth thirty shekels while men are worth fifty—a ratio of 60 percent.[8] For fifty years, from about 1930 to 1980, the value of employed women eerily reflected that biblical ratio: The earnings of full-time working women were only 60 percent of men's earnings. In the 1980s, that ratio began to change. By 1993, women working full-time were earning an average of seventy-seven cents for every dollar men earned. (In 1997, the gap widened again, as the median weekly earnings of full-time working women fell to 75 percent of men's earnings.)

But lo and behold, when we look closer, we find the same old sixty cents to a man's dollar. The usual way to measure the gender wage gap is by comparing the hourly earnings of men and women who work full-time year-round. But this compares only the women who work like men with men—a method that neatly excludes most women. As we have seen, only about half of the mothers of children under eighteen have full-time, year-round paying jobs.[9]

To find the real difference between men's and women's earnings, one would have to compare the earnings of all male and female workers, both full- and part-time. And guess what one discovers? The average earnings of *all* female workers in 1999 were 59 percent of men's earnings.[10] Women who work for pay are still stuck at the age-old biblical value put on their labor.

My research turned up other intriguing reflections of the 60 percent ratio: A survey of 1982 graduates of the Stanford Business School found that ten years after graduation, the median income of the full- and part-time employed female M.B.A.s amounted to $81,300, against the men's median income of $139,100. Again, the women's share is 58 percent. Another study, of 1974 graduates of the University of Michigan Law School, revealed that in the late 1980s the women's average earnings were 61 percent of the men's—despite the fact that 96 percent of the women were working, and that the men and women were virtually identical in terms of training. The authors of this study concluded that the women's family responsibilities were "certainly the most important single cause of sex differences in earnings."[11] . . .

The Cost of Being a Mother

A small group of mostly female academic economists has added another twist to the story. Their research reveals that working mothers not only earn less than men, but also less per hour than childless women, even after such differences as education and experience are factored out. The pay gap between mothers and nonmothers under age thirty-five is now larger than the wage gap between young men and women. . . .

Why do working mothers earn so much less than childless women? Academic researchers have worried over this question like a dog over a bone but haven't turned up a single, definitive answer.[12]

Waldfogel argues that the failure of employers to provide paid maternity leaves is one factor that leads to the family wage gap in the United States. This country is one of only six nations in the world that does not require a paid leave. (The others are Australia, New Zealand, Lesotho, Swaziland, and Papua New Guinea.[13]) With no right to a paid leave, many American mothers who want to stay at home with a new baby simply quit their jobs, and this interruption in employment costs them dearly in terms of lost income. Research in Europe reveals that when paid maternity leaves were mandated, the percentage of women remaining employed rose, and women's wages were higher, unless the leaves lasted more than a few months.[14]

In the United States as well, women who are able to take formal paid maternity leave do not suffer the same setback in their wages as comparably placed women who do not have a right to such leaves. This is a significant benefit to mothers in the five states, including California, New York, and New Jersey, that mandate temporary disability insurance coverage for pregnancy and childbirth.[15]

Paid leaves are so valuable because they don't seem to incur the same penalties that employers impose on even the briefest of unpaid career interruptions. A good example is the experience of the 1974 female graduates of the University of Michigan Law School. During their first fifteen years after law school, these women spent an average of only 3.3 months out of the workplace, compared with virtually no time out for their male classmates. More than one-quarter of the women had worked part-time, for an average of 10.1 months over the fifteen years, compared with virtually no part-time work among the men. While working full-time, the women put in only 10 percent fewer hours than full-time men, again not a dramatic difference.

But the penalties for these slight distinctions between the men's and women's work patterns were strikingly harsh. Fifteen years after graduation, the women's average earnings were not 10 percent lower, or even 20 percent lower, than the men's, but almost 40 percent lower. Fewer than one-fifth of the women in law firms who had worked part-time for more than six months had made partner in their firms, while more than four-fifths of the mothers with little or no part-time work had made partner.[16]

Another survey of almost 200 female M.B.A.s found that those who had taken an average of only 8.8 months out of the job market were less likely to reach upper-middle management and earned 17 percent less than comparable women who had never had a gap in their employment.[17]

Working-class women are also heavily penalized for job interruptions, although these are the very women who allegedly "choose" less demanding occupations that enable them to move in and out of the job market without undue wage penalties. The authors of one study concluded that the negative repercussions of taking a little time out of the labor force were still discernible after twenty years.[18] In blue-collar work, seniority decides who is eligible for better jobs, and who is "bumped" in the event of layoffs. Under current policies, many women lose their seniority forever if they interrupt their employment, as most mothers do. Training programs, required for advancement, often take place after work, excluding the many mothers who can't find child care.[19]

Mandatory overtime is another handicap placed on blue-collar mothers. Some 45 percent of American workers reported in a recent survey that they had to work overtime with little or no notice.[20] In 1994 factory workers put in the highest levels of overtime ever reported by the Bureau of Labor Statistics in its thirty-eight years of tracking the data. Where does that leave a woman who has to be home in time for dinner with the kids? Out of a promotion and maybe out of a job. Increasingly in today's driven workplace, whether she is blue- or white-collar, a woman who goes home when she is supposed to go home is going to endanger her economic well-being.

The fact that many mothers work part-time also explains some of the difference between mothers' and comparable women's hourly pay. (About 65 percent of part-time workers are women, most of whom are mothers.[21] Employers are not required to offer part-time employees equal pay and benefits for equal work. As a result, nonstandard workers earn on average about 40 percent less an hour than full-time workers, and about half of that wage gap persists even for similar workers in similar jobs.

Many bosses privately believe that mothers who work part-time have a "recreational" attitude toward work, as one Maryland businessman assured me. Presumably, this belief makes it easier to justify their exploitation. But the working conditions they face don't sound very much like recreation. A recent survey by Catalyst, a research organization focused on women in business, found that more than half of the people who had switched to part-time jobs and lower pay reported that their workload stayed the same. Ten percent reported an increase in workload after their income had been reduced. Most of these people were mothers.[22]

Another factor in the family wage gap is the disproportionate number of mothers who operate their own small businesses, a route often taken by women who need flexibility during the child-rearing years. Female-owned small businesses have increased twofold over small businesses owned by men in recent years.[23] In 1999, women owned 38 percent of all U.S. businesses, compared with only 5 percent in 1972, a remarkable increase that is frequently cited as evidence of women's economic success. One new mother noted that conversations at play groups "center as much on software and modems as they do on teething and ear infections."[24]

Less frequently mentioned is the fact that many of these women-owned businesses are little more than Mom-minus-Pop operations: one woman trying to earn some money on the side, or keep her career alive, during the years when her children have priority. Forty-five percent of women-owned businesses are home-based. And the more than one-third of businesses owned by women in 1996 generated only 16 percent of the sales of all U.S. businesses in that year.[25]

In 1997, although women were starting new businesses at twice the rate of men, they received only 2 percent of institutional venture capital, a principal source of financing for businesses with serious prospects for growth. Almost one-quarter of female business owners financed their operations the same way that they did their shopping: with their credit cards.[26]

Some researchers have suggested that mothers earn less than childless women because they are less productive. This may be true for some mothers who work at home and are subject to frequent interruptions, or for those who are exhausted from having to do most of the domestic chores, or distracted by creaky child-care arrangements. But the claim that mothers have lower productivity than other workers is controversial and unproven. It is easier to demonstrate that working mothers face the same old problem that has bedeviled women in the workplace for decades: [discrimination]. . . .

How to Lower the Mommy Tax

Until now, narrowing the gender wage gap in the United States has depended almost entirely on what might be called the "be a man" strategy. Women are told to finish school, find a job, acquire skills, develop seniority, get tenure, make partner, and put children off until the very last minute. The longer a woman postpones family responsibilities, and the longer her "preparental" phase lasts, the higher her lifetime earnings will be.

Ambitious women of the baby-boom generation and younger have by and large tried to be a man in this way. A good example is Susan Pedersen, a historian who achieved tenure at Harvard in the mid-1990s. By that time, she was married and in her late thirties, but she had postponed having children until her academic career was secure. Motherhood was something she wanted very much, she commented during an interview, but it posed a serious threat to her professional dreams and had to be delayed.[27]

As Pedersen's success demonstrates, this strategy does work—for the very small number who are able to pull it off. And women who have their children later in life do have higher lifetime earnings and a wider range of opportunities than younger mothers. The advice dished out by writers like Danielle Crittenden—no relation—an antifeminist ideologue who has urged women to marry and have their babies young, ignores this, along with some other hard truths. Crittenden never tells her readers that young parents tend to separate and divorce much more frequently than older couples, leaving young mothers and children vulnerable to poverty. Large numbers of the women who end up on welfare are there because they have done exactly what she recommends: married and had children young and then been left to support them alone.[28]

But trying to be a man has its own risks. Many baby-boomer women postponed families only to discover that when they wanted to become pregnant, it was too late. . . . And millions of women don't feel that being a man is the way they want to live their lives. Increasingly, young women are saying that they don't want to put off children until they almost qualify for membership in AARP.

An alternative strategy is followed in countries like France and Sweden, where the government, private employers, and/or husbands share much more of the costs of raising children. This makes it far easier for women to be mothers and to work. In France, for example, families with two preschool-age children receive about $10,000 worth of annual subsidies, including free health care and housing subsidies and excellent free preschools.[29] As a result, child poverty is unusual, and the pay gap between mothers and others is much smaller in France than in the United States or the United Kingdom.

Whenever Europe is singled out as a model, the usual response is that Americans would never support such generous social policies. But in fact, the United States already does have an extremely generous social welfare state. But unlike the welfare states of western Europe, the American government doesn't protect mothers; it protects soldiers.

Men who postpone or interrupt civilian employment for military service pay a tax on their lifetime earnings that is quite comparable to the mommy tax. White men who were drafted during the Vietnam War, for example, were still earning approximately 15 percent less in the early 1980s than comparable nonveterans.[30] This "warrior wage gap" is strikingly similar to the family wage gap, again indicating that mothers' lower earnings are not entirely attributable to gender discrimination.

But there is unquestionable discrimination in the way the government has responded to the financial sacrifices that soldiers and parents, particularly mothers, make. All Americans are asked to "make it up" to veterans of the military: The damage to a caregiver's pocketbook is unmitigated, while the damage to a veteran's wallet has legitimized a massive relief effort. . . .

The benefits paid to military veterans are so lavish that they are now second only to Social Security in terms of government payments to individuals. And they do an excellent job of reducing the warrior tax. The educational benefits in particular help veterans overcome many of the economic disadvantages they suffer by leaving the workplace for a few years.

A congressional study in the early 1990s concluded that the veterans of World War II who took advantage of the G.I. Bill to earn a college degree enjoyed incomes of up to 10 percent more than they might otherwise have earned. Society was also the beneficiary, for the additional taxes paid by the college-educated veterans during their working lives more than paid for the program.[31]

It hardly needs to be said that there is no G.I. Bill, no health care, no sub-sidized housing, and no job preferences for mothers. As things now stand, millions of women sacrifice their economic independence and risk economic disaster for the sake of raising a child. This says a lot about family values, the nation's priorities, and free riding.

A third way to reduce the mommy tax would be to expand the antidis-crimination laws to cover parents. Joan Williams, a law professor at Ameri-can University's Washington College of Law, argues that the design of work around masculine norms can be reconceptualized as discrimination. As an example, Williams suggests that if a woman works full-time, with good job evaluations for a significant period, then switches to part-time because of family responsibilities and is paid less per hour than full-time employees do-ing similar work, she could claim discrimination under the Equal Pay Act. Williams believes that disparate-action suits could also be filed against em-ployers whose policies (including routine and mandatory overtime, promo-tion tracks, resistance to part-time work) have a disparate impact on women, producing disproportionate numbers of men in top-level positions.[32]

The essential point is that existing laws, and new laws preventing dis-crimination against people with caregiving responsibilities, could go a very long way toward improving mothers' lifetime earnings.

The Ultimate Mommy Tax: Childlessness

The cost of children has become so high that many American women are not having children at all. One of the most striking findings of Claudia Goldin's survey of white female college graduates is their high degree of childlessness (28 percent). Now that the baby-boomer generation is middle-aged, it is clear that more than one-quarter of the educated women in that age group will never have children. Indeed, the percentage of all American women who re-main childless is also steadily rising, from 8 to 9 percent in the 1950s to 10 per-cent in 1976 to 17.5 percent in the late 1990s.

Is this rising childlessness by choice? Goldin thinks not. She found that in 1978, while in their twenties, almost half of the college-educated boomers who would remain childless had said that they did want children. Goldin cal-culated that almost one-fifth of this entire generation (19 percent) of white college graduates was disappointed in not having a child. This is the ultimate price of the "be a man" strategy that has been forced on working women. For women in business, the price is staggering. A recent Catalyst survey of 1,600 M.B.A.s found that only about one-fifth of the women had children, com-pared with 70 percent of the men.[33]

Educated black women have had, if anything, an even harder time com-bining children with their careers. Many of the most accomplished black women now in their forties and fifties, including Oprah Winfrey, Anita Hill,

Eleanor Holmes Norton (the congressional representative for the District of Columbia), and Alexis Herman, secretary of labor in the Clinton administration, have forgone motherhood. These women apparently discovered that the price of success included the lack of parental obligations. And educated black women face an additional problem—an acute shortage of eligible black men.

Americans have a hard time realizing that such deeply personal choices as when or whether to have a child can be powerfully circumscribed by broader social or economic factors. American women, in particular, are stunningly unaware that their "choices" between a career and a family are much more limited than those of women in many European countries, where policies are much more favorable to mothers and children.

ENDNOTES

[1] This calculation was made by economist June O'Neill, using data from the National Longitudinal Survey of Youth. June O'Neill and Solomon Polachek, "Why the Gender Gap in Wages Narrowed in the 1980s," *Journal of Labor Economics* 11 (1993): 205–28. See also June O'Neill, "The Shrinking Pay Gap," *Wall Street Journal,* October 7, 1994.

[2] The concept of the mommy tax was inspired by development economist Gita Sen, who has described the extra economic burden borne by women as a "reproduction tax."

[3] I don't mean to suggest that old-fashioned sex discrimination, even against women who are able to perform as "ideal" workers, is not still alive and well, as numerous recent complaints, from the brokerage offices of Smith Barney to the machine shops of Mitsubishi, can attest. Simply being female still sentences women in virtually every occupation and at every level to lower earnings than men in similar positions. But overt in-your-face discrimination has thankfully declined steadily in recent decades.

[4] Jane Waldfogel, personal communication, October 1996.

[5] Burggraf assumes that the more flexible parent's earnings average $25,750 a year, versus $55,750 for the primary breadwinner. She then multiplies $30,000 (the difference between what the two parents earn) by 45 (the years in a working life-time) to get the $1.350 million. *The Feminine Economy and Economic Man,* p. 61.

[6] Martha Ritchie, personal communication, January 1995.

[7] Sara Rimer, "Study Details Sacrifices in Caring for Elderly Kin," *New York Times,* November 27, 1999. The National Alliance for Caregivers estimates that the number of employed people who provide care for elderly family members will grow to between 11 and 15.6 million in the first decade of the twenty-first century.

[8] Amity Shlaes, "What Does Woman Want?" *Women's Quarterly* (summer 1996): 10.

[9] According to June O'Neill, an economist and former head of the Congressional Budget Office, "Full-time year-round workers are not likely to be representative of all workers. Women are less likely to be in this category than men." See June O'Neill and Solomon Polachek, "Why the Gender Gap in Wages Narrowed in the 1980s," *Journal of Labor Economics* 2, no. 1, pt. 1 (1993): 208–9.

[10] U.S. Bureau of the Census, Current Population Reports, *Money Income in the U.S.: 1995,* Washington, D.C., March 2000, P60-209, pp. 46–49.

[11] Robert G. Wood, Mary E. Corcoran, and Paul N. Courant, "Pay Differentials Among the Highly-Paid: The Male-Female Earnings Gap in Lawyers' Salaries," *Journal of Labor Economics* 11, no. 3 (1993): 417–41.

[12] See Paula England and Michelle Budig, "The Effects of Motherhood on Wages in Recent Cohorts: Findings from the National Longitudinal Survey of Youth," unpublished paper, 1999.

[13] Elizabeth Olson, "U.N. Surveys Paid Leave for Mothers," *New York Times*, February 16, 1998.

[14] Christopher J. Ruhm, "The Economic Consequences of Parental Leave Mandates: Lessons from Europe," *Quarterly Journal of Economics* CXIII, no. 1 (1998): 285–317. Ruhm found that longer leaves (of nine months or more) were associated with a slight reduction in women's relative wages, but Waldfogel discovered that mothers in Britain who exercised their right to a ten-month paid maternity leave and returned to their original employer had wages no different from those of childless women.

[15] Heidi Hartmann, Institute for Women's Policy Research, personal communication, January 8, 1995. Hartmann's research has shown that fully 11 percent of women who have no paid leave have to go on public assistance during their time with a new baby.

[16] Wood, Corcoran, and Courant, "Pay Differentials," pp. 417–28.

[17] This 1993 study was coauthored by Joy Schneer of Rider University's College of Business Administration and Frieda Reitman, professor emeritus at Pace University's Lubin School of Business.

[18] Joyce Jacobsen and Arthur Levin, "The Effects of Intermittent Labor Force Attachment on Female Earnings," *Monthly Labor Review* 118, no. 9 (September 1995): 18.

[19] For a good discussion of the obstacles to mothers' employment in relatively well-paying blue-collar work, see Williams, *Unbending Gender*, pp. 76–81.

[20] This survey of 1,000 workers was conducted by researchers at the University of Connecticut and Rutgers University, and was reported in the *Wall Street Journal*, May 18, 1999.

[21] A survey of more than 2,000 people in four large corporations found that 75 percent of the professionals working part-time were women who were doing so because of child-care obligations. Only 11 percent of the male managers surveyed expected to work part-time at some point in their careers, compared with 36 percent of women managers. *A New Approach to Flexibility: Managing the Work/Time Equation* (New York: Catalyst, 1997), pp. 25–26.

[22] There is other evidence that many so-called part-timers are increasingly working what used to be considered full-time—thirty-five to forty hours a week—for lower hourly pay than regular full-timers. See Reed Abelson, "Part-Time Work for Some Adds Up to Full-Time Job," *New York Times*, November 2, 1998.

[23] In the five years from 1988 through 1992, the number of women-owned sole proprietorships, partnerships, and similar businesses soared 43 percent, compared with overall growth of 26 percent in such businesses. *Wall Street Journal*, January 29, 1996.

[24] Tracy Thompson, "A War Inside Your Head," *Washington Post Magazine*, February 15, 1998, p. 29.

[25] Information on women-owned businesses provided by the National Foundation for Women Business Owners in Washington, D.C., September 2000.

[26] Noelle Knox, "Women Entrepreneurs Attract New Financing," *New York Times*, July 26, 1998.

[27] Susan Pedersen, personal interview, June 1996.

[28] Being a young mother obviously worked for Crittenden, who was affluent enough to have purchased a $1.3-million home in Washington, D.C., while still in her mid-thirties. But not many mothers enjoy such options.

[29] Barbara Bergmann, personal conversation, January 4, 1999.

[30] Joshua D. Angrist, "Lifetime Earnings and the Vietnam Era Draft Lottery: Evidence from Social Security Administrative Records," *American Economic Review* 80, no. 3 (June 1990): 313–31.

[31] David O'Neill, "Voucher Funding of Training Programs: Evidence from the G.I. Bill," *Journal of Human Resources* 12, no. 4 (fall 1977): 425–45; and Joshua D. Angrist, "The Effects of Veterans' Benefits on Education and Earnings," *Industrial and Labor Relations Review* 46, no. 4 (July 1993): 637–57.

[32] Williams, *Unbending Gender,* pp. 101–10.

[33] The theory that much of the childlessness among educated American women is involuntary was supported by an informal class survey of the graduates of Harvard and Radcliffe class of 1971. Roughly one-fifth of both the men and the women were still childless in 1996, when the class was in its mid- to late forties. But many more women than men said they were childless because of "circumstances."

55

THE TIME BIND
When Work Becomes
Home and Home Becomes Work

ARLIE RUSSELL HOCHSCHILD

What are the relationships between work life and family life? How do individuals negotiate the role demands of both social institutions? Arlie Russell Hochschild, a professor of sociology at the University of California at Berkeley, investigates these questions in her three-year study of a large corporation, which she calls "Amerco." Hochschild interviewed 130 employees, including middle and upper management, clerks and factory workers, most of whom were working parents. Hochschild also talked with human resource specialists, psychologists, child-care workers, and homemakers who were married to Amerco employees. In this selection, adapted from her book *The Time Bind: When Work Becomes Home and Home Becomes Work* (1997),

---

Hochschild discusses her findings about the changing relationship between
work life and home life for many working parents.

It's 7:40 A.M. when Cassie Bell, 4, arrives at the Spotted Deer Child-Care
Center, her hair half-combed, a blanket in one hand, a fudge bar in the
other. "I'm late," her mother, Gwen, a sturdy young woman whose
short-cropped hair frames a pleasant face, explains to the child-care worker
in charge. "Cassie wanted the fudge bar so bad, I gave it to her," she adds
apologetically.

"*Pleeese,* can't you take me with you?" Cassie pleads.

"You know I can't take you to work," Gwen replies in a tone that suggests
that she has been expecting this request. Cassie's shoulders droop. But she
has struck a hard bargain—the morning fudge bar—aware of her mother's
anxiety about the long day that lies ahead at the center. As Gwen explains
later, she continually feels that she owes Cassie more time than she gives
her—she has a "time debt."

Arriving at her office just before 8, Gwen finds on her desk a cup of coffee in her personal mug, milk no sugar (exactly as she likes it), prepared by a
co-worker who managed to get in ahead of her. As the assistant to the head
of public relations at a company I will call Amerco, Gwen has to handle responses to any reports that may appear about the company in the press—a
challenging job, but one that gives her satisfaction. As she prepares for her
first meeting of the day, she misses her daughter, but she also feels relief;
there's a lot to get done at Amerco.

Gwen used to work a straight eight-hour day. But over the last three
years, her workday has gradually stretched to eight and a half or nine
hours, not counting the e-mail messages and faxes she answers from home.
She complains about her hours to her co-workers and listens to their complaints—but she loves her job. Gwen picks up Cassie at 5:45 and gives her a
long, affectionate hug.

At home, Gwen's husband, John, a computer programmer, plays with
their daughter while Gwen prepares dinner. To protect the dinner "hour"—
8:00–8:30—Gwen checks that the phone machine is on, hears the phone ring
during dinner but resists the urge to answer. After Cassie's bath, Gwen and
Cassie have "quality time," or "Q.T.," as John affectionately calls it. Half an
hour later, at 9:30, Gwen tucks Cassie into bed.

There are, in a sense, two Bell households: the rushed family they actually are and the relaxed family they imagine they might be if only they had
time. Gwen and John complain that they are in a time bind. What they say
they want seems so modest—time to throw a ball, to read to Cassie, to witness the small dramas of her development, not to speak of having a little fun
and romance themselves. Yet even these modest wishes seem strangely out
of reach. Before going to bed, Gwen has to e-mail messages to her colleagues

in preparation for the next day's meeting; John goes to bed early, exhausted—he's out the door by 7 every morning.

Nationwide, many working parents are in the same boat. More mothers of small children than ever now work outside the home. In 1993, 56 percent of women with children between 6 and 17 worked outside the home full time year-round; 43 percent of women with children 6 and under did the same. Meanwhile, fathers of small children are not cutting back hours of work to help out at home. If anything, they have increased their hours at work. According to a 1993 national survey conducted by the Families and Work Institute in New York, American men average 48.8 hours of work a week, and women 41.7 hours, including overtime and commuting. All in all, more women are on the economic train, and for many—men and women alike—that train is going faster.

But Amerco has "family-friendly" policies. If your division head and supervisor agree, you can work part time, share a job with another worker, work some hours at home, take parental leave or use "flex time." But hardly anyone uses these policies. In seven years, only two Amerco fathers have taken formal parental leave. Fewer than 1 percent have taken advantage of the opportunity to work part time. Of all such policies, only flex time—which rearranges but does not shorten work time—has had a significant number of takers (perhaps a third of working parents at Amerco).

Forgoing family-friendly policies is not exclusive to Amerco workers. A 1991 study of 188 companies conducted by the Families and Work Institute found that while a majority offered part-time shifts, fewer than 5 percent of employees made use of them. Thirty-five percent offered "flex place"—work from home—and fewer than 3 percent of their employees took advantage of it. And an earlier Bureau of Labor Statistics survey asked workers whether they preferred a shorter workweek, a longer one or their present schedule. About 62 percent preferred their present schedule; 28 percent would have preferred longer hours. Fewer than 10 percent said they wanted a cut in hours.

Still, I found it hard to believe that people didn't protest their long hours at work. So I contacted Bright Horizons, a company that runs 136 company-based child-care centers associated with corporations, hospitals and Federal agencies in 25 states. Bright Horizons allowed me to add questions to a questionnaire they sent out to 3,000 parents whose children attended the centers. The respondents, mainly middle-class parents in their early 30s, largely confirmed the picture I'd found at Amerco. A third of fathers and a fifth of mothers described themselves as "workaholic," and 1 out of 3 said their partners were.

To be sure, some parents have tried to shorten their hours. Twenty-one percent of the nation's women voluntarily work part time, as do 7 percent of men. A number of others make under-the-table arrangements that don't show up on surveys. But while working parents say they need more time at home, the main story of their lives does not center on a struggle to get it. Why?

Given the hours parents are working these days, why aren't they taking advantage of an opportunity to reduce their time at work?

The most widely held explanation is that working parents cannot afford to work shorter hours. Certainly this is true for many. But if money is the whole explanation, why would it be that at places like Amerco, the best-paid employees—upper-level managers and professionals—were the least interested in part-time work or job sharing, while clerical workers who earned less were more interested?

Similarly, if money were the answer, we would expect poorer new mothers to return to work more quickly after giving birth than rich mothers. But among working women nationwide, well-to-do new mothers are not much more likely to stay home after 13 weeks with a new baby than low-income new mothers. When asked what they look for in a job, only a third of respondents in a recent study said salary came first. Money is important, but by itself, money does not explain why many people don't want to cut back hours at work.

A second explanation goes that workers don't dare ask for time off because they are afraid it would make them vulnerable to layoffs. With recent downsizings at many large corporations, and with well-paying, secure jobs being replaced by lower-paying, insecure ones, it occurred to me that perhaps employees are "working scared." But when I asked Amerco employees whether they worked long hours for fear of getting on a layoff list, virtually everyone said no. Even among a particularly vulnerable group—factory workers who were laid off in the downturn of the early 1980s and were later rehired—most did not cite fear for their jobs as the only, or main, reason they worked overtime. For unionized workers, layoffs are assigned by seniority, and for nonunionized workers, layoffs are usually related to the profitability of the division a person works in, not to an individual work schedule.

Were workers uninformed about the company's family-friendly policies? No. Some even mentioned that they were proud to work for a company that offered such enlightened policies. Were rigid middle managers standing in the way of workers using these policies? Sometimes. But when I compared Amerco employees who worked for flexible managers with those who worked for rigid managers, I found that the flexible managers reported only a few more applicants than the rigid ones. The evidence, however counterintuitive, pointed to a paradox: workers at the company I studied weren't protesting the time bind. They were accommodating to it.

Why? I did not anticipate the conclusion I found myself coming to: namely, that work has become a form of "home" and home has become "work." The worlds of home and work have not begun to blur, as the conventional wisdom goes, but to reverse places. We are used to thinking that home is where most people feel the most appreciated, the most truly "themselves," the most secure, the most relaxed. We are used to thinking that work is where most people feel like "just a number" or "a cog in a machine." It is where they have to be "on," have to "act," where they are least secure and most harried.

But new management techniques so pervasive in corporate life have helped transform the workplace into a more appreciative, personal sort of social world. Meanwhile, at home the divorce rate has risen, and the emotional demands have become more baffling and complex. In addition to teething, tantrums and the normal developments of growing children, the needs of elderly parents are creating more tasks for the modern family—as are the blending, unblending, reblending of new stepparents, stepchildren, exes and former in-laws.

This idea began to dawn on me during one of my first interviews with an Amerco worker. Linda Avery, a friendly, 38-year-old mother, is a shift supervisor at an Amerco plant. When I meet her in the factory's coffee-break room over a couple of Cokes, she is wearing blue jeans and a pink jersey, her hair pulled back in a long, blond ponytail. Linda's husband, Bill, is a technician in the same plant. By working different shifts, they manage to share the care of their 2-year-old son and Linda's 16-year-old daughter from a previous marriage. "Bill works the 7 A.M. to 3 P.M. shift while I watch the baby," she explains. "Then I work the 3 P.M. to 11 P.M. shift and he watches the baby. My daughter works at Walgreen's after school."

Linda is working overtime, and so I begin by asking whether Amerco required the overtime or whether she volunteered for it. "Oh, I put in for it," she replies. I ask her whether, if finances and company policy permitted, she'd be interested in cutting back on the overtime. She takes off her safety glasses, rubs her face and, without answering my question, explains: "I get home, and the minute I turn the key, my daughter is right there. Granted, she needs somebody to talk to about her day. . . . The baby is still up. He should have been in bed two hours ago, and that upsets me. The dishes are piled in the sink. My daughter comes right up to the door and complains about anything her stepfather said or did, and she wants to talk about her job. My husband is in the other room hollering to my daughter, 'Tracy, I don't ever get any time to talk to your mother, because you're always monopolizing her time before I even get a chance!' They all come at me at once."

Linda's description of the urgency of demands and the unarbitrated quarrels that await her homecoming contrast with her account of arriving at her job as a shift supervisor: "I usually come to work early, just to get away from the house. When I arrive, people are there waiting. We sit, we talk, we joke. I let them know what's going on, who has to be where, what changes I've made for the shift that day. We sit and chitchat for 5 or 10 minutes. There's laughing, joking, fun."

For Linda, home has come to feel like work and work has come to feel a bit like home. Indeed, she feels she can get relief from the "work" of being at home only by going to the "home" of work. Why has her life at home come to seem like this? Linda explains it this way: "My husband's a great help watching our baby. But as far as doing housework or even taking the baby when I'm at home, no. He figures he works five days a week; he's not going to come home and clean. But he doesn't stop to think that I work seven days a week. Why should I have to come home and do the housework without help from anybody else? My husband and I have been through this over and over again. Even if he would just pick up from the kitchen table and stack the dishes for me, that would make a big difference. He does nothing. On his weekends off, he goes fishing. If I want any time off, I have to get a sitter. He'll help out if I'm not here, but the minute I am, all the work at home is mine."

With a light laugh, she continues: "So I take a lot of overtime. The more I get out of the house, the better I am. It's a terrible thing to say, but that's the way I feel."

When Bill feels the need for time off, to relax, to have fun, to feel free, he climbs in his truck and takes his free time without his family. Largely in response, Linda grabs what she also calls "free time"—at work. Neither Linda nor Bill Avery wants more time together at home, not as things are arranged now.

How do Linda and Bill Avery fit into the broader picture of American family and work life? Current research suggests that however hectic their lives, women who do paid work feel less depressed, think better of themselves and are more satisfied than women who stay at home. One study reported that women who work outside the home feel more valued at home than housewives do. Meanwhile, work is where many women feel like "good mothers." As Linda reflects: "I'm a good mom at home, but I'm a better mom at work. At home, I get into fights with Tracy. I want her to apply to a junior college, but she's not interested. At work, I think I'm better at seeing the other person's point of view."

Many workers feel more confident they could "get the job done" at work than at home. One study found that only 59 percent of workers feel their "performance" in the family is "good or unusually good," while 86 percent rank their performance on the job this way.

Forces at work and at home are simultaneously reinforcing this "reversal." This lure of work has been enhanced in recent years by the rise of company cultural engineering—in particular, the shift from Frederick Taylor's principles of scientific management to the Total Quality principles originally set out by W. Edwards Deming. Under the influence of a Taylorist world view, the manager's job was to coerce the worker's mind and body, not to appeal to the worker's heart. The Taylorized worker was de-skilled, replaceable and cheap, and as a consequence felt bored, demeaned and unappreciated.

Using modern participative management techniques, many companies now train workers to make their own work decisions, and then set before their newly "empowered" employees moral as well as financial incentives. At Amerco, the Total Quality worker is invited to feel recognized for job accomplishments. Amerco regularly strengthens the familylike ties of co-workers by holding "recognition ceremonies" honoring particular workers or self-managed production teams. Amerco employees speak of "belonging to the Amerco family," and proudly wear their "Total Quality" pins or "High Performance Team" T-shirts, symbols of their loyalty to the company and of its loyalty to them.

The company occasionally decorates a section of the factory and serves refreshments. The production teams, too, have regular get-togethers. In a New Age recasting of an old business slogan—"The Customer Is Always Right"—Amerco proposes that its workers "Value the Internal Customer." This means: Be as polite and considerate to co-workers inside the company as you would be to customers outside it. How many recognition ceremonies for competent performance are being offered at home? Who is valuing the internal customer there?

Amerco also tries to take on the role of a helpful relative with regard to employee problems at work and at home. The education-and-training division offers employees free courses (on company time) in "Dealing With Anger," "How to Give and Accept Criticism," "How to Cope With Difficult People."

At home, of course, people seldom receive anything like this much help on issues basic to family life. There, no courses are being offered on "Dealing With Your Child's Disappointment in You" or "How to Treat Your Spouse Like an Internal Customer."

If Total Quality calls for "re-skilling" the worker in an "enriched" job environment, technological developments have long been de-skilling parents at home. Over the centuries, store-bought goods have replaced homespun cloth, homemade soap and home-baked foods. Day care for children, retirement homes for the elderly, even psychotherapy are, in a way, commercial substitutes for jobs that a mother once did at home. Even family-generated entertainment has, to some extent, been replaced by television, video games and the VCR. I sometimes watched Amerco families sitting together after their dinners, mute but cozy, watching sitcoms in which television mothers, fathers and children related in an animated way to one another while the viewing family engaged in relational loafing.

The one "skill" still required of family members is the hardest one of all—the emotional work of forging, deepening or repairing family relationships. It takes time to develop this skill, and even then things can go awry. Family ties are complicated. People get hurt. Yet as broken homes become more common—and as the sense of belonging to a geographical community grows less and less secure in an age of mobility—the corporate world has created a sense of "neighborhood," of "feminine culture," of family at work. Life at work can be insecure; the company can fire workers. But workers aren't so secure at home, either. Many employees have been working for Amerco for 20 years but are on their second or third marriages or relationships. The shifting balance between these two "divorce rates" may be the most powerful reason why tired parents flee a world of unresolved quarrels and unwashed laundry for the orderliness, harmony and managed cheer of work. People are getting their "pink slips" at home.

Amerco workers have not only turned their offices into "home" and their homes into workplaces; many have also begun to "Taylorize" time at home, where families are succumbing to a cult of efficiency previously associated mainly with the office and factory. Meanwhile, work time, with its ever longer hours, has become more hospitable to sociability—periods of talking with friends on e-mail, patching up quarrels, gossiping. Within the long workday of many Amerco employees are great hidden pockets of inefficiency while, in the far smaller number of waking weekday hours at home, they are, despite themselves, forced to act increasingly time-conscious and efficient.

The Averys respond to their time bind at home by trying to value and protect "quality time." A concept unknown to their parents and grandparents, "quality time" has become a powerful symbol of the struggle against the growing pressures at home. It reflects the extent to which modern parents feel the flow of time to be running against them. The premise behind "quality time" is that the time we devote to relationships can somehow be separated from ordinary time. Relationships go on during quantity time, of course, but then we are only passively, not actively, wholeheartedly, specializing in our emotional ties. We aren't "on." Quality time at home becomes like an office appointment. You don't want to be caught "goofing off around the water cooler" when you are "at work."

Quality time holds out the hope that scheduling intense periods of togetherness can compensate for an overall loss of time in such a way that a relationship will suffer no loss of quality. But this is just another way of transferring the cult of efficiency from office to home. We must now get our relationships in good repair in less time. Instead of nine hours a day with a child, we declare ourselves capable of getting "the same result" with one intensely focused hour.

Parents now more commonly speak of time as if it is a threatened form of personal capital they have no choice but to manage and invest. What's new here is the spread into the home of a financial manager's attitude toward time. Working parents at Amerco owe what they think of as time debts at home. This is because they are, in a sense, inadvertently "Taylorizing" the house—speeding up the pace of home life as Taylor once tried to "scientifically" speed up the pace of factory life.

Advertisers of products aimed at women have recognized that this new reality provides an opportunity to sell products, and have turned the very pressure that threatens to explode the home into a positive attribute. Take, for example, an ad promoting Instant Quaker Oatmeal: it shows a smiling mother ready for the office in her square-shouldered suit, hugging her happy son. A caption reads: "Nicky is a very picky eater. With Instant Quaker Oatmeal, I can give him a terrific hot breakfast in just 90 seconds. And I don't have to spend any time coaxing him to eat it!" Here, the modern mother seems to have absorbed the lessons of Frederick Taylor as she presses for efficiency at home because she is in a hurry to get to work.

Part of modern parenthood seems to include coping with the resistance of real children who are not so eager to get their cereal so fast. Some parents try desperately not to appease their children with special gifts or smooth-talking promises about the future. But when time is scarce, even the best parents find themselves passing a system-wide familial speed-up along to the most vulnerable workers on the line. Parents are then obliged to try to control the damage done by a reversal of worlds. They monitor mealtime, homework time, bedtime, trying to cut out "wasted" time.

In response, children often protest the pace, the deadlines, the grand irrationality of "efficient" family life. Children dawdle. They refuse to leave places when it's time to leave. They insist on leaving places when it's not time to leave. Surely, this is part of the usual stop-and-go of childhood itself, but perhaps, too, it is the plea of children for more family time and more control over what time there is. This only adds to the feeling that life at home has become hard work.

Instead of trying to arrange shorter or more flexible work schedules, Amerco parents often avoid confronting the reality of the time bind. Some minimize their ideas about how much care a child, a partner or they themselves "really need." They make do with less time, less attention, less understanding and less support at home than they once imagined possible. They _emotionally downsize_ life. In essence, they deny the needs of family members, and they themselves become emotional ascetics. If they once "needed" time with each other, they are now increasingly "fine" without it.

Another way that working parents try to evade the time bind is to buy themselves out of it—an approach that puts women in particular at the heart of a contradiction. Like men, women absorb the work-family speed-up far more than they resist it; but unlike men, they still shoulder most of the workload at home. And women still represent in people's minds the heart and soul of family life. They're the ones—especially women of the urban middle and upper-middle classes—who feel most acutely the need to save time, who are the most tempted by the new "time saving" goods and services—and who wind up feeling the most guilty about it. For example, Playgroup Connections, a Washington-area business started by a former executive recruiter, matches playmates to one another. One mother hired the service to find her child a French-speaking playmate.

In several cities, children home alone can call a number for "Grandma, Please!" and reach an adult who has the time to talk with them, sing to them or help them with their homework. An ad for Kindercare Learning Centers, a for-profit child-care chain, pitches its appeal this way: "You want your child to be active, tolerant, smart, loved, emotionally stable, self-aware, artistic and get a two-hour nap. Anything else?" It goes on to note that Kindercare accepts children 6 weeks to 12 years old and provides a number to call for the

Kindercare nearest you. Another typical service organizes children's birthday parties, making out invitations ("sure hope you can come") and providing party favors, entertainment, a decorated cake and balloons. Creative Memories is a service that puts ancestral photos into family albums for you.

An overwhelming majority of the working mothers I spoke with recoiled from the idea of buying themselves out of parental duties. A bought birthday party was "too impersonal," a 90-second breakfast "too fast." Yet a surprising amount of lunchtime conversation between female friends at Amerco was devoted to expressing complex, conflicting feelings about the lure of trading time for one service or another. The temptation to order flash-frozen dinners or to call a local number for a homework helper did not come up because such services had not yet appeared at Spotted Deer Child-Care Center. But many women dwelled on the question of how to decide where a mother's job began and ended, especially with regard to baby-sitters and television. One mother said to another in the breakroom of an Amerco plant: "Damon doesn't settle down until 10 at night, so he hates me to wake him up in the morning and I hate to do it. He's cranky. He pulls the covers up. I put on cartoons. That way, I can dress him and he doesn't object. I don't like to use TV that way. It's like a drug. But I do it."

The other mother countered: "Well, Todd is up before we are, so that's not a problem. It's after dinner, when I feel like watching a little television, that I feel guilty, because he gets too much TV at the sitter's."

As task after task falls into the realm of time-saving goods and services, questions arise about the moral meanings attached to doing or not doing such tasks. Is it being a good mother to bake a child's birthday cake (alone or together with one's partner)? Or can we gratefully save time by ordering it, and be good mothers by planning the party? Can we save more time by hiring a planning service, and be good mothers simply by watching our children have a good time? "Wouldn't that be nice!" one Amerco mother exclaimed. As the idea of the "good mother" retreats before the pressures of work and the expansion of motherly services, mothers are in fact continually reinventing themselves.

[The final way working parents tried to evade the time bind was to develop what I call "potential selves."]The potential selves that I discovered in my Amerco interviews were fantasy creations of time-poor parents who dreamed of living as time millionaires.

One man, a gifted 55-year-old engineer in research and development at Amerco, told how he had dreamed of taking his daughters on a camping trip in the Sierra Mountains: "I bought all the gear three years ago when they were 5 and 7, the tent, the sleeping bags, the air mattresses, the backpacks, the ponchos. I got a map of the area. I even got the freeze-dried food. Since then the kids and I have talked about it a lot, and gone over what we're going to do. They've been on me to do it for a long time. I feel bad about it. I keep putting it off, but we'll do it, I just don't know when."

Banished to garages and attics of many Amerco workers were expensive electric saws, cameras, skis and musical instruments, all bought with wages it took time to earn. These items were to their owners what Cassie's fudge bar was to her—a substitute for time, a talisman, a reminder of the potential self.

Obviously, not everyone, not even a majority of Americans, is making a home out of work and a workplace out of home. But in the working world, it is a growing reality, and one we need to face. Increasing numbers of women are discovering a great male secret—that work can be an escape from the pressures of home, pressures that the changing nature of work itself are only intensifying. Neither men nor women are going to take up "family-friendly" policies, whether corporate or governmental, as long as the current realities of work and home remain as they are. For a substantial number of time-bound parents, the stripped-down home and the neighborhood devoid of community are simply losing out to the pull of the workplace.

There are several broader, historical causes of this reversal of realms. The last 30 years have witnessed the rapid rise of women in the workplace. At the same time, job mobility has taken families farther from relatives who might lend a hand, and made it harder to make close friends of neighbors who could help out. Moreover, as women have acquired more education and have joined men at work, they have absorbed the views of an older, male-oriented work world, its views of a "real career," far more than men have taken up their share of the work at home. One reason women have changed more than men is that the world of "male" work seems more honorable and valuable than the "female" world of home and children.

So where do we go from here? There is surely no going back to the mythical 1950s family that confined women to the home. Most women don't wish to return to a full-time role at home—and couldn't afford it even if they did. But equally troubling is a workaholic culture that strands both men and women outside the home.

For a while now, scholars on work-family issues have pointed to Sweden, Norway and Denmark as better models of work-family balance. Today, for example, almost all Swedish fathers take two paid weeks off from work at the birth of their children, and about half of fathers and most mothers take additional "parental leave" during the child's first or second year. Research shows that men who take family leave when their children are very young are more likely to be involved with their children as they grow older. When I mentioned this Swedish record of paternity leave to a focus group of American male managers, one of them replied, "Right, we've already heard about Sweden." To this executive, paternity leave was a good idea not for the U.S. today, but for some "potential society" in another place and time.

Meanwhile, children are paying the price. In her book *When the Bough Breaks: The Cost of Neglecting Our Children*, the economist Sylvia Hewlett claims that "compared with the previous generation, young people today are more likely to underperform at school; commit suicide; need psychiatric help; suffer a severe eating disorder; bear a child out of wedlock; take drugs; be the victim of a violent crime." But we needn't dwell on sledgehammer problems like heroin or suicide to realize that children like those at Spotted Deer need more of our time. If other advanced nations with two-job families can give children the time they need, why can't we?

Author's Note: Over three years, I interviewed 130 respondents for a book. They spoke freely and allowed me to follow them through "typical" days, on the understanding that I would protect their anonymity. I have changed the names of the company and of those I interviewed, and altered certain identifying details. Their words appear here as they were spoken.—A.R.H.

PART VIII

Social Change

56

THE McDONALDIZATION OF SOCIETY

GEORGE RITZER

In this reading, the first of five to focus on social change, George Ritzer focuses on the larger consequences of having an organization, such as McDonald's, in society. Ritzer, a professor of sociology at the University of Maryland, argues that societies are being transformed by a process he labels "McDonaldization," in which the principles of the fast-food restaurant have come to influence other aspects of the social structure, such as the family, politics, education, travel, and leisure. Ritzer also summarizes the societal costs and benefits of this widespread social change.

A wide-ranging process of *rationalization* is occurring across American society and is having an increasingly powerful impact in many other parts of the world. It encompasses such disparate phenomena as fast-food restaurants, TV dinners, packaged tours, industrial robots, plea bargaining, and open-heart surgery on an assembly-line basis. As widespread and as important as these developments are, it is clear that we have barely begun a process that promises even more extraordinary changes (e.g., genetic engineering) in the years to come. We can think of rationalization as a historical process and rationality as the end result of that development. As a historical process, rationalization has distinctive roots in the Western world. Writing in the late nineteenth and early twentieth centuries, the great German sociologist Max Weber saw his society as the center of the ongoing process of rationalization and the bureaucracy as its paradigm case. The model of rationalization, at least in contemporary America, is no longer the bureaucracy, but might be better thought of as the fast-food restaurant. As a result, our concern here is with what might be termed the "McDonaldization of Society." While the fast-food restaurant is not the ultimate expression of rationality, it is the current exemplar for future developments in rationalization.

Ritzer, George. "The McDonaldization of Society," *Journal of American Culture* 6, no. 1 (1983): 100–107. Reprinted by permission of Blackwell Publishing.

A society characterized by rationality is one which emphasizes *efficiency, predictability, calculability, substitution of nonhuman for human technology,* and *control over uncertainty.* In discussing the various dimensions of rationalization, we will be little concerned with the gains already made, and yet to be realized, by greater rationalization. These advantages are widely discussed in schools and in the mass media. In fact, we are in danger of being seduced by the innumerable advantages already offered, and promised in the future, by rationalization. The glitter of these accomplishments and promises has served to distract most people from the grave dangers posed by progressive rationalization. In other words, we are ultimately concerned here with the irrational consequences that often flow from rational systems. Thus, the second major theme of this essay might be termed "the irrationality of rationality." . . .

Efficiency

The process of rationalization leads to a society in which a great deal of emphasis is placed on finding the best or optimum means to any given end. Whatever a group of people define as an end, and everything they so define, is to be pursued by attempting to find the best means to achieve the end. Thus, in the Germany of Weber's day, the bureaucracy was seen as the most efficient means of handling a wide array of administrative tasks. Somewhat later, the Nazis came to develop the concentration camp, its ovens, and other devices as the optimum method of collecting and murdering millions of Jews and other people. The efficiency that Weber described in turn-of-the-century Germany, and which later came to characterize many Nazi activities, has become a basic principle of life in virtually every sector of a rational society.

The modern American family, often with two wage earners, has little time to prepare elaborate meals. For the relatively few who still cook such meals, there is likely to be great reliance on cookbooks that make cooking from scratch much more efficient. However, such cooking is relatively rare today. Most families take as their objective quickly and easily prepared meals. To this end, much use is made of prepackaged meals and frozen TV dinners.

For many modern families, the TV dinner is no longer efficient enough. To many people, eating out, particularly in a fast-food restaurant, is a far more efficient way of obtaining their meals. Fast-food restaurants capitalize on this by being organized so that diners are fed as efficiently as possible. They offer a limited, simple menu that can be cooked and served in an assembly-line fashion. The latest development in fast-food restaurants, the addition of drive-through windows, constitutes an effort to increase still further the efficiency of the dining experience. The family now can simply drive through, pick up its order, and eat it while driving to the next, undoubtedly efficiently organized, activity. The success of the fast-food restaurant has come full circle with frozen-food manufacturers now touting products for the home modeled after those served in fast-food restaurants.

Increasingly, efficiently organized food production and distribution systems lie at the base of the ability of people to eat their food efficiently at home, in the fast-food restaurant, or in their cars. Farms, groves, ranches, slaughterhouses, warehouses, transportation systems, and retailers are all oriented toward increasing efficiency. A notable example is chicken production where they are mass-bred, force-fed (often with many chemicals), slaughtered on an assembly line, iced or fast frozen, and shipped to all parts of the country. Some may argue that such chickens do not taste as good as the fresh-killed, local variety, but their complaints are likely to be drowned in a flood of mass-produced chickens. Then there is bacon which is more efficiently shipped, stored, and sold when it is preserved by sodium nitrate, a chemical which is unfortunately thought by many to be carcinogenic. Whatever one may say about the quality or the danger of the products, the fact remains that they are all shaped by the drive for efficiency. . . .

One of the most interesting and important aspects of efficiency is that it often comes to be not a means but an end in itself. This "displacement of goals" is a major problem in a rationalizing society. We have, for example, the bureaucrats who slavishly follow the rules even though their inflexibility negatively affects the organization's ability to achieve its goals. Then there are the bureaucrats who are so concerned with efficiency that they lose sight of the ultimate goals the means are designed to achieve. A good example was the Nazi concentration camp officers who, in devoting so much attention to maximizing the efficiency of the camps' operation, lost sight of the fact that the ultimate purpose of the camps was the murder of millions of people.

Predictability

A second component of rationalization involves the effort to ensure predictability from one place to another. In a rational society, people want to know what to expect when they enter a given setting or acquire some sort of commodity. They neither want nor expect surprises. They want to know that if they journey to another locale, the setting they enter or the commodity they buy will be essentially the same as the setting they entered or product they purchased earlier. Furthermore, people want to be sure that what they encounter is much like what they encountered at earlier times. In order to ensure predictability over time and place, a rational society must emphasize such things as discipline, order, systemization, formalization, routine, consistency, and methodical operation.

One of the attractions of TV dinners for modern families is that they are highly predictable. The TV dinner composed of fried chicken, mashed potatoes, green peas, and peach cobbler is exactly the same from one time to another and one city to another. Home cooking from scratch is, conversely, a notoriously unpredictable enterprise with little assurance that dishes will taste the same time after time. However, the cookbook cannot eliminate all unpredictability. There are often simply too many ingredients and other variables involved. Thus the cookbook dish is far less predictable than the TV dinner or a wide array of other prepared dishes.

Fast-food restaurants rank very high on the dimension of predictability. In order to help ensure consistency, the fast-food restaurant offers only a limited menu. Predictable end products are made possible by the use of similar raw materials, technologies, and preparation and serving techniques. Not only the food is predictable; the physical structures, the logo, the "ambience," and even the personnel are as well.

The food that is shipped to our homes and our fast-food restaurants is itself affected by the process of increasing predictability. Thus our favorite white bread is indistinguishable from one place to another. In fact, food producers have made great efforts to ensure such predictability.

On packaged tours, travelers can be fairly sure that the people they travel with will be much like themselves. The planes, buses, hotel accommodations, restaurants, and at least the way in which the sites are visited are very similar from one location to another. Many people go on packaged tours *because* they are far more predictable than travel undertaken on an individual basis.

Amusement parks used to be highly unpredictable affairs. People could never be sure, from one park to another, precisely what sorts of rides, events, foods, visitors, and employees they would encounter. All of that has changed in the era of the theme parks inspired by Disneyland. Such parks seek to ensure predictability in various ways. For example, a specific type of young person is hired in these parks, and they are all trained in much the same way, so that they have a robot-like predictability.

Other leisure-time activities have grown similarly predictable. Camping in the wild is loaded with uncertainties — bugs, bears, rain, cold, and the like. To make camping more predictable, organized grounds have sprung up around the country. Gone are many of the elements of unpredictability replaced by RVs, paved-over parking lots, sanitized campsites, fences and enclosed camp centers that provide laundry and food services, recreational activities, television, and video games. Sporting events, too, have in a variety of ways been made more predictable. The use of artificial turf in baseball makes for a more predictable bounce of a ball. . . .

Calculability or Quantity Rather than Quality

It could easily be argued that the emphasis on quantifiable measures, on things that can be counted, is *the* most defining characteristic of a rational society. Quality is notoriously difficult to evaluate. How do we assess the quality of a hamburger, or a physician, or a student? Instead of even trying, in an increasing number of cases, a rational society seeks to develop a series of quantifiable measures that it takes as surrogates for quality. This urge to quantify has given great impetus to the development of the computer and has, in turn, been spurred by the widespread use and increasing sophistication of the computer.

The fact is that many aspects of modern rational society, especially as far as calculable issues are concerned, are made possible and more widespread by the computer. We need not belabor the ability of the computer to handle large numbers of virtually anything, but somewhat less obvious is the use of the computer to give the illusion of personal attention in a world made increasingly impersonal in large part because of the computer's capacity to turn virtually everything into quantifiable dimensions. We have all now had many experiences where we open a letter personally addressed to us only to find a computer letter. We are aware that the names and addresses of millions of people have been stored on tape and that with the aid of a number of word processors a form letter has been sent to every name on the list. Although the computer is able to give a sense of personal attention, most people are nothing more than an item on a huge mailing list.

Our main concern here, though, is not with the computer, but with the emphasis on quantity rather than quality that it has helped foster. One of the most obvious examples in the university is the emphasis given to grades and cumulative grade point averages. With less and less contact between professor and student, there is little real effort to assess the quality of what students know, let alone the quality of their overall abilities. Instead, the sole measure of the quality of most college students is their grade in a given course and their grade point averages. Another blatant example is the emphasis on a variety of uniform exams such as SATs and GREs in which the essence of an applicant is reduced to a few simple scores and percentiles.

Within the educational institution, the importance of grades is well known, but somewhat less known is the way quantifiable factors have become an essential part of the process of evaluating college professors. For example, teaching ability is very hard to evaluate. Administrators have difficulty assessing teaching quality and thus substitute quantitative scores. Of course each score involves qualitative judgments, but this is conveniently ignored. Student opinion polls are taken and the scores are summed, averaged, and compared. Those who score well are deemed good teachers while those who don't are seen as poor teachers. There are many problems involved in relying on these scores such as the fact that easy teachers in "gut" courses may well obtain high ratings while rigorous teachers of difficult courses are likely to score poorly. . . .

In the work world we find many examples of the effort to substitute quantity for quality. Scientific management was heavily oriented to turning everything work-related into quantifiable dimensions. Instead of relying on the "rule of thumb" of the operator, scientific management sought to develop precise measures of how much work was to be done by each and every motion of the worker. Everything that could be was reduced to numbers, and all these numbers were then analyzable using a variety of mathematical formulae. The assembly line is similarly oriented to a variety of quantifiable dimensions such as optimizing the speed of the line, minimizing time for each task, lowering the price of the finished product, increasing sales and ultimately increasing profits. The divisional system pioneered by General Motors and thought to be one of the major reasons for its past success was oriented to the reduction of the performance of each division to a few, bottom-line numbers. By monitoring and comparing these numbers, General Motors was able to exercise control over the results without getting involved in the day-to-day activities of each division. . . .

Thus, the third dimension of rationalization, calculability or the emphasis on quantity rather than quality, has wide applicability to the social world. It is truly central, if not the central, component of a rationalizing society. To return to our favorite example, it is the case that McDonald's expends far more effort telling us how many billions of hamburgers it has sold than it does in telling us about the quality of those burgers. Relatedly, it touts the size of its product (the "Big Mac") more than the quality of the product (it is not the "Good Mac"). The bottom line in many settings is the number of customers processed, the speed with which they are processed, and the profits produced. Quality is secondary, if indeed there is any concern at all for it.

Substitution of Nonhuman Technology

In spite of Herculean efforts, there are important limits to the ability to rationalize what human beings think and do. Seemingly no matter what one does, people still retain at least the ultimate capacity to think and act in a variety of unanticipated ways. Thus, in spite of great efforts to make human behavior more efficient, more predictable, more calculable, people continue to act in unforeseen ways. People continue to make home-cooked meals from scratch, to camp in tents in the wild, to eat in old-fashioned diners, and to sabotage the assembly lines. Because of these realities, there is great interest among those who foster increasing rationality in using rational technologies to limit individual independence and ultimately to replace human beings with machines and other technologies that lack the ability to think and act in unpredictable ways.

McDonald's does not yet have robots to serve us food, but it does have teenagers whose ability to act autonomously is almost completely eliminated by techniques, procedures, routines, and machines. There are numerous examples of this including rules which prescribe all the things a counterperson should do in dealing with a customer as well as a large variety of technologies which determine the actions of workers such as drink dispensers which shut themselves off when the cup is full; buzzers, lights, and bells which indicate when food (e.g., french fries) is done; and cash registers which have the prices of each item programmed in. One of the latest attempts to constrain individual action is Denny's use of pre-measured packages of dehydrated food that are "cooked" simply by putting them under the hot water tap. Because of such tools and machines, as well as the elaborate rules dictating worker behavior, people often feel like they are dealing with human robots when they relate to the personnel of a fast-food restaurant. When human robots are found, mechanical robots cannot be far behind. Once people are reduced to a few robot-like actions, it is a relatively easy step to replace them with mechanical robots. Thus, Burgerworld is reportedly opening a prototypical restaurant in which mechanical robots serve the food.

Much of the recent history of work, especially manual work, is a history of efforts to replace human technology with nonhuman technology. Scientific management was oriented to the development of an elaborate and rigid set of rules about how jobs were to be done. The workers were to blindly and obediently follow those rules and not to do the work the way they saw fit. The various skills needed to perform a task were carefully delineated and broken down into a series of routine steps that could be taught to all workers. The skills, in other words, were built into the routines rather than belonging to skilled craftspersons. Similar points can be made about the assembly line, which is basically a set of nonhuman technologies that have the needed steps and skills built into them. The human worker is reduced to performing a limited number of simple, repetitive operations. However, the control of this technology over the individual worker is so great and omnipresent that individual workers have reacted negatively manifesting such things as tardiness, absenteeism, turnover, and even sabotage. We are now witnessing a new stage in this technological development with automated processes now totally replacing many workers with robots. With the coming of robots we have reached the ultimate stage in the replacement of humans with nonhuman technology.

Even religion and religious crusades have not been unaffected by the spread of nonhuman technologies. The growth of large religious organizations, the use of Madison Avenue techniques, and even drive-in churches all reflect the incursion of modern technology. But it is in the electronic church, religion through the TV screens, that replacement of human by nonhuman technology in religion is most visible and has its most important manifestation. . . .

Control

This leads us to the fifth major dimension of rationalization—control. Rational systems are oriented toward, and structured to expedite, control in a variety of senses. At the most general level, we can say that rational systems are set up to allow for greater control over the uncertainties of life—birth, death, food production and distribution, housing, religious salvation, and many, many others. More specifically, rational systems are oriented to gaining greater control over the major source of uncertainty in social life—other people. Among other things, this means control over subordinates by superiors and control of clients and customers by workers.

There are many examples of rationalization oriented toward gaining greater control over the uncertainties of life. The burgeoning of the genetic engineering movement can be seen as being aimed at gaining better control over the production of life itself. Similarly, amniocentesis can be seen as a technique which will allow the parents to determine the kind of child they will have. The efforts to rationalize food production and distribution can be seen as being aimed at gaining greater control over the problems of hunger and starvation. A steady and regular supply of food can make life itself more certain for large numbers of people who today live under the threat of death from starvation.

At a more specific level, the rationalization of food preparation and serving at McDonald's gives it great control over its employees. The automobile assembly line has a similar impact. In fact, the vast majority of the structures of a rational society exert extraordinary control over the people who labor in them. But because of the limits that still exist on the degree of control that rational structures can exercise over individuals, many rationalizing employers are driven to seek to more fully rationalize their operations and totally eliminate the worker. The result is an automated, robot-like technology over which, barring some *2001* rebellion, there is almost total control.

In addition to control over employees, rational systems are also interested in controlling the customer/clients they serve. For example, the fast-food restaurant with its counter, the absence of waiters and waitresses, the limited seating, and the drive-through windows all tend to lead customers to do certain things and not to do others.

Irrationality of Rationality

Although not an inherent part of rationalization, the *irrationality of rationality* is a seemingly inevitable byproduct of the process. We can think of the irrationality of rationality in several ways. At the most general level it can simply be seen as an overarching label for all the negative effects of rationalization. More specifically, it can be seen as the opposite of rationality, at least in some of its senses. For example, there are the inefficiencies and unpredictabilities that are often produced by seemingly rational systems. Thus, although bureaucracies are constructed to bring about greater efficiency in organizational work, the fact is that there are notorious inefficiencies such as the "red tape" associated with the operation of most bureaucracies. Or take the example of the arms race in which a focus on quantifiable aspects of nuclear weapons may well have made the occurrence of nuclear war more, rather than less, unpredictable.

Of greatest importance, however, is the variety of negative effects that rational systems have on the individuals who live, work, and are served by them. We might say that *rational systems are not reasonable systems*. As we've already discussed, rationality brings with it great dehumanization as people are reduced to acting like robots. Among the dehumanizing aspects of a rational society are large lecture classes, computer letters, pray TV, work on the automobile assembly line, and dining at a fast-food restaurant. Rationalization also tends to bring with it disenchantment leaving much of our lives without any mystery or excitement. Production by a hand craftsman is far more mysterious than an assembly-line technology where each worker does a single, very limited operation. Camping in an RV tends to suffer in comparison to the joys to be derived from camping in the wild. Overall a fully rational society would be a very bleak and uninteresting place.

Conclusions

Rationalization, with McDonald's as the paradigm case, is occurring throughout America and, increasingly, other societies. In virtually every sector of society, more and more emphasis is placed on efficiency, predictability, calculability, replacement of human by nonhuman technology, and control over uncertainty. Although progressive rationalization has brought with it innumerable advantages, it has also created a number of problems, the various irrationalities of rationality, which threaten to accelerate in the years to come. These problems, and their acceleration, should not be taken as a case for the return to a less rational form of society. Such a return is not only impossible but also undesirable. What is needed is not a less rational society, but greater control over the process of rationalization involving, among other things, efforts to ameliorate its irrational consequences.

57

HOW WILL THE INTERNET
CHANGE SOCIETY?

CONRAD L. KANAGY • DONALD B. KRAYBILL

This selection is a study of social change written by two sociologists, Conrad L. Kanagy, at Elizabethtown College, and Donald B. Kraybill, at Messiah College. In their research, Kanagy and Kraybill examine how the Internet has changed society. In particular, they investigate how the Internet is changing culture, social structure, and rituals in American society and beyond. Will the Internet create a global community of similar norms and values that transcends national boundaries? What are the limitations of new technologies, such as the Internet, in creating and changing social structure? These and other questions are addressed by Kanagy and Kraybill in this excerpt from their 1999 book, *The Riddles of Human Society.*

On March 14, 1994, police handcuffed Matt Mihaly, a 21-year-old student at Cornell University, and drove him to the Tompkins County Hospital. During the intake process, hospital personnel pressed him: "Do you want to kill yourself? Do you ever hear voices? Are you a danger to yourself?" Matt insisted he was fine. But against his strong protests, an ambulance transported him to the mental health ward of another hospital, where he spent two days in mandatory group therapy sessions. Then he was released.

How did Mihaly get himself into this predicament? Depressed over a broken romance, drunk and reeling in self-pity, he posted the following note to an Internet news group:

> *I am planning on killing myself. . . . I want some information on drugs that induce a relatively painless death. . . . If I can't get the information, I'll probably just try taking a few packs of sleeping pills. . . . Please don't post back stuff about how I shouldn't do it, OK?*

Mihaly insists that he wasn't serious when he sent the message, just angry and depressed. His case initiated serious debate about privacy and free speech on the Internet.[1]

From *The Riddles of Human Society: An Introduction to Society* by Conrad L. Kanagy and Donald B. Kraybill, pp. 260–68, 337–38. Copyright © 1999 Pine Forge Press. Reprinted by permission of Sage Publications, Inc.

The norms of Internet culture remain fuzzy. Technological advances are speeding ahead of social regulation. Are people free to write whatever they want and to anybody they want? How much privacy should we have on the Internet? Should Matt have been hospitalized for his statement? Such gaps between social norms and policy on one hand and technological expertise on the other are typical during rapid social change.

The Social Construction of the Internet

The first Internet exchanges occurred in November 1969 under the authority of the U.S. Department of Defense.[2] The internet was born as ARPANET, a worldwide network of computers linking a few university scientists, military personnel, and computer experts. ARPANET's purpose was to enhance U.S. military prowess in the Cold War against communism. Initial communication was formal and official, some users worried that personal e-mail messages might violate U.S. postal laws. But by the mid-1980s, ARPANET was linked to other networks. The change created near chaos, a "full-scale Mardi Gras parade." By 1990 ARPANET had been shut down, and private companies were overseeing activity in cyberspace.[3]

To many college students today, the Internet is a taken-for-granted part of the objective social world, just like cable TV and Nintendo. They've grown up in a digital world. They've internalized expectations for high-speed communication on the Internet. They watch less television than their parents did, finding its old-fashioned pace too slow. They want technology they can interact with and control. The world has shrunk for these students; it lies at their fingertips.

Clearly, use of the Internet is changing our world. In fact, its effects might parallel the transformations brought about by the invention of the printing press. Both technologies expand exponentially the access of ordinary persons to information once held by experts and elites. Sociologists are beginning to develop a sociology of the Internet to study these social changes, and this subfield is likely to grow rapidly in the next several years.[4]

Culture and the Internet

We already know a few things about the beliefs, norms, and values of Internet culture. For instance, social scientists have been debating for some time the reality of Internet communities, or **virtual communities**.[5] Some have argued that such communities are little more than social networks, because they lack

---

Virtual communities are networks of relationships in which people identify with one another and share feelings for one another but don't share their physical selves or physical space. They share cyberselves and cyberspace.

the typical characteristics of communities—things like residential proximity and economic dependence. However, digital technology has been pressing us to renovate some standard definitions, and the concept of community may be one of them. What do you think? What elements of community are represented in your online relationships? Are chat rooms communities?

In the age of television, many bemoaned the loss of written text as a form of communication. Interestingly, text-based communication has returned on the Internet. The need for writing, reading, and critical expression are as great as, or greater than, ever. But electronic text is extemporaneous, transitory, and soon trashed, unlike the enduring works of Shakespeare and other classic writers.

A problem with text-based communication is the difficulty of expressing emotions and feelings. To counter this difficulty, many Internet users resort to "smileys," combinations of characters that symbolize emotional responses. Besides smileys, people communicating on the Internet are using some new forms of abbreviation and spelling, such as *jc* for "just curious," *bmf* for "biting my fingernails," *brb* for "be right back," *imho* for "in my humble opinion," and *lol* for "laughing out loud."

Internet norms, sometimes referred to as netiquette, are in the process of being defined.[6] Because of the rapid growth and fluidity of the Internet, ambiguity abounds about how people should behave in cyberspace. However, threats of censorship have hastened the development of some norms. Internet users are particularly concerned that outrageous behavior by some will prompt government agencies to censor the Internet. Certain legal norms probably will be defined eventually. In addition, subcultural groups will undoubtedly develop their own particular norms, just as subcultures do in the real world.

What are the values of Internet users that will shape these norms? Don Tapscott, in *Growing Up Digital,* identifies several themes that are important to this subculture. For example, independence, free expression, and inclusion, which are core American values as well. These values are undoubtedly reinforced for Internet users by the freedom and diversity of Internet communication. Other cyberculture values, however, have been socially constructed and reinforced through electronic interaction.

- ▾ Openness characterizes Internet communication.
- ▾ Innovation created the Internet and continues to shape it.
- ▾ An investigative spirit is encouraged by the vast scope of the Internet wilderness.
- ▾ Immediacy is driven by the speed of Internet processing.
- ▾ Internet users, particularly the younger ones, are skeptical of corporate interests and the greed driving some efforts to shape Internet technology.

▾ Authenticity and trust are expected in the open environment of the Internet, where the cooperation of the parts (individuals) is needed to preserve the whole.[7]

Although several of these cyberculture values intersect with more traditional American values, others are relatively new and are likely to influence the cultural values of the larger society in years to come.

Social Structure and the Internet

The changes brought about by the Internet will accelerate as the number of youth who have been socialized into cyberculture grows. Some refer to this generation as the "net generation." These are the children of the baby boomers, the cohort born between 1945 and 1964, who now represent 29% of the U.S. population. The net generation, or "N-geners," born since 1977, comprise 30% of the U.S. population. The baby boomers represent the television generation, their children the digital generation. In their youth, many baby boomers sat staring at programs like *MASH, The Brady Bunch,* and *The Jeffersons.* But N-geners controlled a host of interactive devices, such as Nintendo games and computers. For people who grew up with these technologies, their operation is second nature. The Internet will develop and become more influential as the people who grew up with it become a larger part of the population.[8]

The two cohorts—baby boomers and N-geners—have unique intergenerational problems. In place of a generation gap, where the growing-up experiences of children and parents are simply different, we may have a "generation lap," as children outpace their parents in the race for technological knowledge. Young children often know much more than their parents about the computer. In one study by researchers at Carnegie Mellon University, children were the heaviest computer users in a large majority of families. Two-thirds of children in another survey said they are more proficient on the computer than their parents. In Finland, 5,000 N-geners teach computing to the country's teachers.[9] The "generation lap" turns typical patterns of socialization upside down: The parents, who typically teach their children, are now learning from them. As a result, children and youth have become the gatekeepers of technology and information for their families, teachers, and supervisors. This generational shift means that some entry-level employees will have greater skills and knowledge in some areas than their supervisors, managers, and administrators.

The new generation gap has four themes:

▾ Older people are anxious about the new technology being embraced by youth.

▼ Older people are uneasy about the new media, such as the Internet, which are part of everyday life among youth.

▼ Older media (newspapers, radio, television) are apprehensive about the newer media.

▼ The digital revolution, unlike previous revolutions, is not completely controlled by adults.[10]

Reconciliation between baby boomers and N-geners may lie in the willingness of N-geners to share their knowledge and the humility of baby boomers to receive it.

The digital revolution may create other structural fault lines as well. Some fear that computer technology will exacerbate the existing divide between rich and poor. In fact, only 7% of low-income households have a computer, while among those making more than $50,000 a year, 53% have a computer. Thus economic poverty leads to information poverty, which leads to even greater economic poverty. In addition, racial discrimination in society leads to racial discrimination in media and technology access.[11] Blacks are two-thirds less likely to have a computer than whites, and two-thirds of white students have used the Web as opposed to fewer than half of black students.[12] On the brighter side, the Internet has the potential to equalize without regard to race, sex, or economics. Students in poor, inner-city schools could have access equal to those in wealthy, suburban schools. The challenge for the government and for educators is to ensure such equality. Whether in the final analysis the Internet will increase or diminish social inequality remains to be seen.

Structural differences in technology use also occur in the global arena: . . . developed and developing countries differ substantially in their resources. Information technology will probably heighten those differences. In 1996, 66% of households connected to the Internet were in North America. Even developed countries in Western Europe fall behind the United States in Internet access and use. At the same time, the Internet has the potential to democratize political systems around the world, by giving everyone equal access to information, regardless of cultural or political boundaries. The Internet makes possible the development of a truly global culture, where children in Hong Kong can learn the same information as children in Papua New Guinea. They can also learn about each other.

Ritual and the Internet

Although some social divisions are sharpened by digital technology, the Internet levels the playing field for individuals communicating through e-mail, chat rooms, bulletin boards, and discussion lists. The only symbols of communication are written words; facial expressions, voice intonations, hand gestures, and physical appearance are gone. The context of each individual's social world—family life, occupation, income, residence—is minimized. Such **decontextualization** is quite different from the high context of face-to-face interaction, where we can see the person. The decontextualized nature of Internet culture is the opposite of, say, Amish life, which is a high-context culture that values face-to-face interaction and knowledge of everyone in the community. In a high context culture, social actors know many background details of each other—home, habits, lifestyle, friends, and work. Conversation is embedded in this rich social context.

On the Internet, everyone is alike. The decontextualized space of the Internet brings a new openness in communication and weakens the features that often lead to discrimination and prejudice. People with disabilities, who usually face discrimination, can interact without the scorn of prejudice. Age, beauty, size, body odor, color of hair and eyes, and facial hair lose their power. Labels, stereotypes, and stigmas disappear.

In Goffman's terms, on the Internet the frontstage is the same for everyone, without the typical props, signals, sounds, and appearances of social life. Individuals can create any frontstage that they wish. It may not be real, but who will ever know? Said one 14-year-old: "I'd have to say I'm very shy unless I know a person very well. This doesn't happen though in cyberspace. On the Net, I am one of the most outgoing people I know. Probably why I spend so much time there."[13]

In general, we all have greater control over disclosure and our presentation of self on the Internet than in other social contexts. If we dislike someone, we can break off the communication without serious consequences, especially if we have kept our identity disguised. We'll likely never see the other person, and if we do, we won't recognize each other.

Relationships on the Internet are often disposable, fragile, and superficial. At the same time, however, they can be deeply intimate and personal, because so much contextual baggage is left behind. Some of the values of N-geners arise from these characteristics of ritual interaction on the Internet.[14]

Decontextualized interaction on the Internet poses some interesting dilemmas, which some voice as concerns:

- ▾ Individuals can enter chat rooms or post messages to bulletin boards using multiple identities. Some deliberately create artificial identities to deceive unsuspecting individuals. On-line romances have occasionally resulted in fraud or homicide. Children can be manipulated and harmed by menacing adults.[15]
- ▾ Another danger is Internet addiction, sometimes called "netomania" or "on-lineaholism." Some view this condition as a symptom of a

---

Decontextualization is the loss of identifiable social landmarks in human interaction. In a decontextualized social world like the Internet, we don't have the contextual knowledge—the other person's facial expressions and gestures, a physical setting such as a home or office, and the other person's friends or family—that we usually use to interpret our interaction.

psychiatric disorder; others see it as a disorder in its own right.[16] One analyst, Kimberly Young, has written a self-help guide called *Caught in the Net* to aid those who abandon family, friends, and work to be on-line. She believes up to 5 million Internet users may be addicted.[17] Examples of those with symptoms of Internet addiction include a 31-year-old man who spent more than 100 hours a week on-line, ignoring others and stopping only for sleep. In another case, a 21-year-old college student disappeared, only to be found in the computer lab hooked on seven consecutive days of on-line chat. Some individuals with Internet addiction have reported an average of five psychiatric disorders, including manic-depressive disorder, social phobia, bulimia or binge eating, impulse-control problems, and substance abuse.[18]

▼ Some experts fear that N-geners are losing their social skills. Others are concerned about the short attention span that N-geners may develop through overexposure to interactive communication. Some fear the Internet is stressing children and spreading them too thin. Others worry about the cruelty that children may experience on the Internet. Some argue that the opportunity to create one's homepage leads to vanity — an artificially heightened self-esteem.[19]

All these issues raise a host of ethical questions for an Internet society. How much freedom should Internet users have? How much control should the government and other social institutions exert? Is it ethical to change one's identity on-line? When is on-line deception potentially harmful to individuals and society? Is Internet addiction harmful? Should we have Internet police to regulate activity in chat rooms and discussion groups? Should individuals be held accountable for everything they write on the Internet? How much further will the Internet renovate social relations?[20]

Summary: Internet

Because the development of the Internet is relatively new, we can't really consider its renovation yet. But the recent development of the Internet provides a fascinating opportunity to watch a culture being constructed from scratch.

The construction of the Internet reflects to some extent the cultural norms and structural divisions of the larger society. The Internet has the potential, however, to make the same information available to everyone, regardless of race, class, education, occupation, or residence.

The rituals of interaction on the Internet are still being shaped. It is a de-contextualized environment where we can minimize everyday prejudices by carefully controlling the presentation of self. We can remain relatively anonymous while still being intimate. We can create relationships with few obligations but with high levels of authenticity.

It remains to be seen whether the Internet will remain a communication medium of the middle and upper classes or whether, like television, it will override class lines and serve the masses.

ENDNOTES

[1] Kim Neely, "Caught in the Net," *Rolling Stone,* 1 December 1994.

[2] For on-line resources about the history of the Internet, see <http://info.isoc.org/guest/zakon/Internet/History/Timeline_of_Network_History>; <http://info.isoc.org/guest/zakon/Internet/History/How_the_Internet_came_to_Be>; <http://info.isoc.org/guest/zakon/Internet/History/Brief_History_of_the_Internet>.

[3] Edwin Diamond and Stephen Bates, "The Ancient History of the Internet," *American Heritage* 46 (1995): 34–41.

[4] For related resources, see <http://www.itcs.com/elawley/bourdieu.html> and <http://jefferson.village.virginia.edu/>.

[5] Howard Reingold, *Virtual Communities: Homesteading on the Electronic Frontier* (New York: Harper Perennial, 1993), p. 5.

[6] For an on-line description of netiquette, see <http://rs6000.adm.fau.edu/rinaldi/netiquette.html>. Another valuable resource, titled "A Primer on How to Work with the Usenet Community," is available through the news group news.announce.newusers, with the archive name usernet/primer/part1.

[7] A substantial part of our discussion of the Internet is based on Don Tapscott, *Growing Up Digital* (New York: McGraw-Hill, 1998).

[8] For more on the age profile of Internet users, see Thomas E. Miller, "Segmenting the Internet," *American Demographics* 18 (1996): 48–50.

[9] Don Tapscott, *Growing Up Digital* (New York: McGraw-Hill, 1998).

[10] Ibid., pp. 48–50.

[11] Don Tapscott, *Growing Up Digital* (New York: McGraw-Hill, 1998).

[12] *Time,* "World White Web," 27 April 1998.

[13] Ibid., p. 93.

[14] Don Tapscott, *Growing Up Digital* (New York: McGraw-Hill, 1998).

[15] Ibid.

[16] Ibid.

[17] Vincent Kiernan, "Some Scholars Question Research Methods of Expert on Internet Addiction," *The Chronicle of Higher Education,* 29 May 1998.

[18] Malcolm Ritter, *Associated Press,* 2 June 1998.

[19] Don Tapscott, *Growing Up Digital* (New York: McGraw-Hill, 1998).

[20] Given its recent development, we do not offer any suggestions as to how the Internet will be renovated in the future.

58

THE WILDING OF AMERICA
Iraq and the War against Terrorism

CHARLES DERBER

This reading by Charles Derber is an excerpt from his 2004 book, *The Wilding of America: Money, Mayhem, and the New American Dream*. In his research, Derber, a professor of sociology at Boston College, utilizes the concept of "wilding" to examine aspects of social behavior and change in the United States. By *wilding*, Derber is referring to individualistic behavior that advances or indulges the self by hurting others. Thus, according to Derber, there are many types of wilding, such as *economic wilding*, which is the morally uninhibited pursuit of money by individuals or businesses at the expense of others; *political wilding*, which is the abuse of political office to benefit oneself or one's social class, or the wielding of political authority to inflict morally unacceptable suffering on citizens at home or abroad; and *social wilding*, which ranges from personal or family acts of violence to collective forms of selfishness that weaken society. In the selection that follows, Derber examines two extreme forms of *wilding*: war and terrorism.

The great sociologist Max Weber defined the state as the institution with a monopoly of official violence, and Hans Morganthau, the famous political theorist, argued that states always act in their own self-interest. If states use their monopolies of violence to wage war for naked self-interest or corporate profits, this would appear to make war one of the most catastrophic forms of institutional wilding. We [define] state violence for greed or power at home as political wilding, and in a world exploding with war for power and profit, it is hard to imagine a more dangerous and sociologically important species of wilding.

In this [selection], we consider two American wars: the war against Iraq and the "war on terrorism." In focusing on American-led wars, it is important to keep in mind that the United States is the greatest military power in world history and the sole superpower today. The U.S. spends more on the military—approaching half a trillion dollars annually—than all the other nations of the world combined. Many view the U.S. as an empire, exceeding in its power even the Roman or British empires. Sociologists such as Immanual Wallerstein and Giovanni Arrighi offer a framework known as "world system theory" for understanding the American empire as a wilding system. Looking back on the last 500 years of colonialism, world system theorists argue that the world economy has been organized by a dominant or "hegemonic" power, such as Britain during the late eighteenth and nineteenth centuries, that ruled over much of the world for profit and glory. The U.S. is the successor hegemon to Britain, with even greater power.[1]

Hegemony, as conceived by the Italian social theorist, Antonio Gramsci, is power dressed up in universal values such as freedom and prosperity. Gramsci wrote that governments always use such soothing rhetoric as "the white man's burden" to "manufacture consent," since naked coercion is an expensive and inefficient mode of control. During the British empire, the British claimed to bring civilization to the whole world, as did the ancient Romans to their conquered provinces. During the Cold War, the United States claimed to defend the entire "free world" against the evil of communism. Arrighi and other world system theorists observe that with the collapse of the Soviet Union, American hegemony is increasingly organized around claims to defend the whole civilized world against the evils of terror and chaos.

Hegemons increasingly turn to military force when their economic power and legitimacy begin to wane. The U.S. is in the early phases of hegemonic decline, associated with a long-term crisis in the global economy and the rise of a speculative "casino capitalism" that yields short-term profits at the expense of long-term growth. We can expect that the U.S. may move toward increasing militarism to secure its endangered global wealth and power, leading to the kind of mayhem and wilding witnessed during the decline and fall of the Roman and British empires.[2]

War in Iraq

When Baghdad fell on April 9, 2003, U.S. newspapers and television showed jubilant Iraqis dancing in the streets. Iraqis embraced and kissed American soldiers, stomped on pictures of Saddam Hussein, and with the help of U.S. Marines, toppled the huge iron statue of Saddam in central Baghdad. This was the reaction that President Bush had promised. Although no weapons of mass destruction had been found at this point, the Iraqi celebration seemed to nail down Bush's claim that this was a war of liberation, a just war destroying a barbaric regime and bringing freedom and democracy to a suffering nation.

As I write these words just after Baghdad's collapse, surveys suggest that most Americans agreed with the president. A poll released on April 10, 2003, showed that about 75 percent of Americans supported the war. Even those who had earlier protested the war were rethinking their opposition, wondering whether the end of a horrific despot justified the destruction inevitably wrought by war. One thoughtful student in my class raised his hand and said that the obvious joy of many Iraqis at the downfall of Saddam made him question whether his earlier opposition to the war was ignorant.

But while Americans watched images of Iraqis celebrating in the streets, Arabs were opening newspapers with headlines blazing "Humiliation!" and "Colonialism Is Back!" The images Arabs saw were of dead Iraqi children killed by bombs, starving Iraqi families screaming at U.S. soldiers for water or food, Iraqi soldiers lying dead on the highway, hospitals without electricity or medicine overflowing with wounded Iraqi civilians, widespread looting and mayhem, and fires burning out of control in many Iraqi cities. While there was no love lost on Saddam Hussein, Arabs all over the Mideast were horrified at the prospect of an American military occupation of Iraq.

Talal Salman, publisher of *Al-Safir,* a leading Lebanese moderate newspaper, grieved the loss of the richest Arab civilization to a "colonial power." Iraqis, he wrote, are now moving from "the night of tyranny" under Saddam Hussein to the "night of foreign occupation" under U.S. troops.[3] Ahmed Kamal Aboulmagd, a leading pro-Western member of the Egyptian establishment and a longtime friend of the U.S., said, "Under the present conditions, I cannot think of defending the United States. To most people in this area, the United States is the source of evil on planet earth."[4]

These sentiments were shared by many Iraqis, who were grateful to the U.S. and British soldiers for ousting Saddam but desperate to survive in the wake of the world's most intense bombing campaigns, and viscerally hostile to a new foreign occupation. The majority Shiite population in Iraq mounted huge street protests demanding that American soldiers get out of their country. Iraqis interviewed in Baghdad and Basra told U.S. reporters that they hated Saddam but they equally "resented the foreign troop presence." One Iraqi Shiite cleric said the Iraqis were caught between "two fires"—one, the cruel, fading power of Saddam and the other the looming domination of the Americans. Qabil Khazzal Jumaa, an Iraqi nurse, horrified by the amputated limbs, burned bodies, and rotting corpses among the hundred of civilians he had treated, said that this was "a brutal war. This is not just. This is not accepted by man or God." Iraq did not belong to the Americans who would now govern his country. He said simply, "This is my country."[5]

In the face of these starkly competing images—Iraqis dancing in the streets and a bombed, looted country fearing subjugation to a hegemon occupying its cities and oil fields—how does one decide whether the U.S. war in Iraq was wilding? We can start by asking whether the war was legal and then whether this was a just war. This can be framed from a sociological perspective around the question of hegemony: did the U.S. invade Iraq to tighten its hegemonic control over the Gulf and the entire oil-rich Islamic world?

Legality

According to Article 51 of the U.N. charter (which the U.S. ratified), a country can legally engage in war without U.N. approval if the war is in self-defense. Right after 9/11, on September 12, 2001, President Bush redefined "self-defense" in a more expansive way than the charter implied. Bush asserted that the U.S. could no longer afford to abide by conventional concepts in an age of terrorism. We must be prepared, the president declared, "to strike at moment's notice in any dark corner of the world . . . to be ready for preemptive action when necessary to defend our liberty and to defend our lives." The president was very explicit about preemption: "We must take the battle to the enemy, disrupt his plans and confront the worst threats before they emerge."

In emphasizing that he would act against threats "before they emerge," the president was moving beyond preemption to prevention. A preemptive war occurs when a threat is imminent, for instance, when missiles or planes are detected moving toward one's shores, and there is a plausible concept of "pre-emptive self-defense" within the U.N.'s legal intent. Preventive war is a response to threats not yet visible, and suggests that one nation can use the new Bush doctrine to attack almost any other country that it mistrusts, an application of the wilding precept that "might makes right."

Bush's approach kicked up a firestorm of opposition. Former White House advisor William A. Galston said that Bush's new doctrine "means the end of the system of international institutions, laws, and norms that the United States has worked for more than half a century to build. . . . Rather than continuing to serve as first among equals in the postwar international system, the United States would act as a law unto itself, creating new rules of international engagement without agreement by other nations." Princeton political scientist Richard Falk, a leading authority on international law, writes that "this new approach repudiates the core of the United Nations charter [outlawing wars that are not based on self-defense against overt aggression] . . . it is a doctrine without limits, without accountability to the U.N. or international law, or any dependence on a collective judgment of responsible governments."[6]

When the U.S. invaded Iraq, it claimed that Article 51 made the war legal. The U.N. Security Council disagreed, saying that there was more time for inspection and that the threat was not imminent, meaning that the war could not be viewed as self-defense. France and Germany, along with scores of other countries, repeatedly argued that the war undermined the U.N. charter. Russian President Vladmir Putin declared that the doctrine of preemption meant the world would descend into chronic war and the law of the jungle.

Just a few weeks after Putin's prophecy of a new global anarchy, the government of India announced that it was using the Bush doctrine to consider a preemptive attack against its nuclear-armed adversary, Pakistan, because of Pakistan's incursions into the Indian-controlled part of Kashmir. A central problem with the invasion of Iraq—and the legal doctrine on which it is based—is that it offers a wilding license for international chaos.

Several months after the fall of Baghdad, American forces on the ground had failed to find any nuclear, biological, or chemical weapons. On April 24, 2003, President Bush suggested that weapons of mass destruction (WMD) might never be found and might not exist, raising grave new questions about the legality of the war. The president's legal argument for the war had rested on the premise that such weapons existed and constituted a threat to American and global security. But if no weapons are found, there was no threat and no plausible legal justification, suggesting a war of aggression rather than self-defense.[7]

Whether the president or other members of his administration lied about WMD or about Saddam's relation to Al Qaeda has become a major wilding issue in itself. Lying to create a legal justification for war would be political wilding of the highest order, and widespread suspicion of it has already inspired a mass campaign to impeach Bush led by former Attorney General Ramsey Clark. John Dean, President Nixon's legal advisor during Watergate, has said that if Bush lied about WMD, which he sees as more likely than any other explanation of the failure to find WMD in Iraq, it would be a far more serious impeachable offense than Nixon's cover-up in Watergate. "In the three decades since Watergate," Dean wrote, "this is the first potential scandal I have seen that could make Watergate pale by comparison. . . . To put it bluntly, if Bush has taken Congress and the nation into war based on bogus information, he is cooked. Manipulation or deliberate misuse of national security intelligence data, if proven, could be a 'high crime' under the Constitution's impeachment clause."[8]

In his 2003 State of the Union message, President Bush claimed that Iraq had 30,000 warheads and the materials to produce 38,000 liters of botulinum toxin, 25,000 liters of anthrax, and 500 tons of chemical weapons, none of which have been found at this writing. Bush also told the American public in the State of the Union that Iraq tried to buy uranium from the African country of Niger, even though CIA officials had earlier told Vice President Cheney's office and Bush's National Security Council that the Niger story was an obvious fabrication based on forged documents. The White House acknowledged in July 2003 that Bush should not have included the unfounded allegation about Niger in his speech.[9] The specter of a pattern of lying to create the impression that Iraq posed a nuclear threat is reinforced by Bush's public claim that aluminum tubes in Iraq's possession were intended to enrich uranium after the International Atomic Energy Agency had already publicly concluded that the tubes probably had nothing at all to do with a nuclear program. Bush also claimed that Saddam Hussein was supporting Al Qaeda, when both his own intelligence agencies and the U.N. reported little evidence of this. Bush's statements have led up to 50 percent of Americans to say that they believe that Saddam was behind 9/11, suggesting that Americans were all too ready to believe a president who repeatedly misled them.

One explanation is the soft-pedaling by American media and Congress itself about the official pattern of deception, itself a dangerous form of wilding. In Britain, where the media outrage and public anger have been hotter, two leading cabinet ministers resigned after the Iraqi war, accusing Prime Minister Blair of lying to Britons about WMD. One of the resigning ministers, Claire Short, testified to a parliamentary committee that Blair and Bush concocted a prearranged deal in 2002 to invade Iraq in 2003 no matter what was found about weapons of mass destruction. Blair, at this writing, faces several fierce parliamentary investigations and hard-hitting major media attacks accusing him of lying. But while the *New York Times* headlined the question "Was the intelligence cooked?" the *Times* and other media, as well as the American Congress, have expressed little outrage about the pattern of official deception and the political manipulation of intelligence data. When Vice President Cheney was reported to have walked over to the CIA and spent hours grilling intelligence officials involved with Iraq and other American intelligence officials have disclosed that they felt pressure to come up with results favorable to the administration's case for war, the media gave it little attention. Such political pressure on intelligence analysts, if true, is a horrific form of political wilding, undermining the credibility of the president and endangering democracy, just as the pressure by Wall Street firms on analysts for favorable stock reports endangers the credibility and future of the financial markets. By failing to focus the American public on Bush's distortions and suspected lies that served his war interests, the media have helped normalize such official deception and contributed to a culture of political wilding that has severely damaged our country.

Justice

The question of wilding goes beyond legality to the broader issue of whether the war on Iraq was a just war of liberation. While the argument that the removal of a tryant is indeed a just action is true, three arguments based on historical, economic, and political perspectives suggest other goals were behind this war.

The historical argument is based on planning documents only recently made public. In a 1990 strategy document put together by a team under Dick Cheney in the first Bush administration, the United States announced that it must "preclude the rise of another global rival for the indefinite future," building such an overwhelming military superiority that no other nation could possibly contemplate challenging American power. The Cheney document suggested that the United States needed to create a "democratic zone of peace" in which Americans would be prepared to use force if necessary to ensure "human rights or democracy," even if using force involved violating the sovereignty of another nation that posed no threat to the United States. While Iraq was the test case of the time, the idea of overthrowing Saddam was rejected after the first Gulf War because the U.N. did not authorize a regime change. The Cheney doctrine was shelved as embarrassingly imperialistic.[10] Nonetheless, after 9/11, Cheney's vision became the centerpiece of the new

Bush administration's foreign policy, and the Iraqi war was a crucial first step toward securing the global dominance laid out in the earlier documentary record.[11]

A second argument that the war on Iraq involved wilding centers around the economic goals of the war. Like all prior hegemons, the United States has two economic agendas. The first is to ensure the stable operation of the world economy, including the guarantee of a cheap supply of Mideast oil. In 1990, when Saddam Hussein invaded Kuwait and threatened Saudi Arabia, the United States launched the first Gulf War to stabilize the entire global economic system, protecting the oil supply not only for itself but for European and Asian allies. In the 2003 Gulf War, the United States again acted with broad concern for global economic stability based on securing greater control of Iraq's and its neighbors' oil supplies—still a form of wilding but different than simply grabbing more profit for U.S. oil companies.

Another U.S. economic aim, though, is closer to what the protestors had in mind as they waved their "No Blood for Oil" signs. The corporatized American hegemon sees U.S. national interests as tightly connected to the profitability of politically influential American corporations. The Bush administration, including most notably the president and vice president, is especially close to the energy industries, in which several Bush cabinet members served as corporate executives, as well as to the military-related companies rooted in Texas and throughout the Southwest of the United States. It is predictable that the interests of this sector of American corporations would weigh heavily in the Bush administration's assessment of the national interest.

Evidence that profits for U.S. oil giants and other companies were part of the Iraq war aim comes from the postwar reconstruction contracts, which the U.S. Agency for International Development has begun to award through a closed bidding process.

▾ Halliburton, the Texas-based oil giant formerly headed by Dick Cheney, was awarded the first major contract for servicing of Iraqi oil wells and fire prevention in the oil fields, estimated to be worth up to $7 billion. This is widely seen as a foot in the door for more profitable long-term Iraqi oil contracts, and has led to discussions of a congressional investigation regarding whether Halliburton poses a conflict of interest, since Cheney still receives compensation from the firm.

▾ The United States has also awarded a leading reconstruction role to Bechtel, the vast construction and energy company with ties to Secretary of Defense Donald Rumsfeld and others closely connected to the Bush administration. George Schultz, former president of Bechtel and currently on its board, also sits on Bush's Pentagon's Defense Policy Board, which advises the administration about Iraq and other vital matters. Richard Perle, head of that same board and the leading hawk on Iraq, was forced to resign his chairmanship when concerns about potential conflicts of interest were raised about his own business interests.

At a time when Pentagon planners and the CIA were predicting major new terrorist attacks as a near certainty in the wake of the Iraqi invasion, Perle's company stood to generate lucrative profits from defense and homeland security contracts.[12]

A third argument that the Iraqi war involved wilding concerns domestic political benefits reaped by the Bush administration. Bush entered office without a popular majority and only through a controversial Supreme Court decision about the Florida vote. Even before 9/11 and the Iraq war, critics perceived Bush as a servant of the big corporations whose campaign funding had helped propel him to Washington. In his first moves as president, Bush chose a cabinet led by other former corporate executives, including Cheney, Rumsfeld, and Paul O'Neill, his Secretary of the Treasury. Bush then pushed a domestic agenda centered around the biggest tax cuts to the rich in history, enhancing his image as a political stand-in for his corporate friends.

Such a corporate presidency is inherently vulnerable to a crisis of legitimacy. Bush's social and economic domestic policies have been consistently opposed by a majority of the American electorate. Karl Rove, the president's political guru, has denied in public that foreign policy decisions are made on the basis of domestic political considerations, but he sent a secret memo to Republican activists during the 2002 midterm elections urging them to "focus on the war." He also acknowledged to reporters during the 2002 campaign that he liked the slogan circulating among Republican strategists, "Are you safer now than you were four years ago?"[13]

The domestic political benefits of war in Iraq are too obvious to ignore. While a majority of Americans in polls continue to say they worry about the economy and feel that Bush's domestic agenda is moving the country in the wrong direction, Bush's poll numbers spiked up after the fall of Baghdad. Leaders with unpopular domestic policies have frequently turned to war as a way of countering their slide in the polls, and wars have typically helped presidents regain popularity in the wake of economic downturns. Reliance on war to divert the public from domestic problems has been dubbed the "wag the dog" strategy, and has been widely discussed ever since the popular movie of the same title was made. If even a small part of the Iraq war was driven by political concerns about re-election, this would be a devastating indictment of the war as wilding.

The War on Terrorism

9/11 was a watershed event. When Al Qaeda operatives hijacked the two jumbo jets and crashed them into the twin towers in New York, they showed that the U.S. was vulnerable to the devastating violence that many other countries have suffered for decades. Americans have historically felt protected by the oceans and the enormous power of the U.S. military. We know

now that tiny bands of terrorists can inflict horrific damage on our country, whatever the size of our military or our hegemonic power.

Is the American-led war on terrorism a form of wilding? If it is truly an international struggle to eradicate groups such as Al Qaeda, then diplomatic, police, intelligence, and military actions designed for such aims may be morally legitimate. But the history of hegemonic powers—and of the U.S. in particular—offers cautions. During the Cold War, many wars fought in the name of anticommunism, such as the 1954 overthrow of Guatemela's elected president Jacobo Arbenz, had more to do with protecting the United Fruit Company's banana plantations than fighting Communism. The 1953 CIA overthrow of another democratically elected leader, Iran's President Mohammed Mossadegh, was also an imperialist war. It was called an anticommunist war, but was waged mainly to protect U.S. oil interests. The Cold War developed into a form of hegemonic wilding, involving scores of greed- and power-driven military interventions by the U.S. to build the American empire as well as wars by the Soviet Union to build its own empire.[14]

During the period of Roman hegemonic decline, in the fourth and fifth centuries A.D., the rise of terror from the invading Germanic tribes became a central security issue on the Roman empire's eroding boundaries. Similarly, as the British empire declined, it faced terrorist attacks from African colonies such as Kenya, as well as nationalist attacks from groups such as the Zionists in Israel. If the U.S. is entering a period of hegemonic decline, then we might expect not only disorder and terrorism but a "war on terrorism" that is entirely predictable, since many declining hegemons have waged such a war to preserve their dominance.

What, then, are the real motives driving the war on terrorism that began after 9/11? One is undoubtedly to destroy Al Qaeda and similar violent, criminal groups, and if this were its sole purpose, directed and carried out by the U.N. in coalition with the U.S., the war would not be wilding. But just as the Soviet threat served a useful function for American leaders during the Cold War, the threat of terrorism helps U.S. elites achieve their aims. In fact, the U.S. and its terrorist enemies function like spouses in a long and hostile codependent marriage. They hate each other but need the marriage because it serves crucial functions for each of them. While trying to destroy one another, they also become increasingly reliant on the conflict between them to survive and achieve their own aims.

A key codependent marriage has developed between the U.S. elites and Al Qaeda. Both seek to destroy the other, but at the same time find each other exceedingly useful in promoting their own ends. The American empire provides Al Qaeda with its most potent tool for rallying Arab popular support and undercutting moderate Islamic groups that could make the radicals irrelevant. Similarly, Al Qaeda offers American political leaders their most powerful case for vastly enhanced military spending and wars that bring profit, power, and political legitimacy at home.

A major covert aim of the war on terrorism is to replace the war on communism in order to build the American empire and stem the global tide of
anti-Americanism. Put simply, terrorism (and the war against it) has become
a powerful selling point for the global wilding policies at the heart of empire.
Without Al Qaeda, the Bush administration could not have diverted so much
money to expanding the armed forces, especially in an era of decline in jobs
and domestic social services. Nor could U.S. leaders have explicitly proclaimed the doctrines of preemptive war and unrivalled military dominance.
Al Qaeda has provided U.S. leaders with an argument to introduce American forces in scores of countries as well as to overthrow governments that
have not attacked the U.S., which is perhaps the defining feature of an imperial power. Without their hated terrorist partners, American leaders could
not have attacked Iraq, by falsely linking Saddam Hussein with Al Qaeda, or
pursued so blatantly the new politics of preventive war and empire.

Another unacknowledged aim of the war on terrorism, also suggestive of
systemic political wilding, has been to increase the political standing of the
president at home. As noted earlier, President Bush heads a corporate state.
He has not only proposed huge tax cuts for the rich but increased subsidies
for agribusiness, pharmaceuticals, and other big industries; he has proposed
drilling in the Alaskan wilderness and other energy policies that were a bonanza for the biggest energy giants; and he has supported deregulation that
would enrich telecom, mining, and nearly every other corporate sector. This
has not played well with the American public. By early 2003, as corporations
celebrated the new gifts coming from Washington, half of Americans worried
that they might not have a job in a year. Many saw their pension nest eggs
vanishing, while access to basic health care and education drastically eroded.

The war on terrorism was the answer to the political problem posed by
the inevitable public opposition to the domestic agenda of the corporate state.
Bush's political vulnerability at home would be shared by any president, Democrat or Republican, who presided over the corporate state, since such a
government is structurally committed to policies that do not benefit the majority of Americans. If new corporate presidents continue to rely on the war
on terrorism for their political survival, we may be faced with one wilding
war after another, fought in the name of anti-terrorism, for political benefits
at home. After the fall of Baghdad, rumors surfaced almost immediately of
new potential confrontations with Syria, North Korea, and Iran. Fighting
even one war for domestic political gain is a horrific form of political wilding;
fighting a whole generation of such wars is systemic wilding on a grand scale.

Nations around the world *do* need to come together to try to prevent terrorism. It is precisely because the threat is real and frightening that it is such
a powerful tool for manipulating public opinion. In the face of a very real
threat, we need a more effective and honest approach to stopping terrorism.
What would such an approach look like? First, it would be directed by the
United Nations and the international community rather than by the United

States. Second, it would attack the root causes of terrorism, requiring major changes in U.S. foreign and economic policy. This would include a far more balanced American approach to the Israeli-Palestinian conflict, the most explosive issue in the Middle East. The U.S. could do more to end terror by pushing Israel to ending illegal settlements and accept a viable Palestinian state than by taking any other step, since this would dry up support for Hamas and other Palestinian extremist groups. This will require more pressure on Israel than Bush has exercised since his introduction of his Roadmap to Peace, which most Palestinians correctly perceive as tilted to favor the Israelis. Ending U.S. military occupation of the region and withdrawing U.S. support for the brutal monarchies and sheikdoms there is also essential. This could take place only if the U.S. renounces its aspiration for global hegemony, acknowledging that empire is incompatible with its own democratic ideals as well as with global peace.

An effective anti-terror strategy would imply changing the rules of globalization—which is now the economic expression of American hegemony—such that poor people in the Middle East and around the world are not forced to bear the burden of debt while being denied the means to shape their own development policies. As long as the U.S. imposes a globalization that does not help the 3 billion people who eat fewer calories a day than the ordinary American's cat or dog, we are going to have more anti-American terror.

A war on terrorism that is not wilding would be political, economic, and diplomatic, rather than military. Police and other agents of coercive force may be required to root out violent groups, but the most effective way to do so requires enacting just global policies and involving the full cooperation of other nations and of publics all over the world. The war on terrorism is, of all wars, the one most dependent on winning the hearts and minds of the people.

ENDNOTES

[1] Wallerstein, Immanuel. 2000. *The Essential Wallerstein.* New York: The New Press.

[2] Arrighi, Giovanni. 1994. *The Long Twentieth Century.* London: Verso.

[3] MacFarquhar, Neil. 2002. "Humiliation and Rage Stalk the Arab World." *New York Times,* April 13, Section 4, p. 1.

[4] Sachs, Susan. 2003. "Egyptian Intellectual Speaks of the Arab World's Despair." *New York Times,* April 8, pp. B1–2.

[5] Shadid, Anthony. 2003. "Hospitals Overwhelmed by Living and the Dead." *Washington Post,* April 8, p. A29; Thanassis, Cambanis. 2003. "Iraqis in Basra Weigh Freedom's Cost," *Boston Globe,* April 8, p. B1.

[6] Falk, Richard. 2002. "The New Bush Doctrine." *The Nation,* July 15. Retrieved July 15, 2002 (http://www.thenation.com/doc.mhtml?i=20020715&s=falk).

[7] *Los Angeles Times.* 2003. "Weapons of Mass Destruction May Not Be Found, Bush Says." *Boston Globe,* April 25, p. A17.

[8] Dean, John. 2003. "Is Lying about the Reason for a War an Impeachable Offense?" CNN.com, June 6. Retrieved June 6, 2003 (www.cnn.com/2003/LAW/06/06/find law.analysis.dean.wmd/index.html).

[9] Kristof, Nicholas D. 2003. "White House in Denial." *New York Times,* June 13, p. A33.

[10] Lemann, Nicholas. 2002. "The Next World Order." *The New Yorker,* April 1; Bacevich, Andrew J. 2002. *American Empire: The Realities and Consequences of U.S. Diplomacy.* Cambridge, MA: Harvard University Press, pp. 44–45.

[11] See Lemann, "The Next World Order." See also Project for the New American Century. 2000. "Rebuilding America's Defense." Washington, DC: Author.

[12] See Henriques, Diana B. 2003. "Who Will Put Iraq Back Together?" *New York Times,* March 23, Section 3, p. 1.

[13] Bumiller, Elisabeth and Alison Mitchell. 2002. "Bush Aides See Political Pluses in Security Plan." *New York Times,* June 15, p. A1.

[14] For a recent mainstream discussion of the economic foundations of U.S. military interventions, see Bacevich 2002, *American Empire.* For a more radical view emphasizing many of the same themes, see Chomsky, Noam. 1993. *What Uncle Sam Really Wants.* Tucson, AZ: Odonian Press.

59

COMMUNITY BUILDING
Steps toward a Good Society

AMITAI ETZIONI

In this selection we turn our attention to how society can be improved. Sociologist Amitai Etzioni identifies what he thinks are good steps toward building a good society. A key concept in this article is the *community.* Communities are another type of social structure often studied by sociologists and are defined as being a collection of people in a geographic area or a group of people who share something in common, such as the virtual communities that are created on the Internet. In his 1993 book, *The Spirit of Community,* Etzioni argues that building communities is the key to rebuilding American society. Etzioni believes that a communitarian moral system needs to replace the predominate focus on individualism in the United States. In the article that follows, Etzioni examines two challenges to community building in the contemporary United States.

W ell-formed national societies are not composed of millions of individuals but are constituted as communities of communities. These societies provide a framework within which diverse social groups as well as various subcultures find shared bonds and values. When this framework falls apart, we find communities at each other's throats or even in vicious civil war, as we sadly see in many parts of the world. (Arthur Schlesinger Jr. provides an alarming picture of such a future for our society in his book, *The Disuniting of America*.)

Our community of communities is particularly threatened in two ways that ought to command more of our attention in the next years. First, our society has been growing more diverse by leaps and bounds over recent decades, as immigration has increased and Americans have become more aware of their social and cultural differences. Many on the left celebrate diversity because they see it as ending white European hegemony in our society. Many on the right call for "bleaching out" ethnic differences to ensure a united, homogenous America.

A second challenge to the community of communities emanates from the fact that economic and social inequality has long been rising. Some see a whole new divide caused by the new digital technologies, although others believe that the Internet will bridge these differences. It is time to ask how much inequality the community of communities can tolerate while still flourishing. If we are exceeding these limits, what centrist corrections are available to us?

Diversity within Unity

As a multiethnic society, America has long debated the merit of unity versus pluralism, of national identity versus identity politics, of assimilation of immigrants into mainstream culture versus maintaining their national heritages. All of these choices are incompatible with a centrist, communitarian approach to a good society. Assimilation is unnecessarily homogenizing, forcing people to give up important parts of their selves; unbounded racial, ethnic, and cultural diversity is too conflict-prone for a society in which all are fully respected. The concept of a community of communities provides a third model.

The community of communities builds on the observation that loyalty to one's group, to its particular culture and heritage, is compatible with sustaining national unity as long as the society is perceived not as an arena of conflict but as a society that has some community-like features. (Some refer to a community of communities as an imagined community.) Members of such a society maintain layered loyalties. "Lower" commitments are to one's immediate community, often an ethnic group; "higher" ones are to the community of communities, to the nation as a whole. These include a commitment to a democratic way of life, to a constitution and more generally to a government by law, and above all to treating others—not merely the members of one's group—as ends in themselves and not merely as instruments. Approached this way, one realizes that up to a point, *diversity can avoid being the opposite of unity and can exist within it.*

Moreover, sustaining a particular community of communities does not contradict the gradual development of still more encompassing communities, such as the European Union, a North American community including Canada and Mexico, or, one day, a world community.

During the last decades of the 20th century, the U.S. was racked by identity politics that, in part, have served to partially correct past injustices committed against women and minorities, but have also divided the nation along group lines. Other sharp divisions have appeared between the religious right and much of the rest of the country. One of the merits of the centrist, communitarian approach has been that it has combined efforts to expand the common ground and to cool intergroup rhetoric. Thus communitarians helped call off the "war" between the genders, as Betty Friedan—who was one of the original endorsers of the Communitarian Platform—did in 1997.

New flexibility in involving faith-based groups in the provision of welfare, health care, and other social services, and even allowing some forms of religious activities in public schools, has defused some of the tension between the religious right and the rest of society. The national guidelines on religious expression in public schools, first released by the U.S. Department of Education on the directive of President Clinton in August of 1995, worked to this end. For example, in July of 1996, these guidelines spurred the St. Louis School Board to implement a clearly defined, districtwide policy on school prayer. This policy helped allay the confusion—and litigation—that had previously plagued the role of religion in this school district.

The tendency of blacks and whites not to dialogue openly about racial issues, highlighted by Andrew Hacker, has to some degree been overcome. The main, albeit far from successful, effort in this direction [was] made by President Clinton's Advisory Board on Race. And for the first time in U.S. history, a Jew was nominated by a major political party for the post of vice president.

In the next years, intensified efforts are called for to balance the legitimate concerns and needs of various communities that constitute the American society on one hand, and the need to shore up our society as a community of communities on the other. Prayers truly initiated by students might be allowed in public schools as long as sufficient arrangements are made for students who do not wish to participate to spend time in other organized activities. There are no compelling reasons to oppose "after hours" religious clubs establishing themselves in the midst of numerous secular programs. Renewed efforts for honest dialogues among the races are particularly difficult and needed. None of these steps will cause the differences among various communities—many of which serve to enrich our culture and social life—to disappear. But they may go a long way toward reinforcing the framework that keeps American society together while it is being recast.

Unifying Inequality

Society cannot long sustain its status as a community of communities if general increases in well-being, even including those that trickle down to the

poorest segments of the society, keep increasing the economic distance between the elites and the common people. Fortunately, it seems that at least by
some measures, economic inequality has not increased in the United States
between 1996 and 2000. And by several measures, the federal income tax has
grown surprisingly progressive. (The opposite must be said about rising payroll taxes.) About a third of those who filed income tax returns in 2000 paid
no taxes or even got a net refund from the Internal Revenue Service (IRS).
However, the level of inequality in income at the end of the 20th century was
substantially higher than it was in earlier periods. Between 1977 and 1999,
the after-tax income of the top 1 percent of the U.S. population increased by
115 percent, whereas the after-tax income of the U.S. population's lowest fifth
decreased by 9 percent. There is little reason to expect that this trend will not
continue.

Social Justice

We may debate what social justice calls for; however, there is little doubt
about what community requires. If some members of a community are increasingly distanced from the standard of living of most other members, they
will lose contact with the rest of the community. The more those in charge of
private and public institutions lead lives of hyper-affluence—replete with
gated communities and estates, chauffeured limousines, servants and personal trainers—the less in touch they are with other community members.
Such isolation not only frays social bonds and insulates privileged people
from the moral cultures of the community, but it also blinds them to the realities of the lives of their fellow citizens. This, in turn, tends to cause them to
favor unrealistic policies ("let them eat cake") that backfire and undermine
the trust of the members of the society in those who lead and in the institutions they head.

The argument has been made that for the state to provide equality of outcomes undermines the motivation to achieve and to work, stymies creativity
and excellence, and is unfair to those who do apply themselves. It is also said
that equality of outcomes would raise labor costs so high that a society would
be rendered uncompetitive in the new age of global competition. Equality of
opportunity has been extolled as a substitute. However, to ensure equality of
opportunity, some equality of outcome must be provided. As has often been
pointed out, for all to have similar opportunities, they must have similar
starting points. These can be reached only if all are accorded certain basics.
Special education efforts such as Head Start, created to bring children from
disadvantaged backgrounds up to par, and training for workers released
from obsolescent industries are examples of programs that provide some
equality of results to make equality of opportunity possible.

Additional policies to further curb inequality can be made to work at
both ends of the scale. Policies that ensure a rich basic minimum serve this

goal by lifting those at the lower levels of the economic pyramid. Reference is often made to education and training programs that focus on those most in need of catching up. However, these work very slowly. Therefore, in the short run more effects will be achieved by raising the Earned Income Tax Credit and the minimum wage, and by implementing new intercommunity sharing initiatives.

The poor will remain poor no matter how much they work as long as they own no assets. This is especially damaging because people who own assets, especially a place of residence (even if only an apartment), are most likely to "buy" into a society—to feel and be part of a community. By numerous measures, homeowners are more involved in the life of their communities, and their children are less likely to drop out of school. Roughly one-third of Americans do not own their residence; 73 percent of whites do, compared to 47 percent of African Americans and Hispanics.

Mortgages

Various provisions allowing those with limited resources to get mortgages through federally chartered corporations like Fannie Mae, which helps finance mortgages for many lower-income people, have been helpful in increasing ownership. More needs to be done on this front, especially for those of little means. This might be achieved by following the same model used in the Earned Income Tax Credit in the U.S. and the Working Families Tax Credit in the United Kingdom: providing people who earn below a defined income level with "earned interest on mortgages," effectively granting them two dollars for every dollar set aside to provide seed money for a mortgage. And sweat equity might be used as the future owner's contribution—for instance, if they work on their own housing site. (Those who benefit from the houses that Habitat for Humanity builds are required to either make some kind of a financial contribution themselves or help in the construction of their homes.) Far from implausible, various ideas along these lines were offered by both George W. Bush and Al Gore during the 2000 election campaign, as well as by various policy researchers.

Reducing hard-core unemployment by trying to bring jobs to poor neighborhoods (through "enterprise zones") or by training the long-unemployed in entrepreneurial skills is often expensive and slow, and is frequently unsuccessful. The opposite approach, moving people from poor areas to places where jobs are, often encounters objections by the neighborhoods into which they are moved, as well as by those poor who feel more comfortable living in their home communities. A third approach should be tried much more extensively: providing ready transportation to and from places of employment.

Measures to cap the higher levels of wealth include progressive income taxes, some forms of inheritance tax, closing numerous loopholes in the tax codes, and ensuring that tax on capital is paid as it is on labor. Given that several of these inequality curbing measures cannot be adopted on a significant scale if they seriously endanger the competitive state of a country, steps to introduce many of them should be undertaken jointly with other Organization for Economic Cooperation and Development (OECD) countries, or better yet, among all the nations that are our major competitors and trade partners.

One need not be a liberal—one can be a solid communitarian—and still be quite dismayed to learn that the IRS audits the poor (defined as income below $25,000) more than the rich (defined as income above $100,000). In 1999, the IRS audited 1.36 percent of poor taxpayers, compared to 1.15 percent of rich taxpayers. In 1988, the percentage for the rich was 11.4. In one decade, there was thus a decline of about 90 percent in auditing the rich. This occurred because Congress did not authorize the necessary funds, despite the General Accounting Office's finding that the rich are more likely to evade taxes than are the poor. This change in audit patterns also reflects the concern of Republican members of Congress that the poor will abuse the Earned Income Tax Credit that the Clinton administration has introduced. It should not take a decade to correct this imbalance.

Ultimately, this matter and many others will not be properly attended to until there is a basic change in the moral culture of the society and in the purposes that animate it. Without such a change, a major reallocation of wealth can be achieved only by force, which is incompatible with a democratic society and will cause a wealth flight and other damage to the economy. In contrast, history from early Christianity to Fabian socialism teaches us that people who share progressive values will be inclined to share their wealth voluntarily. A good society seeks to promote such values through a grand dialogue rather than by dictates.

The New Grand Dialogue

The great success of the economy in the 1990s made Americans pay more attention to the fact that there are numerous moral and social questions of concern to the good society that capitalism has never aspired to answer and that the state should not promote. These include moral questions such as what we owe our children, our parents, our friends, and our neighbors, as well as people from other communities, including those in far away places. Most important, we must address this question: What is the ultimate purpose our personal and collective endeavors? Is ever greater material affluence our ultimate goal and the source of meaning? When is enough—enough? What are we considering the good life? *Can a good society be built on ever increasing levels of affluence? Or should we strive to center it around other values, those of mutuality and spirituality?*

The journey to the good society can benefit greatly from the observation, supported by a great deal of social science data, that ever increasing levels of

material goods are not a reliable source of human well-being or contentment—let alone the basis for a morally sound society. To cite but a few studies of a large body of findings: Frank M. Andrews and Stephen B. Withey
found that the level of one's socioeconomic status had meager effects on one's
"sense of well-being" and no significant effect on "satisfaction with life-as-a-
whole." Jonathan L. Freedman discovered that levels of reported happiness
did not vary greatly among the members of different economic classes, with
the exception of the very poor, who tended to be less happy than others.
David G. Myers reported that although per capita disposable (after-tax) income in inflation-adjusted dollars almost exactly doubled between 1960 and
1990, 32 percent of Americans reported that they were "very happy" in 1993,
almost the same proportion as did in 1957 (35 percent). Although economic
growth slowed after the mid-1970s, Americans' reported happiness was remarkably stable (nearly always between 30 and 35 percent) across both high-
growth and low-growth periods.

Happiness

These and other such data help us realize that the pursuit of well-being
through ever higher levels of consumption is Sisyphean. When it comes to
material goods, enough is never enough. This is not an argument in favor of
a life of sackcloth and ashes, of poverty and self-denial. The argument is that
once basic material needs (what Abraham Maslow called "creature comforts") are well sated and securely provided for, additional income does not
add to happiness. On the contrary, hard evidence—not some hippie, touchy-
feely, LSD-induced hallucination—shows that profound contentment is
found in nourishing ends-based relationships, in bonding with others, in
community building and public service, and in cultural and spiritual pur-
suits. Capitalism, the engine of affluence, has never aspired to address the
whole person; typically it treats the person as *Homo economicus*. And of
course, statist socialism subjugated rather than inspired. It is left to the evolving values and cultures of centrist societies to fill the void.

Nobel laureate Robert Fogel showed that periods of great affluence are
regularly followed by what he calls Great Awakenings, and that we are due
for one in the near future. Although it is quite evident that there is a growing
thirst for a purpose deeper than conspicuous consumption, we may not have
the ability to predict which specific form this yearning for spiritual fulfillment will take.

There are some who hold firmly that the form must be a religious one because no other speaks to the most profound matters that trouble the human
soul, nor do others provide sound moral guidance. These believers find good
support in numerous indicators that there was a considerable measure of religious revival in practically all forms of American religion over the last
decades of the 20th century. The revival is said to be evident not merely in the

number of people who participate in religious activities and the frequency of their participation in these activities, but also in the stronger, more involving, and stricter kinds of commitments many are making to religion. (Margaret Talbot has argued effectively that conservative Christians, especially fundamentalists, constitute the true counterculture of our age; they know and live a life rich in fulfillment, not centered around consumer goods.) Others see the spiritual revival as taking more secular forms, ranging from New Age cults to a growing interest in applied ethics.

Priorities

Aside from making people more profoundly and truly content individuals, a major and broadly based upward shift on the Maslovian scale is a prerequisite for being able to better address some of the most tantalizing problems plaguing modern societies, whatever form such a shift may take. That is what is required before we can come into harmony with our environment, because these higher priorities put much less demand on scarce resources than do lower ones. And such a new set of priorities may well be the only conditions under which those who are well endowed would be willing to support serious reallocation of wealth and power, as their personal fortunes would no longer be based on amassing ever larger amounts of consumer goods. In addition, transitioning to a knowledge-based economy would free millions of people (one hopes all of them, gradually) to relate to each other mainly as members of families and communities, thus laying the social foundations for a society in which ends-based relationships dominate while instrumental ones are well contained.

The upward shift in priorities, a return to a sort of moderate counterculture, a turn toward voluntary simplicity—these require a grand dialogue about our personal and shared goals. (A return to a counterculture is not a recommendation for more abuse of controlled substances, promiscuity, and self-indulgence—which is about the last thing America needs—but the realization that one can find profound contentment in reflection, friendship, love, sunsets, and walks on the beach rather than in the pursuit of ever more control over ever more goods.) Intellectuals and the media can help launch such a dialogue and model the new forms of behavior. Public leaders can nurse the recognition of these values by moderating consumption at public events and ceremonies, and by celebrating those whose achievements are compatible with a good society rather than with a merely affluent one.

But ultimately, such a shift lies in changes in our hearts and minds, in our values and conduct—what Robert Bellah called the "habits of the heart." We shall not travel far toward a good society unless such a dialogue is soon launched and advanced to a good, spiritually uplifting conclusion.

60

WHAT CAN WE DO?
Becoming Part of the Solution

ALLAN G. JOHNSON

This last reading is by Allan G. Johnson, a sociologist at the Hartford College for Women of the University of Hartford. Johnson studies the dynamics of privilege, power, and oppression. He is especially interested in understanding how and why systems of privilege are created and maintained in society. In this selection, adapted from *Privilege, Power, and Difference* (2001), Johnson outlines how every individual can be involved in creating solutions to social problems caused by social inequality. He suggests we learn new strategies to effectively become aware of how each of us is privileged and contributes to the oppression of others based on that privilege. With that awareness comes the ability to better affect social change.

The challenge we face is to change patterns of exclusion, rejection, privilege, harassment, discrimination, and violence that are everywhere in this society and have existed for hundreds (or, in the case of gender, thousands) of years. We have to begin by thinking about the trouble and the challenge in new and more productive ways. . . . Here is a summary of the tools we have to start with.

Large numbers of people have sat on the sidelines and seen themselves as neither part of the problem nor the solution. Beyond this shared trait, however, they are far from homogeneous. Everyone is aware of the whites, heterosexuals, and men who intentionally act out in oppressive ways. But there is less attention to the millions of people who know inequities exist and want to be part of the solution. Their silence and invisibility allow the trouble to continue. Removing what silences them and stands in their way can tap an enormous potential of energy for change.

The problem of privilege and oppression is deep and wide, and to work with it we have to be able to see it clearly so that we can talk about it in useful ways. To do that, we have to reclaim some difficult language that names what's going on, language that has been so misused and maligned that it generates more heat than light. We can't just stop using words like *racism, sexism,* and *privilege*, however, because these are tools that focus our awareness on the problem and all the forms it takes. Once we can see and talk about what's going on, we can analyze how it works as a system. We can identify points of leverage where change can begin.

Reclaiming the language takes us directly to the core reality that the problem is privilege and the power that maintains it. Privilege exists when one group has something that is systematically denied to others not because of who they are or what they've done or not done, but because of the social category they belong to.

Privilege is a feature of social systems, not individuals. People have or don't have privilege depending on the system they're in and the social categories other people put them in. To say, then, that I have race privilege says less about me personally than it does about the society we all live in and how it is organized to assign privilege on the basis of a socially defined set of racial categories that change historically and often overlap. The challenge facing me as an individual has more to do with how I participate in society as a recipient of race privilege and how those choices oppose or support the system itself.

In dealing with the problem of privilege, we have to get used to being surrounded by paradox. Very often those who have privilege don't know it, for example, which is a key aspect of privilege. Also paradoxical is the fact that privilege doesn't necessarily lead to a "good life," which can prompt people in privileged groups to deny resentfully that they even have it. But privilege doesn't equate with being happy. It involves having what others don't have and the struggle to hang on to it at their expense, neither of which is a recipe for joy, personal fulfillment, or spiritual contentment. . . .

To be an effective part of the solution, we have to realize that privilege and oppression are not a thing of the past. It's happening right now. It isn't just a collection of wounds inflicted long ago that now need to be healed. The wounding goes on as I write these words and as you read them, and unless people work to change the system that promotes it, personal healing by itself cannot be the answer. Healing wounds is no more a solution to the oppression that causes the wounding than military hospitals are a solution to war. Healing is a necessary process, but it isn't enough. . . .

Since privilege is rooted primarily in systems—such as families, schools, and workplaces—change isn't simply a matter of changing people. People, of course, will have to change in order for systems to change, but the most important point is that changing people isn't enough. The solution also has to include entire systems, such as capitalism, whose paths of least resistance shape how we feel, think, and behave as individuals, how we see ourselves and one another.

As they work for change, it's easy for members of privileged groups to lose sight of the reality of privilege and its consequences and the truth that the trouble around privilege is their trouble as much as anyone else's. This happens in large part because systems of privilege provide endless ways of seeing and thinking about the world that make privilege invisible. These include denying and minimizing the trouble; blaming the victim; calling the trouble something else; assuming everyone prefers things the way they are; mistaking intentions with consequences; attributing the trouble to others and not their own participation in social systems that produce it; and balancing the trouble with troubles of their own. The more aware people can be of how these behaviors limit their effectiveness, the more they can contribute to change both in themselves and the systems where they work and live.

With these tools in hand, we can begin to think about how to make ourselves part of the solution to the problem of privilege and oppression. . . .

STUBBORN OUNCES

(To One Who Doubts the Worth of Doing Anything
if You Can't Do Everything)

You say the little efforts that I make
will do no good; they will never prevail
to tip the hovering scale
where Justice hangs in balance.
                        I don't think
I ever thought they would.
But I am prejudiced beyond debate
In favor of my right to choose which side
shall feel the stubborn ounces of my weight.[1]

Stubborn Ounces: What Can We Do?

There are no easy answers to the question of what can we do about the problem of privilege. There is no twelve-step program, no neat set of instructions. Most important, there is no way around or over it: the only way out is through it. We won't end oppression by pretending it isn't there or that we don't have to deal with it.

Some people complain that those who work for social change are being "divisive" when they draw attention to gender or race or social class and the oppressive systems organized around them. But when members of dominant groups mark differences by excluding or discriminating against subordinate groups and treating them as "other," they aren't accused of being divisive. Usually it's only when someone calls attention to how differences are used for oppressive purposes that the charge of divisiveness comes up.

In a sense, it *is* divisive to say that oppression and privilege exist, but only insofar as it points to divisions that already exist and to the perception that the status quo is normal and unremarkable. Oppression promotes the worst kind of divisiveness because it cuts us off from one another and, by silencing us about the truth, cuts us off from ourselves as well. Not only must we participate in oppression by living in an oppressive society, we also must act as though oppression didn't exist, denying the reality of our own experience and its consequences for people's lives, including our own.

What does it mean to go out by going through? What can we do that will make a difference? I don't have the answers, but I do have some suggestions.

Acknowledge That the Trouble Exists

A key to the continued existence of every oppressive system is unawareness, because oppression contradicts so many basic human values that it invariably arouses opposition when people know about it. The Soviet Union and its East European satellites, for example, were riddled with contradictions so widely known among their people that the oppressive regimes fell apart with an ease and speed that astonished the world. An awareness of oppression compels people to speak out, to break the silence that continued oppression depends on.

This is why most oppressive cultures mask the reality of oppression by denying its existence, trivializing it, calling it something else, blaming it on those most victimized by it, or diverting attention from it. Instead of treating oppression as a serious problem, we go to war or get embroiled in controversial "issues" such as capital gains tax cuts or "family values" or immigrant workers. There would be far more active opposition to racism, for example, if white people lived with an ongoing awareness of how it actually affects the everyday lives of those it oppresses as "not white." As we have seen, however, the vast majority of white people *don't* do this.

It's one thing to become aware and quite another to stay that way. The greatest challenge when we first become aware of a critical perspective on the world is simply to hang on to it. Every system's paths of least resistance invariably lead away from critical awareness of how the system works. In some ways, it's harder and more important to pay attention to systems of privilege than it is to people's behavior and the paths of least resistance that shape it. . . .

Pay Attention

Understanding how privilege and oppression operate and how you participate in them is where the work for change begins. It's easy to have opinions, but it takes work to know what you're talking about. The simplest way to begin is by reading, and making reading about privilege part of your life. Unless you have the luxury of a personal teacher, you can't understand this issue without reading, just as you'd need to read about a foreign country before you traveled there for the first time, or about a car before you tried to work under the hood. Many people assume they already know what they need to know because it's part of everyday life. But they're usually wrong. Just as the last thing a fish would discover is water, the last thing people discover is society itself and something as pervasive as the dynamics of privilege.

We also have to be open to the idea that what we think we know is, if not wrong, so deeply shaped by systems of privilege that it misses most of the truth. This is why activists talk with one another and spend time reading one another's writing: seeing things clearly is tricky. This is also why people who are critical of the status quo are so often self-critical as well: they know how complex and elusive the truth really is and what a challenge it is to work toward it. People working for change are often accused of being orthodox and rigid, but in practice they are typically among the most self-critical people around. . . .

Little Risks: Do Something

The more you pay attention to privilege and oppression, the more you'll see opportunities to do something about them. You don't have to mount an expedition to find those opportunities; they're all over the place, beginning in yourself. As I became aware of how male privilege encourages me to control conversations, for example, I also realized how easily men dominate group meetings by controlling the agenda and interrupting, without women's objecting to it. This pattern is especially striking in groups that are mostly female but in which most of the talking nonetheless comes from a few men. I would find myself sitting in meetings and suddenly the preponderance of male voices would jump out at me, an unmistakable sign of male privilege, in full bloom.

As I've seen what's going on, I've had to decide what to do about this little path of least resistance and my relation to it that leads me to follow it so readily. With some effort, I've tried out new ways of listening more and talking less. At times my methods have felt contrived and artificial, such as telling myself to shut up for a while or even counting slowly to ten (or more) to give others a chance to step into the space afforded by silence. With time and practice, new paths have become easier to follow and I spend less time monitoring myself. But awareness is never automatic or permanent, for paths of least resistance will be there to choose or not as long as male privilege exists.

As you become more aware, questions will arise about what goes on at work, in the media, in families, in communities, in religious institutions, in government, on the street, and at school—in short, just about everywhere. The questions don't come all at once (for which we can be grateful), although they sometimes come in a rush that can feel overwhelming. If you remind yourself that it isn't up to you to do it all, however, you can see plenty of situations in which you can make a difference, sometimes in surprisingly simple ways. Consider the following possibilities:

Make noise, be seen. Stand up, volunteer, speak out, write letters, sign petitions, show up. Every oppressive system feeds on silence. Don't collude in silence. Breaking the silence is especially important for dominant groups, because it undermines the assumption of solidarity that dominance de-

pends on. If this feels too risky, you can practice being aware of how silence reflects your investment in solidarity with other dominant-group
members. This can be a place to begin working on how you participate in
making privilege and oppression happen: "Today I said nothing, colluded in
silence, and this is how I benefited from it. Maybe tomorrow I can try something different."

✗ *Find little ways to withdraw support from paths of least resistance and people's
choices to follow them, starting with yourself.* It can be as simple as not laughing at a racist or heterosexist joke or saying you don't think it's funny, or writing a letter to your senator or representative or the editor of your newspaper,
objecting to an instance of sexism in the media. When my local newspaper ran
an article whose headline referred to sexual harassment as "earthy behavior,"
for example, I wrote a letter pointing out that harassment isn't "earthy."

The key to withdrawing support is to interrupt the flow of business as
usual. We can subvert the assumption that we're all going along with the
status quo by simply not going along. When we do this, we stop the flow, if
only for a moment, but in that moment other people can notice and start to
think and question. It's a perfect time to suggest the possibility of alternatives, such as humor that isn't at someone else's expense, or of ways to think
about discrimination, harassment, and violence that do justice to the reality
of what's going on and how it affects people. . . .

✗ *Dare to make people feel uncomfortable, beginning with yourself.* At the next
local school board meeting, for example, you can ask why principals and
other administrators are almost always white and male (unless your system
is an exception that proves the rule), while the teachers they supervise are
mostly women and people of color. Or look at the names and mascots used
by local sports teams and see if they exploit the heritage and identity of Native Americans; if that's the case, ask principals and coaches and owners
about it.[2] Consider asking similar kinds of questions about privilege and difference in your place of worship, workplace, and local government. . . .

Some will say it isn't "nice" to make people uncomfortable, but oppressive systems do a lot more than make people feel uncomfortable, and there
isn't anything "nice" about allowing that to continue unchallenged. Besides,
discomfort is an unavoidable part of any meaningful process of education.
We can't grow without being willing to challenge our assumptions and take
ourselves to the edge of our competencies, where we're bound to feel uncomfortable. If we can't tolerate ambiguity, uncertainty, and discomfort, then
we'll never get beneath superficial appearances or learn or change anything
of much value, including ourselves.

And if history is any guide, discomfort—to put it mildly—is also an unavoidable part of changing systems of privilege. As sociologist William
Gamson noted in his study of social movements, "the meek don't make it."[3]
To succeed, movements must be willing to disrupt business as usual and
make those in power as uncomfortable as possible. Women didn't win the

right to vote, for example, by reasoning with men and showing them the merits of their position. To even get men's attention, they had to take to the streets in large numbers at considerable risk to themselves. At the very least they had to be willing to suffer ridicule and ostracism, but it often got worse than that. In England, for example, suffragettes were jailed and, when they went on hunger strikes, were force fed through tubes run down their throats. The modern women's movement has had to depend no less on the willingness of women to put themselves on the line in order to make men so uncomfortable that they've had to pay attention and, eventually, to act.

It has been no different with the civil rights movement. Under the leadership of men like Martin Luther King, the movement was dedicated to the principle of nonviolence. As with the movement for women's suffrage, however, they could get white people's attention only through mass demonstrations and marches. Whites typically responded with violence and intimidation.[4] As Douglas McAdam showed in his study of that period, the Federal government intervened and enacted civil rights legislation only when white violence against civil rights demonstrators became so extreme that the government was compelled to act.[5] . . .

Openly choose and model alternative paths. As we identify paths of least resistance, we can identify alternatives and then follow them openly so that other people can see what we're doing. Paths of least resistance become more visible when people choose alternatives, just as rules become more visible when someone breaks them. Modeling new paths creates tension in a system, which moves toward resolution. We don't have to convince anyone of anything. As Gandhi put it, the work begins with us as we try to be the change we want to see happen in the world. If you think this has no effect, watch how people react to the slightest departures from established paths and how much effort they expend trying to ignore or explain away or challenge those who choose alternative paths.

Actively promote change in how systems are organized around privilege. The possibilities here are almost endless, because social life is complicated and privilege is everywhere. You can, for example,

Speak out for equality in the workplace.

Promote diversity awareness and training.

Support equal pay and promotion.

Oppose the devaluing of women and people of color and the work they do, from dead-end jobs to glass ceilings.

Support the well-being of mothers and children and defend women's right to control their bodies and their lives.

Object to the punitive dismantling of welfare and attempts to limit women's access to reproductive health services.

Speak out against violence and harassment wherever they occur, whether at home, at work, or on the street.

Support government and private services for women who are victimized by male violence. Volunteer at the local rape crisis center or battered-women's shelter. Join and support groups that intervene with and counsel violent men.

Call for and support clear and effective anti-harassment policies in workplaces, unions, schools, professional associations, religious institutions, and political parties, as well as public spaces such as parks, sidewalks, and malls.

Object to theaters and video stores that carry violent pornography. This doesn't require a debate about censorship—just the exercise of freedom of speech to articulate pornography's role in the oppression of women and to express how its opponents feel about it.

Ask questions about how work, education, religion, and family are shaped by core values and principles that support race privilege, gender privilege, and other forms of privilege. You might accept women's entry into combat branches of the military or the upper reaches of corporate power as "progress," for example. But you could also raise questions about what happens to people and societies when political and economic institutions are organized around control, domination, "power over," and, by extension, competition and the use of violence. Is it progress to allow selected women to share control with men over oppressive systems?

✗ *Support the right of women and men to love whomever they choose.* Raise awareness of homophobia and heterosexism. For example, ask school officials and teachers about what's happening to gay and lesbian students in local schools. If they don't know, ask them to find out, since it's a safe bet these students are being harassed, suppressed, and oppressed by others at one of the most vulnerable stages of life. When sexual orientation is discussed, whether in the media or among friends, raise questions about its relation to patriarchy. Remember that it isn't necessary to have answers to questions in order to ask them.

✗ *Pay attention to how different forms of oppression interact with one another.* There has been a great deal of struggle within women's movements, for example, about the relationship between gender oppression and other forms of oppression, especially those based on race and social class. White middle- and upper-middle-class feminists have been criticized for pursuing their own agenda to the detriment of women who aren't privileged by class or race. Raising concerns about glass ceilings that keep women out of top corporate and professional positions, for example, does little to help working- or lower-class women. There has also been debate over whether some forms of oppression are more important to attack first or produce more oppressive consequences than other forms.

One way out of this conflict is to realize that patriarchy isn't problematic just because it emphasizes *male* dominance, but because it promotes dominance and control as ends in themselves. In that sense, all forms of oppression draw support from common roots, and whatever we do that calls attention to those roots undermines *all* forms of oppression. If working against patriarchy is seen simply as enabling some women to get a bigger piece of the pie, then some women probably will "succeed" at the expense of others who are disadvantaged by race, class, ethnicity, and other characteristics. One could make the same argument about movements for racial justice: If it just means enabling well-placed blacks to get ahead, then it won't end racial oppression for the vast majority. But if we identify the core problem as *any* society organized around principles of domination and privilege, then changing *that* requires us to pay attention to all the forms of oppression those principles promote. Whether we begin with race or gender or ethnicity or class or the capitalist system, if we name the problem correctly we'll wind up going in the same general direction.

✢ *Work with other people.* This is one of the most important principles of participating in social change. From expanding consciousness to taking risks, being in the company of people who support what you're trying to do makes all the difference in the world. For starters, you can read and talk about books and issues and just plain hang out with other people who want to understand and do something about privilege and oppression. The roots of the modern women's movement were in consciousness-raising groups where women did little more than talk about themselves and try to figure out how they were shaped by a patriarchal society. It may not have looked like much at the time, but it laid the foundation for huge social change. . . .

It is especially important to form alliances across difference—for men to ally with women, whites with people of color, heterosexuals with lesbians and gay men. What does this mean? As Paul Kivel [author of *Uprooting Racism* (1996)] argues, one of the keys to being a good ally is a willingness to listen—for whites to listen to people of color, for example—and to give credence to what people say about their own experience.[6] This isn't easy to do, of course, since whites, heterosexuals, and men may not like what they hear about their privilege from those who are most damaged by it. It is difficult to hear anger about privilege and oppression and not take it personally, but that is what allies have to be willing to do. It's also difficult for members of privileged groups to realize how mistrusted they are by subordinate groups and to not take that personally as well. . . .

✢ *Don't keep it to yourself.* A corollary of looking for company is not to restrict your focus to the tight little circle of your own life. It isn't enough to work out private solutions to social problems like oppression and keep them to yourself. It isn't enough to clean up your own act and then walk away, to find ways to avoid the worst consequences of oppression and privilege at home and inside yourself and think that's taking responsibility. Privilege and oppression aren't a personal problem that can be solved through personal solutions. At some point, taking responsibility means acting in a larger context, even if that means letting just one other person know what you're doing. It makes sense to start with yourself, but it's equally important not to end with yourself.

A good way to convert personal change into something larger is to join an organization dedicated to changing the systems that produce privilege and oppression. Most college and university campuses, for example, have student organizations that focus on issues of gender, race, and sexual orientation. There are also national organizations working for change, often through local and statewide branches. Consider, for example, the National Organization for Women (NOW), the National Association for the Advancement of Colored People (NAACP), the National Conference for Community and Justice (formerly the National Conference of Christians and Jews), the National Gay and Lesbian Task Force, the Southern Poverty Law Center, the National Organization of Men Against Sexism, the Feminist Majority, the National Abortion Rights Action League, the Southern Christian Leadership Conference, and the National Urban League. . . .

✗ *Don't let other people set the standard for you.* Start where you are and work from there. Make lists of all the things you could actually imagine *doing*—from reading another book about inequality to suggesting policy changes at work to protesting against capitalism to raising questions about who cleans the bathroom at home—and rank them from the most risky to the least. Start with the least risky and set reasonable goals ("What small risk for change will I take *today*?"). As you get more experienced at taking risks, you can move up your list. You can commit yourself to whatever the next steps are for you, the tolerable risks, the contributions that offer some way—however small it might seem—to help balance the scales. As long as you do something, it counts.

In the end, taking responsibility doesn't have to involve guilt and blame, letting someone off the hook, or being on the hook yourself. It simply means acknowledging an obligation to make a contribution to finding a way out of the trouble we're all in, and to find constructive ways to act on that obligation. You don't have to do anything dramatic or earth-shaking to help change happen. As powerful as oppressive systems are, they cannot stand the strain of lots of people doing something about it, beginning with the simplest act of naming the system out loud.

What's in It for Me?

It's risky to promote change. You risk being seen as odd, being excluded or punished for asking questions and setting examples that make people uncomfortable or threaten privilege. We've all adapted in one way or another to life in a society organized around competition, privilege, and difference. Paths of least resistance may perpetuate oppression, but they also have the advantage of being familiar and predictable and therefore can seem preferable to untried alternatives and the unknown. There are inner risks—of feeling lost, confused, and scared—along with outer risks of being rejected or worse. Obviously, then, working for change isn't a path of least resistance, which raises the question of why anyone should follow Gandhi's advice and do it anyway.

It's an easier question to answer for subordinate groups than it is for dominants, which helps explain why the former have done most of the work for change. Those on the losing end have much to gain by striving to undo the system that oppresses them, not only for themselves in the short run, but for the sake of future generations. The answer comes less easily for those in dominant groups, but they don't have to look very far to see that they have much to gain—especially in the long run—that more than balances what they stand to lose.[7]

When whites, heterosexuals, and men join the movement against privilege and oppression, they can begin to undo the costs of participating in an oppressive system as the dominant group. Few men, for example, realize how much they deaden themselves in order to support (if only by their silence) a system that privileges them at women's expense, that values maleness by devaluing femaleness, that makes women invisible in order to make men appear larger than life. Most men don't realize the impoverishment to their emotional and spiritual lives, the price they pay in personal authenticity and integrity, how they compromise their humanity, how they limit the connections they can have with other people, how they distort their sexuality to live up to core patriarchal values of control. They don't realize how much they have to live a lie in order to interact on a daily basis with their mothers, wives, sisters, daughters, women friends and co-workers—all members of the group male privilege oppresses. So the first thing men can do is claim a sense of aliveness and realness that doesn't depend on superiority and control, and a connection to themselves and the world—which they may not even realize was missing until they begin to feel its return.

In similar ways, most whites don't realize how much energy it takes to defend against their continuing vulnerability to guilt and blame and to avoid seeing how much trouble the world is in and the central role they play in it. When whites do nothing about racial privilege and oppression, they put themselves on the defensive, in the no-safe-place-to-hide position of every dominator class. But when white people make a commitment to participate in change, to be more than part of the problem, they free themselves to live in the world without feeling open to guilt simply for being white.

In perhaps more subtle ways, homophobia and heterosexism take a toll on heterosexuals. The persecution of lesbians, for example, is a powerful weapon of sexism that encourages women to silence themselves, to disavow feminism, and tolerate male privilege for fear that if they speak out, they'll be labeled as lesbians and ostracized.[8] In similar ways, the fear of being called gay is enough to make men conform to masculine stereotypes that don't reflect who they really are and to go along with an oppressive gender system they may not believe in. And because homosexuals all come from families, parents and siblings may also pay a huge emotional price for the effects of prejudice, discrimination, and persecution directed at their loved ones.

With greater authenticity and aliveness comes the opportunity to go beyond the state of arrested development, the perpetual adolescence that privilege promotes in dominant groups, to move away from unhealthy dependencies on the subordination and undervalued labor of others and toward healthy interdependencies free of oppressive cultural baggage.

When people join together to end any form of oppression, they act with courage to take responsibility to do the right thing, and this empowers them in ways that can extend to every corner of their lives. Whenever we act with courage, a halo effect makes that same courage available to us in other times and places. When we step into our legacies and take responsibility for them, we can see how easily fear keeps us from acting for change in ourselves and in the systems we participate in. As we do the work, we build a growing store of experience to draw on in figuring out how to act with courage again and again. As our inner and outer lives become less bound by the strictures of fear and compromise, we can claim a deeper meaning for our lives than we've known before.

The human capacity to choose how to participate in the world empowers all of us to pass along something different from what's been passed to us. With each strand of the knot of privilege that we help to work loose and unravel, we don't act simply for ourselves, we join a process of creative resistance to oppression that's been unfolding for thousands of years. We become part of the long tradition of people who have dared to make a difference—to look at things as they are, to imagine something better, and to plant seeds of change in themselves, in others, and in the world.

ENDNOTES

[1] Bonaro W. Overstreet, *Hands Laid Upon the Wind* (New York: Norton, 1955), p. 15.

[2] For more on this, see Ward Churchill, "Crimes Against Humanity," *Z Magazine* 6 (March 1993): 43–47. Reprinted in Margaret L. Andersen and Patricia Hill Collins (eds.), *Race, Class, and Gender*, 3d ed. (Belmont, CA: Wadsworth, 1998), pp. 413–20.

[3] William A. Gamson, "Violence and Political Power: The Meek Don't Make It," *Psychology Today* 8 (July 1974): 35–41.

[4] For more on this, see the excellent PBS documentary of the civil rights movement, *Eyes on the Prize.*

[5] Doug McAdam, *Political Process and the Development of Black Insurgency 1930–1970* (Chicago: University of Chicago Press, 1982).

[6] See Kivel, *Uprooting Racism: How White People Can Work for Racial Justice* (Philadelphia: New Society Publishers, 1996), part 3, "Being Allies."

[7] A lot of what follows came out of a brainstorming session with my friend and colleague Jane Tuohy as we worked out the design for a gender workshop.

[8] See Suzanne Pharr, *Homophobia: A Weapon of Sexism* (Inverness, CA: Chardon Press, 1988).